This two-volume work aims to present, as completely as possible, the methods of statistical inference with special reference to their economic applications. It is a well-integrated textbook presenting a wide diversity of models in an entirely coherent and unified framework. The reader will find a description not only of the classical concepts and results of mathematical statistics, but also of concepts and methods recently developed for the specific needs of econometrics. The authors have sought to avoid an overly technical presentation and go to some lengths to encourage an intuitive understanding of the results by providing numerous examples throughout. The breadth of approaches and the extensive coverage of these volumes provide a thorough and entirely self-contained course in modern econometrics.

Volume 1 provides an introduction to general concepts and methods in statistics and econometrics, and goes on to cover estimation, prediction and algorithms. Volume 2 focuses on testing, confidence regions, model selection and asymptotic theory.

Statistics and Econometric Models

VOLUME 1

Themes in Modern Econometrics

Themes in Modern Econometrics is designed to service the large and growing need for explicit teaching tools in econometrics. It will provide an organised sequence of textbooks in econometrics aimed squarely at the student population, and will be the first series in the discipline to have this as its express aim. Written at a level accessible to students with an introductory course in econometrics behind them, each book will address topics or themes that students and researchers encounter daily. While each book will be designed to stand alone as an authoritative survey in its own right, the distinct emphasis throughout will be on pedagogic excellence.

Titles in the series

Statistics and Econometric Models: Volume One
CHRISTIAN GOURIEROUX and ALAIN MONFORT
Translated by QUANG VUONG

Statistics and Econometric Models: Volume Two
CHRISTIAN GOURIEROUX and ALAIN MONFORT
Translated by QUANG VUONG

Time Series and Dynamic Models
CHRISTIAN GOURIEROUX and ALAIN MONFORT
Translated and edited by GIAMPIERO GALLO

Statistics and Econometric Models

VOLUME 1

General Concepts, Estimation, Prediction, and Algorithms

Christian Gourieroux
CREST and CEPREMAP, Paris
Alain Monfort
CREST-INSEE, Paris
Translated by Quang Vuong

Published by the Press Syndicate of the University of Cambridge
The Pitt Building, Trumpington Street, Cambridge CB2 1RP
40 West 20th Street, New York, NY 10011-4211, USA
10 Stamford Road, Oakleigh, Melbourne 3166, Australia

Originally published in French as
Statistique et modèles économétriques Vol 1 by Économica 1989

First published in English by Cambridge University Press 1995
as *Statistics and econometric models Volume 1*

Printed in Great Britain at the University Press, Cambridge

A catalogue record of this book is available from the British Library

Library of Congress cataloguing in publication data applied for

ISBN 0 521 40551 3 (V. 1) 0 521 47162 1 (V. 2)
ISBN 0 521 47744 1 (V. 1 pb) 0 521 47755 X (V. 2 pb)
ISBN 0 521 47837 5 (two volume paperback set)

ISBN 0 521 40551 3 (hardback)
ISBN 0 521 47744 1 (paperback)

TAG

Contents

Preface

The present textbook was motivated by two principles drawn from our teaching experience. First, the application of statistical methods to economic modelling has led to the development of some concepts and tools that are frequently ignored in traditional statistical textbooks. Second, it is possible to introduce these various tools, including the most sophisticated ones, without having recourse to mathematical or probabilistic concepts that are too advanced. Thus the main goal of this book is to introduce these statistical methods by taking into account the specificity of economic modelling and by avoiding a too abstract presentation.

Our first principle has various consequences. Though we discuss problems, concepts, and methods of mathematical statistics in detail, we rely on examples that essentially come from economic situations. Moreover, we analyse the characteristics and contributions of economic methods from a statistical point of view. This leads to some developments in model building but also in concepts and methods. With respect to model building, we address issues such as modelling disequilibrium, agents' expectations, dynamic phenomena, etc. On conceptual grounds, we consider issued such as identification, coherency, exogeneity, causality, simultaneity, latent models, structural forms, reduced forms, residuals, generalized residuals, mixed hypotheses, etc. It is, however, in the field of methods that the economic specificity brings the most important consequences. For instance, this leads to focus on predictions problems, maximum likelihood or pseudo conditional maximum likelihood type estimation methods, M-estimators, moment type estimators, bayesian and recursive methods, specification tests, nonnested tests, model selection criteria, etc.

Our second principle concerns our presentation. In general, we have tried to avoid proofs that are too technical. Instead, we have attempted to emphasize the intuition behind the results, which is a condition necessary to a real understanding. In particular, we have not introduced the concept of σ-algebra and we have systematically left aside issues concerning measurability and negligible sets. We have also tried to strengthen the intuitive understanding of the results by multiplying examples. For the reader interested in technical problems, however, a special chapter (Chapter 24, Volume II) collects rigorous proofs of various asymptotic results. This allows us to lower significantly the mathematical level required for the reading of our book. Lastly, we have included two appendices reviewing basic elements of linear algebra and probability theory. These appendices (A and B, found in Volume II) should provide the reader with a self-contained textbook.

Our textbook can be used in various ways according to the topics covered and levels of difficulty desired. Below, we suggest a three-course sequence. For each course we have defined three sections called "Basic Concepts and Tools," "Estimation and Prediction," and "Tests and Confidence Regions."

Course I

Sections	Chapters
Basic Concepts and Tools	1, 2, 3, and Appendices A, B
Estimation and Prediction	5, 6, 7.1–7.3, 11.1–11.2
Tests and Confidence Regions	14, 15, 16, 20.1–20.5

Course II

Sections	Chapters
Basic Concepts and Tools	4,13.1–13.3
Estimation and Prediction	7.4–7.5, 8.1–8.4, 9, 10, 11.3, 12
Tests and Confidence Regions	17, 18, 20.6–20.8

Course III

Sections	Chapters
Basic Concepts and Tools	13.4–13.6, 22.1, 24
Estimation and Prediction	8.5, 21.1–21.2, 23.1, 23.3
Tests and Confidence Regions	19, 21.3–21.4, 22.2–22.3, 23.2

The first course corresponds to a first-year graduate course in statistical methods for econometrics. The topics covered are indeed the basic ones in statistics. An econometric aspect, however, is provided through the weighting of various topics, the introduction of specific notions, and the choice of examples.

The second course completes the first course by covering asymptotic results. The first two courses should constitute the basic background for a statistician/econometrician wishing to apply the most recent econometric tools.

The third course is the most difficult one on technical grounds. It is also a collection of more advanced topics. A good understanding of the contents of the third level should allow the reading of specialized literature and the beginning of methodological research in good conditions.

We owe a special debt to Martine Germond and Beatrice Lejeune who typed respectively the French and English versions of this book. They both performed promptly and accurately a difficult task. We are also grateful to Quang Vuong for his painstaking translation of our work. Financial support for the publication and translation of this book was provided by the French Ministère de la Recherche et de la Technologie and by the French Ministère de la Culture.

C. Gourieroux
A. Monfort

CHAPTER 1

Models

1.1 Modelling

1.1.1 Principles

The problem of modelling arises as soon as one wants to describe and analyze a real phenomenon. Because reality is often complex, the human mind is unable to comprehend it in its entirety. Thus it is necessary to construct a simplification of reality (or *model*) allowing one to study it partially. This simplification cannot take into account all the characteristics of reality, but only those that seem related to the object of study and that are of sufficient importance. A model suited to a particular purpose often becomes inadequate when the object of study changes (even if the study concerns the same phenomenon) or when there is a need for greater accuracy.

Example 1.1: To predict the result of an election when there are two candidates A and B, one draws with equal probability and replacement a sample of n voters and observes the number Y of individuals in this sample intending to vote for A. The variable Y can be thought of as a random variable distributed as a binomial $B(n, p_A)$, where p_A is the unknown proportion of individuals voting for A on the day of the election.

In this example, the model is given by the family

$$\{B(n, p_A),\ p_A \in [0, 1]\}.$$

Even if this model seems quite natural here, it is only an approximation of reality for it makes several simplifications:

a) For instance, the sample is drawn with a computer using a program to generate random numbers. Since these programs are based on a deterministic algorithm, one only has an approximation of sampling from a uniform distribution.

b) The proportion of individuals voting for A may change between the date of the survey and the date of the election.

c) Some sampled individuals may not divulge their true voting intentions, etc.

Example 1.2: To evaluate the effect on consumption of a change in income, one may propose a model to describe the relationship between these two variables. For instance, one may suppose that they are related through an equality of the form

$$\log C = a \log R + b, \qquad a, b \in \mathbb{R}.$$

The parameter a, called the *consumption elasticity with respect to income*, is equal to the logarithmic derivative $d \log C / d \log R$. If income changes by 1 percent, consumption changes approximately by a percent. The parameter a provides a natural measure of the effect on consumption of a change in income and the model seems appropriate to the study of this effect. The model is clearly an approximation of reality. Indeed time series data (C_t, R_t), $t = 1, \ldots, T$ on consumption and income will not in general be related by an exact equality such as the one proposed.

Example 1.3: A model frequently used to analyze the date of an event is based on the theory of Poisson processes. See Section B.5 in Appendix B, Volume II. The model is more or less suited to the study of unemployment spells (here the event is to find and accept a job). It can be improved and made more realistic by:

a) no longer assuming independence of the past from the present since the probability of an unemployed person finding a job may depend on the length of the unemployment spell,

b) introducing various factors affecting an individual's chances of finding a job. These include general factors such as current economic conditions, and individual factors such as the amount of unemployment benefits received by the individual, whether their spouse is employed, etc.

1.1.2 Stochastic Models

Some of the previous examples have a stochastic character (see Examples 1.1 and 1.3). On the other hand, the model of consumption behavior (1.2) is purely deterministic, which makes it incompatible with the data. One way to solve this difficulty consists in making the model stochastic. Hence the approximate deterministic relation

$$\log C_t = a \log R_t + b, \qquad t = 1, \ldots, T,$$

is replaced by

$$\log C_t = a \log R_t + b + u_t, \qquad t = 1, \ldots, T,$$

where $u_t, t = 1, \ldots, T$, are random variables with zero means called *disturbances* or *error terms.*

A disturbance measures the discrepancy between the observation $\log C$ and the approximate mean $a \log R + b$ proposed by the model. The disturbance may be due to:

(i) the fact that the relation between $\log R$ and $\log C$ is not linear,

(ii) the fact that the coefficients a and b vary over time,

(iii) the omission (voluntary or not) of secondary variables,

(iv) measurement errors on the variables C and R ...

The disturbance is therefore interpreted as a summary of various kinds of ignorance. In fact, the interpretation of the disturbance is important only when hypotheses are made about its distribution. The form of this distribution depends on the kind of ignorance that the disturbance is supposed to represent.

Apart from its interpretation, the introduction of a disturbance has another purpose. As seen later, in a stochastic model it will be possible to construct measures of the error associated with the use of the model. Indeed an evaluation of the accuracy of the results becomes quite essential.

1.1.3 Formulation of a Model

In general, a model has a deterministic component and a random component. How can one obtain an appropriate specification for each of the components? Specifications can rely on observations of the variables or can result from theoretical reasoning based on economic theory or probability theory. Nonetheless, no matter how the model is formulated, the model is ultimately postulated. Its validity only arises from its ability to dominate other models.

Example 1.4: A descriptive analysis of the data may show the presence or absence of correlations among the variables and, hence, may give some ideas about which variables are likely to influence others. Similarly, the study of the empirical distributions of the variables may also suggest suitable families for the probability distributions. For instance, one often uses the families of Pareto distributions or log-normal distributions to describe income distributions. In general, these two families provide good approximations to the observed empirical distributions.

Example 1.5: To explain household consumption expenditures as a function of income and prices, one may rely on the theory of consumption to derive suitable models.

Example 1.6: Some theoretical models can also be derived from probabilistic reasoning. A classical example is the determination of the distribution of the number of events occuring before a certain date under the assumptions of a Poisson process. See Section B.5 in Appendix B.

1.1.4 Descriptive Models and Explanatory Models

A goal of some studies is to know how some variables affect others, i.e., to determine if such effects exist and, if they do, to measure their importance. Models corresponding to such problems are *explanatory.* In contrast, other models are said to be *descriptive.*

Explanatory models are often used to study behavior. They implicitly make a distinction between the variables that are explained and the variables likely to affect the former.

For instance, a study of a firm's production behavior can be based on the *Cobb–Douglas* function relating the level of production Q to the level of capital K and the quantity of labor L

$$Q = AK^{\alpha}L^{\beta},$$

where $A \in \mathbb{R}^+, \alpha \in \mathbb{R}^+, \beta \in \mathbb{R}^+$.

This relation is not only a mathematical equality. In addition to the functional relationship among the variables, it embodies a distinction between the explanatory variables K and L and the explained variable

Q. This distinction intuitively corresponds to a temporal lag where the values for the variables K and L are chosen *before* the value for Q.

Causal relations among variables disappear in descriptive problems. Examples of descriptive problems are the prediction of the outcome of an election from survey data, the determination of the average income of a population and the study of independence between two characteristics.

When many variables are involved in descriptive problems, they are treated symmetrically.

Example 1.7: Psychological tests are used to measure I.Q. level. Each of these tests leads to different measures of I.Q. level. A symmetric and descriptive problem is to study whether two different measures are compatible, i.e., lead to the same ranking, and, if so, to establish a formula linking the two measures.

1.1.5 Sampling Designs

A real phenomenon is frequently studied from data already collected. In some cases, however, it is possible to design a specific sampling. One has so-called *controlled experiments.* In particular, one can devise a simpler, less expensive, and more precise sampling method. Clearly, controlled experiments have important effects on the choice of models.

Example 1.8: Consider again the election Example 1.1. The sample is frequently drawn from a stratified population. The voting population is partitioned into various subpopulations and a sample is randomly drawn from each subpopulation. The whole sample is obtained by pooling the subsamples. The statistician has various options: he can choose the partition, the size of the whole sample, and the distribution of the whole sample over the various subsamples.

Example 1.9: The study of the effects of some variables on others is easier if one can choose the values of the explanatory variables a priori. Such designs are frequent in physics. For instance, to study the dilatation of a liquid, one can choose appropriate levels of temperature and record the corresponding values for the volume. Such designs also exist in economics. They can be set during an experiment. For instance, the effect of the price of electricity on consumption was analyzed by imposing different prices in different areas.

More generally, sampling designs arise when the sample is drawn. A sampling of households, stratified according to their incomes, allows one to fix the income variable. How can one choose the values for the controlled variables? In principle, they should be chosen optimally for the desired study. The optimal design is, however, frequently difficult to implement, and simpler procedures are used. For instance, one can choose some values $x_1, \ldots, x_K$ for the explanatory variables, and, for each of these values, sample independently n observations on the variables to be explained. In this case, one has *repeated observations*.

1.2 Statistical Models

1.2.1 Definitions

Definition 1.1: *A statistical model is a pair $(\mathcal{Y}, \mathcal{P})$, where $\mathcal{Y}$ is the set of possible observations and $\mathcal{P}$ is a family of probability distributions on $\mathcal{Y}$.*

As we saw in the examples of the previous section, the observations generally indicate the values taken for some random variables $Y_1, \ldots, Y_n$. The probability distributions P of the family $\mathcal{P}$ are viewed as possible distributions for the vector $Y = (Y_1, \ldots, Y_n)'$ with values in $\mathcal{Y}$. Different simplifying assumptions can be made about the family $\mathcal{P}$.

a) One can often assume that the support of the distributions is known a priori. In this case, the distributions of the family $\mathcal{P}$ have the same support. Such a condition corresponds to the homogeneity condition that follows.

Definition 1.2:

(i) A model $(\mathcal{Y}, \mathcal{P})$ is dominated if all the distributions in the family $\mathcal{P}$ have densities with respect to the same dominating measure μ.

(ii) A model $(\mathcal{Y}, \mathcal{P})$ is homogeneous if it is dominated and if the measure μ can be chosen so that all the densities are strictly positive.

In both cases, the model can be defined through the family $\mathcal{L}$ of densities associated with $\mathcal{P} = \{P = (\ell(y) \cdot \mu),\ \ell \in \mathcal{L}\}$.

b) Questions concerning real phenomena can frequently be translated into functions of real *parameters*. For instance, in the election example, the proportion p_A of voters in favor of the first candidate arises naturally. When the distributions of the family can be naturally parameterized so that

$$\mathcal{P} = \{P_\theta,\ \theta \in \Theta \subset \mathbb{R}^p\},$$

the problem is said to be *parametric*. It is *nonparametric* otherwise.

Example 1.10: The election problem is parametric. If p_A denotes the proportion of voters for candidate A, the model is

$$(\mathcal{Y} = \{0, 1, \ldots, n\},\ \mathcal{P} = \{B(n, p_A),\ p_A \in [0, 1]\}).$$

Parameterization is clearly not unique. Another parameter that can be readily interpreted is the proportion of voters for candidate B: $p_B = 1 - p_A$. With this new parameterization the model can be written as

$$(\mathcal{Y} = \{0, 1, \ldots, n\},\ \mathcal{P} = \{B(n, 1 - p_B),\ p_B \in [0, 1]\}).$$

Example 1.11: In some surveys firms are asked about their forecasts on some economic variables. Such data allow the study of individual expectations by comparing the forecasts z_i^* to the observed values z_i of the variables. In particular, one can determine whether there is a relationship between these two types of observations or whether these can be viewed as independent. No parameters seem to arise naturally in this problem which is nonparametric in nature.

The distinction often made between parametric and nonparametric problems is not justified mathematically. For, as soon as the observations are real valued, it is always possible to parameterize the family $\mathcal{P}$ with a real parameter $\theta \in I\!R$. See Exercise 1.2. The difficulty, however, is that such a parameter often cannot be interpreted.

In addition, there are situations where parameters arise naturally (for instance, the consumption elasticity with respect to income in a study of consumption behavior) but where knowledge of the values for these parameters is insufficient to characterize the probability law of the observations. Such problems are called *semiparametric.*

Remark 1.1: A dominated parametric model can be defined by the family of its densities $\ell(y;\theta)$ such that $P_\theta = (\ell(y;\theta) \cdot \mu)$. The mapping from θ to $\ell(y;\theta)$ is called the *likelihood function.*

c) Sometimes the observed variables can be assumed to be independent with the same probability law $\tilde{P}$. In this case, $Y_1, \ldots, Y_n$ is a random sample from $\tilde{P}$. If $\tilde{P}$ is known to belong to the family of distributions $\tilde{\mathcal{P}}$ defined on the set $\tilde{\mathcal{Y}}$ of possible values for Y_i, then the model is a *sampling model* and can be written as

$$\left(\mathcal{Y} = \tilde{\mathcal{Y}}^n,\ \mathcal{P} = \{P = \tilde{\mathcal{P}}^{\otimes n},\ \tilde{P} \in \tilde{\mathcal{P}}\}\right),$$

where $\tilde{\mathcal{P}}^{\otimes n}$ denotes the product of the n marginal distributions of the variables $Y_i, i = 1, \ldots, n$.

When the family $\tilde{\mathcal{P}}$ is dominated by a measure $\tilde{\mu}$, the family $\mathcal{P}$ is dominated by $\mu = \tilde{\mu}^{\otimes n}$, and the density ℓ of P is equal to

$$\ell(y) = \prod_{i=1}^{n} f(y_i),$$

where f is the density of $\tilde{\mathcal{P}}$ with respect to $\tilde{\mu}$.

The hypotheses for $\mathcal{P}$ just described can be interpreted easily. Other conditions can be imposed on the family $\mathcal{P}$ to simplify the mathematical derivations associated with the model or the interpretations that can be obtained from it. The importance of *linear models* and *exponential models* is indeed explained by their relative simplicity.

Linear Models

These models are defined by assuming that the mean m of the vector Y of observations belongs to a given linear subspace of $\mathbb{R}^n$. Various formulations are possible if one wants to emphasize different parameters. A coordinate free formulation is

$$Y = m + u, \;\; Eu = 0, \;\; m \in L,$$

where L denotes a linear subspace of $\mathbb{R}^n$.

Parameters can be readily introduced by defining generating systems for the subspace L. If $X_1, \ldots, X_K$ is such a system, where $K \geq \dim L$, the mean m can be decomposed as

$$Y = X_1 b_1 + \cdots + X_K b_K + u, \;\; Eu = 0, \tag{1.1}$$

where $(b_1, \ldots, b_K)$ are the coordinates of m with respect to $X_1, \ldots, X_K$. The decomposition is unique only if the system is a basis for L.

Generating systems arise naturally during the modelling process. For instance, the consumption model studied in Example 1.2 can be written as

$$\begin{pmatrix} \log C_1 \\ \vdots \\ \log C_T \end{pmatrix} = \begin{pmatrix} \log R_1 \\ \vdots \\ \log R_T \end{pmatrix} a + \begin{pmatrix} 1 \\ \vdots \\ 1 \end{pmatrix} b + \begin{pmatrix} u_1 \\ \vdots \\ u_T \end{pmatrix}.$$

The subspace L is generated by the vectors

$$X_1 = \begin{pmatrix} \log R_1 \\ \vdots \\ \log R_T \end{pmatrix}, \qquad X_2 = \begin{pmatrix} 1 \\ \vdots \\ 1 \end{pmatrix}.$$

Note that model (1.1) can be described in a more condensed form using the parameter vector $b = (b_1, \dots, b_K)'$ and a matrix $\mathbf{X}$ of size $n \times K$ of which the column vectors are $X_1, \dots, X_K$. Then we have

$$Y = \mathbf{X}b + u, \qquad Eu = 0. \tag{1.2}$$

Exponential Models

Definition 1.3: *A statistical model $(\mathcal{Y}, \mathcal{P} = \{P_\theta, \theta \in \Theta\})$ is exponential, if the distributions P_θ have densities with respect to the same measure μ of the form*

$$\ell(y; \theta) = C(\theta) h(y) \exp\left(\sum_{j=1}^{r} Q_j(\theta) T_j(y)\right),$$

where the functions Q_j and T_j are real valued. The family $\mathcal{P}$ is an exponential family and the random vector $T = (T_1(y), \dots, T_r(y))'$ is the canonical statistic of the model.

Example 1.12: Let $(Y_1, \dots, Y_n)$ be a random sample from a Poisson distribution with parameter $\lambda \in \mathbb{R}^+$. The distribution of $(Y_1, \dots, Y_n)$ has a density

$$\begin{aligned} \ell(y; \lambda) &= \prod_{i=1}^{n} \exp(-\lambda) \frac{\lambda^{y_i}}{y_i!} \\ &= \left(\prod_{i=1}^{n} \frac{1}{y_i!}\right) \exp(-n\lambda) \exp\left((\log \lambda) \sum_{i=1}^{n} y_i\right) \end{aligned}$$

with respect to the counting measure on $\mathbb{N}^n$. The family is exponential with $r = 1$, $T(Y) = \sum_{i=1}^n Y_i$, $Q_1(\lambda) = \log \lambda$.

Example 1.13: Consider the linear model (1.2) where the vector u of disturbances is assumed to follow a normal distribution $N(0, \sigma^2 \mathbf{I})$. Thus, the vector Y is distributed as $N(\mathbf{X}b, \sigma^2\mathbf{I})$ and its density is

$$\begin{aligned}\ell(y; b, \sigma^2) &= \frac{1}{\sigma^n (2\pi)^{n/2}} \exp\left(-\frac{1}{2\sigma^2}(y - \mathbf{X}b)'\,(y - \mathbf{X}b)\right) \\ &= \frac{1}{\sigma^n (2\pi)^{n/2}} \exp\left(-\frac{b'\mathbf{X}'\mathbf{X}b}{2\sigma^2}\right) \exp\left(-\frac{y'y}{2\sigma^2} + \frac{y'\mathbf{X}b}{\sigma^2}\right).\end{aligned}$$

The model is exponential with $r = K + 1$. A canonical statistic for the model is

$$T_{K+1}(Y) = Y'Y = \|Y\|^2,\ T_k(Y) = Y'X_k,\ k = 1, \ldots, K.$$

1.2.2 A Priori Information

When a priori information on a model is available, it can be introduced through deterministic constraints on the family of distributions $\mathcal{P}$ or through stochastic constraints within a Bayesian framework.

a) Constraints on the Parameters

A study of firm production behavior can lead to a linear model derived from the Cobb–Douglas production function

$$\log Q_t = \log A + \alpha \log K_t + \beta \log L_t + u_t,$$

with $Eu_t = 0,\ t = 1, \ldots, T$. This model corresponds to a family $\mathcal{P}$ of distributions on $\mathbb{R}^T$ of which the means belong to a subspace L of dimension three generated by

$$X_1 = \begin{pmatrix} 1 \\ \vdots \\ 1 \end{pmatrix}, \qquad X_2 = \begin{pmatrix} \log K_1 \\ \vdots \\ log K_T \end{pmatrix}, \qquad X_3 = \begin{pmatrix} \log L_1 \\ \vdots \\ log L_T \end{pmatrix}.$$

If one believes that the production function exhibits constant returns to scale, one needs to impose the constraint

$$\alpha + \beta = 1.$$

The model becomes

$$\log Q_t = \log A + \alpha \log K_t + (1 - \alpha) \log L_t + u_t.$$

The model corresponds to a family $\mathcal{P}_0$ of distributions on $\mathbb{R}^T$ of which the means belong to the affine subspace L_0 of dimension two containing the element $(\log L_1, \dots, \log L_T)'$ and generated by the vectors $(1, \dots, 1)'$ and $(\log K_1 - \log L_1, \dots, \log K_T - \log L_T)'$. Since L_0 is included in L, the family $\mathcal{P}_0$ is included in the family $\mathcal{P}$.

Thus imposing constraints on the parameters is equivalent to specifying a family $\mathcal{P}_0$ that is included in $\mathcal{P}$. In what follows, we shall use the following terminology:

Definition 1.4: *Two models $(\mathcal{Y}, \mathcal{P}_0)$ and $(\mathcal{Y}, \mathcal{P})$ are nested if $\mathcal{P}_0 \subset \mathcal{P}$. Then $(\mathcal{Y}, \mathcal{P}_0)$ is a submodel of $(\mathcal{Y}, \mathcal{P})$ and $(\mathcal{Y}, \mathcal{P})$ is a nesting model for $(\mathcal{Y}, \mathcal{P}_0)$.*

b) Bayesian Approach

Consider a dominated parametric model

$$\mathcal{P} = \{P_\theta = (\ell(y;\theta) \cdot \mu), \ \theta \in \Theta \subset \mathbb{R}^p\}.$$

It may be very restrictive to impose some equality constraints on the parameters, as was done for the Cobb–Douglas model. The Bayesian approach allows a less stringent modelling of available a priori information by assuming that the parameters are random with some probability distribution Π called the *prior distribution.* Instead of specifying with certainty the subspace where the parameters lie (such as $\alpha + \beta = 1$) one simply defines the probability that the parameters lie in various regions.

From a mathematical point of view, this approach has the advantage of treating symmetrically the parameters and the observations. Indeed, defining the family $\mathcal{P}$, i.e., the family of conditional distributions of Y given θ, and defining the marginal distribution Π of θ is equivalent to defining a joint distribution for the pair (Y, θ). This joint distribution is $(\ell(y;\theta) \cdot \mu \otimes \Pi)$. The observations on Y add information on the parameter θ that can be used to modify the a priori information one has on this parameter. Once the observations are drawn, it is natural to consider the conditional distribution of θ given $Y = y$. This conditional distribution denoted $\Pi^{\theta|y}$ is equal to

$$\Pi^{\theta|y} = \frac{\ell(y;\theta)}{\int_\Theta \ell(y;\theta)\Pi(d\theta)} \cdot \Pi \tag{1.3}$$

The distribution $\Pi^{\theta|y}$ is called the *posterior distribution* since it incorporates information from the observed data into the distribution of θ.

c) Empirical Bayesian Approach

A method of modelling that is more flexible than the Bayesian approach consists in introducing more than one possible prior distribution for the parameters. The model is then defined by $(\mathcal{Y}, \mathcal{P} = \{P_\theta, \theta \in \Theta\})$ and the family of possible prior distributions on Θ denoted $\mathbf{\Pi}$,

When the family $\mathbf{\Pi}$ of prior distributions is parametric so that $\mathbf{\Pi} = \{\Pi_\alpha,\ \alpha \in A\}$, the parameter α is called an *hyperparameter.*

This approach is the most general. For if $\mathbf{\Pi}$ is reduced to a single distribution, one obtains the Bayesian approach. If $\mathbf{\Pi}$ consists of degenerate distributions with point mass at θ, i.e. , $\mathbf{\Pi} = \{\varepsilon_\theta,\ \theta \in \Theta\}$, one recovers the initial model $(\mathcal{Y},\ \mathcal{P} = \{P_\theta,\ \theta \in \Theta\})$. Such a two-step approach is useful for formulating models. The following two examples are illustrative.

Example 1.14: Consider an individual consumption model. If one allows households to exhibit different behaviors, one may be naturally led to propose a model of the form

$$\log C_i = a_i logR_i + b_i + u_i, \qquad i = 1, \ldots, n,$$

where i indicates the ith household and where a_i and b_i vary across households. Problems arise, however, from the fact that the number of parameters of the model is $2n$ and hence greater than the number of observed households.

A possible solution consists in assuming that the parameters are independent and, for instance, such that $a_i \sim N(a, \sigma_a^2)$, $b_i \sim N(b, \sigma_b^2)$. The hyperparameter a represents the "average elasticity" of consumption with respect to income. The hyperparameter σ_a^2 measures the dispersion of the individual elasticities. Such a model is said to have *random coefficients.*

Example 1.15: Consider the problem of estimating the mean income of households from a sample of observations on income. The parameter vector is $\theta = (\theta_i,\ i = 1, \ldots, N)$, where θ_i is the income of household i. The function of the parameter θ that is of interest is $\overline{\theta} = \frac{1}{N}\sum_{i=1}^{N} \theta_i$. To simplify, one may assume that the empirical distribution of incomes can be approximated by a log-normal distribution. For instance, one may assume that the parameters θ_i are independent and such that $\log \theta_i \sim N(m, \sigma^2)$ or equivalently, $\theta_i \sim LN(m, \sigma^2)$. The family $\mathbf{\Pi}$ is $\mathbf{\Pi} = \{LN(m, \sigma^2)^{\otimes N},\ m \in I\!R^+\}$. Such a model is sometimes called a *superpopulation model.*

1.2.3 Specification Errors

To study the properties of a model given a set of observations, one can view a model as a good or bad approximation to the "*true*" but unknown distribution P_0 of the observations. In the first case, one assumes that the distribution P_0 generating the observations belongs to the family of distributions associated with the model, i.e., one assumes that $P_0 \in \mathcal{P}$. When the family is parametric so that $\mathcal{P} = \{P_\theta,\ \theta \in \Theta\}$, the distribution P_0 can be defined through a value θ_0 of the parameter, and one has $P_0 = P_{\theta_0}$. This value is called the *true value of the parameter.* The distribution P_0 uniquely defines θ_0 if the mapping $\theta \mapsto P_\theta$ is bijective, i.e., if the model is identified (see Chapter 3).

When one believes a priori that the true distribution P_0 does not belong to $\mathcal{P}$, one says that there may be *specification errors.* Then it is interesting to find the element P_0^* in $\mathcal{P}$ that is closest to P_0 in order to assess the type of specification errors by comparing P_0 to P_0^*. To do this, one must have a measure of the proximity or *discrepancy* between the probability distributions.

In this section, we assume that distributions have strictly positive densities with respect to a common dominating measure μ.

Definition 1.5: *Given two distributions $P = (f(y) \cdot \mu)$ and $P^* = (f^*(y) \cdot \mu)$, the quantity*

$$I\left(P \mid P^*\right) = E^* \log \frac{f^*(y)}{f(y)} = \int_{\mathcal{Y}} \log \frac{f^*(y)}{f(y)} f^*(y)\mu(dy)$$

is called the Kullback discrepancy between P and P^*. This quantity is also called the Kullback discriminating information criterion.

The quantity I is a measure of the discrepancy between the distributions P and P^* because of Property 1.1 below. It is, however, easy to see that the measure I is not a distance in the classical sense since it does not satisfies the symmetry condition and the triangular inequality.

Property 1.1:

(i) $I(P \mid P^*) \geq 0$,

(ii) $I(P \mid P^*) = 0$ if and only if $P = P^*$.

PROOF:

(i) Applying Jensen's Inequality to the convex function $-\log x$ we have

$$\begin{aligned} I(P \mid P^*) &= E^* \log \frac{f^*(Y)}{f(Y)} = E^* \left(-\log \frac{f(Y)}{f^*(Y)} \right) \\ &\geq -\log E^* \frac{f(Y)}{f^*(Y)} = -\log 1 = 0. \end{aligned}$$

(ii) Since the function $-\log x$ is strictly convex, equality in part (i) holds only if $f(Y)/f^*(Y)$ is equal to a constant. Since $E^*(f(Y)/f^*(Y)) = 1$, this constant must be equal to one. □

Definition 1.6:

(i) An element P_0^* in $\mathcal{P}$ is said to be a pseudo true distribution if it satisfies

$$I\left(P_0^* \mid P_0\right) = \min_{P \in \mathcal{P}} I\left(P \mid P_0\right).$$

(ii) The discrepancy between the true distribution and the model is

$$I\left(\mathcal{P} \mid P_0\right) = I\left(P_0^* \mid P_0\right).$$

(iii) When the model is parametric so that $\mathcal{P} = \{P_\theta,\ \theta \in \Theta\}$, a pseudo true distribution P_0^* is associated with some parameter values θ_0^*. These are called pseudo true values for the parameters.

Clearly, the definition of a pseudo true value has meaning only if the minimum is attained for an element of $\mathcal{P}$. This was implicitly assumed. If the model is identified, there is a unique θ_0^* corresponding to each P_0^* (see Chapter 3).

Discrepancy measures other than the Kullback criterion can be introduced. These lead to other pseudo true distributions. See for instance the chi-square discrepancy (Exercise 1.12). The Kullback measure is, however, preferred for it has interesting interpretations, and leads to some natural distances in important special cases as illustrated by the following two examples.

Example 1.16:

(i) Consider two multivariate normal distributions of dimension n with scalar variance covariance matrices, i.e., $P = N(m, \sigma^2 \mathbf{I})$ and $P^* = N(m^*, \sigma^{*2} \mathbf{I})$. We have

$$\log \frac{f^*(Y)}{f(Y)} = \log \frac{\frac{1}{(\sigma^* \sqrt{2\pi})^n} \exp\left(-\frac{1}{2\sigma^{*2}} \|Y - m^*\|^2 \right)}{\frac{1}{(\sigma \sqrt{2\pi})^n} \exp\left(-\frac{1}{2\sigma^2} \|Y - m\|^2 \right)}$$

$$= \quad n \log \frac{\sigma}{\sigma^*} - \frac{1}{2\sigma^{*2}} \|Y - m^*\|^2 + \frac{1}{2\sigma^2} \|Y - m\|^2.$$

Thus

$$\begin{aligned} I(P \mid P^*) &= E^* \log \frac{f^*(Y)}{f(Y)} \\ &= n \log \frac{\sigma}{\sigma^*} - \frac{n}{2} + \frac{n\sigma^{*2} + \|m^* - m\|^2}{2\sigma^2} \\ &= n \log \frac{\sigma}{\sigma^*} - \frac{n}{2} + \frac{n\sigma^{*2}}{2\sigma^2} + \frac{\|m^* - m\|^2}{2\sigma^2}. \end{aligned}$$

In particular, $I(P \mid P^*)$ involves the distance between the means $\|m^* - m\|$ and a measure of discrepancy between the variances

$$\log \frac{\sigma}{\sigma^*} + \frac{\sigma^{*2}}{2\sigma^2} - \frac{1}{2}.$$

(ii) Now suppose that the true distribution is $P_0 = N(m_0, \sigma_0^2 \mathbf{I})$ and that the model is linear

$$\mathcal{P} = \{P = N\left(m, \sigma^2 \mathbf{I}\right) \text{ with } m \in L, \sigma^2 \in \mathbb{R}^{+*}\}.$$

To find the pseudo true values m_0^* and σ_0^{*2} one must minimize the following expression with respect to (m, σ^2) in $L \times \mathbb{R}^{+*}$

$$I(P \mid P_0) = n \log \frac{\sigma}{\sigma_0} - \frac{n}{2} + \frac{n\sigma_0^2}{2\sigma^2} + \frac{\|m_0 - m\|^2}{2\sigma^2}.$$

The minimization with respect to m reduces to the problem of finding the element of the subspace L that is closest to m_0. Thus the solution m_0^* is equal to the orthogonal projection of m_0 on L

$$m_0^* = P_L m_0. \tag{1.4}$$

Then the first-order condition with respect to the variance gives

$$\sigma_0^{*2} = \sigma_0^2 + \frac{\|m_0 - P_L m_0\|^2}{n}. \tag{1.5}$$

Example 1.17:

(i) When the vector of observations is discrete valued, the densities are given by the probability mass functions $P_0 = (p_0(y),\ y \in \mathcal{Y})$,

$P_\theta = (p_\theta(y),\ y \in \mathcal{Y})$, where $\theta \in \Theta$. Then finding the pseudo true values reduces to solving the problem

$$\min_{\theta \in \Theta} \sum_y p_0(y) \log \frac{p_0(y)}{p_\theta(y)},$$

or equivalently

$$\max_{\theta \in \Theta} \sum_y p_0(y) \log p_\theta(y). \tag{1.6}$$

(ii) Now suppose that the observations are on two qualitative variables Y_1, Y_2, each of which can take the values 0 or 1. The true distribution is characterized by the four probabilities

$$\begin{aligned} p_{00}^0 &= p_0\left(Y_1 = 0, Y_2 = 0\right), \\ p_{01}^0 &= p_0\left(Y_1 = 0, Y_2 = 1\right), \\ p_{10}^0 &= p_0\left(Y_1 = 1, Y_2 = 0\right), \\ p_{11}^0 &= p_0\left(Y_1 = 1, Y_2 = 1\right). \end{aligned}$$

Consider a model postulating the independence between the two variables. The corresponding distributions are parameterized by $\alpha = P\left(Y_1 = 0\right)$ and $\beta = P\left(Y_2 = 0\right)$. Under the assumption of independence, we have

$$p_{00} = \alpha\beta,\ p_{01} = \alpha(1-\beta),\ p_{10} = (1-\alpha)\beta,\ p_{11} = (1-\alpha)(1-\beta).$$

The pseudo true values for α and β are obtained by maximizing

$$\begin{aligned} & p_{00}^0 \log\left(\alpha\beta\right) + p_{01}^0 \log\left(\alpha(1-\beta)\right) \\ & \quad + p_{10}^0 \log\left((1-\alpha)\beta\right) + p_{11}^0 \log\left((1-\alpha)(1-\beta)\right) \\ = & \quad (p_{00}^0 + p_{01}^0) \log \alpha + (p_{10}^0 + p_{11}^0) \log(1-\alpha) \\ & \quad + (p_{00}^0 + p_{10}^0) \log \beta + (p_{01}^0 + p_{11}^0) \log(1-\beta). \end{aligned}$$

One obtains

$$\alpha_0^* = p_{00}^0 + p_{01}^0 \text{ and } \beta_0^* = p_{00}^0 + p_{10}^0.$$

Thus $(\alpha_0^*, 1-\alpha_0^*)$ and $(\beta_0^*, 1-\beta_0^*)$ are the true marginal distributions of Y_1 and Y_2 respectively, and the pseudo true distribution, i.e., the distribution satisfying the independence assumption that is closest to P_0, is obtained from the product of the two marginal distributions.

1.3 Intermediate Forms

1.3.1 A Principle for Formulating Explanatory Models

A model can be derived from economic or statistical theoretical reasoning. Frequently one is led to formulate some intermediate forms. In this section we discuss a principle for formulating models in the case where, for each observation i, $i = 1, \ldots, n$, one's goal is to explain the values taken by a vector Y_i of observed or *endogenous* variables as functions of a vector of explanatory variables X_i and a vector of disturbances u_i.

It is sometimes the case that the components of Y_i are functions of a vector of other variables Y_i^*, called *latent variables*, which are easier to explain. Each component of Y_i^* is then explained as a function of some other components of Y_i^* and some variables X_i

$$g\left(Y_i^*, X_i, u_i\right) = 0, \qquad i = 1, \ldots, n, \tag{1.7}$$

where g is a known function.

This system, written in implicit form, is called the *structural form of the latent model.* To be useful, such a form must be able to generate the values of Y_i^*. Thus equation (1.7) must have a unique solution in Y_i^* for every (X_i, u_i). This invertibility condition in Y_i^* is called the *coherency condition.* When this condition is satisfied, one can derive from the structural form an equation for Y_i^* where Y_i^* is expressed as a unique function of X_i and u_i

$$Y_i^* = h(X_i, u_i). \tag{1.8}$$

Equation (1.8) is called the *reduced form of the latent model.*

It remains to specify the relationship between the latent variables Y^* and the observable variables Y. Let

$$Y_i = k(Y_i^*), \tag{1.9}$$

where k is a function that is known or partially known.

The global structural form consists of (1.7) and (1.9). The *observable reduced form* is obtained by replacing Y_i^* in (1.9) by its expression given in (1.8)

$$Y_i = k\left(h(X_i, u_i)\right). \tag{1.10}$$

When the functions g and k depend on unknown parameters, we say that:

- the *structural parameters* are those that naturally appear in (1.7) and (1.9),
- the *latent parameters* are those that appear in (1.7),
- the *reduced form parameters* are those functions of the structural parameters appearing in the observable reduced form (1.10).

In practice, some of the previous forms (structural form, reduced form of the latent model, and observable reduced form) can be identical. To illustrate these various concepts, we now consider some examples where this principle for formulating models is used.

1.3.2 Examples

Example 1.18: In business surveys, firms are asked about the expected directions of changes for some economic variables but not on the magnitudes of those changes. It is interesting to model the qualitative observations with intermediate quantitative latent variables.

Suppose that a question bears on the change in the price of a particular product for the next period. Let the magnitude of this change be Δp. The latter quantity is clearly unknown to the firms. A firm asked about this quantity will provide an answer Y_i^* that is in general different from Δp. For a first step, however, it seems reasonable to assume that firms on average do not make mistakes and that their predictions are independent. Then we can formulate a model of the following type

$$Y_i^* = \Delta p + u_i, \qquad i = 1, \ldots, n,$$

where the disturbances u_i are independent and identically distributed (iid) $N(0, \sigma^2)$.

The parameter σ is interpreted as the firms average error in predicting Δp. The model defined above is a latent model of which the structural and reduced forms are identical.

The model associated with the observed variables can be derived readily. Assume that the questions on the survey allow only two types of answers, such as a "decrease in prices" or an "increase in prices." Then

$$Y_i = k\,(Y_i^*) = \begin{cases} \text{decrease} & \text{if } Y_i^* < 0, \\ \text{increase} & \text{if } Y_i^* \geq 0. \end{cases}$$

In the final model, the observable variables Y_i are iid with common distribution characterized by

$$P(Y_i = \text{decrease}) = P(Y_i^* < 0) = \Phi\left(-\frac{\Delta p}{\sigma}\right),$$

where Φ denotes the cumulative distribution function of the standard normal distribution.

We have here a parametric model where the parameters with a natural interpretation are those of the latent model, namely Δp and σ. The reduced form parameter is $\Delta p/\sigma$.

Example 1.19: Consider two time series, i.e., two sets of data indexed by time, on half-yearly production of some agricultural products. Suppose that in every odd period observations are available on the two series, but that in even periods only the sum of them is observed.

Suppose that the model is defined at the level of the disaggregated time series Y_{1t}^*, Y_{2t}^*, $t = 1, \ldots, 2T$. Then the observed variables are obtained from

$$Y_\tau = \begin{pmatrix} Y_{1,2\tau+1}^* \\ Y_{2,2\tau+1}^* \\ Y_{1,2\tau+2}^* + Y_{2,2\tau+2}^* \end{pmatrix}, \tau = 0, \ldots, T-1.$$

Example 1.20: Description of a Market

Models explaining the quantity Q_t exchanged at time t in a given market and the price p_t for this exchange are formulated by specifying (i) an equation summarizing the behavior of the demand side (the *demand schedule*), (ii) an equation summarizing the behavior of the supply side (*the supply schedule*), and (iii) by describing how the two types of agents interact in the market.

Suppose that the demand at time t is

$$D_t = a_1 p_t + X_{1t} b_1 + u_{1t}, \qquad t = 1, \ldots, T,$$

where X_{1t} denotes the row vector of observations at time t on some macroeconomic variables affecting demand, and where u_{1t} is a random disturbance. Similarly, the supply at time t is given by

$$S_t = a_2 p_t + X_{2t} b_2 + u_{2t}, \qquad t = 1, \ldots, T.$$

(i) An Equilibrium Model

This model is obtained by assuming that prices adjust sufficiently fast to clear the market so that an observation corresponds to the point where demand equals supply.

The observed price is assumed to be equal to the price corresponding to this point (the equilibrium price), while the quantity exchanged is equal to the value common to the demand and the supply (the equilibrium quantity). Thus the model is written as

$$
\begin{aligned}
D_t &= a_1 p_t + X_{1t} b_1 + u_{1t}, \\
S_t &= a_2 p_t + X_{2t} b_2 + u_{2t}, \\
D_t &= S_t.
\end{aligned}
$$

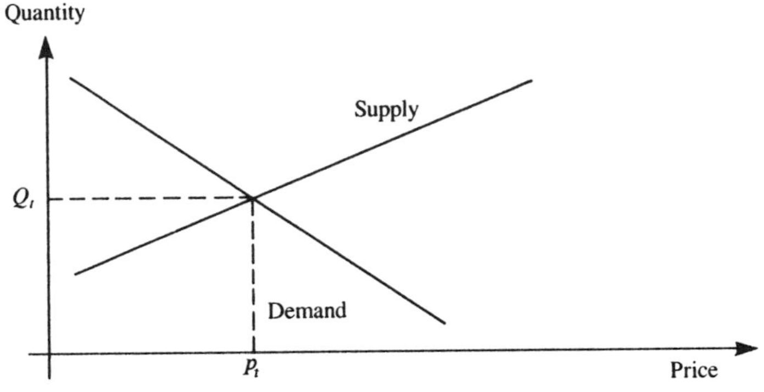

Figure 1.1: Equilibrium Model

From this structural form, one derives the reduced form

$$
\begin{aligned}
p_t &= \frac{X_{1t} b_1 - X_{2t} b_2}{a_2 - a_1} + \frac{u_{1t} - u_{2t}}{a_2 - a_1}, \\
Q_t &= D_t = S_t = \frac{a_2 X_{1t} b_1 - a_1 X_{2t} b_2}{a_2 - a_1} + \frac{a_2 u_{1t} - a_1 u_{2t}}{a_2 - a_1}.
\end{aligned}
$$

In this example there are no latent variables.

(ii) A Disequilibrium or Fixed Price Model

This model contrasts with the previous one. Prices are now fixed. Given fixed prices, demand and supply now differ, and the quantity exchanged cannot be larger than the minimum of demand and supply. In general, one assumes that the quantity exchanged is equal to this minimum value.

From the latent model

$$\begin{aligned} D_t &= a_1 p_t + X_{1t} b_1 + u_{1t}, \\ S_t &= a_2 p_t + X_{2t} b_2 + u_{2t}, \end{aligned}$$

one derives a model for the observed variables using the relationship

$$Q_t = \min(D_t, S_t).$$

Although both models are related to the problem of modelling the same market, they are quite different. In the equilibrium model, the important step is to obtain the reduced form from the structural form. In the disequilibrium model, it is the derivation of the observable model from the latent model that is essential.

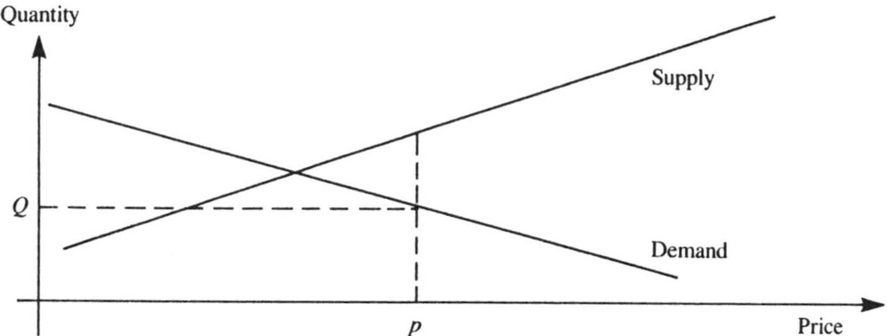

Figure 1.2: Disequilibrium Model

Example 1.21: A Simple Keynesian Model

This model can be used to study the effects of a change in investments on aggregated consumption and production. In its simpler form, the model has four variables which are consumption (C), national income (R), national product (Y), and investment (I). The model has three equations

$$C_t = aR_t + b + u_t,$$

which is the consumption function expressing the dependence of aggregated consumption on national income

$$Y_t = C_t + I_t,$$

which is an identity describing how the national product is distributed over consumption and investment. This identity is analogous to the equilibrium condition in the previous example. Finally

$$R_t = Y_t$$

results from the necessary accounting equality between national product and national income.

This is the structural form of the model where the variables to be explained C, Y, and R are expressed as functions of themselves, the variable I, and the disturbance u

$$\begin{pmatrix} C_t \\ Y_t \\ R_t \end{pmatrix} = \begin{pmatrix} 0 & 0 & a \\ 1 & 0 & 0 \\ 0 & 1 & 0 \end{pmatrix} \begin{pmatrix} C_t \\ Y_t \\ R_t \end{pmatrix} + \begin{pmatrix} b \\ I_t \\ 0 \end{pmatrix} + \begin{pmatrix} u_t \\ 0 \\ 0 \end{pmatrix}. \tag{1.11}$$

The structural form, however, is not well adapted to the evaluation of the effects of a change in investments I on C and Y. To assess these effects, it is convenient to use the reduced form

$$\begin{pmatrix} C_t \\ Y_t \\ R_t \end{pmatrix} = \left(\mathbf{I} - \begin{pmatrix} 0 & 0 & a \\ 1 & 0 & 0 \\ 0 & 1 & 0 \end{pmatrix} \right)^{-1} \begin{pmatrix} b + u_t \\ I_t \\ 0 \end{pmatrix}.$$

This leads to

$$\begin{aligned} C_t &= \frac{a}{1-a} I_t + \frac{b}{1-a} + \frac{u_t}{1-a}, \\ Y_t &= \frac{1}{1-a} I_t + \frac{b}{1-a} + \frac{u_t}{1-a}, \\ R_t &= \frac{1}{1-a} I_t + \frac{b}{1-a} + \frac{u_t}{1-a}. \end{aligned} \tag{1.12}$$

Thus, if investments at time t are modified by ΔI, consumption changes by $\Delta C = \frac{a}{1-a} \Delta I$ and national product by $\Delta Y = \frac{1}{1-a} \Delta I$.

Example 1.22: One may ask whether a given time series is growing linearly or exponentially with time. It may be useful to formulate a model containing both cases. A frequent model is obtained from the *Box–Cox transformation* $T_\lambda : y \mapsto (y^\lambda - 1)/\lambda$, which is a bijective mapping. When $\lambda = 1$ the transformation coincides with a linear affine transformation, and when λ approaches 0 the transformation approaches the logarithmic transformation. The model is

$$\frac{Y_t^\lambda - 1}{\lambda} = at + b + u_t.$$

Since the mapping T_λ can always be inverted, the reduced form is

$$\begin{aligned} Y_t &= T_\lambda^{-1}(at + b + u_t) \\ &= (1 + a\lambda t + b\lambda + \lambda u_t)^{1/\lambda}. \end{aligned}$$

1.3.3 Coherency Conditions

Given a latent structural form $g(Y^*, X, u) = 0$, the reduced form exists if and only if the equation $g(Y^*, X, u) = 0$ has a unique solution in Y^*. Frequently, the structural form is of the type

$$g_0(Y^*) + g_1(X, u) = 0.$$

In this case, the condition is equivalent to the global invertibility of g_0. A simple necessary condition for the invertibility of g_0 is that there are as many independent equations as variables to explain.

This condition is not sufficient. Necessary and sufficient conditions for global invertibility are known only in few cases.

Example 1.23: Suppose that each observation on a vector of latent variables is defined by the linear relation

$$AY_i^* = g_1(X_i, u_i), \qquad i = 1, \ldots, n,$$

where A is a square matrix.

The coherency condition is

$$\det A \neq 0. \tag{1.13}$$

For instance, the reduced form of the Keynesian model of Example 1.21 can be obtained only if $a \neq 1$. For the equilibrium model of Example 1.20, the condition is $a_1 \neq a_2$. This latter condition holds in general since demand is decreasing in prices ($a_1 < 0$) while supply is increasing in prices ($a_2 > 0$).

Example 1.24: When the mapping g_0 is piecewise linear and continuous, i.e., of the form

$$g_0(Y^*) = A_k Y^*, \qquad \text{if } Y^* \in C_k,$$

where the C_k's are cones defined by some linear inequality constraints, and when the cones define a partition of the space for Y^*, one can show that the coherency condition is

The determinants of the mappings A_k have the same sign (1.14)

(see Gourieroux, Laffont, and Monfort (1980)). An illustration of this result is given in Exercise 1.11.

1.4 Conditional Models

1.4.1 Conditioning

Two types of variables appear in the various examples of Section 1.3.2 (consumption or production model, equilibrium or disequilibrium model, Keynesian model). On the one hand, there are variables Y_i or Y_i^* that one seeks to explain, and, on the other hand, there are variables X_i that contribute to the explanation of the former. In addition, it was assumed that the X_i's are deterministic while the disturbances u_i's are stochastic. This implies that the Y_i's and Y_i^*'s are also stochastic. The family of possible distributions for $Y = (Y_1, \dots, Y_n)$ is then determined by a relation of the type (1.10) and the chosen family of distributions for $u = (u_1, \dots, u_n)$. Equivalently, one can suppose that the X_i's are random and that this family of distributions is the family of possible conditional distributions for $(u_1, \dots, u_n)$ given $(X_1, \dots, X_n)$. Then relation (1.10) determines the family of conditional distributions for $Y = (Y_1, \dots, Y_n)$ given $X = (X_1, \dots, X_n)$. Therefore hypotheses on u are actually hypotheses on the conditional distribution of Y given $X = x$.

Definition 1.7: *A conditional model is a pair $(\mathcal{Y}, \mathcal{P}_x)$ where $\mathcal{Y}$ is the set of possible values for a random variable Y, said to be the conditioned variable, and, for any given $x \in \mathcal{X}$, $\mathcal{P}_x$ is a family of conditional distributions for Y given $X = x$, X being the conditioning variables. If $\mathcal{P}_x = \{P_{\theta,x},\ \theta \in \Theta\}$, the conditional model is said to be parametric and, if in addition, $P_{\theta,x} = \ell(y \mid x; \theta) \cdot \mu$, the parametric model is said to be dominated by the measure μ.*

Thus a family of distributions in a parametric conditional model is doubly indexed by x and θ. One should not, however, confuse these two indices. In particular, x is observed while θ is not.

Example 1.25: Consider the consumption model

$$\begin{pmatrix} \log C_1 \\ \vdots \\ \log C_n \end{pmatrix} = \begin{pmatrix} \log R_1 \\ \vdots \\ \log R_n \end{pmatrix} a + \begin{pmatrix} 1 \\ \vdots \\ 1 \end{pmatrix} b + \begin{pmatrix} u_1 \\ \vdots \\ u_n \end{pmatrix},$$

where, conditional upon $(R_1, \ldots, R_n)$, the vector of disturbances $u = (u_1, \ldots, u_n)'$ follows a normal distribution $N(0, \sigma^2 \mathbf{I})$. The family $P_{\theta,x}$ is the family of normal distributions with mean

$$\begin{pmatrix} \log R_1 \\ \vdots \\ \log R_n \end{pmatrix} a + \begin{pmatrix} 1 \\ \vdots \\ 1 \end{pmatrix} b,$$

and with variance covariance matrix $\sigma^2 \mathbf{I}$. Note that this model implies two important hypotheses:

- the conditional expectation $E(\log C_i \mid R_1, \ldots, R_n)$ depends on R_i only;
- the conditional expectation is affine in $\log R_i$ with coefficients a and b independent of i.

The previous example shows that equation (1.10), which is $\log C_i = a \log R_i + b + u_i$ in this example, is asymmetric. Hence, for this example, equation (1.10) defines the conditional distribution of $\log C_i$ given $(\log R_1, \ldots, \log R_n)$. This equation does not, however, determine the conditional distribution of $\log R_i$ given $(\log C_1, \ldots, \log C_n)$. In particular, the conditional expectation of $\log R_i$ given $(\log C_1, \ldots, \log C_n)$ is not in general equal to $(1/a) \log C_i - b/a$ as one might have thought by just solving the equation $\log C_i = a \log R_i + b + u_i$.

1.4.2 Exogeneity

Consider the parametric statistical model $(\mathcal{Y} \times \mathcal{X}, \{P_\theta, \theta \in \Theta\})$. The variables $Y \in \mathcal{Y}$ and $X \in \mathcal{X}$ are observed. It is assumed that the distribution of the pair (Y, X) belongs to the family $\{P_\theta, \theta \in \Theta\}$. It is always possible to "condition" the model upon X, i.e., to consider the parametric conditional model $(\mathcal{Y}, \mathcal{P}_x = \{P_{\theta,x}, \theta \in \Theta\})$ where $\mathcal{P}_x$ is the family of conditional distributions for Y given $X = x$.

It is, however, intuitively clear that consideration of the conditional model leads to a loss of information about θ if the marginal distribution of X, which is ignored in the conditional model, depends on θ. This will be made more precise in Chapter 3.

More generally, if $\Theta = A \times B$, $\theta = (\alpha, \beta)'$, $\alpha \in A$, $\beta \in B$, and if one is interested in α, the *parameter of interest,* but not in β, the *nuisance parameter*, one does not loose information about α when conditioning on X if X is exogenous in the following sense.

Definition 1.8: *Consider the model*

$$(\mathcal{Y} \times \mathcal{X}, \{P_\theta, \theta \in \Theta = A \times B\}).$$

Then X is exogenous for $\alpha \in A$ if the marginal distribution of X does not depend on α and if the conditional distribution of Y given $X = x$ depends only on α and hence not on $\beta \in B$.

In the dominated case where (Y, X) has a density $\ell(y, x; \theta)$ with respect to a measure μ, the exogeneity condition on X for α becomes

$$\ell(y, x; \alpha, \beta) = \ell(y \mid x; \alpha)\ \ell(x; \beta),$$

where $\ell(y, x; \alpha)$ denotes the conditional density of Y given $X = x$ and $\ell(x; \beta)$ denotes the marginal density of X.

Remark 1.2: Definition 1.8 can be readily generalized to a concept of exogeneity of X for $\alpha = g(\theta)$. It suffices that there exists a function $\beta = h(\theta)$ such that θ and (α, β) are in a bijective relationship and such that Definition 1.8 is satisfied for the parameterization $\theta^* = (\alpha, \beta) \in \Theta^* = A \times B$.

Moreover, as illustrated by the next example, the exogeneity condition depends on the chosen parameter of interest.

Example 1.26: Consider the simplified equilibrium model

$$\begin{aligned} D_t &= a + 2P_t + u_{1t}, \\ S_t &= c + u_{2t}, \qquad t = 1, \dots, T, \\ Q_t &= D_t = S_t, \end{aligned}$$

where the T vectors (u_{1t}, u_{2t}) are iid $N(0, \mathbf{I})$. The reduced form of the model is

$$\begin{aligned} P_t &= \frac{c - a}{2} + \frac{u_{2t} - u_{1t}}{2}, \\ Q_t &= c + u_{2t}, \qquad t = 1, \dots, T. \end{aligned}$$

The conditional distribution of $P = (P_1, \dots, P_T)$ given $Q = (Q_1, \dots, Q_T)$ is the product of the normal distributions $N((Q_t - a)/2, 1/4)$, $t = 1, \dots, T$. The marginal distribution of $Q = (Q_1, \dots, Q_T)$ is the product of the normal distributions $N(c, 1)$. It follows that Q is exogenous for a.

The conditional distribution of $Q = (Q_1, \dots, Q_T)$ given $P = (P_1, \dots, P_T)$ is the product of the normal distributions $N(P_t + (c + a)/2; 1/2)$. The marginal distribution of P is the product of the normal distributions $N((c - a)/2, 1/2)$. These two distributions depend on a and c. Thus P is exogenous neither for a nor for c. In contrast, from Remark 1.2, P is exogenous for $c + a$.

1.5 Dynamic Models

1.5.1 Definitions

In the previous example, variables were indexed by time t, t being a date or period index. This particular interpretation of the time index, however, did not affect the development of the proposed models. In contrast, in the models that are considered in this section, the natural ordering of the "time" variable plays an essential role.

Definition 1.9: *A dynamic model is a statistical model $(\mathcal{Y}, \mathcal{P})$ in which the observations $Y = (Y_1, \dots, Y_t, \dots, Y_T)$ are indexed by time and are not independent. If the observations are independent, the model is said to be static.*

The nonindependence assumption implies a temporal or dynamic link between the observed variables. When the dynamic model is parametric and dominated by a measure $\mu = \bigotimes_{t=1}^{T} \mu_t$, a distribution P_θ in the family $\mathcal{P} = \{P_\theta, \theta \in \Theta\}$ is characterized by its density

$$\ell(y; \theta) = \prod_{t=1}^{T} \ell(y_t \mid y_{t-1}, \dots, y_1; \theta),$$

where $\ell(y_t \mid y_{t-1}, \dots, y_1; \theta)$ denotes the conditional density of Y_t given $Y_{t-1} = y_{t-1}, \dots, Y_1 = y_1$, and where the term corresponding to $t = 1$ is, by convention, the marginal density of Y_1.

Now suppose that the vector Y_t is partitioned into two subvectors $Y_t^{(1)}$ and $Y_t^{(2)}$. The conditional density $\ell(y_t \mid y_{t-1}, \dots, y_1; \theta)$ can always be written as

$$\begin{aligned} \ell(y_t \mid y_{t-1}, \dots, y_1; \theta) &= \ell(y_t^{(1)} \mid y_t^{(2)}, y_{t-1}, \dots, y_1; \theta) \\ &\quad \times \ell(y_t^{(2)} \mid y_{t-1}, \dots, y_1; \theta). \end{aligned}$$

If $y_t^{(2)}$ does not appear in the first term of the right-hand side, then $Y_t^{(1)}$ and $Y_t^{(2)}$ are conditionally independent given the past $Y_{t-1}, \dots, Y_1$. See Property B.30. Otherwise, $Y_t^{(1)}$ and $Y_t^{(2)}$ are simultaneously determined, and we say that there is *simultaneity*.

Definition 1.10: *Given a value for the parameter θ, $Y_t^{(1)}$ and $Y_t^{(2)}$ are simultaneous if $Y_t^{(1)}$ and $Y_t^{(2)}$ are not conditionally independent given $Y_{t-1}, \dots, Y_1$.*

Remark 1.3: Definition 1.10 is symmetric in $Y_t^{(1)}$ and $Y_t^{(2)}$ because the concept of independence is. This simultaneity is also called *instantaneous causality* between $Y_t^{(1)}$ and $Y_t^{(2)}$.

Example 1.27: Consider again the equilibrium model

$$\begin{aligned} Q_t &= a + bP_t + u_{1t}, \\ Q_t &= c + u_{2t}, \qquad t = 1, \ldots, T. \end{aligned}$$

If the random vectors $(u_{1t}, u_{2t}), t = 1, \ldots, T$, are independent across time, the model is static. Otherwise, it is dynamic.

The variables Q_t and P_t are simultaneous since the conditional distribution of P_t given $Q_t, P_{t-1}, Q_{t-1}, \ldots, P_1, Q_1$ depends on Q_t. For instance, if (u_{1t}, u_{2t}) is iid $N(0, \mathbf{I})$, this conditional distribution is the normal distribution $N((Q_t - a)/b, 1/b^2)$.

Example 1.28: Now consider the model

$$\begin{aligned} Q_t &= a + bP_{t-1} + u_{1t}, \\ P_t &= c + dP_{t-1} + u_{2t}, \qquad t = 1, \ldots, T, \end{aligned}$$

where (u_{1t}, u_{2t}) are iid $N(0, \mathbf{\Sigma})$ and where P_0 is fixed. The model is dynamic. There is simultaneity if and only if $\mathbf{\Sigma}$ is not diagonal.

1.5.2 Exogeneity and Causality

In a way analogous to what was done in Section 1.4.2, we now consider a dynamic model of the form

$$(\mathcal{Y} \times \mathcal{X}, \{P_\theta, \ \theta \in \Theta\}),$$

where

$$\begin{aligned} Y &= (Y_1, \ldots, Y_T) \in \mathcal{Y}, \\ X &= (X_1, \ldots, X_T) \in \mathcal{X}, \end{aligned}$$

and

$$\Theta = A \times B, \ \theta = (\alpha, \beta)', \ \alpha \in A, \ \beta \in B.$$

Suppose that the parameter of interest is α. Assume that the general Definition 1.8 of exogeneity is satisfied so that

$$\ell(y, x; \ \alpha, \beta) = \ell(y \mid x; \ \alpha) \ \ell(x; \ \beta).$$

One can readily see that this equality can also be written as

$$\ell(y, x; \alpha, \beta) = \prod_{t=1}^{T} \ell(y_t \mid y_{t-1}, \ldots, y_1, x_T, \ldots, x_1; \alpha) \times \prod_{t=1}^{T} \ell(x_t \mid x_{t-1}, \ldots, x_1; \beta). \quad (1.15)$$

Note that all the x variables appear in each term of the first product on the right-hand side.

a) Sequential Exogeneity

There is another definition of exogeneity that is intrinsic to dynamic models.

Definition 1.11: *The variable X is sequentially exogenous for α if for every t*

$$\ell(y_t, x_t \mid y_{t-1}, x_{t-1}, \ldots, y_1, x_1; \alpha, \beta) = \ell(y_t \mid x_t, y_{t-1}, x_{t-1}, \ldots, y_1, x_1; \alpha) \times \ell(x_t \mid y_{t-1}, x_{t-1}, \ldots, y_1, x_1; \beta).$$

This definition implies that the joint density of (x, y) is

$$\ell(y, x; \alpha, \beta) = \prod_{t=1}^{T} \ell(y_t \mid x_t, y_{t-1}, x_{t-1}, \ldots, y_1, x_1; \alpha) \times \prod_{t=1}^{T} \ell(x_t \mid y_{t-1}, x_{t-1}, \ldots, y_1, x_1; \beta). \quad (1.16)$$

As in (1.15), equation (1.16) provides a factorization of $\ell(y, x; \alpha, \beta)$ into two terms of which one depends on α only and the other on β only. Unlike (1.15), however, the two products in (1.16) cannot, in general, be interpreted as densities. In the next examples, we shall also see that exogeneity does not imply sequential exogeneity and vice versa. In fact, it is for such a reason that we have not called sequential exogeneity *weak exogeneity* as is sometimes done.

b) Granger Causality

To relate the previous two notions of exogeneity, it is useful to introduce the following notion of causality due to Granger.

Definition 1.12: *Given a value for the parameter θ, Y does not cause X in the Granger sense if, for every t X_t is conditionally independent of $(Y_{t-1}, \dots, Y_1)$ given $(X_{t-1}, \dots, X_1)$.*

This definition implies that the past of Y does not contain additional information on the current value of X given the past of X. In terms of densities, this definition becomes

$$\forall t, \ \ell(x_t \mid y_{t-1}, x_{t-1}, \dots, y_1, x_1; \theta) = \ell(x_t \mid x_{t-1}, \dots, x_1; \theta).$$

Another definition equivalent to the previous one is given by:

Property 1.2: *The variable Y does not cause the variable X in the Granger sense if and only if Y_t is conditionally independent of $(X_{t+1}, \dots, X_T)$ given $(X_t, Y_{t-1}, X_{t-1}, \dots, Y_1, X_1)$. This latter condition defines an equivalent concept of noncausality due to Sims.*

PROOF: The density $\ell(y, x; \theta)$ can always be written in the following two ways

$$\begin{aligned}
\ell(y, x; \theta) &= \prod_{t=1}^{T} \ell(y_t \mid y_{t-1}, \dots, y_1, x_T, \dots, x_1; \theta) \\
&\quad \times \prod_{t=1}^{T} \ell(x_t \mid x_{t-1}, \dots, x_1; \theta) \\
&= \prod_{t=1}^{T} \ell(y_t \mid x_t, y_{t-1}, x_{t-1}, \dots, y_1, x_1; \theta) \\
&\quad \times \prod_{t=1}^{T} \ell(x_t \mid y_{t-1}, x_{t-1}, \dots, y_1, x_1; \theta).
\end{aligned}$$

If Y does not cause X in the Granger sense, the second term in each of the products are identical. It follows that their first products are equal. Then, by induction, it follows that these products are also equal term by term. Hence Y_t is conditionally independent of $(X_{t+1}, \dots, X_T)$ given $(X_t, Y_{t-1}, X_{t-1}, \dots, Y_1, X_1)$. The converse is proved similarly. □

These two equivalent definitions of causality can be used to establish the following result.

Property 1.3: *If Y does not cause X, then X is sequentially exogenous for α if and only if X is exogenous for α.*

PROOF:

(i) Necessity: Equation (1.16) becomes

$$\begin{aligned} \ell(y,x;\alpha,\beta) &= \prod_{t=1}^{T} \ell(y_t \mid x_t, y_{t-1}, x_{t-1}, \ldots, y_1, x_1; \alpha) \\ &\quad \times \prod_{t=1}^{T} \ell(x_t \mid x_{t-1}, \ldots, x_1; \beta). \end{aligned}$$

Since the second product is the conditional density of X, the first product is the conditional density of Y given X. Hence X is exogenous for α.

(ii) Sufficiency: Using Property 1.2, equation (1.15) can be written as

$$\begin{aligned} \ell(y,x;\alpha,\beta) &= \prod_{t=1}^{T} \ell(y_t \mid y_{t-1}, \ldots, y_1, x_t, \ldots, x_1; \alpha) \\ &\quad \times \prod_{t=1}^{T} \ell(x_t \mid x_{t-1}, \ldots, x_1; \beta). \end{aligned}$$

This implies (by induction) that for every t

$$\begin{aligned} &\ell(y_t, x_t \mid y_{t-1}, x_{t-1}, \ldots, y_1, x_1; \alpha, \beta) \\ &\quad = \ell(y_t \mid x_t, y_{t-1}, x_{t-1} \ldots, y_1, x_1; \alpha) \\ &\quad\quad \times \ell(x_t \mid y_{t-1}, x_{t-1}, \ldots, y_1, x_1; \beta), \end{aligned}$$

which is sequential exogeneity. □

c) Strong Exogeneity

Property 1.3 naturally introduces a third definition of exogeneity.

Definition 1.13: *The variable X is strongly exogenous for α if X is sequentially exogenous for α and if Y does not cause X.*

On the one hand, Property 1.3 shows that X is *a fortiori* exogenous for α if it is strongly exogenous for α. On the other hand, this property shows that an equivalent definition of strong exogeneity for α is the conjunction of exogeneity for α with the noncausality of Y on X.

Example 1.29: Consider the equilibrium model

$$\begin{aligned} Q_t &= a + bP_t + u_{1t}, \\ P_t &= c + dP_{t-1} + u_{2t}, \quad P_0 \text{ fixed}, t = 1, \dots, T, \end{aligned}$$

where (u_{1t}, u_{2t}) is iid $N(0, \mathbf{I})$.

Then $P = (P_1, \dots, P_T)$ is sequentially exogenous for (a, b) because the conditional distribution of Q_t given $(P_t, Q_{t-1}, P_{t-1}, \dots, Q_1, P_1)$ is $N(a + bP_t, 1)$ while the conditional distribution of P_t given $(Q_{t-1}, P_{t-1}, \dots, Q_1, P_1)$ is $N(c + dP_{t-1}, 1)$.

This latter distribution is also the conditional distribution of P_t given $(P_{t-1}, \dots, P_1)$. Thus Q does not cause P. It follows that P is strongly exogenous for (a, b) and hence exogenous for (a, b).

Example 1.30: Now substitute P_{t+1} for P_t in the first equation of the previous example to obtain

$$\begin{aligned} Q_t &= a + bP_{t+1} + u_{1t}, \\ P_t &= c + dP_{t-1} + u_{2t}, \qquad P_0 \text{ fixed}, t = 1, \dots, T, \end{aligned}$$

where (u_{1t}, u_{2t}) is iid $N(0, \mathbf{I})$.

The conditional distribution of $Q = (Q_1, \dots, Q_T)$ given $P = (P_1, \dots, P_{T+1})$ is the distribution $\bigotimes_{t=1}^{T} N(a + bP_{t+1}, 1)$, while the distribution of P is normal with density equal to the product of the densities of $N(c + dP_{t-1}, 1)$. Hence P is exogenous for (a, b).

The conditional distribution of Q_t given P and $(Q_{t-1}, \dots, Q_1)$ is $N(a + bP_{t+1}, 1)$. Hence, from Property 1.2, Q causes P and strong exogeneity does not hold. In addition, the conditional distribution of Q_t given $P_t, Q_{t-1}, P_{t-1}, \dots, Q_1, P_1$ is obtained from

$$Q_t = a + bc + bdP_t + bu_{2,t+1} + u_{1t}.$$

Thus this distribution is $N(a + bc + bdP_t, 1 + b^2)$. It follows that P is not sequentially exogenous for (a, b).

Example 1.31: Lastly, consider the model

$$\begin{aligned} Q_t &= a + bP_t + u_{1t}, \\ P_t &= c + dQ_{t-1} + u_{2t}, \quad Q_0 \text{ fixed}, t = 1, \dots, T, \end{aligned}$$

where (u_{1t}, u_{2t}) is iid $N(0, \mathbf{I})$.

The conditional distribution of Q_t given $(P_t, Q_{t-1}, P_{t-1}, \dots, Q_1, P_1)$ is $N(a+bP_t, 1)$, while the conditional distribution of P_t given $(Q_{t-1}, P_{t-1},$

$\ldots, Q_1, P_1)$ is $N(c + dQ_{t-1}, 1)$. Hence P is sequentially exogenous for (a, b). However, Q causes P since the conditional distribution of P_t given $P_{t-1}, \ldots, P_1$ is $N(c+da+dbP_{t-1}, 1+d^2)$ and differs from the conditional distribution of P_t given $(Q_{t-1}, P_{t-1}, \ldots, Q_1, P_1)$. Thus strong exogeneity does not hold.

Finally, the distribution of P is normal with density equal to the product of the conditional densities of $N(c + da + dbP_{t-1}, 1 + d^2), t = 2, \ldots, T$ and the density of $N(c+dQ_0, 1)$. Since this density depends on (a, b), then P is not exogenous for (a, b).

1.5.3 Formulation of Dynamic Models

In general, the formulation of a dynamic model begins with the choice of variables that are exogenous for the set of parameters of interest θ. For every t, let X_t be the vector of exogenous variables, and let Y_t be the vector of variables to be explained. The variables Y_t are said to be *endogenous.* Then hypotheses on the conditional distribution of $Y = (Y_1, \ldots, Y_T)'$ given $X = (X_1, \ldots, X_T)' = (x_1, \ldots, x_T)'$ are made, i.e., a conditional model is defined where X is viewed as nonstochastic. This conditional model is the basic model within which the concepts of a static model, simultaneity, causality, and exogeneity for some parameters are considered. In general, such a model is defined through a structural form similar to (1.7)–(1.9).

a) Structural Form

To simplify, assume that there are no latent variables. One formulates the observable *structural form*

$$g(Y_t, Y_{t-1}, \ldots, Y_{t-p}, X_t, X_{t-1}, \ldots, X_{t-q}, u_t) = 0, \qquad (1.17)$$

for $t = 1, \ldots, T$, given the initial conditions

$$y_0, \ldots, y_{1-p} \quad \text{and} \quad x_0, \ldots, x_{1-q}.$$

The variables $Y_{t-1}, \ldots, Y_{t-p}$ appearing in (1.17) are called *lagged endogenous variables*, and the disturbances u_t's are unobserved random variables with zero means. Hypotheses on the distribution of $u_t, t = 1, \ldots, T$, are made. A model is parametric if the family of possible distributions for $u = (u_1, \ldots, u_T)$ and the family of functions g both depend on a finite number of parameters only. Let θ denote the parameter vector.

b) Reduced Form

The coherency condition ensures that (1.17) can be solved for Y_t uniquely to obtain the *reduced form*

$$Y_t = h(Y_{t-1}, \ldots, Y_{t-p}, X_t, X_{t-1}, \ldots, X_{t-q}, u_t), \tag{1.18}$$

which defines Y_t as a function of the lagged endogenous variables, the exogenous variables, and the disturbance at time t.

c) Final Form

If one eliminates $Y_{t-1}, \ldots, Y_{t-p}$ recursively from (1.18), one can express Y_t as a function of $u_t, u_{t-1}, \ldots, u_1, X_t, X_{t-1}, \ldots, X_1$ and the initial conditions as follows

$$Y_t = f_t(X_t, X_{t-1}, \ldots, X_1, u_t, \ldots, u_1). \tag{1.19}$$

d) Multipliers

When g is a linear function, then h and f_t are also linear functions. In this case

$$h^*(y_{t-1}, \ldots, y_{t-p}, x_t, \ldots, x_{t-q}) = h(y_{t-1}, \ldots, y_{t-p}, x_t, \ldots, x_{t-q}, 0)$$

is interpreted as the conditional expectation of Y_t given $Y_{t-1} = y_{t-1}$, $\ldots, Y_{t-p} = y_{t-p}$, and one can define *short-term multipliers* as partial derivatives of h^* with respect to the components of x_t. Similarly

$$f_t^*(x_t, x_{t-1}, \ldots, x_t) = f_t(x_t, x_{t-1}, \ldots, x_1, 0, \ldots, 0)$$

is interpreted as the mathematical expectation of Y_t, and the partial derivative of f_t^* with respect to a component of x_{t-i} measures the effect of a unit change in that component of x_{t-i} on this expectation. These partial derivatives are called *dynamic multipliers.* Lastly, if one sets all the x_t's to some given values x and, if all the u_t's are zero, then y_t may converge to some limit y called *long-run equilibrium* that satisfies

$$g(y, \ldots, y, x, \ldots, x, 0) = 0, \tag{1.20}$$

or

$$y = h(y, \ldots, y, x, \ldots, x, 0), \tag{1.21}$$

or

$$y = \lim_{t \to \infty} f_t(x, \ldots, x, 0, \ldots, 0). \tag{1.22}$$

The latter equation, also written $y = F(x)$, is the *long-run form* of the model, and the partial derivative of F with respect to the components of x are called *long-term multipliers.*

Given linearity of g, multipliers only depend on those parameters in θ that define g. In particular, hypotheses on multipliers imply constraints on θ.

Example 1.32: Consider the equilibrium model

$$\begin{aligned} D_t &= a + bP_t + u_{1t}, \\ S_t &= c + dP_{t-1} + ex_t + fx_{t-1} + u_{2t}, \\ Q_t &= D_t = S_t, \qquad t = 1, \ldots, T, \end{aligned}$$

where x_t is an exogenous variable, and P_0 and x_0 are fixed.

The model can also be written as

$$\begin{aligned} Q_t &= a + bP_t + u_{1t}, \\ Q_t &= c + dP_{t-1} + ex_t + fx_{t-1} + u_{2t}, \quad t = 1, \ldots, T. \end{aligned}$$

This is the (observable) structural form where Q_t and P_t are the endogenous variables.

The reduced form is

$$\begin{aligned} P_t &= \frac{c-a}{b} + \frac{d}{b}P_{t-1} + \frac{e}{b}x_t + \frac{f}{b}x_{t-1} + \frac{u_{2t} - u_{1t}}{b}, \\ Q_t &= c + dP_{t-1} + ex_t + fx_{t-1} + u_{2t}. \end{aligned}$$

Thus the short-term multipliers are

$$\begin{aligned} e/b \quad &\text{for} \quad P_t, \\ e \quad &\text{for} \quad Q_t. \end{aligned}$$

The final form is

$$\begin{aligned} P_t &= \sum_{i=0}^{t-1} \left(\frac{c-a}{b} + \frac{e}{b}x_{t-i} + \frac{f}{b}x_{t-1-i} + \frac{1}{b}(u_{2,t-i} - u_{1,t-i}) \right) \left(\frac{d}{b} \right)^i \\ &\quad + p_0 \left(\frac{d}{b} \right)^t, \end{aligned}$$

$$\begin{aligned}
Q_t &= c + p_0 d\left(\frac{d}{b}\right)^{t-1} + ex_t + fx_{t-1} + u_{2t} \\
&\quad + d\sum_{i=0}^{t-2}\left(\frac{c-a}{b} + \frac{e}{b}x_{t-1-i} + \frac{f}{b}x_{t-2-i}\right. \\
&\quad \left. + \frac{1}{b}(u_{2,t-1-i} - u_{1,t-1-i})\right)\left(\frac{d}{b}\right)^{i}.
\end{aligned}$$

Hence the dynamic multipliers for P_t, for example, are

$$\frac{e}{b}, \frac{ed}{b^2} + \frac{f}{b}, \ldots, \left(\frac{d}{b}\right)^{i-1}\left(\frac{ed}{b^2} + \frac{f}{b}\right), \ldots$$

If $\mid d/b \mid < 1$, there is a long-run equilibrium characterized by

$$\begin{aligned}
Q &= a + bP, \\
Q &= c + dP + (e+f)x.
\end{aligned}$$

Thus the long-run form is

$$\begin{aligned}
P &= \frac{c-a}{b-d} + \frac{e+f}{b-d}x, \\
Q &= \frac{bc-ad}{b-d} + \frac{b(e+f)}{b-d}x,
\end{aligned}$$

and the long-term multipliers are $(e+f)/(b-d)$ for P and $b(e+f)/(b-d)$ for Q.

One can readily check that the long-term multipliers are equal to the infinite sums of dynamic multipliers. Thus each multiplier can be viewed as measuring the effect of a permanent change in one unit of an exogenous variable on an endogenous variable.

1.6 Exercises

EXERCISE 1.1: Let $(\mathcal{Y}, \mathcal{P})$ be a homogenous model. Show that

$$\forall A \subset \mathcal{Y}, \forall P, Q \in \mathcal{P} : P(A) = 0 \Leftrightarrow Q(A) = 0.$$

EXERCISE 1.2:

a) Verify that the cumulative distribution function of a probability distribution P on $\mathbb{R}$ is right continuous when it is defined by $F(x) = P((-\infty, x])$.

b) Prove that a cumulative distribution function can be characterized by its values at the rational numbers, and that the set of cumulative distribution functions on $\mathbb{R}$ has the cardinality of the continuum. Conclude that any family of distributions on $\mathbb{R}$ can be indexed by a real parameter.

EXERCISE 1.3: Let $Y_1, \ldots, Y_n$ be a random sample from the exponential distribution of which the density is

$$(\mathbf{1}_{y \geq \theta}) \exp\left(-(y-\theta)\right), \theta \in \mathbb{R}.$$

a) Find the joint density of the n observations.

b) For $n = 1$ and $n = 2$, graph the density and the likelihood function.

EXERCISE 1.4: To explain the diffusion of a durable good among households one specifies the logistic model

$$y_t = \frac{1}{1 + \exp(at + b)}, \quad t = 1, \ldots, T,$$

where y_t is the percentage of households having the durable good at time t and where a and b are unknown parameters.

a) Study how y changes with t and discuss the expected sign of the parameter a.

b) Show that $\log\left(y_t/(1-y_t)\right)$ is a linear function in the parameters. Conclude that the following model is linear

$$y_t = \frac{1}{1 + \exp(at + b + u_t)} \quad t = 1, \ldots, T,$$

where u_t is a disturbance with zero mean.

c) Consider the model

$$y_t = \frac{k}{1 + \exp(at + b + u_t)},$$

where k is a parameter between 0 and 1.

(i) Interpret k.

(ii) Can this model be made linear in a, b, and k by a suitable transformation of the variable y?

EXERCISE 1.5: Consider the linear model $Y = X_1 b_1 + \cdots + X_K b_K + u$, $Eu = 0$, where the parameters $b_1, \ldots, b_K$ satisfy some linear constraints. Show that the model thus obtained is also linear.

EXERCISE 1.6: For each of the following deterministic models relating a variable y to another variable x, indicate those that can be reduced to linear models. Also indicate where disturbances should appear.

$$
\begin{array}{rlr}
i) & y_t = a(x_t - 2) & a \in \mathbb{R}. \\
ii) & y_t = a_0 + a_1 x_t + a_2 x_t^2 & a_0, a_1, a_2 \in \mathbb{R}. \\
iii) & y_t = a_0 x_t^{a_1} & a_0, a_1 \in \mathbb{R}. \\
iv) & y_t = \exp(a_0 + a_1 x_t + a_2 \log x_t) & a_0, a_1, a_2 \in \mathbb{R}. \\
v) & y_t = (a_0 x_t - a_1)/(a_2 x_t - a_3) & a_0, a_1, a_2, a_3 \in \mathbb{R}. \\
vi) & y_t = \min(a_0 x_t + a_1, a_2 x_t + a_3) & a_0, a_1, a_2, a_3 \in \mathbb{R}.
\end{array}
$$

EXERCISE 1.7: Consider an exponential model. The family of densities with respect to a measure μ is

$$
\ell(y; \theta) = C(\theta) h(y) \exp\left(\sum_{j=1}^{r} Q_j(\theta) T_j(y) \right).
$$

Establish the following properties:

a) Since one can use another dominating measure, one can always assume that $h(y) = 1$.

b) The distribution of $T(Y) = (T_1(Y), \ldots, T_r(Y))'$ also belongs to an exponential family.

c) The distribution of $S(Y)$ belongs to an exponential family when S is a bijective differentiable mapping from $\mathcal{Y} \subset \mathbb{R}^n$ into $S(\mathcal{Y}) \subset \mathbb{R}^n$ with a differentiable inverse function.

d) Property c) is not necessarily satisfied if S is not bijective.

EXERCISE 1.8: Consider the sampling model

$$
(\mathcal{Y} = \tilde{\mathcal{Y}}^n, \mathcal{P} = \{P = \tilde{P}^{\otimes n}, \tilde{P} \in \tilde{\mathcal{P}}\}),
$$

where the distributions in the family $\tilde{\mathcal{P}}$ have densities of the form

$$f(y_i;\theta) = \tilde{C}(\theta)\tilde{h}(y_i)\exp\left(\sum_{j=1}^{r} \tilde{Q}_j(\theta)\tilde{T}_j(y_i)\right).$$

Show that this sampling model is exponential and determine its canonical statistics.

EXERCISE 1.9: Consider the dynamic consumption model

$$c_t = b_0 + b_1 c_{t-1} + b_2 r_t + b_3 r_{t-1},$$

where:

- c_t denotes the logarithm of consumption at time t,
- r_t denotes the logarithm of income at time t,
- b_0, b_1, b_2, and b_3 are parameters.

Suppose that the long-run propensity to consume dc/dr is constant. Show that this hypothesis can be formally written as the linear constraint $1 - b_1 = b_2 + b_3$.

EXERCISE 1.10: Given the two distributions $P = f(y) \cdot \mu$ and $P^* = f^*(y) \cdot \mu$, one defines the quantity

$$\mathcal{X}^2(P \mid P^*) = \int_{\mathcal{Y}} \frac{(f(y) - f^*(y))^2}{f^*(y)} \mu(dy) = E^*\left(\frac{f(Y)}{f^*(Y)} - 1\right)^2.$$

a) Show that $\mathcal{X}^2(P \mid P^*) \geq 0$ and that $\mathcal{X}^2(P \mid P^*) = 0$ if and only if $P = P^*$.

b) Verify that

$$\mathcal{X}^2(P \mid P^*) = E^*\left(\frac{f^2(Y)}{f^{*2}(Y)}\right) - 1.$$

c) Compute the value of this quantity when P and P^* are normal distributions. Compare it to the value of the Kullback–Leibler information criterion obtained from Example 1.16. (In particular, one could study the behavior of these two quantities when σ^* and m^* converge to σ and m, respectively.)

EXERCISE 1.11: Consider the disequilibrium model

$$\begin{aligned} D_t &= a_1 P_t + X_{1t} b_1 + u_{1t}, \\ S_t &= a_2 P_t + X_{2t} b_2 + u_{2t}, \\ Q_t &= \min(D_t, S_t), \end{aligned}$$

in which prices can adjust instantaneously at positive rates λ_1 and λ_2 depending on which regime one is in

$$P_t - P_{t-1} = \begin{cases} \lambda_1(D_t - S_t), & \text{if } D_t > S_t, \\ \lambda_2(D_t - S_t), & \text{if } D_t < S_t. \end{cases}$$

The observable variables are X_1, X_2, P, and Q.

a) Which are the endogenous latent variables? Which are the observable endogenous variables?

b) Show that the reduced form exists if the following coherency condition is satisfied: $1 + \lambda_1(a_2 - a_1)$ and $1 + \lambda_2(a_2 - a_1)$ have the same sign. Under what conditions is this satisfied in practice?

c) Determine the observable reduced form of the system.

1.7 References

Brown, B.W. and Mariano, R.S. (1984). "Residual-Based Procedure for Prediction and Estimation in Nonlinear Simultaneous System," *Econometrica*, 52, 321–343.

Chamberlain, G. (1982). "The General Equivalence of Granger and Sims Causality," *Econometrica*, 50, 569–581.

Engle, R.F., Hendry, D.F., and Richard, J.F. (1988). "Exogeneity," *Econometrica*, 51, 277–304.

Ferguson, T.S. (1967). *Mathematical Statistics*, Academic Press.

Florens, J.P. and Mouchart, M. (1982). "A Note on Noncausality," *Econometrica*, 50, 583–591.

Gourieroux, C., Laffont, J.J., and Monfort, A. (1980). "Coherency Conditions in Simultaneous Linear Equation Models with Endogeneous Switching Regimes," *Econometrica*, 48, 675–695.

Granger, C.W.J. (1969). "Investigating Causal Relations by Econometric Models and Cross Spectral Methods, " *Econometrica*, 37, 424–439.

Haavelmo, T. (1944). "The Probability Approach to Economics," supplement to *Econometrica*, 12, 1–118.

Hood, W.C. and Koopmans, T.C. (1953). *Studies in Econometric Method*, Yale University Press.

Kullback, S. (1959). *Information Theory and Statistics*, Wiley.

Sawa, T. (1982). "Information Criteria for Discriminating Among Alternative Regression Models," *Econometrica*, 50, 27–41.

Sims, C. (1972). "Money Income and Causality," *American Economic Review*, 62, 540–552.

CHAPTER 2

Statistical Problems and Decision Theory

2.1 Examples of Statistical Problems

In general, the study of a real phenomenon translates into a number of particular questions to which a researcher wishes answer. For instance, consider the diffusion of a durable good based on answers to surveys at various dates t. A number of related questions can be raised:

- What approximate value can one give to the proportion p_t of households having the durable good at date t. Such a problem is called a *point estimation problem.*

- Instead of looking for a point approximation, it might be preferable to find an interval of "likely"values for p_t. The search for such an interval is referred to as a problem of *interval estimation* or *estimation by confidence regions.*

- Another natural question is whether the quantity bought at time t is larger than that bought at time $t-1$. This reduces to whether $p_t - p_{t-1}$ is larger than $p_{t-1} - p_{t-2}$. Such a question, which has two possible answers, is an example of a *testing problem.*

- Lastly, one might examine the buying behavior at time $t+1$ of a household not possessing the durable good at time t. Because such a behavior can be represented by a random variable indicating the occurrence of the event "buys at time $t+1$," the problem is that of approximating this random variable. Such a problem is called a *prediction problem.*

In the following sections we formalize these problems and we review the methods that have been proposed. The theoretical framework constitutes what is called *Decision Theory.* It is assumed that answers to various questions are based on observations Y generated from a statistical model $(\mathcal{Y}, \mathcal{P})$.

2.2 Decision Rules

2.2.1 Space of Decisions

A statistical problem can be viewed as a problem of choices among various possible responses. In what follows, we call a *decision* such a response. A decision is denoted d and the set of possible decisions is denoted $\mathcal{D}$. Below, we define the spaces of decisions associated with the various statistical problems introduced in the previous section.

a) Point Estimation of the True Value of a Parameter

Because the statistical model is not necessarily parametric, a parameter is defined *via* a mapping g from $\mathcal{P}$ to G that associates a value in G to every distribution in $\mathcal{P}$. The true value g_0 of the parameter corresponds to the true distribution $P_0 \in \mathcal{P}$. In point estimation, the object is to propose an approximate value to the true but unknown value g_0. The possible decisions are the elements of $\mathcal{D} = G$. Here the space of decisions agrees with the parameter space G.

In some cases, to simplify the theoretical analysis, decisions outside G may be considered. For instance, in the case of an election (see Example 1.1), the size N of the population of voters is finite. Hence the possible values for the parameter p_A are $0/N, 1/N, 2/N, \ldots, N/N = 1$. Nonetheless, one usually considers as valid any decision in $\mathcal{D} = [0,1]$.

b) Interval Estimation of g_0

In this case, one proposes a set of approximate values for g_0. A decision is a subset of G and the space of decisions is the set of all subsets of G.

c) Test of an Hypothesis about P_0

There are two possible decisions:

d_0: "I think that the hypothesis is true,"

d_1: "I think that the hypothesis is false."

The space of decisions has two elements only: $\mathcal{D} = \{d_0, d_1\}$.

Sometimes, the space of decisions can be extended to allow for a third response:

d_2: "I cannot decide," or

d_2': "I need additional observations to decide."

d) Choice among Models

Sometimes one has to choose among many competing models $(\mathcal{Y}, \mathcal{P}_k), k = 1, \ldots, K$, where $\mathcal{P}_k \cap \mathcal{P}_\ell = \emptyset$, $\forall\ k \neq \ell$. In this case, a possible response is:

d_k: "I think that the model $(\mathcal{Y}, \mathcal{P}_k)$ is the most adequate description of the observations."

The space of decisions is $\mathcal{D} = \{d_1, \ldots, d_K\}$.

With respect to the decision space, there are only small differences between a testing problem, a problem of model choice, and an estimation problem of a parameter with values in a finite space. In every case, the space of decisions has a finite number of elements.

e) Prediction

Here one wants to approximate a random variable. The possible decisions are the values that can be taken by the variable one wants to predict.

2.2.2 Nonrandomized Decision Rules

Given a statistical problem, a researcher must provide an answer based on the observations. Thus, the researcher must be able to associate a response $\delta(y) \in \mathcal{D}$ to every possible $y \in \mathcal{Y}$.

Definition 2.1: *A nonrandomized decision rule is a mapping δ from the set of observations $\mathcal{Y}$ to the set of decisions $\mathcal{D}$.*

A decision rule δ provides a decision for every set of observations. Thus, it corresponds to an *ex ante* notion, i.e., to a notion prior to the observations. Once the observations are available, the decision that is taken is $\delta(y)$. Thus $\delta(y)$, which is the value of the mapping δ at y, corresponds to an *ex post* notion. Usually some specific names are given to decision rules associated with usual statistical problems. This terminology is summarized in the Table 2.1.

Table 2.1

Problem	δ	$\delta(y)$
Point estimation	Estimator	Estimate
Interval estimation	Confidence region	
Test	Test	Test outcome
Model choice	Criterion	
Prediction	Predictor	Prediction

Example 2.1: Consider again the example of the diffusion of a durable good. Suppose that one draws with equal probability and replacement a sample of size n at time t, and that one observes the response of every household sampled

$$Y_i = \begin{cases} 1, & \text{if the } i\text{th household has the durable good,} \\ 0, & \text{otherwise.} \end{cases}$$

The statistical model is $(\mathcal{Y} = \{0,1\}^n, \mathcal{P} = \{B(1,p_t)^{\otimes n}, p_t \in [0,1]\})$.

Consider the problem of point estimating p_t. The space of decisions is $\mathcal{D} = [0,1]$. A natural approximation for p_t is the proportion of households having the durable good in the sample. The corresponding decision rule (or estimator) is the mapping $\delta = \hat{p}_t$ defined by

$$\delta(y_1, \ldots, y_n) = \hat{p}_t(y_1, \ldots, y_n) = \frac{y_1 + \cdots + y_n}{n} = \overline{y}_n.$$

This mapping takes its values in $\mathcal{D} = [0, 1]$.

If the size of the sample is $n = 1000$ and, if 700 households have the durable good, then the corresponding estimate is $\hat{p}_t(y) = 0.7$.

Example 2.2: Consider now the problem of testing the hypothesis that "more than half of the households have the durable good." This hypothesis can be translated in terms of the parameter p_t. It is satisfied if $g = p_t \in G_0 = (0.5, 1]$, i.e., if $p_t > 0.5$. It is not satisfied otherwise. A decision rule (or test) may be to consider that the hypothesis is true if and only if $\hat{p}_t > 0.5$. Thus, with this rule, if $\hat{p}_t(y) = 0.7$, one is led to accept the hypothesis.

Remark 2.1: The value taken by the decision rule must be known as soon as y is. In particular, the decision rule δ cannot depend on the distribution P_0 (or on a parameter associated to it) since the true distribution P_0 is unknown.

The central problem of statistical decision theory consists in searching for decision rules. The theory provides decision rules before the observations are available. The only information *ex ante* that one has about the observations is that they are generated by a distribution P_0 in the family $\mathcal{P}$. *Ex ante*, the observation Y is random, and the decision $\delta(Y)$, which is a function of Y, is also random. Its distribution, which is the induced distribution of P_0 by the mapping δ, is unknown since P_0 is known to belong to $\mathcal{P}$ only. At this stage, one can note that a decision does not depend on the unknown distribution P_0 (see Remark 2.1), but its distribution does. In contrast, *ex post*, the value $\delta(y)$ taken by the decision rule is deterministic.

For a given statistical problem there is a large number of possible decision rules (as many as measurable mappings from $\mathcal{Y}$ to $\mathcal{D}$). Among these, some are of little interest.

Example 2.3: In the example of the diffusion of a durable good one may propose the estimator $\tilde{p}_t$ of p_t which is defined by the constant mapping $\tilde{p}_t(y) = 0.7$, $\forall\ y \in \mathcal{Y}$. This decision rule does not take into account the observations, and is therefore not very interesting. Note, however, that this decision rule may turn out (by chance) to be correct. For instance, if the true value of the parameter p_t happens to be equal to 0.7, this estimator gives the correct answer for any set of observations.

2.2.3 Randomized Decision Rules

Instead of taking a unique decision for each set y of observations, one can extend the space of decision rules by associating a probability distribution defined on $\mathcal{D}$ to every y.

Definition 2.2: *A randomized decision rule is a mapping from $\mathcal{Y}$ to the set of probability distributions defined on $\mathcal{D}$.*

If m denotes a randomized decision rule, $m_y(D)$ is interpreted as the probability of choosing a decision d in D when the observation is y. Thus a randomized decision rule defines a distribution on $\mathcal{D}$ conditional upon each value of Y.

Clearly, the set of possible randomized decision rules contains the set of possible nonrandomized decision rules. A nonrandomized decision rule δ can be viewed as a randomized decision rule m where m_y is the point mass distribution at $\delta(y)$

$$m_y = \varepsilon_{\delta(y)}, \ \forall \ y \in \mathcal{Y}.$$

This generalization of the notion of decision rules is mainly for mathematical convenience. The set of randomized decision rules is convex, and some optimization problems, such as those arising in the theory of testing, are easier to solve when sets are convex. In practice, however, it does not seem attractive to give a sponsor of a statistical study a random answer such as "the proportion of households having the durable good is 0.4 with probability 1/2 and 0.7 with probability 1/2."

2.3 Ordering Decision Rules

The developments of decision theory, which are presented in this section, are well suited to problems of estimation, testing, and model choice (see Exercise 2.5). The search for a confidence region, however, can be reduced to the search for a test (see Chapter 19, Volume II), and the search for good predictors can be studied directly (see Chapter 20, Volume II).

2.3.1 Correct Decisions

When the true distribution P_0 is known and belongs to $\mathcal{P}$, it is straightforward to take a correct decision (provided there is no identification problem – see Chapter 3). Such a response is called a *correct decision* and is denoted $\tilde{d}(P_0)$.

a) Point Estimation of g_0

We have $\tilde{d}(P_0) = g_0$.

b) Test of an Hypothesis about P_0

The correct decision is

$$\begin{aligned}\tilde{d}(P_0) &= d_0, \text{ if the hypothesis is satisfied by } P_0,\\ \tilde{d}(P_0) &= d_1, \text{ otherwise.}\end{aligned}$$

Let $\mathcal{P}_0$ be the set of distributions of $\mathcal{P}$ for which the hypothesis is satisfied, and let $\mathcal{P}_1$ be its complement in $\mathcal{P}$. We have

$$\tilde{d}(P_0) = d_0 \mathbb{1}_{P_0 \in \mathcal{P}_0} + d_1 \mathbb{1}_{P_0 \in \mathcal{P}_1}.$$

c) Model Choice

Let d_k denote the decision of asserting that the kth model is correct. We have

$$\tilde{d}(P_0) = d_k, \text{ if } P_0 \in \mathcal{P}_k, \; k = 1, \ldots, K.$$

From these examples we can see that the correct decisions depend on the true but unknown distribution P_0. Hence the correct decisions are infeasible. In the next subsection, we shall retain only decision rules that are "closest" to the correct decisions.

2.3.2 Loss Functions

To solve the problem of finding an appropriate decision rule, one must introduce a measure of loss incurred when the decision taken is d while the true distribution is P_0 and the correct decision is $\tilde{d}_0 = \tilde{d}(P_0)$.

Definition 2.3: *A loss function is a nonnegative real mapping L defined on $\mathcal{D} \times \mathcal{P}$.*

$L(d, P)$ measures the loss incurred from taking the decision d when the true distribution is equal to P. For a given statistical problem, there may exist many loss functions. Loss functions, however, must satisfy some natural conditions. For instance, the loss must be zero if and only if d is a correct decision

$$\forall \; P \in \mathcal{P} : L(d, P) = 0 \Leftrightarrow d = \tilde{d}(P).$$

For the statistical problems introduced earlier, we now present some common loss functions satisfying such a condition.

a) Point Estimation of a Scalar Parameter

To simplify, we consider a parametric model $(\mathcal{Y}, \mathcal{P} = \{P_\theta, \theta \in \Theta\})$ and a scalar function g. The possible decisions are the elements of $G = g(\Theta) \subset I\!R$. The correct decision associated with the distribution P_θ is $\tilde{d}(P_\theta) = g(\theta)$. Thus it seems natural to consider the loss to be a measure of the discrepancy between d and $g(\theta)$. The loss function that is most frequently used is given by the square of the euclidean norm. It is the *quadratic loss function* or *squared error loss function* and is defined by

$$L(d, \theta) = (d - g(\theta))^2 .$$

In the parametric case, one uses the notation $L(d, \theta)$ instead of $L(d, P_\theta)$. The loss function is then defined on $\mathcal{D} \times \Theta$.

Other loss functions are possible. For instance, sometimes one uses the loss function associated with the absolute norm

$$L_1(d, \theta) = \mid d - g(\theta) \mid .$$

Also, one may use truncated versions of the preceding loss functions such as

$$L_1^*(d, \theta) = \begin{cases} \mid d - g(\theta) \mid, & \text{if } \mid d - g(\theta) \mid \leq c, \\ c, & \text{if } \mid d - g(\theta) \mid \geq c. \end{cases}$$

b) Point Estimation of a Parameter Vector

Consider now the case where $g(\theta) \in G \subset I\!R^q$. The most natural generalizations of the quadratic loss function introduced above for the scalar case are the *scalar quadratic loss function*

$$L(d, \theta) = \|d - g\|^2 = \sum_{j=1}^{q} (d_j - g_j(\theta))^2 ,$$

and the family of loss functions

$$L_u(d, \theta) = (u'd - u'g(\theta))^2 ,$$

where $u \in I\!R^q$. The quantity $L_u(d, \theta)$ measures the loss incurred when estimating the linear form $u'g(\theta)$. Considering the losses $L_u(d, \theta)$ for all vectors u allows us to assess the loss in all directions simultaneously.

Similarly, one can extend the loss function L_1 associated with the absolute norm to

$$L_1(d, \theta) = \|d - g(\theta)\|_1 = \sum_{j=1}^{q} \mid d_j - g_j(\theta) \mid ,$$

or

$$L_{1,u}(d,\theta) = \mid u'd - u'g(\theta) \mid,$$

where $u \in I\!R^q$.

c) Test of an Hypothesis about θ

We assume that the hypothesis is true if $\theta \in \Theta_0$ and that the hypothesis is false otherwise. A possible loss function is

$$L(d_0,\theta) = \begin{cases} 0, & \text{if } \theta \in \Theta_0, \\ a_0(\theta) > 0, & \text{otherwise.} \end{cases}$$

$$L(d_1,\theta) = \begin{cases} a_1(\theta) > 0, & \text{if } \theta \in \Theta_0, \\ 0, & \text{otherwise.} \end{cases}$$

This loss function corresponds to the idea that there is no loss if the decision is correct, and a strictly positive loss otherwise.

d) Model Choice

To simplify, we assume that each model $\mathcal{P}_k$ is defined by means of some constraints on θ

$$P \in \mathcal{P}_k \Leftrightarrow \theta \in \Theta_k.$$

The subsets $\Theta_k, k = 1,\ldots,K$ constitute a partition of Θ. The loss function introduced for the testing problem can be readily generalized to

$$L(d_k,\theta) = \begin{cases} 0, & \text{if } \theta \in \Theta_k, \\ a_k(\theta) > 0, & \text{if } \theta \notin \Theta_k, \end{cases}$$

with $k = 1,\ldots,K$.

2.3.3 Ordering Nonrandomized Decision Rules

Given a nonrandomized decision rule δ, the loss resulting from the use of δ is $L(\delta(y), P)$ when the observation is y and the true distribution is P. Prior to the observations, the quantity $L(\delta(Y), P)$ is random. Then one considers the average loss or *risk function*.

Definition 2.4: *The risk function associated with the nonrandomized decision rule δ is the mapping $R(\delta, .)$ from $\mathcal{P}$ to $I\!R^+$ defined by*

$$R(\delta, P) = E_P L(\delta(Y), P) = \int_{\mathcal{Y}} L(\delta(y), P)\, dP(y).$$

When the model is parametric, we use the notation $R(\delta, \theta)$ instead of $R(\delta, P_\theta)$, and we consider $R(\delta, .)$ as a mapping from Θ to $\mathbb{R}^+$.

Using the risk function, we can rank nonrandomized decision rules. A decision rule dominates another one if its average loss is smaller for every possible distribution P.

Definition 2.5: *A decision rule δ_1 (weakly) dominates another decision rule δ_2, i.e., $\delta_1 \succeq \delta_2$, if $R(\delta_1, P) \leq R(\delta_2, P), \forall P \in \mathcal{P}$.*

The relation $\succeq$ is a partial preordering. We shall see that two decision rules may not be comparable. This is the case when there exist some distributions $P_1, P_2 \in \mathcal{P}$ such that

$$R(\delta_1, P_1) < R(\delta_2, P_1) \text{ and } R(\delta_1, P_2) > R(\delta_2, P_2).$$

We now examine the risk functions associated with the usual loss functions introduced earlier. To simplify, we consider the case where the model is parametric $(\mathcal{Y}, \mathcal{P} = \{P_\theta, \theta \in \Theta\})$.

a) Point Estimation of a Scalar Parameter

Consider a point estimator of $g(\theta) \in G \subset \mathbb{R}$. The risk function associated with the quadratic loss function is called the *quadratic risk function* and is given by

$$R(\delta, \theta) = E_\theta \left(\delta(Y) - g(\theta)\right)^2,$$

where E_θ denotes the expectation with respect to the distribution P_θ.

b) Point Estimation of a Parameter Vector

The *scalar quadratic risk function* is defined by

$$R(\delta, \theta) = E_\theta \|\delta(Y) - g(\theta)\|^2 = E_\theta \left(\sum_{j=1}^{q} (\delta_j(Y) - g_j(\theta))^2 \right).$$

c) Test of an Hypothesis about θ

Suppose that the hypothesis is true when $\theta \in \Theta_0$ and is false when $\theta \in \Theta_1 = {}^c\Theta_0$. If the loss function is given by

$$L(d_k, \theta) = \begin{cases} 0, & \text{if } \theta \in \Theta_k, \\ a_k(\theta), & \text{otherwise,} \end{cases}$$

with $k = 0, 1$, then the corresponding risk function is obtained by integration and is given by

$$R(\delta(Y), \theta) = \begin{cases} a_1(\theta) P_\theta(\delta(Y) = d_1), & \text{if } \theta \in \Theta_0, \\ a_0(\theta) P_\theta(\delta(Y) = d_0), & \text{if } \theta \in \Theta_1. \end{cases}$$

This formula shows the dependence of the risk function on the probabilities of taking incorrect decisions, namely on:

- the probabilities of stating that the hypothesis is false when it is true
$$P_\theta(\delta(Y) = d_1),$$
where $\theta \in \Theta_0$,
- the probabilities of stating that the hypothesis is true when it is false
$$P_\theta(\delta(Y) = d_0),$$
where $\theta \in \Theta_1 = {}^c\Theta_0$.

These probabilities are called probabilities of *Type I error* and *Type II error*, respectively.

The problem of model choice is treated in a similar fashion.

2.3.4 Ordering Randomized Decision Rules

The ordering discussed in the preceding section can be extended to randomized decision rules. Consider a randomized decision rule m. Given the observation y, m_y defines a distribution on $\mathcal{D}$. Thus, when the true distribution is P, the average loss given y is

$$\int_{\mathcal{D}} L(d, P) dm_y(d).$$

Ex ante only the distribution of Y is given. Thus *ex ante* the average loss or risk is

$$R(m, P) = \int_{\mathcal{Y}} \left(\int_{\mathcal{D}} L(d, P) dm_y(d) \right) dP(y). \tag{2.1}$$

Thus the risk is obtained by integrating the loss function successively with respect to the distribution of d conditional upon $Y = y$ and the marginal distribution of Y.

When the randomized decision rule m corresponds to the nonrandomized decision rule δ, we have $m_y = \varepsilon_{\delta(y)}$, which is the distribution with mass point at $\delta(y)$. Thus

$$\begin{aligned} R(m,P) &= \int_{\mathcal{Y}} \left(\int_{\mathcal{D}} L(d,P)\; d\varepsilon_{\delta(y)}(d) \right) P(y) \\ &= \int_{\mathcal{Y}} L\left(\delta(y),P\right) dP(y) \\ &= R(\delta,P). \end{aligned}$$

Hence the two definitions agree, and the ordering of the randomized decision rules extends that of the nonrandomized decision rules.

Definition 2.6: *The randomized decision rule m_1 (weakly) dominates the randomized decision rule m_2, i.e., $m_1 \succeq m_2$, if $R(m_1,P) \leq R(m_2,P)$, $\forall\ P \in \mathcal{P}$.*

2.3.5 Admissible Decision Rules

As the example in the next section illustrates, there does not exist in general an *optimal decision rule*, i.e., a rule that dominates any other rule. The preceding preordering, however, can eliminate some decision rules for which there exists a dominating rule.

Definition 2.7: *A decision rule m^* is admissible if there does not exist a decision rule m that strictly dominates it, i.e., if there does not exist a rule m such that $R(m,P) \leq R(m^*,P)$ for all $P \in \mathcal{P}$ with at least a strict inequality for some P.*

Clearly, one should retain only decision rules that are admissible. The problem of selecting a decision rule, however, is not completely resolved for there may exist a large number of admissible decision rules. As we shall see, for the partial preordering to become a total preordering, either additional criteria must be imposed or the partial preordering must be modified appropriately.

2.4 An Example

With the help of an example, we now illustrate the definitions that have been introduced.

2.4.1 The Model

Let Y be one observation on a random variable following a Bernoulli distribution $B(1, \theta)$, i.e., $f(y; \theta) = \theta^y (1-\theta)^{1-y}$, where the parameter θ can take only the two possible values 1/3 or 1/2. Thus the parameter space is $\Theta = \{1/3, 1/2\}$.

2.4.2 The Estimation Problem

We are interested in point estimation of the parameter θ. Here the space of decisions agrees with the parameter space: $\mathcal{D} = \Theta = \{1/3, 1/2\}$. A nonrandomized decision rule is a mapping from $\mathcal{Y} = \{0, 1\}$ to $\mathcal{D} = \{1/3, 1/2\}$. There are $2^2 = 4$ nonrandomized decision rules, which are given by

$$\begin{aligned} \delta_1(y) &= 1/3, \qquad & \delta_3(y) &= 1/3y + 1/2(1-y), \\ \delta_2(y) &= 1/2, \qquad & \delta_4(y) &= 1/3(1-y) + 1/2y. \end{aligned}$$

Because the first two decision rules are constant, these rules do not depend on the observation.

There is an infinity of randomized decision rules. Each one is characterized by the probability assigned to the value 1/3 when $y = 0$ and by the probability assigned to the value 1/3 when $y = 1$. We denote these two probabilities by $m(0)$ and $m(1)$ respectively. We have $0 \leq m(0) \leq 1$ and $0 \leq m(1) \leq 1$.

The nonrandomized decision rules correspond to the cases where $m(0)$ and $m(1)$ are equal to 0 or 1.

2.4.3 Risks Associated with Nonrandomized Decision Rules

For each decision rule, the risk function is characterized by its values for all possible values of the parameter. Thus, in the present example, it is completely defined by two values. If we consider the quadratic loss function $L(d, \theta) = (d - \theta)^2$, the risk function associated with a nonrandomized decision rule δ is

$$R(\delta, \theta) = E_\theta \left(\delta(Y) - \theta\right)^2,$$

i.e.

$$R(\delta, \theta) = \begin{cases} E_{1/3}\left(\delta(Y) - 1/3\right)^2, & \text{if } \theta = 1/3, \\ E_{1/2}\left(\delta(Y) - 1/2\right)^2, & \text{if } \theta = 1/2. \end{cases}$$

Table 2.2

Decision rules	Parameter values	
	$\theta = 1/3$	$\theta = 1/2$
δ_1	0	1/36
δ_2	1/36	0
δ_3	1/54	1/72
δ_4	1/108	1/72

Hence we obtain Table 2.2.

The estimator δ_4 strictly dominates δ_3 since the two values of the risk function 1/108 and 1/72 are smaller than 1/54 and 1/72, respectively. The estimators $\delta_1, \delta_2, \delta_4$ are not comparable. They are admissible non-randomized decision rules.

In the present example, each estimator can be associated with a point in $\mathbb{R}^2$ of which the coordinates are the values of the corresponding risk function. An estimator is admissible if the negative orthant drawn from the corresponding point does not contain any other point.

2.4.4 Risks Associated with Randomized Decision Rules

A randomized decision rule m_y associates a distribution with probabilities

$$\{m(0), (1 - m(0))\}, \quad \text{when } y = 0,$$

and a distribution with probabilities

$$\{m(1), (1 - m(1))\}, \quad \text{when } y = 1.$$

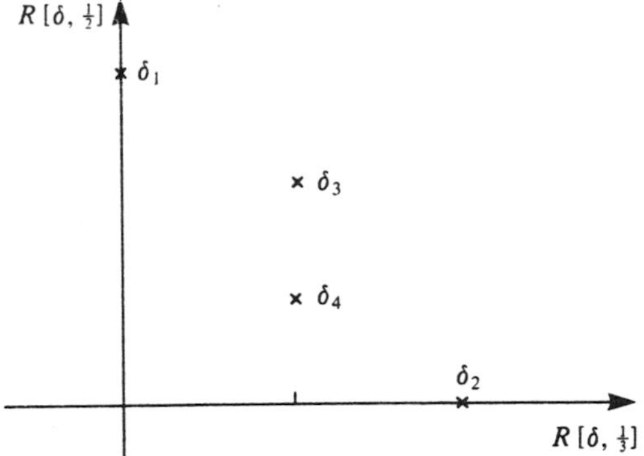

Figure 2.1: Nonrandomized Decision Rules

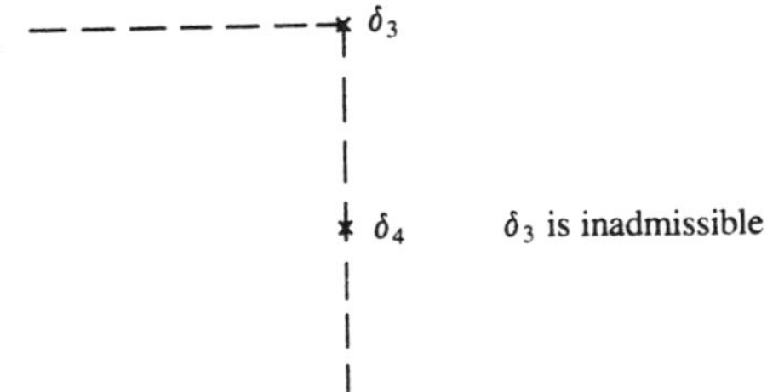

Figure 2.2: Inadmissible Decision Rules

The loss function is

$$L(m_y, \theta) = \int_{\mathcal{D}} (d - \theta)^2 dm_y(d),$$

i.e.

$$L(m_y, \theta) = \begin{cases} m(0)(1/3 - \theta)^2 + (1 - m(0))\,(1/2 - \theta)^2, & \text{if } y = 0, \\ m(1)(1/3 - \theta)^2 + (1 - m(1))\,(1/2 - \theta)^2, & \text{if } y = 1. \end{cases}$$

More compactly, the loss function can be written as

$$\begin{aligned} L(m_y, \theta) &= (1 - y)\left[m(0)(1/3 - \theta)^2 + (1 - m(0))\,(1/2 - \theta)^2\right] \\ &\quad + y\left[m(1)(1/3 - \theta)^2 + (1 - m(1))\,(1/2 - \theta)^2\right]. \end{aligned}$$

The risk function is obtained by integrating the loss function with respect to the Bernoulli distribution $B(1, \theta)$, i.e., by taking the expectation of the loss. Since $E_\theta Y = \theta$, we obtain

$$\begin{aligned} R(m,\theta) &= (1-\theta)\left[m(0)(1/3-\theta)^2 + (1-m(0))\,(1/2-\theta)^2\right] \\ &\quad +\theta\left[m(1)(1/3-\theta)^2 + (1-m(1))\,(1/2-\theta)^2\right]. \end{aligned}$$

Note that the risk associated with a nonrandomized decision rule is obtained by considering the limit case where $m(0)$ and $m(1)$ are equal to 0 or 1. For instance, δ_3, which corresponds to $m(0) = 0$ and $m(1) = 1$, gives a risk function

$$R(\delta_3, \theta) = (1-\theta)(1/2-\theta)^2 + \theta(1/3-\theta)^2.$$

Similarly, δ_4, which corresponds to $m(0) = 1$ and $m(1) = 0$, gives a risk function

$$R(\delta_4, \theta) = (1-\theta)(1/3-\theta)^2 + \theta(1/2-\theta)^2.$$

When $m(0)$ and $m(1)$ vary between 0 and 1, the points in $\mathbb{R}^2$ associated with the randomized decision rules generate a convex set. One can verify that its vertices correspond to the limit cases where $m(0)$ and $m(1)$ are equal to 0 or 1. Thus this convex set is also the convex hull based on the four points associated with the four nonrandomized decision rules.

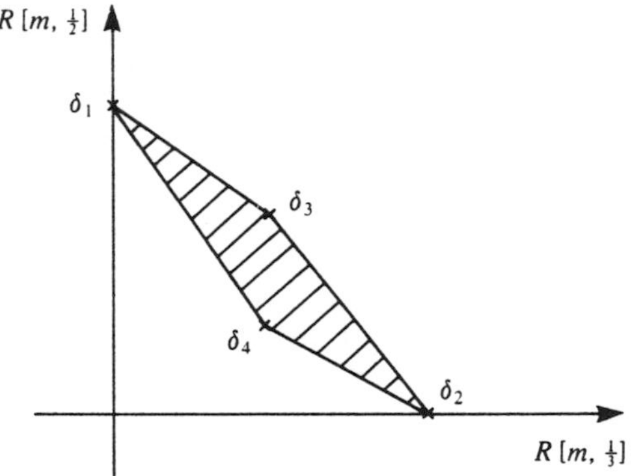

Figure 2.3: Randomized Decision Rules

In the class of randomized decision rules, the admissible rules are those rules that are associated with the points on the lower left frontier of the convex set, i.e., to $([\delta_1, \delta_4] \cup [\delta_4, \delta_2])$. For the negative orthant drawn from each of the points on this frontier (and only from those points) contains no other point of the convex set. Hence the admissible randomized decision rules are the convex combinations of δ_1 and δ_4 or δ_4 and δ_2. These rules correspond to $m(0) = 1$ or $m(1) = 0$.

2.5 Other Orderings of Decision Rules

2.5.1 Bayesian Approach

To simplify, we assume that the model is parametric. In the Bayesian approach a prior distribution Π on the parameter is available. Then the risk function can be integrated with respect to Π.

Definition 2.8: *The Bayes risk denoted R_Π is the expectation of the risk function with respect to the prior distribution.*

For a nonrandomized decision rule, the Bayes risk is given by

$$\begin{aligned} R_\Pi(\delta) &= E_\Pi R(\delta,\theta) = E_\Pi E_\theta L\left(\delta(Y),\theta\right) \\ &= \int_\Theta \int_\mathcal{Y} L\left(\delta(y),\theta\right) dP_\theta(y) d\Pi(\theta). \end{aligned}$$

For a randomized decision rule, the Bayes risk is given by

$$R_\Pi(m) = \int_\Theta \int_\mathcal{Y} \int_\mathcal{D} L(d,\theta) dm_y(d) dP_\theta(y) d\Pi(\theta). \qquad (2.2)$$

Thus, one needs to integrate the loss function with respect to the conditional distribution of d given (Y,θ) which is here independent of θ, then with respect to the conditional distribution of Y given θ, and finally with respect to the prior distribution of θ.

In the Bayesian approach, the decision rules are ranked according to the Bayes risk R_Π.

Definition 2.9: *The decision rule m_1 (weakly) dominates the decision rule m_2 in the Bayesian sense, i.e., $m_1 \succeq_\Pi m_2$ if and only if $R_\Pi(m_1) \leq R_\Pi(m_2)$.*

The Bayesian approach associates a real value R_Π, which is the Bayesian risk, to every decision rule. As a consequence one clearly obtains a *total preordering.* Hence the choice of a prior distribution allows one to solve the problem of the nonexistence of an optimal decision rule mentioned in the previous sections.

There is a relationship between the Bayesian and the classical approaches.

Property 2.1: $m_1 \succeq m_2 \Rightarrow m_1 \succeq_\Pi m_2$.

PROOF: If $m_1 \succeq m_2$, we have $\forall\, \theta, R(m_1,\theta) \leq R(m_2,\theta)$. Taking expectation with respect to the prior distribution, we obtain

$$E_\Pi R(m_1,\theta) \leq E_\Pi R(m_2,\theta) \Leftrightarrow R_\Pi(m_1) \leq R_\Pi(m_2). \square$$

Property 2.2: *If Θ is discrete and if the prior distribution Π assigns a strictly positive probability to every value of Θ, then a decision rule m^* that is optimal in the Bayesian sense is admissible.*

PROOF: Suppose that m^* is not admissible. Then there would exist another decision rule m such that $R(m, \theta_j) \leq R(m^*, \theta_j)$, $\forall\ \theta_j \in \Theta$ with at least one strict inequality. In this case we would have

$$\begin{aligned} R_\Pi(m) &= \sum_j \pi(\theta_j) R(m, \theta_j), \\ &< \sum_j \pi(\theta_j) R(m, \theta_j) = R_\Pi(m^*). \end{aligned}$$

Hence m^* would not be optimal in the Bayesian sense, which is a contradiction. □

The preceding property can be generalized to a parameter space Θ that is not discrete, provided additional regularity conditions are imposed on the prior distribution and on the loss function (see Exercise 2.6). A natural question is whether the set of admissible rules is identical to the set of decision rules that are optimal in the Bayesian sense when Π varies.

Example 2.4: The aforementioned result is true for the example of Section 2.4. The Bayes risk is equal to

$$\pi(1/3) R(m, 1/3) + (1 - \pi(1/3))\, R(m, 1/2).$$

Given a prior distribution, i.e., given a value π_0 of $\pi(1/3)$, we can consider the family of straight lines

$$\pi_0 R(., 1/3) + (1 - \pi_0) R(., 1/2) = k.$$

The estimator that is optimal in the Bayesian sense is obtained by taking the intersection of the convex set defined in Section 2.4 with the lowest straight line in the preceding family.

Changing π_0 is equivalent to considering all possible negative slopes. Therefore the set of decision rules that are optimal in the Bayesian sense is identical to the set of decision rules that are admissible in the classical sense.

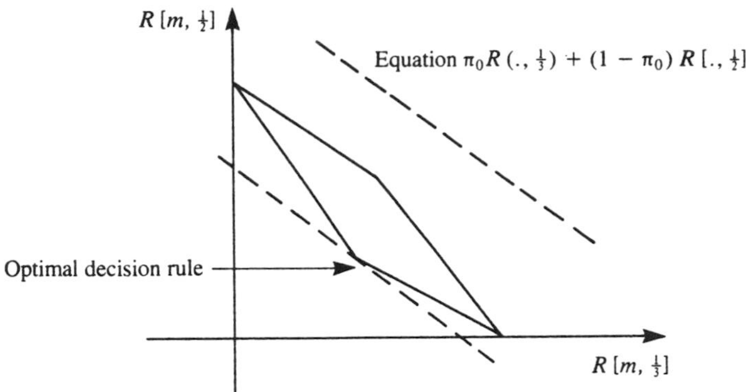

Figure 2.4: Optimal Decision Rules

2.5.2 Empirical Bayesian Approach

We now consider a family $\mathbf{\Pi}$ of possible prior distributions. Then the expectation of the risk function can be computed with respect to each of the prior distributions

$$R_{\Pi}(m) = E_{\Pi} R(m, \theta), \ \forall \ \Pi \in \mathbf{\Pi}.$$

Definition 2.10: *The empirical Bayesian ordering of decision rules is defined by* $m_1 \succeq_{\mathbf{\Pi}} m_2 \Leftrightarrow R_{\Pi}(m_1) \leq R_{\Pi}(m_2), \ \forall \ \Pi \in \mathbf{\Pi}$.

The total preordering in the Bayesian approach is obtained when $\mathbf{\Pi}$ is reduced to one element.

The partial preordering in the classical approach is obtained when $\mathbf{\Pi}$ has enough elements. This is illustrated by the following cases:

a) If $\mathbf{\Pi} = \{\varepsilon_\theta, \theta \in \Theta\}$ is the set of all point mass distributions, then $R_{\varepsilon_\theta}(m) = R(m, \theta)$. Thus the empirical Bayesian and classical preorders are clearly identical.

b) If $\mathbf{\Pi}$ is the set of all possible distributions on Θ, then these two preorders are again identical as a consequence of a) and Property 2.1.

c) The empirical Bayesian and classical preorders are also identical if the family $\mathbf{\Pi}$ is sufficiently large to recover the point mass distributions. This is the case when ε_θ can be written as

$$\varepsilon_\theta = \lim_{N \to \infty} \sum_{n=1}^{N} \alpha_{nN} \Pi_{nN}, \text{ with } \alpha_{nN} > 0 \text{ and } \Pi_{nN} \in \mathbf{\Pi}.$$

2.5.3 Conditional Approach

When one is interested in a conditional model, one can consider the *conditional risk* or the *unconditional risk* depending on the case at hand. These concepts are now discussed within a classical framework.

The model is defined *via* the conditional distribution of Y given $X = x$. A randomized decision rule m associates a probability distribution $m_{x,y}$ on $\mathcal{D}$ to every value of the observation (x, y).

The conditional risk given $X = x$ is obtained by integrating the loss function with respect to the conditional distribution of Y given $X = x$. We obtain

$$R_x(m, \theta) = \int_{\mathcal{Y}} L(m_{x,y}, \theta) P_\theta(dy \mid x).$$

As many values of the conditional risk are obtained as values for x.

The preorder is defined as

$$m_1 \succeq m_2 \Leftrightarrow R_x(m_1, \theta) \leq R_x(m_2, \theta), \forall\ \theta \in \Theta, \forall\ x \in \mathcal{X}. \tag{2.3}$$

In some cases, a priori information about the marginal distribution of X is available. For instance, we can assume that this distribution belongs to a family $\mathcal{E}$ of distributions ξ. Given ξ, we can evaluate the conditional risk as

$$R_\xi(m, \theta) = \int_{\mathcal{X}} \left(\int_{\mathcal{Y}} L(m_{x,y}, \theta) P_\theta(dy \mid x) \right) d\xi(x).$$

Then the decision rules are ranked according to

$$m_1 \geq_\xi m_2 \Leftrightarrow R_\xi(m_1, \theta) \leq R_\xi(m_2, \theta), \forall\ \theta \in \Theta, \forall\ \xi \in \mathcal{E}. \tag{2.4}$$

2.6 Exercises

EXERCISE 2.1: A *complete class* of decision rules is a subset C of the set of randomized decision rules such that

$$\forall m' \notin C, \ \ \exists m \in C, \ m \ \text{ strictly dominates } m'.$$

Show that every admissible decision rule belongs to C. Show that C may contain some decision rules that are not admissible.

EXERCISE 2.2: A *minimal complete class* is a complete class (as defined in Exercise 2.1) such that no proper subset is a complete class. Show that a minimal complete class is necessarily equal to the set of admissible decision rules.

EXERCISE 2.3: Consider a statistical model defined by $\mathcal{Y} = \{0,1\}, \mathcal{P} = \{P_\theta, \theta \in [0,1]\}$ where P_θ is the Bernoulli distribution with parameter θ satisfying $P_\theta(1) = \theta, P_\theta(0) = 1 - \theta$, and $\mathcal{D} = \{d_1, d_2\}$. The loss function is defined by $L(d_1, \theta) = \theta$, and $L(d_2, \theta) = 1 - \theta$.

a) Find the nonrandomized decision rules. Compute the risk functions associated with these rules, and illustrate them on a diagram.

b) Find the nonrandomized decision rule that has the smallest Bayes risk when the prior distribution is the uniform distribution on $[0,1]$.

EXERCISE 2.4 Consider the statistical model of Exercise 2.3. We now consider randomized decision rules.

a) Determine the risk function associated with a randomized decision rule m. Show that the family of curves representing these functions is a family of parabolas going through the point $(1/2, 1/2)$.

b) Find the admissible decision rules and the decision rule with minimal Bayes risk when the prior distribution is the uniform distribution on $[0,1]$.

EXERCISE 2.5: Consider a parametric statistical model

$$(\mathcal{Y}, \mathcal{P} = \{P_\theta, \theta \in \mathbb{R}\}) .$$

One wants to obtain an interval estimate of θ. Specifically, one wants to associate an interval I of $\mathbb{R}$ to every outcome $y \in \mathcal{Y}$. Let the loss function be $L(I, \theta) = 0$ if $\theta \in I$ and $L(I, \theta) = 1$ if $\theta \notin I$. Find the optimal decision rule. Discuss your result. How would you modify the loss function?

EXERCISE 2.6: Consider the statistical model and decision problem defined by $\mathcal{Y} = \mathbb{R}, P_\theta = N(\theta, 1), \Theta = \mathcal{D} = [0,1]$ and $L(d, \theta) = (d - \theta)^2$. Show that the risk function $R(m, \theta)$ associated with a randomized decision rule m is continuous in θ. Let Π be a prior distribution on Θ with strictly positive density with respect to Lebesgue measure. Show that the optimal Bayes rule is admissible.

EXERCISE 2.7: Consider the statistical decision problem defined by

$$\begin{aligned}
&\Theta = \{\theta_1, \theta_2\}, \quad \theta_1 = 0.4, \quad \theta_2 = 0.6, \\
&\mathcal{D} = \{d_1, d_2\}, \\
&L(d_1, \theta_1) = L(d_2, \theta_2) = 0, \\
&L(d_2, \theta_1) = 10, \quad L(d_1, \theta_2) = 20.
\end{aligned}$$

Two independent and identically distributed observations Y_1, Y_2 are available from the Bernoulli distribution with parameter θ with $P(Y = 1) = \theta$ and $P(Y = 0) = 1 - \theta$. Decision rules based on $X = Y_1 + Y_2$ are considered.

a) Find the nonrandomized decision rules.

b) Illustrate in $\mathbb{R}^2$ every nonrandomized decision rule δ by a point with coordinates $(R(\delta, \theta_1),\ R(\delta, \theta_2))$.

c) Find the optimal Bayes rule for at least one prior distribution.

EXERCISE 2.8: Within the framework of Exercise 2.7, consider the randomized decision rules. Specifically, answer the next questions.

a) Identify the set of points with coordinates $(R(m, \theta_1), R(m, \theta_2))$ associated with the randomized decision rules.

b) Find the admissible randomized decision rules. Find the optimal Bayes rule for at least one prior distribution.

2.7 References

Aczel, J. and Caroczy, Z. (1975). *On Measures of Information and their Characterizations*, Academic Press.

Barra, J.R. (1971). *Notions Fondamentales de Statistique Mathématique*, Dunod.

De Groot, M. (1970). *Optimal Statistical Decisions*, McGraw Hill.

Ferguson, T.S. (1967). *Mathematical Statistics*, Academic Press.

Lehmann, E.L. (1959). *Testing Statistical Hypotheses*, Wiley.

Lehmann, E.L. (1983). *Theory of Point Estimation*, Wiley.

Monfort, A. (1982). *Cours de Statistique Mathématique*, Economica.

Raiffa, H. and Schlaifer, R. (1961). *Applied Statistical Decision Theory*, Harvard University Press.

Silvey, S.D. (1970). *Statistical Inference*, Chapman and Hall.

CHAPTER 3

Statistical Information: Classical Approach

As discussed in the previous chapter, on the one hand, problems of estimation and testing are defined with respect to a function of the parameters. On the other hand, methods that answer these problems are based on functions of the observations. In the present chapter, we shall focus on the "information" on a given function of the parameters that is contained in a function of the observations, i.e., in a statistic. We shall study successively the following four issues:

a) Characterize the statistics that contain all the available information regarding the parameter function of interest. These are called *sufficient statistics.*

b) Characterize the statistics that contain no information regarding the parameter function of interest. These are called *ancillary statistics.*

c) Measure the loss of information associated with a given statistic that is neither sufficient nor ancillary.

d) Characterize the functions or the values of the parameters for which it is impossible to be completely informed. This is the so-called *identification problem.*

In this chapter, we shall study these issues within a classical framework, i.e., within a decision theoretical framework without a prior distribution on the parameters. Similar results are established in Chapter 4 within the Bayesian and empirical Bayesian frameworks.

3.1 Sufficiency

3.1.1 Definition

Suppose that an entrepreneur receives an important shipment of industrial parts. The shipment contains an unknown proportion θ of defective parts. Because a systematic quality control is too expensive, the entrepreneur only checks a sample of n parts. It is assumed that each part is randomly drawn with equal probability and replacement. Let $Y_i, \quad i = 1, \ldots, n$ denote the variable defined as

$$\begin{aligned} Y_i &= 1, \quad \text{if the } i\text{th part is defective,} \\ Y_i &= 0, \quad \text{otherwise.} \end{aligned}$$

The statistical model associated with this experiment is the sampling model

$$\left(\{0,1\}^n, B(1,\theta)^{\otimes n}\right).$$

It is natural to expect that information on θ contained in the n-tuple $(Y_1, \ldots, Y_n)$ is summarized in the number of defective parts in the sample, i.e., in $S(Y) = Y_1 + Y_2 + \cdots + Y_n$. We can formalize this idea by considering the conditional distribution of Y given $S(Y) = s$. We have

$$\begin{aligned} P_\theta\left(Y = y \mid S(Y) = s\right) &= P_\theta(Y_1 = y_1, \ldots, Y_n = y_n \mid \sum_{i=1}^{n} Y_i = s) \\ &= \begin{cases} 0, & \text{if } \sum_{i=1}^n y_i \neq s, \\ \dfrac{\theta^s(1-\theta)^{n-s}}{\binom{n}{s}\theta^s(1-\theta)^{n-s}} = \dfrac{1}{\binom{n}{s}}, & \text{if } \sum_{i=1}^n y_i = s. \end{cases} \end{aligned}$$

The density of the observations Y, which is $\ell(y;\theta) = \theta^s(1-\theta)^{n-s}$, can be decomposed as

$$\ell(y;\theta) = \ell_S(s;\theta)\ \ell(y \mid S = s),$$

where

$$\ell_S(s;\theta) = \binom{n}{s}\theta^s(1-\theta)^{n-s}$$

is the density of S and $\ell(y \mid S = s)$ is the conditional density of Y given $S = s$ with $s = S(y)$.

Note that θ does not appear in the conditional distribution. Thus the information about θ contained in Y is contained in the statistic S. Another interpretation of the above decomposition is that the knowledge of the realized value s of S is sufficient for simulating a realization of Y even when the parameter θ is unknown. Indeed, Y can be simulated by drawing from the *known* conditional distribution of Y given $S = s$.

The preceding example leads to the following definition of a sufficient statistic in the case of a parametric model.

Definition 3.1: *Let* $(\mathcal{Y}, \mathcal{P} = \{P_\theta, \theta \in \Theta\})$ *be a parametric model, and* S *be a statistic with values in* $\mathcal{S}$. *The statistic* S *is sufficient for* θ *if the conditional distribution of* Y *given* S *does not depend on* $\theta \in \Theta$.

In fact, the notion of sufficiency is independent of the chosen parameterization: if $\tilde{\theta} = \tilde{g}(\theta)$, where $\tilde{g}$ is bijective from Θ on to $\tilde{g}(\Theta)$, then a statistic that is sufficient for θ is also sufficient for $\tilde{\theta}$.

Example 3.1: The *identity* statistic $S(Y) = Y = (Y_1, \dots, Y_n)$ is sufficient. The conditional distribution of Y given $S(Y) = s$ is equal to the distribution with mass point at s. Clearly, such a distribution is independent of θ.

Example 3.2: Let $Y_1, \dots, Y_n$ be a random sample from an absolutely continuous distribution on $I\!R$ with density $f(y; \theta)$. Consider the *order statistics* obtained by ranking the observations in increasing order

$$S(Y) = \left(Y_{(1)}, \dots, Y_{(n)}\right),$$

with

$$\begin{aligned}
Y_{(1)} &= \min\nolimits_{Y \in \{Y_1, \dots, Y_n\}} Y &&= \min_{i=1,\dots,n} Y_i, \\
Y_{(2)} &= \min\nolimits_{Y \in \{Y_1, \dots, Y_n\} - Y_{(1)}} Y, && \\
&\vdots && \\
Y_{(n)} &= \min\nolimits_{Y \in \{Y_1, \dots, Y_n\} - \{Y_{(1)}, \dots, Y_{(n-1)}\}} Y &&= \max_{i=1,\dots,n} Y_i.
\end{aligned}$$

The conditional distribution of Y given $S = s$ is the discrete distribution with equal probability on the set of values $(y_1, \dots, y_n)$ obtained from s *via* the $n!$ possible permutations (see Exercise 3.1). Such a distribution is independent of θ. Thus the statistic S is sufficient, and the ordering of the observations is irrelevant for the knowledge of θ.

Example 3.3: Consider a random sample $Y_1, \ldots, Y_n$ from the normal distribution $N(0, \sigma^2)$. The population variance $\sigma^2 = EY_i^2$ can be approximated by the quantity $\frac{1}{n}\sum_{i=1}^n y_i^2$. It is natural to ask whether the statistic $S(Y) = \sum_{i=1}^n Y_i^2$ is sufficient. Now S/σ^2 follows a chi-square distribution with n degrees of freedom. Moreover, because the distribution of $(Y_1, \ldots, Y_n)$ is invariant to rotations, the conditional distribution of Y given $S = s$ is uniform on the sphere defined by the equation $\sum_{i=1}^n y_i^2 = s$. Such a distribution is independent of σ^2. Therefore S is sufficient for σ^2. Note also that the distribution of S is absolutely continuous with density

$$\ell_S(s;\sigma^2) = \exp\left(-\frac{s}{2\sigma^2}\right)\frac{s^{\frac{n}{2}-1}}{(2\sigma^2)^{\frac{n}{2}}\Gamma(\frac{n}{2})}\mathbb{1}_{\mathbb{R}^+}(s).$$

3.1.2 Characterization of Sufficiency

It is frequently difficult to derive the conditional distribution of Y given S and hence to determine whether S is sufficient. The criterion given below is particularly useful.

Theorem 3.1: Factorization Criterion. *Let $(\mathcal{Y}, \mathcal{P} = \{P_\theta, \theta \in \Theta\})$ be a dominated parametric model. A necessary and sufficient condition for a statistic $S(Y)$ to be sufficient is that the density $\ell(y;\theta)$ can be decomposed as*

$$\ell(y;\theta) = \psi\left(S(y);\theta\right)\lambda(y).$$

PROOF: A general proof is complicated. Here we shall give a simple proof in the case where the family $\mathcal{P}$ consists of discrete distributions.

(i) Necessity: Suppose that S is sufficient. We can write

$$\ell(y;\theta) = P_\theta(Y = y) = P_\theta\left(S(Y) = S(y)\right)P_\theta\left(Y = y \mid S(Y) = S(y)\right).$$

Let

$$\psi\left(S(y);\theta\right) = P_\theta\left(S(Y) = S(y)\right) \text{ and } \lambda(y) = P_\theta\left(Y = y \mid S(Y) = S(y)\right).$$

Then the quantity $\lambda(y)$ is independent of θ because S is sufficient.

(ii) Sufficiency: Conversely, suppose that the distribution of Y can be decomposed as

$$P_\theta\left(Y = y\right) = \psi\left(S(y);\theta\right)\lambda(y).$$

We have

$$P_\theta(Y = y \mid S(Y) = s) = \frac{P_\theta(Y = y, S(Y) = s)}{P_\theta(S(Y) = s)}$$

$$= \begin{cases} 0, & \text{if } S(y) \neq s, \\ \dfrac{P_\theta(Y = y)}{\sum_{y:S(y)=s} P_\theta(Y = y)} = \dfrac{\lambda(y)}{\sum_{y:S(y)=s} \lambda(y)}, & \text{if } S(y) = s. \end{cases}$$

Hence the conditional distribution of Y given S is independent of θ. □

The previous proof also provides an interpretation of the function λ. The restriction of this function to $\{y : S(y) = s\}$ is proportional to the conditional density of Y given $S = s$.

The decomposition appearing in the factorization criterion is not unique. One changes from one decomposition to another by modifying the proportionality factor. This means that, given two decompositions

$$\psi(S(y); \theta)\lambda(y) = \tilde{\psi}(S(y); \theta)\tilde{\lambda}(y),$$

there exists a function h such that

$$\tilde{\lambda}(y) = h(S(y))\,\lambda(y) \text{ and } \psi(S(y); \theta) = h(S(y))\,\tilde{\psi}(S(y); \theta).$$

Example 3.4: Consider an exponential model of which the densities are

$$\ell(y; \theta) = C(\theta)h(y)\exp\left(\sum_{j=1}^{r} Q_j(\theta)T_j(y)\right).$$

Applying the factorization criterion shows immediately that the statistic $T(Y) = (T_1(Y), \ldots, T_r(Y))$ is sufficient for θ (take $\lambda(y) = h(y)$).

Example 3.5: Consider a random sample from a translated exponential distribution. The density for an observation is given by

$$f(y_i; \theta) = \exp(-(y_i - \theta))\,\mathbb{1}_{y_i \geq \theta}.$$

We have

$$\begin{aligned} \ell(y; \theta) &= \prod_{i=1}^{n} f(y_i; \theta) = \exp\left(-\sum_{i=1}^{n} y_i + n\theta\right)\prod_{i=1}^{n} \mathbb{1}_{y_i \geq \theta} \\ &= \exp\left(-\sum_{i=1}^{n} y_i\right)\exp(n\theta)\mathbb{1}_{\inf y_i \geq \theta}. \end{aligned}$$

The term involving both the parameter and the observations depend on the latter only through the statistic $S(Y) = \inf_{i=1,\ldots,n} Y_i$. Thus this statistic is sufficient.

3.1.3 Set of Sufficient Statistics

Property 3.1: *Given a dominated parametric model with parameter θ, let S_1 and S_2 be two statistics such that $S_1 = h(S_2)$. If S_1 is sufficient for θ, then S_2 is also sufficient for θ.*

The result is expected. When $S_1 = h(S_2)$, knowledge of S_2 implies knowledge of S_1. Thus, if S_1 contains all the information on θ, then S_2 also contains all the information on θ.

PROOF: If S_1 is sufficient, we have from the factorization criterion

$$\ell(y;\theta) = \psi\left(S_1(y);\theta\right)\lambda(y).$$

Since $S_1 = h(S_2)$, it follows that

$$\ell(y;\theta) = \psi^*\left(S_2(y);\theta\right)\lambda(y),$$

with $\psi^*\left(S_2(y);\theta\right) = \psi\left(h(S_2(y));\theta\right)$. This implies that S_2 is also sufficient. □

Property 3.1 defines a preordering on the set of sufficient statistics

$$S_1 \Re S_2 \Leftrightarrow \exists h : S_1 = h(S_2).$$

If S_1 and S_2 satisfy the preceding relation where the function h is not bijective, S_1 is preferred since it retains all the relevant information on θ in a more concise form. Then it is natural to ask whether all relevant information can be summarized in an even more concise statistic.

Definition 3.2: *A statistic S is minimal sufficient if it is sufficient and if there exists a function h such that $S = h(T)$ for any other sufficient statistic T.*

In general, minimal sufficient statistics are found by applying the factorization criterion. For instance, consider a random sample $Y_1, \ldots, Y_n$ from a uniform distribution $U_{[0,\theta]}$. The joint density is given by

$$\ell(y;\theta) = \frac{1}{\theta^n}\mathbb{1}_{\inf y_i \geq 0}\mathbb{1}_{\sup y_i \leq \theta}.$$

If $T(Y)$ is another sufficient statistic, it follows from the factorization criterion that

$$\ell(y;\theta) = \frac{1}{\theta^n}\mathbb{1}_{\inf y_i \geq 0}\mathbb{1}_{\sup y_i \leq \theta} = \lambda(y)\psi\left(T(y);\theta\right).$$

The value $\sup y_i$ can be interpreted as the largest value of θ for which $\psi(T(y);\theta) = 0$. Hence $\sup Y_i$ is a function of $T(Y)$. Since T is an arbitrary sufficient statistic, then $\sup Y_i$ is a minimal sufficient statistic.

Property 3.2: *Two minimal sufficient statistics must be related by a bijective function.*

PROOF: Let, if they exist, S and S^* be two minimal sufficient statistics. Since they are sufficient, there exist functions h and h^* such that

$$S = h(S^*) \text{ and } S^* = h^*(S),$$

i.e.

$$\forall\ y,\ S(y) = h\left(S^*(y)\right) \text{ and } S^*(y) = h^*\left(S(y)\right).$$

This implies that h, considered as a function from $\mathcal{S}^* = S^*(\mathcal{Y})$ to $\mathcal{S} = S(\mathcal{Y})$, is invertible with inverse function $h^{-1} = h^*$. □

Property 3.3: *If S is a minimal sufficient statistic, any sufficient statistic of the form $S^* = h^*(S)$ is also minimal sufficient.*

PROOF: Let T be a sufficient statistic. We have $S = h(T)$. Thus $S^* = h^*\left(h(T)\right)$, which shows that S^* is minimal sufficient. □

From Property 3.2, note that the function h^* is necessarily bijective. Hence, if S is a minimal sufficient statistic, any other minimal sufficient statistic can be obtained by transforming S *via* an arbitrary bijective function.

It remains to consider the problem of existence of minimal sufficient statistics.

Property 3.4: *Consider an exponential model*

$$\ell(y;\theta) = C(\theta)h(y)\exp\sum_{j=1}^{r} Q_j(\theta)T_j(y).$$

If the smallest affine subspace of $\mathbb{R}^r$ that contains all the points with coordinates $Q(\theta) = (Q_1(\theta),\ldots,Q_r(\theta))'$, $\theta \in \Theta$, is $\mathbb{R}^r$ itself, then the statistic $T(Y) = (T_1(Y),\ldots,T_r(Y))'$ is minimal sufficient.

PROOF: First, note that if μ denotes the dominating measure, then the function C is given by

$$C(\theta)^{-1} = \int_{\mathcal{Y}} h(y)\exp\left(\sum_{j=1}^{r} Q_j(\theta)T_j(y)\right) d\mu(y).$$

Thus this function depends on the parameter θ through $Q(\theta)$. Hereafter, we let $C(\theta) = C^*(Q(\theta))$. We know already that the statistic $T(Y)$ is sufficient (see Example 3.4). Thus it suffices to show that it is minimal.

Let S be a sufficient statistic. From the factorization criterion, we obtain

$$\begin{aligned} \psi(S(y), q)\,\lambda(y) &= C^*(q)h(y)\exp\sum_{j=1}^{r} q_j T_j(y) \\ &= C^*(q)h(y)\exp < q, T(y) >, \end{aligned}$$

$\forall\ q \in Q(\Theta)$, where $< \cdot, \cdot >$ denotes the usual scalar product in $I\!R^r$.

Let $q^0, q^1, \ldots, q^r \in Q(\Theta)$ such that $q^1 - q^0, \ldots, q^r - q^0$ are linearly independent. It follows that

$$\log\frac{\psi(S(y), q^j)}{\psi(S(y), q^0)} = \log\frac{C^*(q^j)}{C^*(q^0)} + < q^j - q^0, T(y) >,$$

$\forall\ \ j = 1, \ldots, r$, or with obvious notations

$$a(S(y)) = b + \mathbf{M}T(y),$$

where the square matrix $\mathbf{M}$ is nonsingular. Hence T can be expressed as a function of S

$$T(y) = \mathbf{M}^{-1}(a(S(y)) - b).$$

Thus T is minimal. □

In particular, note that the condition of Property 3.4 is satisfied when the interior of $Q(\Theta)$ is nonempty.

Example 3.6: Consider a random sample $Y_1, \ldots, Y_n$ from the normal distribution $N(\theta_1, \theta_2), \theta_1 \in I\!R^{+*}, \theta_2 \in I\!R^{+*}$. The joint density of the observations is

$$\ell(y; \theta_1, \theta_2) = \frac{1}{(2\pi)^{\frac{n}{2}}(\theta_2)^{\frac{n}{2}}}\exp -\frac{n\theta_1^2}{2\theta_2}\exp\left(\frac{n\bar{Y}\theta_1}{\theta_2} - \frac{\sum_{i=1}^n Y_i^2}{2\theta_2}\right).$$

The model is exponential with $T_1(Y) = \bar{Y}, T_2(Y) = \sum_{i=1}^n Y_i^2$, $Q_1(\theta) = n\theta_1/\theta_2, Q_2(\theta) = -1/(2\theta_2)$.

The image of $\Theta = (I\!R^{+*})^2$ by the mapping Q is $Q(\Theta) = I\!R^{+*} \times I\!R^{-*}$. Since this set has a nonempty interior, the statistic $(T_1(Y), T_2(Y))'$ is minimal sufficient.

When the additional constraint $\theta_1 = \theta_2$ is imposed, it can readily be seen from the form of $\ell(y; \theta_1, \theta_1)$ that $T_2(Y)$ is minimal sufficient for θ_1. On the other hand, because $(T_1(Y), T_2(Y))$ is not a bijective function of $T_2(Y)$, this pair of statistics is no longer minimal. In addition, we note that the sufficient condition given in Property 3.4 is no longer satisfied since $Q(\Theta)$ is a half line in $\mathbb{R}^2$.

3.1.4 Some Properties of Sufficient Statistics

a) Improving Decision Rules

The concept of sufficiency is useful for it allows us to focus on decision rules that are functions of sufficient statistics.

Theorem 3.2: *Consider a statistical decision problem with a set of decisions $\mathcal{D}$ and a loss function L. Given any sufficient statistic S and any randomized decision rule m, there exists a randomized decision rule m^* that is a function of S and that has the same risk as m.*

PROOF: Consider the decision rule m^* defined by

$$m_y^*(D) = E_\theta \left(m_y(D) \mid S(Y) = S(y) \right),$$

$\forall\, y,\ \forall\, D \subset \mathcal{D}$, where

$$E_\theta \left(m_y(D) \mid S(Y) = s \right) = \int_{\mathcal{Y}} \left(\int_{\mathcal{D}} dm_y(d) \right) dP_\theta^{Y|S(Y)=s}(y).$$

Since S is sufficient, then the conditional distribution of Y given $S(Y) = S(y)$ is independent of θ. Thus we have defined a randomized decision rule that is clearly a function of $S(y)$, and we can introduce the notation $\bar{m}_{S(y)} = m_y^*$.

The risk associated with m^* is

$$\begin{aligned} R(m^*, \theta) &= \int_{\mathcal{Y}} \left(\int_{\mathcal{D}} L(d, \theta) dm_y^*(d) \right) dP_\theta(y) \\ &= \int_{\mathcal{S}} \left(\int_{\mathcal{D}} L(d, \theta) d\bar{m}_S(d) \right) dP_\theta^S(s) \\ &= \int_{\mathcal{S}} \left(\int_{\mathcal{Y}} \left(\int_{\mathcal{D}} L(d, \theta) dm_y(d) \right) dP_\theta^{Y|S=s}(y) \right) dP_\theta^S(s) \\ &= \int_{\mathcal{Y}} \left(\int_{\mathcal{D}} L(d, \theta) dm_y(d) \right) dP_\theta(y) \\ &= R(m, \theta). \end{aligned}$$

Hence the two decision rules have the same risk function. □

b) Sufficiency and Nested Models

Property 3.5: *If S is a sufficient statistic for θ in the model $(\mathcal{Y}, \mathcal{P} = \{P_\theta, \theta \in \Theta\})$, then S is a sufficient statistic for θ in the nested model $(\mathcal{Y}, \mathcal{P}^* = \{P_\theta, \theta \in \Theta^*\})$, where $\Theta^* \subset \Theta$.*

PROOF: The conditional distribution of Y given $S(Y)$ is independent of θ when $\theta \in \Theta$. Thus it is also independent of θ when $\theta \in \Theta^* \subset \Theta$. □

The converse of Property 3.5 is clearly false (see Exercise 3.2).

3.1.5 Conditioning

a) Conditional Models

The definitions and results of the preceding sections can be easily generalized to conditional models (see Section 1.4). Let Y be the conditioned variables and X be the conditioning variables. A conditional model is of the form $(\mathcal{Y}, \mathcal{P}_x = \{P_{\theta,x}, \theta \in \Theta\}, x \in \mathcal{X})$, where $P_{\theta,x}$ is interpreted as one possible conditional distribution for Y given $X = x$.

Here a statistic S is a function of the observations (X, Y).

Definition 3.3: *A statistic $S(X, Y)$ is sufficient conditionally on X if the conditional distribution of Y given X and $S(X, Y)$ is independent of $\theta \in \Theta$.*

To study the properties of conditionally sufficient statistics it suffices to apply the previous arguments for fixed $X = x$, $x \in \mathcal{X}$. Thus, from the factorization criterion 3.1, S is conditionally sufficient if the conditional density of Y given $X = x$ can be decomposed as

$$\ell(y \mid x; \theta) = \psi\,(S(x,y), x; \theta)\, \lambda(x,y), \;\; \forall\, x \in \mathcal{X}, \;\; y \in \mathcal{Y}, \;\; \theta \in \Theta.$$

Example 3.7: Consider a linear conditional model where the conditional distribution of Y is $P_{\theta,\mathbf{X}} = N(\mathbf{X}\theta, \mathbf{I})$ and the dimensions of $Y, \mathbf{X}, \theta$ are $n \times 1, n \times K, K \times 1$ respectively. The conditional density is

$$\begin{aligned} \ell(y \mid \mathbf{X}; \theta) &= \frac{1}{(2\pi)^{n/2}} \exp -\frac{1}{2}(y - \mathbf{X}\theta)'(y - \mathbf{X}\theta) \\ &= \frac{1}{(2\pi)^{n/2}} \exp\left(-\frac{1}{2} y'y - \frac{1}{2}\theta'\mathbf{X}'\,\mathbf{X}\theta + y'\mathbf{X}\theta \right). \end{aligned}$$

Let

$$\psi\,(S(x,y), x; \theta) = \exp\left(-1/2\ \theta'\mathbf{X}'\mathbf{X}\theta + y'\mathbf{X}\theta\right).$$

It follows that $S(\mathbf{X}, Y) = \mathbf{X}'Y$ is sufficient conditionally on $\mathbf{X}$.

Results concerning minimal sufficiency can be generalized similarly. A minimal sufficient statistic conditional on X is a statistic $S(X, Y)$ that is a function of every other conditionally sufficient statistic $T(X, Y)$

$$S(x, y) = h\left(x, T(x, y)\right), \ \forall \ (x, y) \in \mathcal{X} \times \mathcal{Y}. \tag{3.1}$$

For instance, such statistics exist for models that are exponential conditionally on X, i.e., for which the conditional densities are of the form

$$\ell(x, y; \theta) = C(x, \theta) h(x, y) \exp\left(\sum_{j=1}^{r} Q_j(\theta) T_j(x, y)\right).$$

Provided the condition of Property 3.4 is satisfied, the statistic

$$T(X, Y) = (T_1(X, Y), \ldots, T_r(X, Y))' \tag{3.2}$$

is minimal sufficient conditionally on X.

Example 3.8: Consider again the linear exponential model of Example 3.7. The conditional model is exponential with conditional sufficient statistic $T(\mathbf{X}, Y) = \mathbf{X}'Y$. The condition of Property 3.4 is satisfied since θ is unconstrained. Thus the statistic $T(\mathbf{X}, Y) = \mathbf{X}'Y$ is minimal sufficient conditionally on $\mathbf{X}$. Any bijective function of T (for a given $\mathbf{X}$) has the same property. If $\mathbf{X}$ is of full column rank K, then $(\mathbf{X}'\mathbf{X})^{-1}\mathbf{X}'Y$ is minimal sufficient.

b) Partial Sufficiency

Now consider the case where the parameter vector θ is partitioned into two subvectors α and β that can vary independently from each other. Thus the parameter space Θ has the product form $\Theta = A \times B$. One is interested in the value of α, called *the parameters of interest*, but not in β, called *the nuisance parameters.* In this case, it is useful to have statistics that summarize all the information on α contained in the observations Y. One may also want to construct statistics summarizing all the information on β.

Definition 3.4: *A dominated parametric model with a cut is a model where the parameter $\theta = (\alpha, \beta)' \in \Theta = A \times B$ and where the densities can be decomposed as*

$$\ell(y; \alpha, \beta) = \ell(y \mid S(Y) = S(y); \alpha) \ \ell_S(S(y); \beta).$$

That is, the marginal density of $S(Y)$ depends on θ through β only. On the other hand, since the conditional density does not depend on β, then $S(Y)$ is a sufficient statistic for β *for every fixed* α. We say that $S(Y)$ is *partially sufficient* for β.

Although the marginal distribution of $S(Y)$ does not depend on α, the conditional distribution of Y given $S(Y)$ depends on θ through α. Intuitively, the conditional distribution will be used for questions concerning α. We say that $S(Y)$ is *exogenous for* α. Note that this definition is compatible with Definition 1.8.

Example 3.9: In studies of consumption behavior, the parameters α of interest are frequently those that charaterize the quantity Y consumed conditionally on the values of other variables X, such as prices. When the determination of price levels does not depend on consumption behavior, one adopts frequently a decomposition of the form

$$\ell(y, x; \alpha, \beta) = \ell(y \mid x; \alpha)\ \ell(x; \beta).$$

Thus it is natural to focus one's attention on the conditional model when answering questions about α. That is, one is led to consider conditional models where X is exogenous for the parameter of interest.

Example 3.10: Consider the equilibrium model defined by

$$\begin{cases} Q_t = aP_t + X_t b + u_t, & a < 0, \\ Q_t = \alpha P_t + Z_t\beta + v_t, & \alpha > 0, \end{cases}$$

with $t = 1, \dots, T$, where u_t and v_t are independent of each other conditionally on X and Z, and distributed as $N(0, \sigma_u^2)$ and $N(0, \sigma_v^2)$ respectively. This model, where each equation corresponds to some structural behavior, is a model conditional on $X = x$ and $Z = z$.

Can we condition on either one of the two variables Q or P? The density of the observations (Q_t, P_t), $t = 1, \dots, T$, is given by

$$\begin{aligned} &\prod_{t=1}^{T} \ell(q_t, p_t \mid x_t, z_t; a, b, \alpha, \beta, \sigma_u^2, \sigma_v^2) \\ &\quad = \prod_{t=1}^{T} \frac{(\alpha - a)}{2\pi\sigma_u\sigma_v} \exp\left(-\frac{1}{2\sigma_u^2}(q_t - ap_t - x_t b)^2 \right) \\ &\qquad \times \exp\left(-\frac{1}{2\sigma_v^2}(q_t - \alpha p_t - z_t\beta)^2 \right). \end{aligned}$$

If $\alpha = 0$, the likelihood function can be decomposed as

$$\prod_{t=1}^{T} \frac{(-a)}{\sigma_u\sqrt{2\pi}} \exp\left(-\frac{1}{2\sigma_u^2}(q_t - ap_t - x_t b)\right)^2$$
$$\times \prod_{t=1}^{T} \frac{1}{\sigma_v\sqrt{2\pi}} \exp\left(-\frac{1}{2\sigma_v^2}(q_t - z_t\beta)^2\right).$$

The second term corresponds to the marginal density of $Q_1, \ldots, Q_T$, while the first term corresponds to the conditional density of $P_1, \ldots, P_T$ given $Q_1, \ldots, Q_T$. Thus $(Q_1, \ldots, Q_T)$ is partially sufficient for (β, σ_v^2), and is exogenous for the other parameters (a, b, σ_u^2), under $\alpha = 0$.

3.2 Ancillarity

3.2.1 Ancillary Statistics

Definition 3.5: *Let $(\mathcal{Y}, \mathcal{P} = \{P_\theta, \theta \in \Theta\})$ be a statistical model. A statistic $S(Y)$ is ancillary if its distribution does not depend on the parameter θ.*

Thus, when a model is dominated and $S(Y)$ is ancillary, there exists a cut of the form

$$\ell(y;\theta) = \ell\,(y \mid S(Y) = S(y);\theta)\,\ell_S(S(y)).$$

All the information on θ is contained in the conditional distribution of Y given $S(Y)$.

Remark 3.1: The previous definition applies to parametric models. It can, however, be easily extended to an arbitrary model $(\mathcal{Y}, \mathcal{P})$. Namely, a statistic is ancillary if its distribution does not depend on $P \in \mathcal{P}$.

Example 3.11: Let $Y_1, \ldots, Y_n$ be a random sample from $N(m, 1)$. The statistic $S(Y) = \sum_{i=1}^n (Y_i - \bar{Y})^2$ follows a $\chi^2(n-1)$ distribution. Since this distribution does not depend on m, $S(Y)$ and the empirical variance $\frac{1}{n-1}\sum_{i=1}^n (Y_i - \bar{Y})^2$ are ancillary statistics for the mean m. Other ancillary statistics are

$$Y_1 - \bar{Y}, Y_2 - Y_1, (Y_1 - \bar{Y}, \ldots, Y_n - \bar{Y}), \text{ etc.}$$

3.2.2 Ancillarity and Sufficiency

Definition 3.6: *A statistic S is complete if and only if*

$$E_\theta g\left(S(Y)\right) = 0, \quad \forall\, \theta \in \Theta \Rightarrow g = 0.$$

Remark 3.2: A statistic that is complete for a given model is also complete for a nesting model.

Property 3.6: *Let S and T be two statistics. If S is sufficient and complete and if T is ancillary, then S and T are independent $\forall\, \theta \in \Theta$.*

PROOF: Let $h(T)$ be a function of T. Since S is sufficient, therefore $E_\theta\left(h(T) \mid S\right)$ is independent of θ, i.e., $E_\theta\left(h(T) \mid S\right) = E\left(h(T) \mid S\right)$. Since T is ancillary, $E_\theta h(T)$ is also independent of θ, i.e., $E_\theta h(T) = Eh(T)$.

It now suffices to note that

$$E_\theta\left(E(h(T) \mid S) - Eh(T)\right) = E_\theta E_\theta(h(T) \mid S) - E_\theta E_\theta h(T) = 0,\ \forall\, \theta \in \Theta.$$

Since S is complete, it follows that

$$\begin{aligned} E(h(T) \mid S) &= Eh(T),\ \forall\, h \quad \text{or} \\ E_\theta(h(T) \mid S) &= E_\theta h(T),\ \forall\, h,\ \forall\ \theta \in \Theta. \end{aligned}$$

This implies the independence of T and S for every value of the parameter. □

Property 3.7: *Let S and T be two statistics defined on an homogeneous model $(\mathcal{Y}, \mathcal{P} = \{P_\theta, \theta \in \Theta\})$. If S is sufficient, and, if S and T are independent, then T is ancillary.*

SKETCH OF THE PROOF: Because S and T are independent

$$E_\theta\left(h(T) \mid S\right) = E_\theta h(T).$$

Because S is sufficient, $E_\theta\left(h(T) \mid S\right)$ does not depend on θ. Hence, for any given h, $E_\theta h(T)$ does not depend on θ. This implies that T is ancillary. □

Example 3.12: From Example 3.11 where $Y_1, \ldots, Y_n$ is a random sample from $N(m, 1)$, the statistic $T(Y) = \sum_{i=1}^n (Y_i - \bar{Y})^2$ is ancillary. On the other hand, we know that the empirical mean $S(Y) = \bar{Y}$ is sufficient. It can be readily checked that $\bar{Y}$ is complete (see Exercise 3.3). Thus the two statistics $S(Y)$ and $T(Y)$ are independent. As is well known, this is Fisher's theorem (see Theorem B.5 in Appendix B).

3.3 Information Measures

In Sections 3.1 and 3.2, we saw that a sufficient statistic retains all the relevant information, while an ancillary statistic loses all that information. In general, a statistic is neither sufficient nor ancillary. In this section, we consider measures of the information on a parameter that is contained in a statistic.

To simplify, we consider the case of a parametric model $\big(\mathcal{Y}, \mathcal{P} = \{P_\theta, \theta \in \Theta\}\big)$. The information on θ contained in a statistic S is denoted $I^S(\theta)$. As a measure of information, the function I must satisfy several desirable properties. These are:

(i) $I^S(\theta)$ is either a nonnegative real number or a positive semidefinite symmetric matrix for every θ and S.

(ii) S is a sufficient statistic if and only if $I^S(\theta) = I^Y(\theta)$ where $I^Y(\theta)$ denotes the information contained in the identity statistic $Y \mapsto Y$.

(iii) $I^S(\theta)$ is minimal if and only if S is an ancillary statistic.

(iv) if S_1 and S_2 are two independent statistics

$$I^{(S_1,S_2)}(\theta) = I^{S_1}(\theta) + I^{S_2}(\theta), \ \forall \ \theta.$$

(v) if $S^* = h(S)$, then $I^{S^*}(\theta) \preceq I^S(\theta)$.

It is possible to construct information measures that satisfy such properties. Here, we adopt another approach. First, we present the Fisher information measure, which is one of the most common information measures, and we verify that it satisfies the preceding desired properties. Then we study the relationship between Fisher information and Kullback information measures.

3.3.1 Fisher Information

a) Definition

We assume that the parametric model is dominated. Let μ be a dominating measure. We also assume that the following conditions are satisfied:

H1 : Θ is open and convex,

H2 : $\ell(y;\theta) > 0, \quad \forall \ y \in \mathcal{Y}, \ \forall \ \theta \in \Theta,$

H3 : $\partial \ell(y;\theta)/\partial\theta$ and $\partial^2 \ell(y;\theta)/\partial\theta\partial\theta'$ exist $\forall\, y \in \mathcal{Y}$, $\forall\, \theta \in \Theta$,

H4 : $\partial \log \ell(y;\theta)/\partial\theta$ is square integrable with respect to P_θ, $\forall\, \theta \in \Theta$,

H5 : $\forall\, \theta \in \Theta$, $\forall\, A \subset \mathcal{Y}$, one can twice differentiate $\int_A \ell(y;\theta)d\mu(y)$ under the integral with respect to the components of θ.

Definition 3.7: *Fisher Information, which is denoted $\mathcal{I}(\theta)$, is the variance covariance matrix of the score vector $\partial \log \ell(Y;\theta)/\partial\theta$.*

Since $\int_{\mathcal{Y}} l(y;\theta)d\mu(y) = 1$, we obtain by differentiating with respect to θ

$$0 = \int \frac{\partial \ell(y;\theta)}{\partial\theta} d\mu(y) = \int \frac{\partial \log \ell(y;\theta)}{\partial\theta} \ell(y;\theta) d\mu(y),$$

i.e.

$$E_\theta \frac{\partial \log \ell(Y;\theta)}{\partial\theta} = 0, \ \forall\theta.$$

It follows that

$$\begin{aligned} \mathcal{I}(\theta) &= V_\theta\left(\frac{\partial \log \ell(Y;\theta)}{\partial\theta}\right) \\ &= E_\theta\left(\frac{\partial \log \ell(Y;\theta)}{\partial\theta}\frac{\partial \log \ell(Y;\theta)}{\partial\theta'}\right). \end{aligned} \tag{3.3}$$

Remark 3.3: If the dominating measure μ is replaced by another measure $\tilde{\mu}$ such that $\mu = h(y)\tilde{\mu}$, the new density is $\tilde{\ell}(y;\theta) = \ell(y;\theta)h(y)$. Thus $\partial \log \tilde{\ell}(y;\theta)/\partial\theta = \partial \log \ell(y;\theta)/\partial\theta'$. Hence Definition 3.7 does not depend on the chosen dominating measure.

Example 3.13: Consider n random variables $Y_1, \ldots, Y_n$ that are independent and identically distributed $B(1,p)$. The logarithm of the likelihood function is

$$\log \ell(y;p) = \sum_{i=1}^n y_i \log \frac{p}{1-p} - n\log(1-p).$$

Thus

$$\frac{\partial \log \ell(y;p)}{\partial p} = \sum_{i=1}^n y_i \frac{1}{p(1-p)} + \frac{n}{1-p},$$

$$\mathcal{I}(p) = V_p\left(\frac{\partial \log \ell(Y;p)}{\partial p}\right) = \frac{1}{p^2(1-p)^2} V_p\left(\sum_{i=1}^n Y_i\right) = \frac{n}{p(1-p)}.$$

Computation of the variance of the score vector is not always as simple. Then the next property may be useful.

Property 3.8:

$$\mathcal{I}(\theta) = E_\theta \left(-\frac{\partial^2 \log \ell(Y;\theta)}{\partial\theta\, \partial\theta'} \right).$$

PROOF: We saw that $\int_{\mathcal{Y}} \partial \ell(y;\theta)/\partial\theta d\mu(y) = 0, \ \forall\, \theta \in \Theta$. Differentiating once more under the integral gives

$$\int_{\mathcal{Y}} \frac{\partial^2 \ell(y;\theta)}{\partial\theta\, \partial\theta'} d\mu(y) = E_\theta \left(\frac{1}{\ell(Y;\theta)} \frac{\partial^2 \ell(Y;\theta)}{\partial\theta\, \partial\theta'} \right) = 0, \quad \forall\, \theta \in \Theta.$$

Since

$$\begin{aligned} \frac{\partial^2 \log \ell(y;\theta)}{\partial\theta\partial\theta'} &= \frac{\partial}{\partial\theta'} \left(\frac{1}{\ell(y;\theta)} \frac{\partial \ell(y;\theta)}{\partial\theta} \right) \\ &= \frac{1}{\ell(y;\theta)} \frac{\partial^2 \ell(y;\theta)}{\partial\theta\partial\theta'} - \frac{1}{\ell^2(y;\theta)} \frac{\partial \ell(y;\theta)}{\partial\theta} \frac{\partial \ell(y;\theta)}{\partial\theta'}, \end{aligned}$$

the desired result follows by integrating with respect to the distribution $P_\theta = \ell(y;\theta) \cdot \mu$. □

Example 3.14: Consider the linear model $Y \sim N(\mathbf{X}\theta, \mathbf{I})$. The log-likelihood function is

$$\log \ell(y;\theta) = -\frac{n}{2} \log 2\pi - \frac{1}{2}(y - \mathbf{X}\theta)'(y - \mathbf{X}\theta).$$

Hence

$$-\frac{\partial^2 \log(y;\theta)}{\partial\theta\partial\theta'} = \mathbf{X}'\mathbf{X}.$$

Therefore $\mathcal{I}(\theta) = E_\theta(\mathbf{X}'\mathbf{X}) = \mathbf{X}'\mathbf{X}$, which is independent of θ. Throughout, distributions and expectations are conditional upon $\mathbf{X}$.

Example 3.15: Consider the exponential model with likelihood function

$$\ell(y;\theta) = h(y) \exp \left(\sum_{j=1}^{p} \theta_j T_j(y) + A(\theta) \right).$$

We have

$$\frac{\partial^2 \log \ell(y;\theta)}{\partial\theta\partial\theta'} = \frac{\partial^2 A(\theta)}{\partial\theta\partial\theta'}.$$

Thus

$$\mathcal{I}(\theta) = E_\theta \left(-\frac{\partial^2 A(\theta)}{\partial\theta\partial\theta'} \right) = -\frac{\partial^2 A(\theta)}{\partial\theta\partial\theta'}.$$

In particular, the matrix $\partial^2 A(\theta)/\partial\theta\partial\theta'$ is negative semidefinite.

b) Fisher Information for a Nested Model

Given a parametric model $(\mathcal{Y}, \mathcal{P}=\{P_\theta, \theta \in \Theta\})$, we can restrict the parameters θ by considering that they are functions of another parameter vector α of lower dimension, i.e., $\theta = a(\alpha), \alpha \in A$. Hence, we obtain a model nested in the original model

$$\left(\mathcal{Y}, \mathcal{P}^* = \{P_{a(\alpha)}, \alpha \in A\}\right).$$

For this new model, Fisher information for α is easily computed provided a is differentiable. Namely, we have

$$\begin{aligned}
\mathcal{I}^*(\alpha) &= E_\alpha\left(\frac{\partial \log \ell(Y; a(\alpha))}{\partial \alpha}\frac{\partial \log \ell(Y; a(\alpha))}{\partial \alpha'}\right) \\
&= E\left(\frac{\partial a'}{\partial \alpha}\frac{\partial \log \ell(Y; a(\alpha))}{\partial a}\frac{\partial \log \ell(Y; a(\alpha))}{\partial a'}\frac{\partial a}{\partial \alpha'}\right),
\end{aligned}$$

i.e.

$$\mathcal{I}^*(\alpha) = \frac{\partial a'}{\partial \alpha} I(a(\alpha)) \frac{\partial a}{\partial \alpha'}.$$

Remark 3.4: If $a(\alpha) = (\alpha, 0)'$, i.e., if the nested model is obtained by restricting the last components of θ to be zero, then $\mathcal{I}^*(\alpha)$ is simply the upper diagonal block $\mathcal{I}_{\alpha\alpha}$ of the matrix $\mathcal{I}(\theta)$ evaluated at $\theta = (\alpha, 0)'$.

Remark 3.5: If the mapping a is bijective, the new model is identical to the original model with a new parameterization. Then the above equation shows that the Fisher information matrix is not invariant to reparameterization.

c) Fisher Information Associated with a Statistic

Given a statistic S, we can consider the model associated with it, namely, $\left(\mathcal{S}, \mathcal{P}_S = \{P_\theta^S, \theta \in \Theta\}\right)$. This model is said to be the *model induced by* S.

Definition 3.8: *The Fisher information matrix, denoted $\mathcal{I}^S(\theta)$, associated with a statistic S is the Fisher information matrix for the model induced by S.*

When the induced model is dominated, we let $\ell_S(S; \theta)$ denote the density of the distribution of S, and we assume that the conditions H1

– H5 are satisfied. Then

$$\mathcal{I}^S(\theta) = V_\theta\left(\frac{\partial \log \ell_S(S;\theta)}{\partial\theta}\right) = E_\theta\left(-\frac{\partial^2 \log \ell_S(S;\theta)}{\partial\theta\partial\theta'}\right).$$

This information measure is a symmetric matrix. It satisfies the positive semidefinite property (i) mentioned earlier. The other desired properties are also satisfied in view of the next property, which is established by decomposing the density of Y as

$$\ell(y;\theta) = \ell_S(S(y);\theta)\, \ell(y \mid S(Y) = S(y);\theta),$$

(see Property B.15 in Appendix B).

Property 3.9: *Fisher information $\mathcal{I}(\theta)$ can be decomposed as*

$$\mathcal{I}(\theta) = \mathcal{I}^S(\theta) + E_\theta \mathcal{I}^{Y|S}(\theta),$$

where

$$\begin{aligned}\mathcal{I}^{Y|S}(\theta) &= V_\theta\left(\frac{\partial \log \ell(Y \mid S(Y);\theta)}{\partial\theta} \mid S(Y)\right)\\ &= E_\theta\left(-\frac{\partial^2 \log \ell(Y \mid S(Y);\theta)}{\partial\theta\partial\theta'} \mid S(Y)\right)\\ &= V_\theta\left(\frac{\partial \log \ell(Y;\theta)}{\partial\theta} \mid S(Y)\right),\end{aligned}$$

is the Fisher information matrix for the conditional model for Y given S. Moreover

$$\mathcal{I}^S(\theta) = V_\theta E_\theta\left(\frac{\partial \log \ell(Y;\theta)}{\partial\theta} \mid S(Y)\right).$$

PROOF: From the preceding decomposition of the density, it follows that

$$\log \ell(Y;\theta) = \log \ell_S(S(Y);\theta) + \log \ell(Y \mid S(Y);\theta).$$

Hence

$$-\frac{\partial^2 \log \ell(Y;\theta)}{\partial\theta\partial\theta'} = -\frac{\partial^2 \log \ell_S(S(Y);\theta)}{\partial\theta\partial\theta'} - \frac{\partial^2 \log \ell(Y \mid S(Y);\theta)}{\partial\theta\partial\theta'}.$$

Taking expectation, we obtain

$$\begin{aligned}\mathcal{I}(\theta) &= \mathcal{I}^S(\theta) + E_\theta\left(-\frac{\partial^2 \log \ell(Y \mid S(Y);\theta)}{\partial\theta\partial\theta'}\right)\\ &= \mathcal{I}^S(\theta) + E_\theta E_\theta\left(-\frac{\partial^2 \log \ell(Y \mid S(Y);\theta)}{\partial\theta\partial\theta'} \mid S(Y)\right)\\ &= \mathcal{I}^S(\theta) + E_\theta \mathcal{I}^{Y|S}(\theta).\end{aligned}$$

Note also that

$$\begin{aligned}\mathcal{I}^{Y|S}(\theta) &= V_\theta\left(\frac{\partial \log \ell(Y \mid S(Y);\theta)}{\partial \theta} \mid S(Y)\right)\\ &= V_\theta\left(\frac{\partial \log \ell(Y;\theta)}{\partial \theta} - \frac{\partial \log \ell_S(S(Y);\theta)}{\partial \theta} \mid S(Y)\right)\\ &= V_\theta\left(\frac{\partial \log(Y;\theta)}{\partial \theta} \mid S(Y)\right).\end{aligned}$$

Hence

$$\begin{aligned}\mathcal{I}^{S}(\theta) &= \mathcal{I}(\theta) - E_\theta \mathcal{I}^{Y|S}(\theta)\\ &= V_\theta\left(\frac{\partial \log \ell(Y;\theta)}{\partial \theta}\right) - E_\theta V_\theta\left(\frac{\partial \log \ell(Y;\theta)}{\partial \theta} \mid S(Y)\right)\\ &= V_\theta E_\theta\left(\frac{\partial \log(Y;\theta)}{\partial \theta} \mid S(Y)\right),\end{aligned}$$

where the last equality follows from the well-known analysis of variance formula. □

The decomposition given by Property 3.9 is readily interpreted. The first term $\mathcal{I}^S(\theta)$ corresponds to the information contained in S, i.e., in the distribution ℓ_S. The second term corresponds to the information contained in the conditional distribution of Y given S. Note also that the expression for $\mathcal{I}^S(\theta)$ can be directly obtained from the property

$$\frac{\partial \log \ell_S(S;\theta)}{\partial \theta} = E_\theta\left(\frac{\partial \log \ell(Y;\theta)}{\partial \theta} \mid S\right),$$

which is established in the appendix to Chapter 11.

We can now establish the remaining desirable properties for $\mathcal{I}^S(\theta)$.

Corollary 3.1:

(i) $\mathcal{I}^S(\theta) \ll \mathcal{I}(\theta),\ \forall\ \theta$.

(ii) $\mathcal{I}^S(\theta) = 0,\ \forall\ \theta \Leftrightarrow S$ *is ancillary.*

(iii) $\mathcal{I}^S(\theta) = \mathcal{I}(\theta),\ \forall\ \theta \Leftrightarrow S$ *is sufficient.*

(iv) If S *and* T *are two independent statistics, then* $\mathcal{I}^{(S,T)}(\theta) = \mathcal{I}^S(\theta) + \mathcal{I}^T(\theta),\ \forall\ \theta$.

PROOF:

(i) This follows from the positive semidefiniteness of

$$E_\theta V_\theta \left(\frac{\partial \log \ell(Y \mid S(Y); \theta)}{\partial \theta} \mid S(Y) \right).$$

(ii) $\mathcal{I}^S(\theta) = 0, \ \forall\ \theta$ if and only if

$$V_\theta \left(\frac{\partial \log \ell_S(S(Y); \theta)}{\partial \theta} \right) = 0, \ \forall\ \theta,$$

i.e., if and only if

$$\frac{\partial \log \ell_S(S(Y); \theta)}{\partial \theta} = 0, \ \forall\ \theta.$$

(We have used the fact that the latter vector has zero mean, as can be readily seen by differentiating under the integral $\int_S \ell_S(s;\theta) d\mu^S(s) = 1$.) Thus $\log \ell_S(S(Y);\theta)$ is independent of θ. Hence the statistic S is ancillary.

(iii) The proof is similar to the proof of (ii). In this case, the second term in the decomposition given by Property 3.9 is zero. This arises if and only if

$$\frac{\partial \log \ell(Y \mid S(Y); \theta)}{\partial \theta} = 0, \ \forall\ \theta,$$

i.e., if and only if $\ell(Y \mid S(Y); \theta)$ is independent of θ.

(iv) The last property follows from

$$\log \ell_{S,T}(S, T; \theta) = \log \ell_S(S; \theta) + \log \ell_T(T; \theta).$$

This completes the proof. □

Remark 3.6: Similar definitions can be given for a conditional model $(\mathcal{Y}, \{\mathcal{P}_x, x \in \mathcal{X}\})$ provided statistics of the form $S(X,Y)$ are used and one argues conditionally on X.

3.3.2 Kullback Information

The Fisher information matrix introduced in the previous section is related to the Kullback measure of discrepancy between distributions discussed in Section 1.2.3. Given two densities f and f^*, the Kullback discrepancy is $\tilde{I}(f \mid f^*) = E_* \log [f^*(Y)/f(Y)]$.

Consider a parametric model $(\mathcal{Y}, \mathcal{P} = \{P_\theta, \ \theta \in \Theta\})$. We may ask whether the distribution associated with the value θ of the parameter can be distinguished easily from any other distribution in the model. This leads naturally to the function

$$\theta_1 \to \tilde{I}(\theta_1 \mid \theta) = E_\theta \log \frac{\ell(Y;\theta)}{\ell(Y;\theta_1)}.$$

Then the question reduces to whether the Kullback measure of discrepancy increases sufficiently fast as θ_1 differs from θ. Since $\tilde{I}(\theta_1 \mid \theta)$ is minimized at $\theta_1 = \theta$, a second-order expansion of the preceding function in the neighborhood of θ gives

$$\tilde{I}(\theta_1 \mid \theta) = \frac{1}{2}(\theta_1 - \theta)' \left(\frac{\partial^2}{\partial\theta_1 \partial\theta_1'} \tilde{I}(\theta_1 \mid \theta) \right)_{\theta_1 = \theta} (\theta_1 - \theta) + o(\|\theta_1 - \theta\|^2).$$

The curvature of this function at θ is given by the matrix

$$\left(\frac{\partial^2 \tilde{I}(\theta_1 \mid \theta)}{\partial\theta_1 \, \partial\theta_1'} \right)_{\theta_1 = \theta}.$$

Property 3.10:

$$\left(\frac{\partial^2 \tilde{I}(\theta_1 \mid \theta)}{\partial\theta_1 \, \partial\theta_1'} \right)_{\theta_1 = \theta} = \mathcal{I}(\theta), \ \forall \ \theta.$$

PROOF: $\tilde{I}(\theta_1 \mid \theta) = E_\theta \log \ell(Y;\theta) - E_\theta \log \ell(Y;\theta_1)$. Hence

$$\frac{\partial^2 \tilde{I}(\theta_1 \mid \theta)}{\partial\theta_1 \, \partial\theta_1'} = -E_\theta \frac{\partial^2 \log \ell(Y;\theta_1)}{\partial\theta_1 \, \partial\theta_1'}.$$

It suffices to compute this derivative at $\theta_1 = \theta$ to obtain the Fisher information matrix. □

Property 3.10 shows that the comparison of Fisher information matrices reduces to the comparison of the curvatures of Kullback discrepancy measures in the neighborhood of a parameter value.

3.4 Identification

Sometimes parameters or parameter values cannot be determined or known perfectly even in the most favorable situation where the maximum amount of information is available, i.e., when the true distribution P_0 is known. Such a difficulty, which is referred as *the identification problem*, is studied in this section.

3.4.1 Definitions

Definition 3.9:

(i) *A parameter value* θ_1 *is said to be identified if there does not exist another parameter value* θ_2 *of* θ *such that* $P_{\theta_2} = P_{\theta_1}$.

(ii) *A parameter value* θ_1 *is said to be locally identified if there exists a neighborhood* $\mathcal{V}(\theta_1)$ *of* θ_1 *such that*

$$\forall\ \theta_2 \neq \theta_1,\ \theta_2 \in \mathcal{V}(\theta_1) : P_{\theta_2} \neq P_{\theta_1}.$$

If θ_1 is identified and if the true distribution is $P_0 = P_{\theta_1}$, then the true value of the parameter is θ_1. Hence the identification condition allows us to interchange freely the true distribution and the true value of the parameter.

Example 3.16: Consider the sampling model

$$\left(\mathcal{Y} = \mathbb{R}^n, \mathcal{P} = \{N(a^2, 1)^{\otimes n}, a \in \mathbb{R}\}\right).$$

The value zero of the parameter a is identified. The other parameter values are not identified since the values a and $-a$ give the same distribution. These values are, however, locally identified.

Definition 3.10: *A parametric model is said to be identified if every value of the parameters are identified, i.e., if the mapping* $\theta \mapsto P_\theta$ *is injective on* Θ.

In this case, one frequently says that the *parameter* θ *is identified.* The above definitions easily extend to functions of the parameters, and, in particular, to subvectors of the parameter vector.

Definition 3.11: *A function* $g(\theta)$ *of the parameter is identified if and only if*

$$\forall\ \theta_1, \theta_2 : g(\theta_1) \neq g(\theta_2) \Rightarrow P_{\theta_1} \neq P_{\theta_2},$$

or equivalently if and only if

$$\forall\ \theta_1, \theta_2 : P_{\theta_1} = P_{\theta_2}, \Rightarrow g(\theta_1) = g(\theta_2).$$

Thus a function of the parameter is identified if and only if the value $g(\theta)$ can be recovered uniquely from the distribution P_θ. In other words, $g(\theta)$ is a function of P_θ. It follows that any function of an identified parameter such as a mean, a variance, a covariance, etc. is also identified.

3.4.2 Some Examples

Example 3.17: Consider a linear model $Y \sim N(\mathbf{X}b, \mathbf{I}), b \in I\!R^K$. We want to find the linear functions of b that are identified. Arguments are made conditionally on $\mathbf{X}$, i.e., as if $\mathbf{X}$ is a constant matrix. The normal distribution depends on b through $\mathbf{X}b$. Thus the identification condition for $\lambda' b$ where $\lambda \in I\!R^K$ becomes

$$\begin{aligned} & \forall \quad b_1, b_2 : \mathbf{X}b_1 = \mathbf{X}b_2 \Rightarrow \lambda' b_1 = \lambda' b_2 \\ \Leftrightarrow & \forall \quad b_1, b_2 : \mathbf{X}(b_1 - b_2) = 0 \Rightarrow \lambda'(b_1 - b_2) = 0 \\ \Leftrightarrow & \forall \quad \beta : \beta \in \text{Ker } \mathbf{X} \Rightarrow \lambda' \beta = 0 \\ \Leftrightarrow & \qquad \lambda \in (\text{Ker } \mathbf{X})^{\perp} = Im\ \mathbf{X}'. \end{aligned}$$

In particular, all linear functions of the parameter are identified if and only if Ker $\mathbf{X} = \{0\}$, i.e., if $\mathbf{X}$ is of full column rank K . This is the so-called *rank condition*. Hence a necessary condition for identification of b is that $n \geq K$, i.e., that there are more observations than parameters. This is the so-called *order condition.*

Example 3.18: Let $Y_1^*, \ldots, Y_n^*$ be independent random variables from $N(m, \sigma^2)$. Suppose that only the signs of these observations are observed. The sign of Y_i^* is a qualitative variable defined by

$$Y_i = \begin{cases} +, & \text{if } Y_i^* \geq 0, \\ -, & \text{if } Y_i^* < 0. \end{cases}$$

Its distribution is given by

$$P(Y_i = +) = P(Y_i^* \geq 0) = P\left(\frac{Y_i^* - m}{\sigma} \geq -\frac{m}{\sigma}\right) = \Phi\left(\frac{m}{\sigma}\right),$$

where Φ denotes the cumulative standard normal distribution function. It is easy to see that m and σ are not identified, but that m/σ is. The nonidentification of the parameters of interest m and σ arises from the fact that these parameters pertain to the latent model and that the latent variables are not observed.

Example 3.19: Consider the equilibrium model

$$\begin{aligned} D_t &= aP_t + b + u_t, a < 0, \\ S_t &= \alpha P_t + \beta + v_t, \alpha > 0, \\ Q_t &= D_t = S_t, \end{aligned}$$

where the errors u_t, v_t are assumed to be mutually independent with respective distributions $N(0, \sigma_u^2)$ and $N(0, \sigma_v^2)$. The reduced form (see Equation 1.10) is

$$\begin{aligned} P_t &= \frac{b-\beta}{\alpha - a} + \frac{u_t - v_t}{\alpha - a}, \\ Q_t &= \frac{\alpha b - \beta a}{\alpha - a} + \frac{\alpha u_t - a v_t}{\alpha - a}. \end{aligned}$$

The functions $(b-\beta)/(\alpha - a)$ and $(\alpha b - \beta a)/(\alpha - a)$, which are the means of P_t and Q_t, are identified. Similarly, the variances and covariance of P_t and Q_t are identified. They are given by

$$\begin{aligned} VP_t &= \frac{1}{(\alpha - a)^2}(\sigma_u^2 + \sigma_v^2), \\ VQ_t &= \frac{1}{(\alpha - a)^2}(\alpha^2\sigma_u^2 + a^2\sigma_v^2), \\ \mathrm{Cov}(P_t, Q_t) &= \frac{1}{(\alpha - a)^2}(\alpha\sigma_u^2 + a\sigma_v^2). \end{aligned}$$

Because it is normal, the distribution of (P_t, Q_t) depends on the structural parameters only through the five preceding functions. Since these five functions depend on six parameters $(a, b, \alpha, \beta, \sigma_u^2, \sigma_v^2)$, the mapping that associates structural parameters to distributions is not injective. Hence the structural parameters are not identified.

In this example the identification problem arises from simultaneity. The parameters of interest are the structural parameters, while the distributions in the model are derived from the reduced form.

Any model nested in an identified model is also identified. But a nested model can be identified without the nesting model being identified. Thus, imposing constraints on parameters can resolve some identification problems. Such constraints are said to be *identifying*. For instance, in Example 3.18, the constraint $\sigma = 1$ is identifying.

Example 3.20: Time series often present some regularities. A frequent modelling method consists in assuming that the value Y_t at date t of a time series is the sum of a component Z_t called the *trend*, a component S_t representing the cyclical variations called the *seasonal component*, and a random term or *error*. For instance, suppose that we have a quarterly time series. We assume that the trend is linear, i.e., $Z_t = at + b$, and that the seasonality is of the form $S_t = S_1 \, \mathbb{1}_{t=1} + S_2 \, \mathbb{1}_{t=2} + S_3 \, \mathbb{1}_{t=3} + S_4 \, \mathbb{1}_{t=4}$, where $1\!\!1_{t=j}$ is the variable indicating that t corresponds to the jth quarter while $S_j, j = 1, \ldots, 4$ are parameters.

The model can be written as $Y_t = at + b + S_1 \; 1\!\!1_{t=1} + S_2 \; 1\!\!1_{t=2} + S_3 \; 1\!\!1_{t=3} + S_4 \; 1\!\!1_{t=4} + u_t$, where the errors u_t are assumed to be independently distributed $N(0, \sigma^2)$. The model is linear with matrix $\mathbf{X}$ that is not of full column rank since $\forall \; t, \; 1\!\!1_{t=1} + 1\!\!1_{t=2} + 1\!\!1_{t=3} + 1\!\!1_{t=4} = 1$. The only identified functions are those that depend on the parameters through $a, b + S_1, b + S_2, b + S_3,$ and $b + S_4$. An identifying constraint is obtained by assuming that the sum of the seasonal coefficients S_j is zero: $S_1 + S_2 + S_3 + S_4 = 0$. That is, it is assumed that the seasonal effect averaged over the whole year is null.

3.4.3 Application to Exponential Models

In this subsection, we consider an exponential model indexed by p parameters $\theta = (\theta_1, \ldots, \theta_p)'$ belonging to an open subset Θ of $I\!\!R^p$. The family of densities is

$$\ell(y; \theta) = C(\theta) h(y) \exp \left(\sum_{j=1}^{r} Q_j(\theta) T_j(y) \right).$$

Property 3.11: *Suppose that the statistics $T_j(Y), j = 1, \ldots, r$ are linearly independent (in the affine sense), i.e.*

$$\sum_{j=1}^{r} a_j T_j(Y) = a_0 \Rightarrow a_j = 0, \quad \forall \; j = 0, 1, \ldots, r.$$

Then $P_{\theta_1} = P_{\theta_2}$ if and only if

$$Q_j(\theta_1) = Q_j(\theta_2), \quad \forall j = 1, \ldots, r.$$

PROOF: $P_{\theta_1} = P_{\theta_2}$ if and only if

$$C(\theta_1) \exp \sum_{j=1}^{r} Q_j(\theta_1) T_j(y) = C(\theta_2) \exp \sum_{j=1}^{r} Q_j(\theta_2) T_j(y),$$

which implies that $\sum_{j=1}^{r} \left(Q_j(\theta_2) - Q_j(\theta_1) \right) T_j(y)$ is a function that is constant in y. Hence, from the assumption of linear independence, it follows that

$$Q_j(\theta_2) - Q_j(\theta_1) = 0, \quad \forall \; j.$$

Conversely, if $Q_j(\theta_2) - Q_j(\theta_1) = 0, \quad \forall\, j$, the condition

$$1 = \int_{\mathcal{Y}} \ell(y;\theta_1)d\mu(y) = \int_{\mathcal{Y}} \ell(y;\theta_2)d\mu(y)$$

implies that $C(\theta_2) = C(\theta_1)$. Equality between the distributions P_{θ_1} and P_{θ_2} follows. □

Remark 3.7: From Property 3.11, it follows that the parameter θ is identified if and only if the mapping $\theta \mapsto Q(\theta) = (Q_1(\theta), \ldots, Q_r(\theta))'$ is injective. More generally, the function $g(\theta)$ is identified if and only if

$$Q(\theta_1) = Q(\theta_2) \Rightarrow g(\theta_1) = g(\theta_2),$$

i.e., if and only if g depends on θ through $Q(\theta)$ only.

Suppose that the affine subspace generated by the points with coordinates $Q(\theta), \theta \in \Theta$, is of dimension r. From Property 3.4, we know that $T(y) = (T_1(y), \ldots, T_r(y))'$ is minimal sufficient. Analogously, $Q(\theta) = (Q_1(\theta), \ldots, Q_r(\theta))'$ can be viewed as the most condensed "summary" of the parameter.

Two cases can be considered:

(i) If $r < p$, the mapping Q is, in general, not injective. The model is said to be *underidentified* and *the degree of underidentification* is $p - r$.

(ii) If the mapping Q is injective, we have $r \geq p$ in general. The model is said to be *just identified* when $r = p$, and *overidentified* if $r > p$. In the latter case, $r - p$ measures *the degree of overidentification.*

Example 3.21: Consider the conditional model given (x, z) defined by

$$\begin{aligned} y_{1i} &= y_{2i}a + x_i b + u_i, \\ y_{2i} &= x_i \pi_1 + z_i \pi_2 + v_i, \end{aligned}$$

$i = 1, \ldots, n$, where y_{1i} and y_{2i} are random variables, x_i' and z_i' are vectors of dimensions H and L that can be considered nonstochastic, and a, b, π_1, π_2 are parameters. The vectors $(u_i, v_i)'$ are assumed to be independently and identically distributed with the bivariate normal distribution

$$N\left(0, \begin{pmatrix} \eta_u & \eta_{uv} \\ \eta_{uv} & \eta_v \end{pmatrix}^{-1}\right).$$

Using the inverse of the variance covariance matrix allows a simple expression for the density

$$
\begin{aligned}
&\ell(y;\theta)\\
&= \frac{1}{(2\pi)^n}(\eta_u\eta_v-\eta_{uv}^2)^{\frac{n}{2}}\\
&\quad \times \exp\{-\frac{1}{2}(\eta_u\sum_{i=1}^n(y_{1i}-y_{2i}\ a-x_ib)^2+\eta_v\sum_{i=1}^n(y_{2i}-x_i\pi_1-z_i\pi_2)^2\\
&\quad +2\eta_{uv}\sum_{i=1}^n(y_{1i}-y_{2i}\ a-x_ib)(y_{2i}-x_i\pi_1-z_i\pi_2))\}.
\end{aligned}
$$

It is easy to see that the model is exponential. The cross term is

$$
\begin{aligned}
&\sum_{j=1}^r Q_j(\theta)T_j(y)\\
&= -\frac{1}{2}\eta_u\sum_{i=1}^n y_{1i}^2+\sum_{i=1}^n y_{2i}^2\left(-\frac{a^2\eta_u}{2}-\frac{\eta_v}{2}+a\eta_{uv}\right)\\
&\quad +\left(\sum_{i=1}^n y_{1i}y_{2i}\right)(a\eta_u-\eta_{uv})+\sum_{h=1}^H\left(\sum_{i=1}^n y_{1i}x_{hi}\right)(\eta_u b_h+\eta_{uv}\pi_{1h})\\
&\quad +\sum_{l=1}^L\left(\sum_{i=1}^n y_{1i}z_{li}\right)\eta_{uv}\pi_{2l}\\
&\quad +\sum_{h=1}^H\left(\sum_{i=1}^n y_{2i}x_{hi}\right)(\eta_v\pi_{1h}-a\eta_{uv}\pi_{1h}-\eta_u a b_h+\eta_{uv}b_h)\\
&\quad +\sum_{l=1}^L\left(\sum_{i=1}^n y_{2i}z_{li}\right)(\eta_v\pi_{2l}-\eta_{uv}a\pi_{2l}).
\end{aligned}
$$

The number of terms in this decomposition is $r = 3 + 2H + 2L$. The number of initial parameters is $p = 3 + 1 + 2H + L$. The affine independence condition on the the statistics $T_j(Y)$ is satisfied provided the variables x and z are linearly independent. Thus we can distinguish the following cases:

(i) If $L = 0$, the model is underidentified and the degree of underidentification is one.

(ii) If $L = 1$, the model is just identified.

(iii) If $L > 1$ the model is overidentified and the degree of overidentification is equal to $L - 1$.

3.4.4 Identification and Information

Since the Kullback discrepancy is equal to zero if and only if two distributions are identical, i.e., $\tilde{I}(\theta_1 \mid \theta_2) = 0 \Leftrightarrow P_{\theta_1} = P_{\theta_2}$, we can characterize identification by means of the function $\tilde{I}$.

Property 3.12: *θ is identified if and only if*

$$\forall\, \theta_1, \theta_2 : \tilde{I}(\theta_1 \mid \theta_2) = 0 \Rightarrow \theta_1 = \theta_2.$$

From the expression for the Kullback information criterion and the fact that $\tilde{I}(\theta_1 \mid \theta_2)$ reaches a minimum in θ_1 at $\theta_1 = \theta_2$, we obtain the following equivalent characterization.

Property 3.13: *θ_1 is identified if and only if for every θ_1 the function $\theta_2 \mapsto E_{\theta_1} \log \ell(Y; \theta_2)$ is maximized uniquely at $\theta_2 = \theta_1$.*

From a Taylor expansion of the function $\tilde{I}$, it is easy to obtain a criterion for local identification.

Property 3.14: *If the Fisher information matrix $\mathcal{I}(\theta_0)$ is nonsingular, θ is locally identified at θ_0.*

PROOF: In a neighborhood of θ_0, a Taylor expansion of the function $\tilde{I}(\theta \mid \theta_0)$ gives

$$\tilde{I}(\theta \mid \theta_0) = \frac{1}{2}(\theta - \theta_0)'\mathcal{I}(\theta_0)(\theta - \theta_0) + 0(\|\theta - \theta_0\|^2).$$

Since the matrix $\mathcal{I}(\theta_0)$ is symmetric positive definite, the function $\tilde{I}(\theta \mid \theta_0)$ is locally strictly convex, and therefore minimized uniquely at θ_0 in this neighborhood. □

In some models, nonsingularity of the Fisher information matrix at any point implies global identification.

Property 3.15: *An exponential model with densities of the form*

$$\ell(y; \theta) = h(y) \exp\left(\sum_{j=1}^{p} \theta_j T_j(y) + A(\theta) \right),$$

where θ belongs to an open subset Θ of $I\!R^p$, is globally identified if and only if $\mathcal{I}(\theta)$ is nonsingular, $\forall\ \theta \in \Theta$.

PROOF: The information matrix is equal to

$$\mathcal{I}(\theta) = V_\theta\left(\frac{\partial \log \ell(Y;\theta)}{\partial \theta}\right) = V_\theta\left(T(Y) + \frac{\partial A(\theta)}{\partial \theta}\right) = V_\theta T(Y).$$

If the matrix $\mathcal{I}(\theta)$ is nonsingular, then the variance covariance matrix of the statistic $T(Y)$ is nonsingular. Thus the components of $T(Y)$ are linearly independent in the affine sense. See B.27 in Appendix B. The desired result follows from applying Property 3.11 to the function $Q(\theta) = \theta$.

Conversely, if $\mathcal{I}(\theta)$ is nonsingular at θ_0, then T belongs to an affine subspace of dimension smaller than p. Thus the densities associated with values θ and θ^* such that $\theta - \theta^*$ are orthogonal to this subspace are identical. Hence the model is not identified. □

Example 3.22: The linear model $Y \sim N(\mathbf{X}\theta, \mathbf{I})$ is an exponential model with $Q(\theta) = \theta$ and information matrix $\mathcal{I}(\theta) = \mathbf{X}'\mathbf{X}$. Thus the model is identified if and only if $\mathbf{X}'\mathbf{X}$ is nonsingular, i.e., if and only if $\mathbf{X}$ is of full column rank. Compare this result with that found in Example 3.16.

3.5 Exercises

EXERCISE 3.1: Let S be the mapping that associates the vector of order statistics $S(Y) = \left(Y_{(1)}, \ldots, Y_{(n)}\right)'$ to a vector of random variables $Y = (Y_1, \ldots, Y_n)'$ (see Example 3.2).

a) Verify that each value $S(y)$ can be obtained from $n!$ different y's obtained by considering all the possible permutations of the components of $S(y)$.

b) When the variables Y_i are absolutely continuous with density $f(y;\theta)$, use Property B.9 in Appendix B to show that the vector $S(Y)$ is absolutely continuous with density on $I\!R^n$ given by

$$\ell_S(s;\theta) = \mathbb{1}_{s_1 < s_2, \ldots < s_n} n! \prod_{i=1}^{n} f(s_i;\theta).$$

c) Find the conditional distribution of Y given $S(Y)$.

EXERCISE 3.2: Let $Y_1, \ldots, Y_n$ be n random variables independently and identically normally distributed $N(m, \sigma^2)$. Show that the statistic $\frac{1}{n}\sum_{i=1}^n Y_i^2$ is sufficient when $m = 0$, and that it is not sufficient when the parameter m is unknown.

EXERCISE 3.3: Let $Y_1, \ldots, Y_n$ be a random sample from a normal distribution $N(m, 1), m \in \mathbb{R}$.

a) Find the distribution of the sample mean $\overline{Y}$.

b) Using Theorem B.1 in Appendix B of the Laplace transform, conclude that $E_m h(\overline{Y}) = 0, \ \forall \ m$ implies that $h = 0$.

EXERCISE 3.4: Let $g(\theta)$ be an identified function of the parameter θ. Show that, for any function $h, \ h(g(\theta))$ is also identified.

EXERCISE 3.5: Let $Y_1, \ldots, Y_n$ be n random variables independently and identically distributed from the Poisson distribution $P(\lambda)$.

a) Find the distribution of $S(Y) = \sum_{i=1}^n Y_i$.

b) Show that the conditional distribution of $Y_1, \ldots, Y_n$ given $S(Y) = s$ is the multinomial distribution $M(s, \frac{1}{n}, \ldots, \frac{1}{n})$, and conclude that $S(Y)$ is sufficient.

c) Use some general properties of exponential models to show that $S(Y)$ is minimal sufficient.

EXERCISE 3.6: Let S and T be two statistics such that $\mathcal{I}^{(S,T)}(\theta) = \mathcal{I}^S(\theta) + \mathcal{I}^T(\theta), \ \forall \ \theta$. Show that S and T are not necessarily independent. Hint: Show that if they were independent then any statistic would be equal to a constant.

EXERCISE 3.7: Let $Y_1 \ldots, Y_n$ be n random variables independently and identically distributed Q_θ, where θ is an unknown parameter belonging to a finite parameter space $\Theta = \{\theta_1, \ldots, \theta_p\}$.

a) Show that the model is dominated.

b) Let f_θ denote the density of Q_θ with respect to a dominating measure. Show that the statistic with values in $\mathbb{R}^p$ of which the components are $\prod_{i=1}^n f_{\theta_j}(Y_i), j = 1, \ldots, p$, is sufficient.

EXERCISE 3.8: Consider the sampling model $\left(\mathbb{R}^2, N(\mu, \Omega)\right)^{\otimes n}$, where the parameter vector $\mu' = (\mu_1, \mu_2)$ is unknown and the matrix Ω is known. Let $Y_i' = (Y_{1i}, Y_{2i}), \ i = 1, \ldots, n$, denote the observations.

a) Let $\bar{Y}_j = \frac{1}{n}\sum_{i=1}^{n} Y_{ji}, j = 1, 2$. Show that $(\bar{Y}_1, \bar{Y}_2)'$ is a minimal sufficient statistic.

b) Suppose that $\mu_1 = 0$. Is $\bar{Y}_2$ sufficient ? Find a linear combination of $\bar{Y}_1$ and $\bar{Y}_2$ that is sufficient. Show that this sufficient statistic is independent of $\bar{Y}_1$.

EXERCISE 3.9:

a) Given the assumptions of Property 3.7, show that for every pair θ_1, θ_2 one has

$$E_{\theta_1}(h(T) \mid S) = E_{\theta_1}(h(T)) \quad P_{\theta_1} \ \ a.s.$$

$$E_{\theta_2}(h(T) \mid S) = E_{\theta_2}(h(T)) \quad P_{\theta_2} \ \ a.s.$$

Conclude that $E_{\theta_1}(h(T)) = E_{\theta_2}(h(T))$ if there does not exist A_1 and A_2 such that $P_{\theta_1}(A_1) = 1,\ P_{\theta_2}(A_2) = 1$, and $A_1 \cap A_2 = \phi$.

b) Show that the latter condition holds if the model is homogenous.

EXERCISE 3.10: Let S be a complete statistic. Show that any statistic T that is a function of S is complete.

EXERCISE 3.11: Prove that the quantity $E_\theta \mathcal{I}^{Y|S}(\theta)$ appearing in Property 3.9 can be written as $V_\theta\left(\partial \log \ell(Y \mid S; \theta)/\partial\theta\right)$.

3.6 References

Bahadur, R. (1954). "Sufficiency and Statistical Decision Functions," *Annals of Mathematical Statistics*, 25, 423–462.

Barra, J.R. (1971). *Notions Fondamentales de Statistique Mathématique*, Dunod.

Basu, A.P. (1955). "On Statistics Independent of Complete Sufficiency," *Sankhya*, 15, 377–380.

Fisher, F. (1966). *The Identification Problem in Econometrics*, McGraw Hill.

Lehmann, E.L. (1959). *Testing Statistical Hypotheses*, Wiley.

Lehmann, E.L. (1983). *Theory of Point Estimation*, Wiley.

Monfort, A. (1982). *Cours de Statistique Mathématique*, Economica.

Richmond, J. (1974). "Identifiability in Linear Models," *Econometrica*, 42, 731–736.

Rothenberg, T.J. (1971). "Identification in Parametric Models," *Econometrica*, 39, 577–592.

CHAPTER 4

Bayesian Interpretations of Sufficiency, Ancillarity, and Identification

Throughout this chapter, we consider a dominated parametric model

$$(\mathcal{Y}, \mathcal{P} = \{P_\theta = \ell(y;\theta)\cdot\mu,\ \theta \in \Theta\})$$

with a prior distribution Π defined on the parameter space Θ. It is assumed that the prior distribution Π is absolutely continuous with respect to a measure ν with density $\pi(\theta)$. It follows that the joint distribution of the pair (Y, θ) has a density with respect to the product measure $\mu \otimes \nu$. The joint density is $\ell(y;\theta)\pi(\theta)$. In addition, the posterior distribution, which is the conditional distribution of θ given Y, has a density with respect to ν given by

$$\pi(\theta \mid y) = \frac{\ell(y;\theta)\pi(\theta)}{\int_\Theta \ell(y;\theta)\pi(\theta)\nu(d\theta)}.$$

The posterior distribution is denoted $\Pi^{\theta|Y=y}$.

4.1 Sufficiency

4.1.1 Definition

According to the classical Definition 3.1 of sufficiency, a statistic S with values in $\mathcal{S}$ is sufficient if the conditional distribution of Y given $S(Y)$ does not depend on θ. When θ is a random variable, as in this case, such a definition is equivalent to the conditional independence of θ and Y given $S(Y)$ (see Property B.30 in Appendix B).

Definition 4.1: *A statistic S is sufficient in the Bayesian sense if θ and Y are conditionally independent given $S(Y)$. We use the notation*

$$\theta \perp Y \mid S(Y).$$

Note, however, that the preceding definition is equivalent to Definition 3.1 only if difficulties arising from the possible presence of negligible sets are not taken into account. For instance, if Θ is an open subset of $\mathbb{R}^p$ and if Π is the Dirac distribution with mass point at θ^* (say) in Θ, then θ and Y are conditionally independent given any statistic $S(Y)$. But the statistic S is not necessarily sufficient in the classical sense (see Exercises 4.1 and 4.2). This counterexample, however, is of little practical interest since the prior distribution assigns a positive probability only to the subset $\bar{\Theta} = \{\theta^*\}$ of Θ. Hence, in the Bayesian approach, the actual parameter space is not Θ but $\bar{\Theta}$.

The properties of conditional independence allow a third characterization of Bayesian sufficiency.

Property 4.1: *A statistic S is sufficient in the Bayesian sense if and only if the conditional distribution of θ given Y, i.e., the posterior distribution, is identical to that of θ given $S(Y)$.*

Property 4.1 is intuitive. It requires that $S(Y)$ and Y contain the same information about θ.

Example 4.1: Consider a random sample $Y_1, \dots, Y_n$ drawn from a normal distribution $N(m, 1)$. Suppose that the prior distribution for m is the standard normal distribution. The joint distribution of the pair (Y, m) is normal

$$N\left(\begin{pmatrix} 0 \\ 0 \end{pmatrix}, \begin{pmatrix} \Sigma_{yy} & \Sigma_{ym} \\ \Sigma_{my} & \Sigma_m \end{pmatrix} \right),$$

where

$$\Sigma_{yy} = VY = \begin{pmatrix} 2 & 1 & \cdots & 1 \\ 1 & 2 & \cdots & 1 \\ & & \vdots & \\ 1 & 1 & \cdots & 2 \end{pmatrix},$$

$$\Sigma_{ym} = \Sigma'_{my} = \begin{pmatrix} 1 \\ 1 \\ \vdots \\ 1 \end{pmatrix}, \text{ and } \Sigma_m = Vm = 1.$$

From Property B.44 in Appendix B, it follows that the conditional distribution of m given Y is the normal distribution

$$N(\Sigma_{my}\Sigma_{yy}^{-1}Y, \Sigma_m - \Sigma_{my}\Sigma_{yy}^{-1}\Sigma_{ym}).$$

The posterior distribution depends on Y only through the conditional mean $\Sigma_{my}\Sigma_{yy}^{-1}Y$. The latter is equal to $1/(n+1)\Sigma_{i=1}^{n}Y_i$. Hence the sample mean $\bar{Y} = 1/n\Sigma_{i=1}^{n}Y_i$ is sufficient in the Bayesian sense.

4.1.2 Minimal Sufficiency

A statistic S^* is said to be *minimal sufficient in the Bayesian sense* if it is sufficient (in the Bayesian sense) and if it is a function of every other sufficient statistic (in the Bayesian sense).

When a minimal sufficient statistic S^* exists, then knowing S^* becomes equivalent to knowing the posterior distribution $\Pi^{\theta|Y=y}, y \in \mathcal{Y}$. Indeed, since S^* is sufficient, then $\Pi^{\theta|Y=y}$ depends on y through S^*. Thus $\Pi^{\theta|Y=\cdot}$ is a function of S^*. It remains to verify the converse, i.e., that S^* is a function of $\Pi^{\theta|Y=\cdot}$. To simplify, we consider the case where Y is discrete. Suppose that $S^*(y)$ is not a function of $\Pi^{\theta|Y=y}$. Then there exist two values y_1 and y_2 such that $\Pi^{\theta|Y=y_1} = \Pi^{\theta|Y=y_2}$ with $S^*(y_1) \neq S^*(y_2)$. Then, define the statistic

$$\tilde{S}(y) = \begin{cases} S^*(y), & \text{if } y \neq y_2, \\ S^*(y_1), & \text{if } y = y_2. \end{cases}$$

It is easy to see that $\tilde{S}$ is sufficient and that S^* is not a function of $\tilde{S}$. This contradicts the hypothesis that S^* is minimal sufficient. The preceding result is a special case of the following general property.

Property 4.2: *A statistic $S(Y)$ that is minimal sufficient in the Bayesian sense is in a bijective relationship with the posterior distribution $\Pi^{\theta|Y}$.*

Example 4.2: In Example 4.1, the posterior distribution was

$$N\left(\Sigma_{my}\Sigma_{yy}^{-1}Y, \Sigma_m - \Sigma_{my}\Sigma_{yy}^{-1}\Sigma_{ym}\right).$$

A minimal sufficient statistic in the Bayesian sense is

$$\Sigma_{my}\Sigma_{yy}^{-1}Y = \frac{n}{n+1}\overline{Y}.$$

Since $\overline{Y}$ is in a bijective relationship with this statistic, then $\overline{Y}$ is also minimal sufficient.

Example 4.3: Consider a parameter space with two elements only, i.e., $\Theta = \{\theta_1, \theta_2\}$. The posterior probabilities are

$$\pi(\theta_1 \mid y) = \frac{\ell(y;\theta_1)\pi(\theta_1)}{\ell(y;\theta_1)\pi(\theta_1) + \ell(y;\theta_2)\pi(\theta_2)} = 1 - \pi(\theta_2 \mid y).$$

Hence the statistic $\pi(\theta_1 \mid Y)$ is minimal sufficient in the Bayesian sense.

It is also clear that if $\ell(y;\theta_1)$ and $\ell(y;\theta_2)$ are strictly positive, then the statistic $\ell(Y;\theta_2)/\ell(Y;\theta_1)$ is well defined and is in a bijective relationship with $\pi(\theta_1 \mid Y)$. Therefore this statistic is also minimal sufficient in the Bayesian sense.

4.1.3 Improving Decision Rules

Theorem 3.1 states that if S is sufficient in the Bayesian sense and if m is a randomized decision rule, then there exists a randomized decision rule m^* with a risk function equal to that of m : $R(m^*,\theta) = R(m,\theta)$. From this result it follows immediately that m^* has the same Bayesian risk as m since

$$\begin{aligned} R_\pi(m^*) &= E_\pi R(m^*,\theta) \\ &= E_\pi R(m,\theta) \\ &= R_\pi(m). \end{aligned}$$

4.1.4 Partial Sufficiency and Bayesian Cut

Defintion 4.1 can be generalized straightforwardly to functions $g(\theta)$ of the parameter.

Definition 4.2: *A statistic S is partially sufficient in the Bayesian sense for $g(\theta)$ if*

$$g(\theta) \perp Y \mid S(Y).$$

In particular, from some general properties of conditional independence, it follows that, if S is sufficient, then S is partially sufficient for every function $g(\theta)$.

Example 4.4: Consider the estimation of m^2 in Example 4.1. The conditional distribution of m^2 given Y is, up to a known proportional factor, a noncentral χ^2 distribution with one degree of freedom and noncentrality parameter proportional to $\bar{Y}^2$. Hence $\bar{Y}^2$ is partially sufficient for m^2. From Example 4.2, it is also clear that $\bar{Y}^2$ is not minimal.

A more precise concept that is related to partial sufficiency is the concept of Bayesian cut.

Definition 4.3: *Let $S(Y)$ be a statistic and $\theta = (\alpha, \beta)'$ be a partitioning of the parameter vector. A Bayesian cut occurs if the following three conditions are satisfied:*

(i) α and β are independent, i.e., $\alpha \perp \beta$.

(ii) θ and $S(Y)$ are conditionally independent given α, i.e., $\theta \perp S(Y) \mid \alpha$.

(iii) θ and Y are conditionally independent given β and $S(Y)$, i.e., $\theta \perp Y \mid (\beta, S(Y))$.

To understand such a definition, it is useful to write the preceding conditions in terms of densities. The joint density of the pair (Y, θ) can be decomposed as $\ell(y;\theta)\pi(\theta)$ where $\ell(y;\theta)$ is the conditional density of Y given θ, and $\pi(\theta)$ is the marginal density of θ. Moreover, by conditioning on $S(Y)$, the density $\ell(y;\theta)$ can be decomposed as

$$\ell(y;\theta) = \ell_S(S(y);\theta)\ell(y \mid S(Y) = S(y);\theta).$$

Consider now the conditions of Definition 4.3. Condition (i) says that $\pi(\theta)$ can be decomposed as

$$\pi(\theta) = \pi_1(\alpha)\pi_2(\beta).$$

Condition (ii) implies that the conditional distribution of $S(Y)$ given θ is equal to the conditional distribution of $S(Y)$ given α , i.e.

$$\ell_S(S(y);\theta) = \ell_S(S(y);\alpha).$$

Condition (iii) implies that the conditional distribution of Y given $(S(Y), \theta)$ is identical to the conditional distribution of Y given $(S(Y), \beta)$. This can be written as

$$\ell(y \mid S(Y) = S(y);\theta) = \ell(y \mid S(Y) = S(y);\beta).$$

From these conditions, it follows that the joint density of the pair (Y, θ) can be decomposed as

$$\ell_S(S(y);\alpha)\ \ell(y \mid S(Y) = S(y);\beta)\pi_1(\alpha)\pi_2(\beta). \tag{4.1}$$

Note first that such a decomposition implies that the conditional distribution of (Y, θ) given $(S(Y), \alpha)$ is

$$\ell(y \mid S(Y) = S(y);\beta)\pi_2(\beta).$$

This density does not depend on α. Hence

$$(Y, \theta) \perp \alpha \mid S(Y),$$

which implies

$$Y \perp \alpha \mid S(Y).$$

The preceding argument shows that S is partially sufficient in the Bayesian sense for α. In addition, the decomposition (4.1) is similar to the one established in the classical framework (see Definition 3.4). The only difference comes from condition (i). This condition implies that the concept of partial sufficiency (of $S(Y)$ for α) and the concept of exogeneity (of $S(Y)$ for β) are relevant only when the parameters α and β can vary independently from each other. Such a condition replaces the condition $\Theta = A \times B$ in the classical framework.

4.2 Ancillarity

From Definition 3.5, a statistic T is ancillary if its distribution does not depend on θ. In the Bayesian framework where θ is a random variable, such a definition is equivalent to the independence of θ and T (see Exercise 4.3).

Definition 4.4: *A statistic T is ancillary in the Bayesian sense if θ and $T(Y)$ are mutually independent. This is denoted $T(Y) \perp \theta$. More generally, T is partially ancillary in the Bayesian sense for a function $g(\theta)$ of the parameter if $T(Y)$ and $g(\theta)$ are mutually independent, i.e., $T(Y) \perp g(\theta)$.*

Obviously, an ancillary statistic is partially ancillary in the Bayesian sense for every function $g(\theta)$.

Property 4.3: *Any statistic $T(Y)$ that is independent in the Bayesian sense of a partially sufficient statistic $S(Y)$ for $g(\theta)$ is partially ancillary for $g(\theta)$.*

PROOF: Mutual independence in the Bayesian sense of $T(Y)$ and $S(Y)$ means that the equality $E[k(T(Y)) \mid S(Y)] = E[k(T(Y))]$ holds for every function k. Here expectation is taken with respect to the marginal distribution of Y. This contrasts with the classical case where expectation is taken with respect to the conditional distribution of Y given θ.

Consider two functions of $g(\theta)$ and Y, denoted $h(g(\theta))$ and $k(T(Y))$, respectively. We have

$$\begin{aligned}
&E[h(g(\theta))k(T(Y))] \\
&\quad = EE[h(g(\theta))k(T(Y)) \mid S(Y)] \\
&\quad = E[E[k(g(\theta)) \mid S(Y)] \cdot E[k(T(Y)) \mid S(Y)]] \\
&\qquad \text{(from partial sufficiency)} \\
&\quad = E[E[h(g(\theta)) \mid S(Y)]E[k(T(Y))]] \\
&\qquad \text{(from Bayesian independence of } S(Y) \text{ and } T(Y)) \\
&\quad = E[h(g(\theta))] \cdot E[k(T(Y))].
\end{aligned}$$

Hence $g(\theta)$ and $T(Y)$ are independent. □

Example 4.5: (Examples 4.1 and 4.4 continued.) We have seen that $S(Y) = \bar{Y}^2$ is partially sufficient in the Bayesian sense for m^2. Consider the statistic $T(Y) = \text{sign } \bar{Y}$. Since the marginal distribution of $\bar{Y}$ is normal with zero mean, the conditional distribution of $T(Y)$ given $S(Y)$ is the known distribution $1/2\varepsilon_{(-)} + 1/2\varepsilon_{(+)}$. Hence $T(Y)$ and $S(Y)$ are independent. Therefore, from Property 4.3, $T(Y)$ is an ancillary statistic for m^2.

Property 4.4: *If there is a Bayesian cut, then $S(Y)$ is partially sufficient for β.*

PROOF:

$$\begin{aligned} E[h(\beta)k(S(Y))] &= EE[h(\beta)k(S(Y)) \mid \alpha] \\ &= E[E(h(\beta) \mid \alpha)E(k(S(Y)) \mid \alpha)], \end{aligned}$$

because of the conditional independence of θ and $S(Y)$ given α. Then, from the independence of α and β, we obtain

$$E[h(\beta)k(S(Y))] = E(h(\beta)) \cdot EE(k(S(Y)) \mid \alpha).$$

Thus β and $S(Y)$ are independent. □

4.3 Identification

In the Bayesian framework, there is a complete symmetry between the observation Y and the parameter θ from a mathematical point of view (but not from a statistical point of view). Thus it is possible to define a concept of sufficiency for functions of the parameter θ. We shall see that such a concept is closely related to the concept of identification discussed in Chapter 3.

Definition 4.5: *A function $g(\theta)$ of the parameter is said to be sufficient in the Bayesian sense if the conditional distribution of Y given θ is equal to that of Y given $g(\theta)$.*

Note that independence of Y and θ is conditional upon $g(\theta)$

$$Y \perp \theta \mid g(\theta). \tag{4.2}$$

This means that the distribution P_θ depends on θ through the function $g(\theta)$ (up to a Π-negligible set, see Exercise 4.6).

Moreover, a function $g(\theta)$ of the parameter is said to be minimal sufficient if it is sufficient and if it is a function of any other sufficient function. Provided there exists a minimal sufficient function, then from a property analogous to Property 4.2, it follows that the function $\theta \mapsto P_\theta$ is minimal sufficient and hence that θ is minimal sufficient if and only if the function $\theta \mapsto P_\theta$ is injective. Thus from Definition 3.10 of identification, we obtain the following property.

Property 4.5: *θ is identified if and only if θ is minimal sufficient in the Bayesian sense.*

Remark 4.1: In the Bayesian framework, the nonidentification of a parameter does not prevent, in general, the computation of usual estimators. These estimators, however, may have undesired properties. For instance, consider a random sample $Y_1, \ldots, Y_n$ drawn from the normal distribution $N(a+b, 1)$ where a and b are independent parameters, each distributed as $N(0,1)$. The posterior means of these parameters are

$$E(a \mid \bar{Y}) = E(b \mid \bar{Y}) = \frac{n}{1+2n}\bar{Y}.$$

Thus these estimators can be computed although a and b are not identified. If, however, we examine the consistency properties of such estimators, we see that $E(a \mid \bar{Y})$ and $E(b \mid \bar{Y})$ both converge to $(a+b)/2$ and not to the true values of the parameters. Consistency is satisfied only for identified linear combinations of the parameters since

$$\forall \lambda \in I\!R,\ E(\lambda(a+b) \mid \bar{Y}) = \lambda \frac{2n}{1+2n}\bar{Y},$$

which converges to $\lambda(a+b)$.

4.4 Exercises

EXERCISE 4.1: Show directly that a sufficient statistic S in the classical sense (see Definition 3.1) is also sufficient in the Bayesian sense. Hint: Consider the case where there are densities $\ell(y;\theta)$, and show that the posterior density $\pi(\theta \mid y)$ depends on y through $S(y)$. Then use Property 4.1.

EXERCISE 4.2: Let Π and Π^* be two prior distributions on Θ that are absolutely continuous with respect to each other. Show that sufficiency properties using Π and Π^* are identical. Answer the same question for ancillarity properties.

EXERCISE 4.3: Consider the limiting case where the prior distribution is the distribution Π with point mass at θ_0. Show that any statistic $S(Y)$ is simultaneously ancillary and sufficient in the Bayesian sense.

EXERCISE 4.4: Consider Example 4.1, and let the prior distribution for m be $N(m_0, \sigma_0^2)$ with m_0 and σ_0^2 known. Find the posterior distribution. Conclude that the posterior mean of m is a minimal sufficient statistic. Study how such a posterior mean depends on m_0 and σ_0^2. What happens if σ_0^2 increases to infinity or converges to zero ?

EXERCISE 4.5: Let $Y_i = (Y_i^1, Y_i^2)'$, $i = 1, \ldots, n$, be n pairs of observations independently and identically distributed

$$N\left(\begin{pmatrix} 0 \\ 0 \end{pmatrix}, \begin{pmatrix} 1 & \theta \\ \theta & 1 \end{pmatrix}\right).$$

Show that $Y^1 = (Y_1^1, \ldots, Y_n^1)'$ and $Y^2 = (Y_1^2, \ldots, Y_n^2)'$ are ancillary in the Bayesian sense whenever the support of the prior distribution is $(-1, 1)$. Determine the prior distributions for which the statistic $Y = (Y_1', \ldots, Y_n')'$ is ancillary in the Bayesian sense.

EXERCISE 4.6: Let $Y_1, \ldots, Y_n$ be n vectors independently and identically distributed $N((\theta_1, \theta_1\theta_2)', \mathbf{I})$. The prior distribution for the parameter $(\theta_1, \theta_2)'$ is $N((1,1)', \mathbf{I})$.

a) Is the parameter vector $(\theta_1, \theta_2)'$ minimal sufficient?

b) Is it identified?

EXERCISE 4.7: Let $Y_1, \ldots, Y_n$ be a random sample from the uniform distribution on the interval $[0, \theta]$. Suppose that the prior distribution for the parameter θ is the uniform distribution on $[1, 2]$.

a) Find the posterior distribution of θ given Y.

b) Show that this distribution depends on $Y_1, \ldots, Y_n$ only through $\max(\max Y_i, 1)$.

c) Contrast minimal sufficiency in the classical sense to minimal sufficiency in the Bayesian sense.

4.5 References

Dreze, J. (1974). "Bayesian Theory of Identification in Simultaneous Equations Models," in S.E. Fienberg and A. Zellner, eds. *Studies in Bayesian Econometrics and Statistics*, North-Holland.

Florens, J., Mouchart, M., and Rolin, J. (1983). "Elements of Bayesian Statistics," CORE, University of Louvain.

Kadane, J. (1974). "The Role of Identification in Bayesian Theory," in S.E. Fienberg and A. Zellner, eds. *Studies in Bayesian Econometrics and Statistics*, North-Holland.

Lindley, D.V. (1965). *Introduction to Probability and Statistics from a Bayesian Viewpoint*, Cambridge University Press.

Zellner, A. (1971). *An Introduction to Bayesian Inference in Econometrics*, Wiley.

CHAPTER 5

Elements of Estimation Theory

5.1 Consequences of Decision Theory

From Chapter 2 a nonrandomized estimator of a function $g(\theta)$ of the parameters is a mapping $\delta(Y)$ from $\mathcal{Y}$ to $g(\Theta)$, and a randomized estimator of $g(\theta)$ is a mapping m_Y from $\mathcal{Y}$ to the set of probability distributions on $g(\Theta)$. The comparison of these estimators is based on risk functions associated with loss functions that are frequently convex (see Section 2.3.2).

5.1.1 Improving Nonrandomized Decision Rules

Because common loss functions are convex, estimation problems are greatly simplified. Indeed, as the next property states, any randomized estimator is (weakly) dominated by a nonrandomized estimator. Thus it suffices to consider nonrandomized estimators. In fact, as seen later, it suffices to consider nonrandomized estimators that are functions of a sufficient statistic.

Property 5.1: *Suppose that $g(\Theta)$ is convex and that the loss function $L(d, \theta)$ is convex in $d \in g(\Theta)$. Then every randomized estimator is (weakly) dominated by a nonrandomized estimator.*

PROOF: Let m be a randomized estimator of $g(\theta)$. Since $g(\Theta)$ is convex, the mean $\int_{g(\Theta)} d \, dm_Y(d) = \delta(Y)$ is an element of $g(\Theta)$. Thus the mapping δ can be interpreted as a nonrandomized estimator. Since L is convex, it follows from B.46 that

$$\int_{g(\Theta)} L(d,\theta)dm_Y(d) \geq L(\int_{g(\Theta)} d\, dm_Y(d), \theta) = L(\delta(Y), \theta).$$

Integrating with respect to the distribution P_θ gives $R(m,\theta) \geq R(\delta,\theta)$, $\forall\theta$. □

Property 5.2: *Under the assumptions of Property 5.1, suppose that S is a sufficient statistic. Then every nonrandomized or randomized estimator is (weakly) dominated by a nonrandomized estimator that is a function of S.*

PROOF: This follows immediately from Theorem 3.1 and Property 5.1. □

In the case of a nonrandomized estimator δ, the estimator in question is $\delta^*(S(Y)) = E_\theta(\delta(Y) \mid S(Y))$, which is independent of θ because S is sufficient. Such an estimator is called the *Rao–Blackwell improved estimator* of δ.

5.1.2 Quadratic Risk Functions

When estimating a scalar function of the parameter $g(\theta)$, one frequently uses the quadratic loss function

$$L(d,\theta) = (d - g(\theta))^2.$$

When $g(\theta)$ is a vector function, i.e., $g(\theta) \in \mathbb{R}^q$, a frequent generalization is *the matrix quadratic loss function*

$$L(d,\theta) = (d - g(\theta))(d - g(\theta))'.$$

It is important to note that such a loss function takes its values in the set of symmetric matrices.

Definition 5.1: *An estimator δ^* weakly dominates another estimator δ in the matrix risk sense if and only if $\forall\ \theta \in \Theta$*

$$\begin{aligned} & R(\delta^*,\theta) = E_\theta(\delta^*(Y) - g(\theta))(\delta^*(Y) - g(\theta))' \\ \preceq\ & R(\delta,\theta) = E_\theta(\delta(Y) - g(\theta))(\delta(Y) - g(\theta))'. \end{aligned}$$

In fact, comparing estimators based on their matrix risk functions is equivalent to comparing estimators based on the family of scalar risk functions associated with loss functions $L_u(d, \theta) = [u'(d - g(\theta))]^2$ for every $u \in I\!R^q$.

Property 5.3: *An estimator δ^* dominates another estimator δ in the matrix quadratic risk sense if and only if δ^* dominates δ for every scalar risk function associated with the loss function*

$$L_u(d, \theta) = [u'(d - g(\theta))]^2, \; u \in I\!R^q.$$

PROOF: $R(\delta^*, \theta) \preceq R(\delta, \theta)$ if and only if

$$E_\theta(\delta^*(Y) - g(\theta))(\delta^*(Y) - g(\theta))' \preceq E_\theta(\delta(Y) - g(\theta))(\delta(Y) - g(\theta))', \; \forall \; \theta.$$

By the definition of the preordering for symmetric matrices, it follows that the preceding statement is equivalent to

$$\begin{aligned} \forall \; \theta, \; \forall \; u \in I\!R^q, \qquad & u'E_\theta(\delta^*(Y) - g(\theta))(\delta^*(Y) - g(\theta))'u \\ & \leq u'E_\theta(\delta(Y) - g(\theta))(\delta(Y) - g(\theta))'u, \end{aligned}$$

i.e.

$$\forall \; \theta, \; \forall \; u \in I\!R^q, E_\theta L_u(\delta^*(Y), \theta) \leq E_\theta L_u(\delta(Y), \theta),$$

i.e.

$$\forall \; \theta, \; \forall \; u \in I\!R^q, R_u(\delta^*, \theta) \leq R_u(\delta, \theta),$$

where R_u denotes the risk function associated with L_u. □

Thus the estimator δ^* dominates δ in the matrix risk sense if, for every u, the linear form $u'\delta^*(Y)$ dominates $u'\delta(Y)$ when estimating $u'g(\theta)$. In other words, the matrix risk function takes into account all possible directions. Note, however, that the condition $R_u(\delta^*, \theta) \leq R_u(\delta, \theta)$, $\forall \; \theta$, for the vectors u of a given basis of $I\!R^q$, is not sufficient to ensure that δ^* dominates δ in the matrix sense (see Exercise 5.1).

Property 5.4:

$$R(\delta, \theta) = V_\theta \delta(Y) + (E_\theta \delta(Y) - g(\theta)) (E_\theta \delta(Y) - g(\theta))'.$$

PROOF: We have

$$\begin{aligned} R(\delta, \theta) &= E_\theta(\delta(Y) - g(\theta))(\delta(Y) - g(\theta))' \\ &= E_\theta(\delta(Y) - E_\theta\delta(Y) + E_\theta\delta(Y) - g(\theta)) \\ & \quad \times(\delta(Y) - E_\theta\delta(Y) + E_\theta\delta(Y) - g(\theta))' \end{aligned}$$

$$\begin{aligned} = \quad & E_\theta(\delta(Y) - E_\theta\delta(Y))(\delta(Y) - E_\theta\delta(Y))' \\ & + E_\theta(E_\theta\delta(Y) - g(\theta))(E_\theta\delta(Y) - g(\theta))' \\ & + E_\theta(\delta(Y) - E_\theta\delta(Y))(E_\theta\delta(Y) - g(\theta))' \\ & + E_\theta(E_\theta\delta(Y) - g(\theta))(\delta(Y) - E_\theta\delta(Y))'. \end{aligned}$$

Because the cross terms are equal to zero, we obtain

$$R(\delta, \theta) = V_\theta\delta(Y) + (E_\theta\delta(Y) - g(\theta))(E_\theta\delta(Y) - g(\theta))'.$$

□

Thus the risk can be written as the sum of the variance covariance matrix $V_\theta\delta(Y)$ of the estimator and *the squared bias*

$$(E_\theta\delta(Y) - g(\theta))(E_\theta\delta(Y) - g(\theta))'.$$

Hence the fact that $\delta(Y)$ does not coincide with $g(\theta)$ results from the variability of the estimator and the average discrepancy between the estimator and the true value.

Example 5.1: Consider two estimators δ^* and δ of $\theta \in \mathbb{R}^p$ such that δ^* dominates δ in the matrix risk sense. Partition the vectors δ^*, δ, and θ into subvectors of dimensions p_1 and $p - p_1$

$$\delta^* = \begin{pmatrix} \delta_1^* \\ \delta_2^* \end{pmatrix}, \delta = \begin{pmatrix} \delta_1 \\ \delta_2 \end{pmatrix}, \theta = \begin{pmatrix} \theta_1 \\ \theta_2 \end{pmatrix}.$$

The risk functions can be partitioned similarly. For instance, we have

$$R(\delta, \theta) = \begin{pmatrix} E_\theta(\delta_1(Y) - \theta_1)(\delta_1(Y) - \theta_1)' & E_\theta(\delta_1(Y) - \theta_1)(\delta_2(Y) - \theta_2)' \\ E_\theta(\delta_2(Y) - \theta_2)(\delta_1(Y) - \theta_1)' & E_\theta(\delta_2(Y) - \theta_2)(\delta_2(Y) - \theta_2)' \end{pmatrix}.$$

The condition $R(\delta^*, \theta) \preceq R(\delta, \theta)$ implies an analogous condition for the quadratic form that is restricted to the subspace generated by the p_1 first components. Thus we have

$$\forall\, \theta : \; E_\theta(\delta_1^*(Y) - \theta_1)(\delta_1^*(Y) - \theta_1)' \preceq E_\theta(\delta_1(Y) - \theta_1)(\delta_1(Y) - \theta_1).$$

Hence δ_1^* dominates δ_1 in the matrix risk sense when estimating the parameter function $g(\theta) = \theta_1$.

Example 5.2: Sometimes, one considers the scalar quadratic risk function

$$\begin{aligned} R_1(\delta,\theta) &= E_\theta(\delta(Y)-g(\theta))'(\delta(Y)-g(\theta)) \\ &= \sum_{j=1}^{q} E_\theta(\delta_j(Y)-g_j(\theta))^2 \\ &= \text{Tr } R(\delta,\theta). \end{aligned}$$

From Property A.8, it follows immediately that δ^* dominates δ according to the scalar risk function R_1 if δ^* dominates δ in the matrix risk sense.

Example 5.3: Consider two independent observations Y_1 and Y_2 from the Poisson distribution $\mathcal{P}(\lambda)$. The parameter λ is equal to the mean and the variance of the Poisson distribution. Hence it is natural to consider the following estimators for λ:

– the sample mean

$$\delta_1(Y) = \frac{Y_1+Y_2}{2},$$

– the sample variance

$$\begin{aligned} \delta_2(Y) &= \frac{1}{2-1}\left(\left(Y_1-\frac{Y_1+Y_2}{2}\right)^2+\left(Y_2-\frac{Y_1+Y_2}{2}\right)^2\right) \\ &= \frac{(Y_1-Y_2)^2}{2}. \end{aligned}$$

It is easy to compute the risk associated with each estimator using the next formulae, which give the moments up to the fourth order of the Poisson distribution with parameter λ

$$\begin{aligned} &E_\lambda Y=\lambda, \quad E_\lambda Y^2=\lambda+\lambda^2, \; E_\lambda Y^3=\lambda+3\lambda^2+\lambda^3, \\ &E_\lambda Y^4=\lambda+7\lambda^2+6\lambda^3+\lambda^4. \end{aligned}$$

(i) Risk for δ_1: We have

$$\begin{aligned} E_\lambda\delta_1(Y) &= E\left(\frac{Y_1+Y_2}{2}\right)=\frac{2\lambda}{2}=\lambda, \\ V_\lambda\delta_1(Y) &= V_\lambda\left(\frac{Y_1+Y_2}{2}\right)=\frac{1}{4}(V_\lambda Y_1+V_\lambda Y_2)=\frac{\lambda}{2}. \end{aligned}$$

Thus the risk for δ_1 is $R(\delta_1, \lambda) = \lambda/2$. The risk function is a straight line passing through the origin.

(ii) Risk for δ_2: We have

$$\begin{aligned} E_\lambda \delta_2(Y) &= \frac{1}{2} E_\lambda (Y_1 - Y_2)^2 = \frac{1}{2} V_\lambda (Y_1 - Y_2) \\ &= \frac{1}{2}(V_\lambda Y_1 + V_\lambda Y_2) = \lambda, \end{aligned}$$

$$\begin{aligned} E_\lambda \delta_2(Y)^2 &= \frac{1}{4} E_\lambda (Y_1 - Y_2)^4 \\ &= \frac{1}{4}\left(2E_\lambda Y^4 - 8E_\lambda Y E_\lambda Y^3 + (6E_\lambda Y^2)^2\right) \\ &= \frac{1}{2}\left(E_\lambda Y^4 - 4E_\lambda Y\ E_\lambda Y^3 + 3(E_\lambda Y^2)^2\right) \\ &= \frac{1}{2}(\lambda + 7\lambda^2 + 6\lambda^3 + \lambda^4 - 4\lambda^2 - 12\lambda^3 - 4\lambda^4 \\ &\qquad + 3\lambda^2 + 3\lambda^4 + 6\lambda^3) \\ &= \frac{1}{2}(\lambda + 6\lambda^2). \end{aligned}$$

Thus

$$V_\lambda \delta^2(Y) = \frac{1}{2}(\lambda + 6\lambda^2) - \lambda^2 = \frac{\lambda}{2} + 2\lambda^2.$$

The risk function is here equal to the variance $R(\delta_2, \lambda) = \lambda/2 + 2\lambda^2$. It is a part of a parabola.

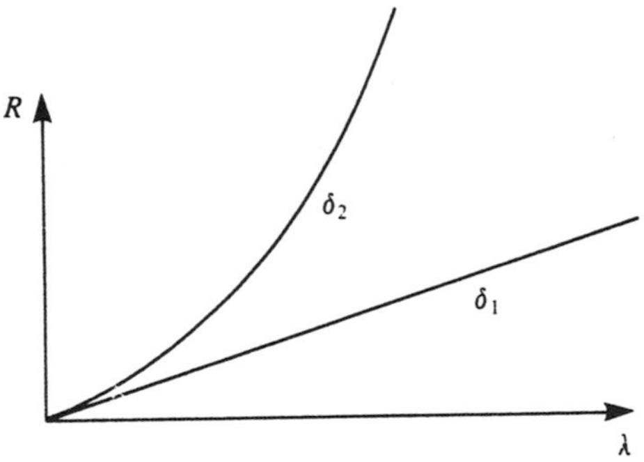

Figure 5.1: Risk Functions

Since the risk function associated with δ_1 is always below the one associated with δ_2, i.e., $\forall\ \lambda \in \mathbb{R}^+,\ R(\delta_1, \lambda) \leq R(\delta_2, \lambda)$, the sample mean estimator dominates the sample variance estimator.

A comparison based on quadratic risks defines a preordering. The preordering is not total, for two estimators may not be comparable. We may, however, ask whether there exists an estimator δ^* of $g(\theta)$ that dominates every other estimator.

Example 5.4: Nonexistence of an Optimal Estimator

Suppose that an optimal estimator δ^* exists. This estimator must dominate the estimator δ_{g_o} for $g(\theta)$ that associates the constant value g_o

$$\forall\, \theta \in \Theta,\ R(\delta^*, \theta) \preceq R(\delta_{g_o}, \theta).$$

In particular, this inequality must hold for the parameter values θ_o satisfying $g(\theta_o) = g_o$. But

$$\begin{aligned} R(\delta_{g_o}, \theta_o) &= E_{\theta_o}(\delta_{g_o}(Y) - g_{(\theta_o)})(\delta_{g_o}(Y) - g(\theta_o))' \\ &= E_{\theta_o}(g_o - g_o)(g_o - g_o)' = 0. \end{aligned}$$

Therefore

$$R(\delta^*, \theta_o) = E_{\theta_o}(\delta^*(Y) - g_o)(\delta^*(Y) - g_o)' = 0.$$

Since the matrix under the expectation sign is symmetric positive definite, we have $\delta^*(Y) = g_o$. Since g_o is arbitrary, the latter equality must hold for every value $g_o \in g(\Theta)$. These equalities are compatible only if the set $g(\Theta)$ is reduced to one element hence only if the estimation problem can be solved perfectly without any observations – a case without much interest.

5.2 Estimation Principles

Since an optimal estimator does not exist, except in the degenerate case, one must consider some appropriate methods for selecting an estimator. In particular, it is useful to examine some additional desirable properties that could be imposed on estimators.

5.2.1 Invariance Principle

A natural idea consists in considering estimators that are tractable. Often, one is led to consider:

- estimators that are *linear* in the observations when estimating parameters such as means

$$\delta(Y_1, \ldots, Y_n) = \sum_{i=1}^{n} a_i Y_i,$$

- estimators that are *quadratic* in the observations when estimating parameters such as variances

$$\delta(Y_1, \ldots, Y_n) = \sum_{i,j} a_{ij} Y_i Y_j.$$

Frequently, constraints imposed on estimators are interpreted as invariance properties with respect to a group of transformations. This explains the name of *invariance principle.* For instance, linear estimators can be viewed as estimators satisfying an invariance property with respect to linear combinations since such estimators satisfy

$$\delta(\alpha Y + \alpha^* Y^*) = \alpha \delta(Y) + \alpha^* \delta(Y^*)$$

for every vector Y and Y^* of $\mathbb{R}^n$ and every scalars α and α^*.

Example 5.5: Suppose that a researcher wishes to know the average income of a given population. Suppose that n observations on household incomes are available. Let $y_1, \ldots, y_n$ denote the observed incomes measured in dollars (say). The unknown average income m in the population is estimated by $\delta(y_1, \ldots, y_n)$. Now suppose the estimation problem is considered in another unit such as cents. Then the average income is $100m$, the observations are $100y_1, \ldots, 100y_n$, and the estimator becomes $\delta(100y_1, \ldots, 100y_n)$. It is desirable that the change of measurement units does not modify the result, i.e., that

$$\delta(100y_1, \ldots, 100y_n) = 100\delta(y_1, \ldots, y_n), \ \forall\ y_1, \ldots, y_n.$$

In Example 5.5, requiring independence of measurement units is equivalent to assuming that

$$\forall\ \lambda > 0, \ \delta(\lambda Y_1, \ldots, \lambda Y_n) = \lambda \delta(Y_1, \ldots, Y_n).$$

That is, the estimator is invariant with respect to the set of positive scalar transformations.

Similarly, when observations are dates of events, one may impose that estimation results are not modified by a change of time origin. In this case, one considers invariance properties with respect to translations

$$\forall\ \alpha, \ \delta(Y_1 + \alpha, \ldots, Y_n + \alpha) = \delta(Y_1, \ldots, Y_n) + \alpha.$$

5.2.2 Unbiasedness Principle

Definition 5.2: *An estimator δ is an unbiased estimator of $g(\theta)$ if and only if $E_\theta \delta(Y) = g(\theta),\ \forall\ \theta \in \Theta$.*

Thus an estimator is unbiased if, on average, the estimated value is equal to the value of the parameter, for every value of this parameter. In Example 5.3, the estimators δ_1 and δ_2 are unbiased.

5.2.3 Asymptotic Criteria

When the number of observations is large, one frequently requires that estimators satisfy some so-called asymptotic properties, i.e., properties that are defined when the sample size n increases to infinity.

Then, it is necessary to alter the usual statistical framework. In particular, we now consider a sequence of models indexed by the number n of observations: $(\mathcal{Y}_n,\ \mathcal{P}_n = \{P_{n,\theta},\ \theta \in \Theta\})$. These models depend on n, but the parameter θ is independent of n.

To estimate a function $g(\theta)$ of the parameter, one considers a sequence of estimators $\{\delta_n, n \in \mathbf{N}\}$, where δ_n is a mapping from $\mathcal{Y}_n$ to $g(\Theta)$. Thus unbiasedness can be defined for the limiting case where n is infinitely large.

Definition 5.3: *The sequence of estimators $\{\delta_n,\ n \in \mathbf{N}\}$ is asymptotically unbiased if*

$$\lim_{n \mapsto \infty} E_\theta \delta_n(Y) = g(\theta),\ \forall\ \theta \in \Theta.$$

The expectation $E_\theta(\cdot)$ is taken with respect to the distribution $P_{n,\theta}$. Hence, in principle, the expectation should also be indexed by n. We shall say that *an estimator δ_n is asymptotically unbiased* when the sequence of estimators δ_n is asymptotically unbiased.

Definition 5.4: *A sequence of estimators $\{\delta_n,\ n \in \mathbf{N}\}$ is said to be:*

(i) weakly consistent if, for every θ, $\delta_n(Y)$ converges in probability to $g(\theta)$, i.e.

$$\forall\ \varepsilon > 0,\ P_{n,\theta}(\|\delta_n(Y) - g(\theta)\| > \varepsilon) \overset{n\to\infty}{\to} 0,\ \forall\ \theta \in \Theta;$$

(ii) consistent in quadratic mean, which is denoted $\delta_n \overset{qm}{\to} g(\theta)$, if

$$E_\theta \|\delta_n(Y) - g(\theta)\|^2 \overset{n\to\infty}{\to} 0,\ \forall\ \theta \in \Theta;$$

(iii) strongly consistent if $\delta_n(Y)$ converges P_θ almost surely to $g(\theta)$ for every $\theta \in \Theta$.

Clearly some relations exist among these consistency concepts. Two of them are:

- strong consistency implies weak consistency,
- consistency in quadratic mean implies weak consistency.

Weak and strong consistency properties are maintained when estimators are transformed through continous mappings (see Property B.68).

Property 5.5: *Let h be a continous mapping on $g(\Theta)$. If δ_n is a weakly (or strongly) consistent estimator of $g(\theta)$ then $h(\delta_n)$ is a weakly (or strongly) consistent estimator of $h(g(\theta))$.*

In general, the property that is easiest to verify is consistency in quadratic mean, which implies weak consistency. This follows from the next property.

Property 5.6: $\delta_n \overset{qm}{\to} g(\theta)$ *if and only if*

$$
\begin{aligned}
&E_\theta \delta_n(Y) \to g(\theta), \\
&V_\theta \delta_n(Y) \to 0,
\end{aligned}
$$

$\forall\ \theta \in \Theta$, *i.e., if and only if the estimator is asymptotically unbiased and its variance converges to zero.*

Proof: The result follows from

$$
E_\theta \|\delta_n(Y) - g(\theta)\|^2 = E_\theta(\delta_n(Y) - g(\theta))'(\delta_n(Y) - g(\theta)),
$$

which is equal to

$$
\|E_\theta \delta_n(Y) - g(\theta)\|^2 + \mathrm{Tr}\ V_\theta \delta_n(Y),
$$

and the fact that each term of the latter decomposition is nonnegative.□

5.3 Search for Good Estimators

There are many methods for finding "good estimators." Within the classical framework, we can distinguish:

- methods that consist in finding the best estimator in a restricted class of estimators that satisfy some desirable properties,

- methods that consist in selecting the best estimator by maximizing or minimizing a criterion and then by examining whether the estimator thus obtained satisfies some appropriate properties.

An alternative approach is to adopt the Bayesian framework, which leads, in general, to a unique optimal estimator.

5.3.1 Search Within a Subclass

The most common method consists in searching for the *best unbiased estimator* or the *best linear unbiased estimator*. In Chapter 6, we shall see that optimal estimators exist within such classes for some problems. In particular, these methods will be applied to exponential models and linear models.

Another method consists in introducing a natural family of estimators for $g(\theta)$ and then in finding the best estimator in this family. This approach leads to *methods of moments* and their generalizations. Examples are *asymptotic least squares* and *generalized methods of moments*, which will be studied in Chapter 9.

5.3.2 Criterion Optimization

The most well-known method based on a criterion optimization is the *maximum likelihood (ML) method.* This method consists in maximizing the likelihood function $\ell(y;\cdot)$ of the model with respect to $\theta \in \Theta$. A solution of $\max_{\theta\in\Theta} \ell(y;\theta)$, if it exists, is retained as an estimator of θ. This method will be studied in Chapter 7.

Other objective functions can be considered. These are studied in Chapters 8 and 10. Examples are *ordinary least squares* and *pseudo maximum likelihood* methods.

5.3.3 Bayesian Methods

The methods described in Sections 5.3.1 and 5.3.2 belong to the classical framework. As mentioned earlier, in the Bayesian approach, one minimizes the Bayesian risk

$$R_\Pi(\delta) = E_\Pi R(\delta, \theta).$$

While uniform minimization over classical risk functions does not have a solution, minimization of the Bayesian risk produces, in general, a solution. When the quadratic risk function is used, the solution can be obtained explicitly.

Property 5.7: *The posterior expectation of $g(\theta)$, i.e.*

$$\delta_\Pi = E(g(\theta) \mid Y) = \int_\Theta g(\theta) d\Pi(\theta \mid Y),$$

minimizes the quadratic Bayesian matrix risk function

$$R_\Pi(\delta) = E_\Pi E_\theta(\delta(Y) - g(\theta))(\delta(Y) - g(\theta))'.$$

PROOF: We have

$$R_\Pi(\delta) = E(\delta(Y) - g(\theta))(\delta(Y) - g(\theta))',$$

where E denotes the expectation with respect to the joint distribution of the pair (θ, Y). An argument similar to that given in the proof of Property 5.4 implies that

$$\begin{aligned} & E[(\delta(Y) - g(\theta))(\delta(Y) - g(\theta))' \mid Y] \\ = \; & V(g(\theta) \mid Y) + E[(\delta(Y) - E(g(\theta) \mid Y))(\delta(Y) - E(g(\theta) \mid Y))' \mid Y] \\ \succeq \; & V(g(\theta) \mid Y) = E[(\delta_\Pi(Y) - g(\theta))(\delta_\Pi(Y) - g(\theta))' \mid Y]. \end{aligned}$$

Now it suffices to take the expectation with respect to Y of both terms of the preceding inequality to obtain

$$R_\Pi(\delta) \succeq EV(g(\theta) \mid Y) = E(\delta_\Pi(Y) - g(\theta))(\delta_\Pi(Y) - g(\theta))',$$

i.e.

$$R_\Pi(\delta) \succeq R_\Pi(\delta_\Pi).$$

□

The Bayesian approach to estimation problems will be studied in Chapter 12.

5.4 Exercises

EXERCISE 5.1: Let Y_1, Y_2, and Y_3 be three observations jointly normally distributed as $N((a, b, a)', \mathbf{I})$. Consider estimating the pair $(a, b)'$. Determine the matrix risk function associated with each of the following two estimators

$$\delta = \begin{pmatrix} \delta_1 \\ \delta_2 \end{pmatrix} = \begin{pmatrix} Y_1 \\ Y_2 \end{pmatrix} \text{ and } \delta^* = \begin{pmatrix} \delta_1^* \\ \delta_2^* \end{pmatrix} = \begin{pmatrix} Y_1 \\ Y_2 - Y_1 + Y_3 \end{pmatrix}.$$

Verify that the two matrix risk functions are not comparable even though

$$V\delta_1^* = V\delta_1, \; V\delta_2^* > V\delta_2.$$

EXERCISE 5.2: For the model described in Exercise 5.1, verify that

$$\text{Tr } R(\delta^*, \theta) \geq \text{Tr } R(\delta, \theta), \; \forall \, \theta = (a, b)' \in \mathbb{R}^2.$$

EXERCISE 5.3: Prove that an estimator δ^* of $g(\theta) \in \mathbb{R}^q$ dominates another estimator δ in the matrix risk sense if and only if δ^* dominates δ for every scalar risk associated with a loss function of the form

$$L_\Omega(d, \theta) = (d - g(\theta))'\Omega(d - g(\theta)),$$

where Ω is an arbitrary positive definite matrix. Does the result hold if the matrix Ω is a function of the parameter θ ?

EXERCISE 5.4: Let $Y_1, \ldots, Y_n$ be n independent and identically distributed observations. Justify the use of estimators δ that are symmetric in $Y_1, \ldots, Y_n$. Verify that such estimators are characterized by their invariance property with respect to the set of permutations.

EXERCISE 5.5: Given the sequence of statistical models

$$(\mathcal{Y}_n, \mathcal{P}_n = \{P_{n,\theta}, \; \theta \in \Theta\}),$$

let δ_n be an estimator of $g(\theta)$ which is consistent in quadratic mean. Show that there exists an infinity of estimators that are consistent in quadratic mean for $g(\theta)$.

EXERCISE 5.6: Prove that consistency in quadratic mean of an estimator is preserved by linear transformations.

EXERCISE 5.7: Let $\delta_n(Y)$ be an estimator of $g(\theta) \in \mathbb{R}$ that is consistent in quadratic mean.

a) Prove the inequality

$$P_{n,\theta}(|\delta_n(Y) - g(\theta)| > \varepsilon) \leq \frac{V_\theta \delta_n(Y) + (E_\theta \delta_n(Y) - g(\theta))^2}{\varepsilon^2}.$$

b) In addition, suppose that $\sqrt{n}(\delta_n(Y) - g(\theta))$ converges in distribution to the normal distribution $N(0, \sigma^2(\theta))$. Find an asymptotic approximation to $P_{n,\theta}(|\delta_n(Y) - g(\theta)| > \varepsilon)$.

c) Compare the approximation in b) to the upper bound obtained in a).

EXERCISE 5.8: Consider the dynamic model

$$Y_t = a_0 + a_1 X_{t-1} + \cdots + a_p X_{t-p} + u_t, \ t = 1, \ldots, T,$$

where the errors u_t are independent identically distributed $N(0, \sigma^2)$ and p is assumed unknown. Determine the set of possible values for the parameter vector $\theta = (a_0, a_1, \ldots, a_p, p, \sigma^2)'$. Is such a set convex? Can the Rao–Blackwell method be used to improve upon any given nonrandomized estimator (see Section 5.1) ?

EXERCISE 5.9: Let δ and δ^* be two estimators of the parameter function $g(\theta)$. These estimators could be compared as follows: δ^* is considered to dominate δ if and only if

$$\det R(\delta^*, \theta) \leq \det R(\delta, \theta), \ \forall \ \theta \in \Theta,$$

where R denotes the matrix risk function defined in Section 5.3.

a) Interpret the criterion function $\det R(\cdot, \theta)$.

b) Does such a criterion correspond to a scalar loss function?

c) Compare the preceding ordering to the preordering associated with the matrix risk.

5.5 References

Barra, J.R. (1971). *Notions Fondamentales de Statistique Mathématique*, Dunod.

Cox, D.R. and Hinkley, D.V. (1974). *Theoretical Statistics*, Chapman and Hall.

Ferguson, T.S. (1967). *Mathematical Statistics*, Academic Press.

Monfort, A. (1982). *Cours de Statistique Mathématique*, Economica.

CHAPTER 6

Unbiased Estimation

6.1 Definitions

6.1.1 Unbiased Estimators

In Chapter 5 unbiased estimation was introduced as one of the various principles for reducing the class of estimators considered.

Definition 6.1: *Given a parametric model $(\mathcal{Y}, \{P_\theta, \theta \in \Theta\})$, an estimator $T(Y)$ is unbiased for a function $g(\theta) \in \mathbb{R}^q$ of the parameter θ if*

$$E_\theta T(Y) = g(\theta), \ \forall \ \theta \in \Theta.$$

In particular, unbiased estimators of the parameter θ itself are frequently considered.

Example 6.1: Let $Y_1, \ldots, Y_n$ be a random sample from the uniform distribution $U_{[0,\theta]}$. The mean of each random variable is $\theta/2$. Thus an unbiased estimator of θ is

$$T(Y) = \frac{2}{n} \sum_{i=1}^{n} Y_i.$$

Example 6.2: If $T(Y)$ is an unbiased estimator of $g(\theta)$, then every linear transformation $\mathbf{A}T(Y) + \mathbf{B}$ where $\mathbf{A}$ and $\mathbf{B}$ are constant matrices of dimension $r \times q$ and $r \times 1$ is an unbiased estimator for the function $\mathbf{A}g(\theta) + \mathbf{B}$. This follows from

$$E_\theta(\mathbf{A}T(Y) + \mathbf{B}) = \mathbf{A}E_\theta T(Y) + \mathbf{B} = \mathbf{A}g(\theta) + \mathbf{B}, \ \forall \ \theta \in \Theta.$$

Example 6.3: Let $Y_1, \ldots, Y_n$ be uncorrelated observations from possibly nonidentical distributions with the same mean m and the same variance σ^2. Unbiased estimators of these two parameters are easily obtained. For instance, $\bar{Y}$ is an unbiased estimator of m since

$$E_{m,\sigma^2}\bar{Y} = \frac{1}{n}\sum_{i=1}^{n} E_{m,\sigma^2}Y_i, \ = m, \quad \forall\, m, \sigma^2.$$

To construct an unbiased estimator of σ^2, it is useful to consider the statistic $\sum_{i=1}^{n} (Y_i - \bar{Y})^2$. This statistic is the square length of the orthogonal projection of $Y = (Y_1, \ldots, Y_n)'$ on to the subspace orthogonal to the vector e of which all the components are equal to one. Let $\mathbf{I} - \mathbf{P}$ denote the corresponding orthogonal projection operator. From Property A.1, Corollary A.4, and B.20 we have

$$\begin{aligned}
E_{m,\sigma^2}\left(\sum_{i=1}^{n}(Y_i - \bar{Y})^2\right) &= E_{m,\sigma^2}\|(\mathbf{I}-\mathbf{P})Y\|^2 \\
&= E_{m,\sigma^2}(Y'(\mathbf{I}-\mathbf{P})Y) \\
&= E_{m,\sigma^2}(\text{Tr } Y'(\mathbf{I}-\mathbf{P})Y) \\
&= E_{m,\sigma^2}(\text{Tr } (\mathbf{I}-\mathbf{P})YY') \\
&= \text{Tr } \left((\mathbf{I}-\mathbf{P})(\sigma^2\mathbf{I}+m^2ee')\right) \\
&= \sigma^2 \text{Tr } (\mathbf{I}-\mathbf{P}) \\
&= (n-1)\sigma^2.
\end{aligned}$$

Hence $\hat{\sigma}^2 = \frac{1}{n-1}\sum_{i=1}^{n}(Y_i - \bar{Y})^2$ is an unbiased estimator of σ^2.

Remark 6.1: It is important to note that the unbiasedness condition

$$E_\theta T(Y) = g(\theta),$$

must hold for *every* possible value of the parameter and not only for some of these values. Thus, if $\theta_0 \in \Theta$, then $T(Y) = \theta_0$ is an estimator satisfying the condition $E_\theta T(Y) = \theta$ when $\theta = \theta_0$. However, because the unbiasedness condition is not satisfied for every other parameter value, this estimator is not unbiased.

When an estimator is unbiased, its matrix quadratic risk function reduces to its variance covariance matrix since

$$\begin{aligned}
R_\theta(T(Y), g(\theta)) &= E_\theta\left[(T(Y) - g(\theta))(T(Y) - g(\theta))'\right] \\
&= V_\theta T(Y) + (E_\theta T(Y) - g(\theta))(E_\theta T(Y) - g(\theta))' \\
&= V_\theta T(Y).
\end{aligned}$$

Thus comparing two unbiased estimators of $g(\theta)$ becomes equivalent to comparing their variance covariance matrices.

Property 6.1: *If T_1 and T_2 are two unbiased estimators, then T_1 dominates T_2 if and only if*

$$V_\theta T_2(Y) \succeq V_\theta T_1(Y), \quad \forall\, \theta \in \Theta,$$

i.e., if and only if $V_\theta T_2(Y) - V_\theta T_1(Y)$ is a positive semidefinite matrix for every possible value of the parameter.

6.1.2 Existence of Unbiased Estimators

Property 6.2: *If $g(\theta)$ is a nonidentified parameter function, then there does not exist an unbiased estimator of $g(\theta)$.*

PROOF: The proof is by contradiction. Suppose there exists an unbiased estimator T of $g(\theta)$. Consider two parameter values θ_1 and θ_2 such that the corresponding distributions are identical, i.e., such that $P_{\theta_1} = P_{\theta_2}$. Then we have

$$\begin{aligned} g(\theta_1) &= E_{\theta_1} T(Y) = \int_{\mathcal{Y}} T(y)\, dP_{\theta_1}(y) \\ &= \int_{\mathcal{Y}} T(y)\, dP_{\theta_2}(y) = E_{\theta_2} T(Y) = g(\theta_2). \end{aligned}$$

Thus the condition $P_{\theta_1} = P_{\theta_2}$ implies that $g(\theta_1) = g(\theta_2)$. This means that $g(\theta)$ is identified.□

Thus a necessary condition for the existence of an unbiased estimator is the identification of the parameter function to be estimated. This condition, however, is not sufficient as the following example illustrates.

Example 6.4: Suppose that there is only one observation Y_1 from a Bernoulli distribution $B(1,p)$. An estimator is of the form $T(Y_1)$, and its mean is

$$\begin{aligned} E_p T(Y_1) &= T(0)P(Y_1 = 0) + T(1)P(Y_1 = 1) \\ &= T(0)(1-p) + T(1)p \\ &= T(0) + (T(1) - T(0))p. \end{aligned}$$

Therefore, only linear functions of the parameter p can be estimated in an unbiased fashion.

6.1.3 Unbiased Estimation and Sufficiency

Property 6.3: *If $T(Y)$ is an unbiased estimator of $g(\theta)$, and if $S(Y)$ is a sufficient statistic for θ, then the Rao–Blackwell improved estimator $E(T(Y) \mid S(Y))$ is unbiased for $g(\theta)$.*

PROOF: This is a direct consequence of the property

$$E_\theta E(T(Y) \mid S(Y)) = E_\theta T(Y) = g(\theta), \quad \forall\, \theta \in \Theta.$$

□

The Rao–Blackwell estimator has a smaller variance than the original estimator (see Theorem 3.1 and Property 5.2). In fact, this property follows directly from

$$\begin{aligned} V_\theta T(Y) &= V_\theta E(T(Y) \mid S(Y)) + E_\theta V_\theta(T(Y) \mid S(Y)) \\ &\succeq V_\theta E(T(Y) \mid S(Y)). \end{aligned}$$

Example 6.5: Consider the sampling model of Example 6.1. The unbiased estimator $T(Y) = (2/n)\sum_{i=1}^n Y_i$ of θ is not a function of the sufficient statistic $S(Y) = \sup_{i=1,\ldots,n}(Y_i)$.

To determine the Rao–Blackwell improved estimator, we note that

$$\begin{aligned} & E(Y_1 \mid \sup_{i=1,\ldots,n} Y_i = z) \\ &= P(\sup_{i=1,\ldots,n} Y_i = Y_1)E(Y_1 \mid Y_1 = z, \sup_{i=1,\ldots,n} Y_i = Y_1) \\ &\quad + \sum_{j=2}^n P(\sup_{i=1,\ldots,n} Y_i = Y_j)E(Y_1 \mid Y_j = z, Y_1 < z,\ Y_i < z,\ i \neq 1, j) \\ &= \frac{1}{n}z + \frac{n-1}{n}E(Y_1 \mid Y_1 < z) \\ &= \frac{1}{n}(z + (n-1)\frac{z}{2}) \\ &= \frac{(n+1)z}{2n}. \end{aligned}$$

Hence

$$E\left(\frac{2}{n}\sum_{i=1}^n Y_i \mid \sup_{i=1,\ldots,n} Y_i = z\right) = \frac{2}{n}\frac{(n+1)z}{2} = \frac{n+1}{n}z.$$

Thus the Rao–Blackwell estimator is $((n+1)/n)\sup_{i=1,\ldots,n} Y_i$. The reader can verify directly that this estimator is unbiased as expected (see Exercise 6.3).

6.1.4 Conditional Models

When the model is conditional, i.e., when the probability distributions in the model depend on the values taken by some exogenous variables, it is frequent to use a definition of unbiasedness that is stronger than Definition 6.1.

Definition 6.2: *$T(X,Y)$ is an estimator (conditionally) unbiased for $g(\theta)$ if and only if*

$$E_\theta(T(Y,X) \mid X = x) = g(\theta), \ \forall\, \theta \in \Theta, \ \forall\, x \in \mathcal{X}.$$

It is equivalent to require that estimators are unbiased for every possible marginal distribution of the exogenous variables. For, if the marginal distribution of X is ν, we have

$$\begin{aligned} E_\theta T(Y,X) &= \int_{\mathcal{X}} E_\theta(T(Y,X) \mid X = x)\, d\nu(x) \\ &= \int_{\mathcal{X}} g(\theta)\, d\nu(x) \\ &= g(\theta), \ \forall\, \theta \in \Theta, \end{aligned}$$

which is nothing else than the unbiased condition relative to the joint distribution of the pair (X,Y). Conversely, if the estimator is unbiased for every marginal distribution ν, it must be unbiased for every marginal distribution with point mass $\varepsilon_{(x)}$.

Estimators that are conditionally unbiased for $g(\theta)$ are compared by means of their variance covariance matrices conditional upon X.

6.2 Frechet–Darmois–Cramer–Rao Inequality

The Frechet–Darmois–Cramer–Rao (FDCR) inequality provides a lower bound to the variance covariance matrices of unbiased estimators for $g(\theta)$. This inequality holds under suitable regularity conditions. In order not to complicate the statement of the theorem, we begin by stating these conditions.

Definition 6.3: *A dominated parametric model with densities $\ell(y;\theta)$, $\theta \in \Theta$, is said to be regular if:*

(i) Θ is an open subset of $\mathbb{R}^p$,

(ii) $\ell(y;\theta)$ *is differentiable with respect to* θ,

(iii) $\int_{\mathcal{Y}} \ell(y;\theta)d\mu(y)$ *as a function of* θ *is differentiable, and*

$$\frac{\partial}{\partial\theta}\int_{\mathcal{Y}} \ell(y;\theta)d\mu(y) = \int_{\mathcal{Y}} \frac{\partial}{\partial\theta}\,\ell(y;\theta)d\mu(y),$$

(iv) The Fisher information matrix

$$\mathcal{I}(\theta) = E_\theta\left(\frac{\partial \log \ell(Y;\theta)}{\partial\theta}\frac{\partial \log \ell(Y;\theta)}{\partial\theta'}\right)$$

exists and is nonsingular (i.e., positive definite) for every $\theta \in \Theta$.

Models encountered in classical statistical problems are frequently regular. Examples of nonregular models arise when models are not identified (condition (iv) is not satisfied) or are such that the support of their distributions depends on the parameter. For instance, consider a random sample $Y_1, \ldots, Y_n$ drawn from a uniform distribution $U_{(0,\theta)}$, $\theta \in I\!R^{+*}$. Then the likelihood function is

$$\ell(y;\theta) = \frac{1}{\theta^n}\; 1\!\!1_{\sup_{i=1,\ldots,n} y_i < \theta}.$$

Because the support depends on θ in this case, the likelihood is not differentiable at $\theta = \sup_{i=1,\ldots,n} y_i$. Hence condition (ii) is not satisfied.

It is also necessary to impose some regularity conditions on unbiased estimators. An estimator $T(Y)$ is said to be *regular* if it is square integrable, i.e., if

$$E_\theta \|T(Y)\|^2 < +\infty, \quad \forall\, \theta \in \Theta,$$

and if $\int_{\mathcal{Y}} T(y)\; \ell(y;\theta)\; d\mu(y)$, as a function of θ, is differentiable with a derivative satisfying

$$\frac{\partial}{\partial\theta}\int_{\mathcal{Y}} T(y)\; \ell(y;\theta)\; d\mu(y) = \int_{\mathcal{Y}} T(y)\frac{\partial}{\partial\theta}\; \ell(y;\theta)\; d\mu(y).$$

Theorem 6.1: *Given a regular parametric model, every estimator* $T(Y)$ *that is regular and unbiased for* $g(\theta) \in I\!R^q$ *has a variance covariance matrix satisfying*

$$V_\theta T(Y) \succeq \frac{\partial g(\theta)}{\partial\theta'}\mathcal{I}(\theta)^{-1}\frac{\partial g(\theta)'}{\partial\theta},\ \forall\,\theta\ \in \Theta,$$

where $\partial g(\theta)/\partial\theta'$ is the $q \times p$ matrix of first partial derivatives of the components of g with respect to the components of θ.

In particular, if $g(\theta) = \theta$, then $V_\theta T(Y) \succeq \mathcal{I}(\theta)^{-1}$. The quantity $(\partial g(\theta)/\partial\theta')\mathcal{I}(\theta)^{-1}(\partial g(\theta)')/\partial\theta)$, which is independent of the estimator considered, is called the *Frechet–Darmois–Cramer–Rao* lower bound.

PROOF: Differentiating the unbiasedness condition

$$E_\theta T(Y) = \int_{\mathcal{Y}} T(y)\, \ell(y;\theta)\, d\mu(y) = g(\theta), \quad \forall\, \theta \in \Theta,$$

with respect to θ, we obtain

$$\begin{aligned} \frac{\partial g(\theta)}{\partial\theta'} &= \int_{\mathcal{Y}} T(y) \frac{\partial \ell(y;\theta)}{\partial\theta'}\, d\mu(y) \\ &= \int_{\mathcal{Y}} T(y) \frac{\partial \log \ell(y;\theta)}{\partial\theta'}\, \ell(y;\theta)\, d\mu(y) \\ &= E_\theta \left(T(Y) \frac{\partial \log \ell(Y;\theta)}{\partial\theta'} \right). \end{aligned}$$

From Section 3.3.1, we know that the score vector $\partial \log \ell(Y;\theta)/\partial\theta$ has zero mean. Hence

$$\frac{\partial g(\theta)}{\partial\theta'} = \mathrm{Cov}_\theta \left(T(Y), \frac{\partial \log \ell(Y;\theta)}{\partial\theta} \right).$$

In addition, from the multivariate version of Schwarz inequality (see Property B.20), it follows that the matrix

$$\begin{aligned} &V_\theta T(Y) - \mathrm{Cov}_\theta \left(T(Y), \frac{\partial \log \ell(Y;\theta)}{\partial\theta} \right) \\ &\times V_\theta \left(\frac{\partial \log \ell(Y;\theta)}{\partial\theta} \right)^{-1} \mathrm{Cov}_\theta \left(\frac{\partial \log \ell(Y;\theta)}{\partial\theta}, T(Y) \right), \end{aligned}$$

is symmetric positive semidefinite. Since $V_\theta\left(\partial \log \ell(Y;\theta)/\partial\theta\right)$ is nothing else than Fisher information matrix, it follows that

$$V_\theta T(Y) \succeq \frac{\partial g(\theta)}{\partial\theta'} \mathcal{I}(\theta)^{-1} \frac{\partial g(\theta)'}{\partial\theta}.$$

□

6.3 Best Unbiased Estimators

The unbiasedness condition allows us to restrict the class of estimators under consideration. Thus the question of existence of a best estimator can be reconsidered.

6.3.1 Efficient Estimators

Definition 6.4: *Given a regular parametric model, a regular unbiased estimator of $g(\theta)$ is efficient if its variance covariance matrix is equal to the FDCR lower bound, i.e., if*

$$V_\theta T(Y) = \frac{\partial g(\theta)}{\partial \theta'} \mathcal{I}(\theta)^{-1} \frac{\partial g(\theta)'}{\partial \theta}, \ \forall \, \theta \in \Theta.$$

In particular, an efficient estimator of θ is an estimator of which the variance covariance matrix is equal to the inverse of the Fisher information matrix.

Property 6.4: *An efficient estimator of $g(\theta)$ is optimal in the class of regular unbiased estimators.*

PROOF: This is a straightforward consequence of the FDCR inequality. □

The next property characterizes the cases where there exists an efficient estimator of $g(\theta)$.

Property 6.5: Converse of FDCR Inequality

Consider a regular parametric model and a function $g(\theta)$ of the parameter θ such that:

a) $\partial \ell(y;\theta)/\partial\theta$ is continuous in θ for every y,

b) $\partial g(\theta)/\partial\theta'$ is a nonsingular square matrix for every $\theta \in \Theta$.

Then $T(Y)$ is an efficient regular estimator of $g(\theta)$ if and only if $\ell(y;\theta)$ can be written as

$$\ell(y;\theta) = h(y) \exp\left(\sum_{j=1}^{p} Q_j(\theta) T_j(y) + b(\theta) \right),$$

where the functions $Q' = (Q_1, \ldots, Q_p)$ and b are such that:

(i) Q *and* b *are differentiable,*

(ii) $\partial Q(\theta)/\partial\theta'$ *is nonsingular,*

(iii) $g(\theta) = -\left(\partial Q'(\theta)/\partial\theta\right)^{-1} \partial b(\theta)/\partial\theta$.

PROOF: First, consider the case where equality holds in the FDCR inequality, i.e., suppose that

$$V_\theta T(Y) - \mathrm{Cov}_\theta\left(T(Y), \frac{\partial \log \ell(Y;\theta)}{\partial\theta}\right)$$
$$V_\theta\left(\frac{\partial \log \ell(Y;\theta)}{\partial\theta}\right)^{-1} \mathrm{Cov}_\theta\left(\frac{\partial \log \ell(Y;\theta)}{\partial\theta}, T(Y)\right) = 0.$$

Since this matrix is the variance covariance matrix of the residuals in the population regression of $T(Y)$ on the components of $\partial \log \ell(Y;\theta)/\partial\theta$, equality holds if and only if the residuals, which have zero mean, are identically null. (Technical difficulties due to the presence of negligible sets are avoided because of condition (a).) Thus we have

$$T(y) - \mathrm{Cov}_\theta\left(T(Y), \frac{\partial \log \ell(Y;\theta)}{\partial\theta}\right)$$
$$V_\theta\left(\frac{\partial \log \ell(Y;\theta)}{\partial\theta}\right)^{-1} \frac{\partial \log \ell(y;\theta)}{\partial\theta} - g(\theta) = 0, \ \forall\, y,\theta.$$

This can also be written as

$$T(y) - \frac{\partial g(\theta)}{\partial\theta'}\mathcal{I}(\theta)^{-1}\frac{\partial \log l(y;\theta)}{\partial\theta} = g(\theta), \ \forall\, y,\theta.$$

It follows that

$$\frac{\partial \log \ell(y;\theta)}{\partial\theta} = \mathcal{I}(\theta)\left(\frac{\partial g(\theta)}{\partial\theta'}\right)^{-1}(T(y) - g(\theta)), \ \forall\, y,\theta.$$

Integrating with respect to θ given y shows that the logarithm of the density is of the form

$$\log \ell(y;\theta) = Q'(\theta)T(y) + b(\theta) + \log h(y), \quad \forall\, y,\theta,$$

where $Q(\theta)$ and $b(\theta)$ are of dimensions $p \times 1$ and 1×1 respectively. Moreover, $Q(\theta)$ and $b(\theta)$ are differentiable, and their derivatives are

$$\frac{\partial Q'(\theta)}{\partial\theta} = \mathcal{I}(\theta)\left(\frac{\partial g(\theta)}{\partial\theta'}\right)^{-1},$$
$$\frac{\partial b(\theta)}{\partial\theta} = -\mathcal{I}(\theta)\left(\frac{\partial g(\theta)}{\partial\theta'}\right)^{-1} g(\theta).$$

Hence $\partial Q'(\theta)/\partial\theta$ is nonsingular, and

$$\frac{\partial b(\theta)}{\partial\theta} = -\frac{\partial Q'(\theta)}{\partial\theta} g(\theta),$$

i.e.

$$g(\theta) = -\left(\frac{\partial Q'(\theta)}{\partial\theta}\right)^{-1} \frac{\partial b(\theta)}{\partial\theta}.$$

Conversely, if the family is exponential and satisfies conditions (i) – (iii), then we can let

$$g(\theta) = -\left(\frac{\partial Q'(\theta)}{\partial\theta}\right)^{-1} \frac{\partial b(\theta)}{\partial\theta}.$$

Then it is easy to see that $T(Y)$ is an unbiased estimator of $g(\theta)$. For, differentiating the identity $\int \ell(y;\theta)d\mu(y) = 1$ with respect to θ gives

$$\frac{\partial Q'(\theta)}{\partial\theta} \int_{\mathcal{Y}} T(y)\ \ell(y;\theta)\ d\mu(y) + \frac{\partial b(\theta)}{\partial\theta} \int_{\mathcal{Y}} \ell(y;\theta)\ d\mu(y) = 0,$$

i.e.

$$\frac{\partial Q'(\theta)}{\partial\theta} E_\theta T(Y) + \frac{\partial b(\theta)}{\partial\theta} = 0,$$

i.e.

$$E_\theta T(Y) = -\left(\frac{\partial Q'(\theta)}{\partial\theta}\right)^{-1} \frac{\partial b(\theta)}{\partial\theta} = g(\theta).$$

To compute the variance covariance matrix of $T(Y)$, we note that

$$\int_{\mathcal{Y}} T'(y)\ \ell(y;\theta)\ d\mu(y) - g'(\theta) = 0.$$

Hence the function g is differentiable. Differentiating again with respect to θ gives, after some algebra

$$E_\theta(T(Y)T'(Y)) - g(\theta)g(\theta)' - \left(\frac{\partial Q'(\theta)}{\partial\theta}\right)^{-1} \frac{\partial g(\theta)}{\partial\theta} = 0,$$

i.e.

$$V_\theta T(Y) = \left(\frac{\partial Q'(\theta)}{\partial\theta}\right)^{-1} \frac{\partial g'(\theta)}{\partial\theta}.$$

To complete the proof, it remains to compute the Fisher information matrix. Since the score is

$$\begin{aligned}\frac{\partial \log \ell(y;\theta)}{\partial \theta} &= \frac{\partial Q'(\theta)}{\partial \theta} T(y) + \frac{\partial b(\theta)}{\partial \theta} \\ &= \frac{\partial Q'(\theta)}{\partial \theta}(T(y) - E_\theta T(Y)),\end{aligned}$$

it follows that

$$\begin{aligned}\mathcal{I}(\theta) &= V_\theta \frac{\partial \log \ell(Y;\theta)}{\partial \theta} \\ &= \frac{\partial Q'(\theta)}{\partial \theta} V_\theta T(Y) \frac{\partial Q(\theta)}{\partial \theta'} \\ &= \frac{\partial g'(\theta)}{\partial \theta}\frac{\partial Q(\theta)}{\partial \theta'}.\end{aligned}$$

Because the parametric model is regular, then the information matrix $\mathcal{I}(\theta)$ and therefore $\partial g'(\theta)/\partial\theta$ and $\partial Q(\theta)/\partial\theta'$ are nonsingular. Hence we can write

$$\begin{aligned}\frac{\partial Q'(\theta)}{\partial \theta} &= \mathcal{I}(\theta)\left(\frac{\partial g(\theta)}{\partial \theta'}\right)^{-1}, \\ V_\theta T(Y) &= \left(\frac{\partial Q'(\theta)}{\partial \theta}\right)^{-1}\frac{\partial g'(\theta)}{\partial \theta} \\ &= \frac{\partial g(\theta)}{\partial \theta'}(\mathcal{I}(\theta))^{-1}\frac{\partial g'(\theta)}{\partial \theta}.\end{aligned}$$

Thus $T(Y)$ is an efficient estimator. □

Corollary 6.1: *Under the assumptions of Property 6.5, the exponential model is of minimal order p in the sense that the statistics* $T_1(Y),\ldots,$ $T_p(Y)$ *and the functions* $Q_1(\theta),\ldots,Q_p(\theta)$ *are each independent in the affine sense.*

PROOF: The independence of $T_i(Y)$, $i = 1,\ldots,p$, follows from the nonsingularity of $V_\theta T(Y)$. The independence of the functions $Q_j(\theta)$, $j = 1,\ldots,p$ follows from the nonsingularity of $\partial Q(\theta)/\partial\theta'$. □

Property 6.6: *If* $T(Y)$ *is a* $q \times 1$ *efficient estimator of its mean and if* $\mathbf{A}$ *and* $\mathbf{B}$ *are two constant matrices of dimensions* $r \times q$ *and* $r \times 1$ *respectively, then the estimator* $\mathbf{A}T(Y)+\mathbf{B}$ *is also an efficient estimator of its mean.*

PROOF: Since $T(Y)$ is efficient, its variance covariance matrix is equal to the FDCR lower bound for the parameter $g(\theta) = E_\theta T(Y)$

$$V_\theta T(Y) = \frac{\partial g(\theta)}{\partial \theta'} \mathcal{I}(\theta)^{-1} \frac{\partial g(\theta)'}{\partial \theta}.$$

On the other hand, $\mathbf{A}T(Y) + \mathbf{B}$ is an unbiased estimator of $\mathbf{A}g(\theta) + \mathbf{B}$, and its variance covariance matrix is

$$\begin{aligned} V_\theta(\mathbf{A}T(Y) + \mathbf{B}) &= \mathbf{A}V_\theta(T(Y))\mathbf{A}' \\ &= \mathbf{A}\frac{\partial g(\theta)}{\partial \theta'} \mathcal{I}(\theta)^{-1} \frac{\partial g(\theta)'}{\partial \theta}\mathbf{A}' \\ &= \frac{\partial(\mathbf{A}g(\theta) + \mathbf{B})}{\partial \theta'} \mathcal{I}(\theta)^{-1} \frac{\partial(\mathbf{A}g(\theta) + \mathbf{B})'}{\partial \theta}, \end{aligned}$$

which is equal to the FDCR lower bound for the parameter function $\mathbf{A}g(\theta) + \mathbf{B}$. Thus $\mathbf{A}T(Y) + \mathbf{B}$ is efficient. □

It is straightforward to obtain a converse to Property 6.6.

Property 6.7: *Given a regular exponential model of minimal order p with density*

$$\ell(y;\theta) = h(y) \exp\left(\sum_{j=1}^{p} Q_j(\theta) T_j(y) + b(\theta)\right),$$

every efficient regular estimator is an affine function of the statistic $T(Y)$. Thus only affine functions of $E_\theta T(Y)$ can be estimated efficiently.

PROOF: If $T^*(Y)$ is an efficient estimator of $g^*(\theta)$, then the residuals in the population regression of $T^*(Y)$ on $\partial \log \ell(Y;\theta)/\partial\theta$ are null

$$T^*(Y) - \frac{\partial g^*(\theta)}{d\theta'} \mathcal{I}(\theta)^{-1} \frac{\partial \log \ell(Y;\theta)}{\partial \theta} = g^*(\theta).$$

Now it suffices to note that the score vector is an affine function of $T(Y)$. □

Property 6.8: *If $T(Y)$ and $T^*(Y)$ are two efficient estimators of $g(\theta)$ and $g^*(\theta)$, respectively, then the statistic $(T(Y), T^*(Y))'$ is an efficient estimator of $(g(\theta), g^*(\theta))'$.*

PROOF: Let

$$\mathbf{B} = \begin{pmatrix} \mathbf{B}_{gg} & \mathbf{B}_{gg^*} \\ \mathbf{B}_{g^*g} & \mathbf{B}_{g^*g^*} \end{pmatrix},$$

be the partitioned FDCR lower bound for the parameter vector $(g(\theta), g^*(\theta))'$. The estimator $(T(Y), T^*(Y))'$ is unbiased for $(g(\theta), g^*(\theta))'$. Hence, from FDCR inequality, we obtain

$$V_\theta \begin{pmatrix} T \\ T^* \end{pmatrix} - \mathbf{B} \succeq 0,$$

i.e.

$$\begin{pmatrix} 0 & \mathrm{Cov}_\theta(T(Y), T^*(Y)) - \mathbf{B}_{gg^*} \\ \mathrm{Cov}_\theta(T^*(Y), T(Y)) - \mathbf{B}_{g^*g} & 0 \end{pmatrix} \succeq 0,$$

i.e.

$$\mathrm{Cov}_\theta(T(Y), T^*(Y)) = \mathbf{B}_{gg^*}.$$

Thus $V_\theta(T, T^*)' = \mathbf{B}$ and the estimator $(T, T^*)'$ is efficient. □

6.3.2 Examples of Efficient Estimators

Example 6.6: Consider a random sample of size n drawn from a Bernoulli distribution $B(1, p)$. The model is exponential of minimal order one with

$$\ell(y; p) = \exp\left(n \log\left(\frac{p}{1-p}\right) \bar{y} + n \log(1-p)\right).$$

The functions $Q(p)$ and $b(p)$ are

$$Q(p) = n \log \frac{p}{1-p}, \quad b(p) = n \log(1-p).$$

The sufficient statistic $T(Y) = \bar{Y}$ is an efficient estimator of its mean $g(p) = p = -(db(p)/dp)(dQ(p)/dp)$. The efficiency of $T(Y) = \bar{Y}$ for p can be verified directly since

$$V\bar{Y} = \frac{VY_1}{n} = \frac{p(1-p)}{n},$$

which is the inverse of the Fisher information matrix (see Example 3.13).

On the other hand, the estimator $n/(n-1)((\bar{Y})^2 - (\bar{Y}/n))$ is unbiased for p^2 but is not efficient because it is a nonlinear function of $\bar{Y}$.

Example 6.7: Consider a random sample of size n drawn from a normal distribution $N(m, \sigma^2)$. The density is

$$\ell(y; m, \sigma^2) = \exp\left(-n\frac{\sum_{i=1}^n y_i^2/n}{2\sigma^2} + \frac{mn}{\sigma^2}\bar{y} - \frac{nm^2}{2\sigma^2} - \frac{n}{2}\log 2\pi\sigma^2\right).$$

A sufficient statistic is $T(Y) = (\bar{Y^2}, \bar{Y})'$ where $\bar{Y^2} = \frac{1}{n}\sum_{i=1}^{n} Y_i^2$. Moreover, $T(Y)$ is an efficient estimator of its mean

$$E_{m,\sigma^2}T(Y) = \begin{pmatrix} E_{m,\sigma^2}Y_1^2 \\ E_{m,\sigma^2}Y_1 \end{pmatrix} = \begin{pmatrix} \sigma^2 + m^2 \\ m \end{pmatrix}.$$

Thus, in such a model, only parameter functions that are affine transformations of $(\sigma^2 + m^2, m)'$ can be estimated efficiently. In particular, the mean m can be estimated efficiently, but the variance cannot.

Example 6.8: The preceding example can be readily generalized to the linear model with normal errors

$$Y = \mathbf{X}b + u,$$

where the conditional distribution of u given $\mathbf{X}$ is $N(0, \sigma^2\mathbf{I})$. The density is

$$\begin{aligned} \ell(Y; b, \sigma^2 \mid \mathbf{X}) &= \exp\{\frac{b'(\mathbf{X}'\mathbf{X})}{\sigma^2}(\mathbf{X}'\mathbf{X})^{-1}\mathbf{X}'Y - \frac{Y'Y}{2\sigma^2} \\ &\quad -\frac{b'\mathbf{X}'\mathbf{X}b}{2\sigma^2} - \frac{n}{2}\log 2\pi\sigma^2\}. \end{aligned}$$

A sufficient statistic is

$$T(Y) = \begin{pmatrix} (\mathbf{X}'\mathbf{X})^{-1}\mathbf{X}'Y \\ Y'Y \end{pmatrix},$$

which is an efficient estimator of

$$g\begin{pmatrix} b \\ \sigma^2 \end{pmatrix} = \begin{pmatrix} b \\ n\sigma^2 + b'\mathbf{X}'\mathbf{X}b \end{pmatrix}.$$

As in Example 6.7, there exists an efficient estimator of the parameter b. The variance σ^2, however, cannot be estimated efficiently.

6.3.3 Lehmann–Scheffé Theorem

Every efficient estimator is optimal in the class of unbiased regular estimators. See Definition 6.4 and Property 6.4. The converse, however, is not true. This is a consequence of the next property, which, in addition, establishes the existence of best unbiased estimators in some cases and provides a method for constructing such estimators.

Lehmann–Scheffé Theorem 6.2: *Suppose that there exists a complete sufficient statistic $S(Y)$. An unbiased estimator of $g(\theta)$, which is* *a function of this statistic, i.e., is of the form $T(Y) = h(S(Y))$, is best in the class of unbiased estimators.*

PROOF: In view of the Rao–Blackwell construction (see Section 6.1.3), it suffices to restrict our comparison to unbiased estimators that are functions of $S(Y)$. Thus let $T^*(Y)$ be another unbiased estimator of this type, i.e., such that $T^*(Y) = h^*(S(Y))$. We have

$$\begin{aligned} E_\theta(T(Y) - T^*(Y)) &= E_\theta[h(S(Y)) - h^*(S(Y))] \\ &= g(\theta) - g(\theta) = 0. \end{aligned}$$

It follows from the completeness of S (see Definition 3.6) that $h(S(Y))= h^*(S(Y))$. Hence, the two estimators T and T^* are identical. That is, there exists only one unbiased estimator that is a function of $S(Y)$. Moreover, this estimator is best by the Rao–Blackwell property. □

Under the assumptions of Theorem 6.2 it suffices to have an unbiased estimator $T(Y)$ of $g(\theta)$ in order to construct the best unbiased estimator. Namely, it suffices to consider the Rao–Blackwell estimator $E(T(Y) \mid S(Y))$, which is best unbiased.

Exponential models constitute an important class of models for which there exist complete sufficient statistics.

Property 6.9: *Consider the exponential model*

$$\ell(y;\theta) = C(\theta)h(y)\exp\sum_{j=1}^{r} Q_j(\theta)T_j(y),$$

where the mapping Q is bijective and the interior of $Q(\Theta)$ is nonempty. Then the statistic $T(Y) = (T_1(Y), \ldots, T_r(Y))'$ is complete.

PROOF: We need to show that

$$E_\theta g(T(Y)) = 0, \ \ \forall\, \theta \Rightarrow g(T(Y)) = 0.$$

Since this condition does not depend on the chosen parameterization, we can work with the canonical parameters $q = Q(\theta) = (q_1, \ldots, q_r)'$. Now consider a function $g(T(Y))$ of the statistic T. Its mean is

$$E_q g(T(Y)) = \int_{\mathcal{Y}} g(T(y))C^*(q)h(y)\exp < q, T(y) > d\mu(y),$$

with $C^*(q) = C(Q^{-1}(q))$.

Let μ^{*T} denote the measure induced by T of $\mu^* = h\cdot\mu$. The preceding equation becomes

$$E_q g(T(Y)) = C^*(q) \int_{T(\mathcal{Y})} g(t) \exp < q, t > d\mu^{*^T}(t).$$

Supposing that this expectation is zero for every value of q implies that

$$\int_{T(\mathcal{Y})} g(t) \exp < q, t > d\mu^{*^T}(t) = 0, \quad \forall\, q.$$

The left-hand term is the Laplace transform of the measure $g \cdot \mu^{*T}$. This transform is null only if the measure $g \cdot \mu^{*T}$ is null in view of Theorem B.1 on Laplace transforms. That is, $g = 0$. □

Example 6.9: From Theorem 6.2 and Property 6.9, it follows that, in an exponential model satisfying the conditions of Property 6.9, every function of $T(Y)$ with a (finite) mean is a best unbiased estimator of its mean. Although best unbiased, this estimator is, in general, not efficient unless it is a linear function of $T(Y)$. That is, the risk is not, in general, equal to the FDCR lower bound. In some cases the risk can be larger than the bound for every value of the parameter.

Example 6.10: Consider a random sample of size n drawn from a normal distribution $N(m, \sigma^2)$. The estimator

$$s^2 = \frac{1}{n-1} \sum_{i=1}^{n} (Y_i - \bar{Y})^2 = \frac{n}{n-1} \left((\bar{Y^2}) - (\bar{Y})^2 \right),$$

is a function of the complete sufficient statistic $T(Y) = ((\bar{Y^2}), \bar{Y})'$. Thus it is best unbiased for its mean $Es^2 = \sigma^2$. Its variance, which is equal to $2\sigma^4/(n-1)$, is always larger than the FDCR lower bound, which is equal to $2\sigma^4/n$ (see Exercise 6.6).

Example 6.11: Consider a random sample $Y_1, \ldots, Y_n$ drawn from a uniform distribution $U_{[0,\theta]}, \theta \in \mathbb{R}^{+*}$. The statistic $S(Y) = \sup_{i=1,\ldots,n} Y_i$ is sufficient. To see that it is also complete, we can determine its distribution, which is given by

$$\begin{aligned} P_\theta(S(Y) \leq s) &= P_\theta(Y_i \leq s, \ \forall\, i) \\ &= \prod_{i=1}^{n} P_\theta(Y_i \leq s) = \left(\frac{s}{\theta}\right)^n, \end{aligned}$$

where $s \in [0, \theta]$. The density is obtained by differentiating. It is

$$\ell_S(s;\theta) = \frac{ns^{n-1}}{\theta^n} \mathbb{1}_{0 \leq s \leq \theta}.$$

Now consider a continuous function (to simplify) of the statistic $S(Y)$ that has zero mean for every θ, i.e.

$$E_\theta g(S(Y)) = 0, \quad \forall\, \theta > 0,$$

i.e.

$$\int_0^\theta \frac{ns^{n-1}}{\theta^n} g(s)\, ds = 0, \ \forall\, \theta > 0,$$

i.e.

$$\int_0^\theta s^{n-1} g(s)\, ds = 0, \ \forall\, \theta > 0.$$

Differentiating with respect to θ, we obtain

$$\theta^{n-1} g(\theta), \quad \forall\, \theta > 0,$$

i.e.

$$g(\theta) = 0, \quad \forall\, \theta > 0.$$

Thus the statistic $S(Y)$ is complete. The best unbiased estimator of θ is the function of $S(Y)$ with mean θ that is given in Example 6.5, namely, $(n+1)/n \sup_{i=1,\ldots,n} Y_i$.

6.3.4 Uniqueness of the Best Unbiased Estimator

Property 6.10: *A best unbiased estimator $T^*(Y)$ of $g(\theta)$ is uncorrelated with the difference between itself and every other unbiased estimator of $g(\theta)$.*

PROOF: It is equivalent to show that every linear combination $u'T^*$ of T^* is uncorrelated with every linear combination $v'(T - T^*)$ of $(T - T^*)$, where T is an arbitrary unbiased estimator. Consider the estimator

$$S_\alpha(Y) = u'T^*(Y) + \alpha v'(T(Y) - T^*(Y)).$$

This estimator is unbiased for $u'g(\theta)$. Its variance is

$$\begin{aligned} V_\theta S_\alpha(Y) &= V_\theta(u'T^*(Y)) + 2\alpha \operatorname{Cov}_\theta[u'T^*(Y), v'(T(Y) - T^*(Y))] \\ &\quad + \alpha^2 V_\theta[v'(T(Y) - T^*(Y))], \end{aligned}$$

which is larger than the variance of $u'T^*(Y)$ because the latter is best unbiased. Hence

$$\begin{aligned}\forall\, \alpha, \qquad & \alpha^2 V_\theta[v'(T(Y) - T^*(Y))] \\ & +2\alpha \operatorname{Cov}_\theta[u'T^*(Y), v'(T(Y) - T^*(Y))] \geq 0.\end{aligned}$$

This second degree polynomial in α is nonnegative only if

$$\operatorname{Cov}_\theta[u'T^*(Y), v'(T(Y) - T^*(Y))] = 0.$$

□

Property 6.10 implies that if $T^*(Y)$ is best unbiased and $T(Y)$ unbiased, then

$$\begin{aligned}V_\theta T(Y) &= V_\theta[T^*(Y) + (T(Y) - T^*(Y))] \\ &= V_\theta T^*(Y) + V_\theta(T(Y) - T^*(Y)).\end{aligned}$$

Hence

$$V_\theta(T(Y) - T^*(Y)) = V_\theta T(Y) - V_\theta T^*(Y). \tag{6.1}$$

Property 6.11: *The best unbiased estimator of $g(\theta)$ is unique.*

PROOF: If $T(Y)$ and $T^*(Y)$ are two best unbiased estimators, then we have $V_\theta T^*(Y) = V_\theta T(Y)$, $\forall\, \theta$. From equation (6.1), it follows that

$$V_\theta(T^*(Y) - T(Y)) = 0, \quad \forall\, \theta,$$

which implies

$$\begin{aligned}T^*(Y) - T(Y) &= E_\theta(T^*(Y) - T(Y)) \\ &= g(\theta) - g(\theta) = 0.\end{aligned}$$

□

In particular, an efficient estimator of $g(\theta)$ is necessarily unique.

6.4 Best Invariant Unbiased Estimators

The results of Section 6.3 can be used to find best unbiased estimators in models that are parametric. These theorems no longer apply to semiparametric models such as models in which only the first two moments are parameterized. Nonetheless, in some cases, it is possible to find best unbiased estimators by imposing additional invariance conditions on estimators.

In this section, we consider such an approach:

a) when the parameters of interest appear linearly in the first moment, and when the class of estimators is restricted to estimators that are linear in the observations, or

b) when the parameters of interest appear in the second moment and the class of estimators is restricted to quadratic estimators.

6.4.1 Gauss–Markov Theorem

It is assumed that the observations satisfy the linear model

$$Y = \mathbf{X}b + u, \; E(u \mid \mathbf{X}) = 0, \; V(u \mid \mathbf{X}) = \sigma^2 \mathbf{I},$$

where Y is an n-dimensional vector and $\mathbf{X}$ is an $n \times K$ matrix of rank K. The model is conditional on $\mathbf{X}$. Contrary to Example 6.8, no other assumptions are made on the conditional distribution of the errors.

The parameter of interest is the K-dimensional vector b, which is linearly related to the conditional mean of Y given $\mathbf{X}$. We consider unbiased estimators that are linear in Y. The reasoning is conditional on $\mathbf{X}$.

Gauss–Markov Theorem 6.3: *The Ordinary Least Squares (OLS) estimator $\hat{b}(Y) = (\mathbf{X}'\mathbf{X})^{-1}\mathbf{X}'Y$ is best in the class of linear unbiased estimators of b. Its variance is $V\hat{b}(Y) = \sigma^2(\mathbf{X}'\mathbf{X})^{-1}$.*

PROOF: The OLS estimator is clearly linear and unbiased. Its variance covariance matrix is

$$V\hat{b}(Y) = \sigma^2(\mathbf{X}'\mathbf{X})^{-1}.$$

Consider another linear estimator of b. It is of the form $\tilde{b}(Y) = \mathbf{A}Y$. It is unbiased (conditionally on $\mathbf{X}$) if

$$E_{b,\sigma^2}\tilde{b}(Y) = \mathbf{A}\mathbf{X}b = b \quad \forall \; b, \sigma^2,$$

i.e., if $\mathbf{AX} = \mathbf{I}$.

We now establish a property analogous to Property 6.10, i.e., that $\hat{b}(Y)$ is uncorrelated with $\hat{b}(Y) - \tilde{b}(Y)$. We have

$$\begin{aligned}
&\mathrm{Cov}_{b,\sigma^2}\left(\hat{b}(Y), \hat{b}(Y) - \tilde{b}(Y)\right) \\
&= \mathrm{Cov}_{b,\sigma^2}\left((\mathbf{X}'\mathbf{X})^{-1}\mathbf{X}'Y, (\mathbf{X}'\mathbf{X})^{-1}\mathbf{X}'Y - \mathbf{A}Y\right) \\
&= \sigma^2\left((\mathbf{X}'\mathbf{X})^{-1} - (\mathbf{X}'\mathbf{X})^{-1}\mathbf{X}'\mathbf{A}'\right) \\
&= \sigma^2\left((\mathbf{X}'\mathbf{X})^{-1} - (\mathbf{X}'\mathbf{X})^{-1}\right) \\
&\quad \text{(since } \mathbf{AX} = \mathbf{I}) \\
&= 0.
\end{aligned}$$

The desired result follows from

$$V\tilde{b}(Y) = V\hat{b}(Y) + V(\tilde{b}(Y) - \hat{b}(Y)) \succeq V\hat{b}(Y).$$

□

Corollary 6.2: *Consider the conditional model*

$$y = \mathbf{X}b + u \text{ with } E(u \mid \mathbf{X}) = 0,\ V(u \mid \mathbf{X}) = \sigma^2\mathbf{\Omega}_0,$$

where $\mathbf{\Omega}_0$ is known positive definite and $\mathbf{X}$ is of full colummn rank. The Generalized Least Squares (GLS) estimator $\hat{b}(Y) = (\mathbf{X}'\mathbf{\Omega}_0^{-1}\mathbf{X})^{-1}$ $\mathbf{X}'\mathbf{\Omega}_0^{-1}Y$ is best in the class of linear unbiased estimators of b. Its variance is $V\hat{b}(Y) = \sigma^2(\mathbf{X}'\mathbf{\Omega}_0^{-1}\mathbf{X})^{-1}$.

Proof: It suffices to apply the preceding result after an appropriate transformation. Specifically, we want to find the best estimator of the form $\tilde{b}(Y) = \mathbf{A}Y$. Using the matrix $\mathbf{\Omega}_0^{-1/2}$, we have $\tilde{b}(Y) = \mathbf{A}\mathbf{\Omega}_0^{1/2}\mathbf{\Omega}_0^{-1/2}Y = \mathbf{A}^*Y^*$, where $\mathbf{A}^* = \mathbf{A}\mathbf{\Omega}_0^{1/2}$ and $Y^* = \mathbf{\Omega}_0^{-1/2}Y$. Thus the problem becomes equivalent to finding $\mathbf{A}^*$, i.e., the best unbiased estimator that is linear in Y^*. Since Y^* satisfies the model

$$\begin{aligned} Y^* &= \mathbf{X}^*b + u^*, \text{ with } \mathbf{X}^* = \mathbf{\Omega}_0^{-1/2}\mathbf{X}, \\ u^* &= \mathbf{\Omega}_0^{-1/2}u,\ V(u^* \mid \mathbf{X}) = \sigma^2\mathbf{I}, \end{aligned}$$

it follows that the solution is

$$\hat{b}(Y) = (\mathbf{X}^{*\prime}\mathbf{X}^*)^{-1}\mathbf{X}^{*\prime}Y^* = (\mathbf{X}'\mathbf{\Omega}_0^{-1}\mathbf{X})^{-1}\mathbf{X}'\mathbf{\Omega}_0^{-1}Y.$$

□

Because the reasoning is conditional on $\mathbf{X}$, the condition that $\mathbf{\Omega}_0$ is known means that $\mathbf{\Omega}_0$ does not depend on unknown parameters although it may depend on $\mathbf{X}$.

6.4.2 Best Quadratic Unbiased Estimators

It is assumed that the observations satisfy the linear model

$$Y = \mathbf{X}b + u,$$

where, conditionally on $\mathbf{X}$, the errors $u_i, i = 1, \ldots, n$, are independent with $E(u_i \mid \mathbf{X}) = 0,\ E(u_i^2 \mid \mathbf{X}) = \sigma^2,\ E(u_i^3 \mid \mathbf{X}) = 0,\ E(u_i^4 \mid \mathbf{X}) = 3\sigma^4$.

For instance, the latter assumption on the fourth-order moment is satisfied when the errors are normal. The parameter of interest is now σ^2, and we consider estimators that are unbiased and quadratic, i.e., that are second-order homogeneous polynomials in the observations Y_i. In particular, this implies that estimators of the variance are multiplied by λ^2 when the observation vector Y is multiplied by λ. These estimators are of the form $\sigma^2(Y) = Y'\mathbf{A}Y$ where $\mathbf{A}$ is a matrix that can be chosen to be symmetric. Moreover, since σ^2 is a nonnegative parameter, the matrix $\mathbf{A}$ must be positive semidefinite so that the corresponding variance estimator remains nonnegative.

Now such an estimator is unbiased if

$$E(Y'\mathbf{A}Y) = \sigma^2, \ \forall\, b, \sigma^2.$$

Since

$$\begin{aligned} E(Y'\mathbf{A}Y) &= E \text{ Tr } (Y'\mathbf{A}Y) \\ &= E \text{ Tr } (\mathbf{A}YY') \\ &= \text{ Tr } (\mathbf{A}EYY') \\ &= (\text{Tr } (\mathbf{A}\mathbf{X}b(\mathbf{X}b)') + \text{ Tr } \sigma^2\mathbf{A} \\ &= b'\mathbf{X}'\mathbf{A}\mathbf{X}b + \sigma^2 \text{ Tr } \mathbf{A}, \end{aligned}$$

the unbiasedness condition implies

$$\begin{cases} \mathbf{X}'\mathbf{A}\mathbf{X} = 0, \\ \text{Tr } \mathbf{A} = 1. \end{cases}$$

Next consider the second-order moment of the above estimator. Since the estimator is unbiased, its variance is the expectation of the square of the estimator. Hence searching for the best quadratic unbiased estimator becomes equivalent to solving the following optimization problem

$$\min_{\mathbf{A}} E(Y'\mathbf{A}Y)^2,$$

subject to $\mathbf{A}$ being symmetric positive definite, $\mathbf{X}'\mathbf{A}\mathbf{X} = 0$, and Tr $\mathbf{A} =$ 1.

Consider the quantity $E(Y'\mathbf{A}Y)^2$. Since $\mathbf{A}$ is symmetric positive definite and since $\mathbf{X}'\mathbf{A}\mathbf{X} = 0$, it follows that $\mathbf{A}\mathbf{X} = 0$. Hence, subject to the constraints of the problem, $Y'\mathbf{A}Y$ is equal to $(Y - \mathbf{X}b)'\mathbf{A}(Y - \mathbf{X}b) = u'\mathbf{A}u$. Moreover

$$E(u'\mathbf{A}u)^2 = E\left(\sum_{i=1}^{n}\sum_{j=1}^{n} a_{ij}u_iu_j \sum_{k=1}^{n}\sum_{l=1}^{n} a_{kl}u_ku_l\right)$$

$$= \sum_{i=1}^{n}\sum_{j=1}^{n}\sum_{k=1}^{n}\sum_{l=1}^{n} a_{ij}a_{kl}E(u_iu_ju_ku_l).$$

Consider each term of this sum. If the index i (say) appears only once, then

$$E(u_iu_ju_ku_l) = Eu_iE(u_ju_ku_l) = 0.$$

Thus, only in the following cases, the quantity $E(u_iu_ju_ku_l)$ is nonzero, in which case it is given by

$$\begin{aligned} Eu_i^4 = 3\sigma^4 &\quad \text{if} \quad i = u = k = l, \\ E(u_i^2u_k^2) = Eu_i^2Eu_k^2 = \sigma^4 &\quad \text{if} \quad i = j,\ k = l\ (i \neq k), \\ \sigma^4 &\quad \text{if} \quad i = k,\ j = l\ (i \neq j), \\ \sigma^4 &\quad \text{if} \quad i = l,\ j = k\ (i \neq j). \end{aligned}$$

From these expressions we obtain

$$\begin{aligned} E(u'\mathbf{A}u)^2 &= \sum_{i=1}^{n} a_{ii}^2\ 3\sigma^4 + \sum_{\substack{i=1\\ i\neq j}}^{n}\sum_{j=1}^{n} a_{ii}a_{jj}\sigma^4 \\ &\quad +2\sum_{\substack{i=1\\ i\neq j}}^{n}\sum_{j=1}^{n} a_{ij}^2\sigma^4 \\ &= \sigma^4\left(\sum_{i=1}^{n}\sum_{j=1}^{n} a_{ii}a_{jj} + 2\sum_{i=1}^{n}\sum_{j=1}^{n} a_{ij}^2\right) \\ &= \sigma^4\left((\text{Tr }\mathbf{A})^2 + 2\text{ Tr }\mathbf{A}^2\right) \\ &= \sigma^4\left(1 + 2\text{ Tr }(\mathbf{A}^2)\right), \end{aligned}$$

where we have used the constraint Tr $\mathbf{A} = 1$.

Therefore the optimization problem becomes

$$\min_{\mathbf{A}}\ \text{Tr }(\mathbf{A}^2),$$

subject to $\mathbf{A}$ being symmetric positive definite, $\mathbf{X}'\mathbf{A}\mathbf{X} = 0$, and Tr $\mathbf{A} =$ 1. The condition $\mathbf{X}'\mathbf{A}\mathbf{X} = 0$ means that the column vectors of $\mathbf{X}$ are eigenvectors of $\mathbf{A}$ associated with the zero eigenvalue. Let $\mathbf{Q}$ be the orthogonal matrix of which the first K column vectors are the eigenvectors of $\mathbf{A}$ belonging to the subspace generated by the column vectors of $\mathbf{X}$, and the last $n - K$ column vectors are the eigenvectors of $\mathbf{A}$ belonging to the subspace orthogonal to $\mathbf{X}$. Thus $\mathbf{A}$ can be written as

$$\mathbf{A} = \mathbf{Q}\ \mathbf{\Delta}\ \mathbf{Q}', \text{ with } \mathbf{\Delta} = \begin{pmatrix} 0 & & & 0 \\ & 0 & & \\ & & \lambda_{K+1} & \\ 0 & & & \lambda_n \end{pmatrix}.$$

Since Tr $\mathbf{A}$ = Tr $\mathbf{\Delta}$ and Tr $\mathbf{A}^2$ = Tr $\mathbf{\Delta}^2$, the optimization problem can be written in terms of the eigenvalues of $\mathbf{A}$

$$\begin{aligned} \min \text{ Tr } \mathbf{\Delta}^2 &= \sum_{i=K+1}^{n} \lambda_i^2, \\ \text{subject to Tr } \mathbf{\Delta} &= \sum_{i=K+1}^{n} \lambda_i = 1. \end{aligned}$$

This problem has a unique solution, which is

$$\lambda_i = \frac{1}{n-K}, \ i = K+1, \ldots, n.$$

Thus the matrix $\mathbf{A}$ corresponding to the optimal estimator is

$$\mathbf{A} = \frac{1}{n-K} \mathbf{Q} \begin{pmatrix} 0 & 0 \\ 0 & \mathbf{I}_{n-K} \end{pmatrix} \mathbf{Q}' = \frac{1}{n-K}(\mathbf{I} - \mathbf{P}),$$

where $\mathbf{P}$ is the orthogonal projection on to the subspace generated by the column vectors of $\mathbf{X}$. Hence the optimal estimator is

$$\begin{aligned} s^2 &= \frac{1}{n-K} Y'(\mathbf{I} - \mathbf{P})Y \\ &= \frac{\hat{u}'\hat{u}}{n-K}, \end{aligned}$$

where $\hat{u}$ denote the vector of OLS residuals

$$\hat{u} = (\mathbf{I} - \mathbf{P})Y = Y - \mathbf{X}\hat{b}.$$

Property 6.12: *Consider the linear model defined at the beginning of Section 6.4.2. Then the estimator*

$$s^2 = \frac{1}{n-K} Y'(\mathbf{I} - \mathbf{P})\ Y = \frac{\hat{u}'\hat{u}}{n-K},$$

is the best quadratic unbiased estimator of σ^2.

6.5 Biased and Unbiased Estimators

6.5.1 Nonlinear Functions of an Unbiased Estimator

We have seen that if $T(Y)$ is an unbiased estimator of $g(\theta)$ then $\mathbf{A}T(Y)+\mathbf{B}$ is an unbiased estimator of $\mathbf{A}g(\theta)+\mathbf{B}$. What happens if the mapping is no longer affine ? In general, if h is a nonlinear function then $E_\theta h(T(Y)) = h(E_\theta T(Y))$ no longer holds. That is, a nonlinear function of an unbiased estimator is no longer an unbiased estimator of the corresponding nonlinear function of the parameter.

More precise results can be obtained when the function is convex or concave. To simplify, suppose that $g(\theta)$ is a scalar function, and let h be a convex function from $I\!R$ to $I\!R$. From Jensen's inequality (see B.9), we have

$$E_\theta h(T(Y)) \geq h(E_\theta T(Y)), \quad \forall\ \theta,$$

i.e.

$$E_\theta h(T(Y)) \geq h(g(\theta)), \quad \forall \theta,$$

where equality holds only if h is linear. Hence, there is overestimation on average of the corresponding transformation of the parameter. Similarly, underestimation is obtained when the function h is concave.

Property 6.13: *Let $T(Y)$ be an unbiased estimator of $g(\theta) \in I\!R$:*

a) If h is convex, then $h(T(Y))$ overestimates $h(g(\theta))$ on average,

b) If h is concave, then $h(T(Y))$ underestimates $h(g(\theta))$ on average.

Example 6.12: Let $Y_1, \ldots, Y_n$ be a random sample from a common distribution with mean m and variance σ^2. Then

$$s^2 = \frac{1}{n-1}\sum_{i=1}^{n}(Y_i - \bar{Y})^2$$

is an unbiased estimator of σ^2. Since the square root function is concave, then the estimator $s = \sqrt{s^2}$ underestimates the standard error $\sigma = \sqrt{\sigma^2}$.

The fact that unbiased properties are not preserved by nonlinear transformations suggests that unbiased properties should not be required at all costs. A more important criterion is that of risk minimization.

6.5.2 Inadmissible Best Unbiased Estimators

A best unbiased estimator is, by definition, better than any other unbiased estimator. It may, however, happen that a best unbiased estimator is inadmissible, in which case any estimator that (strictly) dominates it must be biased.

Property 6.14: *A best unbiased estimator may be inadmissible.*

PROOF: It suffices to find an example where the best unbiased estimator is (strictly) dominated by a biased estimator.

Let $Y_1, \ldots, Y_n$ be a random sample from $N(0, \sigma^2)$. The estimator $S(Y) = \frac{1}{n}\sum_{i=1}^n Y_i^2$ of σ^2 is efficient and hence best unbiased. This estimator is such that $nS(Y)/\sigma^2 \sim \chi^2(n)$. Thus its risk function is

$$R(S, \sigma^2) = \frac{2\sigma^4}{n}.$$

Now consider the estimator defined by

$$T(Y) = \frac{1}{n}\sum_{i=1}^n (Y_i - \bar{Y})^2.$$

The statistic $nT(Y)/\sigma^2$ follows a $\chi^2(n-1)$. Hence

$$E_{\sigma^2}T(Y) = \sigma^2\frac{(n-1)}{n}, \quad V_{\sigma^2}T(Y) = 2\sigma^4\frac{(n-1)}{n^2}.$$

The statistic T is biased, and its risk function is

$$\begin{aligned} R(T, \sigma^2) &= 2\sigma^4\frac{(n-1)}{n^2} + \left(\sigma^2\frac{(n-1)}{n} - \sigma^2\right)^2 \\ &= 2\sigma^4\frac{(n-1)}{n^2} + \frac{\sigma^4}{n^2} \\ &= \sigma^4\frac{(2n-1)}{n^2}. \end{aligned}$$

It is easy to see that $R(T, \sigma^2) < R(S, \sigma^2)$. Therefore the biased estimator $T(Y)$ strictly dominates the efficient estimator $S(Y)$. □

Example 6.13: James–Stein Estimator.

Another well-known example is the inadmissibility of the OLS estimator when the number of parameters is strictly larger than two. We shall verify this statement in the simple case where the observations vector Y follows a normal distribution $N(\theta, \mathbf{I})$ with $\theta \in \mathbb{R}^p$.

The OLS estimator of θ is $\hat{\theta} = Y$. This estimator is efficient and hence best unbiased for θ. Note, however, that the squared length of the estimator, i.e., $\|\hat{\theta}\|^2 = \|Y\|^2$, overestimates $\|\theta\|^2$ (see Property 6.13) and that the bias can be substantial. Indeed, $E\|\hat{\theta}\|^2 - \|\theta\|^2 = p$ and the smaller $\|\theta\|^2$ the larger the relative bias on $\|\theta\|^2$. This suggests to transform the OLS estimator by multiplying it by a *shrinkage factor* that decreases with $\|\theta\|^2$. Since $\|\theta\|^2$ is unknown, it can be replaced by $\|\hat{\theta}\|^2$.

For instance, consider the estimator defined by

$$\tilde{\theta}_c = \left(1 - \frac{c}{\|\hat{\theta}\|^2}\right)\hat{\theta},$$

where c is a positive constant. This choice gives a shrinkage factor equal to $1 - c/\|\hat{\theta}\|^2$. The shrinkage factor is not always positive. It could be replaced by $\max\left(1 - c/\|\hat{\theta}\|^2, 0\right)$. Now consider the *scalar* quadratic risk associated to $\tilde{\theta}_c$. We have

$$\begin{aligned} E_\theta\|\tilde{\theta}_c - \theta\|^2 &= E_\theta\|\hat{\theta} - \theta - \frac{c\hat{\theta}}{\|\hat{\theta}\|^2}\|^2 \\ &= E_\theta\|\hat{\theta} - \theta\|^2 - 2cE_\theta\left(\frac{(\hat{\theta}-\theta)'\hat{\theta}}{\|\hat{\theta}\|^2}\right) + c^2E_\theta\left(\frac{1}{\|\hat{\theta}\|^2}\right). \end{aligned}$$

Thus the difference between the risk associated with $\tilde{\theta}_c$ and that of the OLS estimator is

$$\begin{aligned} &-2cE_\theta\left(\frac{(\hat{\theta}-\theta)'\hat{\theta}}{\|\hat{\theta}\|^2}\right) + c^2E_\theta\left(\frac{1}{\|\hat{\theta}\|^2}\right) \\ &= -2cE_\theta\left(\frac{\|\hat{\theta}\|^2 - \|\theta\|^2 - \theta'(\hat{\theta}-\theta)}{\|\hat{\theta}\|^2}\right) + c^2E_\theta\left(\frac{1}{\|\hat{\theta}\|^2}\right) \\ &= -2c + (2c\|\theta\|^2 + c^2)E_\theta\left(\frac{1}{\|\hat{\theta}\|^2}\right) + 2c\theta'E_\theta\left(\frac{\hat{\theta}-\theta}{\|\hat{\theta}\|^2}\right). \end{aligned}$$

We must determine whether this difference is positive or negative. Recall that, if X and Z are two random variables such that the marginal distribution of Z is $P(\|\theta\|^2/2)$, i.e., Poisson with parameter $\|\theta\|^2/2$, and the conditional distribution of X given Z is $\chi^2(p+2Z)$, then the marginal distribution of X is a noncentral chi-square $\chi^2(p, \|\theta\|^2)$ (see Property

B.53). This result is useful here since $\|\hat{\theta}\|^2 \sim \chi^2(p, \|\theta\|^2)$. We have

$$E_\theta\left(\frac{1}{\|\hat{\theta}\|^2}\right) = E_\theta E_\theta\left(\frac{1}{\|\hat{\theta}\|^2} \mid Z\right) = E_\theta\left(\frac{1}{p-2+2Z}\right).$$

On the other hand, we have

$$E_\theta\left(\frac{1}{\|\hat{\theta}\|^2}\right) = \int \frac{1}{\|y\|^2}\frac{1}{(2\pi)^{p/2}}\exp -\frac{1}{2}\|y-\theta\|^2 dy$$

and

$$E_\theta\left(\frac{1}{p-2+2Z}\right) = \sum_z \left(\frac{1}{p-2+2z}\frac{1}{z!}\left(\frac{\|\theta\|^2}{2}\right)^z\right)\exp -\left(\frac{\|\theta\|^2}{2}\right).$$

Differentiating both expressions with respect to θ gives

$$\frac{\partial}{\partial\theta}E_\theta\left(\frac{1}{\|\hat{\theta}\|^2}\right) = \frac{\partial}{\partial\theta}E_\theta\left(\frac{1}{p-2+2Z}\right),$$

i.e.

$$E_\theta\left(\frac{\hat{\theta}-\theta}{\|\hat{\theta}\|^2}\right) = \frac{\theta}{\|\theta\|^2}E_\theta\left(\frac{2Z-\|\theta\|^2}{p-2+2Z}\right).$$

Hence the difference between the two risk functions is

$$\begin{aligned} & R(\tilde{\theta}_c,\theta) - R(\hat{\theta},\theta) \\ &= -2c + (2c\|\theta\|^2 + c^2)E_\theta\left(\frac{1}{p-2+2Z}\right) + 2cE_\theta\left(\frac{2Z-\|\theta\|^2}{p-2+2Z}\right) \\ &= (c^2 - 2c(p-2))E_\theta\left(\frac{1}{p-2+2Z}\right). \end{aligned}$$

When p is larger or equal to two, the quantity $E_\theta\left(1/(p-2+2Z)\right)$ is positive since Z is positive. Hence it is possible to choose c so that $c^2 - 2c(p-2) < 0$. We can even find an optimal value for c. This value c_0, is the solution that maximizes $(-c^2+2c(p-2))$. Hence $c_0 = p-2$. The corresponding estimator, $\tilde{\theta} = \left(1-(p-2)/\|\hat{\theta}\|^2\right)\hat{\theta}$ is called the *James–Stein estimator.*

6.6 Exercises

EXERCISE 6.1: Consider a statistical model $\mathcal{M} = (\mathcal{Y}, \{P_\theta,\ \theta \in \Theta\})$, and a nested model $\mathcal{M}_0 = (\mathcal{Y}, \{P_\theta,\ \theta \in \Theta_0\})$ where $\Theta_0 \subset \Theta$. Show that an unbiased estimator for θ in the model $\mathcal{M}_0$ is not necessarily unbiased for θ in the model $\mathcal{M}$.

EXERCISE 6.2: Consider a random sample $Y_1, \ldots, Y_n$ drawn from a discrete distribution that assigns 0.5 probabilities to the points θ_1 and θ_2, $\theta_1 < \theta_2$, $\theta_1, \theta_2 \in I\!R$. Verify that there does not exist unbiased estimators for θ_1 and θ_2. Characterize the functions of the parameters that can be estimated in an unbiased fashion.

EXERCISE 6.3: Let $Y_1, \ldots, Y_n$ be a random sample drawn from a uniform distribution $U_{[0,\theta]}$, $\theta > 0$.

a) Verify that $P_\theta(\sup Y_i < z) = (z/\theta)^n$.

b) Show that the mean of a positive real random variable Z with cumulative distribution function $F(z)$ is

$$EZ = \int_0^\infty (1 - F(z))dz.$$

c) Find the mean of $Z = \sup Y_i$, and compare the result to that of Example 6.5.

EXERCISE 6.4: Consider a random sample $Y_1, \ldots, Y_n$ drawn from a Poisson distribution with parameter θ. Consider the estimation of $g(\theta) = \exp(-\theta)$.

a) Verify that the estimator

$$T(Y) = 1\!\!1_{(Y_1=0)} = \begin{cases} 1 \text{ if } Y_1 = 0, \\ 0 \text{ otherwise,} \end{cases}$$

is unbiased for $g(\theta)$.

b) Determine the conditional distribution of Y_1 given the sufficient statistic $S = \sum_{i=1}^n Y_i$.

c) Conclude that the Rao–Blackwell improved estimator of $T(Y)$ is $\left(1 - \frac{1}{n}\right)^S$.

d) Show that the estimator obtained in c) is best unbiased. Show that it is not efficient.

EXERCISE 6.5: Consider a model parameterized by $\theta = (\alpha, \beta)'$. Let $\hat{\alpha}$ be an efficient estimator of α and $\hat{\beta}$ be an unbiased estimator of β. Verify that the covariance $\text{Cov}_\theta(\hat{\alpha}, \hat{\beta})$ does not depend on the choice of $\hat{\beta}$. Conclude that, in the normal case, the sample mean $\bar{Y}$ is uncorrelated with every unbiased estimator of the variance σ^2.

EXERCISE 6.6: Let $Y_1, \ldots, Y_n$ be a random sample drawn from a normal distribution $N(m, \sigma^2)$. Find the Fisher information matrix and compute its inverse. Determine the variance of

$$S^2 = \frac{1}{n-1} \sum_{i=1}^{n} (Y_i - \bar{Y})^2.$$

Hint: Use the fact that $(n-1)S^2/\sigma^2 \sim \chi^2(n-1)$.

EXERCISE 6.7: Consider a random sample $Y_1, \ldots, Y_n$ drawn from a normal distribution $N(m, \sigma^2)$. Characterize the estimators of σ^2 that are unbiased, quadratic, and invariant with respect to permutations. What do you conclude ?

EXERCISE 6.8: Consider the simple linear regression model

$$y_i = b_0 + b_1 x_i + u_i, \; E(u_i \mid x_i) = 0, \; i = 1, \ldots, n.$$

This model can also be written as

$$y_i = c_0 + b_1 x_i^* + u_i \text{ where } x_i^* = x_i - \bar{x} \text{ and } c_0 = b_0 + b_1 \bar{x}.$$

Verify that the explanatory variables x^* is orthogonal to the constant term. Conclude that

$$\hat{b}_1 = \frac{\sum_{i=1}^n y_i x_i^*}{\sum_{i=1}^n x_i^{*2}},$$

is equal to the OLS estimator of b_1, and hence that it is unbiased.

EXERCISE 6.9: Consider the model

$$Y = \mathbf{X}b + u \text{ where } E(u \mid \mathbf{X}) = 0, \; V(u \mid \mathbf{X}) = \sigma^2 \mathbf{\Omega}_0.$$

a) Verify that the OLS estimator of b, which is $\tilde{b} = (\mathbf{X}'\mathbf{X})^{-1}\mathbf{X}'Y$ is unbiased for b. Conclude that its variance is larger (in the matrix sense) than that of the GLS estimator (see Corollary 6.2).

b) Give a necessary and sufficient condition for these two estimators to have the same variance covariance matrix.

EXERCISE 6.10: Consider a homogeneous model parameterized by $\theta \in \Theta \subset I\!R$. One wants to find a lower bound for the variances of unbiased estimators of θ that is more stringent than the FDCR lower bound.

a) Differentiate twice the equality $1 = \int_{\mathcal{Y}} \ell(y;\theta) d\mu(y)$ and the unbiasedness condition $E_\theta T(Y) = \int_{\mathcal{Y}} T(y)\ell(y;\theta)d\mu(y) = \theta$ with respect to θ.

b) Let

$$G(Y;\theta) = \frac{\partial \log \ell(Y;\theta)}{\partial \theta} - EL\left(\frac{\partial \log \ell(Y;\theta)}{\partial \theta} \mid \frac{1}{\ell(Y;\theta)} \frac{\partial^2 \ell(Y;\theta)}{\partial \theta^2}\right),$$

where EL denotes the population linear regression. Verify that

$$E_\theta G(Y;\theta) = 0 \text{ and } E_\theta(T(Y)G(Y;\theta)) = 1.$$

c) Conclude that

$$V_\theta T(Y) \geq \frac{1}{V_\theta G(Y;\theta)}.$$

Verify that

$$V_\theta G(Y;\theta) < V_\theta\left(\frac{\partial \log \ell(Y;\theta)}{\partial \theta}\right).$$

What do you conclude ?

6.7 References

Barndorff-Nielsen, O. (1978). *Information and Exponential Families in Statistical Theory*, Wiley.

McCullagh, P. and Nelder, J. (1983). *Generalized Linear Models*, Chapman and Hall.

James, W. and Stein, C. (1961). "Estimation with Quadratic Loss," *Proceedings of the Fourth Berkley Symposium*, 1, 361–397.

Lehmann, E.L. (1983). *Theory of Point Estimation*, Wiley.

Malinvaud, E. (1964). *Méthodes Statistiques de l'Econométrie*, Dunod.

Rao, C.R. (1973). *Linear Statistical Inference and its Applications*, Wiley.

Silvey, S.D. (1970). *Statistical Inference*, Chapman and Hall.

Stein, C. (1956). "Inadmissibility of the Usual Estimator for the Mean of a Multivariate Normal Distribution," *Proceedings of the Third Berkeley Symposium*, 1, 197–206.

Theil, H. (1971). *Principles of Econometrics*, Wiley.

Wilks, S.S. (1962). *Mathematical Statistics*, Wiley.

CHAPTER 7

Maximum Likelihood Estimation

7.1 Principle

7.1.1 Definition

We consider a parametric model in which the joint distribution of $Y = (Y_1, \ldots, Y_n)$ has a density $\ell(y;\theta)$ with respect to a measure μ. Thus $P_\theta = \ell(y;\theta)\cdot\mu$ where $\theta \in \Theta \subset \mathbb{R}^p$. Once $y = (y_1, \ldots, y_n)$ is observed, the maximum likelihood method consists in retaining as an estimate of the parameter θ a value $\hat{\theta}(y)$ that maximizes the likelihood function $\theta \mapsto \ell(y;\theta)$. *Ex ante*, i.e., prior to the observations, y is unknown. Nonetheless, we can determine the mapping $\hat{\theta}$ and hence study the estimator $\hat{\theta}(y)$, which is called the *maximum likelihood* (ML) *estimator*.

Definition 7.1: *A maximum likelihood estimator of θ is a solution to the maximization problem*

$$\max_{\theta\in\Theta} \ell(Y;\theta).$$

Because the solutions to an optimization problem remain unchanged when the objective function is transformed by a strictly increasing mapping, a maximum likelihood estimator is also obtained as a solution to

$$\max_{\theta\in\Theta} \log \ell(Y;\theta). \tag{7.1}$$

Using the logarithm of the likelihood often allows some simplifications in the numerical determination of the maximum likelihood estimator as well as in the study of the properties of the estimator. This is because the logarithm function changes products into sums and removes exponential functions that appear in probability density functions.

Remark 7.1: By definition, *the maximum likelihood estimator of a function* $g(\theta)$ *of the parameter* is $g(\hat{\theta})$, where $\hat{\theta}$ is the maximum likelihood estimator of θ. See also Property 7.7 below.

Remark 7.2: In the case of conditional models defined by families of conditional densities $\ell(y \mid x; \theta)$, a (conditional) maximum likelihood estimator is defined as a solution to $\max_{\theta \in \Theta} \ell(Y \mid X; \theta)$. In general, a solution depends on both Y and X.

7.1.2 Three Difficulties

Although intuitive, Definition 7.1 raises a few difficulties which we now discuss.

a) Nonuniqueness of the Likelihood Function

When the observations are discrete, the likelihood function is the mapping that associates $\ell(y;\theta) = P_\theta(Y = y)$ to every θ. In this case the likelihood function is defined unambiguously. This is not so when the distribution of the observations has a continuous part. For instance, suppose that $Y_1, \ldots, Y_n$ is a random sample drawn from the normal distribution $N(\theta, 1)$. Usually, one considers the joint density

$$\ell_1(y;\theta) = \frac{1}{(2\pi)^{n/2}} \left(\exp -\frac{1}{2} \sum_{i=1}^{n} (y_i - \theta)^2 \right).$$

Other choices of densities that lead to the same family of distributions are possible. For instance, we can use

$$\ell_2(y;\theta) = \begin{cases} \ell_1(y;\theta), & \text{if } \sum_{i=1}^n y_i^2 \neq \theta, \\ 100, & \text{if } \sum_{i=1}^n y_i^2 = \theta. \end{cases}$$

The likelihood function is modified on the set $\left\{\sum_{i=1}^n y_i^2 = \theta\right\}$, which has zero probability. Hence ℓ_2 is another density for P_θ with respect to the Lebesgue measure.

A direct application of the maximum likelihood method to the family ℓ_1 leads to $\hat{\theta}_1(Y) = \bar{Y}$. On the other hand, the same method applied to the family ℓ_2 gives $\hat{\theta}_2(Y) = \sum_{i=1}^{n} Y_i^2$.

Thus, modifying the density on a negligible set may change the resulting estimator. To avoid such a difficulty, whenever possible, one may require densities to be continuous in y or piecewise continuous on compact sets with nonempty interiors.

b) Nonexistence of a Solution to the Maximization Problem

The nonexistence of $\hat{\theta}(y)$ may occur for all values of y or for some of them. In general, this is due either to the fact that the parameter space Θ is open or that the log-likelihood function is discontinuous in θ.

Example 7.1: Consider a random variable Y_1 that follows a binomial distribution $B(1, 1/(1+\exp\theta))$ where $\theta \in \Theta = \mathbb{R}$. If the observation is $y_1 = 1$, then $\ell(1;\theta) = 1/(1+\exp\theta)$. The likelihood function is decreasing, and its maximum is not attained on Θ. A maximum would be reached if the parameter space is closed, which is the case if $\Theta = \bar{\mathbb{R}} = \mathbb{R} \cup \{\pm\infty\}$. Then the maximum likelihood estimate would be $\hat{\theta}(1) = -\infty$. A similar reasoning applies to $\ell(0;\theta)$, i.e., when $y_1 = 0$.

Example 7.2: Now suppose that one has two independent random variables Y_1 and Y_2, each distributed as $B(1, 1/(1+\exp\theta))$. As in Example 7.1, it is easy to see that there does not exist a maximum likelihood estimate when the observations are $y = (0,0)$ or $y = (1,1)$. On the other hand, the maximum likelihood estimate exists when $y = (0,1)$ or $y = (1,0)$. Specifically, we have

$$\ell((1,0);\theta) = \ell((0,1);\theta) = \frac{\exp\theta}{(1+\exp\theta)^2}.$$

This function attains a unique maximum at $\theta = 0$. Thus we have $\hat{\theta}((1,0)) = \hat{\theta}((0,1)) = 0$.

A sufficient condition for the existence of a maximum likelihood estimator is given next.

Property 7.1: Sufficient Condition for Existence

If the parameter space Θ is compact and if the likelihood function $\theta \mapsto \ell(y;\theta)$ is continuous on Θ, then there exists a maximum likelihood estimator.

c) Multiple Solutions to the Maximization Problem

Multiple solutions may arise for all values of y or for some of them.

Example 7.3: One reason for multiple solutions is the nonidentification of the parameter θ. Specifically, consider a nonidentified model where each value θ of the parameter is associated with another value $\theta^* \neq \theta$ that leads to the same distribution $\ell(Y;\theta) = \ell(Y;\theta^*)$. Let h denote the mapping that associates $\theta^* = h(\theta)$ to θ. Thus if $\hat{\theta}(Y)$ is a maximum likelihood estimator, then $\hat{\theta}^*(Y) = h(\hat{\theta}(Y))$ is another maximum likelihood estimator because it leads to the same value of the likelihood function. If, however, the parameter function $g(\theta)$ is identified in this model, then we have $g(\theta) = g(\theta^*)$ and $g(\hat{\theta}(Y)) = g(\hat{\theta}^*(Y))$. Therefore multiple solutions due to nonidentification disappear for maximum likelihood estimations of identified functions of the parameters.

Example 7.4: To illustrate the case of multiple solutions due to nonidentification of the parameter, consider a linear model $Y \sim N(\mathbf{X}b, \mathbf{I})$ where the matrix $\mathbf{X}$ is of size $n \times p$ and of rank strictly smaller than p. The likelihood function is

$$\ell(y \mid \mathbf{X}; b) = \frac{1}{(2\pi)^{n/2}} \exp\left\{-\frac{1}{2}(y - \mathbf{X}b)'(y - \mathbf{X}b)\right\},$$

which is maximized at values of b satisfying $\mathbf{X}'\mathbf{X}b = \mathbf{X}'y$, i.e., at values that are associated with vectors in $\mathbb{R}^p$ that are in a subspace of dimension $p - \operatorname{rank} \mathbf{X}'\mathbf{X}$.

Multiple solutions may also arise when the model is identified.

Example 7.5: Let $Y_1, \ldots, Y_n$ be a random sample drawn from the uniform distribution $U_{[\theta,\theta+1]}$. The likelihood function is

$$\begin{aligned} \ell(y;\theta) &= \prod_{i=1}^{n} f(y_i;\theta) = \prod_{i=1}^{n} \mathbb{1}_{\theta \le y_i \le 1+\theta} \\ &= \mathbb{1}_{\inf y_i \ge \theta} \quad \mathbb{1}_{\sup y_i \le 1+\theta}. \end{aligned}$$

The solutions to the maximization of $\ell(y;\theta)$ are all the values $\hat{\theta}$ between $\sup y_i - 1$ and $\inf y_i$. In this example there is an infinity of solutions to the maximization problem.

Example 7.6: Sometimes there may exist a finite number of different solutions to the maximization problem for different observations. Consider two independent random variables Y_1 and Y_2 following each a translated

Cauchy distribution with density $(1/\pi)(1/(1+(y-\theta)^2))$. The likelihood function is

$$\ell(y_1, y_2; \theta) = \frac{1}{\pi^2} \frac{1}{1+(y_1-\theta)^2} \frac{1}{1+(y_2-\theta)^2}.$$

The likelihood function converges to zero when θ converges to $\pm\infty$. It is symmetric about $\tilde{\theta} = (y_1+y_2)/2$, i.e., $\ell(y_1, y_2; \theta) = \ell(y_1, y_2; y_1+y_2-\theta)$.

To determine the maximizing values of this function, we consider the values at which the first derivative is null. We have

$$\begin{aligned}
&\frac{\partial \ell}{\partial \theta}(y_1, y_2; \theta) \\
&= \ell(y_1, y_2; \theta) \left[\frac{2(y_1-\theta)}{1+(y_1-\theta)^2} + \frac{2(y_2-\theta)}{1+(y_2-\theta)^2} \right] \\
&= 2\ell(y_1, y_2; \theta) \frac{(y_1+y_2-2\theta)(\theta^2-(y_1+y_2)\theta+1+y_1y_2)}{(1+(y_1-\theta)^2)(1+(y_2-\theta)^2)}.
\end{aligned}$$

The discriminant of the second-order equations $\theta^2-(y_1+y_2)\theta+1+y_1y_2 = 0$ is $(y_1-y_2)^2-4$. If it is negative, then the shape of the likelihood function is of the form pictured below. Moreover, there is a unique maximum at $\tilde{\theta}(y) = (y_1+y_2)/2$.

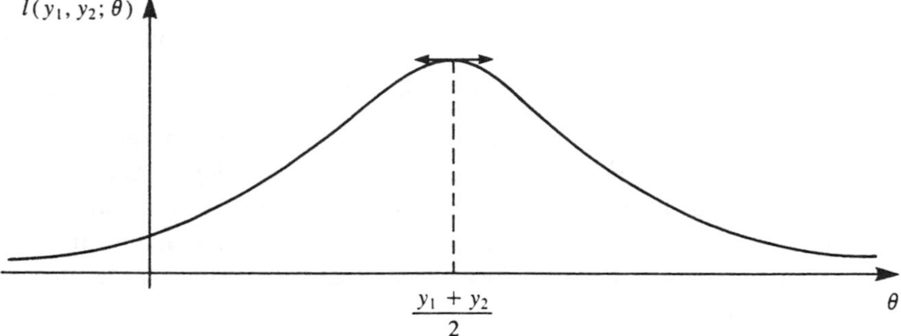

Figure 7.1: Unimodal Likelihood Function

On the other hand, if the discriminant is positive, the shape of the likelihood function is of the form pictured below. The maximization problem has two solutions $\hat{\theta}_1(y)$ and $\hat{\theta}_2(y)$ that are symmetric about $(Y_1+Y_2)/2$.

A sufficient condition for the uniqueness of the maximum likelihood estimator is given next.

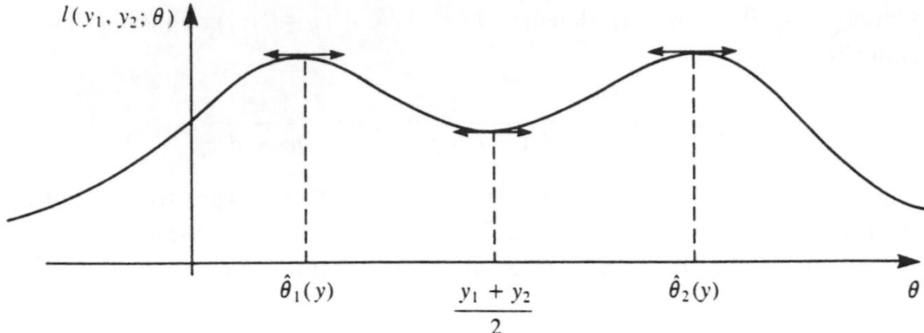

Figure 7.2: Bimodal Likelihood Function

Property 7.2: *If the parameter space Θ is convex and if the log-likelihood function is strictly concave in $\xi = h(\theta)$, where $h(\cdot)$ is a bijective transformation of the parameter, then the maximum likelihood estimator is unique when it exists.*

PROOF: Suppose the contrary. There would exist at least two distinct solutions $\hat{\theta}_1(y)$ and $\hat{\theta}_2(y)$. Since the function $\log \ell(y;\theta)$ is strictly concave in $\xi = h(\theta)$, we would have

$$\forall\ \lambda \in (0,1) \quad \log \ell(y;\hat{\theta}) > \lambda \log(y;\hat{\theta}_1) + (1-\lambda)\log \ell(y;\hat{\theta}_2),$$

where $\hat{\theta}(y) = h^{-1}\left(\lambda h(\hat{\theta}_1(y)) + (1-\lambda)h(\hat{\theta}_2(y))\right)$. This contradicts the property that $\hat{\theta}_1$ and $\hat{\theta}_2$ give the same maximal log-likelihood value. □

Example 7.7: A model, which is frequently used to explain how unemployment spells depend on the ages of the unemployed individuals, relies on Poisson processes. Specifically, suppose that, conditionally on ages $x_1, \ldots, x_n$, unemployment spells $y_1, \ldots, y_n$ are independent and exponentially distributed with a mean that depends exponentially on the age of the individual

$$f(y_i \mid x_i; b_0, b_1) = \exp(b_0 + b_1 x_i)\ \exp(-y_i \exp(b_0 + b_1 x_i)).$$

The log-likelihood function is

$$\sum_{i=1}^{n} \log f(y_i \mid x_i; b_0, b_1) = \sum_{i=1}^{n}(b_0 + b_1 x_i) - \sum_{i=1}^{n} y_i \exp(b_0 + b_1 x_i).$$

Since y_i is nonnegative, the log-likelihood function is strictly concave in

b_0 and b_1 as soon as one y_i is nonzero. It follows that the maximum likelihood estimate is unique on $\bigcup_{i=1}^{n}(y_i \neq 0)$.

7.1.3 An Interpretation of ML Estimation

To simplify, we consider a random sample of size n drawn from a discrete distribution with probabilities $p_k(\theta)$ and values $\tilde{y}_k, k = 1, \ldots, K$. Let n_k denote the number of observations with value $\tilde{y}_k$. The log-likelihood function is given by

$$L(y;\theta) = \sum_{k=1}^{K} n_k \log p_k(\theta).$$

The maximum likelihood estimator is obtained by maximizing $L(Y;\theta)$, where $\frac{1}{n}L(y;\theta) = \sum_{k=1}^{K} \frac{n_k}{n} \log p_k(\theta)$, or by minimizing $I(P_\theta \mid \hat{P})$, where $\hat{P}$ denotes the empirical distribution $\hat{P} = \left(\frac{n_k}{n},\ k = 1, \ldots, K\right)$ and I is the Kullback discrepancy measure (see Definition 1.5). Hence the maximum likelihood method reduces to the search for the distribution in the model that is closest to the empirical distribution according to the Kullback discrepancy measure I.

7.2 Likelihood Equations

7.2.1 General Remarks

Maximum likelihood estimators are frequently found by solving the first-order conditions of the maximization problem. For instance, this method was used in Example 7.6. It is, however, important to note that the first-order conditions are neither sufficient nor necessary unless additional assumptions are satisfied.

Example 7.8: To illustrate that the first-order conditions are not necessary, consider a random sample $Y_1, \ldots, Y_n$ drawn from a distribution with density

$$f(y;\theta) = \exp -(y-\theta)\mathbb{1}_{y \geq \theta}, \quad \theta \in \mathbb{R}.$$

The likelihood function is

$$\ell(y;\theta) = \prod_{i=1}^{n} f(y_i;\theta)$$

$$= \exp\left(-\sum_{i=1}^{n} y_i + n\theta\right) \mathbb{1}_{\theta \leq \inf y_i}.$$

The likelihood function $\theta \mapsto \ell(y;\theta)$ is graphed below.

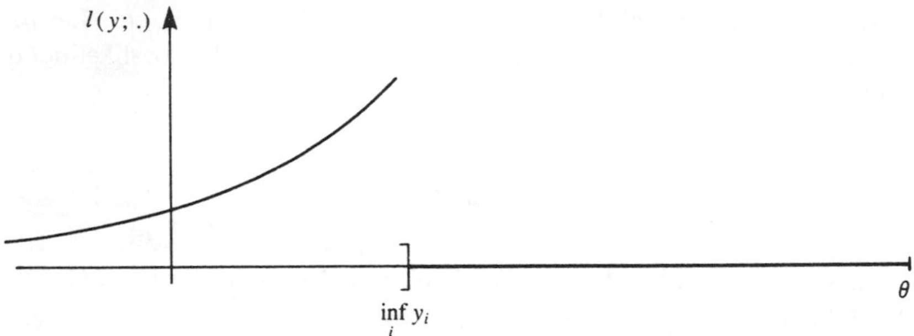

Figure 7.3: Likelihood Function

The likelihood function attains a unique maximum at $\hat{\theta}(y) = \inf_i y_i$. The left derivative of the likelihood function, however, is not zero at this point.

Example 7.9: Conversely, consider a value $\tilde{\theta}(y)$ at which the first derivative is zero. Then $\tilde{\theta}(y)$ does not correspond necessarily to a maximum of the likelihood function. For instance, $\tilde{\theta}(y)$ may lead to a minimum (see Example 7.6) or to an inflexion point. These cases are easy to distinguish by examining the matrix of second partial derivatives. Note, however, that, even if the matrix of second partial derivatives is negative definite, the value $\tilde{\theta}(y)$ may correspond to a local maximum and not to a global maximum.

In practice, to determine the ML estimator $\hat{\theta}(y)$, one finds the values at which the first partial derivatives are zero. Then, one determines the local maxima $\tilde{\theta}_j$ among those values and the corresponding values $\tilde{\ell}_j$ of the function ℓ (or $\tilde{L}_j$ of the function $L = \log \ell$). The values $\tilde{\theta}_j$ corresponding to the maximum value $\tilde{\ell} = \max_j \tilde{\ell}_j$ (or $\tilde{L} = \max_j \tilde{L}_j$) are retained. It is then necessary to compare this value $\tilde{\ell}$ to the maximum value attained by ℓ on the boundary of Θ.

It is frequently difficult to determine all the local maxima. The preceding procedure greatly simplifies when ℓ or L satisfy some concavity properties, in which case the first-order conditions become sufficient for a global maximum, or when the likelihood function converges to zero at infinity, in which case maxima belong to a bounded set.

7.2.2 Unconstrained Maxima

The first-order conditions are necessary in the well-known case considered in the next property, which is thus given without proof.

Property 7.3: *If $\theta = (\theta_1, \ldots, \theta_p)' \in \Theta \subset I\!\!R^p$, if the log-likelihood function is differentiable in θ, and if $\hat{\theta}(y)$ belongs to the interior of Θ, then the maximum likelihood estimator satisfies*

$$\frac{\partial L(y;\hat{\theta})}{\partial \theta} = \frac{\partial \log \ell(y;\hat{\theta})}{\partial \theta} = 0.$$

These equations are called the *likelihood equations.*

Example 7.10: Let $Y_1, \ldots, Y_n$ be a random sample drawn from a translated logistic distribution with density

$$f(y;\theta) = \frac{\exp(y-\theta)}{(1+\exp(y-\theta))^2}, \quad \theta \in I\!\!R.$$

The log-likelihood function is

$$\begin{aligned} L(y;\theta) &= \sum_{i=1}^n \log f(y_i;\theta) \\ &= \sum_{i=1}^n (y_i - \theta) - 2\sum_{i=1}^n \log(1+\exp(y_i-\theta)). \end{aligned}$$

The log-likelihood function is continuous in θ. Moreover, when θ diverges to $\pm\infty$, then $L(y;\theta)$ diverges to $-\infty$. Hence the likelihood function attains a global maximum on $I\!\!R$, which is a solution to the likelihood equation

$$0 = \frac{\partial L(y;\theta)}{\partial \theta} = -n + 2\sum_{i=1}^n \frac{\exp(y_i-\theta)}{1+\exp(y_i-\theta)}.$$

It is known that such an equation has at least one solution. This solution, however, cannot be determined in closed form. Thus it is necessary to use some numerical algorithms to solve the likelihood equation (see Chapter 13).

Example 7.11: Let $Y_1, \ldots, Y_n$ be a random sample drawn from a Poisson distribution $P(\lambda)$. The log-likelihood function is

$$L(y;\lambda) = -n\lambda + \sum_{i=1}^{n} y_i \log \lambda - \sum_{i=1}^{n} \log(y_i!).$$

This function is strictly concave in λ provided there exists at least one nonzero observed y_i. It attains a maximum at $\hat{\lambda}$ satisfying

$$0 = \frac{\partial L(y;\hat{\lambda})}{\partial \lambda} = -n + \sum_{i=1}^{n} \frac{y_i}{\hat{\lambda}}.$$

Hence $\hat{\lambda} = \bar{y}$.

7.2.3 Constrained Maxima

Statistical models are frequently defined through explicit constraints on parameters. The most common ones are equality constraints. Then the log-likelihood function $\theta \mapsto L(y;\theta) = \log \ell(y;\theta)$ is defined on $\Theta = \Theta^* \cap \{g(\theta) = 0\}$, where Θ^* is, for instance, an open subset of $I\!R^p$ and g is a function from $I\!R^p$ to $I\!R^r$ with $r \leq p$. As a consequence, maximization of the likelihood function must take into account the constraints $g(\theta) = 0$. To do so, we can introduce a vector λ of r Lagrange multipliers and the maximization of the Lagrangian function $L(y;\theta) - \lambda' g(\theta)$. The first-order conditions are obtained by differentiating the latter function with respect to θ and λ. Setting the derivatives equal to zero, we obtain the system

$$\begin{cases} \dfrac{\partial L(y;\hat{\theta})}{\partial \theta} - \dfrac{\partial g'(\hat{\theta})}{\partial \theta} \cdot \hat{\lambda} = 0, \\ \\ g(\hat{\theta}) = 0. \end{cases} \tag{7.2}$$

Example 7.12: Consider a vector Y of which the components are doubly indexed: $Y = (Y_{ij},\ i = 1, \ldots, I,\ j = 1, \ldots, J)$. Suppose that Y follows a multinomial distribution $M(n; p_{ij} = p_{i\cdot}\ p_{\cdot j},\ i = 1, \ldots, I,\ j = 1, \ldots, J)$. The parameters $p_{i\cdot}$ and $p_{\cdot j}$ satisfy $\sum_{i=1}^{I} p_{i\cdot} = 1$, $\sum_{j=1}^{J} p_{\cdot j} = 1$, $p_{i\cdot} \geq 0,\ i = 1, \ldots, I$ and $p_{\cdot j} \geq 0,\ j = 1, \ldots, J$.

Leaving aside the inequality constraints for the moment, we must introduce two Lagrange multipliers λ_1 and λ_2. The Lagrangian function is

$$\begin{aligned}
\Lambda(p) &= L(y;p) - \lambda_1 \left(\sum_{i=1}^{I} p_{i\cdot} - 1 \right) - \lambda_2 \left(\sum_{j=1}^{J} p_{\cdot j} - 1 \right) \\
&= \log \left(\frac{n!}{\prod_{i=1}^{I} \prod_{j=1}^{J} y_{ij}!} \right) + \sum_{i=1}^{I} \sum_{j=1}^{J} y_{ij} \log(p_{i\cdot} p_{\cdot j}) \\
&\quad - \lambda_1 \left(\sum_{i=1}^{I} p_{i\cdot} - 1 \right) - \lambda_2 \left(\sum_{j=1}^{J} p_{\cdot j} - 1 \right).
\end{aligned}$$

Equating to zero the first partial derivatives with respect to $p_{i\cdot}, p_{\cdot j}, \lambda_1, \lambda_2$ gives

$$\begin{aligned}
\frac{\partial \Lambda}{\partial p_{i\cdot}} &= \left(\sum_{j=1}^{J} y_{ij} \right) \frac{1}{p_{i\cdot}} - \lambda_1 = 0, \quad i = 1, \ldots, I, \\
\frac{\partial \Lambda}{\partial p_{\cdot j}} &= \left(\sum_{i=1}^{I} y_{ij} \right) \frac{1}{p_{\cdot j}} - \lambda_2 = 0, \quad j = 1, \ldots, J, \\
\frac{\partial \Lambda}{\partial \lambda_1} &= \sum_{i=1}^{I} p_{i\cdot} - 1 = 0, \\
\frac{\partial \Lambda}{\partial \lambda_2} &= \sum_{j=1}^{J} p_{\cdot j} - 1 = 0.
\end{aligned}$$

Let $y_{i\cdot} = \sum_{j=1}^{J} y_{ij}$ and $y_{\cdot j} = \sum_{i=1}^{I} y_{ij}$. From the first I equations we obtain $y_{i\cdot} = \lambda_1 p_{i\cdot}$, $i = 1, \ldots, I$ and $\lambda_1 = \sum_{i=1}^{n} y_{i\cdot} = n$. Similarly, we have $\lambda_2 = n$. Thus there exists a unique solution to the likelihood equations, namely

$$\begin{aligned}
\hat{p}_{i\cdot} &= \frac{y_{i\cdot}}{n}, \quad i = 1, \ldots, I, \\
\hat{p}_{\cdot j} &= \frac{y_{\cdot j}}{n}, \quad j = 1, \ldots, J.
\end{aligned}$$

Note that this solution satisfies the constraints $\hat{p}_{i\cdot} \geq 0$ and $\hat{p}_{\cdot j} \geq 0$. This solution corresponds to a global maximum since the log-likelihood function is strictly concave and the constraints are linear.

7.2.4 Concentrated Likelihood Function

The numerical determination of maximum likelihood estimators can be simplified by considering successive maximizations. Specifically, consider a partition of the parameter vector θ into two subvectors α and β so that $\theta = (\alpha', \beta')'$.

Property 7.4: *The solutions* $\hat{\theta} = (\hat{\alpha}', \hat{\beta}')'$ *to the maximization problem* $\max_{\alpha,\beta} \log \ell(y; \alpha, \beta)$ *can be obtained* via *the following two-step procedure:*

a) *In a first step, maximize the log-likelihood function with respect to* α *given* β. *The maximum value is attained for values of* α *in a set* $\hat{A}(\beta)$ *depending on the parameter* β. *Thus, if* $\alpha \in \hat{A}(\beta)$, *the log-likelihood value is*

$$\log \ell_c(y; \beta) = \max_{\alpha} \log \ell(y; \alpha, \beta).$$

The mapping $\log \ell_c$ *is called the concentrated (in* α*) log-likelihood function.*

b) *In a second step, maximize the concentrated log-likelihood function with respect to* β. *The maximum value is attained on a set* $\hat{B}$ *of* β *values.*

Then the solutions $\hat{\theta} = (\hat{\alpha}', \hat{\beta}')'$ *belong to the set* $\bigcup_{\beta \in \hat{B}} \{\hat{A}(\beta) \times \beta\}$.

PROOF: Let $(\hat{\alpha}', \hat{\beta}')'$ be a maximum likelihood estimator. We have

$$\forall\ \alpha, \beta, \quad \log \ell(y; \hat{\alpha}, \hat{\beta}) \geq \log \ell(y; \alpha, \beta).$$

In particular, we have

$$\forall\ \alpha, \quad \log \ell(y; \hat{\alpha}, \hat{\beta}) \geq \log \ell(y; \alpha, \hat{\beta}),$$

i.e., $\hat{\alpha} \in \hat{A}(\hat{\beta})$ and $\log \ell_c(y; \hat{\beta}) = \log \ell(y; \hat{\alpha}, \hat{\beta})$. Moreover, since the first inequality holds for every β and every $\alpha \in \hat{A}(\beta)$, it follows that

$$\forall\ \beta, \quad \log \ell_c(y; \hat{\beta}) \geq \log \ell_c(y; \beta),$$

i.e., that $\hat{\beta} \in \hat{B}$.

Conversely, let $(\tilde{\alpha}', \tilde{\beta}')'$ be an element of $\bigcup_{\beta \in \hat{B}} \{\hat{A}(\beta) \times \beta\}$. We have

$$\forall\ \beta, \quad \log \ell_c(y; \tilde{\beta}) \geq \log \ell_c(y; \beta).$$

By definition of the concentrated log-likelihood function, we have

$$\forall\ \alpha,\quad \log \ell_c(y;\beta) \geq \log \ell(y;\alpha,\beta).$$

It follows that

$$\forall\ \alpha,\beta,\quad \log \ell_c(y;\tilde{\beta}) = \log \ell(y;\tilde{\alpha},\tilde{\beta}) \geq \log \ell(y;\alpha,\beta).$$

Hence $(\tilde{\alpha}', \tilde{\beta}')'$ is a maximum likelihood estimator. □

The above two-step procedure is useful when the correspondence $\beta \mapsto \hat{A}(\beta)$ can be determined explicitly, in which case the original maximization problem reduces to a maximization with respect to a subvector β of which the dimension is smaller than that of θ.

Note also that this two-step procedure can be generalized to a partition of θ in a large number of subvectors: $\theta = (\alpha_1', \ldots, \alpha_J')'$. Namely, one begins with the maximization with respect to α_1 given $(\alpha_2', \ldots, \alpha_J')'$. One obtains a set of solutions $\hat{A}_1(\alpha_2, \ldots, \alpha_J)$ and a concentrated (in α_1) log-likelihood function $\log \ell_{1c}(y;\alpha_2, \ldots, \alpha_J)$. In a second step, one obtains a set of solutions $\hat{A}_2(\alpha_3, \ldots, \alpha_J)$ and a log-likelihood function $\log \ell_{2c}(y;\alpha_3, \ldots, \alpha_J)$ concentrated in α_1 and α_2. Continuing in this manner until the Jth step where one maximizes, with respect to α_J, the log-likelihood function concentrated in $(\alpha_1, \ldots, \alpha_{J-1})$. The elements of $\hat{A}_J$ are the maximum likelihood estimators of α_J. The procedure is completed by substituting recursively the successive estimates into the correspondences $\hat{A}_j$.

Example 7.13: Consider the random variables $Y_t, t = 1, \ldots, T$, defined by the model

$$Y_t = at + u_t, \text{ with } u_t = \rho u_{t-1} + \varepsilon_t,$$

where the errors $\varepsilon_t, t = 1, \ldots, T$ are independent and identically distributed $N(0, \sigma^2)$. We can write

$$Y_t = \rho Y_{t-1} + at - a\rho(t-1) + \varepsilon_t.$$

Conditionally on Y_0 assumed to be known, the density of the observations is

$$\ell(y;a,\rho,\sigma^2) = \frac{1}{(2\pi)^{T/2}\sigma^T} \exp -\frac{1}{2\sigma^2} \sum_{t=1}^{T} (y_t - \rho y_{t-1} - at + a\rho(t-1))^2.$$

Thus the log-likelihood function is

$$\begin{aligned} L(y; a, \rho, \sigma^2) &= -\frac{T}{2}\log 2\pi - \frac{T}{2}\log\sigma^2 \\ &\quad -\frac{1}{2\sigma^2}\sum_{t=1}^{T}(y_t - \rho y_{t-1} - a(t - \rho t + \rho))^2. \end{aligned}$$

Concentrating a out gives

$$\begin{aligned} \tilde{a}(\rho, \sigma^2) &= \frac{\sum_{t=1}^{T}(y_t - \rho y_{t-1})(t - \rho t + \rho)}{\sum_{t=1}^{T}(t - \rho t + \rho)^2} = \tilde{a}(\rho), \\ L_{1c}(y; \rho, \sigma^2) &= -\frac{T}{2}\log 2\pi - \frac{T}{2}\log\sigma^2 \\ &\quad -\frac{1}{2\sigma^2}\sum_{t=1}^{T}(y_t - \rho y_{t-1} - \tilde{a}(\rho)(t - \rho t + \rho))^2. \end{aligned}$$

Now concentrating σ^2 out gives

$$\tilde{\sigma}^2(\rho) = \frac{1}{T}\sum_{t=1}^{T}(y_t - \rho y_{t-1} - \tilde{a}(\rho)(t - \rho t + \rho))^2.$$

Thus the log-likelihood function concentrated in a and σ^2 is

$$L_{2c}(y; \rho) = -\frac{T}{2}\log 2\pi - \frac{T}{2} - \frac{T}{2}\log\tilde{\sigma}^2(\rho).$$

Hence we are led to minimize with respect to ρ the function

$$\begin{aligned} T\tilde{\sigma}^2(\rho) &= \sum_{t=1}^{T}(y_t - \rho y_{t-1} \\ &\quad - \frac{\sum_{t=1}^{T}(y_t - \rho y_{t-1})(t - \rho\, t + \rho)}{\sum_{t=1}^{T}(t - \rho\, t + \rho)^2}(t - \rho\, t + \rho))^2 \\ &= \sum_{t=1}^{T}(y_t - \rho y_{t-1})^2 \\ &\quad - \frac{\left(\sum_{t=1}^{T}(y_t - \rho y_{t-1})(t - \rho\, t + \rho)\right)^2}{\sum_{t=1}^{T}(t - \rho\, t + \rho)^2}. \end{aligned}$$

Example 7.14: Frish–Waugh Theorem

Consider a linear model with two sets of explanatory variables $\mathbf{X}_1$ and $\mathbf{X}_2$

$$Y = \mathbf{X}_1 b_1 + \mathbf{X}_2 b_2 + u, \text{ where } u \sim N(0, \mathbf{I}).$$

Concentrating b_2 out is equivalent to considering a model with a fixed b_1, i.e., a linear model with endogenous variable $Y - \mathbf{X}_1 b_1$ and exogenous variables $\mathbf{X}_2$

$$Y - \mathbf{X}_1 b_1 = \mathbf{X}_2 b_2 + u.$$

The optimal value $\tilde{b}_2(b_1)$ is

$$\tilde{b}_2(b_1) = (\mathbf{X}_2' \, \mathbf{X}_2)^{-1} \, \mathbf{X}_2'(Y - \mathbf{X}_1 b_1).$$

Substituting this expression for b_2 in the original model leads to the maximization of the concentrated likelihood function, which corresponds to the linear model

$$Y = \mathbf{X}_1 b_1 + \mathbf{X}_2 (\mathbf{X}_2' \, \mathbf{X}_2)^{-1} \mathbf{X}_2' (Y - \mathbf{X}_1 b_1) + v.$$

or

$$(\mathbf{I} - \mathbf{X}_2(\mathbf{X}_2'\mathbf{X}_2)^{-1}\mathbf{X}_2')Y = (\mathbf{I} - \mathbf{X}_2(\mathbf{X}_2'\mathbf{X}_2)^{-1}\mathbf{X}_2')\mathbf{X}_1 b_1 + v.$$

Thus the maximum likelihood estimator $\hat{b}_1$ is the OLS estimator in this model, i.e.

$$\hat{b}_1 = \left(\mathbf{X}_1'(\mathbf{I} - \mathbf{X}_2(\mathbf{X}_2'\mathbf{X}_2)^{-1}\mathbf{X}_2')\mathbf{X}_1\right)^{-1} \mathbf{X}_1' \left(\mathbf{I} - \mathbf{X}_2(\mathbf{X}_2'\mathbf{X}_2)^{-1}\mathbf{X}_2'\right) Y,$$

where we have used the fact that $\mathbf{X}_2(\mathbf{X}_2'\mathbf{X}_2)^{-1}\mathbf{X}_2'$ is an orthogonal projection operator. The latter expression is equal to the first components of the vector

$$\hat{b} = (\mathbf{X}'\mathbf{X})^{-1}\mathbf{X}'Y = \left(\begin{pmatrix} \mathbf{X}_1' \\ \mathbf{X}_2' \end{pmatrix} (\mathbf{X}_1, \mathbf{X}_2) \right)^{-1} \begin{pmatrix} \mathbf{X}_1' \\ \mathbf{X}_2' \end{pmatrix} Y.$$

Properties of the concentrated log-likelihood function can be easily derived from those of the original log-likelihood function. Hereafter, it is assumed that concentrating leads to a unique value, i.e., $\hat{A}(\beta) = \{\tilde{\alpha}(\beta)\}$.

Property 7.5: *If the log-likelihood function*

$$L(\alpha, \beta) = \log \ \ell(y; \alpha, \beta)$$

is differentiable in $(\alpha', \beta')'$*, then the function* $\tilde{\alpha}(\beta)$ *and the concentrated log-likelihood function* $L_c(\beta) = \log \ell_c(y; \beta)$ *are differentiable in* β*, and we have*

$$\frac{\partial L_c(\beta)}{\partial \beta} = \frac{\partial L(\tilde{\alpha}(\beta), \beta)}{\partial \beta}.$$

PROOF: Differentiability properties follow from the implicit function theorem. Moreover, since $L_c(\beta) = L(\tilde{\alpha}(\beta), \beta)$, we have

$$\begin{aligned} \frac{\partial L_c(\beta)}{\partial \beta} &= \frac{\partial \tilde{\alpha}(\beta)'}{\partial \beta} \frac{\partial L(\tilde{\alpha}(\beta), \beta)}{\partial \alpha} + \frac{\partial L(\tilde{\alpha}(\beta), \beta)}{\partial \beta} \\ &= \frac{\partial L(\tilde{\alpha}(\beta), \beta)}{\partial \beta}, \end{aligned}$$

where the second equality follows from the fact that the derivatives $\partial L / \partial \alpha$ evaluated at $(\tilde{\alpha}(\beta), \beta)$ are null because $\tilde{\alpha}(\beta)$ maximizes $L(\alpha, \beta)$ with respect to α. □

Property 7.5 is useful in practice for finding β, especially when the derivatives $\partial L / \partial \beta$ are simpler than those of the concentrated log-likelihood function L_c.

Property 7.6: *If the log-likelihood function* $L(\alpha, \beta)$ *is twice differentiable in* $\theta = (\alpha', \beta')'$*, then the function* $\tilde{\alpha}(\beta)$ *and the concentrated log-likelihood function is twice differentiable in* β*, and we have*

$$\frac{\partial^2 L_c(\beta)}{\partial \beta \, \partial \beta'} = \left(\left(\frac{\partial^2 L(\tilde{\alpha}(\beta), \beta)}{\partial \theta \, \partial \theta'} \right)^{\beta\beta} \right)^{-1},$$

where $(\cdot)^{\beta\beta}$ *denotes the block corresponding to the parameter* β *of the inverse of the partitioned matrix* $(\cdot)$.

PROOF: Differentiability properties follows from the implicit function theorem. Moreover, by definition of $\tilde{\alpha}(\beta)$, we have

$$\frac{\partial L(\tilde{\alpha}(\beta), \beta)}{\partial \alpha} = 0, \quad \forall \; \beta.$$

Differentiating with respect to β, we obtain

$$\frac{\partial^2 L(\tilde{\alpha}(\beta), \beta)}{\partial \alpha \, \partial \beta'} + \frac{\partial^2 L(\tilde{\alpha}(\beta), \beta)}{\partial \alpha \, \partial \alpha'} \frac{\partial \tilde{\alpha}(\beta)}{\partial \beta'} = 0, \quad \forall \; \beta,$$

or equivalently

$$\frac{\partial \tilde{\alpha}(\beta)}{\partial \beta'} = - \left(\frac{\partial^2 L(\tilde{\alpha}(\beta), \beta)}{\partial \alpha \, \partial \alpha'} \right)^{-1} \frac{\partial^2 L(\tilde{\alpha}(\beta), \beta)}{\partial \alpha \, \partial \beta'}, \ \ \forall \, \beta.$$

On the other hand, differentiating with respect to β the equality established in Property 7.5, we have

$$\frac{\partial^2 L_c(\beta)}{\partial \beta \, \partial \beta'} = \frac{\partial^2 L(\tilde{\alpha}(\beta), \beta)}{\partial \beta \, \partial \alpha'} \frac{\partial \tilde{\alpha}(\beta)}{\partial \beta'} + \frac{\partial^2 L(\tilde{\alpha}(\beta), \beta)}{\partial \beta \, \partial \beta'},$$

Using the above expression for $\partial \tilde{\alpha}(\beta) / \partial \beta'$, we obtain

$$\begin{aligned} \frac{\partial^2 L_c(\beta)}{\partial \beta \partial \beta'} &= \frac{\partial^2 L(\tilde{\alpha}(\beta), \beta)}{\partial \beta \, \partial \beta'} \\ & \quad - \frac{\partial^2 L(\tilde{\alpha}(\beta), \beta)}{\partial \beta \, \partial \alpha'} \left(\frac{\partial^2 L(\tilde{\alpha}(\beta), \beta)}{\partial \alpha \, \partial \alpha'} \right)^{-1} \frac{\partial^2 L(\tilde{\alpha}(\beta), \beta)}{\partial \alpha \, \partial \beta'}. \end{aligned}$$

Hence, from the partitioned matrix inverse formula, we obtain

$$\left(\frac{\partial^2 L_c(\beta)}{\partial \beta \, \partial \beta'} \right)^{-1} = \left(\frac{\partial^2 L(\tilde{\alpha}(\beta), \beta)}{\partial \theta \, \partial \theta'} \right)^{\beta\beta}.$$

□

Note that, when the log-likelihood function is concave in (α, β), the preceding property implies that the matrix $\partial^2 L_c(\beta) / \partial \beta \, \partial \beta'$ is negative semidefinite. Thus the concentrated log-likelihood function is concave in β.

7.3 Finite Sample Properties

7.3.1 Functional Invariance

Property 7.7: *Consider a dominated parametric model* $(\mathcal{Y}, \mathcal{P} = \{P_\theta = \ell(y; \theta) \cdot \mu, \ \theta \in \Theta\})$ *and a bijective function* g *from* Θ *on to a set* Λ. *If* $\hat{\theta}$ *is a maximum likelihood estimator of* θ, *then* $\hat{\lambda} = g(\hat{\theta})$ *is a maximum likelihood estimator of* λ *in the model*

$$(\mathcal{Y}, \mathcal{P}^* = \{P_\lambda^* = P_{g^{-1}(\lambda)}, \ \lambda \in \Lambda\}).$$

PROOF: By definition of $\hat{\theta}$, we have

$$\hat{\theta} \in \Theta \text{ and } \ell(y; \hat{\theta}(y)) \geq \ell(y; \theta), \ \forall \, \theta \in \Theta,$$

or equivalently, letting $\hat{\lambda} = g(\hat{\theta})$ and $\lambda = g(\theta)$, we have

$$\hat{\lambda} \in \Lambda \text{ and } \ell(y; g^{-1}(\hat{\lambda})(y)) \geq \ell(y; g^{-1}(\lambda)), \ \forall\, \lambda \in \Lambda.$$

The latter condition means that $\hat{\lambda}$ is a maximum likelihood estimator of λ in a model with densities $\ell(y; g^{-1}(\lambda))$. □

Thus maximum likelihood estimation is invariant to parameterization. Note also that Property 7.7 agrees with Remark 7.1, which defines the maximum likelihood estimator of a function of the parameter.

Example 7.15: Reparameterization can be used to generate strictly concave log-likelihood functions. For instance, consider T random variables $Y_1^*, \ldots, Y_T^*$ that are normally distributed $N(at+b, \sigma^2)$, $t = 1, \ldots, T$, where a, b, and σ^2 are unknown parameters. Suppose that these variables are not completely observed. Namely, suppose that only $Y_1, \ldots, Y_T$ are observed where Y_t is related to the latent variable Y_t^* by

$$Y_t = \begin{cases} Y_t^*, & \text{if } Y_t^* > 0, \\ 0, & \text{otherwise.} \end{cases}$$

This model, called the *Tobit model*, corresponds to a family of distributions that have a probability mass at zero and that are absolutely continuous on $\mathbb{R}^+$. The log-likelihood function is

$$\begin{aligned} L(y;\theta) &= \log \ell(y;\theta) \\ &= \sum_{t=1}^{T} (\mathbb{1}_{y_t=0} \log P_\theta(Y_t^* < 0) + \mathbb{1}_{y_t>0} \log f_t(y_t;\theta)), \end{aligned}$$

where f_t denotes the density of Y_t. Hence

$$\begin{aligned} L(y;\theta) &= \sum_{t=1}^{T} \left\{ \mathbb{1}_{y_t=0} \log \Phi\left(-\frac{at}{\sigma} - \frac{b}{\sigma} \right) \right. \\ &\quad \left. + \mathbb{1}_{y_t>0} \left(-\log(\sigma\sqrt{2\pi}) - \frac{1}{2}\frac{(y_t - at - b)^2}{\sigma^2} \right) \right\}, \end{aligned}$$

where Φ is the standard normal cumulative distribution function.

Let $\lambda_1 = a/\sigma$, $\lambda_2 = b/\sigma$ and $\lambda_3 = 1/\sigma$. We have

$$\begin{aligned} \log \ell(y; g^{-1}(\lambda)) &= \sum_{t=1}^{T} \mathbb{1}_{y_t=0} \log \Phi(-\lambda_1 t - \lambda_2) \\ &\quad + \mathbb{1}_{y_t=0}(-\log\sqrt{2\pi} + \log \lambda_3 - \frac{1}{2}(\lambda_3 y_t - \lambda_1 t - \lambda_2)^2). \end{aligned}$$

Since

$$\frac{d^2 \log \Phi(x)}{dx^2} = \frac{d}{dx}\left(\frac{\phi(x)}{\Phi(x)}\right) = \frac{\phi(x)}{\Phi(x)^2}(\phi(x) + x\Phi(x)) \leq 0$$

(see Property B.33), the function $\lambda \mapsto \log \ell(y; g^{-1}(\lambda))$ is strictly concave in λ. Thus the maximum likelihood estimator $\hat{\lambda}$ is unique and is characterized by the first-order conditions. The maximum likelihood estimator of the original parameters is obtained as

$$\hat{\sigma} = \frac{1}{\hat{\lambda}_3},\ \hat{b} = \frac{\hat{\lambda}_2}{\hat{\lambda}_3},\ \hat{a} = \frac{\hat{\lambda}_1}{\hat{\lambda}_3}.$$

Example 7.16: Consider an equilibrium model where demand and supply depend on one explanatory variable x in addition to prices

$$\begin{aligned} d_t &= ap_t + b + u_t, \\ s_t &= \alpha p_t + \beta x_t + v_t, \\ q_t &= d_t = s_t. \end{aligned}$$

The error vectors $(u_t, v_t)'$ are assumed to be independent over time and identically distributed $N\left(\begin{pmatrix} 0 \\ 0 \end{pmatrix}, \begin{pmatrix} \sigma_u^2 & \sigma_{uv} \\ \sigma_{uv} & \sigma_v^2 \end{pmatrix}\right)$. The reduced form is

$$\begin{aligned} p_t &= -\frac{b}{a-\alpha} + \frac{\beta x_t}{a-\alpha} + \frac{-u_t + v_t}{a-\alpha}, \\ q_t &= -\frac{\alpha b}{a-\alpha} + \frac{a\beta x_t}{a-\alpha} + \frac{-\alpha u_t + a v_t}{a-\alpha}. \end{aligned}$$

This can be written as

$$\begin{aligned} p_t &= \pi_{11} + \pi_{12} x_t + \varepsilon_t, \\ q_t &= \pi_{21} + \pi_{22} x_t + \eta_t, \end{aligned}$$

where

$$\begin{pmatrix} \varepsilon_t \\ \eta_t \end{pmatrix} \sim N\left(\begin{pmatrix} 0 \\ 0 \end{pmatrix}, \begin{pmatrix} \sigma_\varepsilon^2 & \sigma_{\varepsilon\eta} \\ \sigma_{\varepsilon\eta} & \sigma_\eta^2 \end{pmatrix}\right).$$

The reduced form parameters are related to the structural parameters by

$$\pi_{11} = -\frac{b}{a-\alpha},\ \pi_{12} = \frac{\beta}{a-\alpha}, \pi_{21} = -\frac{\alpha b}{a-\alpha},\ \pi_{22} = +\frac{a\beta}{a-\alpha},$$

$$\begin{aligned}\sigma_\varepsilon^2 &= \frac{\sigma_u^2 + \sigma_v^2 - 2\sigma_{uv}}{(a-\alpha)^2}, \\ \sigma_\eta^2 &= \frac{\alpha^2\sigma_u^2 + a^2\sigma_v^2 - 2a\alpha\sigma_{uv}}{(a-\alpha)^2}, \\ \sigma_{\varepsilon\eta} &= \frac{+\alpha\sigma_u^2 + a\sigma_v^2 - (a+\alpha)\sigma_{uv}}{(a-\alpha)^2}.\end{aligned}$$

It is easy to verify that the mapping that associates the reduced form parameters to the structural parameters is bijective. The model is said to be *just identified* (see Section 3.4.3).

The maximum likelihood estimator can be obtained by determining $\hat{\pi}$'s and $\hat{\sigma}_\varepsilon^2, \hat{\sigma}_\eta^2$ and $\hat{\sigma}_{\varepsilon\eta}$ in a first step. For instance, $\hat{\pi}_{11}$ and $\hat{\pi}_{12}$ are the OLS estimators in a regression of p_t on the constant term and x_t. In a second step, the maximum likelihood estimator of the structural parameters is obtained by solving back the preceding equations. For instance, we have $\hat{\alpha} = \hat{\pi}_{21}/\hat{\pi}_{11}$. Such a two-step procedure is called *indirect least squares.*

7.3.2 Relationship with Sufficiency

Property 7.8: *Under the assumptions of the factorization criterion (Theorem 3.1), a maximum likelihood estimator is a function of every sufficient statistic.*

PROOF: Let $S(Y)$ be a sufficient statistic. From the factorization criterion (Theorem 3.1), we have $\ell(y;\theta) = \Psi(S(y);\theta)h(y)$, i.e.

$$\log \ell(y;\theta) = \log \Psi(S(y);\theta) + \log h(y).$$

Hence maximizing $\log \ell(y;\theta)$ with respect to θ is equivalent to maximizing $\log \Psi(S(y);\theta)$. Therefore a maximum likelihood estimator depends on Y through $S(Y)$. □

7.3.3 Exponential Models

Property 7.9: *Under the assumptions of the converse to the FDCR inequality (Property 6.5), an unbiased estimator $T(Y)$ that is efficient for $\theta \in \Theta \subset I\!R^p$ is the unique solution to the likelihood equations.*

PROOF: From the converse to the FDCR inequality it follows that, if

$T(Y)$ is an efficient unbiased estimator of θ, the density is of the form

$$\ell(y;\theta) = h(y) \exp\left(\sum_{j=1}^{p} Q_j(\theta)\, T_j(y) + b(\theta)\right).$$

The vector functions $Q(\theta) = (Q_1(\theta), \ldots, Q_p(\theta))'$ and $b(\theta)$ are related to the mean of $T(Y) = (T_1(Y), \ldots, T_p(Y))'$ by

$$E_\theta T(Y) = \theta = -\left(\frac{dQ'(\theta)}{d\theta}\right)^{-1} \frac{db(\theta)}{d\theta}, \ \forall\, \theta \in \Theta.$$

Now solutions to the likelihood equations are obtained from

$$\frac{\partial \log \ell(y;\hat{\theta})}{\partial \theta} = 0,$$

i.e.

$$\frac{\partial}{\partial \theta}\left(\sum_{j=1}^{p} Q_j(\hat{\theta}) T_j(y) + b(\hat{\theta})\right) = 0,$$

i.e.

$$\frac{dQ'(\hat{\theta})}{d\theta} T(y) + \frac{db(\hat{\theta})}{d\theta} = 0,$$

i.e.

$$T(y) = -\left(\frac{dQ'(\hat{\theta})}{d\theta}\right)^{-1} \frac{db(\hat{\theta})}{d\theta} = \hat{\theta}(y).$$

Hence the likelihood equations have a unique solution which is $\hat{\theta}(y) = T(y)$. □

One can ask whether the above solution to the likelihood equations corresponds to a maximum of the likelihood function. If the mapping Q is invertible, one can define new parameters q by $q = Q(\theta)$. In terms of q the log-likelihood function can be written as

$$\begin{aligned} \log \ell^*(y;q) &= \log \ell(y; Q^{-1}(q)) \\ &= q' \cdot T(y) + \beta(q) + \log h(y), \end{aligned}$$

where $\beta(q) = b(Q^{-1}(q))$. Hence the second-order derivatives of the log-likelihood function are equal to the second-order derivatives of $\beta(q)$. Since the latter do not depend on the observations, they are equal to their expectations, i.e., to the Fisher information matrix for q. Therefore, the matrix of second partial derivatives, which is symmetric, is negative definite. Thus the (unique) solution to the likelihood equations corresponds to a global maximum. To complete the argument, it suffices to invoke Property 7.7 so as to establish that the (unique) solution to the likelihood equations in θ corresponds to a global maximum of the likelihood function.

7.4 Asymptotic Properties

We now study the properties of maximum likelihood estimators when the number of observations is large. Under suitable regularity conditions, ensuring for instance that the model is close to a sampling model, the maximum likelihood estimator exists and converges to the true unknown parameter value as the number of observations increases. In addition, the maximum likelihod estimator is asymptotically normally distributed and its variance covariance matrix is equal to the FDCR bound, i.e., it is *asymptotically efficient.*

There are different proofs of such properties. Each one corresponds to different regularity conditions. The main purpose of this section is to present the main steps of these proofs and to discuss the regularity conditions. To simplify, we consider a sampling model although the results of this section can be extended to more general situations where the observations are neither independent nor identically distributed. Such situations are illustrated by some examples that can be studied directly.

The reader who would like more rigorous proofs of the next asymptotic theorems may consult Chapter 24, Volume II. Also, the concept of asymptotic efficiency introduced here is discussed in Chapter 23, Volume II in more detail.

Consistency and asymptotic efficiency of maximum likelihood estimators constitute an important justification for the use of this estimation method when the sample size is large. There are, however, some cases where these "good" asymptotic properties do not hold. Some examples are given in Section 7.4.5.

7.4.1 Existence and Strong Consistency

We consider a sequence of observations $Y_i, i = 1, 2, \ldots$ satisfying a parametric model. It is assumed that the following regularity conditions hold.

Regularity Conditions:

A1: The variables $Y_i, i = 1, 2, \ldots$ are independent and identically distributed with density $f(y;\theta)$, $\theta \in \Theta \subset I\!R^p$.

A2: The parameter space Θ is compact.

A3: The true but unknown parameter value θ_0 is identified.

A4: The log-likelihood function

$$L_n(y;\theta) = \sum_{i=1}^{n} \log f(y_i;\theta)$$

is continuous in θ.

A5: $E_{\theta_0} \log f(Y_i;\theta)$ exists.

A6: The log-likelihood function is such that $(1/n)L_n(y;\theta)$ converges almost surely to $E_{\theta_0} \log f(Y_i;\theta)$ uniformly in $\theta \in \Theta$.

Property 7.10: *Under Assumptions A1–A6, there exists a sequence of maximum likelihood estimators converging almost surely to the true parameter value* θ_0.

SKETCH OF THE PROOF: Assumptions A2 and A4 ensure the existence of a maximum likelihood estimator $\hat{\theta}_n$. It is obtained by maximizing $L_n(\theta)$ or equivalently by maximizing $\frac{1}{n}L_n(\theta)$. Since $\frac{1}{n}L_n(\theta) = \frac{1}{n}\sum_{i=1}^{n} \log f(Y_i;\theta)$ can be interpreted as the sample mean of the random variables $\log f(Y_i;\theta)$, which are independent and identically distributed, the objective function converges almost surely to $E_{\theta_0} \log f(Y;\theta)$ by the Strong Law of Large Numbers.

To complete the proof, one uses the fact that, when the latter convergence is uniform (see Assumption A6), then the solution $\hat{\theta}_n$ converges to the solution to the limit problem

$$\max_{\theta} E_{\theta_0} \log f(Y;\theta),$$

i.e.

$$\max_{\theta} \int_{\mathcal{Y}} \log f(y;\theta) f(y;\theta_0) d\mu(y).$$

Now, properties of the Kullback information measure together with the identification condition on θ_0 (see Assumption A3) imply that the solution to the limit problem is unique and equal to θ_0. Hence $\hat{\theta}_n$ converges almost surely to θ_0. □

Clearly, the assumption that is difficult to verify is the uniform requirement on the almost sure convergence in Assumption A6. On the other hand, the other hypotheses are easily verifiable. They can also be weakened provided the statement of the theorem is modified appropriately (see Chapter 25, Volume II for more details). For instance, the compactness requirement of the parameter space can be replaced by:

A2′: The interior of Θ is nonempty and θ_0 belongs to the interior of Θ.

Property 7.11: *Under Assumptions A1, A2′, A3–A6, there exists a sequence of local maxima of the log-likelihood function that converges almost surely to θ_0.*

SKETCH OF THE PROOF: The basic idea is to consider a compact subset of the parameter space and to apply Property 7.10. Specifically, consider a closed sphere with radius $r > 0$ centered at θ_0 and strictly included in Θ. Let $V(\theta_0, r)$ denote such a sphere. Consider the constrained maximum likelihood estimation problem, i.e.

$$\max_{\theta \in V(\theta_0, r)} L(\theta).$$

Since $V(\theta_0, r)$ is compact, Property 7.10 implies that there exists a sequence of solutions $\tilde{\theta}_n$ to this problem that converges almost surely to θ_0. Convergence implies that, for n sufficiently large, $\tilde{\theta}_n$ belongs to the interior of $V(\theta_0, r)$. Thus $\tilde{\theta}_n$ corresponds to a local maximum of the log-likelihood function. □

The preceding property remains valid if Assumption A6 is replaced by:

A6′: There exist a neighborhood of θ_0 on which $(1/n)L_n(\theta)$ converges almost surely and uniformly.

Corollary 7.1: *If in addition to the assumptions of Property 7.11 the likelihood function is differentiable, then there exists a sequence of solutions to the likelihood equations that converges almost surely to θ_0.*

PROOF: This is a straightforward consequence of the fact that a local maximum on the open sphere $V^0(\theta_0, r)$ must satisfy the likelihood equations. □

When Θ is open, a consistent sequence of local maxima may not be a sequence of global maxima.

Example 7.17: Suppose that the observed variables $Y_i, i = 1, \ldots, n$, are defined by $Y_i = \min(Y_{1i}, Y_{2i})$, where Y_{1i} and Y_{2i} are independent variables following the normal distributions $N(m_1, \sigma_1^2)$ and $N(m_2, \sigma_2^2)$, respectively. The marginal density of Y_i is

$$\begin{aligned} f(y_i) &= \frac{1}{\sigma_1}\phi\left(\frac{y_i - m_1}{\sigma_1}\right)\left(1 - \Phi\left(\frac{y_i - m_2}{\sigma_2}\right)\right) \\ &\quad + \frac{1}{\sigma_2}\phi\left(\frac{y_i - m_2}{\sigma_2}\right)\left(1 - \Phi\left(\frac{y_i - m_1}{\sigma_1}\right)\right), \end{aligned}$$

where ϕ and Φ denote the density and the cumulative distribution functions of the standard normal distribution.

The likelihood function is

$$\begin{aligned} \ell(y;\theta) &= \left\{\prod_{i=1}^{n} \frac{1}{\sigma_1}\phi\left(\frac{y_i - m_1}{\sigma_1}\right)\left(1 - \Phi\left(\frac{y_i - m_2}{\sigma_2}\right)\right)\right. \\ &\quad \left. + \frac{1}{\sigma_2}\phi\left(\frac{y_i - m_2}{\sigma_2}\right)\left(1 - \Phi\left(\frac{y_i - m_1}{\sigma_1}\right)\right)\right\}. \end{aligned}$$

Using

$$\lim_{\sigma \to 0} \frac{1}{\sigma}\phi\left(\frac{y - m}{\sigma}\right) = \begin{cases} 0, \text{ if } m \neq y, \\ +\infty, \text{ if } m = y, \end{cases}$$

$$\lim_{\sigma \to 0} \Phi\left(\frac{y - m}{\sigma}\right) = \begin{cases} 0, \text{ if } y < m, \\ 1/2, \text{ if } y = m, \\ 1, \text{ if } y > m, \end{cases}$$

it is seen that the likelihood function diverges to $+\infty$ when m_2 and σ_2 are fixed, $m_1 = \max y_i$ and σ_1 converges to zero. These solutions correspond to global maxima. They are, however, not consistent since $\hat{\sigma}_1$ converges to zero, which is not the true value σ_1.

From Property 7.11, however, there exists a consistent sequence of local maxima. These local maxima are not global maxima since the likelihood is finite everywhere on $\mathbb{R}^2 \times \mathbb{R}^{+2}$. This example is due to Quandt.

7.4.2 Asymptotic Distribution

Since the sequence $\hat{\theta}_n$ converges to θ_0, it is useful to consider the asymptotic behavior of $\hat{\theta}_n - \theta_0$. In particular, it is interesting to determine its rate of convergence toward zero. This allows us to establish the asymptotic normality of the ML estimator.

We need additional regularity conditions.

Regularity conditions:

A7: The log-likelihood function $L_n(\theta)$ is twice continously differentiable in an open neighborhood of θ_0.

A8: The matrix

$$\mathcal{I}_1(\theta_0) = E_{\theta_0}\left(-\frac{\partial^2 \log f(Y_1;\theta_0)}{\partial\theta\,\partial\theta'}\right)$$

exists and is nonsingular.

Property 7.12: *Under the assumptions of Property 7.11, suppose that Assumptions A7–A8 hold. Then a consistent sequence $\hat{\theta}_n$ of local maxima is such that $\sqrt{n}(\hat{\theta}_n - \theta_0)$ converges in distribution to a normal distribution with mean zero and variance covariance matrix $\mathcal{I}_1(\theta_0)^{-1}$, i.e.*

$$\sqrt{n}(\hat{\theta}_n - \theta_0) \xrightarrow{d} N(0, \mathcal{I}_1(\theta_0)^{-1}).$$

Sketch of the Proof: Since the sequence $\hat{\theta}_n$ satisfies the likelihood equations $\partial L(\hat{\theta}_n)/\partial\theta = 0$ and since $\hat{\theta}_n$ converges to θ_0, a Taylor expansion of the score vector $\partial L_n(\theta)/\partial\theta$ in a neighborhood of $\theta = \theta_0$ gives

$$\frac{\partial L_n(\theta)}{\partial\theta} \# \frac{\partial L_n(\theta_0)}{\partial\theta} + \frac{\partial^2 L_n(\theta_0)}{\partial\theta\partial\theta'}(\theta - \theta_0),$$

where the symbol # means that the difference between the left-hand side and the right-hand side is an $o_P(1)$ (see Chapter 24, Volume II). Letting $\theta = \hat{\theta}_n$ and using the likelihood equations, it follows that

$$-\frac{\partial^2 L_n(\theta_0)}{\partial\theta\,\partial\theta'}(\hat{\theta}_n - \theta_0) \# \frac{\partial L_n(\theta_0)}{\partial\theta},$$

or equivalently

$$\left(-\frac{1}{n}\frac{\partial^2 L_n(\theta_0)}{\partial\theta\,\partial\theta'}\right)\sqrt{n}(\hat{\theta}_n - \theta_0) \# \frac{1}{\sqrt{n}}\frac{\partial L_n(\theta_0)}{\partial\theta}.$$

Now, on the one hand

$$-\frac{1}{n}\frac{\partial^2 L_n(\theta_0)}{\partial\theta\,\partial\theta'} = \frac{1}{n}\sum_{i=1}^{n}\frac{\partial^2 \log f(Y_i;\theta_0)}{\partial\theta\,\partial\theta'}$$

converges almost surely to

$$\mathcal{I}_1(\theta_0) = E_{\theta_0}\left(-\frac{\partial^2 \log f(Y_i;\theta_0)}{\partial\theta\,\partial\theta'}\right),$$

by the Strong Law of Large Numbers. Thus we have

$$\mathcal{I}_1(\theta_0)\sqrt{n}(\hat{\theta}_n - \theta_0) \# \frac{1}{\sqrt{n}}\frac{\partial L_n(\theta_0)}{\partial\theta}.$$

On the other hand, we have

$$\begin{aligned}\frac{1}{\sqrt{n}}\frac{\partial L_n(\theta_0)}{\partial\theta} &= \frac{1}{\sqrt{n}}\sum_{i=1}^{n}\frac{\partial \log f(Y_i;\theta_0)}{\partial\theta} \\ &= \frac{1}{\sqrt{n}}\sum_{i=1}^{n}\left(\frac{\partial \log f(Y_i;\theta_0)}{\partial\theta} - E_{\theta_0}\frac{\partial \log f(Y_i;\theta_0)}{\partial\theta}\right),\end{aligned}$$

which converges in distribution to

$$N\left(0, V_{\theta_0}\left(\frac{\partial \log f(Y_i;\theta_0)}{\partial\theta}\right)\right) = N(0, \mathcal{I}_1(\theta_0)),$$

by the Central Limit Theorem.

Collecting the preceding results and premultiplying by $\mathcal{I}_1(\theta_0)^{-1}$, we obtain the desired result. □

Property 7.12 gives an approximation to the sampling distribution of the ML estimator $\hat{\theta}_n$ for large n. Specifically, the approximation is

$$\hat{\theta}_n \approx N\left(\theta_0, \frac{1}{n}\mathcal{I}_1(\theta_0)^{-1}\right).$$

Since

$$\frac{1}{n}\mathcal{I}_1(\theta_0)^{-1} = (n\mathcal{I}_1(\theta_0))^{-1} = \mathcal{I}_n(\theta_0)^{-1},$$

where $\mathcal{I}_n(\theta_0)$ is the Fisher information matrix for n observations, we obtain

$$\hat{\theta}_n \approx N\left(\theta_0, \mathcal{I}_n(\theta_0)^{-1}\right).$$

This means that the distribution of $\hat{\theta}_n$ can be approximated by a normal distribution centered around the true parameter value θ_0 with variance covariance matrix equal to the FDCR lower bound. We shall say that the ML estimator $\hat{\theta}_n$ is *asymptotically unbiased* and *asymptotically efficient.*

The Fisher information matrix $\mathcal{I}_1(\theta_0)$ depends on the unknown parameter value θ_0. It can, however, be estimated consistently when $\mathcal{I}_1(\theta)$ is continuous in θ. For instance, some consistent estimators are

$$\mathcal{I}_1(\hat{\theta}_n),$$

or

$$-\frac{1}{n}\frac{\partial^2 \log \ell_n(Y;\hat{\theta}_n)}{\partial\theta\,\partial\theta'},$$

or

$$\frac{1}{n}\sum_{i=1}^{n}\frac{\partial \log f(Y_i;\hat{\theta}_n)}{\partial\theta}\frac{\partial \log f(Y_i;\hat{\theta}_n)}{\partial\theta'}. \tag{7.3}$$

The asymptotic properties of the ML estimator of a function $g(\theta_0)$ of the parameter are easily derived from those of the ML estimator $\hat{\theta}_n$.

Property 7.13: *Let g be a continuously differentiable function of $\theta \in I\!R^p$ with values in $I\!R^q$. Then, under the assumptions of Property 7.12:*

(i) $g(\hat{\theta}_n)$ converges almost surely to $g(\theta_0)$,

(ii) $\sqrt{n}\left(g(\hat{\theta}_n) - g(\theta_0)\right)$ converges in distribution to the normal distribution

$$N\left(0, \frac{dg(\theta_0)}{d\theta'}I_1(\theta_0)^{-1}\frac{dg'(\theta_0)}{d\theta}\right).$$

PROOF: This follows straightforwardly from Properties B.68 and B.69. □

7.4.3 Concentrated Likelihood Function

In Section 7.2.4 we saw that, in some cases, concentrating out a subvector α of $\theta = (\alpha', \beta')'$ from the likelihood function may be useful. The next property states that a consistent estimator of the variance covariance matrix of the ML estimator $\hat{\beta}_n$ of β can be readily obtained from the concentrated log-likelihood function.

Property 7.14: *For every β, suppose that the log-likelihood function $L_n(\alpha,\beta) = \log \ell_n(y;\alpha,\beta)$ has a unique global maximum in α, denoted $\tilde{\alpha}(\beta)$. Suppose also that the assumptions of Properties 7.6 and 7.12 hold.*

Then the asymptotic variance covariance matrix of $\sqrt{n}(\hat{\beta}_n - \beta_0)$ *can be estimated consistently by*

$$\left(-\frac{1}{n}\frac{\partial^2 L_{nc}(\hat{\beta}_n)}{\partial\beta\,\partial\beta'}\right)^{-1}.$$

PROOF: This readily follows from the equality

$$\begin{aligned}\left(\frac{\partial^2 L_{nc}(\hat{\beta}_n)}{\partial\beta\,\partial\beta'}\right)^{-1} &= \left(\frac{\partial^2 L_n(\tilde{\alpha}(\hat{\beta}_n),\hat{\beta}_n)}{\partial\theta\,\partial\theta'}\right)^{\beta\beta} \\ &= \left(\frac{\partial^2 L_n(\hat{\alpha}_n,\hat{\beta}_n)}{\partial\theta\,\partial\theta'}\right)^{\beta\beta},\end{aligned}$$

(see Property 7.6) and the fact that the asymptotic variance covariance matrix of $\sqrt{n}(\hat{\beta}_n - \beta_0)$ is estimated consistently by

$$\left(-\frac{1}{n}\frac{\partial^2 L_n(\hat{\alpha}_n,\hat{\beta}_n)}{\partial\theta\,\partial\theta'}\right)^{\beta\beta}.$$

□

7.4.4 Direct Derivation of Asymptotic Properties

The general framework presented in Sections 7.4.1 and 7.4.2 will be used to derive further asymptotic properties when studying, for instance, some large sample tests. This general framework, however, imposes conditions that are sometimes too strong for particular statistical problems. In addition, it may be more interesting and sometimes easier to establish directly the asymptotic properties of the ML estimator. Some examples are given below.

Example 7.18: Consider a random sample $Y_1, \ldots, Y_n$ drawn from a Poisson distribution $P(\lambda)$. The maximum likelihood estimator of λ is $\hat{\lambda}_n = \bar{Y}_n$. This estimator is such that $n\hat{\lambda}_n = \sum_{i=1}^n Y_i$ follows a Poisson distribution $P(n\lambda)$. A direct application of the Strong Law of Large Numbers shows that $\hat{\lambda}_n = \bar{Y}_n$ converges almost surely to $EY_i = \lambda$. In addition, from the Central Limit Theorem it follows that

$$\sqrt{n}(\bar{Y}_n - \lambda) \xrightarrow{d} N(0, V_\lambda Y_i) = N(0, \lambda).$$

Example 7.19: A similar reasoning can be used in a multiparameter context. Consider a population classified into K mutually exhaustive and exclusive subpopulations. Let $p_1, \dots, p_K$ denote the corresponding proportions, where $p_k \geq 0$, $k = 1, \dots, K$ and $\sum_{k=1}^{K} p_k = 1$. A random sample of size n is drawn with equal probability and replacement from the whole population. Let $(n_1, \dots, n_K)'$ denote the observation vector, where n_k denotes the number of individuals in the sample belonging to the kth subpopulation. The observation vector follows a multinomial distribution $M(n, p_1, \dots, p_K)$. The maximum likelihood estimator is

$$\hat{p} = (\hat{p}_1, \dots, \hat{p}_K)' = \left(\frac{n_1}{n}, \dots, \frac{n_K}{n}\right)'.$$

Applying the Strong Law of Large Numbers and the multivariate Central Limit Theorem (see Property B.63 and Theorem B.8) establishes that $\hat{p}$ is a strongly consistent estimator of $(p_1, \dots, p_K)'$ and that

$$\sqrt{n}(\hat{p} - p) \xrightarrow{d} N(0, \ \text{diag}\ p - pp').$$

The preceding examples are straightforward applications of basic classical asymptotic theorems. In more complex situations it may be necessary to invoke more powerful versions of these theorems.

Example 7.20: Let $Y_1, \dots, Y_n$ be a random sample drawn from a gamma distribution $\gamma(1, 1/\theta)$, where $\theta \in I\!R^{+*}$. The maximum likelihood estimator of $1/\theta$ is $\bar{Y}_n$. Thus from Property 7.7, the maximum likelihood estimator of θ is $\hat{\theta}_n = 1/\bar{Y}_n$. Hence the asymptotic properties of $\hat{\theta}_n$ follow from those of $\bar{Y}_n$ using Properties B.68 and B.69. Specifically, since $\bar{Y}_n$ is a strongly consistent estimator of $1/\theta$, then $\hat{\theta}_n = 1/\bar{Y}_n$ is a strongly consistent estimator of $1/(1/\theta) = \theta$. Since $\bar{Y}_n$ is asymptotically normal, i.e.

$$\sqrt{n}(\bar{Y}_n - \frac{1}{\theta}) \xrightarrow{d} N(0, V_\theta Y_i),$$

it follows that

$$\sqrt{n}(\hat{\theta}_n - \theta) \xrightarrow{d} N\left(0, \left(\frac{d(1/\theta)}{d\theta}\right)^2 V_\theta Y_i\right),$$

i.e.

$$\sqrt{n}(\hat{\theta}_n - \theta) \xrightarrow{d} N\left(0, \frac{1}{\theta^4} V_\theta Y_i\right),$$

i.e.

$$\sqrt{n}(\hat{\theta}_n - \theta) \xrightarrow{d} N\left(0, \frac{1}{\theta^6}\right).$$

Example 7.21: Suppose that the observations $Y_t, t = 0, 1, \ldots$ are defined by $Y_t = \rho Y_{t-1} + u_t$ where the errors u_t are independent and identically distributed $N(0,1)$. Let T denote the sample size. Conditionally upon Y_0, the joint density of $Y_1, \ldots, Y_T$ is

$$\frac{1}{(2\pi)^{T/2}} \exp -\frac{1}{2} \sum_{t=1}^{T} (y_t - \rho y_{t-1})^2.$$

Maximizing the log-likelihood function (conditional upon Y_0) gives $\hat{\rho}_T = \frac{1}{T}\sum_{t=1}^{T} y_t\, y_{t-1}$. In this example, the observations Y_t are neither independent nor identically distributed. Nonetheless, invoking stronger versions of the basic classical asymptotic theorems (Properties B.65 and B.66), it can be shown that $\hat{\rho}_T$ is a strongly consistent estimator of ρ and that $\sqrt{T}(\hat{\rho}_T - \rho)$ follows asymptotically the normal distribution $N(0, 1 - \rho^2)$ (see Example B.6).

7.4.5 On the Regularity Conditions

The good asymptotic properties of the maximum likelihood estimator, namely, its strong convergence, its asymptotic efficiency, and its approximate normality, hold under some regularity conditions. It is important to examine whether such properties are robust when the regularity conditions are weakened.

a) The Number of Parameters Increases with the Number of Observations

Up to now we have implicitly assumed that the number of parameters is equal to a fixed constant p. In some cases, the number of parameters increases naturally with the number of observations. In such cases, the ML estimator (i) may no longer converge, (ii) may converge to a parameter value different from the true value θ_0, or (iii) may still converge to θ_0. In general, the outcome depends on the importance of the number of parameters relative to the number of observations.

Example 7.22: Let $Y_1, Y_2, \ldots$ be independent random variables, each following a Poisson distribution with parameter θ_i, $i = 1, 2, \ldots$. For any sample size n there are as many parameters as observations. For a sample size n the maximum likelihood estimator of θ_i is $\hat{\theta}_{in} = Y_i$, $\forall i < n$. Thus the ML estimator does not depend on n and converges to the random variable $Y_i \neq \theta_i$.

Example 7.23: Consider independent pairs of observations $(Y_{1t}, Y_{2t})'$, $t = 1, 2 \ldots$, each drawn from

$$N\left(\begin{pmatrix} \mu_{0t} \\ \mu_{0t} \end{pmatrix}, \begin{pmatrix} \sigma_0^2 & 0 \\ 0 & \sigma_0^2 \end{pmatrix}\right).$$

Let T be the sample size. There are $T+1$ parameters for $2T$ observations. The maximum likelihood estimator of μ_{0t} is

$$\hat{\mu}_{tT} = \frac{1}{2}(Y_{1t} + Y_{2t}).$$

The maximum likelihood estimator of σ_0^2 is

$$\begin{aligned} \hat{\sigma}_T^2 &= \frac{1}{2T}\sum_{t=1}^{T}\left((Y_{1t} - \hat{\mu}_{tT})^2 + (Y_{2t} - \hat{\mu}_{tT})^2\right) \\ &= \frac{1}{T}\sum_{t=1}^{T}\left(\frac{Y_{1t} - Y_{2t}}{2}\right)^2 \\ &= \frac{1}{4T}\sum_{t=1}^{T}(Y_{1t} - Y_{2t})^2. \end{aligned}$$

Thus $\hat{\mu}_{tT}$ converges to the random variable $(Y_{1t} + Y_{2t})/2$ when T increases to infinity. Moreover, from the Strong Law of Large Numbers, $\hat{\sigma}_T^2$ converges almost surely to

$$\frac{1}{4}E(Y_{1t} - Y_{2t})^2 = \frac{1}{4}V(Y_{1t} - Y_{2t}) = \frac{\sigma_0^2}{2},$$

i.e., to a constant different from σ_0^2.

Example 7.24: Now suppose that one has independent observations $Y_{t\tau}$, $t = 1, \ldots, T$, $\tau = 1, \ldots, T$, $T = 1, 2, \ldots$, each following a normal distribution $N(\mu_{0t}, \sigma_0^2)$. We have

$$\hat{\mu}_{tT} = \frac{1}{T}\sum_{\tau=1}^{T} Y_{t\tau} = \bar{Y}_t \xrightarrow{\text{as}} \mu_{0t}.$$

Moreover

$$\begin{aligned}\hat{\sigma}_T^2 &= \frac{1}{T^2}\sum_{t=1}^{T}\sum_{\tau=1}^{T}(Y_{t\tau}-\bar{Y}_{t\cdot})^2\\ &= \frac{1}{T}\sum_{t=1}^{T}\frac{1}{T}\sum_{\tau=1}^{T}(Y_{t\tau}-\bar{Y}_{t\cdot})^2.\end{aligned}$$

Each sequence $\frac{1}{T}\sum_{\tau=1}^{T}(Y_{t\tau}-\bar{Y}_{t\cdot})^2$ converges almost surely to σ_0^2. Hence the average of these sequences, namely $\hat{\sigma}_T^2$, converges to σ_0^2.

b) The True Parameter Value θ_0 Does Not Belong to Θ

The model is misspecified in the sense that it does not contain the true distribution generating the observations. This important case is studied in Chapter 8 in detail. In general, there is strong convergence to a parameter value that is different from the true value.

c) The Support of P_θ Depends on the Parameter

This arises when the distributions in the model have a nonstrictly positive density with respect to a measure that is independent of the parameter. In this case the maximum likelihood estimator is frequently consistent but is not asymptotically normal.

Example 7.25: The likelihood function of an independent and identically distributed sample drawn from a translated exponential distribution with density

$$f(y;\theta) = (\exp-(y-\theta))\,\mathbb{1}_{y\geq\theta}$$

is given by

$$\begin{aligned}\ell(y;\theta) &= \prod_{i=1}^{n}(\exp-(y_i-\theta)\mathbb{1}_{y_i\geq\theta})\\ &= \left(\exp-\sum_{i=1}^{n}(y_i-\theta)\right)\mathbb{1}_{\inf_i y_i\geq\theta}.\end{aligned}$$

The maximum is attained at

$$\hat{\theta}_n = \inf_i Y_i,$$

where the likelihood function is not differentiable.

The estimator $\hat{\theta}_n$ converges almost surely to θ_0. To see this note that

$$
\begin{aligned}
P_{\theta_0}\left(\bigcup_{m\geq n}(|\hat{\theta}_m - \theta_0| > \varepsilon)\right) &= P_{\theta_0}\left(\bigcup_{m\geq n}(\hat{\theta}_m > \theta_0 + \varepsilon)\right) \\
&\qquad (\text{ since } \hat{\theta}_m > \theta_0) \\
&= P_{\theta_0}(\hat{\theta}_n > \theta_0 + \varepsilon) \\
&\qquad (\text{ since } \hat{\theta}_n \text{ is decreasing}) \\
&= P_{\theta_0}(\forall\, i \leq n, Y_i > \theta_0 + \varepsilon) \\
&= \prod_{i=1}^{n} P_{\theta_0}(Y_i > \theta_0 + \varepsilon) \\
&= \left(\int_{\theta_0+\varepsilon}^{+\infty} \exp -(y - \theta_0)dy\right)^n \\
&= \exp(-n\varepsilon).
\end{aligned}
$$

This quantity converges to zero when n increases to infinity. The strong convergence of $\hat{\theta}_n$ to θ_0 follows.

In addition, it is easy to see that $\sqrt{n}(\hat{\theta}_n - \theta_0)$ cannot converge to a centered distribution because $\hat{\theta}_n$ is always larger than θ_0. More precisely, the cumulative distribution function of $\hat{\theta}_n$ is given by

$$P_{\theta_0}(\hat{\theta}_n < z) = 1 - \exp -(n(z - \theta_0)).$$

Thus the random variable $n(\hat{\theta}_n - \theta_0)$ follows a gamma distribution $\gamma(1)$. Note that the rate of convergence is $1/n$ instead of $1/\sqrt{n}$. Moreover, the asymptotic distribution is $\gamma(1)$ instead of a normal distribution.

d) θ_0 Belongs to Θ but not to the Interior of Θ

This case arises when the parameter space Θ is not open.

Example 7.26: Consider the model associated with the *Box–Cox transformation*

$$\frac{y_t^\lambda - 1}{\lambda} = ax_t + b + u_t, \quad t = 1, \ldots, T,$$

where the errors u_t are independent and identically distributed $N(0, \sigma^2)$. The parameter λ is, in general, constrained to be between zero and one. The limit cases correspond to a log-linear formulation ($\lambda = 0$) and a linear formulation ($\lambda = 1$). When $\lambda_0 = 1$, the maximum likelihood estimator of λ is consistent but its asymptotic distribution is not centered normal because $\hat{\lambda}_T - 1$ is always negative.

e) Correlated Observations

Properties of consistency and asymptotic normality hold only when the observations are not strongly correlated.

Example 7.27: Let the observation vector $Y = (Y_1, \dots, Y_n)'$ be jointly normally distributed with mean $EY = me$ and variance covariance matrix $VY = (1 - \rho_0)\mathbf{I} + \rho_0 ee'$, where e denotes the vector of which all the components are equal to one and $\rho_0 \in (0, 1)$. Thus every pair of observations is correlated with identical correlation ρ_0. The model is called an *equi-correlation model.*

The maximum likelihood estimator of m is $\hat{m}_n = \bar{Y}_n$. Its distribution is normal $N(m, (1 + (n-1)\rho_0)/n)$. This estimator does not converge in quadratic mean since

$$V\bar{Y}_n \to \rho_0 \neq 0.$$

f) Nonidentically Distributed Observations

Example 7.28: Consider independent random variables $Y_i, i = 1, 2 \dots$, each following a normal distribution $N(ax_i, 1)$ where a is a parameter and $x_i, i = 1, 2 \dots$ are given constants. Let n be the sample size. The maximum likelihood estimator of a is

$$\hat{a} = \frac{\sum_{i=1}^n x_i Y_i}{\sum_{i=1}^n x_i^2}.$$

Its distribution is normal $N(a, 1/\sum_{i=1}^n x_i^2)$. This estimator may not be consistent. For instance, if $\sum_{i=1}^n x_i^2$ converges to one, then $\hat{a}_n$ converges in distribution to $N(a, 1)$. Therefore the ML estimator is not weakly consistent and *a fortiori* not strongly consistent for a.

On the other hand, if $\sum_{i=1}^n x_i^2$ diverges to infinity, then

$$V\hat{a}_n = \frac{1}{\sum_1^n x_1^2} \to 0.$$

Since $E\hat{a}_n = a$, the ML estimator converges to a in quadratic mean. However, $\hat{a}_n - a$ does not converge necessarily to a normal distribution at the rate $1/\sqrt{n}$. More precisely, we have

$$\sqrt{\sum_{i=1}^{n} x_i^2}(\hat{a}_n - a) \xrightarrow{d} N(0,1),$$

and the appropriate rate of convergence is $1/\sqrt{\sum_{i=1}^{n} x_i^2}$.

g) Discontinuity of the Likelihood Function

When the support of the distributions P_θ remains constant when θ varies, a discontinuity of the likelihood function is unlikely in practice. This explains the artificial nature of the next example which is due to Basu.

Example 7.29: Consider independent and identically distributed random variables drawn from

$$\begin{cases} B(1,\theta), & \text{if } \theta \in \mathbb{Q} \cap [0,1], \\ B(1,1-\theta), & \text{if } \theta \in \mathbb{Q}^c \cap [0,1], \end{cases}$$

where $\mathbb{Q}$ denotes the set of rational numbers and $\mathbb{Q}^c$ its complement. The likelihood function is

$$\ell(y;\theta) = \begin{cases} \theta^{n\bar{y}}(1-\theta)^{n-n\bar{y}}, & \text{if } \theta \in \mathbb{Q} \cap [0,1], \\ \theta^{n-n\bar{y}}(1-\theta)^{n\bar{y}}, & \text{if } \theta \in \mathbb{Q}^c \cap [0,1], \end{cases}$$

where $\bar{y} = \frac{1}{n}\sum_{i=1}^{n} y_i$. Maximizing the likelihood function gives $\hat{\theta}_n = \bar{Y}$ since $\bar{Y}$ is always a rational number. From the Strong Law of Large Numbers, it follows that

$$\hat{\theta}_n \xrightarrow{\text{as}} \begin{cases} \theta, & \text{if } \theta \in \mathbb{Q} \cap [0,1], \\ 1-\theta, & \text{if } \theta \in \mathbb{Q}^c \cap [0,1]. \end{cases}$$

7.5 Marginal and Conditional ML Estimation

7.5.1 Principles

For computational reasons, it is sometimes interesting not to use all the information contained in the observations. This is the topic of this section.

To simplify, we assume that the pairs of observations $(Y_i', X_i')'$, $i = 1, \ldots, n$ are independent and identically distributed. For the nonindependent and nonidentically distributed case, see Chapter 24, Volume II. The joint distribution of each pair can be decomposed as the product of the conditional distribution of Y_i given X_i and the marginal distribution of X_i

$$f(y_i, x_i; \theta) = f(y_i \mid x_i; \theta) f(x_i; \theta).$$

Definition 7.2:

(i) A marginal maximum likelihood estimator of θ is a solution $\hat{\theta}_{m,n}$ to the problem

$$\max_{\theta \in \Theta} \sum_{i=1}^{n} \log f(X_i; \theta).$$

(ii) A conditional maximum likelihood estimator of θ is a solution $\hat{\theta}_{c,n}$ to the problem

$$\max_{\theta \in \Theta} \sum_{i=1}^{n} \log f(Y_i \mid X_i; \theta).$$

Clearly, the roles of the variables X and Y can be interchanged. For instance, we can define a marginal maximum likelihood estimator associated with Y.

In practice, it frequently happens that some components of θ do not appear in either the marginal distribution or the conditional distribution. Thus, although the true parameter value θ_0 is identified in the joint model for $(Y_i', X_i')', i = 1, ..., n$, it may not be identified in the marginal model or in the conditional model. To take into account such a difficulty, we assume that θ can be partitioned as $\theta = (\alpha', \beta', \gamma')'$, where $(\alpha', \beta')'$ appears in the conditional model and $(\beta', \gamma')'$ appears in the marginal model

$$f(Y_i, X_i; \theta) = f(Y_i \mid X_i; \alpha, \beta) \ f(X_i; \beta, \gamma).$$

An important case arises when there is a *cut.* Then there are no common parameters β.

Property 7.15: *Suppose that there is a cut so that*

$$f(y_i, x_i; \theta) = f(y_i \mid x_i; \alpha) \ f(x_i; \gamma), \quad (\alpha; \gamma) \in A \times C.$$

The maximum likelihood estimator of θ is

$$\hat{\theta}_n = \begin{pmatrix} \hat{\alpha}_{c,n} \\ \hat{\gamma}_{m,n} \end{pmatrix}.$$

PROOF: Since

$$\sum_{i=1}^{n} \log f(y_i, x_i; \theta) = \sum_{i=1}^{n} \log f(y_i \mid x_i; \alpha) + \sum_{i=1}^{n} \log f(x_i; \gamma),$$

then maximizing the joint log-likelihood function with respect to $\theta = (\alpha', \gamma')'$ is equivalent to maximizing separately the conditional log-likelihood function with respect to α and the marginal log-likelihood function with respect to γ. □

Thus, if the parameter vector of interest is α, then we can neglect the marginal distribution of the variables X_i when estimating α by maximum likelihood methods.

7.5.2 Examples

The determination of a conditional maximum likelihood estimator is similar to the determination of the unconditional maximum likelihood estimator.

Example 7.30: Consider a family of densities defined on $I\!R$, parameterized by a mean m, and given by

$$\tilde{f}(y, m) = \exp(A(m) + B(y) + C(m)y),$$

where A and C are continuously differentiable real functions.

It is easy to verify that m being the mean implies

$$\frac{\partial A}{\partial m} + m \frac{\partial C}{\partial m} = 0.$$

In addition, the derivative $\partial C / \partial m$ is the inverse of the variance associated with the density $\tilde{f}$. Thus, if this variance is strictly positive, then the function C is strictly increasing and hence bijective.

Now suppose that the variables $Y_1, \ldots, Y_T$ are mutually independent conditionally on $X_1, \ldots, X_T$. Suppose also that the conditional density of Y_t given $X = (x_1, \ldots, x_T)$ is $f(y_t \mid x_t, \theta) = \tilde{f}(y_t, C^{-1}(x_t'\theta))$ with $\theta \in I\!R^p$. The log-likelihood function is

$$\log \ell(y \mid x; \theta) = \sum_{t=1}^{T} \left(A(C^{-1}(x_t \theta)) + B(y_t) + x_t' \theta y_t \right).$$

The first-order conditions are

$$\begin{aligned}
0 &= \frac{\partial \log \ell(y \mid x; \hat{\theta}_c)}{\partial \theta} \\
&= \sum_{t=1}^{T} \left(\frac{1}{\frac{\partial C}{\partial m}(C^{-1}(x_t'\hat{\theta}_c))} \frac{\partial A}{\partial m}(C^{-1}(x_t'\hat{\theta}_c)) + y_t \right) x_t \\
&= \sum_{t=1}^{T} \left(-(C^{-1}(x_t'\hat{\theta}_c)) + y_t \right) x_t \\
&= \sum_{t=1}^{T} x_t \left(y_t - E_{\hat{\theta}_c}(Y_t \mid x_t) \right).
\end{aligned}$$

These conditions express the orthogonality between the explanatory variables and the estimated residuals $y_t - E_{\hat{\theta}_c}(Y_t \mid x_t)$. For this reason, the previous system is called the system of *normal equations.*

Example 7.31: Constrained Maximum

An important example is given by the linear model $Y \sim N(\mathbf{X}\theta, \sigma_0^2 \mathbf{I})$, where $\mathbf{X}$ is a $n \times K$ matrix of rank K, σ_0^2 is known, and θ is subject to some linear constraints. The linear constraints are of the form $\mathbf{G}\theta = g$, where $\mathbf{G}$ is a known $r \times K$ matrix of full row rank r and g is a known $r \times 1$ vector. We have

$$L(y; \theta) = -\frac{n}{2} \log(\sigma_0^2 2\pi) - \frac{1}{2} \frac{(y - \mathbf{X}\theta)'(y - \mathbf{X}\theta)}{\sigma_0^2},$$

$$\frac{\partial L(y; \theta)}{\partial \theta} = \frac{\mathbf{X}'(y - \mathbf{X}\theta)}{\sigma_0^2}.$$

If $\hat{\lambda}$ denotes the vector of Lagrange multipliers associated with the r constraints, the first-order conditions are

$$\begin{aligned}
-\frac{\mathbf{X}'(y - \mathbf{X}\hat{\theta}_c)}{\sigma_0^2} - \mathbf{G}'\hat{\lambda} &= 0, \\
\mathbf{G}\hat{\theta}_c &= g.
\end{aligned}$$

From the first set of equations, we obtain

$$\mathbf{X}'\mathbf{X}\hat{\theta}_c = \mathbf{X}'y + \sigma_0^2 \mathbf{G}'\hat{\lambda},$$

or

$$\hat{\theta}_c = (\mathbf{X}'\mathbf{X})^{-1}\mathbf{X}'y + \sigma_0^2 (\mathbf{X}'\mathbf{X})^{-1}\mathbf{G}'\hat{\lambda}.$$

Using the second set of equations, we obtain

$$\sigma_0^2 \mathbf{G}(\mathbf{X}'\mathbf{X})^{-1}\mathbf{G}'\hat{\lambda} = g - \mathbf{G}(\mathbf{X}'\mathbf{X})^{-1}\mathbf{X}'y.$$

Hence

$$\hat{\lambda} = \frac{1}{\sigma_0^2}(\mathbf{G}(\mathbf{X}'\mathbf{X})^{-1}\mathbf{G}')^{-1}(g - \mathbf{G}(\mathbf{X}'\mathbf{X})^{-1}\mathbf{X}'y), \tag{7.4}$$

and

$$\begin{aligned} \hat{\theta}_c &= (\mathbf{X}'\mathbf{X})^{-1}\mathbf{X}'y \\ &\quad + (\mathbf{X}'\mathbf{X})^{-1}\mathbf{G}'(\mathbf{G}(\mathbf{X}'\mathbf{X})^{-1}\mathbf{G}')^{-1}(g - \mathbf{G}(\mathbf{X}'\mathbf{X})^{-1}\mathbf{X}'y). \end{aligned} \tag{7.5}$$

The log-likelihood function is strictly concave because the matrix $\partial^2 L(y;\theta)/\partial\theta\,\partial\theta' = -\mathbf{X}'\mathbf{X}$ is negative definite. Moreover the constraints are linear. It follows that the constrained ML estimator $\hat{\theta}_c$ is the maximum likelihood estimator.

7.5.3 Asymptotic Properties

The approach is similar to that used for establishing the consistency and asymptotic normality of $\hat{\theta}$ (see Section 7.4). Here, we need to impose suitable regularity assumptions on the distribution of the pair $(Y_i', X_i')'$. To simplify, we assume that these pairs are independent and identically distributed. In particular, this implies that, conditionally on $X_1, \ldots, X_n$, the conditional distribution of Y_i depends on X_i only and that these conditional distributions are identical across i

$$P^{Y_i|X_1,\ldots,X_n} = P^{Y_i|X_i},$$

and

$$P^{Y_i|X_i=x} = P^{Y_j|X_j=x}, \ \forall\, i, j.$$

In addition, the conditioning variables must be mutually independent and identically distributed. Although such an assumption is not likely to be satisfied in practice, we shall maintain this assumption to simplify the exposition. The next results, however, hold under weaker conditions (see Chapter 24, Volume II).

Identification conditions must also be modified so as to allow for:

(i) identification of the true values α_0 and β_0 in the conditional model, namely

$$f(y \mid x; \alpha, \beta) = f(y \mid x; \alpha_0, \beta_0), \ \forall\, x, y,$$

implies $\alpha = \alpha_0$ and $\beta = \beta_0$,

(ii) identification of the true values β_0 and γ_0 in the marginal model, namely

$$f(x;\beta,\gamma) = f(x;\beta_0,\gamma_0), \ \forall \ x,$$

implies $\beta = \beta_0$ and $\gamma = \gamma_0$.

The remaining regularity conditions are similar to those given in Section 7.4. The reader can also find a set of sufficient conditions by invoking the general results of Chapter 24, Volume II.

Thereafter, $E_X(\cdot)$ denotes expectation with respect to the marginal distribution of X_i while $E(\cdot \mid x)$ denotes expectation with respect to the conditional distribution of Y_i given $X_i = x$. Also, let $\theta_m = (\beta', \gamma')'$ and $\theta_c = (\alpha', \beta')$.

Property 7.16: Marginal Maximum Likelihood Estimation

Under the regularity conditions discussed in Section 7.4, the estimators $\hat{\beta}_{m,n}$ and $\hat{\gamma}_{m,n}$:

(i) exist asymptotically,

(ii) are strongly consistent for the true values β_0 and γ_0,

(iii) are asymptotically normally distributed with

$$\sqrt{n}\left(\left(\begin{array}{c}\hat{\beta}_{mn}\\ \hat{\gamma}_{mn}\end{array}\right) - \left(\begin{array}{c}\beta_0\\ \gamma_0\end{array}\right)\right) \xrightarrow{d} N\left(0, \tilde{\mathcal{I}}_m^{-1}(\theta_0)\right),$$

where

$$\tilde{\mathcal{I}}_m(\theta_0) = E_X\left(-\frac{\partial^2 \log f(X;\beta_0,\gamma_0)}{\partial\theta_m\,\partial\theta_m'}\right).$$

PROOF: See Chapter 24, Volume II. □

Property 7.17: Conditional Maximum Likelihood Estimation

Under the regularity conditions discussed in Section 7.4, the estimators $\hat{\alpha}_{c,n}$ and $\hat{\beta}_{c,n}$:

(i) exist asymptotically,

(ii) are strongly consistent for the true values α_0 and β_0,

(iii) are asymptotically normally distributed with

$$\sqrt{n}\left(\left(\begin{array}{c}\hat{\alpha}_{cn}\\ \hat{\beta}_{cn}\end{array}\right) - \left(\begin{array}{c}\alpha_0\\ \beta_0\end{array}\right)\right) \xrightarrow{d} N\left(0, \tilde{\mathcal{I}}_c^{-1}(\theta_0)\right),$$

where

$$\tilde{\mathcal{I}}_c(\theta_0) = E_{\theta_0}\left(-\frac{\partial^2 \log f(Y \mid X; \alpha_0, \beta_0)}{\partial\theta_c\, \partial\theta_c'}\right).$$

PROOF: See Chapter 24, Volume II. □

Note that $\tilde{\mathcal{I}}_c(\theta_0)$ depends in general on γ_0 since it is necessary to take expectation with respect to the true marginal distribution of X.

The corresponding Fisher information matrices can be expressed as variance covariance matrices of the marginal and conditional scores respectively. Namely, we have

$$\begin{aligned}\tilde{\mathcal{I}}_m(\theta_0) &= V_X\left(\frac{\partial \log f(X; \beta_0, \gamma_0)}{\partial\theta_m}\right)\\ &= E_X\left(\frac{\partial \log f(X; \beta_0, \gamma_0)}{\partial\theta_m}\frac{\partial \log f(X; \beta_0, \gamma_0)}{\partial\theta_m'}\right),\end{aligned}$$

$$\begin{aligned}\tilde{\mathcal{I}}_c(\theta_0) &= E_X V_{\theta_0}\left(\frac{\partial \log f(Y \mid X; \beta_0, \gamma_0)}{\partial\theta_c} \mid X\right)\\ &= V_{\theta_0}\left(\frac{\partial \log f(Y \mid X; \beta_0, \gamma_0)}{\partial\theta_c}\right)\\ &= E_{\theta_0}\left(\frac{\partial \log f(Y \mid X; \beta_0, \gamma_0)}{\partial\theta_c}\frac{\partial \log f(Y \mid X; \beta_0, \gamma_0)}{\partial\theta_c'}\right).\end{aligned}$$

Property 7.18: *The estimators $\hat{\alpha}_{c,n}$, $\hat{\beta}_{c,n}$, $\hat{\beta}_{m,n}$, and $\hat{\gamma}_{m,n}$ are asymptotically at most as efficient as the maximum likelihood estimators $\hat{\alpha}_n$, $\hat{\beta}_n$, and $\hat{\gamma}_n$.*

PROOF: It suffices to compare the information matrices associated with the joint model, the marginal model, and the conditional model. Partition these matrices according to $(\alpha', \beta', \gamma')'$. We have

$$\mathcal{I}(\theta_0) = \begin{pmatrix} \mathcal{I}_{\alpha\alpha} & \mathcal{I}_{\alpha\beta} & \mathcal{I}_{\alpha\gamma} \\ \mathcal{I}_{\beta\alpha} & \mathcal{I}_{\beta\beta} & \mathcal{I}_{\beta\gamma} \\ \mathcal{I}_{\gamma\alpha} & \mathcal{I}_{\gamma\beta} & \mathcal{I}_{\gamma\gamma} \end{pmatrix},$$

$$\tilde{\mathcal{I}}_m(\theta_0) = \begin{pmatrix} \mathcal{I}_{\beta\beta,m} & \mathcal{I}_{\beta\gamma,m} \\ \mathcal{I}_{\gamma\beta,m} & \mathcal{I}_{\gamma\gamma,m} \end{pmatrix},$$

$$\tilde{\mathcal{I}}_c(\theta_0) = \begin{pmatrix} \mathcal{I}_{\alpha\alpha,c} & \mathcal{I}_{\alpha\beta,c} \\ \mathcal{I}_{\beta\alpha,c} & \mathcal{I}_{\beta\beta,c} \end{pmatrix}.$$

From Property 3.9, we have

$$\mathcal{I}(\theta_0) = \begin{pmatrix} 0 & 0 \\ 0 & \tilde{\mathcal{I}}_m(\theta_0) \end{pmatrix} + \begin{pmatrix} \tilde{\mathcal{I}}_c(\theta_0) & 0 \\ 0 & 0 \end{pmatrix}.$$

Thus the difference

$$\begin{pmatrix} \mathcal{I}_{\alpha\alpha} & \mathcal{I}_{\alpha\beta} & \mathcal{I}_{\alpha\gamma} \\ \mathcal{I}_{\beta\alpha} & \mathcal{I}_{\beta\beta} & \mathcal{I}_{\beta\gamma} \\ \mathcal{I}_{\gamma\alpha} & \mathcal{I}_{\gamma\beta} & \mathcal{I}_{\gamma\gamma} \end{pmatrix} - \begin{pmatrix} \mathcal{I}_{\alpha\alpha,c} & \mathcal{I}_{\alpha\beta,c} & 0 \\ \mathcal{I}_{\beta\alpha,c} & \mathcal{I}_{\beta\beta,c} & 0 \\ 0 & 0 & 0 \end{pmatrix}$$

is a symmetric positive semidefinite matrix. Then it suffices to show that

$$V\begin{pmatrix} \hat{\alpha}_{cn} \\ \hat{\beta}_{cn} \end{pmatrix} = \begin{pmatrix} \mathcal{I}_{\alpha\alpha,c} & \mathcal{I}_{\alpha\beta,c} \\ \mathcal{I}_{\beta\alpha,c} & \mathcal{I}_{\beta\beta,c} \end{pmatrix}^{-1}$$
$$\succeq V\begin{pmatrix} \hat{\alpha}_{n} \\ \hat{\beta}_{n} \end{pmatrix} = \left(\begin{pmatrix} \mathcal{I}_{\alpha\alpha} & \mathcal{I}_{\alpha\beta} \\ \mathcal{I}_{\beta\alpha} & \mathcal{I}_{\beta\beta} \end{pmatrix} - \begin{pmatrix} \mathcal{I}_{\alpha\gamma} \\ \mathcal{I}_{\beta\gamma} \end{pmatrix} \mathcal{I}_{\gamma\gamma}^{-1}(\mathcal{I}_{\gamma\alpha}\mathcal{I}_{\gamma\beta})\right)^{-1},$$

or equivalently that

$$\begin{pmatrix} \mathcal{I}_{\alpha\alpha,c} & \mathcal{I}_{\alpha\beta,c} \\ \mathcal{I}_{\beta\alpha,c} & \mathcal{I}_{\beta\beta,c} \end{pmatrix} \preceq \begin{pmatrix} \mathcal{I}_{\alpha\alpha} & \mathcal{I}_{\alpha\beta} \\ \mathcal{I}_{\beta\alpha} & \mathcal{I}_{\beta\beta} \end{pmatrix} - \begin{pmatrix} \mathcal{I}_{\alpha\gamma} \\ \mathcal{I}_{\beta\gamma} \end{pmatrix} \mathcal{I}_{\gamma\gamma}^{-1}(\mathcal{I}_{\gamma\alpha}\mathcal{I}_{\gamma\beta}).$$

But from Definition A.2–(viii), if $\mathbf{A}$ and $\mathbf{B}$ are two symmetric matrices satisfying $\mathbf{A} \succeq \mathbf{B}$, then we have $\mathbf{PAP}' \succeq \mathbf{PBP}'$ for every matrix $\mathbf{P}$ of which the number of columns is equal to the common dimension of $\mathbf{A}$ and $\mathbf{B}$. Applying this property with

$$\mathbf{A} = \mathcal{I}(\theta_0),\ \mathbf{B} = \begin{pmatrix} \tilde{\mathcal{I}}_c(\theta_0) & 0 \\ 0 & 0 \end{pmatrix},\ \mathbf{P} = \left(\mathbf{I}, -\begin{pmatrix} \mathcal{I}_{\alpha\gamma} \\ \mathcal{I}_{\beta\gamma} \end{pmatrix} \mathcal{I}_{\gamma\gamma}^{-1}\right)$$

gives the desired result. A similar proof establishes the asymptotic inefficiency of the marginal maximum likelihood estimator. □

Corollary 7.2:

(i) The conditional ML estimator $\hat{\alpha}_{c,n}$ is asymptotically as efficient as the ML estimator $\hat{\alpha}_n$ in the following two cases:

- *where there are no common parameters β,*
- *where $\hat{\alpha}_n$ and $\hat{\beta}_n$ are uncorrelated asymptotically.*

(ii) The marginal ML estimator $\hat{\gamma}_{m,n}$ is asymptotically as efficient as the ML estimator $\hat{\gamma}_n$ in the following two cases:

– *where there are no common parameters β,*
– *where $\hat{\beta}_n$ and $\hat{\gamma}_n$ are uncorrelated asymptotically.*

PROOF: The conditional ML estimator $\hat{\alpha}_{c,n}$ is asymptotically as efficient as the ML estimator $\hat{\alpha}_n$ if and only if

$$\left(\mathcal{I}_{\alpha\alpha,c} - \mathcal{I}_{\alpha\beta,c}(\mathcal{I}_{\beta\beta,c})^{-1}\mathcal{I}_{\beta\alpha,c}\right)^{-1}$$
$$= \left(\mathcal{I}_{\alpha\alpha} - (\mathcal{I}_{\alpha\beta}, \mathcal{I}_{\alpha\gamma})\begin{pmatrix} \mathcal{I}_{\beta\beta} & \mathcal{I}_{\beta\gamma} \\ \mathcal{I}_{\gamma\beta} & \mathcal{I}_{\gamma\gamma} \end{pmatrix}^{-1}\begin{pmatrix} \mathcal{I}_{\beta\alpha} \\ \mathcal{I}_{\gamma\alpha} \end{pmatrix}\right)^{-1}.$$

But the above partitioning of $\mathcal{I}(\theta_0)$ shows that

$$\mathcal{I}_{\alpha\alpha} = \mathcal{I}_{\alpha\alpha,c},\ \mathcal{I}_{\alpha\beta} = \mathcal{I}_{\alpha\beta,c},\ \mathcal{I}_{\alpha\gamma} = 0,\ \mathcal{I}_{\beta\beta} = \mathcal{I}_{\beta\beta,c} + \mathcal{I}_{\beta\beta,m}.$$

Hence we obtain

$$\left(\mathcal{I}_{\alpha\alpha} - \mathcal{I}_{\alpha\beta}(\mathcal{I}_{\beta\beta,c})^{-1}\mathcal{I}_{\beta\alpha}\right)^{-1}$$
$$= \left(\mathcal{I}_{\alpha\alpha} - (\mathcal{I}_{\alpha\beta}, 0)\begin{pmatrix} \mathcal{I}_{\beta\beta} & \mathcal{I}_{\beta\gamma} \\ \mathcal{I}_{\gamma\beta} & \mathcal{I}_{\gamma\gamma} \end{pmatrix}^{-1}\begin{pmatrix} \mathcal{I}_{\beta\alpha} \\ 0 \end{pmatrix}\right)^{-1}.$$

Two cases arise:

a) There are no parameters β. Then terms containing β disappear and the preceding equality becomes

$$\mathcal{I}_{\alpha\alpha}^{-1} = (\mathcal{I}_{\alpha\alpha} - 0\,\mathcal{I}_{\gamma\gamma}^{-1}0)^{-1},$$

which is trivially satisfied.

b) There are some common parameters β. The preceding equality is equivalent to

$$\mathcal{I}_{\alpha\beta}(\mathcal{I}_{\beta\beta,c})^{-1}\mathcal{I}_{\beta\alpha} = (\mathcal{I}_{\alpha\beta}, 0)\begin{pmatrix} \mathcal{I}_{\beta\beta} & \mathcal{I}_{\beta\gamma} \\ \mathcal{I}_{\gamma\beta} & \mathcal{I}_{\gamma\gamma} \end{pmatrix}^{-1}\begin{pmatrix} \mathcal{I}_{\beta\alpha} \\ 0 \end{pmatrix},$$

i.e.

$$\mathcal{I}_{\alpha\beta}\,\mathcal{I}_{\beta\beta,c}^{-1}\,\mathcal{I}_{\beta\alpha} = \mathcal{I}_{\alpha\beta}\left(\mathcal{I}_{\beta\beta} - \mathcal{I}_{\beta\gamma}\,\mathcal{I}_{\gamma\gamma}^{-1}\mathcal{I}_{\gamma\beta}\right)^{-1}\mathcal{I}_{\beta\alpha}.$$

Since

$$\mathcal{I}_{\beta\beta} - \mathcal{I}_{\beta\gamma}\,\mathcal{I}_{\gamma\gamma}^{-1}\,\mathcal{I}_{\gamma\beta} = \mathcal{I}_{\beta\beta,c} + \mathcal{I}_{\beta\beta,m} - \mathcal{I}_{\beta\gamma,m}\,\mathcal{I}_{\gamma\gamma,m}^{-1}\,\mathcal{I}_{\gamma\beta,m},$$

is strictly larger in the matrix sense than $\mathcal{I}_{\beta\beta,c}$, equality holds if and only if $\mathcal{I}_{\alpha\beta} = 0$.

This establishes (i). The proof is similar for (ii). □

The marginal and conditional information matrices $\tilde{\mathcal{I}}_m(\theta_0)$ and $\tilde{\mathcal{I}}_c(\theta_0)$ defined in Properties 7.16 and 7.17 can be estimated consistently in various ways. For instance, the conditional information matrix $\tilde{\mathcal{I}}_c(\theta_0)$ can be estimated consistently by:

(i) $\tilde{\mathcal{I}}_c(\tilde{\theta}_n)$ where $\tilde{\theta}_n$ is a consistent estimator of $\theta_0 = (\alpha_0', \beta_0', \gamma_0')'$. In particular, this requires that a consistent estimator of γ_0 is available and hence that a parametric marginal model for X is specified and estimated, or by

(ii) other estimators that do not require the specification and estimation of the marginal model for X. One of these is

$$-\frac{1}{n}\frac{\partial^2 \log \ell_n(y \mid x; \hat{\alpha}_{cn}, \hat{\beta}_{cn})}{\partial\theta_c \, \partial\theta_c'},$$

where $\ell_n(y \mid x)$ denotes the conditional density of $Y_1, \ldots, Y_n$ given $X_1, \ldots, X_n$. Another estimator is

$$\frac{1}{n}\sum_{i=1}^{n} \frac{\partial \log f(y_i \mid x_i; \hat{\alpha}_{cn}, \hat{\beta}_{cn})}{\partial\theta_c} \frac{\partial \log f(y_i \mid x_i; \hat{\alpha}_{cn}, \hat{\beta}_{cn})}{\partial\theta_c'}.$$

7.6 Exercises

EXERCISE 7.1: Consider the linear model $Y \sim N(\mathbf{X}\theta, \sigma^2\mathbf{I})$, where θ and σ^2 are unknown parameters. Suppose that θ is subject to some linear constraints $\mathbf{G}\theta = g$.

a) Determine the constrained maximum likelihood estimator of θ and σ^2 and the Lagrange multipliers associated with the linear constraints.

b) Compare your results to those obtained in Example 7.31.

EXERCISE 7.2: Consider a linear model with explanatory variables $\mathbf{X}_1$ and $\mathbf{X}_2$, namely, $Y \sim N(\mathbf{X}_1 b_1 + \mathbf{X}_2 b_2, \mathbf{I})$. Determine the log-likelihood function $L_c(b_1)$ concentrated in b_2. Derive an expression for the matrix $-\left(\partial^2 \log \ell_c(b_1)/\partial b_1 \partial b_1'\right)^{-1}$. Compare this expression to the variance covariance matrix of the maximum likelihood estimator of b_1.

EXERCISE 7.3:

a) Determine the log-likelihood function of the equilibrium model

$$\begin{aligned} D_t &= ap_t + x_t b_1 + u_t, \\ S_t &= z_t b_2 + v_t, \\ Q_t &= D_t = S_t, \end{aligned}$$

where the error terms u_t and v_t are independent and distributed $N(0, \sigma_u^2)$ and $N(0, \sigma_v^2)$, respectively.

b) Concentrate out the likelihood function with respect to b_2, σ_v^2, b_1 and σ_u^2, successively. Conclude that the maximum likelihood estimator of a is given by

$$\hat{a} = \frac{V_{emp}(Q - \hat{Q})}{\mathrm{Cov}_{emp}(Q - \hat{Q}, p - \hat{p})},$$

where $V_{emp}(\cdot)$ and Cov_{emp} denote the empirical variance and covariance and

$$\begin{aligned} \hat{Q}_t &= x_t \left(\sum_{t=1}^{T} x_t' x_t \right)^{-1} \sum_{t=1}^{T} x_t' Q_t, \\ \hat{p}_t &= x_t \left(\sum_{t=1}^{T} x_t' x_t \right)^{-1} \sum_{t=1}^{T} x_t' p_t. \end{aligned}$$

Interpret $\hat{Q}_t$, $\hat{p}_t$, $Q_t - \hat{Q}_t$, $p_t - \hat{p}_t$, and $1/\hat{a}$.

c) Find a new parameterization such that the log-likelihood function can be maximized directly. Hint: Note that the demand equation can be replaced by the inverse demand equation

$$p_t = \frac{D_t}{a} - x_t \frac{b_1}{a} - \frac{u_t}{a}.$$

EXERCISE 7.4: Consider a random sample of size n drawn from a bivariate normal distribution

$$N\left(\begin{pmatrix} m_1 \\ m_2 \end{pmatrix}, \begin{pmatrix} \sigma_1^2 & \rho\sigma_1\sigma_2 \\ \rho\sigma_1\sigma_2 & \sigma_2^2 \end{pmatrix} \right).$$

Determine the maximum likelihood estimator of the correlation coefficient ρ:

a) when the parameters m_1, m_2, σ_1, and σ_2 are known,

b) when these parameters are unknown.

EXERCISE 7.5: Error terms can be introduced in a model in various ways. Consider the following two versions of a disequilibrium model:
Model 1:

$$\begin{aligned} D_t &= ap_t + x_t b + u_t, \\ S_t &= \alpha p_t + z_t \beta + v_t, \\ Q_t &= \min(D_t, S_t). \end{aligned}$$

Model 2:

$$\begin{aligned} D_t &= ap_t + x_t b + u_t, \\ S_t &= \alpha p_t + z_t \beta + v_t, \\ Q_t &= \min(D_t, S_t) + \varepsilon_t. \end{aligned}$$

In each model it is assumed that the errors u_t and v_t are independent and distributed $N(0, \sigma_u^2)$ and $N(0, \sigma_v^2)$, respectively. In the second model it is also assumed that ε_t is distributed $N(0, \sigma_\varepsilon^2)$ independently from u_t and v_t.

a) Interpret the error terms in each model.

b) Determine the likelihood function of each model assuming that the observed endogenous variable is the quantity exchanged Q_t. Which likelihood function is easier to maximize?

c) Propose a model containing both models as special cases.

EXERCISE 7.6: The disequilibrium model

$$\begin{aligned} D_t &= ap_t + x_t b + u_t, \quad u_t \sim N(0, \sigma_u^2), \\ S_t &= \alpha p_t + z_t \beta + v_t, \quad v_t \sim N(0, \sigma_u^2), \\ Q_t &= \min(D_t, S_t), \end{aligned}$$

is augmented by a price equation

$$p_t - p_{t-1} = \lambda(D_t - S_t), \quad \lambda \geq 0.$$

a) Determine the joint distribution of p_t, Q_t for $t = 1, \ldots, T$.

b) Find the limit of the likelihood function when the parameter λ increases to infinity.

c) Verify that this limit is equal to the likelihood function associated with the equilibrium model

$$\begin{aligned} Q_t &= ap_t + x_t b + u_t, \\ Q_t &= \alpha p_t + z_t \beta + v_t. \end{aligned}$$

d) Interpret the parameter λ and discuss the result obtained in c).

EXERCISE 7.7: Consider a consumption function of the form

$$\log C_t = a_0 \log R_t + a_1 \log C_{t-1} + a_2 \log R_{t-1} + a_3 + u_t,$$

where the errors are independent and identically distributed $N(0, \sigma^2)$. Suppose that the model is estimated by maximum likelihood (conditionally upon the first observation C_1).

a) Find the long-run income elasticity of consumption as a function of a_0, a_1, and a_2.

b) Find an expression for the asymptotic variance of the maximum likelihood estimate of this elasticity as a function of the variances and covariances of the maximum likelihood estimates $\hat{a}_0$, $\hat{a}_1$, and $\hat{a}_2$.

EXERCISE 7.8: Consider a parametric model $\{P_\theta, \theta \in \Theta\}$ where the parameter space is reduced to one element θ only. What is the maximum likelihood estimator of θ? Discuss its asymptotic properties.

EXERCISE 7.9: Let $Y_t^* \sim N(m, 1)$, $t = 1, \ldots, T$, be an independent and identically distributed sample drawn from a normal distribution $N(m, 1)$. We consider three models where the observed variable is defined by:

a) $Y_{1t} = Y_t^*$,

b) $Y_{2t} = Y_t^* \mathbb{1}_{Y_t^* > 0}$,

c) $Y_{3t} = \mathbb{1}_{Y_t^* > 0}$.

In each case, find the asymptotic variance of the maximum likelihood estimator of m. Discuss the information loss due to the partial observability of Y_t^* as a function of m.

EXERCISE 7.10: Show that concentrating the likelihood function in Example 7.13 leads to the same results if one consider the distribution of the observations $Y_0, Y_1, \ldots, Y_T$ unconditionally upon Y_0.

7.7 References

Amemiya, T. (1979). "The Estimation of a Simultaneous Equation Tobit Model," *International Economic Review*, 20, 169–182.

Amemiya, T. (1985). *Advanced Econometrics*, Blackwell.

Cox, D.R. and Hinkley, D.V. (1974). *Theoretical Statistics*, Chapman and Hall.

Heckman, J. (1979). "Sample Selection Bias as a Specification Error," *Econometrica*, 47, 153–161.

Jennrich, R. (1969). "Asymptotic Properties of Nonlinear Least Squares Estimators," *Annals of Mathematical Statistics*, 40, 633–643.

Kendall, M. and Stuart, A. (1973). *The Advanced Theory of Statistics*, Griffin.

Kiefer, N. (1979). "On the Value of Sample Separation Information," *Econometrica*, 47, 997–1004.

Quandt, R. (1982). "Econometric Disequilibrium Models," *Econometric Review*, 2, 1–63.

Silvey, S.D. (1970). *Statistical Inference*, Chapman and Hall.

Wilks, S.S. (1962). *Mathematical Statistics*, Wiley.

CHAPTER 8

M-Estimation

As seen in the previous chapter, the maximum likelihood method consists in estimating parameters by maximizing the log-likelihood function. Similar methods can be defined by optimizing other objective functions. The corresponding estimators are frequently called *M-estimators* where M indicates either a minimization or a maximization.

In Section 1 we derive the general asymptotic properties of such estimators. Then these general results are applied to various estimation methods such as nonlinear least squares methods (Section 3), pseudo-maximum likelihood methods (Section 4), and L_1 estimation methods (Section 5). These methods are especially useful when estimating semiparametric models defined *via* moments conditions (Section 2).

8.1 Definition and Asymptotic Properties

8.1.1 Definition

We consider a parametric or semiparametric model where the parameter θ is unknown. To include conditional models, we assume that the observed variables can be partitioned into a set of endogenous variables denoted Y and a set of exogenous variables denoted X. Observations are pairs (Y_i, X_i), $i = 1, 2, \ldots$ and n denotes the sample size.

Definition 8.1: *An M-estimator of a function $g(\theta)$ of the parameter is* *a solution to the optimization problem*

$$\text{opt}_{g\in g(\Theta)=G} \quad \sum_{i=1}^{n} \Psi(Y_i, X_i; g),$$

where Ψ *is a given real function.*

In what follows, we assume that the objective function is maximized, i.e., we consider the problem

$$\max_{g\in G} \sum_{i=1}^{n} \Psi(Y_i, X_i; g). \tag{8.1}$$

Note that it is always possible to consider a maximization problem since a minimization problem can be transformed into a maximization problem by considering the function $-\Psi$.

In some simple cases, the function Ψ is differentiable in g. Then an M-estimator $\tilde{g}_n(X, Y)$, when it exists and belongs to the interior of G, must satisfy the first-order conditions

$$\sum_{i=1}^{n} \frac{\partial \Psi(Y_i, X_i; \tilde{g}_n)}{\partial g} = 0. \tag{8.2}$$

8.1.2 Existence and Consistency of M-Estimators

The study of the general asymptotic properties of M-estimators is similar to the study of maximum likelihood estimators presented in the preceding chapter. The basic idea consists in replacing the optimization problem (8.1) by an appropriate limit problem. To simplify, we assume that the pairs (Y_i, X_i) are identically distributed. The objective function is

$$\sum_{i=1}^{n} \Psi(Y_i, X_i; g),$$

or equivalently

$$\frac{1}{n} \sum_{i=1}^{n} \Psi(Y_i, X_i; g).$$

From the Strong Law of Large Numbers, it can be seen that the objective function can be approximated asymptotically by the mathematical expectation of the function $\Psi(Y, X; g)$. Thus the limit problem is

$$\max_{g\in G} E_X E_0 \Psi(Y, X; g), \tag{8.3}$$

where E_0 denotes the expectation with respect to the true conditional distribution of Y given X and E_X denotes the expectation with respect to the true marginal distribution of X. Under suitable regularity conditions, the set of solutions to the finite sample optimization problem converges to the set of solutions to the limit problem. More precisely, we have the next result of which a proof relies on the general theorems of Chapter 24, Volume II.

Property 8.1: *Suppose that:*

(i) The pairs (Y_i, X_i) are independent and identically distributed,

(ii) G is compact,

(iii) Ψ is continuous in g and integrable with respect to the true distribution of (Y_i, X_i) for every g,

(iv) $(1/n)\sum_{i=1}^{n} \Psi(Y_i, X_i; g)$ converges almost surely and uniformly on G to $E_X E_0 \Psi(Y, X; g)$,

(v) the limit problem has a unique solution $g_\infty^0 = g_\infty(\theta_0)$, where θ_0 is the parameter value associated with the true distribution of (Y_i, X_i).

Then there exists an M-estimator $\tilde{g}_n(X, Y)$ converging almost surely to $g_\infty(\theta_0) = g_\infty^0$.

As in maximum likelihood estimation, assumption (ii) that G is compact can be replaced by assumption (ii') that G is open. In this case we have:

Property 8.2: *Suppose that Ψ is continuously differentiable in g and that assumptions (i), (ii'), (iii)–(v) hold. Then there exists asymptotically a solution to the first-order conditions that converges almost surely to $g_\infty(\theta_0) = g_\infty^0$. This solution corresponds to a local maximum of the objective function.*

Thereafter, such a solution converging to g_∞^0 is called an M-estimator as well.

Although M-estimators converge, the preceding two properties show that their limits are not necessarily equal to the value $g(\theta_0)$ of interest. A necessary and sufficient condition for the consistency of M-estimators is given in the next property.

Property 8.3: *Under the assumptions of Property 8.1 or Property 8.2, there exists an M-estimator converging almost surely to $g(\theta)$, $\theta \in \Theta$, if and only if $g_\infty(\theta) = g(\theta)$, $\forall\, \theta \in \Theta$.*

Thus, provided suitable regularity conditions are satisfied, it suffices to show that the solution to the limit problem is equal to the value of interest so as to establish the strong consistency of an M-estimator.

8.1.3 Asymptotic Normality

Asymptotic normality of an M-estimator is established by taking a Taylor expansion of the first-order conditions in a neighborhood of the limit value $g_\infty(\theta_0)$. We have

$$\sum_{i=1}^{n} \frac{\partial \Psi(Y_i, X_i; \tilde{g}_n)}{\partial g} = 0,$$

which gives

$$\frac{1}{\sqrt{n}} \sum_{i=1}^{n} \frac{\partial \Psi(Y_i, X_i; g_\infty(\theta_0))}{\partial g} + \frac{1}{\sqrt{n}} \sum_{i=1}^{n} \frac{\partial^2 \Psi(Y_i, X_i; g_\infty(\theta_0))}{\partial g \, \partial g'} (\tilde{g}_n - g_\infty(\theta_0)) \# 0,$$

where # means that the left-hand side and the right-hand side differ by a quantity converging to zero in probability. Hence

$$\begin{aligned} &\sqrt{n}(\tilde{g}_n - g_\infty(\theta_0)) \\ &\# \left(-\frac{1}{n} \sum_{i=1}^{n} \frac{\partial^2 \Psi(Y_i, X_i; g_\infty(\theta_0))}{\partial g \, \partial g'} \right)^{-1} \frac{1}{\sqrt{n}} \sum_{i=1}^{n} \frac{\partial \Psi(Y_i, X_i; g_\infty(\theta_0))}{\partial g} \\ &\# \left(E_X E_0 - \frac{\partial^2 \Psi(Y, X; g_\infty(\theta_0))}{\partial g \, \partial g'} \right)^{-1} \frac{1}{\sqrt{n}} \sum_{i=1}^{n} \frac{\partial \Psi(Y_i, X_i; g_\infty(\theta_0))}{\partial g}, \end{aligned}$$

where we have used the Strong Law of Large Numbers applied to the sample means of second partial derivatives.

Now we have

$$E_X E_0 \frac{\partial \Psi(Y_i, X_i; g_\infty(\theta_0))}{\partial g} = \left(\frac{\partial}{\partial g} E_X E_0 \Psi(Y_i, X_i; g_\infty(\theta_0) \right) = 0,$$

because $g_\infty(\theta_0)$ is the solution of the limit problem. Thus the vectors $\partial \Psi(Y_i, X_i; g_\infty(\theta_0))/\partial g$ are independent and identically distributed with mean zero and variance covariance matrix

$$\mathcal{I} = E_X E_0 \left(\frac{\partial \Psi(Y, X; g_\infty(\theta_0))}{\partial g} \frac{\partial \Psi(Y, X; g_\infty(\theta_0))}{\partial g',} \right).$$

From the Central Limit Theorem it follows that

$$\frac{1}{\sqrt{n}} \sum_{i=1}^{n} \frac{\partial \Psi(Y_i, X_i; g_\infty(\theta_0))}{\partial g} \xrightarrow{d} N(0, \mathcal{I}).$$

Hence the vector $\sqrt{n}(\tilde{g}_n - g_\infty(\theta_0))$, which is a linear transformation of the preceding vector, is asymptotically normally distributed with zero mean and variance covariance matrix $\mathcal{J}^{-1}\mathcal{I}\mathcal{J}^{-1}$, where

$$\mathcal{J} = E_X E_0 \left(- \frac{\partial^2 \Psi(Y, X; g_\infty(\theta_0))}{\partial g \, \partial g'} \right).$$

Of course, this result holds provided a Taylor expansion is justified. Suitable regularity conditions are given in the next property.

Property 8.4: *Suppose that the assumptions of Property 8.2 hold and that:*

(vi) Ψ *is twice continuously differentiable in* g,

(vii) the matrix $\mathcal{J} = E_X E_0 \left(-\partial^2 \Psi(Y, X; g_\infty(\theta_0)) / \partial g \, \partial g' \right)$ *exists and is nonsingular.*

Then $\sqrt{n}(\tilde{g}_n - g_\infty(\theta_0))$ *is asymptotically normally distributed* $N(0, \mathcal{J}^{-1}\mathcal{I} \mathcal{J}^{-1})$, *where*

$$\mathcal{I} = E_X E_0 \left(\frac{\partial \Psi(Y, X; g_\infty(\theta_0))}{\partial g} \frac{\partial \Psi(Y, X; g_\infty(\theta_0))}{\partial g'} \right).$$

PROOF: See Chapter 24, Volume II. □

The variance covariance matrix $\mathcal{J}^{-1}\mathcal{I}\mathcal{J}^{-1}$ depends on the unknown true distribution of the pair (Y_i, X_i). It must be estimated when evaluating the precision of the estimator $\tilde{g}_n$. To do so, it suffices to replace mathematical expectations by their corresponding sample means and $g_\infty(\theta_0)$ by the consistent estimator $\tilde{g}_n$. Thus a consistent estimator of the matrix $\mathcal{J}^{-1}\mathcal{I}\mathcal{J}^{-1}$ is

$$\hat{V} \left[\sqrt{n}(\tilde{g}_n - g_\infty(\theta_0)) \right] = \hat{\mathcal{J}}^{-1} \hat{\mathcal{I}} \hat{\mathcal{J}}^{-1}, \tag{8.4}$$

where

$$\hat{\mathcal{J}} = -\frac{1}{n} \sum_{i=1}^{n} \frac{\partial^2 \Psi(Y_i, X_i; \tilde{g}_n)}{\partial g \, \partial g'},$$

and

$$\hat{\mathcal{I}} = \frac{1}{n}\sum_{i=1}^{n}\left(\frac{\partial\Psi(Y_i, X_i; \tilde{g}_n)}{\partial g}\frac{\partial\Psi(Y_i, X_i; \tilde{g}_n)}{\partial g'}\right).$$

Remark 8.1: In the special case of maximum likelihood estimation (see Chapter 7), the function Ψ is equal to the log-likelihood function for one observation, $g(\theta) = \theta$, and the matrices $\mathcal{J}$ and $\mathcal{I}$ are equal since they are equivalent expressions of the Fisher information matrix. Specifically, in this case, the asymptotic variance covariance matrix simplifies to

$$\mathcal{J}^{-1}\mathcal{I}\mathcal{J}^{-1} = \mathcal{J}^{-1} = \mathcal{I}^{-1}.$$

As expected, we obtain the inverse of the Fisher information matrix.

8.1.4 Quasi Generalized M-Estimators

M-estimation can be generalized to cases where objective functions depend on nuisance parameters. These cases are frequent and naturally arise when searching for optimal M-estimators.

Specifically, the objective function is now of the form

$$\sum_{i=1}^{n}\Psi(Y_i, X_i; g, \tilde{c}_n),$$

where $\tilde{c}_n$ is a function of the observations that converges almost surely to a limit c_0 depending on the true distribution of the observations.

Definition 8.2: *A quasi generalized M-estimator $\tilde{g}_n$ is a solution to the optimization problem*

$$\max_{g\in G}\sum_{i=1}^{n}\Psi(Y_i, X_i; g, \tilde{c}_n).$$

Existence and consistency properties are obtained by considering, as before, the corresponding limit problem where sample means are replaced by their expectations and $\tilde{c}_n$ by c_0

$$\max_{g\in G} E_X E_0 \Psi(Y, X; g, c_0). \tag{8.5}$$

Under suitable regularity conditions (see Chapter 24, Volume II), the estimator $\tilde{g}_n$ converges almost surely to the unique solution $g_\infty(\theta_0) = g_\infty^0$

to the limit problem (8.5). Thus the presence of consistent estimators of nuisance parameters in the objective function does not introduce new difficulties in terms of consistency. In general, however, such a presence will modify the asymptotic variance covariance matrix of an M-estimator.

To see this, we now consider a Taylor expansion of the first-order conditions in a neighborhood of the point $(g_\infty(\theta_0), c_0) = (g_\infty^0, c_0)$. From

$$\sum_{i=1}^{n} \frac{\partial \Psi(Y_i, X_i; \tilde{g}_n, \tilde{c}_n)}{\partial g} = 0,$$

we obtain

$$\begin{aligned}
&\frac{1}{\sqrt{n}} \sum_{i=1}^{n} \frac{\partial \Psi(Y_i, X_i; g_\infty^0, c_0)}{\partial g} \\
&\qquad + \frac{1}{\sqrt{n}} \sum_{i=1}^{n} \frac{\partial^2 \Psi(Y_i, X_i; g_\infty^0, c_0)}{\partial g \, \partial g'} (\tilde{g}_n - g_\infty^0) \\
&\qquad + \frac{1}{\sqrt{n}} \sum_{i=1}^{n} \frac{\partial^2 \Psi(Y_i, X_i; g_\infty^0, c_0)}{\partial g \, \partial c'} (\tilde{c}_n - c_0) \# 0.
\end{aligned}$$

Hence

$$\begin{aligned}
&\frac{1}{\sqrt{n}} \sum_{i=1}^{n} \frac{\partial \Psi(Y_i, X_i; g_\infty^0, c_0)}{\partial g} \\
&\qquad + E_X E_0 \left(\frac{\partial^2 \Psi(Y, X; g_\infty^0, c_0)}{\partial g \, \partial g'} \right) \sqrt{n}(\tilde{g}_n - g_\infty^0) \\
&\qquad + E_X E_0 \left(\frac{\partial^2 \Psi(Y, X; g_\infty^0, c_0)}{\partial g \, \partial c'} \right) \sqrt{n}(\tilde{c}_n - c_0) \# 0.
\end{aligned}$$

It follows that

$$\sqrt{n}(\tilde{g}_n - g_\infty^0) \# \mathcal{J}^{-1} \left(\frac{1}{\sqrt{n}} \sum_{i=1}^{n} \frac{\partial \Psi(Y_i, X_i; g_\infty^0, c_0)}{\partial g} + \mathcal{H} \sqrt{n}(\tilde{c}_n - c_0) \right),$$

where

$$\mathcal{J} = E_X E_0 \left(- \frac{\partial^2 \Psi(Y, X; g_\infty^0, c_0)}{\partial g \, \partial g'} \right)$$

and

$$\mathcal{H} = E_X E_0 \left(\frac{\partial^2 \Psi(Y, X; g_\infty^0, c_0)}{\partial g \, \partial c'} \right).$$

If the vector of random variables

$$\begin{pmatrix} \frac{1}{\sqrt{n}}\sum_{i=1}^{n} \frac{\partial \Psi(Y_i, X_i; g_\infty^0, c_0)}{\partial g} \\ \sqrt{n}(\tilde{c}_n - c_0) \end{pmatrix}$$

is asymptotically normally distributed with mean zero and variance covariance matrix

$$\begin{pmatrix} \mathcal{I} & \mathcal{I}_{0c} \\ \mathcal{I}_{c0} & \mathcal{I}_{cc} \end{pmatrix},$$

then the quasi generalized estimator $\tilde{g}_n$ is asymptotically normally distributed. Namely, we have

$$\sqrt{n}(\tilde{g}_n - g_\infty^0) \xrightarrow{d} N(0, \mathbf{V}), \tag{8.6}$$

where

$$\mathbf{V} = \mathcal{J}^{-1}\left((\mathbf{I}, \mathcal{H}) \begin{pmatrix} \mathcal{I} & \mathcal{I}_{0c} \\ \mathcal{I}_{c0} & \mathcal{I}_{cc} \end{pmatrix}, \begin{pmatrix} \mathbf{I} \\ \mathcal{H}' \end{pmatrix} \right) \mathcal{J}^{-1}.$$

Thus, with the exception of the special case considered below, this variance covariance matrix is different from that of the M-estimator that treats $\tilde{c}_n$ as given.

Property 8.5: *If*

$$\mathcal{H} = E_X E_0 \left(\frac{\partial^2 \Psi(Y, X; g_\infty^0, c_0)}{\partial g \, \partial c'} \right) = 0,$$

then the quasi generalized M-estimator $\tilde{g}_n$ satisfies

$$\sqrt{n}(\tilde{g}_n - g_\infty^0) \xrightarrow{d} N(0, \mathcal{J}^{-1} \, \mathcal{I} \, \mathcal{J}^{-1}),$$

where

$$\begin{aligned} \mathcal{J} &= E_X E_0 \left(-\frac{\partial^2 \Psi(Y, X; g_\infty^0, c_0)}{\partial g \, \partial g'} \right), \\ \mathcal{I} &= E_X E_0 \left(\frac{\partial \Psi(Y, X; g_\infty^0, c_0)}{\partial g} \frac{\partial \Psi(Y, X; g_\infty^0, c_0)}{\partial g'} \right). \end{aligned}$$

Thus the condition $E_X E_0 \left(\partial^2 \Psi(Y, X; g_\infty^0, c_0) / \partial g \, \partial c' \right) = 0$ greatly simplifies the asymptotic variance covariance matrix. In particular, it implies that the asymptotic properties of the quasi generalized M-estimator $\tilde{g}_n$ can be obtained without taking into account the asymptotic distribution of the nuisance parameter estimator $\tilde{c}_n$. After having estimated c_0 by $\tilde{c}_n$ in a first step, one can use this estimate in a second step for obtaining an estimate $\tilde{g}_n$ of g.

8.2 Nonlinear Regression Models of Order 1 and 2

8.2.1 Definitions

Let $Y_1, \ldots, Y_n$ be n observations on an endogenous random variable with values in $I\!R$. It is assumed that Y_i has a conditional mean given some exogenous variables $X_1, \ldots, X_n$ of the form $h(X_i, b_0)$, where b_0 is a $K \times 1$ vector of unknown parameters. Thus the statistical model is a semiparametric conditional model given by

$$Y_i = h(X_i, b_0) + u_i, \tag{8.7}$$

where

$$E_0(u_i \mid X_1, \ldots, X_n) = 0, \quad \forall\, i.$$

Such a model is called a *regression model of order 1.*

Our goal is to find consistent estimators of the parameters b_0 appearing in the conditional mean. It is clear that the conditional distribution of $Y_1, \ldots, Y_n$ in such a model is not completely specified since only the conditional mean is considered. Hence maximum likelihood estimation as well as properties of exponential families cannot be invoked. It is necessary to introduce other estimation methods.

The precision in model (8.7) can be assessed through the conditional variance covariance matrix of the vector of errors $(u_1, \ldots, u_n)'$. Thereafter it is assumed that these errors are conditionally independent. Moreover, we let

$$V_0(u_i \mid X_1, \ldots, X_n) = \omega^2(X_i) \tag{8.8}$$

denote the conditional variance. In general, this variance is unknown.

When additional information on the form of the conditional variance is available, it is frequently possible to construct more efficient estimators. In this case, the conditional model is defined by its first two moments. Namely, we have

$$Y_i = h(X_i, b_0) + u_i, \tag{8.9}$$

where

$$\begin{aligned} E_0(u_i \mid X_1, \ldots, X_n) &= 0, \\ V_0(u_i \mid X_1, \ldots, X_n) &= \omega^2(X_i, \beta_0), \end{aligned}$$

and β_0 is an $L \times 1$ vector of unknown parameters. We say that we have a *regression model of order 2.*

8.2.2 Special Cases and Examples

In some applications the first two moments may have some simple expressions.

Example 8.1: When $h(X, b) = F(X)'b$, where F is a vector function with values in $\mathbb{R}^K$, it is easy to see that a change of exogenous variables, namely $Z = F(X)$, gives the model

$$Y_i = Z_i' b + u_i,$$

where

$$E_0(u_i \mid Z_1, \ldots, Z_n) = 0.$$

That is, we have a linear model.

Example 8.2: More generally, the search for consistent estimators is frequently facilitated in the case of *decomposable models of order 1*, i.e., models for which

$$h(X, b) = F(X)' H(b).$$

Let $Z = F(X)$. We have

$$Y_i = Z_i' H + u_i,$$

where $H = H(b)$ and

$$E_0(u_i \mid Z_1, \ldots, Z_n) = 0.$$

Such models can be viewed as models that are linear in H where the natural parameters H are subject to the constraints $H = H(b)$.

Example 8.3: Some specific forms for the conditional variance may turn out to be useful. In some cases the conditional variance:

(i) is known up to a proportional factor

$$\omega^2(X_i, \beta) = \beta\, \omega^2(X_i),$$

where $\omega^2(X_i)$ is known and β is an unknown positive constant,

(ii) is a linear combination (with nonnegative weights) of positive parameters

$$\omega^2(X_i, \beta) = \beta_1 \omega_1^2(X_i) + \ldots + \beta_L \omega_L^2(X_i),$$

where $\omega_\ell^2(X_i), l = 1, \ldots, L$ are known and $\beta_\ell \geq 0$, $l = 1, \ldots, L$ are unknown nonnegative constants,

(iii) is a transformation of a linear combination of the parameters

$$\omega^2(X_i, \beta) = k\left(\sum_{l=1}^{L} \beta_l k_l(X_i)\right),$$

where the functions k and k_l, $l = 1, \ldots, L$ are known, and β_l, $l = 1, \ldots, L$ are unknown constants.

Econometric models are often derived from economic theory which suggests some deterministic relations between the variables Y and X. Such relations are made probabilistic by introducing suitable error terms. Econometric models are more or less simple depending on how the errors are introduced.

Example 8.4: Consider a constant elasticity of substitution (CES) production function

$$Y_t = (aK_t^r + bL_t^r)^{\frac{1}{r}}.$$

There exist various ways for introducing error terms.

First, error terms can be introduced directly in the right-hand side. In this case, error terms are interpreted as measurement errors on Y and we have

$$Y_t = (aK_t^r + bL_t^r)^{\frac{1}{r}} + u_t.$$

The model is not decomposable.

Another method consists in introducing error terms inside the parentheses so that

$$Y_t = (aK_t^r + bL_t^r + u_t)^{\frac{1}{r}},$$

which is equivalent to

$$Y_t^r = aK_t^r + bL_t^r + u_t.$$

Hence, if r is known, the model is linear after a suitable transformation.

Example 8.5: Consider a simultaneous equation model. Its reduced form consists of equations of the form

$$Y_{jt} = X_t \Pi_j(\theta) + \nu_{jt}, \quad j = 1, \ldots, J, \quad t = 1, \ldots, T,$$

where Y_{jt} is the tth observation on the jth endogenous variable, $\Pi_j(\theta)$ is the vector of reduced form parameters in the jth equation which is a function of the structural parameters θ, and ν_{jt} is the error term in the reduced form with mean zero. The reduced form model is a decomposable nonlinear regression model. Thus it may be useful to consider all the endogenous variables simultaneously, i.e., to write an equation of the form (8.7) with possibly an equation of the form (8.8), where Y_t is now a vector. This extension, which is straightforward, is left to the reader.

Example 8.6: The number of registered patents of a firm i during a given period is a discrete variable Y_i. It is natural to propose a conditional model based on the Poisson distribution. For instance, suppose that the variables Y_i are conditionally independent given some firms characteristics X_i. Suppose also that the conditional distribution of Y_i is

$$Y_i \sim P(\lambda_i),$$

where $\lambda_i = \exp(X_i b)$. Note that the exponential form implies that λ_i is positive as required.

The previous model, however, may not be fully satisfying for it implies a strong relationship between the conditional mean and the conditional variance. This is because $E(Y_i \mid X_i) = V(Y_i \mid X_i) = \exp(X_i b)$. To solve such a problem, a method consists in introducing an error term ε_i in the expression for λ_i, namely

$$\lambda_i = \exp(X_i b + \varepsilon_i).$$

The unobserved error term ε_i can be due to omitted variables. Then assuming that $E(\exp \varepsilon_i \mid X_i) = 1$ and $V(\exp \varepsilon_i \mid X_i) = \sigma^2$, we obtain

$$\begin{aligned} E(Y_i \mid X_i) &= E(\exp(X_i b + \varepsilon_i) \mid X_i) \\ &= \exp X_i b, \end{aligned}$$

and

$$\begin{aligned} V(Y_i \mid X_i) &= V(E(Y_i \mid X_i, \varepsilon_i) \mid X_i) + E(V(Y_i \mid X_i, \varepsilon_i) \mid X_i) \\ &= V(\exp(X_i b + \varepsilon_i) \mid X_i) + E(\exp(X_i b + \varepsilon_i) \mid X_i) \\ &= \sigma^2 \exp(2X_i b) + \exp(X_i b). \end{aligned}$$

In particular, the parameters appearing in the conditional mean and the conditional variance are related to each others.

8.2.3 First-Order and Second-Order Identification

In general, the parameters b and β are functions of a same set of parameters $\theta \in \Theta$, i.e., $b = b(\theta)$ and $\beta = \beta(\theta)$.

Definition 8.3:

(i) The parameter vector b is first-order identified if, for every value b_0

$$h(x,b) = h(x,b_0), \ \forall \ x \in \mathcal{X}, \Rightarrow b = b_0,$$

(ii) The parameter vector θ is first-order identified if, for every value θ_0

$$h(x,b(\theta)) = h(x,b(\theta_0)), \ \forall \ x \in \mathcal{X}, \Rightarrow \theta = \theta_0,$$

(iii) The parameter vector θ is second-order identified if, for every value θ_0

$$\left\{ \begin{array}{l} h(x,b(\theta))) = h(x,b(\theta_0)), \ \forall \ x \in \mathcal{X} \\ \omega^2(x,\beta(\theta)) = \omega^2(x,\beta(\theta_0)), \ \forall \ x \in \mathcal{X}, \end{array} \right. \Rightarrow \theta = \theta_0.$$

First-order identification of θ clearly implies first-order identification of b. Hence θ is not first-order identified if b is not. A parameter that is first-order identified is known if the first-order conditional moment is known. Similarly, a second-order identified parameter is known if the first two conditional moments are known.

Definition 8.3 is related to the definitions of identification introduced in Chapter 3. Specifically, it suffices to introduce an appropriate family of distributions for the endogenous variables. For instance, consider the family of normal distributions. We have the following result.

Property 8.6:

(i) The parameter θ is first-order identified if θ is identified in the conditional model

$$\left(I\!R^n, \left\{ \bigotimes_{i=1}^{n} N(h(X_i,b(\theta)),1), \theta \in \Theta \right\} \right),$$

(ii) The parameter θ is second-order identified if θ is identified in the conditional model

$$\left(I\!R^n, \left\{ \bigotimes_{i=1}^{n} N(h(X_i,b(\theta)),\omega^2(X_i,\beta(\theta))), \theta \in \Theta \right\} \right).$$

PROOF: This follows from the fact that two normal distributions are identical if and only if their means and variances are equal. □

From the proof, it is clear that we could have chosen other families of distributions that are completely characterized by their first two moments.

8.3 Nonlinear Least Squares

8.3.1 The Method

We consider the nonlinear regression model

$$Y_i = h(X_i, b_0) + u_i,$$

where $E_0(u_i \mid X_1, \ldots, X_n) = 0$ and $b_0 \in \mathcal{B}$.

Definition 8.4:

(i) A nonlinear least squares estimator of b is a solution to the optimization problem

$$\min_{b \in \mathcal{B}} \sum_{i=1}^{n} (Y_i - h(X_i, b))^2.$$

(ii) A weighted nonlinear least squares estimator of b is a solution to the optimization problem

$$\min_{b \in \mathcal{B}} \sum_{i=1}^{n} (Y_i - h(X_i, b))^2 a(X_i),$$

where a is a given strictly positive function.

The weighted nonlinear least squares estimator is obtained by minimizing a weighted sum of squared errors $Y_i - h(X_i, b)$. This estimator clearly depends on the chosen weights a. It is denoted $\hat{b}_n(a)$. The ordinary least squares estimator $\hat{b}_n(1)$ corresponds to the weights $a = 1$.

Least squares estimators have the usual geometric interpretation. Namely, let $Y = (Y_1, \ldots, Y_n)'$ denote the vector of observations on the endogenous variable, and let $\mathcal{L}$ denote the manifold associated with the specified model

$$\mathcal{L} = \left\{ (h(X_1, b), \ldots, h(X_n, b))', \; b \in \mathcal{B} \right\}.$$

The vector $\hat{Y}(a) = \left(h(X_1, \hat{b}_n(a)), \ldots, h(X_n, \hat{b}_n(a)) \right)'$ is the element of $\mathcal{L}$ that is closest to Y in the metric associated with the scalar product defined by a. Thus $\hat{Y}(a)$ is the orthogonal projection of Y on to $\mathcal{L}$.

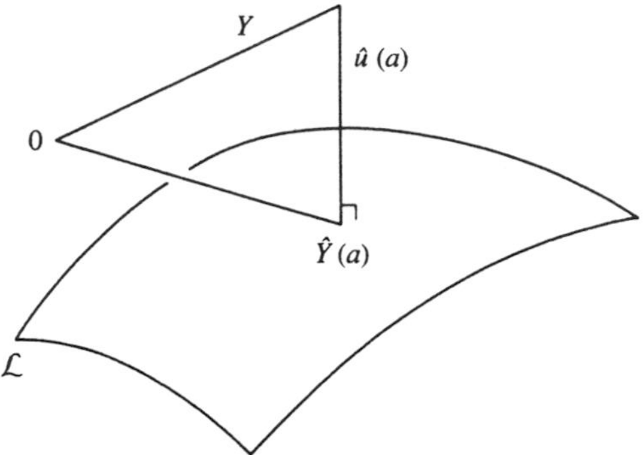

Figure 8.1: Nonlinear Least Squares Estimation

Definition 8.5:

(i) $\hat{Y}_i(a) = h(X_i, \hat{b}_n(a))$ *is called the predicted value of* Y_i,

(ii) $\hat{u}_i(a) = Y_i - \hat{Y}_i(a)$ *is called the ith residual of the nonlinear regression.*

Note that $\hat{Y}_i(a)$ is the prediction of Y_i based on the model and $\hat{u}_i(a)$ is the predicted value for u_i.

The estimator $\hat{b}_n(a)$ is found by solving the first-order conditions

$$\frac{\partial}{\partial b}\left(\sum_{i=1}^{n}[Y_i - h(X_i, \hat{b}_n(a))]^2 a(X_i)\right) = 0,$$

i.e.

$$\sum_{i=1}^{n} a(X_i)[Y_i - h(X_i, \hat{b}_n(a))]\frac{\partial h(X_i, \hat{b}_n(a))}{\partial b} = 0. \tag{8.10}$$

These equations are nonlinear in $\hat{b}_n(a)$. They are solved using numerical algorithms (see Chapter 13). For some decomposable models, however, they can be solved analytically.

Example 8.7: If $h(X, b) = F(X)'b$, the model is linear and $\hat{b}_n(a)$ is the weighted (linear) least squares estimator (see Corollary 6.2). Specifically, we have

$$\hat{b}_n(a) = \left(\sum_{i=1}^{n} F(X_i)F'(X_i)a(X_i)\right)^{-1} \sum_{i=1}^{n} F(X_i)Y_i a(X_i),$$

provided the first matrix is nonsingular.

Example 8.8: Suppose that the conditional mean can be written as $h(X, b) = F(X)'H(b)$, where H is a bijective mapping. Then the weighted nonlinear least squares estimator is

$$\hat{b}_n(a) = H^{-1}\left(\left(\sum_{i=1}^{n} F(X_i)F'(X_i)a(X_i)\right)^{-1} \sum_{i=1}^{n} F(X_i)Y_i a(X_i)\right).$$

That is, it suffices to apply the inverse mapping H^{-1} to the solution obtained in Example 8.7.

The first-order conditions (8.10) express the orthogonality between the residual vector $(\hat{u}_1(a), \ldots, \hat{u}_n(a))'$ and the hyperplane that is tangent to the surface $\mathcal{L}$ at the point $\hat{Y}(a)$. This hyperplane is generated by the $K \times 1$ vectors

$$\left(\frac{\partial h(X_i, \hat{b}_n(a))}{\partial b}\right)_{i=1,\ldots,n}.$$

Here, orthogonality is defined with respect to the scalar product

$$(z_1, z_2) = \sum_{i=1}^{n} a(X_i) z_{1i} z_{2i}.$$

8.3.2 Asymptotic Properties

The asymptotic properties of nonlinear least squares estimators follow directly from the general results given in Section 8.1. The objective function is defined by

$$\Psi(Y_i, X_i; b) = -\frac{1}{2} a(X_i)(Y_i - h(X_i, b))^2.$$

The limit problem associated with the least squares method is

$$\min_{b \in \mathcal{B}} E_X E_0 \left[a(X)(Y - h(X, b))^2\right].$$

Since E_0 denotes the expectation conditional on X, we have

$$\begin{aligned}
&E_X E_0 \left[a(X)(Y - h(X, b))^2\right] \\
&= E_X E_0 \left[a(X)(Y - h(X, b_0) + h(X, b_0) - h(X, b))^2\right] \\
&= E_X \left[a(X) E_0(Y - h(X, b_0) + h(X, b_0) - h(X, b))^2\right] \\
&= E_X \left[a(X)[V_0 Y + (h(X, b_0) - h(X, b))^2]\right] \\
&= E_X \left(a(X)\omega_0^2(X)\right) + E_X\left[a(X)(h(X, b_0) - h(X, b))^2\right],
\end{aligned}$$

where $V_0 Y = \omega_0^2(X)$ is the conditional variance of Y given X. Only the the second term depends on b. Since this term is nonnegative and equal to zero when $b = b_0$, the solutions to the limit problem satisfy

$$a(x)(h(x, b_0) - h(x, b))^2 = 0, \ \forall \ x \in \mathcal{X}.$$

Since $a(x) > 0$, the latter condition is equivalent to

$$h(x, b_0) - h(x, b) = 0, \ \forall \ x \in \mathcal{X}.$$

Thus b_0 is the unique solution to the limit problem if and only if the parameter b is first-order identified.

Property 8.7: *Under the regularity conditions (i)–(iv) of Property 8.1, if b is first-order identified, then there exists a nonlinear least squares estimator $\hat{b}_n(a)$ converging almost surely to the true value b_0.*

The determination of the asymptotic variance covariance matrix requires the computation of the following matrices

$$\mathcal{J} = E_X E_0 \left(-\frac{\partial^2 \Psi(Y, X; b_0)}{\partial b \, \partial b'} \right)$$

and

$$\mathcal{I} = E_X E_0 \left(\frac{\partial \Psi(Y, X; b_0)}{\partial b} \frac{\partial \Psi(Y, X; b_0)}{\partial b'} \right).$$

We have

$$\begin{aligned} \frac{\partial^2 \Psi(Y, X; b_0)}{\partial b \, \partial b'} &= a(X)(Y - h(X, b_0)) \frac{\partial^2 h(X, b_0)}{\partial b \, \partial b'} \\ &\quad - a(X) \frac{\partial h(X, b_0)}{\partial b} \frac{\partial h(X, b_0)}{\partial b'}. \end{aligned}$$

Taking conditional expectation given X and noting that $E_0(Y - h(X, b_0)) = 0$, we obtain

$$\mathcal{J} = E_X \left(a(X) \frac{\partial h(X, b_0)}{\partial b} \frac{\partial h(X, b_0)}{\partial b'} \right). \tag{8.11}$$

The other matrix is given by

$$\mathcal{I} = E_X E_0 \left(a(X)^2 \frac{\partial h(X, b_0)}{\partial b} \frac{\partial h(X, b_0)}{\partial b'} (Y - h(X, b_0))^2 \right),$$

i.e.

$$\mathcal{I} = E_X\left(a(X)^2 \frac{\partial h(X,b_0)}{\partial b}\frac{\partial h(X,b_0)}{\partial b'} E_0(Y - h(X,b_0))^2\right).$$

Hence

$$\mathcal{I} = E_X\left(a(X)^2 \frac{\partial h(X,b_0)}{\partial b}\frac{\partial h(X,b_0)}{\partial b'} \omega_0^2(X)\right). \tag{8.12}$$

We have established the following property.

Property 8.8: *Under the regularity conditions of Property 8.4, there exists a nonlinear least squares estimator $\hat{b}_n(a)$ that is asymptotically normal with*

$$\sqrt{n}(\hat{b}_n(a) - b_0) \xrightarrow{d} N(0, \mathcal{J}^{-1}\mathcal{I}\mathcal{J}^{-1}),$$

where the matrices $\mathcal{J}$ and $\mathcal{I}$ are given in equations (8.11) and (8.12).

Example 8.9: Consider a decomposable model where

$$h(X,b) = F(X)'H(b).$$

We have

$$\frac{\partial h(X,b)}{\partial b} = \frac{\partial H'(b)}{\partial b} \cdot F(X).$$

The first-order conditions are

$$\sum_{i=1}^n a(X_i)[Y_i - F(X_i)'H(\hat{b}_n(a))]\frac{\partial H'(\hat{b}_n(a))}{\partial b}F(X_i) = 0,$$

i.e.

$$\frac{\partial H'(\hat{b}_n(a))}{\partial b}\sum_{i=1}^n a(X_i)Y_iF(X_i)$$
$$-\frac{\partial H'(\hat{b}_n(a))}{\partial b}\sum_{i=1}^n a(X_i)F(X_i)F(X_i)'H(\hat{b}_n(a)) = 0.$$

Hence the first-order conditions are separable in terms that are functions of $\hat{b}_n(a)$ and terms that are functions of the observations Y_i. This separability property remains when we consider the asymptotic variance covariance matrix since

$$\mathcal{J} = \frac{\partial H'(b_0)}{\partial b}E_X(a(X)F(X)F(X)')\frac{\partial H(b_0)}{\partial b'}$$

and

$$\mathcal{I} = \frac{\partial H'(b_0)}{\partial b}E_X(a^2(X)\omega_0^2(X)F(X)F(X)')\frac{\partial H(b_0)}{\partial b'}.$$

8.3.3 Quasi Generalized Nonlinear Least Squares

In general, different choices of weights lead to estimators with different asymptotic variance covariance matrices. In this subsection we consider the choice of optimal weights.

Property 8.9: *The asymptotic variance covariance matrix of the estimator $\hat{b}_n(a)$ is minimized when $a(X)$ is proportional to $1/\omega_0^2(X)$.*

PROOF: Consider the following two random vectors

$$Z_1 = E_X\left(a(X)\frac{\partial h(X,b_0)}{\partial b}\frac{\partial h(X,b_0)}{\partial b'}\right)^{-1} a(X)\frac{\partial h(X,b_0)}{\partial b}(Y - h(X,b_0)),$$

$$\begin{aligned} Z_2 &= E_X\left(\frac{1}{\omega_0^2(X)}\frac{\partial h(X,b_0)}{\partial b}\frac{\partial h(X,b_0)}{\partial b'}\right)^{-1} \\ &\quad \frac{1}{\omega_0^2(X)}\frac{\partial h(X,b_0)}{\partial b}(Y - h(X,b_0)). \end{aligned}$$

The two vectors Z_1 and Z_2 are centered. Moreover, we have:

(i) $VZ_1 = E_X V_0 Z_1 + V_X E_0 Z_1 = E_X V_0 Z_1 = \mathcal{J}^{-1}\mathcal{I}\mathcal{J}^{-1}$,

(ii) $VZ_2 = \mathcal{J}_0^{-1}\mathcal{I}_0\mathcal{J}_0^{-1} = \mathcal{J}_0^{-1}$ because $\mathcal{J}_0 = \mathcal{I}_0$ where $\mathcal{J}_0$ and $\mathcal{I}_0$ denote the matrices $\mathcal{J}$ and $\mathcal{I}$ when $a(X) = 1/\omega_0^2(X)$,

(iii) $\text{Cov}\ (Z_1, Z_2) = E_X \text{Cov}_0\ (Z_1, Z_2)$

$$\begin{aligned} &= E_X\left(\mathcal{J}^{-1}a(X)\frac{\partial h(X,b_0)}{\partial b}V_0 Y\frac{\partial h(X,b_0)}{\partial b'}\frac{1}{\omega_0^2(X)}\mathcal{J}_0^{-1}\right) \\ &= \mathcal{J}^{-1}E_X\left(a(X)\frac{\partial h(X,b_0)}{\partial b}\frac{\partial h(X,b_0)}{\partial b'}\right)\mathcal{J}_0^{-1} \\ &= \mathcal{J}^{-1}\mathcal{J}\mathcal{J}_0^{-1} \\ &= \mathcal{J}_0^{-1} \\ &= VZ_2. \end{aligned}$$

It follows that

$$\begin{aligned} V(Z_1 - Z_2) &= VZ_1 - \text{Cov}\ (Z_1, Z_2) - \text{Cov}\ (Z_2, Z_1) + VZ_2 \\ &= VZ_1 - VZ_2 - VZ_2 + VZ_2 \\ &= \mathcal{J}^{-1}\mathcal{I}\mathcal{J}^{-1} - \mathcal{J}_0^{-1}. \end{aligned}$$

Hence $\mathcal{J}^{-1}\mathcal{I}\mathcal{J}^{-1} - \mathcal{J}_0^{-1}$ is a positive semidefinite matrix for any choice of a, i.e.

$$\forall\, a > 0,\ \mathcal{J}^{-1}\mathcal{I}\mathcal{J}^{-1} \gg \mathcal{J}_0^{-1} = \mathcal{J}_0^{-1}\mathcal{I}_0\mathcal{J}_0^{-1}.$$

Therefore the asymptotic variance covariance matrix is minimized when $a(X) = 1/\omega_0^2(X)$. More generally, if $a(X)$ is proportional to $1/\omega_0^2(X)$, then the estimators $\hat{b}_n(a)$ and $\hat{b}_n(1/\omega_0^2)$ are identical. Thus the choice of such a function a allows us to attain the smallest possible asymptotic variance covariance matrix. □

Property 8.10: *Suppose that the conditional variance is either known, i.e., $\omega^2(x,\beta) = \omega^2(x)$, or is known up to a positive scalar, i.e, $\omega^2(x,\beta) = \beta\omega^2(X)$. Then the estimator obtained by minimizing*

$$\sum_{i=1}^{n} \frac{1}{\omega^2(X_i)}(Y_i - h(X_i, b))^2$$

is asymptotically optimal in the class of weighted nonlinear least squares estimators. This estimator is called the generalized nonlinear least squares estimator.

PROOF: This follows immediately from Property 8.9. □

When the conditional variance is neither known nor known up to a scalar, the optimality property 8.9 cannot be applied directly. Specifically, one would like to choose a function $a(X)$ that is proportional to $1/\omega^2(X, \beta_0)$, which is, however, unknown since β_0 is unknown.

A natural idea consists in replacing, when possible, β_0 by a consistent estimator $\hat{\beta}_n$.

Definition 8.6: *A quasi generalized nonlinear least squares estimator is a solution $\hat{b}_n$ to the problem*

$$\min_{b\in\mathcal{B}} \sum_{i=1}^{n} \frac{1}{\omega^2(X_i, \hat{\beta}_n)}(Y_i - h(X_i, b))^2,$$

where $\hat{\beta}_n$ is a consistent estimator of β_0.

Property 8.11: *Under the regularity conditions given in Section 8.1.4, there exists a quasi generalized nonlinear least squares estimator $\hat{b}_n$ converging almost surely to b_0 and asymptotically normally distributed with*

$$\sqrt{n}(\hat{b}_n - b_0) \xrightarrow{d} N(0, \mathcal{J}_0^{-1}).$$

In particular, this estimation method achieves the lower bound for the asymptotic variance covariance matrices of weighted nonlinear least squares estimators.

PROOF: We need to verify the condition given in Property 8.5, namely

$$\mathcal{H} = E_X E_0 \frac{\partial^2 \Psi(Y, X; b_0, \beta_0)}{\partial b \, \partial \beta'} = 0.$$

Since

$$\frac{\partial^2 \Psi(Y, X; b_0, \beta_0)}{\partial b \, \partial \beta'} = \frac{\partial}{\partial \beta'} \left(\frac{1}{\omega^2(X, \beta_0)} (Y - h(X, b_0)) \frac{\partial h(X, b_0)}{\partial b} \right)$$

and since $E_0(Y - h(X, b_0)) = 0$, it is easily seen that the above condition is satisfied. Therefore the asymptotic distribution of the quasi generalized least squares estimator is identical to that of the generalized least squares estimator that assumes β_0 to be known. □

8.3.4 Linearizing a Nonlinear Model

Estimating a nonlinear econometric model of the type $Y_i = h(X_i, b_0) + u_i$ reduces to solving a system of nonlinear equations which do not have, in general, some closed form solutions. In practice, to simplify the computation of the nonlinear least squares estimator, it is frequent to replace the original nonlinear model by a linear approximation that is more tractable. Such a linearization can be performed with respect to either the exogenous variables or the parameters.

a) Linearizing With Respect to the Explanatory Variables

The basic idea consists in replacing the regression curve $x \mapsto h(x, b_0)$ by its tangent at a point x^0. Letting x be a row vector, this leads to

$$Y_i \approx h(x^0, b_0) + (X_i - x^0) \frac{\partial h(x^0, b_0)}{\partial x'} + u_i,$$

i.e.

$$Y_i \approx h(x^0, b_0) - x^0 \frac{\partial h(x^0, b_0)}{\partial x'} + X_i \frac{\partial h(x^0, b_0)}{\partial x'} + u_i.$$

Thus the endogenous variable satisfies approximately the linear model

$$Y_i \approx \alpha + X_i \beta + u_i,$$

where the "true values" of the parameters α and β correspond to the intercept and the slope of the tangent at x^0 to the regression curve when X_i is a scalar variable. These "true values" are given by

$$\begin{aligned}\alpha_0 &= h(x^0, b_0) - x^0 \frac{\partial h(x^0, b_0)}{\partial x'}, \\ \beta_0 &= \frac{\partial h(x^0, b_0)}{\partial x'}.\end{aligned}$$

Then it may seem natural to estimate the unknown values α_0 and β_0 by regressing Y_i on the constant term and X_i by ordinary least squares methods. As we shall see in the next example, however, these estimators do not converge to α_0 and β_0.

Example 8.10: Consider the quadratic specification

$$\begin{aligned}Y_i &= h(X_i, b_0) + u_i \\ &= b_{00} + X_i b_{10} + X_i^2 b_{20} + u_i.\end{aligned}$$

The model obtained by linearization is

$$Y_i \approx b_{00} + (x^0)^2 b_{20} + X_i(b_{10} + 2x^0 b_{20}) + u_i.$$

The sample correlation coefficient between Y_i and X_i is equal to

$$\hat{\rho} = \frac{\mathrm{Cov}_{\mathrm{emp}}(Y_i, X_i)}{V_{\mathrm{emp}}(X_i)}.$$

It converges to

$$\rho_\infty = \frac{\mathrm{Cov}_X(Xb_{10} + X^2 b_{20}, X)}{V_X(X)} = b_{10} + b_{20} \frac{\mathrm{Cov}_X(X^2, X)}{V_X(X)}.$$

This limit is equal to the desired value $b_{10} + 2x^0 b_{20}$ if and only if either $b_{20} = 0$ or $\mathrm{Cov}_X(X^2, X) = 2x^0 V_X(X)$.

The condition $b_{20} = 0$ corresponds to an original model that is linear and hence for which there is no need for linearization. In the general case where $b_{20} \neq 0$, there is convergence to the desired value only if the value x^0 is equal to half the coefficient of a regression of X^2 on X. Such a condition is unlikely to be satisfied in practice.

Example 8.10 shows that the estimation of a linear model when the regression curve is nonlinear does not lead, contrary to intuition, to the estimation of a tangent to this curve. Nonetheless, it is easy to interpret the estimated regression line obtained from the above linearization.

Property 8.12: *When the regression curve of Y on X is nonlinear and given by $E(Y \mid X) = h(X, b_0)$, the estimation of a misspecified linear model $Y_i = X_i\beta + u_i$ by ordinary least squares (OLS) leads to the consistent estimation of the hyperplane defined by $y = x\beta_0$, where β_0 satisfies*

$$E_X(h(X, b_0) - X\beta_0)^2 = \min_\beta E_X(h(X, b_0) - X\beta)^2.$$

PROOF: The OLS estimator is obtained by minimizing

$$\frac{1}{n}\sum_{i=1}^{n}(Y_i - X_i\beta)^2.$$

It converges to the solution to the limit problem

$$\min_\beta E(Y - X\beta)^2.$$

Then it suffices to note that

$$E(Y - X\beta)^2 = E(Y - h(X, b_0))^2 + E_X(h(X, b_0) - X\beta)^2.$$

The desired result follows. □

Hence linearizing the original model with respect to the explanatory variables leads to estimating the hyperplane $y = x\beta_0$ that is closest to the regression curve according to the mean square error criterion.

b) Linearizing With Respect to the Parameters

It is also possible to take a Taylor expansion of the original model with respect to the parameters. Let $\tilde{b}_0$ be a parameter value chosen a priori. A Taylor expansion of the original model gives

$$\begin{aligned} Y_i &= h(X_i, b_0) + u_i \\ &\approx h(X_i, \tilde{b}_0) + \frac{\partial h(X_i, \tilde{b}_0)}{\partial b'}(b_0 - \tilde{b}_0) + u_i, \end{aligned}$$

i.e.

$$Y_i - h(X_i, \tilde{b}_0) + \frac{\partial h(X_i, \tilde{b}_0)}{\partial b'}\tilde{b}_0 \approx \frac{\partial h(X_i, \tilde{b}_0)}{\partial b'} b_0 + u_i.$$

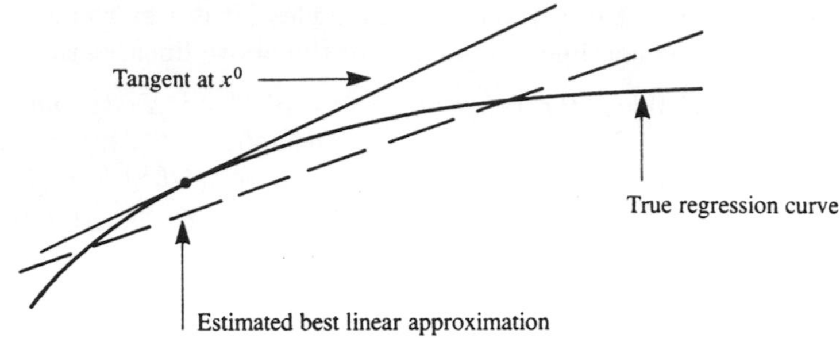

Figure 8.2: Approximated Linear Model

The second equation can be viewed as a linear model with "endogenous variable"

$$\tilde{Y}_i = Y_i - h(X_i, \tilde{b}_0) + \frac{\partial h(X_i, \tilde{b}_0)}{\partial b'} \tilde{b}_0,$$

and "exogenous variables"

$$\tilde{X}_i = \frac{\partial h(X_i, \tilde{b}_0)}{\partial b'}.$$

Then it may seem natural to estimate the unknown parameter b_0 from an OLS regression of $\tilde{Y}_i$ on $\tilde{X}_i$. The estimator is

$$\begin{aligned} \hat{b}_n &= \left(\sum_{i=1}^{n} \frac{\partial h'(X_i, \tilde{b}_0)}{\partial b} \frac{\partial h(X_i, \tilde{b}_0)}{\partial b'} \right)^{-1} \\ &\quad \sum_{i=1}^{n} \frac{\partial h'(X_i, \tilde{b}_0)}{\partial b} \left(Y_i - h(X_i, \tilde{b}_0) + \frac{\partial h(X_i, \tilde{b}_0)}{\partial b'} \tilde{b}_0 \right). \end{aligned}$$

In general, this estimator does not converge to the true parameter value b_0.

Example 8.11: Suppose that the original model is exponential, i.e., $Y_i = \exp X_i b_0 + u_i$ where X is a scalar exogenous variable. A Taylor expansion around $\tilde{b}_0 = 0$ gives

$$Y_i \approx 1 + X_i b_0 + u_i.$$

The OLS estimator in this linearized model is

$$\hat{b} = \frac{\sum_{i=1}^{n} X_i (Y_i - 1)}{\sum_{i=1}^{n} X_i^2}.$$

It converges to

$$b_\infty = \frac{E[X(Y-1)]}{E_X(X^2)} = \frac{E_X[X(\exp(Xb_0)-1)]}{E_X(X^2)}.$$

Since $\exp(Xb_0) - 1 > Xb_0$, it is easily seen that $b_\infty > b_0$. Hence in this example, the OLS estimator in the linearized model overestimates the true parameter value.

Although a Taylor expansion around a fixed value of b produces, in general, inconsistent estimators, this may not be the case when a Taylor expansion is performed around a random value. More precisely, we have the following result.

Property 8.13: *Let $\tilde{b}_n$ be a consistent estimator of b_0. The OLS estimator of b_0 in a model linearized around $\tilde{b}_n$ is also consistent for b_0.*

PROOF: The OLS estimator in the linearized model is

$$\begin{aligned} \hat{b}_n &= \left(\sum_{i=1}^n \frac{\partial h'(X_i,\tilde{b}_n)}{\partial b}\frac{\partial h(X_i,\tilde{b}_n)}{\partial b'}\right)^{-1} \\ & \sum_{i=1}^n \frac{\partial h'(X_i,\tilde{b}_n)}{\partial b}\left(Y_i - h(X_i,\tilde{b}_n) + \frac{\partial h(X_i,\tilde{b}_n)}{\partial b'}\tilde{b}_n\right). \end{aligned}$$

Hence

$$\begin{aligned} \hat{b}_n \# \tilde{b}_n &+ \left(E_X\left(\frac{\partial h'(X,b_0)}{\partial b}\frac{\partial h(X,b_0)}{\partial b'}\right)\right)^{-1} \\ & \times E_X\left(\frac{\partial h'(X,b_0)}{\partial b}(Y - h(X,b_0))\right), \end{aligned}$$

where # means that the left-hand side and the right-hand side differ by a quantity converging to zero in probability.

Since $h(X, b_0)$ is the regression curve of Y on X, we have

$$E(Y - h(X,b_0))^2 = \min_b E(Y - h(X,b))^2.$$

The corresponding first-order conditions are

$$E\left(\frac{\partial h'(X,b_0)}{\partial b}(Y - h(X,b_0))\right) = 0.$$

It follows that $\hat{b}_n \# \tilde{b}_n \# b_0$. □

8.4 Pseudo Maximum Likelihood Estimation

8.4.1 ML Estimation With Specification Errors

To study the relationship between an endogenous variable Y and some exogenous variables X, one considers a conditional model specifying the form of the conditional distribution of $Y_1, \dots, Y_n$ given $X_1, \dots, X_n$. To simplify, it is assumed that the model is parameterized by $\theta \in \Theta$ which is an open subset of $\mathbb{R}^p$, that the model is dominated and that the densities can be written as

$$\ell(y_1, \dots, y_n \mid x_1, \dots, x_n; \theta) = \prod_{i=1}^{n} f(y_i \mid x_i; \theta), \quad \theta \in \Theta.$$

Thus the model implies the mutual independence of the variables $Y_1, \dots,$ Y_n conditionally on $X_1, \dots, X_n$ and the equality of the conditional densities $f(y_i \mid x_i; \theta)$ across observations.

Throughout this subsection, we shall consider the case where the model is misspecified. The true distribution of the observations is given by the density

$$\ell_0(y_1, \dots, y_n \mid x_1, \dots, x_n) = \prod_{i=1}^{n} f_0(y_i \mid x_i),$$

where $f_0(y \mid x)$ does not belong to the specified family, i.e.

$$f_0(y \mid x) \notin \{f(y \mid x; \theta),\ \theta \in \Theta\}. \tag{8.13}$$

In such a misspecified context we saw in Chapter 1 that it is possible to evaluate the discrepancy between the true density f_0 and the model $\{f(y \mid x; \theta),\ \theta \in \Theta\}$ by the Kullback information measure. This leads naturally to the concept of *pseudo true* (or *quasi true*) value θ_0^* of the parameter θ that corresponds to the distribution in the model that is closest to f_0. This pseudo true value is a solution to

$$\max_{\theta \in \Theta} E_X E_0 \log f(Y \mid X; \theta),$$

where E_0 denotes the conditional expectation of Y given X under f_0. Thereafter it is assumed that θ_0^* is unique.

Definition 8.7: *A pseudo (or quasi) maximum likelihood (PML) estimator* $\hat{\theta}_n$ *of* θ *is a solution* $\hat{\theta}_n$ *to*

$$\max_{\theta \in \Theta} \sum_{i=1}^{n} \log f(Y_i \mid X_i; \theta).$$

Thus $\hat{\theta}_n$ is a maximum likelihood estimator based on a misspecified model.

Property 8.14: *Under the regularity conditions of Property 8.1, the pseudo maximum likelihood estimator converges almost surely to the pseudo true value* θ_0^*.

PROOF: It suffices to note that the asymptotic optimization problem is

$$\max_{\theta \in \Theta} E_X E_0 \log f(Y \mid X; \theta).$$

This problem has a unique solution which is the pseudo true value θ_0^*. □

The previous result some useful in practice for evaluating the direction and the magnitude of some asymptotic biases.

Example 8.12: Sample Selection Bias.

To determine the average income in a population of households, a researcher has n available observations on income $R_1, \ldots, R_n$. It is assumed that the observations are independent and identically distributed with density $f(R, m)$ on $\mathbb{R}^+$, where $m \in \mathbb{R}^+$ is an unknown mean.

However, individuals with high income, for instance those with income larger than a threshold $\bar{R}$, do not answer the survey. This fact is not taken into account by the researcher. If m_0 denotes the true population mean income, then the true density of each observation is

$$f_0(R) = \frac{f(R, m_0)}{\int_0^{\bar{R}} f(r, m_0) dr} \mathbb{1}_{R < \bar{R}},$$

which coincides with the conditional density of R given that there is a response to the survey, i.e., given $R < \bar{R}$. The pseudo maximum likelihood estimator is a solution to

$$\max_{m \in \mathbb{R}^+} \sum_{i=1}^{n} \log f(R_i, m).$$

It converges to the pseudo true value which is the solution to

$$\max_{m \in I\!R^+} E_0 \log f(R, m),$$

i.e.

$$\max_{m \in I\!R^+} \frac{\int_0^{\bar{R}} f(r, m_0) \log f(r, m) dr}{\int_0^{\bar{R}} f(r, m_0) dr},$$

i.e.

$$\max_{m \in I\!R^+} \int_0^{\bar{R}} f(r, m_0) \log f(r, m) dr.$$

In general, the solution m_0^* is not equal to the true value m_0.

For instance, consider the case where the family f is the family of exponential densities

$$f(r, m) = \frac{1}{m} \exp\left(-\frac{r}{m}\right) \mathbb{1}_{r>0}.$$

The limit problem is

$$\max_m \int_0^{\bar{R}} \frac{1}{m_0} \exp\left(-\frac{r}{m_0}\right) \left(-\log m - \frac{r}{m}\right) dr,$$

i.e.

$$\begin{aligned} &\max_m \log m \left(\exp(-\bar{R}/m_0) - 1\right) \\ &\quad + \frac{m_0}{m} \frac{\bar{R}}{m_0} \exp(-\bar{R}/m_0) + \frac{m_0}{m} \left(\exp(-\bar{R}/m_0) - 1\right). \end{aligned}$$

The first-order condition gives

$$\begin{aligned} 0 &= \frac{1}{m_0^*} \left(\exp(-\bar{R}/m_0) - 1\right) \\ &\quad - \frac{1}{m_0^{*2}} \left(\bar{R} \exp(-\bar{R}/m_0) + m_0 \left(\exp(-\bar{R}/m_0) - 1\right)\right), \end{aligned}$$

i.e.

$$m_0^* = \frac{\bar{R} \exp(-\bar{R}/m_0)}{\exp(-\bar{R}/m_0) - 1} + m_0.$$

Thus, in general, specification errors lead to an asymptotic bias. The latter is given by

$$\begin{aligned} m_0^* - m_0 &= \frac{\bar{R}\exp(-\bar{R}/m_0)}{\exp(-\bar{R}/m_0) - 1} \\ &= m_0 \frac{u\exp(-u)}{\exp(-u) - 1}, \end{aligned}$$

where $u = \bar{R}/m_0$. It is easy to see that the asymptotic bias is always negative and decreases in absolute value when the threshold $\bar{R}$ increases.

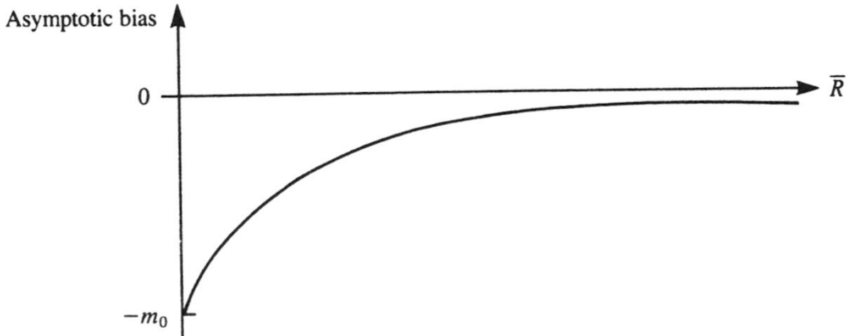

Figure 8.3: Asymptotic Bias

Property 8.15: *Under the regularity conditions of Property 8.4, the pseudo maximum likelihood estimator is asymptotically normally distributed with*

$$\sqrt{n}(\hat{\theta}_n - \theta_0^*) \xrightarrow{d} N(0, \mathcal{J}^{-1}\mathcal{I}\mathcal{J}^{-1}),$$

where

$$\begin{aligned} \mathcal{J} &= E_X E_0 \left(-\frac{\partial^2 \log f(Y \mid X; \theta_0^*)}{\partial\theta\, \partial\theta'} \right), \\ \mathcal{I} &= E_X E_0 \left(\frac{\partial \log f(Y \mid X; \theta_0^*)}{\partial\theta} \frac{\partial \log f(Y \mid X; \theta_0^*)}{\partial\theta'} \right). \end{aligned}$$

PROOF: This is a straightforward application of Property 8.4 with the function Ψ being the individual log-likelihood, i.e., $\Psi = \log f$. □

It is important to note that the matrices $\mathcal{J}$ and $\mathcal{I}$ are not, in general, equal when specification errors are present. Thus comparing estimates of the two matrices $\mathcal{J}$ and $\mathcal{I}$ can be useful for detecting specification errors (see the information matrix test discussed in Chapter 18, Volume II).

Example 8.13: Omitted Heteroskedasticity.
Consider an heteroskedastic linear model with known variances

$$Y_i = X_i b_0 + u_i, \quad i = 1, \ldots, n,$$

where the errors u_i are independent and distributed $N(0, \omega^2(X_i))$ and X_i is a $K \times 1$ row vector.

Suppose that the parameter vector b is estimated by OLS or equivalently by maximum likelihood of the misspecified model, where u_i is assumed $N(0,1)$. The pseudo maximum likelihood estimator of b is

$$\hat{b}_n = (\mathbf{X}'\mathbf{X})^{-1}\mathbf{X}'Y = \left(\sum_{i=1}^{n} X_i' X_i \right)^{-1} \sum_{i=1}^{n} X_i' Y_i.$$

It converges to the true value b_0, which is here equal to the pseudo true value b_0^*. The specified density used for determining $\hat{b}_n$ is

$$\log f(Y_i \mid X_i; b) = -\frac{1}{2} \log 2\pi - \frac{1}{2}(Y_i - X_i b)^2.$$

We have

$$\frac{\partial \log f(Y \mid X; b)}{\partial b} = X'(Y - Xb),$$

and

$$\frac{\partial^2 \log f(Y \mid X; b)}{\partial b \, \partial b'} = -X'X.$$

Hence

$$\mathcal{J} = E_X(X'X) \text{ and } \mathcal{I} = E_X(\omega^2(X) X'X).$$

Although equal when $\omega^2(X) = 1$, these two matrices are, in general, different.

8.4.2 Consistent PML Estimation of Order 1

a) Definition

We consider a regression model of order 1. Thus the model focuses on the relationship between X and Y *via* the conditional mean of Y given X

$$Y_i = h(X_i, b_0) + u_i, \quad \text{where } E_X(u_i \mid X_1, \ldots, X_n) = 0. \qquad (8.14)$$

Here Y and h can be multidimensional of size G.

The model is assumed to be first-order identified. Since maximum likelihood estimation is possible only if the form of the distribution of Y_i given X_i is specified, various families of conditional distributions for Y_i given X_i can be proposed. Our goal is to find those families that lead to consistent estimators of b_0 even if the resulting models are misspecified.

More precisely, we consider a family of densities parameterized by a mean m. The densities are denoted $f(y,m)$, $m \in M$. The set M is assumed to contain all possible values for $h(x,b)$. We are interested in pseudo maximum likelihood estimators of b obtained as if the variables $Y_1,\ldots,Y_n$ are conditionally independent given $X_1,\ldots,X_n$ with a conditional distribution of Y_i given $Y_1,\ldots Y_n,\ldots$ given by the density

$$f(y_i;h(x_i,b)).$$

The corresponding pseudo maximum likelihood estimator $\hat{b}_n$ is a solution to

$$\max_b \sum_{i=1}^{n} \log f(Y_i;h(X_i,b)). \tag{8.15}$$

b) Consistency

From Section 8.4.1 the estimator $\hat{b}_n$ converges almost surely to the pseudo true value b_0^*, which is the solution to the limit problem

$$\max_b E_X E_0 \log f(Y;h(X,b)).$$

In general, the pseudo true value b_0^* depends on the limiting distribution ν of the exogenous variables. Hence, in principle, it should be denoted $b_0^*(\nu)$.

Property 8.16: *Under the assumptions of Property 8.1, the pseudo maximum likelihood estimator $\hat{b}_n$ is consistent for b_0 for any possible value of the parameter, any functional form of the conditional mean, any limiting distribution ν of the exogenous variables, and any conditional distribution satisfying (8.14) if and only if the pseudo true densities are of the form*

$$f(y;m) = \exp(A(m) + B(y) + C(m)y),$$

where m is the mean of the density $f(y;m)$. Such a density is called a linear exponential density.

That is, it is necessary and sufficient to specify a family that is a linear exponential family. The proof of this proposition relies on the following lemma, which is proved in the appendix to this chapter.

Lemma 8.1: *Let* $g_1, \ldots, g_K$ *and* h *be real scalar functions from* $\mathbb{R}^G$ *to* $\mathbb{R}$ *satisfying the following two conditions:*

(i) For every index $k = 1, \ldots, K$*, there exists two probability distributions* P_{1k} *and* P_{2k} *such that*

$$\int_{\mathcal{Y}} g_k(y)dP_{1k}(y) > 0, \int_{\mathcal{Y}} g_k(y)dP_{2k}(y) < 0,$$

$$\int_{\mathcal{Y}} g_j(y)dP_{1k}(y) = 0, \int_{\mathcal{Y}} g_j(y)dP_{2k}(y) = 0, \quad \forall\, j \neq k,$$

(ii) For every probability distribution P *satisfying*

$$\int_{\mathcal{Y}} g_k(y)dP(y) = 0, \quad \forall\, k = 1, \ldots, K,$$

we have

$$\int_{\mathcal{Y}} h(y)dP(y) = 0,$$

Under these two conditions, there exist real numbers λ_k, $k = 1, \ldots, K$ *such that*

$$h(y) = \sum_{k=1}^{K} \lambda_k g_k(y), \quad \forall\, y \in \mathbb{R}^G.$$

PROOF OF PROPOSITION 8.16:

(i) Necessity: The pseudo maximum likelihood estimator is consistent if the solution to the limit optimization problem

$$\max_b E_X E_0 \log f(Y; h(X, b))$$

is the true parameter value b_0, i.e., the value defined by

$$E_X E_0 Y = E_X h(X, b_0).$$

In other words, if

$$E_X E_0 (Y - h(X, b_0)) = 0,$$

then we must have

$$E_X E_0 \frac{\partial \log f(Y; h(X, b_0))}{\partial b} = 0,$$

where we have used the first-order conditions associated with the solution to the limit optimization problem.

The preceding property must hold for any functional form of the conditional mean. In particular, it must hold when $h(X, b) = b$. In addition, the above equality must hold for any marginal distribution of X and any conditional distribution of Y given X. Thus the preceding property reduces to

$$E_0(Y - b_0) = 0 \Rightarrow E_0 \frac{\partial \log f(Y; b_0)}{\partial b} = 0$$

for any conditional distribution of Y given X.

We now apply Lemma 8.1 with $g_1(y) = y_1 - b_{01}, \ldots, g_G(y) = y_G - b_{0G}$ and h successively equal to the partial derivatives $\partial \log f(y; b_0)/\partial b_j$, $j = 1, \ldots, G$. It follows that there exists a square matrix $\mathbf{\Lambda}$ of size G, which is a function of X and b_0 such that

$$\frac{\partial \log f(y; b_0)}{\partial b} = \mathbf{\Lambda}(X, b_0)(y - b_0).$$

Since the family of conditional distributions of Y given X has been chosen independent of X, then $\mathbf{\Lambda}$ is also independent of X so that

$$\frac{\partial \log f(y; b)}{\partial b} = \mathbf{\Lambda}(b)(y - b).$$

Now it suffices to integrate this equation to obtain the desired result

$$f(y; m) = \exp(A(m) + B(y) + C(m)y),$$

where $dA(m)/dm = -\mathbf{\Lambda}(m)m$ and $dC(m)/dm = \mathbf{\Lambda}(m)$.

(ii) Sufficiency: Conversely, suppose that the pseudo maximum likelihood estimator corresponds to the linear exponential model

$$f(y; m) = \exp(A(m) + B(y) + C(m)y).$$

The limit problem is

$$\max_b E_X E_0 \log f(Y; h(X, b)),$$

i.e.

$$\max_b E_X E_0[A(h(X,b)) + B(Y) + C(h(X,b))Y],$$

i.e.

$$\max_b E_X E_0[A(h(X,b)) + C(h(X,b))Y].$$

Now, from Kullback inequality (see Property 1.1) it follows that the integral

$$\int \log f(y; h(X,b)) f(y; h(X,b_0)) d\mu(y)$$

is maximized at $h(X,b) = h(X,b_0)$. But this integral is equal to

$$A(h(X,b)) + C(h(X,b))h(X,b_0) + \int B(y) f(y; h(X,b_0)) d\mu(y),$$

where the last term does not depend on b. Hence the maximum value of $E_X E_0[A(h(X,b)) + C(h(X,b))Y]$ is attained at a point b_0^* satisfying $h(x,b_0^*) = h(x,b_0)$, $\forall\ x$. Thus we have $b_0^* = b_0$ since b_0 is first-order identified. □

Remark 8.2: The preceding proof shows that it is possible to select a family of the form $f(y,x;m)$, i.e., a family that also depends on the exogenous variables. In this case the linear exponential model becomes

$$f(y,x;m) = \exp(A(x,m) + B(x,y) + C(x,m)y),$$

where

$$\frac{\partial A(x,m)}{\partial m} + \frac{\partial C(x,m)}{\partial m} m = 0.$$

Property 8.16 shows that there exists a large number of pseudo true distributions leading to consistent pseudo maximum likelihood estimators. The objective functions associated with these consistent pseudo maximum likelihood estimators are of the form

$$\sum_{i=1}^{n} [A(h(x_i,b)) + B(y_i) + C(h(x_i,b))y_i].$$

Since the second term does not depend on parameters, the optimization problem reduces to the maximization of

$$\sum_{i=1}^{n} [A(h(x_i,b)) + C(h(x_i,b))y_i].$$

In particular, it follows that the observations Y_i need not have the same support as that of the pseudo true distributions. For instance, a pseudo true family of Poisson distributions can be used even when the variables y are not positive integer-valued.

In contrast, it is crucial to take into account the constraint $h(x, b) \in M$ on the conditional mean. Consider again the previous example. The pseudo true family of Poisson distributions can be used only if the conditional mean $h(x, b)$ is positive valued.

The objective functions that are maximized in pseudo maximum likelihood estimation depend on the chosen families of pseudo true distributions. Those associated with the most important linear exponential families are given in the next table. It can be seen that the nonlinear least squares estimator can be viewed as a pseudo maximum likelihood estimator associated with the family of normal distributions.

Consistent pseudo maximum likelihood estimators are found by solving first-order conditions of the form

$$\sum_{i=1}^{n} \frac{\partial \log f(Y_i; h(X_i, \hat{b}_n))}{\partial b} = 0$$

i.e.

$$\sum_{i=1}^{n} \frac{\partial h'(X_i, \hat{b}_n)}{\partial b} \left(\frac{dA(h(X_i, \hat{b}_n))}{dm} + \frac{dC(h(X_i, \hat{b}_n))}{dm} Y_i \right) = 0.$$

Using the fact that

$$\frac{dA(m)}{dm} + \frac{dC(m)}{dm} m = 0,$$

the first-order conditions can be written as

$$\sum_{i=1}^{n} \frac{\partial h'(X_i, \hat{b}_n)}{\partial b} \frac{dC(h(X_i, \hat{b}_n))}{dm} (Y_i - h(X_i, \hat{b}_n)) = 0.$$

Since dC/dm is the inverse of the variance covariance matrix $\mathbf{\Sigma}(m)$ associated with the pseudo true distribution (see Exercise 8.1), the latter equality is equivalent to

$$\sum_{i=1}^{n} \frac{\partial h'(X_i, \hat{b}_n)}{\partial b} \mathbf{\Sigma}^{-1}(h(X_i, \hat{b}_n))(Y_i - h(X_i, \hat{b}_n)) = 0. \tag{8.16}$$

This equation can be interpreted as an orthogonality condition between the residual vector $\hat{u}_i = Y_i - h(X_i, \hat{b}_n)$, $i = 1, \ldots, n$ and the hyperplane

Table 8.1
Pseudo Maximum Likelihood Estimation and Objective Functions

Family	Set M	Density	Objective Function
Binomial (n given)	(0,n)	$\frac{\Gamma(n+1)}{\Gamma(y+1)\Gamma(n-y+1)} \left(\frac{m}{n}\right)^y \left(1-\frac{m}{n}\right)^{n-y}$	$\max \sum_i \left\{y_i \log \frac{h(x_i,b)}{n} + (n-y_i)\log\left(1-\frac{h(x_i,b)}{n}\right)\right\}$
Poisson	$I\!R^{+*}$	$\frac{\exp(-m)m^y}{y!}$	$\max \sum_i (y_i \log h(x_i,b) - h(x_i,b))$
Negative Binomial (α given)	$I\!R^{+*}$	$\frac{\Gamma(\alpha+y)}{\Gamma(\alpha)\Gamma(y+1)} \left(\frac{m}{\alpha}\right)^y \left(1+\frac{m}{\alpha}\right)^{-\alpha-y}$	$\max \sum_i \left\{y_i \log \frac{h(x_i,b)}{\alpha} + (-\alpha-y_i)\log\left(1+\frac{h(x_i,b)}{\alpha}\right)\right\}$
Gamma (α given)	$I\!R^{+*}$	$\frac{y^{\alpha-1}\exp-\frac{\alpha y}{m}}{\Gamma(\alpha)\left(\frac{m}{\alpha}\right)^{\alpha}}$	$\max \sum_i \left\{(\alpha-1)\log y_i - \alpha\frac{y_i}{h(x_i,b)} - \alpha \log h(x_i,b)\right\}$
Normal (σ^2 given)	$I\!R$	$\frac{1}{\sigma\sqrt{2\pi}} \exp -\frac{1}{2\sigma^2}(y-m)^2$	$\min \sum_i (y_i - h(x_i,b))^2$
Multinomial (n given)	$m_k \geq 0, \forall k$ and $\sum_{j=1}^K m_k = n$	$\frac{n!}{y_1!\dots y_k!} \left(\frac{m_1}{n}\right)^{y_1} \dots \left(\frac{m_K}{n}\right)^{y_K}$	$\max \Sigma_i \Sigma_k y_{ik} \log h_k(x_i,b)$

tangent to the manifold

$$\mathcal{L} = \{(h(X_1, b), \ldots, h(X_n, b))', b \in \mathcal{B}\}$$

at the point corresponding to the estimated value $\hat{b}_n$ of the parameter. This orthogonality condition is defined with respect to the scalar product associated with the block diagonal matrix of which the ith diagonal block is $\mathbf{\Sigma}^{-1}(h(X_i, \hat{b}_n))$.

Example 8.14: In the special case where the model does not have exogenous variables, i.e., $Y_i = b + u_i$, the first-order condition is

$$\sum_{i=1}^{n} \mathbf{\Sigma}^{-1}(\hat{b}_n)(Y_i - \hat{b}_n) = 0,$$

i.e.

$$\sum_{i=1}^{n} (Y_i - \hat{b}_n) = 0.$$

Hence

$$\hat{b}_n = \bar{Y}_n.$$

Thus all consistent pseudo maximum likelihood estimators are identical and equal to the sample mean of the observations.

c) Asymptotic Distribution

Under the regularity conditions of Property 8.4, a pseudo maximum likelihood estimator associated with a linear exponential model is asymptotically normal. Its variance covariance matrix is obtained from the first and second partial derivatives of the objective function.

We have

$$\frac{\partial \log f(y, h(x,b))}{\partial b} = \frac{\partial h'(x,b)}{\partial b} \frac{dC(h(x,b))}{dm} (y - h(x,b)),$$

and

$$\frac{\partial^2 \log f(y, h(x,b))}{\partial b \, \partial b'} = \sum_{k=1}^{G} \frac{\partial^2 h_k(x,b)}{\partial b \, \partial b'} \frac{\partial C(h(x,b))}{\partial m_k} (y - h(x,b))$$

$$+ \frac{\partial h'(x,b)}{\partial b} \left(\sum_{k=1}^{G} \frac{d^2 C_k(h(x,b))}{dm \, dm'} (y_k - h_k(x,b)) - \frac{dC(h(x,b))}{dm} \right) \frac{\partial h(x,b)}{\partial b'}.$$

Hence, upon integration, we obtain

$$\begin{aligned}\mathcal{I} &= E_X E_0\left(\frac{\partial \log f}{\partial b}\frac{\partial \log f}{\partial b'}\right)\\ &= E_X\left(\frac{\partial h'}{\partial b}\frac{dC}{dm}E_0(Y-h)(Y-h)'\frac{dC'}{dm'}\frac{\partial h}{\partial b'}\right)\\ &= E_X\left(\frac{\partial h'}{\partial b}\boldsymbol{\Sigma}^{-1}\boldsymbol{\Omega}\boldsymbol{\Sigma}^{-1}\frac{\partial h}{\partial b'}\right),\end{aligned}$$

where $\boldsymbol{\Omega}$ denotes the true variance covariance matrix of Y conditional on X, and $\boldsymbol{\Sigma}$ denotes the conditional variance covariance matrix associated with the chosen pseudo true family. All these quantities are evaluated at the true value of the parameter.

Similarly, we have

$$\begin{aligned}\mathcal{J} &= E_X E_0\left(\frac{-\partial^2 \log f(Y \mid X; b_0)}{\partial b\, \partial b'}\right)\\ &= E_X E_0\left(\frac{\partial h'}{\partial b}\frac{dC}{dm}\frac{\partial h}{\partial b'}\right) \quad (\text{since } E_0(Y-h)=0)\\ &= E_X\left(\frac{\partial h'}{\partial b}\boldsymbol{\Sigma}^{-1}\frac{\partial h}{\partial b'}\right).\end{aligned}$$

Hence we can state the following property.

Property 8.17: *Under the regularity conditions of Property 8.4, a consistent pseudo maximum likelihood estimator associated with a linear exponential family is asymptotically normally distributed with*

$$\sqrt{n}(\hat{b}_n - b_0) \xrightarrow{d} N(0, \mathcal{J}^{-1}\mathcal{I}\mathcal{J}^{-1}),$$

where

$$\begin{aligned}\mathcal{I} &= E_X\left(\frac{\partial h'}{\partial b}\boldsymbol{\Sigma}^{-1}\boldsymbol{\Omega}\boldsymbol{\Sigma}^{-1}\frac{\partial h}{\partial b'}\right),\\ \mathcal{J} &= E_X\left(\frac{\partial h'}{\partial b}\boldsymbol{\Sigma}^{-1}\frac{\partial h}{\partial b'}\right),\end{aligned}$$

$\boldsymbol{\Omega}$ *is the true variance covariance matrix of* Y *conditional on* X*, and* $\boldsymbol{\Sigma}$ *is the conditional variance covariance matrix associated with the chosen pseudo true family.*

Thus the precision of a PML estimator depends on the associated family of pseudo true distributions through the second-order moment $\boldsymbol{\Sigma}$ only.

Example 8.15: Consider the generalized Poisson model introduced in Example 8.6. We have $h(X, b) = \exp(Xb)$ and $\boldsymbol{\Omega} = \sigma^2 \exp(2Xb) + \exp(Xb)$, where X is a row vector.

(i) If the family of pseudo true distributions is chosen to be the family of Poisson distributions $P(h(X, b)) = P(\exp Xb)$, we obtain

$$\frac{\partial h'}{\partial b} = X' \exp Xb \text{ and } \boldsymbol{\Sigma} = \exp(Xb).$$

The corresponding pseudo maximum likelihood estimator is a solution to

$$\max_b - \sum_{i=1}^{n} \exp X_i b + \sum_{i=1}^{n} Y_i X_i b.$$

Its asymptotic variance covariance matrix is

$$\begin{aligned} \mathcal{J}^{-1}\mathcal{I}\mathcal{J}^{-1} &= (E_X(X'X \exp Xb_0))^{-1} \\ &\quad E_X(X'X(\exp Xb_0 + \sigma_0^2 \exp 2Xb_0)) \\ &\quad (E_X(X'X \exp Xb_0))^{-1}, \end{aligned}$$

which gives

$$\mathcal{J}^{-1}\mathcal{I}\mathcal{J}^{-1} = (E_X(X'X \exp Xb_0))^{-1}$$

$$+\sigma_0^2 (E_X(X'X \exp Xb_0))^{-1} E_X(X'X \exp 2Xb_0)(E_X(X'X \exp Xb_0))^{-1}.$$

(ii) If the family of pseudo true distributions is the family of normal distributions $N(\exp Xb, 1)$, the pseudo maximum likelihood estimator is the nonlinear least squares estimator, which is solution to

$$\max_b \sum_{i=1}^{n} (Y_i - \exp X_i b)^2.$$

Its variance covariance matrix is

$$\begin{aligned} \tilde{\mathcal{J}}^{-1}\tilde{\mathcal{I}}\tilde{\mathcal{J}}^{-1} &= (E_X(X'X \exp 2Xb_0))^{-1} \\ &\quad E_X(X'X \exp 2Xb_0(\exp Xb_0 + \sigma_0^2 \exp 2Xb_0)) \\ &\quad (E_X(X'X \exp 2Xb_0))^{-1}. \end{aligned}$$

The two variance covariance matrices $\mathcal{J}^{-1}\mathcal{I}\mathcal{J}^{-1}$ and $\tilde{\mathcal{J}}^{-1}\tilde{\mathcal{I}}\tilde{\mathcal{J}}^{-1}$ are not, in general, comparable. Hence neither estimator is clearly more efficient asymptotically than the other. It is, however, possible to show that the first estimator dominates uniformly the second estimator for certain distributions of the exogenous variables (see Exercise 8.2).

The next property provides a lower bound to the asymptotic variance covariance matrices of pseudo maximum likelihood estimators.

Property 8.18: *The variance covariance matrice of a pseudo maximum likelihood estimators is at least as large as*

$$\mathcal{K} = \left(E_X \left(\frac{\partial h'}{\partial b} \mathbf{\Omega}^{-1} \frac{\partial h}{\partial b'} \right) \right)^{-1},$$

i.e., $\mathcal{J}^{-1}\mathcal{I}\mathcal{J}^{-1} \succeq \mathcal{K}$.

PROOF: The result follows from the equality

$$\begin{aligned} &\mathcal{J}^{-1}\mathcal{I}\mathcal{J}^{-1} - \mathcal{K} \\ &= E_X\Big(\left(\mathcal{K}\frac{\partial h'}{\partial b}\mathbf{\Omega}^{-1}\mathbf{\Sigma}^{1/2} - \mathcal{J}^{-1}\frac{\partial h'}{\partial b}\mathbf{\Sigma}^{-1/2} \right) \\ &\quad \mathbf{\Sigma}^{-1/2}\mathbf{\Omega}\mathbf{\Sigma}^{-1/2} \left(\mathbf{\Sigma}^{1/2}\mathbf{\Omega}^{-1}\frac{\partial h}{\partial b'}\mathcal{K} - \mathbf{\Sigma}^{-1/2}\frac{\partial h}{\partial b'}\mathcal{J}^{-1} \right) \Big) \succeq 0. \end{aligned}$$

□

The lower bound $\mathcal{K}$ is a function of the moments of the true but unknown distribution. It is independent of the chosen family of pseudo true distributions.

8.4.3 Quasi Generalized PML Estimation

The existence of a lower bound $\mathcal{K}$ raises the question of whether it is possible to find a consistent estimator of which the asymptotic variance covariance matrix attains the lower bound $\mathcal{K}$. Such an estimator, if it exists, would be asymptotically better than any other consistent pseudo maximum likelihood estimator. The purpose of this section is to present some two-step methods producing such estimators when the functional form of the second-order conditional moment is known and given by

$$V(Y_i \mid X_1, \ldots, X_n) = \mathbf{\Omega}(X_i, \beta_0). \tag{8.17}$$

In a first step, the basic idea consists in estimating consistently the parameter β_0 appearing in the second-order moment. Then, in a second step, the method consists in estimating the parameter b_0 using an appropriate pseudo maximum likelihood method based on a family of pseudo true distributions with a "good" variance. To do so, it is necessary to define a doubly parameterized family of pseudo true distributions

$$f(y; m, \eta) = \exp(A(m, \eta) + B(\eta, y) + C(m, \eta)y), \tag{8.18}$$

where $\eta = \eta(m, \mathbf{\Sigma})$ and m denotes the mean of each distribution so that $\partial A/\partial m + (\partial C/\partial m)m = 0$. The additional parameter η, which is a function of the mean m, and the variance covariance matrix $\mathbf{\Sigma}$, is assumed to be in a bijective relationship with $\mathbf{\Sigma}$ whenever m is fixed.

Examples of such doubly parameterized families are the family of normal distributions ($\eta = \sigma^2$), the family of binomial distributions ($\eta = \alpha$), and the family of gamma distributions ($\eta = \alpha$), which are given in the table of Section 8.4.2.

Property 8.19: *Under the conditions of Section 8.1.4, let $\tilde{b}_n$ and $\tilde{\beta}_n$ be two consistent estimators of b_0 and β_0, respectively, such that*

$$(\sqrt{n}(\tilde{b}_n - b_0)', \sqrt{n}(\tilde{\beta}_n - \beta_0)')'$$

converges in distribution to a normal distribution. The estimator of b_0 defined as a solution to

$$\max_b \sum_{i=1}^{n} \log f[Y_i; h(X_i, b), \eta(h(X_i, \tilde{b}_n), \mathbf{\Omega}(X_i, \tilde{\beta}_n))],$$

is called a quasi generalized pseudo maximum likelihood estimator. This estimator, denoted $\hat{b}_n$, is consistent and asymptotically normal with

$$\sqrt{n}(\hat{b}_n - b_0) \xrightarrow{d} N(0, \mathcal{K}).$$

PROOF: The result follows from the general properties of quasi generalized M-estimators obtained in Section 8.1.4.

(i) Consistency: When n increases, the objective function

$$\frac{1}{n} \sum_{i=1}^{n} \log f[Y_i; h(X_i, b), \eta(h(X_i, \tilde{b}_n), \mathbf{\Omega}(X_i, \tilde{\beta}_n))],$$

converges to

$$E_X E_0 \log f[Y; h(X, b), \eta(h(X, b_0), \mathbf{\Omega}(X, \beta_0))].$$

From Kullback inequality, this quantity is maximized when $h(X, b) = h(X, b_0)$. Thus, provided the model is first-order identified, the quasi generalized pseudo maximum likelihood estimator is consistent.

(ii) Asymptotic normality: First, we verify that the condition of Property 8.5, namely

$$H = E_X E_0 \left(\frac{\partial^2 \Psi(Y, X; g_\infty^0, c_0)}{\partial g \, \partial c'} \right) = 0,$$

is satisfied. This condition holds because

$$\begin{aligned}
E_0 \left(\frac{\partial^2 \log f(Y; m, \eta)}{\partial m \, \partial \eta} \right) &= E_0 \left(\frac{\partial}{\partial \eta'} \left(\frac{\partial A(m,\eta)}{\partial m} + \frac{\partial C(m,\eta)}{\partial m} Y \right) \right) \\
&= \frac{\partial}{\partial \eta'} E_0 \left(\frac{\partial A(m,\eta)}{\partial m} + \frac{\partial C(m,\eta)}{\partial m} Y \right) \\
&= \frac{\partial}{\partial \eta'} \left(\frac{\partial A(m,\eta)}{\partial m} + \frac{\partial C(m,\eta)}{\partial m} m \right) \\
&= \frac{\partial}{\partial \eta'} (0) \\
&= 0,
\end{aligned}$$

where we have used the equality $\partial A / \partial m + (\partial C / \partial m) \, m = 0$.

It follows that the asymptotic variance covariance matrix of the quasi generalized pseudo maximum likelihood estimator is identical to that of the corresponding pseudo maximum likelihood estimator. Now the variance covariance matrix $\mathbf{\Sigma}_0$ of the limiting pseudo true distribution is such that

$$\eta(h(X, b_0), \mathbf{\Sigma}_0) = \eta(h(X, b_0), \mathbf{\Omega}(X, \beta_0)).$$

Since η is bijective for every given $h(X, b_0)$, it follows that $\mathbf{\Sigma}_0 = \mathbf{\Omega}(X, \beta_0) = \mathbf{\Omega}_0$.

Hence we have

$$\begin{aligned}
\mathcal{J}^{-1} \mathcal{I} \mathcal{J}^{-1} &= \left(E_X \left(\frac{\partial h'}{\partial b} \mathbf{\Sigma}_0^{-1} \frac{\partial h}{\partial b'} \right) \right)^{-1} E_X \left(\frac{\partial h'}{\partial b} \mathbf{\Sigma}_0^{-1} \mathbf{\Omega}_0 \mathbf{\Sigma}_0^{-1} \frac{\partial h}{\partial b'} \right) \\
&\quad \left(E_X \left(\frac{\partial h'}{\partial b} \mathbf{\Sigma}_0^{-1} \frac{\partial h}{\partial b'} \right) \right)^{-1} \\
&= \left(E_X \left(\frac{\partial h'}{\partial b} \mathbf{\Omega}_0^{-1} \frac{\partial h}{\partial b'} \right) \right)^{-1} \\
&= \mathcal{K}.
\end{aligned}$$

Note also that we have $\mathcal{I} = \mathcal{J}$. □

Example 8.16: Consider the linear regression model of order 2 defined by

$$Y_i = h(X_i, b_0) + u_i,$$

where

$$E(u_i \mid X_1, \ldots, X_n) = 0,$$
$$V(u_i \mid X_1, \ldots, X_n) = \gamma_0 \, \omega^2(X_i, b_0).$$

In such a model, the parameter b_0 can be estimated consistently by the nonlinear least squares estimator. Let $\tilde{b}_n$ denote such an estimator. The parameter γ_0 can be estimated from the associated residuals

$$\tilde{\gamma}_n = \frac{1}{n} \sum_{i=1}^{n} \frac{(Y_i - h(X_i, \tilde{b}_n))^2}{\omega^2(X_i, \tilde{b}_n)}.$$

In a second step we can base a quasi generalized pseudo maximum likelihood method on the family of normal or gamma distributions.

For the family of normal distributions, the estimator $\hat{b}_n$ is obtained by solving

$$\min_b \sum_{i=1}^{n} \frac{(Y_i - h(X_i, b))^2}{\omega^2(X_i, \tilde{b}_n)\tilde{\gamma}_n},$$

i.e., by solving

$$\min_b \sum_{i=1}^{n} \frac{(Y_i - h(X_i, b))^2}{\omega^2(X_i, \tilde{b}_n)}.$$

For the family of gamma distributions, the optimization problem is

$$\max_b \sum_{i=1}^{n} -\eta(h(X_i, \tilde{b}_n), \tilde{\gamma}_n \omega^2(X_i, \tilde{b}_n)) \left(\log h(X_i, b) + \frac{Y_i}{h(X_i, b)} \right),$$

i.e.

$$\max_b \sum_{i=1}^{n} -\frac{h^2(X_i, \tilde{b}_n)}{\tilde{\gamma}_n \omega^2(X_i, \tilde{b}_n)} \left(\log h(X_i, b) + \frac{Y_i}{h(X_i, b)} \right).$$

These two quasi generalized PML estimators differ from each other. They have, however, the same asymptotic variance covariance matrix.

8.4.4 Consistent PML Estimation of Order 2

a) Definition

The pseudo maximum likelihood approach presented above can be easily generalized to the case where one wishes to estimate jointly the parameters appearing in the first two moments.

Specifically, we consider a univariate regression model of order 2 defined by

$$Y_i = h(X_i, b_0) + u_i, \tag{8.19}$$

where

$$E(u_i \mid X_0, \dots, X_n) = 0,$$
$$V(u_i \mid X_1, \dots, X_n) = \omega^2(X_i, \beta_0).$$

The parameters b_0 and β_0 are assumed to be second-order identifed.

The families of pseudo true distributions are parameterized by their first two moments m and σ^2. Their densities are denoted $f(y; m, \sigma^2)$.

A *pseudo maximum likelihood estimator of order 2* of b_0 and β_0 is defined as a solution to

$$\max_{b,\beta} \sum_{i=1}^{n} \log f(Y_i; h(X_i, b), \omega^2(X_i, \beta)). \tag{8.20}$$

Property 8.20: *Under the assumptions of Property 8.1, the pseudo maximum likelihood estimator of order 2, denoted $(\hat{b}_n, \hat{\beta}_n)$, is consistent for (b_0, β_0) for any possible value of the parameters, any functional form of the conditional mean and variance, any limiting distribution ν of the exogenous variables, and any conditional distribution satisfying (8.19) if and only if the pseudo true densities are of the form*

$$f(y; m, \sigma^2) = \exp(A(m, \sigma^2) + B(y) + C(m, \sigma^2)y + D(m, \sigma^2)y^2)),$$

where m and σ^2 are the mean and the variance of the density $f(y; m, \sigma^2)$. Such a density is called a quadratic exponential density.

PROOF: The proof is similar to the proof of Property 8.16 and relies on Lemma 8.1.

Specifically, the conditions on the first two moments imply that b_0 and β_0 must be the solutions to the limit problem. Using the particular functional forms and parameterization $b_0 = E_0 Y$ and $\beta_0 = E_0 Y^2$, then the condition

$$\forall\, b_0, \beta_0, \quad E_0(Y - b_0) = 0 \quad \text{and} \quad E_0(Y^2 - \beta_0) = 0,$$

must imply

$$E_0 \left(\frac{\partial \log f(Y; b_0, \beta_0)}{\partial (b'\beta')'} \right) = 0.$$

From Lemma 8.1 it follows that

$$\frac{\partial \log f(Y; b_0, \beta_0)}{\partial (b'\beta')'} = \lambda(b_0, \beta_0)(Y - b_0) + \mu(b_0, \beta_0)(Y^2 - \beta_0).$$

Now it suffices to integrate the latter equation so as to obtain the required form for the pseudo true densities. This establishes necessity.

The proof of sufficiency is similar to that given for Property 8.16. It is left to the reader (see Exercise 8.4). □

Example 8.17: The family of normal distributions $N(m, \sigma^2)$ is a family of quadratic exponential distributions. Thus it can be used in a pseudo maximum likelihood estimation method of order 2. Estimators are obtained as solutions to

$$\max_{b,\beta} - \sum_{i=1}^{n} \left(\log \omega^2(X_i, \beta) + \frac{(Y_i - h(X_i, b))^2}{\omega^2(X_i, \beta)} \right).$$

Note that these estimators are consistent even if some constraints exist among the parameters b and β appearing in the conditional mean and variance.

b) Asymptotic Distribution

From the general results on M-estimators (see Property 8.4) it follows that pseudo maximum likelihood estimators of order 2 are asymptotically normally distributed. Here, we shall give an expression for their asymptotic variance covariance matrices when the pseudo true distributions are normal and the parameters b and β are unconstrained.

The objective function is defined by

$$\Psi(y, x; b, \beta) = - \log \omega^2(x, \beta) - \frac{(y - h(x, b))^2}{\omega^2(x, \beta)}.$$

The first partial derivatives of Ψ are

$$\begin{aligned}
\frac{\partial \Psi}{\partial b} &= 2\frac{y-h(x,b)}{\omega^2(x,\beta)}\frac{\partial h(x,b)}{\partial b}, \\
\frac{\partial \Psi}{\partial \beta} &= \left(-\frac{1}{\omega^2(x,\beta)} + \frac{(y-h(x,b))^2}{\omega^4(x,\beta)}\right)\frac{\partial \omega^2(x,\beta)}{\partial \beta}.
\end{aligned}$$

Let μ_3 and μ_4 be the central moments of order 3 and 4

$$\mu_3 = E_0(Y-h(X,b_0))^3, \quad \mu_4 = E_0(Y-h(X,b_0))^4.$$

The matrix $\mathcal{I}$ is given by

$$\mathcal{I} = E_X E_0 \begin{pmatrix} \frac{\partial \Psi}{\partial b}\frac{\partial \Psi}{\partial b'} & \frac{\partial \Psi}{\partial b}\frac{\partial \Psi}{\partial \beta'} \\ \frac{\partial \Psi}{\partial \beta}\frac{\partial \Psi}{\partial b'} & \frac{\partial \Psi}{\partial \beta}\frac{\partial \Psi}{\partial \beta'} \end{pmatrix},$$

i.e.

$$\mathcal{I} = E_X \begin{pmatrix} \frac{4}{\omega^2}\frac{\partial h}{\partial b}\frac{\partial h}{\partial b'} & \frac{2\mu_3}{\omega^6}\frac{\partial h}{\partial b}\frac{\partial \omega^2}{\partial \beta'} \\ \frac{2\mu_3}{\omega^6}\frac{\partial \omega^2}{\partial \beta}\frac{\partial h}{\partial b'} & \left(-\frac{1}{\omega^4}+\frac{\mu_4}{\omega^8}\right)\frac{\partial \omega^2}{\partial \beta}\frac{\partial \omega^2}{\partial \beta'} \end{pmatrix}.$$

All functions appearing in the above matrix are evaluated at b_0 and β_0.

To find an expression for the matrix $\mathcal{J}$, we need the second partial derivatives of the objective function. We have

$$\begin{aligned}
\frac{\partial^2 \Psi}{\partial b\, \partial b'} &= \frac{-2}{\omega^2}\frac{\partial h}{\partial b}\frac{\partial h}{\partial b'} + 2\frac{y-h}{\omega^2}\frac{\partial^2 h}{\partial b\, \partial b'}, \\
\frac{\partial^2 \Psi}{\partial b\, \partial \beta'} &= -2\frac{y-h}{\omega^4}\frac{\partial h}{\partial b}\frac{\partial \omega^2}{\partial \beta'}, \\
\frac{\partial^2 \Psi}{\partial \beta\, \partial \beta'} &= \left(-\frac{1}{\omega^2} + \frac{(y-h)^2}{\omega^4}\right)\frac{\partial^2\, \omega^2}{\partial \beta\, \partial \beta'} \\
&\quad + \left(\frac{1}{\omega^4} - \frac{2}{\omega^6}(y-h)^2\right)\frac{\partial \omega^2}{\partial \beta}\frac{\partial \omega^2}{\partial \beta'}.
\end{aligned}$$

It follows that

$$\mathcal{J} = E_X E_0 \begin{pmatrix} -\frac{\partial^2 \Psi}{\partial b\, \partial b'} & -\frac{\partial^2 \Psi}{\partial b\, \partial \beta'} \\ -\frac{\partial^2 \Psi}{\partial \beta \partial b'} & -\frac{\partial^2 \Psi}{\partial \beta \partial \beta'} \end{pmatrix}$$

$$= \quad E_X \begin{pmatrix} \frac{2}{\omega^2} \frac{\partial h}{\partial b} \frac{\partial h}{\partial b'} & 0 \\ 0 & \frac{1}{\omega^4} \frac{\partial \omega^2}{\partial \beta} \frac{\partial \omega^2}{\partial \beta'} \end{pmatrix}.$$

8.5 Estimation of a Conditional Median

8.5.1 The Model

In the nonlinear regression model of Section 8.2 the conditional distribution of the endogenous variable Y given the exogenous variables X is summarized by the conditional mean $E(Y \mid X)$. Other measures of central tendency such as the conditional median can be used. The conditional median has the advantage of being less dependent on the tails of the conditional distribution of Y given X. Thus an estimation method based on the conditional median is likely to be relatively insensitive to specification errors in the tails of the conditional distribution or to the presence of outliers.

The model that we shall study is similar to the regression model (8.7). Specifically, we assume

$$Y_i = h(X_i, b_0) + u_i, \tag{8.21}$$

where the error term u_i has, conditionally on $X_1, \ldots, X_n$, a continuous distribution with median zero.

The difference between this model and model (8.7) arises essentially from the assumption on the error term u_i. Here the error term is assumed to have median zero while in the other model it was assumed to have mean zero. These two assumptions are clearly identical when the conditional distribution of the error term u_i is symmetric and the conditional mean exists. For instance, this is the case when the conditional distribution of u_i is normal.

8.5.2 Least Absolute Deviations Estimation

Following the least squares method for regression models, we can define an estimation method for the parameter b appearing in the conditional median.

Definition 8.8: *A least absolute deviations (LAD) estimator of* b *is a solution to the problem*

$$\min_b \sum_{i=1}^n |Y_i - h(X_i, b)|.$$

Hence the discrepancy between the endogenous variable Y_i and its approximation $h(X_i, b)$ provided by the model is now measured by the L_1-distance instead of the usual L_2-distance.

A difficulty with the LAD method arises from the nondifferentiability of the objective function. This function, however, is continuous and continuously differentiable at every point except at zero, where there exist a left and a right derivative. Because of such properties, an approach similar to the previous one can be followed provided the derivative at every point is replaced by the right derivative. The latter derivative is given by

$$\frac{\partial^+ |x|}{\partial x} = \mathbb{1}_{x \geq 0} - \mathbb{1}_{x<0}. \tag{8.22}$$

Hence a solution to the preceding optimization problem is obtained by solving the first-order conditions. In the favorable case (defined below) the first conditions are

$$\frac{\partial^+}{\partial b} \sum_{i=1}^n |Y_i - h(X_i, \hat{b}_n)| = 0,$$

i.e.

$$\sum_{i=1}^n \frac{\partial h(X_i, \hat{b}_n)}{\partial b} \left(\mathbb{1}_{(Y_i - h(X_i, \hat{b}_n) \geq 0)} - \mathbb{1}_{(Y_i - h(X_i, \hat{b}_n) < 0)} \right) = 0. \tag{8.23}$$

In the unfavorable case where zero does not belong to the set of possible values of $\partial^+ \sum_{i=1}^n |Y_i - h(X_i, b)| / \partial b$ when b varies, the first-order conditions are replaced by inequalities. Specifically, assuming that the function $\partial^+ \sum_{i=1}^n |Y_i - h(X_i, b)| / \partial b$ is right continuous, the first-order conditions become

$$\frac{\partial^+}{\partial b} \sum_{i=1}^n |Y_i - h(X_i, \hat{b}_n^-)| \leq 0,$$

and

$$\frac{\partial^+}{\partial b} \sum_{i=1}^n |Y_i - h(X_i, \hat{b}_n)| \geq 0.$$

Example 8.18: In the simple case of an iid sample drawn from a distribution with median b, the objective function is

$$\sum_{i=1}^{n} \Psi(Y_i, b) = \sum_{i=1}^{n} |Y_i - b|.$$

This function is convex in b so that the first-order condition is necessary and sufficient. The first-order conditions are

$$\sum_{i=1}^{n} \left(\mathbb{1}_{(Y_i - \hat{b}_n^- > 0)} - \mathbb{1}_{(Y_i - \hat{b}_n^- \leq 0)} \right) \geq 0,$$

and

$$\sum_{i=1}^{n} \left(\mathbb{1}_{(Y_i - \hat{b}_n > 0)} - \mathbb{1}_{(Y_i - \hat{b}_n \leq 0)} \right) \leq 0,$$

i.e.

$$\sum_{i=1}^{n} \mathbb{1}_{(Y_i > \hat{b}_n^-)} \geq \sum_{i=1}^{n} \mathbb{1}_{(Y_i \leq \hat{b}_n^-)},$$

and

$$\sum_{i=1}^{n} \mathbb{1}_{(Y_i > \hat{b}_n)} \leq \sum_{i=1}^{n} \mathbb{1}_{(Y_i \leq \hat{b}_n)}.$$

A LAD estimator is such that there are as many observations above $\hat{b}_n$ as observations below $\hat{b}_n$. Thus LAD estimators are the empirical medians associated with the empirical distribution of the observations. This example suggests that the L_1-norm is well adapted to the estimation of a median. Moreover, the LAD estimator is unique if the number of observations n is odd. On the other hand, there is an infinity of LAD estimators when n is even. (This property clearly holds because the distribution of the observations Y_i is assumed to be continuous so that observations are unlikely to be identical.)

Example 8.19: The convexity of the objective function noted above still holds when the conditional median is a linear function of the parameters, i.e., when $h(X_i, b) = X_i b$. In general, however, it is no longer possible to obtain explicitly the solutions to the first-order conditions. Moreover, in the general case, it may be easier to solve directly the optimization problem using linear programming techniques. Specifically, the original optimization problem which is $\min_b \sum_{i=1}^{n} |Y_i - X_i b|$ has the same solutions as the optimization problem

$$\min_{b, r_i^+, r_i^-} \sum_{i=1}^{n} (r_i^+ + r_i^-),$$

subject to

$$\begin{cases} Y_i = X_i b + r_i^+ - r_i^-, & i = 1, \ldots, n, \\ r_i^+ \geq 0, \\ r_i^- \geq 0. \end{cases}$$

The consistency and asymptotic normality of LAD estimators can be established in a manner similar to that used in the preceding sections.

a) Consistency

Under suitable regularity conditions we can replace the optimization problem in finite samples by its asymptotic problem. Thus we need to study the limit objective function. In particular, if the pairs (X_i, Y_i) are assumed to be mutually independent and identically distributed and if the mean of $Y - h(X, b)$ exists, we have

$$\frac{1}{n} \sum_{i=1}^{n} |Y_i - h(X_i, b)| \stackrel{as}{\to} E_X E_0 |Y - h(X, b)|.$$

Hence $\hat{b}_n$ converges to b_0 if and only if b_0 is the unique solution to the problem $\min_b \Psi_\infty(b) = E_X E_0 |Y - h(X, b)|$.

If u denotes the error term, we have

$$\Psi_\infty(b) = E_X E_0 |u + h(X, b_0) - h(X, b)|.$$

Property 8.21: *Suppose that the conditional distribution of Y given X has a unique median $h(X, b_0)$ and that the parameter b is identified from the conditional median, i.e.*

$$h(x, b) = h(x, b_0), \ \forall \ x \Rightarrow b = b_0.$$

Then b_0 is the unique solution to the problem $\min_b \Psi_\infty(b)$.

The proof of Property 8.21 uses the following two lemmas.

Lemma 8.2: *We have*

$$E|u - a| = \int_{-\infty}^{+\infty} ((1 - 2F(t)) \mathbb{1}_{t > a} + F(t)) \, dt,$$

where F is the cumulative distribution function of u.

PROOF: We have

$$
\begin{aligned}
E|u-a| &= E((u-a)\mathbb{1}_{u>a}) + E((a-u)\mathbb{1}_{u\leq a}) \\
&= \int_{-\infty}^{+\infty}\left(\int_{-\infty}^{+\infty}\mathbb{1}_{u>t>a}dt\right)dF(u) \\
&\quad + \int_{-\infty}^{+\infty}\left(\int_{-\infty}^{+\infty}\mathbb{1}_{u\leq t\leq a}dt\right)dF(u) \\
&= \int_{-\infty}^{+\infty}(1-F(t))\mathbb{1}_{t>a}dt + \int_{-\infty}^{+\infty}F(t)\mathbb{1}_{t\leq a}dt.
\end{aligned}
$$

using Fubini Theorem. Since $\mathbb{1}_{t\leq a} = 1 - \mathbb{1}_{t>a}$ we obtain

$$E|u-a| = \int_{-\infty}^{+\infty}((1-2F(t))\mathbb{1}_{t>a} + F(t))\,dt.$$

□

Lemma 8.3: *If u is a random variable with a continuous distribution, then the minimum in a of $E|u-a|$ is attained at the medians of the distribution of u, i.e., at real values a for which $F(a) = 1/2$.*

PROOF: Minimizing $E \mid u-a \mid$ is equivalent to minimizing

$$H(a) = \int_{-\infty}^{+\infty}\left(\left(\frac{1}{2}-F(t)\right)\mathbb{1}_{t>a} + \frac{1}{2}F(t)\right)dt$$

(see Lemma 8.2). Since the function F is continuous and nondecreasing, the set of values a such that $F(a) = 1/2$ is a closed interval $[a_0, a_1]$ (the median interval). Since $1/2 - F(t)$ is strictly positive when $t < a_0$ and strictly negative when $t > a_1$, it is easily seen that the function H attains its minimum at every point in $[a_0, a_1]$. □

PROOF OF PROPERTY 8.21: Lemma 8.3 can be used to solve the optimization problem of $\Psi_\infty(b)$. Since the conditional median of the error u is zero, the minimum of $E \mid u + h(x, b_o) - h(x, b) \mid$ is attained at every value of b such that $h(x, b) = h(x, b_0)$. Thus the minimum of the function Ψ_∞ is attained at every parameter value such that

$$h(x, b_0) = h(x, b), \quad \forall\ x.$$

The identifiability of b from the conditional median implies that b_0 is the unique solution to the limit problem $\min_b \Psi_\infty(b)$. □

b) Asymptotic Normality

The asymptotic distribution of the LAD estimator is obtained by a Taylor expansion of the first-order conditions. Such a Taylor expansion, however, cannot be obtained in the same manner as in Section 8.1.3. This is because the first-order conditions are not continuous in the parameters. We shall sketch an approach due to Huber (1967).

The first-order conditions can be written as

$$\frac{1}{n}\sum_{i=1}^{n}\frac{\partial^+\Psi(Y_i,X_i;\hat{b}_n)}{\partial b}=0 \tag{8.24}$$

(in the favorable case). From the regularity conditions, the strong convergence of $(1/n)\sum_{i=1}^{n}\partial^+\Psi(Y_i,X_i;b)\ /\partial b$ to $E_X E_0 \partial^+\Psi(Y,X;b)\ /\partial b$, which follows from the Strong Law of Large Numbers, is uniform in the parameter b. Hence, if $\hat{b}_n$ converges to b_0, we obtain

$$\frac{1}{n}\sum_{i=1}^{n}\frac{\partial^+\Psi(Y_i,X_i;\hat{b}_n)}{\partial b}\rightarrow E_X E_0\frac{\partial^+\Psi(Y,X;b_0)}{\partial b}$$

(see Chapter 24, Volume II for a proof). Hence we can write

$$\begin{aligned}
0 &= \frac{1}{\sqrt{n}}\sum_{i=1}^{n}\frac{\partial^+\Psi(Y_i,X_i;\hat{b}_n)}{\partial b}\\
&\# \frac{1}{\sqrt{n}}\sum_{i=1}^{n}\frac{\partial^+\Psi(Y_i,X_i;b_0)}{\partial b}\\
&\quad+\sqrt{n}\left(\left(E_X E_0\frac{\partial^+\Psi(Y,X;b)}{\partial b}\right)_{b=\hat{b}_n}\right.\\
&\quad\left.-\left(E_X E_0\frac{\partial^+\Psi(Y,X;b)}{\partial b}\right)_{b=b_0}\right).
\end{aligned}$$

Now, since b_0 corresponds to a minimum of the function $\Psi_\infty(b) = E_X E_0\Psi(Y,X,b)$, the first-order conditions $\partial\Psi_\infty(b_0)/\partial b = 0$ must be satisfied. Assuming that it is possible to interchange expectations and differentiations, the first-order conditions give

$$\begin{aligned}
0 &= \frac{\partial\Psi_\infty(b_0)}{\partial b}\\
&= \left(\frac{\partial^+ E_X E_0\Psi(X,Y;b)}{\partial b}\right)_{b=b_0}
\end{aligned}$$

$$= \left(E_X E_0 \frac{\partial^+ E_X E_0 \Psi(X,Y;b)}{\partial b} \right)_{b=b_0}.$$

Hence we obtain an expansion of the form

$$\begin{aligned} 0 &= \frac{1}{\sqrt{n}} \sum_{i=1}^{n} \frac{\partial^+ \Psi(Y_i, X_i; \hat{b}_n)}{\partial b} \\ &\# \frac{1}{\sqrt{n}} \sum_{i=1}^{n} \frac{\partial^+ \Psi(Y_i, X_i; b_0)}{\partial b} + \sqrt{n} \left(E_X E_0 \frac{\partial^+ \Psi(Y,X;b)}{\partial b} \right)_{b=\hat{b}_n} \end{aligned} \quad (8.25)$$

This expansion can be pursued provided $E_X E_0 \partial^+ \Psi(Y,X;b)/\partial b$ is differentiable in b. Since $\hat{b}_n$ converges to b_0, we can write

$$\begin{aligned} 0 \quad \# \quad & \frac{1}{\sqrt{n}} \sum_{i=1}^{n} \frac{\partial^+ \Psi(Y_i, X_i; b_0)}{\partial b} \\ & + \left(\frac{\partial}{\partial b} \left(E_X E_0 \frac{\partial^+ \Psi(Y,X;b)}{\partial b'} \right) \right)_{b=b_0} \sqrt{n}(\hat{b}_n - b_0). \end{aligned}$$

If the matrix

$$\left(\frac{\partial}{\partial b} \left(E_X E_0 \frac{\partial^+ \Psi(Y,X;b)}{\partial b'} \right) \right)_{b=b_0}$$

is nonsingular, this implies

$$\begin{aligned} \sqrt{n}(\hat{b}_n - b_0) \quad \# \quad & - \left[\left(\frac{\partial}{\partial b} \left(E_X E_0 \frac{\partial^+ \Psi(Y,X;b)}{\partial b'} \right) \right)_{b=b_0} \right]^{-1} \\ & \frac{1}{\sqrt{n}} \sum_{i=1}^{n} \frac{\partial^+ \Psi(Y_i, X_i; b_0)}{\partial b}. \end{aligned}$$

Now, from the Central Limit Theorem

$$\frac{1}{\sqrt{n}} \sum_{i=1}^{n} \frac{\partial^+ \Psi(Y_i, X_i; b_0)}{\partial b},$$

follows asymptotically a central normal distribution with variance covariance matrix

$$\mathcal{I} = E_X E_0 \left(\frac{\partial^+ \Psi(Y,X;b_0)}{\partial b} \frac{\partial^+ \Psi(Y,X;b_0)}{\partial b'} \right).$$

Hence the asymptotic distribution of $\hat{b}_n$ is also normal. It is given by

$$\sqrt{n}(\hat{b}_n - b_0) \xrightarrow{d} N(0, \mathcal{J}^{-1}\mathcal{I}\mathcal{J}^{-1}), \tag{8.26}$$

where

$$\mathcal{I} = E_X E_0 \left(\frac{\partial^+ \Psi(Y, X; b_0)}{\partial b} \frac{\partial^+ \Psi(Y, X; b_0)}{\partial b'} \right)$$

and

$$\mathcal{J} = \left(\frac{\partial}{\partial b} \left(E_X E_0 \frac{\partial^+ \Psi(Y, X; b)}{\partial b'} \right) \right)_{b=b_0}$$

This asymptotic result is readily applied to our case. We have

$$\frac{\partial^+ \Psi(Y, X; b)}{\partial b} = \frac{\partial h(X, b)}{\partial b} \left(-\mathbb{1}_{(Y - h(X,b) \geq 0)} + \mathbb{1}_{(Y - h(X,b) < 0)} \right).$$

It follows that

$$\begin{aligned}
\mathcal{I} &= E_X E_0 \left(\frac{\partial^+ \Psi(Y, X; b_0)}{\partial b} \frac{\partial^+ \Psi(Y, X; b_0)}{\partial b'} \right) \\
&= E_X \Bigg[\left(\frac{\partial h(X, b_0)}{\partial b} \frac{\partial h(X, b_0)}{\partial b'} \right) \\
&\qquad E_0 (\mathbb{1}_{(Y - h(X,b_0) \geq 0)} - \mathbb{1}_{(Y - h(X,b_0) < 0)})^2 \Bigg] \\
&= E_X \Bigg[\left(\frac{\partial h(X, b_0)}{\partial b} \frac{\partial h(X, b_0)}{\partial b'} \right) \\
&\qquad E_0 (\mathbb{1}_{(Y - h(X,b_0) \geq 0)} + \mathbb{1}_{(Y - h(X,b_0) < 0)}) \Bigg] \\
&= E_X \left[\left(\frac{\partial h(X, b_0)}{\partial b} \frac{\partial h(X, b_0)}{\partial b'} \left(\frac{1}{2} + \frac{1}{2} \right) \right) \right] \\
&= E_X \left(\frac{\partial h(X, b_0)}{\partial b} \frac{\partial h(X, b_0)}{\partial b'} \right).
\end{aligned}$$

Similarly, we obtain

$$\mathcal{J} = \frac{\partial}{\partial b} \left(E_X E_0 \frac{\partial^+ \Psi(Y, X; b)}{\partial b'} \right)_{b=b_0}$$

$$
\begin{aligned}
&= \frac{\partial}{\partial b}\left(E_X - \left(\frac{\partial h(X,b)}{\partial b'} \left(P_0(Y - h(X,b) \geq 0) \right.\right.\right. \\
&\qquad \left.\left.\left. - P_0(Y - h(X,b) < 0) \right)\right)\right)_{b=b_0} \\
&= E_X - \left(\frac{\partial^2 h(X,b)}{\partial b \, \partial b'} \left(P_0(Y - h(X,b_0) \geq 0) - P_0(Y - h(X,b_0) < 0) \right) \right) \\
&\quad - E_X\left(\left(\frac{\partial (P_0(Y - h(X,b) \geq 0) - P_0(Y - h(X,b) < 0))}{\partial b} \right)_{b=b_0} \right. \\
&\qquad \left. \frac{\partial h(X,b_0)}{\partial b'} \right).
\end{aligned}
$$

The first term is equal to zero since

$$P_0(Y - h(X,b_0) \geq 0) = P_0(Y - h(X,b_0) < 0) = \tfrac{1}{2}.$$

If f_0 denotes the density of the error term u, then the second term can be written as

$$\mathcal{J} = E_X \left(\frac{\partial h(X,b_0)}{\partial b} \frac{\partial h(X,b_0)}{\partial b'} 2 f_0(0) \right).$$

To summarize, we have established the following property which gives the asymptotic distribution of $\hat{b}_n$.

Property 8.22: *Under suitable regularity conditions, the LAD estimator of the parameter vector appearing in the conditional median satisfies*

$$\sqrt{n}(\hat{b}_n - b_0) \xrightarrow{d} N\left(0, \frac{1}{4 f_0(0)^2} E_X \left(\frac{\partial h(X,b_0)}{\partial b} \frac{\partial h(X,b_0)}{\partial b'} \right)^{-1} \right).$$

Example 8.20: Consider a linear regression model $Y_i = X_i b_0 + u_i$ in which the distribution of the error term is symmetric with mean zero. The parameter vector b_0 can be estimated either by ordinary least squares or by least absolute deviations.

The OLS estimator is given by

$$\tilde{b}_n = \left(\sum_{i=1}^{n} X_i' X_i \right)^{-1} X_i' Y_i.$$

Its asymptotic distribution is $N(0, \sigma_0^2 E_X(X'X)^{-1})$.

The LAD estimator, which is a solution to $\min_b \sum_{i=1}^n |Y_i - X_i b|$ is asymptotically distributed as $N(0, E_X(X'X)^{-1}/(4f_0(0)^2))$.

Hence the least absolute deviations estimator is asymptotically more efficient than the ordinary least squares estimator if the distribution of the error term is such that

$$4f_0(0)^2 \geq \frac{1}{\sigma_0^2} \Leftrightarrow 2f_0(0) \geq \frac{1}{\sigma_0}.$$

Example 8.21: If the error term is normally distributed, the OLS estimator is asymptotically efficient. The ratio of the asymptotic variances of $\hat{b}_n$ and $\tilde{b}_n$ must be at least as large as one. In fact, it is

$$\frac{V_{as}\hat{b}_n}{V_{as}\tilde{b}_n} = \frac{1}{4f_0(0)^2\sigma_0^2} = \frac{1}{4\sigma_0^2\left(\frac{1}{\sqrt{2\pi\sigma_0^2}}\right)^2} = \frac{\pi}{2}.$$

In particular, this ratio is independent of the value of the variance σ_0^2.

Example 8.22: As expected, the case of normal errors is clearly quite favorable to ordinary least squares estimation. An opposite case is obtained when the errors are Cauchy distributed with density

$$f_0(u) = \frac{1}{\pi\lambda_0}\frac{1}{1+\left(\frac{u}{\lambda_0}\right)^2}, \quad \lambda_0 \in \mathbb{R}^{+*}.$$

For such a distribution, the OLS estimator is such that $E\|\tilde{b}_n - b_0\|^2 = +\infty$. Thus the OLS estimator is quite ill-behaved in the quadratic precision sense. On the other hand, generalizing Properties 8.21 and 8.22 to the case where the mean of u does not exist, one can see that the asymptotic variance of the LAD estimator is given by

$$V_{as}\sqrt{n}(\hat{b}_n - b_0) = E_X(X'X)^{-1}\frac{\pi^2\lambda_0^2}{4}.$$

8.5.3 Maximum Score Estimation˙

Other methods based on alternative criterion functions can be used to define consistent estimators of parameters appearing in the conditional median. Maximum score estimation is one of such methods.

The basic idea of the method is to compare the sign of the endogenous variable Y_i to the sign of its approximation $h(X_i, b)$ provided by the model. To do so, one introduces the *score function* which counts the number of observations for which the signs of these two quantities agree. The score vector is

$$S(b) = \sum_{i=1}^{n} \left(\mathbb{1}_{(h(X_i,b)>0)} \mathbb{1}_{(Y_i>0)} + \mathbb{1}_{(Y_i<0)} \mathbb{1}_{(h(X_i,b)<0)} \right). \qquad (8.27)$$

Definition 8.9: *A maximum score estimator of b is a solution to the problem* $\max_b S(b)$.

Hence one seeks a value of the parameter that maximizes the number of times the sign of Y_i agrees with the sign of its approximation $h(X_i, b)$. The maximum score estimator is an M-estimator since the objective function can be written as

$$S(b) = \sum_{i=1}^{n} \Psi(Y_i, X_i; b), \qquad (8.28)$$

where $\Psi(Y, X; b) = \mathbb{1}_{(y>0)} \mathbb{1}_{(h(X,b)>0)} + \mathbb{1}_{(Y<0)} \mathbb{1}_{(h(X,b)<0)}$.

Remark 8.3: An advantage of this method is that it relies on the sign of Y_i only. Thus the method is especially adapted to dichotomous qualitative models, where the latent model is $Y_i^* = X_i b + u_i$ and the observed variable is $Y_i = \mathbb{1}_{(Y_i^*>0)}$. Clearly, when the latent quantitative variable can be observed, an estimation method based on the sign of Y_i may lead to a possibly substantial loss of precision.

a) Consistency

Under suitable regularity conditions allowing the consideration of the corresponding asymptotic problem, it is possible to establish the consistency of the maximum score estimator whenever the conditional distribution of Y given X is continuous with a unique median $h(X, b_0)$ and the parameter b is identified from the sign of the conditional median, i.e.

$$h(x, b)h(x, b_0) \geq 0, \quad \forall\, x \Rightarrow b = b_0.$$

For instance, such an identification condition is satisfied if $h(x, b_0) = 1 + \sum_{k=1}^{K-1} b_{0k} x_k$.

We have

$$\begin{aligned}\Psi_\infty(b) &= \lim_n \frac{1}{n}\sum_{i=1}^{n}\left(\mathbb{1}_{(Y_i>0)}\mathbb{1}_{(h(X_i,b)>0)} + \mathbb{1}_{(Y_i<0)}\mathbb{1}_{(h(X_i,b)<0)}\right)\\ &= E_X E_0\left(\mathbb{1}_{(Y>0)}\mathbb{1}_{(h(X,b)>0)} + \mathbb{1}_{(Y<0)}\mathbb{1}_{(h(X,b)<0)}\right)\\ &= E_X E_0\left(\mathbb{1}_{(u>-h(X,b_0)}\mathbb{1}_{(h(X,b)>0)}+\mathbb{1}_{(u<-h(X,b_0))}\right)\left(\mathbb{1}_{h(X,b)<0)}\right).\end{aligned}$$

Let F_0 denote the cumulative distribution function of minus the error term. The limit objective function becomes

$$\Psi_\infty(b) = E_X\left(F_0(h(X,b_0))\mathbb{1}_{(h(X,b)>0)} + [1 - F_0(h(X,b_0))]\,\mathbb{1}_{(h(X,b)<0)}\right).$$

Lemma 8.4: *We have $\Psi_\infty(b) \leq \Psi(b_0)$, $\forall b$, with a strict inequality if $b \neq b_0$.*

PROOF: We have

$$\begin{aligned}\Psi_\infty(b_0) - \Psi_\infty(b) &= E_X\big((\mathbb{1}_{(h(X,b_0)>0)} - \mathbb{1}_{(h(X,b)>0)})F_0(h(X,b_0))\\ &\quad +(\mathbb{1}_{(h(X,b_0)<0)} - \mathbb{1}_{(h(X,b)<0)})[1 - F_0(h(X,b_0))]\big)\end{aligned}$$

$$\begin{aligned}&= E_X\big((\mathbb{1}_{(h(X,b_0)>0)}\mathbb{1}_{(h(X,b)<0)} - \mathbb{1}_{(h(X,b_0)<0)}\mathbb{1}_{(h(X,b)>0)})F_0(h(X,b_0))\\ &+(\mathbb{1}_{(h(X,b_0)<0)}\mathbb{1}_{(h(X,b)>0)} - \mathbb{1}_{(h(X,b_0)>0)}\mathbb{1}_{(h(X,b)<0)})[1 - F_0(h(X,b_0))]\big).\end{aligned}$$

Hence

$$\begin{aligned}\Psi_\infty(b_0) - \Psi_\infty(b) &= E_X\big(\mathbb{1}_{(h(X,b_0)<0)}\mathbb{1}_{(h(X,b)>0)}[1 - 2F_0(h(X,b_0))]\\ &\quad +\mathbb{1}_{(h(X,b_0)>0)}\mathbb{1}_{(h(X,b)<0)}[2F_0(h(X,b_0)) - 1]\big).\end{aligned}$$

Since the median of the cdf F_0 is unique and equal to zero, we have

$$F_0(h(X,b_0)) < \frac{1}{2}, \quad \text{if } h(X,b_0) < 0,$$

$$F_0(h(X,b_0)) > \frac{1}{2}, \quad \text{if } h(X,b_0) > 0.$$

Hence we have established the nonnegativity of $\Psi_\infty(b_0) - \Psi_\infty(b)$.

This quantity is equal to zero if and only if

$$\begin{aligned}\mathbb{1}_{(h(x,b_0)<0)}\mathbb{1}_{(h(x,b)>0)} &= 0\\ \mathbb{1}_{(h(x,b_0)>0)}\mathbb{1}_{(h(x,b)<0)} &= 0, \quad \forall\, x.\end{aligned}$$

Since b is identified from the sign of the conditional mean, this implies that $b = b_0$. □

Consistency of the maximum score estimator follows directly from Lemma 8.4.

b) Asymptotic Distribution

The asymptotic distribution of the maximum score estimator is not normal and its rate of convergence is of the order $n^{-1/3}$. This can be explained by the fact that the proof used for establishing the asymptotic distribution (8.26) of the least absolute deviations estimator is no longer applicable here. This is so because that proof relies on the first-order conditions which require that the criterion function is continuous and right differentiable. Here the objective function is given by

$$\Psi(Y, X; b) = \mathbb{1}_{(Y>0)}\mathbb{1}_{(h(X,b)>0)} + \mathbb{1}_{(Y<0)}\mathbb{1}_{(h(X,b)<0)}, \tag{8.29}$$

which is discontinuous at values of b such that $h(X, b) = 0$.

8.5.4 Consistent Estimators of Parameters Appearing in the Conditional Median

In Section 8.4.2 we have characterized the pseudo maximum likelihood estimators that are consistent for the parameters appearing in the conditional mean of Y given X. A similar analysis can be followed to characterize the estimators that are consistent for the parameters appearing in the conditional median. As before, we require that consistency holds for any conditional distribution of the error term, any distribution of the exogenous variables, and any possible value of the parameters. When b is identified, the true parameter value b_0 is characterized by the condition

$$E_0\left(1_{Y\leq h(X,b_0)} - \frac{1}{2}\right) = 0.$$

If the M-estimator that is based on the function $\Psi(Y, h(X, b))$ is consistent, then b_0 must be a solution to the first-order conditions associated with the corresponding asymptotic problem. That is, b_0 must satisfy

$$E_X E_0 \frac{\partial^+ \Psi(Y, h(X, b_0))}{\partial b} = 0.$$

In the special case where there are no exogenous variables and the parameter of interest is the median itself, it is readily seen that the functions Ψ leading to consistent M-estimators must satisfy the property

$$E_0\left(1_{Y\leq b_0} - \frac{1}{2}\right) = 0 \Rightarrow E\frac{\partial^+ \Psi(Y, b_0)}{\partial b} = 0,$$

for every continuous distribution with median b_0. From Lemma 8.1 it follows that there must exists a function λ of the parameter b such that

$$\frac{\partial^+ \Psi(Y,b)}{\partial b} = \lambda(b)\left(1_{Y \leq b} - \frac{1}{2}\right), \quad \forall\, y, b.$$

In addition, note that the first derivative of the objective function is given asymptotically by

$$\frac{\partial E_0 \Psi(Y,b)}{\partial b} = E_0 \frac{\partial^+ \Psi(Y,b)}{\partial b} = \lambda(b)\left(P_0(Y \leq b) - \frac{1}{2}\right).$$

Assuming to simplify that λ is differentiable in b, the second-order conditions associated with an extremum imply that

$$\begin{aligned} \frac{\partial^2 E_0 \Psi(Y,b_0)}{\partial b^2} &= \frac{\partial \lambda(b_0)}{\partial b}\left(P_0(Y \leq b_0) - \frac{1}{2}\right) + \lambda(b_0) f_0(0) \\ &= \lambda(b_0) f_0(0) \geq 0, \end{aligned}$$

where f_0 is the density of the error term $Y - b_0$. This second partial derivative is nonnegative when the function λ is. To summarize, we have obtained a neccessary form for the objective function.

Property 8.23: *Under suitable regularity conditions, criterion functions Ψ leading to M-estimators that are consistent for the parameters appearing in the conditional median must be of the form*

$$\frac{\partial^+ \Psi(y,h)}{\partial h} = \lambda(h)\left(\mathbb{1}_{y \leq h} - \frac{1}{2}\right),$$

where $\lambda(h) \geq 0$.

Integrating both sides of the preceding equality, we can obtain an equivalent condition on the criterion function Ψ itself. Specifically, being nonnegative, the function λ can be interpreted as a density with respect to Lebesgue measure of a nonnegative measure with cumulative function Λ. Then we can write

$$\frac{\partial^+ \Psi(y,h)}{\partial h} = \begin{cases} -\frac{1}{2}\lambda(h), & \text{if } h < y, \\ \frac{1}{2}\lambda(h), & \text{if } h \geq y. \end{cases}$$

Integrating with respect to h gives

$$\Psi(y,h) = \begin{cases} -\frac{1}{2}\Lambda(h) + C(y), & \text{if } h < y, \\ \frac{1}{2}\Lambda(h) - \Lambda(y) + C(y), & \text{if } h \geq y, \end{cases}$$

where $C(y)$ denotes an integration constant which is a function of y but independent of h. Changing this integration constant gives

$$\Psi(y,h) = \begin{cases} -\frac{1}{2}(\Lambda(h) - \Lambda(y)) + C^*(y), & \text{if } h < y, \\ \frac{1}{2}(\Lambda(h) - \Lambda(y)) + C^*(y), & \text{if } h \geq y, \end{cases}$$

where $C^*(y) = C(y) - \Lambda(y)/2$.

The function Λ is nondecreasing. Thus the criterion function Ψ can be written as

$$\Psi(y,h) = \frac{1}{2}|\Lambda(h) - \Lambda(y)| + C^*(y). \tag{8.30}$$

It is easily verified that these forms for Ψ are sufficient in the sense that they lead to M-estimators that are consistent. To summarize, we have established the following property.

Property 8.24: *M-estimators that are consistent for the parameter b appearing in the conditional median $h(X,b)$ are obtained as solutions to*

$$\min_b \sum_{i=1}^{n} |\Lambda(Y_i) - \Lambda(h(X_i,b))|,$$

where Λ is the cumulative function of a nonnegative measure on $\mathbb{R}$.

Remark 8.4: If the median of Y_i is $h(X_i, b_0)$, it follows from B.15 that the median of $\Lambda(Y_i)$ is $\Lambda(h(X_i, b_0))$ because Λ is nondecreasing. Hence the consistent M-estimators are the least absolute deviations estimators applied to the variables $\Lambda(Y_i)$.

Example 8.23: When the measure associated to Λ is the Lebesgue measure, the criterion function is $\sum_{i=1}^{n} |Y_i - h(X_i, b)|$. Thus we obtain the usual LAD estimator.

Example 8.24: In the limiting case where the measure associated with Λ is the distribution with mass point at zero, then the criterion function is

$$\begin{aligned} & \sum_{i=1}^{n} |\mathbb{1}_{(Y_i \geq 0)} - \mathbb{1}_{(h(X_i,b) \geq 0)}| \\ &= \sum_{i=1}^{n} \left(\mathbb{1}_{(Y_i \geq 0)} \mathbb{1}_{(h(X_i,b)<0)} + \mathbb{1}_{(Y_i<0)} \mathbb{1}_{(h(X_i,b) \geq 0)}\right) \\ &= n - \sum_{i=1}^{n} \left(\mathbb{1}_{(Y_i \geq 0)} \mathbb{1}_{(h(X_i,b) \geq 0)} + \mathbb{1}_{(Y_i<0)} \mathbb{1}_{(h(X_i,b)<0)}\right) \\ &= n - S(b). \end{aligned}$$

Hence minimizing this criterion function is equivalent to maximizing the score function. Thus we obtain the maximum score estimator.

8.6 Appendix

Proof of Lemma 8.1:
Step 1: Let Q be a probability distribution on $\mathbb{R}^G$ such that $E_Q g_k = \int g_k dQ$ exists for every $k = 1, \ldots, K$. Let $\varepsilon_k = +1$ if $E_Q g_k \leq 0$ and $\varepsilon_k = +2$ otherwise. Consider the probability distribution defined by

$$\Pi = \alpha_0 Q + \sum_{k=1}^{K} \alpha_k P_{\varepsilon_k, k}, \quad \sum_{k=0}^{K} \alpha_k = 1, \ \alpha_k \geq 0, \ k = 0, \ldots, K.$$

Given the definition of the probability distributions $P_{\varepsilon_k, k}$ (Lemma 8.1-(i)), we have

$$E_\Pi g_k = \alpha_0 E_Q g_k + \alpha_k \, E_{P_{\varepsilon_k, k}} g_k.$$

Thus we can choose α_k such that

$$\frac{\alpha_k}{\alpha_0} = -\frac{E_Q g_k}{E_{P_{\varepsilon_k, k}} g_k}, \quad k = 1, \ldots, K \quad \text{and} \sum_{k=0}^{k} \alpha_k = 1.$$

With this choice of α_k's, we obtain

$$E_\Pi g_k = 0, \quad k = 1, \ldots, K,$$

and from assumption (ii) of Lemma 8.1

$$E_\Pi h = 0.$$

The latter equality can be written as

$$E_Q h + \sum_{k=1}^{K} \frac{\alpha_k}{\alpha_0} E_{P_{\varepsilon_k, k}} \, h = 0,$$

or equivalently as

$$E_Q h - \sum_{k=1}^{K} \frac{E_Q g_k}{E_{P_{\varepsilon_k, k}} g_k} \, E_{P_{\varepsilon_k, k}} h = 0,$$

or equivalently as

$$E_Q\left(h - \sum_{k=1}^{K} \lambda_k g_k\right) = 0,$$

where

$$\lambda_k = \frac{E_{P_{\varepsilon_k,k}} h}{E_{P_{\varepsilon_k,k}} g_k}.$$

Step 2: We shall show that every λ_k does not depend on the value taken by ε_k. Consider a convex combination of P_{1k} and P_{2k}

$$P = \alpha P_{1k} + (1-\alpha)P_{2k}, \quad 0 < \alpha < 1.$$

By definition of P_{ik}, $i = 1, 2$, we have

$$E_P g_j = 0, \quad \forall\, j \neq k.$$

But

$$E_P g_k = \alpha E_{P_{1k}} g_k + (1-\alpha) E_{P_{2k}} g_k$$

is equal to zero by choosing α such that

$$\frac{\alpha}{1-\alpha} = -\frac{E_{P_{2k}} g_k}{E_{P_{1k}} g_k}.$$

Hence, with this choice of α, we have

$$E_p h = 0.$$

i.e.

$$\alpha E_{P_{1k}} h + (1-\alpha) E_{P_{2k}} h = 0.$$

This implies

$$\frac{E_{P_{2k}} h}{E_{P_{1k}} h} = -\frac{\alpha}{1-\alpha} = \frac{E_{P_{2k}} g_k}{E_{P_{1k}} g_k}.$$

It follows immediately that the two possible values for λ_k are equal for every $k = 1, \ldots, K$.

Step 3: Steps 1 and 2 imply that for every probability distribution Q such that the expectations $E_Q g_k$, $k = 1, \ldots, K$ exist, we have

$$E_Q\left(h - \sum_{k=1}^{K} \lambda_k g_k\right) = 0,$$

where the λ_k's are some constants independent of Q. Considering Dirac mass distributions for instance, it follows that

$$h(y) = \sum_{k=1}^{K} \lambda_k g_k(y)$$

for every y.

8.7 Exercises

EXERCISE 8.1: Let $f(y;m) = \exp(A(m) + B(y) + C(m)y)$ be a linear exponential density with mean m. Differentiating with respect to m the equalities $\int f(y;m)d\mu(y) = 1$ and $\int yf(y;m)d\mu(y) = m$, prove that $dC/dm = \mathbf{\Sigma}^{-1}(m)$, where $\mathbf{\Sigma}(m)$ is the variance covariance matrix of the probability density $f(y;m)$.

EXERCISE 8.2: Consider a Poisson model of the form

$$Y_i \sim P(\exp(a_0 + X_i^* b_0^* + \varepsilon_i)),$$

where $E \exp \varepsilon_i = 1$, $V \exp \varepsilon_i = \eta_0^2$, and X_i^* is a row vector. Suppose that the variables X_i^* are independent and identically normally distributed $N(0, \mathbf{I})$.

a) Compute the matrix $\mathbf{A}$ defined by

$$\mathbf{A} = E\left(\begin{pmatrix} 1 \\ X^{*\prime} \end{pmatrix} (1, X^*) \exp\theta(a_0 + X^* b_0^*)\right),$$

and show that

$$\mathbf{A} = \exp\left(-\theta a_0 - \frac{\theta^2 \|b_0^*\|^2}{2}\right) \begin{pmatrix} 1 + \theta^2\|b_0^*\|^2 & -\theta b_0^{*\prime} \\ -\theta b_0^* & \mathbf{I} \end{pmatrix}.$$

b) Find the asymptotic variance covariance matrices of the PML estimators of b_0^* based on (i) the normal distribution, (ii) the Poisson distribution, and (iii) the Gamma distribution.

c) Conclude that the nonlinear least squares estimator is dominated by PML estimators of the type (ii) or (iii). Give a necessary and sufficient condition on a_0, b_0^*, and η_0^2 for the PML estimator based on the Poisson distribution to be asymptotically more efficient than the PML estimator based on the Gamma distribution.

EXERCISE 8.3: Consider the model

$$\begin{aligned}
&Y_i = h(X_i, b) + u_i,\\
&E(u_i \mid X_i) = 0,\\
&V(u_i \mid X_i) = \omega^2(X_i, b)\gamma.
\end{aligned}$$

Prove that if $\omega^2(X_i, b) = 1$ or $\omega^2(X_i, b) = h^2(X_i, b)$, then a quasi generalized PML estimator can be obtained as an appropriate (one step) PML estimator.

EXERCISE 8.4: Consider an econometric model defined by its first two moments

$$Y_i = h(X_i, b_0) + u_i, \quad \text{with} \quad Eu_i = 0, \quad \text{and } Vu_i = \omega^2(X_i, \beta_0).$$

The parameters are estimated by a PML method based on the family of densities

$$f(y; m, \sigma^2) = \exp(A(m, \sigma^2) + B(y) + C(m, \sigma^2)y + D(m, \sigma^2)y^2),$$

with mean m and variance σ^2.

a) Determine the limit of the objective function

$$\frac{1}{n}\sum_{i=1}^{n} f(Y_i; h(X_i, b), \omega^2(X_i, \beta)),$$

when n increases to infinity.

b) Find conditions on the functions A, C, and D for m and σ^2 to be the mean and variance of the density $f(y; m, \sigma^2)$.

c) Show that the limit objective function is maximized when we have $h(X, b) = h(X, b_0)$ and $\omega^2(X, \beta) = \omega^2(X, \beta_0)$. Conclude.

EXERCISE 8.5: Give a sufficient condition for a quasi generalized PML estimator to be asymptotically efficient.

EXERCISE 8.6: Let θ be a real number between zero and one. Let Y_i, $i = 1, \ldots, n$, be independent and identically distributed random variables with an absolutely continuous distribution F_0 on $\mathbb{R}$ and a strictly positive density.

Consider a solution $\hat{b}_n$ to the problem

$$\min_b \sum_{i=1}^{n} (Y_i - b) \left(\theta \mathbb{1}_{Y_i > b} - (1-\theta)\mathbb{1}_{Y_i < b}\right).$$

a) Verify that, under suitable regularity conditions, such an estimator is consistent for the quantile of the distribution F_0 associated with θ, i.e., for $F_0^{-1}(\theta)$.

b) What can be said in the special case $\theta = 1/2$?

c) Verify that the asymptotic distribution of this estimator is normal and find its asymptotic variance.

EXERCISE 8.7: Consider a regression model $Y_i = h(X_i, b_0) + u_i$, $i = 1, \ldots, n$, where the variables (X_i, Y_i) are independent and identically distributed and the distribution of u_i is symmetric about zero.

a) Let Ψ be an even function. Find conditions on Ψ which ensure that an estimator which is a solution to

$$\min_b \sum_{i=1}^{n} \Psi(Y_i - h(X_i, b)),$$

is consistent.

b) Discuss the use of a PML estimator of b based on a (misspecified) distribution of the error term that belongs to the family of *Sargan distributions*. These distributions are absolutely continuous on $\mathbb{R}$ with densities of the form

$$f(u) = \frac{\alpha}{4}(1 + \alpha|u|)\exp(-\alpha|u|).$$

Study how the asymptotic variance of such an estimator varies as the nuisance parameter α varies.

8.8 References

Amemiya, T. (1982). "Two Stage Least Absolute Deviations Estimators," *Econometrica*, 50, 689–711.

Amemiya, T. (1985). *Advanced Econometrics*, Blackwell.

Bassett, G.J. and Koenker, R. (1978). "Asymptotic Theory of Least Absolute Error Regression," *Journal of the American Statistical Association*, 73, 618–622.

Burguete, J., Gallant, R., and Souza, G. (1982). "On Unification of the Asymptotic Theory of Nonlinear Econometric Methods," *Econometric Review*, 1, 151–190.

Cosslett, S. (1983). "Distribution Free Maximum Likelihood Estimator of the Binary Choice Model," *Econometrica*, 51, 765–782.

Gallant, R.A. (1987). *Nonlinear Statistical Models*, Wiley.

Goldfeld, S. and Quandt, R. (1972). *Nonlinear Methods in Econometrics*, North-Holland.

Gourieroux, C., Monfort, A., and Renault, E. (1987). "Consistent M-Estimators in a Semi–Parametric Model," CEPREMAP DP 8720.

Gourieroux, C., Monfort, A., and Trognon, A. (1984). "Pseudo Maximum Likelihood Methods: Theory," *Econometrica*, 52, 681–700.

Huber, P.J. (1965). "The Behavior of Maximum Likelihood Estimates under Nonstandard Conditions," in J. Neyman, ed., *Proceedings of the Fifth Berkeley Symposium*, 1, 221–233. Berkeley: University of California Press.

Huber, P.J. (1981). *Robust Statistics*, Wiley.

Jennrich, R. (1969). "Asymptotic Properties of Nonlinear Least Squares Estimators," *The Annals of Mathematical Statistics*, 40, 633–643.

Malinvaud, E. (1970). "The Consistency of Nonlinear Regressions," *The Annals of Mathematical Statistics*, 41, 956–969.

Manski, C.F. (1975). "The Maximum Score Estimation of the Stochastic Utility Model of Choice," *Journal of Econometrics*, 3, 205–228.

Manski, C.F. (1985). "Semiparametric Analysis of Discrete Response: Asymptotic Properties of the Maximum Score Estimator," *Journal of Econometrics*, 27, 313–333.

White, H. (1981). "Consequences and Detection of Misspecified Nonlinear Regression Models," *Journal of the American Statistical Association*, 76, 419–433.

White, H. (1981). "Maximum Likelihood Estimation of Misspecified Models," *Econometrica*, 50, 1–25.

CHAPTER 9

Methods of Moments and Their Generalizations

It is frequently difficult to estimate directly the parameters of interest. An alternative method consists in:

- finding functions of the parameters, i.e., *auxiliary parameters* that can be easily estimated consistently,
- combining appropriately the estimates of the auxiliary parameters to approximate the parameters of interest.

This method is illustrated in the next examples, which concern sampling models, i.e., models where the observations $Y_1, \ldots, Y_n$ are independent and identically distributed P_θ, $\theta \in \Theta \subset I\!R^p$. To estimate θ, the auxiliary parameters are typically chosen to be the first moments of the observations. This explains the name of the method.

Specifically, if the first p moments $b_1(\theta) = E_\theta\, Y, \ldots, b_p(\theta) = E_\theta(Y^p)$ are in a bijective relationship with θ, then, in a first step, we can estimate the auxiliary parameters $b_1, \ldots, b_p$ by the sample moments

$$\hat{b}_{1n} = \frac{1}{n}\sum_{i=1}^{n} Y_i, \ldots, \hat{b}_{pn} = \frac{1}{n}\sum_{i=1}^{n} Y_i^p.$$

Then, in a second step, we can obtain a consistent estimator of θ by

$$\hat{\theta}_n = b^{-1}(\hat{b}_n).$$

Such a method is a *method of moments.*

Example 9.1: Consider the logistic distribution P_θ with density

$$\frac{\exp -(y-\theta)}{(1+\exp -(y-\theta))^2}.$$

The maximum likelihood estimator of θ cannot be determined explicitly. An alternative estimation method consists in using the first-order moment which is $b_1 = E_\theta Y = \theta$. Thus the method of moments estimator based on b_1 is

$$\hat{\theta}_n = \hat{b}_{1n} = \bar{Y}_n.$$

Example 9.2: Let P_θ be the uniform distribution $U_{[\theta_1,\theta_2]}$. Its first two moments are

$$b_1 = E_\theta Y = \frac{\theta_1+\theta_2}{2},$$

and

$$b_2 = E_\theta(Y^2) = \frac{\theta_2^2+\theta_1^2+\theta_1\,\theta_2}{3}.$$

The method of moments estimators are by solving

$$\begin{aligned}
\hat{b}_{1n} &= \bar{Y}_n = \frac{\hat{\theta}_{1n}+\hat{\theta}_{2n}}{2},\\
\hat{b}_{2n} &= (\bar{Y^2})_n = \frac{\hat{\theta}_{2n}^2+\hat{\theta}_{1n}^2+\hat{\theta}_{1n}\,\hat{\theta}_{2n}}{3},
\end{aligned}$$

where $\hat{\theta}_{1n} < \hat{\theta}_{2n}$. They are given by

$$\begin{aligned}
\hat{\theta}_{1n} &= \hat{b}_{1n} - \sqrt{3(\hat{b}_{2n}-\hat{b}_{1n}^2)},\\
\hat{\theta}_{2n} &= \hat{b}_{1n} + \sqrt{3(\hat{b}_{2n}-\hat{b}_{1n}^2)}.
\end{aligned}$$

Consideration of the first p moments may lead to a substantial loss of information and hence to estimators of θ that are relatively inefficient asymptotically. Thus it may be preferable to retain a number H of moments that is larger than the number p of parameters of interest. Then the main difficulty is to find a suitable method for solving approximately the system of equations relating the parameters of interest to the estimates $\hat{b}_n$ of the auxiliary parameters since this system has more equations (H) than unknowns (p).

In the following sections, we shall propose two methods that extend the method of moments. These are the *asymptotic least squares method* and the *generalized method of moments.*

9.1 Asymptotic Least Squares

9.1.1 Parameters of Interest and Auxiliary Parameters

Let $Y_1, \ldots, Y_n$ be n observations of which the distribution belongs to a family indexed by a parameter vector $\theta \in \Theta \subset \mathbb{R}^p$. We are interested in estimating a K-dimensional function of the parameter vector θ

$$a = a(\theta) \in \mathcal{A} = a(\Theta) \subset \mathbb{R}^K. \tag{9.1}$$

To do so, we introduce the H auxiliary parameters

$$b = b(\theta) \in \mathcal{B} = b(\Theta) \subset \mathbb{R}^H. \tag{9.2}$$

The latter parameters are related to the parameters of interest through a system of implicit equations. This system is of the form

$$g(b, a) = 0, \tag{9.3}$$

and contains G equations satisfying

$$g(b(\theta), a) = 0 \Rightarrow a = a(\theta), \; \forall\, \theta \in \Theta. \tag{9.4}$$

The latter condition simply means that the parameters of interest a must be determined without ambiguity from the auxiliary parameters b. The system (9.3) is sometimes called the *system of estimating equations.*

Estimators of the auxiliary parameters are assumed to exist and to be consistent and asymptotically normally distributed. That is, we assume that there exists a sequence of estimators $\hat{b}_n$ of b such that

$$\begin{cases} \hat{b}_n \overset{n\to\infty}{\to} b_0 = b(\theta_0) \quad P_{\theta_0}\text{--almost surely} \\[2ex] \sqrt{n}(\hat{b}_n - b(\theta_0)) \xrightarrow{d} N(0, \mathbf{\Omega}(\theta_0)), \end{cases} \tag{9.5}$$

as $n \to \infty$, where θ_0 denotes the true parameter value.

9.1.2 The Estimation Principle

The estimation principle consists in estimating the parameters of interest a by forcing the G constraints

$$g(\hat{b}_n, a) = 0,$$

to be satisfied approximately.

Definition 9.1: *Let* $\mathbf{S}_n$ *be a symmetric positive definite matrix that possibly depends on the observations. An asymptotic least squares estimator associated with* $\mathbf{S}_n$ *is a solution* $\tilde{a}_n(\mathbf{S}_n)$ *to the problem*

$$\min_{a \in \mathcal{A}} g(\hat{b}_n, a)' \, \mathbf{S}_n \, g(\hat{b}_n, a).$$

Thus the asymptotic least squares estimator $\tilde{a}_n(\mathbf{S}_n)$ renders the constraints $g(\hat{b}_n, a)$ closest to zero in the metric associated with the scalar product defined by $\mathbf{S}_n$.

Theorem 9.1: *Under the following conditions:*

H1: $\mathcal{A}$ *is a compact set,*

H2: as $n \to \infty$, $\mathbf{S}_n \to \mathbf{S}_0$, P_{θ_0}−almost surely, *where* $\mathbf{S}_0$ *is a nonstochastic positive definite matrix,*

H3: $a(\theta_0)$ *satisfies*

$$g(b(\theta_0), a)'\mathbf{S}_0 g(b(\theta_0), a) = 0 \Rightarrow a = a(\theta_0),$$

H4: the function g *is continuous,*

then the asymptotic least squares estimator $\tilde{a}_n(\mathbf{S}_n)$ *exists and strongly converges to* $a(\theta_0)$.

PROOF: Under the assumptions of the theorem the function $a \mapsto g(\hat{b}_n, a)' \mathbf{S}_n g(\hat{b}_n, a)$ is continuous on the compact set $\mathcal{A}$. It follows that the estimator $\tilde{a}_n(\mathbf{S}_n)$ exists because the associated optimization problem has a solution.

Next, consider the sequence $\tilde{a}_n(\mathbf{S}_n)$ for a given sequence of observations $y_1, \ldots, y_n$. Since the sequence $\tilde{a}_n(\mathbf{S}_n)$ belongs to the compact set $\mathcal{A}$, there exists a subsequence $\tilde{a}_{n_j}(\mathbf{S}_{n_j})$ converging to a value $a_\infty(y) \in \mathcal{A}$. Since

$$g(\hat{b}_{n_j}, \tilde{a}_{n_j}(\mathbf{S}_{n_j}))'\mathbf{S}_{n_j} g(\hat{b}_{n_j}, \tilde{a}_{n_j}(\mathbf{S}_{n_j})) \leq g(\hat{b}_{n_j}, a(\theta_0))'\mathbf{S}_{n_j} g(\hat{b}_{n_j}, a(\theta_0))$$

because $\tilde{a}_{n_j}(\mathbf{S}_{n_j})$ is a solution to the minimization problem, taking the limit, it follows that

$$g(b(\theta_0), a_\infty)'\mathbf{S}_0 g(b(\theta_0), a_\infty) \leq g(b(\theta_0), a(\theta_0))'\mathbf{S}_0 g(b(\theta_0), a(\theta_0)).$$

Because the right-hand side of the latter inequality is zero, it follows that the left-hand side must also be equal to zero. Then Assumption H3 implies that $a_\infty = a(\theta_0)$. In particular, $a_\infty(y)$ is nonrandom. Finally, it suffices to note that every converging subsequence of $\tilde{a}_n(\mathbf{S}_n)$ converges to the same limit $a(\theta_0)$. Because $\mathcal{A}$ is compact, it follows that the sequence $\tilde{a}_n(\mathbf{S}_n)$ itself converges to $a(\theta_0)$. □

Theorem 9.2: *If in addition to the conditions of Theorem 9.1, it is assumed that*

H5: g is twice continuously differentiable,

H6: the true value θ_0 is such that $a(\theta_0)$ belongs to the interior of $\mathcal{A}$,

H7: the matrix $\partial g'(b(\theta_0), a(\theta_0))/\partial a\ \mathbf{S}_0 \partial g(b(\theta_0), a(\theta_0))/\partial a'$ is nonsingular, which implies that $K \leq G$,

then the estimator $\tilde{a}_n(\mathbf{S}_n)$ is asymptotically normally distributed with

$$\sqrt{n}(\tilde{a}_n(\mathbf{S}_n) - a(\theta_0)) \xrightarrow{d} N(0, \mathbf{\Sigma}(\mathbf{S}_0)),$$

as $n \to \infty$, where

$$\mathbf{\Sigma}(\mathbf{S}_0) = \left(\frac{\partial g'}{\partial a}\mathbf{S}_0\frac{\partial g}{\partial a'}\right)^{-1}\frac{\partial g'}{\partial a}\mathbf{S}_0\frac{\partial g}{\partial b'}\mathbf{\Omega}\frac{\partial g'}{\partial b}\mathbf{S}_0\frac{\partial g}{\partial a'}\left(\frac{\partial g'}{\partial a}\mathbf{S}_0\frac{\partial g}{\partial a'}\right)^{-1},$$

and the various matrices are evaluated at θ_0, $a(\theta_0)$ and $b(\theta_0)$.

PROOF: When the number of observations n is sufficiently large, the estimator $\tilde{a}_n(\mathbf{S}_n)$ satisfies the first-order conditions

$$\left[\frac{\partial g(\hat{b}_n, a)'\mathbf{S}_n g(\hat{b}_n, a)}{\partial a}\right]_{a=\tilde{a}_n(\mathbf{S}_n)} = 0,$$

i.e.

$$\frac{\partial g'(\hat{b}_n, \tilde{a}_n(\mathbf{S}_n))}{\partial a}\mathbf{S}_n g(\hat{b}_n, \tilde{a}_n(\mathbf{S}_n)) = 0.$$

Now we can take a Taylor expansion of these equations because $\mathbf{S}_n$, $\hat{b}_n$, and $\tilde{a}_n(\mathbf{S}_n)$ converge to

$$\mathbf{S}_0, \quad b_0 = b(\theta_0), \quad a_0 = a(\theta_0),$$

respectively, as n increases to infinity. Using the fact that $g(b(\theta_0), a(\theta_0)) = 0$, we obtain

$$\sqrt{n}\left(\frac{\partial g'}{\partial a}\mathbf{S}_0\frac{\partial g}{\partial a'}(\tilde{a}_n(\mathbf{S}_n) - a_0) + \frac{\partial g'}{\partial a}\mathbf{S}_0\frac{\partial g}{\partial b'}(\hat{b}_n - b_0)\right) \# 0,$$

or equivalently

$$\sqrt{n}\,(\tilde{a}_n(\mathbf{S}_n) - a_0) \# - \left(\frac{\partial g'}{\partial a}\mathbf{S}_0\frac{\partial g}{\partial a'}\right)^{-1}\frac{\partial g'}{\partial a}\mathbf{S}_0\frac{\partial g}{\partial b'}\sqrt{n}(\hat{b}_n - b_0).$$

Then it suffices to use the asymptotic normality of $\sqrt{n}(\hat{b}_n - b_0)$ to establish that $\sqrt{n}(\tilde{a}_n(\mathbf{S}_n) - a_0)$ is asymptotically normally distributed with mean zero and variance covariance matrix $\mathbf{\Sigma}(\mathbf{S}_0)$. □

The preceding results show that there is a large number of consistent and asymptotically normally distributed estimators, each one corresponding to a particular sequence of matrices $\mathbf{S}_n$. It is interesting to know whether there exists an optimal sequence of matrices $\mathbf{S}_n$.

9.1.3 Best Asymptotic Least Squares Estimators

Property 9.1 *Under Assumptions H1–H7, if*

H8: the matrices

$$\frac{\partial g}{\partial b'}\mathbf{\Omega}\frac{\partial g'}{\partial b} \quad \text{and} \quad \frac{\partial g'}{\partial a}\left(\frac{\partial g}{\partial b'}\mathbf{\Omega}\frac{\partial g'}{\partial b}\right)^{-1}\frac{\partial g}{\partial a'}$$

are nonsingular where $\mathbf{\Omega}$, $\partial g'/\partial a$, and $\partial g'/\partial b$ are evaluated at θ_0 (this implies that $K \leq G \leq H$),

then best asymptotic least squares estimators exist. They correspond to sequences of matrices $\mathbf{S}_n^*$ converging to

$$\mathbf{S}_0^* = \left(\frac{\partial g}{\partial b'}\mathbf{\Omega}\frac{\partial g'}{\partial b}\right)^{-1}.$$

Their asymptotic variance covariance matrices are equal and given by

$$\mathbf{\Sigma}(\mathbf{S}^*) = \left(\frac{\partial g'}{\partial a}\left(\frac{\partial g}{\partial b'}\mathbf{\Omega}\frac{\partial g'}{\partial b}\right)^{-1}\frac{\partial g}{\partial a'}\right)^{-1}.$$

PROOF: We need to prove that $\mathbf{\Sigma}(\mathbf{S}_0^*) \preceq \mathbf{\Sigma}(\mathbf{S}_0)$ for every other symmetric positive matrix $\mathbf{S}_0$. This condition can be written as

$$\left(\frac{\partial g'}{\partial a}\left(\frac{\partial g}{\partial b'}\mathbf{\Omega}\frac{\partial g'}{\partial b}\right)^{-1}\frac{\partial g}{\partial a'}\right)^{-1}$$
$$\preceq \left(\frac{\partial g'}{\partial a}\mathbf{S}_0\frac{\partial g}{\partial a'}\right)^{-1}\frac{\partial g'}{\partial a}\mathbf{S}_0\frac{\partial g}{\partial b'}\mathbf{\Omega}\frac{\partial g'}{\partial b}\mathbf{S}_0\frac{\partial g}{\partial a'}\left(\frac{\partial g'}{\partial a}\mathbf{S}_0\frac{\partial g}{\partial a'}\right)^{-1}.$$

Let

$$\mathbf{A} = \left(\frac{\partial g}{\partial b'}\mathbf{\Omega}\frac{\partial g'}{\partial b}\right)^{-1/2}\frac{\partial g}{\partial a'},$$

and

$$\mathbf{B} = \left(\frac{\partial g}{\partial b'}\mathbf{\Omega}\frac{\partial g'}{\partial b}\right)^{1/2}\mathbf{S}_0\frac{\partial g}{\partial a'}.$$

The above condition becomes

$$(\mathbf{A}'\mathbf{A})^{-1} \preceq (\mathbf{A}'\mathbf{B})^{-1}\mathbf{B}'\mathbf{B}(\mathbf{A}'\mathbf{B})^{-1},$$

i.e.

$$\mathbf{A}'\mathbf{A} \succeq \mathbf{A}'\mathbf{B}(\mathbf{B}'\mathbf{B})^{-1}\mathbf{B}'\mathbf{A},$$

i.e.

$$\mathbf{A}'(\mathbf{I} - \mathbf{B}(\mathbf{B}'\mathbf{B})^{-1}\mathbf{B}')\mathbf{A} \succeq 0.$$

The latter inequality is satisfied because $\mathbf{I}-\mathbf{B}(\mathbf{B}'\mathbf{B})^{-1}\mathbf{B}'$ is an orthogonal projection matrix. □

Remark 9.1: When b is estimated, the equations $g(b_0, a_0) = 0$ linking the two types of parameters a and b can be replaced by

$$0 = g(\hat{b}_n, a_0) + u_n.$$

The error term u_n is asymptotically normally distributed with

$$\sqrt{n}u_n = -\sqrt{n}g(\hat{b}_n, a_0) \xrightarrow{d} N(0, (\mathbf{S}_0^*)^{-1}).$$

Thus the optimal asymptotic least squares estimation method reduces to a quasi generalized least squares method applied to the *approximate model*

$$0 = g(\hat{b}_n, a) + u_n, \quad Eu_n = 0, \quad Vu_n = (\mathbf{S}_n^*)^{-1}/n.$$

Indeed, the minimization of the objective function

$$nu_n'\mathbf{S}_n^*u_n \text{ with } \mathbf{S}_n^* \to \mathbf{S}_0^*$$

is identical to the minimization of

$$g(\hat{b}_n, a)'\mathbf{S}_n^* g(\hat{b}_n, a).$$

This interpretation motivates the name of *asymptotic least squares* given to the estimation method.

9.2 Examples

9.2.1 Relations of the Form $b = h(a)$

Since $g(b, a) = -b + h(a)$, the partial derivatives $\partial g/\partial b'$ and $\partial g/\partial a'$ are given by

$$\frac{\partial g}{\partial b'} = -\mathbf{I} \quad \text{and} \quad \frac{\partial g}{\partial a'} = \frac{\partial h}{\partial a'}.$$

Then best asymptotic least squares estimators $\hat{a}_n$ are obtained by minimizing

$$(h(a) - \hat{b}_n)'\mathbf{\Omega}_n^{-1}(h(a) - \hat{b}_n)$$

since $\mathbf{S}_0^* = \mathbf{\Omega}^{-1}$. Their asymptotic variance covariance matrices are

$$V_{as}\sqrt{n}(\hat{a}_n - a_0) = \left(\frac{\partial h'}{\partial a}\mathbf{\Omega}^{-1}\frac{\partial h}{\partial a'}\right)^{-1}. \tag{9.6}$$

9.2.2 Estimation Using the Laplace Transform

Consider a random sample $Y_1, \ldots, Y_n$ drawn from a distribution P_θ, $\theta \in \Theta \subset \mathbb{R}^p$. It is assumed that this distribution has a Laplace transform

$$\Psi(t, \theta) = E_\theta(\exp tY),$$

where t belongs to an interval of $\mathbb{R}$ containing zero.

Clearly, every value of the Laplace transform can be consistently estimated by the corresponding sample moment

$$\hat{\Psi}(t) = \frac{1}{n}\sum_{i=1}^{n}\exp(tY_i).$$

Then, select H points $t_1, \ldots, t_H$ and take as auxiliary parameters the quantities

$$b_h = \Psi(t_h, \theta), \ h = 1, \ldots, H.$$

The corresponding estimators $\hat{b}_h = \hat{\Psi}(t_h)$, $h = 1, \ldots, H$, are consistent and asymptotically normally distributed. The (h, ℓ)-th element of their asymptotic variance covariance matrix $\mathbf{\Omega}$ is

$$\begin{aligned}\mathbf{\Omega}_{h\ell} &= E_\theta(\exp t_h Y \exp t_\ell Y) - E_\theta(\exp t_h Y) E_\theta(\exp t_\ell Y) \\ &= \Psi(t_h + t_\ell, \theta) - \Psi(t_h, \theta)\Psi(t_\ell, \theta).\end{aligned}$$

An optimal asymptotic least squares estimator of θ is obtained as a solution $\theta^*(t_1, \ldots, t_H)$ to the problem

$$\begin{bmatrix} \hat{\Psi}(t_1) - \Psi(t_1, \theta) \\ \vdots \\ \hat{\Psi}(t_H) - \Psi(t_H, \theta) \end{bmatrix}' \hat{\mathbf{\Omega}}^{-1} \begin{bmatrix} \hat{\Psi}(t_1) - \Psi(t_1, \theta) \\ \vdots \\ \hat{\Psi}(t_H) - \Psi(t_H, \theta) \end{bmatrix}, \tag{9.7}$$

where $\hat{\mathbf{\Omega}}_{h\ell} = \hat{\Psi}(t_h + t_\ell) - \hat{\Psi}(t_h)\hat{\Psi}(t_\ell)$.

The method only requires the estimated values $\hat{\Psi}(t)$. The asymptotic variance covariance matrix of the resulting estimator is

$$V_{as}[\sqrt{n}(\hat{\theta}_n(t_1, \ldots, t_H) - \theta)] = \left(\frac{\partial \Psi(t, \theta)'}{\partial \theta} \mathbf{\Omega}^{-1} \frac{\partial \Psi(t, \theta)}{\partial \theta'} \right)^{-1}, \tag{9.8}$$

where

$$\frac{\partial \Psi(t, \theta)}{\partial \theta'} = \left[\frac{\partial \Psi(t_1, \theta)}{\partial \theta}, \ldots, \frac{\partial \Psi(t_H, \theta)}{\partial \theta} \right]'.$$

9.2.3 Exponential Families

Consider a random sample $Y_1, \ldots, Y_n$ drawn from an exponential family with densities

$$f(y; \theta) = C(\theta) h(y) \exp(Q(\theta) T(y)),$$

where $\theta \in \Theta \subset \mathbb{R}^p$.

The (row) function Q takes its values in $\mathbb{R}^H$. It is also assumed that θ is identified. To estimate the parameter vector of interest θ, we can choose the means of the canonical statistics, i.e.

$$b_1 = E_\theta T_1(Y), \ldots, b_H(\theta) = E_\theta T_H(Y),$$

as auxiliary parameters. These auxiliary parameters can be estimated consistently by

$$\hat{b}_n = \frac{1}{n} \sum_{i=1}^{n} T(Y_i). \tag{9.9}$$

Moreover, $\hat{b}_n$ is asymptotically normally distributed with

$$\sqrt{n}(\hat{b}_n - b(\theta)) \xrightarrow{d} N(0, V_\theta T(Y)).$$

We can invoke the properties of exponential families to determine $\partial b'(\theta)/\partial\theta$ and $V_\theta T(Y)$. Specifically, since $\int_\mathcal{Y} \partial f(y;\theta)/\partial\theta \, d\mu(y) = 0$ we have

$$\frac{\partial Q(\theta)}{\partial\theta} E_\theta T(Y) + \frac{\partial \log C(\theta)}{\partial\theta} = 0.$$

It follows that

$$\frac{1}{f(y;\theta)} \frac{\partial f(y;\theta)}{\partial\theta} = \frac{\partial Q(\theta)}{\partial\theta}(T(y) - E_\theta T(Y)).$$

Taking the variance of each side, we obtain the Fisher information matrix

$$\begin{aligned}\mathcal{I}(\theta) &= V_\theta\left[\frac{\partial \log f(Y;\theta)}{\partial\theta}\right] \\ &= \frac{\partial Q(\theta)}{\partial\theta} V_\theta T(Y) \frac{\partial Q'(\theta)}{\partial\theta'}.\end{aligned}$$

On the other hand

$$\begin{aligned}\frac{\partial E_\theta T(Y)'}{\partial\theta} &= \int_\mathcal{Y} \frac{\partial f(y;\theta)}{\partial\theta} T(y)' d\mu(y) \\ &= E_\theta\left(\frac{\partial Q(\theta)}{\partial\theta}(T(Y) - E_\theta T(Y))T(Y)'\right) \\ &= \frac{\partial Q(\theta)}{\partial\theta} V_\theta T(Y).\end{aligned}$$

Therefore the asymptotic variance covariance matrix of the best asymptotic least squares estimator of θ is

$$\begin{aligned}V_{as}\sqrt{n}(\hat{\theta}_n(Y) - \theta) &= \left(\frac{\partial E_\theta T(Y)'}{\partial\theta}(V_\theta T(Y))^{-1}\frac{\partial E_\theta T(Y)}{\partial\theta'}\right)^{-1} \\ &= \left(\frac{\partial Q(\theta)}{\partial\theta} V_\theta T(Y) \frac{\partial Q'(\theta)}{\partial\theta'}\right)^{-1} \\ &= (\mathcal{I}(\theta))^{-1}.\end{aligned}$$

We have established the following property.

Property 9.2: *Best asymptotic least squares estimators of θ based on the means of the canonical statistics are asymptotically efficient, i.e.*

$$V_{as}\left[\sqrt{n}(\hat{\theta}_n(Y) - \theta)\right] = (\mathcal{I}(\theta))^{-1}.$$

In particular, Property 9.2 says that, asymptotically, all relevant information is contained in the mean $E_\theta T(Y)$.

Example 9.3: One has available repeated observations Y_{ik}, $i = 1, \dots, n$, $k = 1, \dots, K$, on a binary $(0-1)$ variable, where K denotes the number of experimental designs $x_k = (x_{k1}, \dots, x_{kp})$, $k = 1, \dots, K$.

It is assumed that the observations are mutually independent with

$$P[Y_{ik} = 1] = \frac{1}{1 + \exp -(x_k\theta)} = p_k(\theta),$$

where θ is a p-dimensional vector, with $p \leq K$. The distribution of $Y_i = (Y_{i1}, \dots, Y_{ik})'$ has density

$$\begin{aligned} f(y;\theta) &= \prod_{k=1}^{K} \left[\frac{1}{1+\exp-(x_k\theta)}\right]^{y_k} \left[\frac{\exp-(x_k\theta)}{1+\exp(-x_k\theta)}\right]^{1-y_k} \\ &= C(\theta)h(y)\exp Q(\theta)T(y), \end{aligned}$$

where

$$\begin{aligned} Q(\theta) &= (Q_1(\theta), \dots, Q_K(\theta)) \\ &= (x_1\theta, \dots, x_K\theta) \\ &= \theta'\mathbf{X}', \end{aligned}$$

$\mathbf{X}' = (x_1', \dots, x_K')$ and $T(y) = (y_1, \dots, y_K)' = y$.

We have

$$\begin{aligned} E_\theta T(Y) &= E_\theta Y \\ &= (p_1(\theta), \dots, p_K(\theta))' \\ &= p(\theta), \end{aligned}$$

and

$$V_\theta T(Y) = \text{diag}\ [p_k(\theta)(1 - p_k(\theta))].$$

For every $k = 1, \dots, K$, the auxiliary parameter $\hat{p}_k(\theta)$ can be estimated by the observed relative frequency $\hat{p}_k = (1/n)\sum_{i=1}^{n} Y_{ik}$, which is the relative number of observations equal to 1 in the kth cell.

Thus a best asymptotic least squares estimator is a solution to

$$\min_\theta\ (\hat{p} - p(\theta))'(\hat{V}_\theta T(Y))^{-1}(\hat{p} - p(\theta)),$$

i.e.

$$\min_\theta \sum_{k=1}^{K} \frac{(\hat{p}_k - p_k(\theta))^2}{\hat{p}_k(1-\hat{p}_k)} = \sum_{k=1}^{K} \left[\frac{(\hat{p}_k - p_k(\theta))^2}{\hat{p}_k} + \frac{(1 - \hat{p}_k - 1 + p_k(\theta))^2}{1 - \hat{p}_k}\right]$$

The objective function is identical to a sum of usual chi-square measures. Thus, in this example, the method reduces to finding the value of the parameter θ for which the distributions $[p_k(\theta), 1 - p_k(\theta)]$ are closest to the empirical distributions $[\hat{p}_k, 1 - \hat{p}_k]$ according to the usual chi-square measure. The latter method is known as the *minimum chi-square method.* From Property 9.2, this method gives an asymptotically efficient estimator.

Example 9.4: Berkson Method

Instead of using the auxiliary parameters $p_k(\theta) = 1/(1+\exp -(x_k\theta))$, one can base an asymptotic least squares method on $b_k(\theta) = x_k\theta = \log(p_k(\theta)/(1 - p_k(\theta)))$.

Consistent estimators of $(b_k(\theta))$ are

$$\hat{b}_k = \log \frac{\hat{p}_k}{1 - \hat{p}_k}.$$

These estimators are mutually independent and asymptotically normally distributed with asymptotic variances

$$\begin{aligned} V_{as}[\sqrt{n}(\hat{b}_k - b_k(\theta))] &= \left(\frac{\partial \log(p_k/(1 - p_k))}{\partial p_k}\right)^2 V_{as}(\sqrt{n}(\hat{p}_k - p_k)) \\ &= \frac{1}{p_k(1 - p_k)}. \end{aligned}$$

See Property B.69.

A best asymptotic least squares estimator based on $b(\theta)$ can be obtained as a solution to

$$\min_\theta \sum_{k=1}^{K} \hat{p}_k(1 - \hat{p}_k) \left(\log \frac{\hat{p}_k}{1 - \hat{p}_k} - x_k\theta\right)^2.$$

It is equal to the weighted least squares estimator in a regression of $\log(\hat{p}_k/(1 - \hat{p}_k))$ on x_k with weights $\hat{p}_k(1 - \hat{p}_k)$. Its explicit expression is

$$\hat{\hat{\theta}}_n = \left(\sum_{k=1}^{K} \hat{p}_k(1 - \hat{p}_k)x'_k x_k\right)^{-1} \sum_{k=1}^{K} \hat{p}_k(1 - \hat{p}_k)x'_k \log \frac{\hat{p}_k}{1 - \hat{p}_k}. \quad (9.10)$$

The reader may verify that this estimator is asymptotically efficient. See Exercises 9.1 and 9.2.

9.2.4 Estimating Equations Linear in the Parameters of Interest

Suppose that the estimating equations are of the form $b_1 = b_2 a$, where b_1 and b_2 are a G-dimensional vector and a $G \times K$ matrix of auxiliary parameters, respectively. Substituting the estimator $\hat{b}_n$ for b, we obtain the approximate system

$$\hat{b}_{1n} = \hat{b}_{2n} a + u_n,$$

where $V_{as}(\sqrt{n} u_n) = V_{as}[\sqrt{n}(\hat{b}_{1n} - \hat{b}_{2n} a)]$.

A best asymptotic least squares estimator can be obtained as a quasi generalized least squares estimator applied to this approximate system.

Example 9.5: Consider the linear model

$$Y_i = X_i a + u_i,\ i = 1, \ldots, n,$$

where $E(u_i \mid X_i) = 0$ and $V(u_i \mid X_i) = \sigma^2$. The parameter a is interpreted as the coefficient vector in the population regression of Y on X. Suppose that the variables (X_i, Y_i), $i = 1, \ldots, n$, are independent and identically distributed. Then the parameter vector a is given by

$$E(X'Y) = E(X'X)a.$$

The cross moments between X and Y can be used as auxiliary parameters. They are estimated consistently by

$$\frac{1}{n}\sum_{i=1}^{n} X_i' Y_i \text{ and } \frac{1}{n}\sum_{i=1}^{n} X_i' X_i.$$

A best asymptotic least squares estimator of a is

$$\begin{aligned} \hat{a}_n &= \left(\frac{1}{n}\sum_{i=1}^{n} X_i' X_i\right)^{-1} \frac{1}{n}\sum_{i=1}^{n} X_i' Y_i \\ &= \left(\sum_{i=1}^{n} X_i' X_i\right)^{-1} \sum_{i=1}^{n} X_i' Y_i. \end{aligned}$$

It is equal to the ordinary least squares estimator of a.

Example 9.6: Consider a stationary process $\{Y_t\}$ with an autoregressive representation of order two, i.e.

$$Y_t = \phi_1 Y_{t-1} + \phi_2 Y_{t-2} + \varepsilon_t,$$

where $\{\varepsilon_t\}$ is a sequence of uncorrelated random variables with mean zero and identical variance. The coefficients ϕ_1 and ϕ_2 are such that the polynomial $1 - \phi_1 z - \phi_2 z^2$ has its roots outside the unit circle. The coefficients ϕ_1 and ϕ_2 can be interpreted as the coefficients in a population regression. They satisfy the system of normal equations

$$\begin{aligned} E(Y_t Y_{t-1}) &= \phi_1 E Y_{t-1}^2 + \phi_2 E(Y_{t-1} Y_{t-2}), \\ E(Y_t Y_{t-2}) &= \phi_1 E(Y_{t-1} Y_{t-2}) + \phi_2 E(Y_{t-2}^2). \end{aligned}$$

Let $\rho(1)$ and $\rho(2)$ denote the first two values of the autocorrelation function of the process Y_t

$$\begin{aligned} \rho(1) &= \frac{E(Y_t Y_{t-1})}{E Y_t^2}, \ \forall\, t, \\ \rho(2) &= \frac{E(Y_t Y_{t-2})}{E Y_t^2}, \ \forall\, t. \end{aligned}$$

The parameters of interest ϕ_1 and ϕ_2 are related to the auxiliary parameters $\rho(1)$ and $\rho(2)$ through the system

$$\begin{aligned} \rho(1) &= \phi_1 + \phi_2 \rho(1), \\ \rho(2) &= \phi_1 \rho(1) + \phi_2. \end{aligned}$$

Let $\hat\rho(1)$ and $\hat\rho(2)$ be consistent estimators of $\rho(1)$ and $\rho(2)$ respectively. For instance

$$\begin{aligned} \hat\rho(1) &= \frac{\sum_2^T Y_t Y_{t-1}}{\sum_1^T Y_t^2}, \\ \hat\rho(2) &= \frac{\sum_3^T Y_t Y_{t-2}}{\sum_1^T Y_t^2}. \end{aligned}$$

Then consistent estimators of ϕ_1 and ϕ_2 can be obtained by solving the so-called *Yule–Walker equations*

$$\begin{aligned} \hat\rho(1) &= \hat\phi_1 + \hat\phi_2 \hat\rho(1), \\ \hat\rho(2) &= \hat\phi_1 \hat\rho(1) + \hat\phi_2. \end{aligned}$$

This gives

$$\begin{aligned} \hat\phi_1 &= \frac{\hat\rho(1) - \hat\rho(1)\hat\rho(2)}{1 - \hat\rho(1)^2}, \\ \hat\phi_2 &= \frac{\hat\rho(2) - \hat\rho(1)^2}{1 - \hat\rho(1)^2}. \end{aligned}$$

Clearly it is possible to improve upon these estimates by considering higher-order autocorrelations. See Exercise 9.3.

9.3 Seemingly Linear Models

One may be tempted to apply ordinary least squares as soon as the relationship between the explained variable and the explanatory variables is linear, i.e., of the form

$$\begin{aligned} Y_i &= \sum_{k=1}^{K} X_{ik} b_{k0} + u_i \\ &= X_i b_0 + u_i, \quad E u_i = 0, \ i = 1, \ldots, n, \end{aligned} \tag{9.11}$$

where Y_i and X_{ik} denote the ith observations on the explained variable and the kth explanatory variable, respectively, b_0 denotes the "true value" of the parameter vector of interest, and the error term u_i associated with the ith observation has mean zero *unconditionally* on X.

Ordinary least squares methods, however, can lead to bad estimators, in particular to inconsistent estimators, even if the relationship between Y and X is of the preceding type. The purpose of this section is to study conditions under which ordinary least squares (OLS) estimators are consistent. In addition, some examples are given where these conditions are not satisfied. In Section 9.4, we shall apply the method of asymptotic least squares estimators to these examples so as to obtain appropriate estimation methods.

9.3.1 Consistency of OLS Estimators

The OLS estimator of b_0, which it is natural to consider in this case, is obtained by regressing Y on X using the n available observations. It is given by

$$\hat{b}_n = (\mathbf{X}_n' \mathbf{X}_n)^{-1} \mathbf{X}_n' Y_n,$$

where the subscript n indicates that the matrix $\mathbf{X}_n$ and the vector Y_n are based on the first n observations. This estimator can also be written as

$$\hat{b}_n = \left(\sum_{i=1}^{n} X_i' X_i \right)^{-1} \sum_{i=1}^{n} X_i' Y_i$$

$$= \left(\frac{1}{n} \sum_{i=1}^{n} X_i' X_i \right)^{-1} \frac{1}{n} \sum_{i=1}^{n} X_i' Y_i,$$

where X_i is a row vector.

To simplify, suppose that the observations (X_i, Y_i), $i = 1, \ldots, n$, are independent and identically distributed with finite second-order moments $EX'X$ and $EX'Y$. Suppose also that $EX'X$ is nonsingular. Then it is readily seen that the OLS estimator converges to

$$b_\infty = (E(X'X))^{-1} E(X'Y). \tag{9.12}$$

That is, $\hat{b}_n$, which is the empirical linear regression coefficient vector of Y_i on X_i, converges to the population linear regression coefficient vector b_∞ of Y on X.

Therefore consistency of the OLS estimator obtains if and only if

$$b_\infty = b_0. \tag{9.13}$$

Substituting $Xb_0 + u$ for Y in the expression for b_∞ gives

$$\begin{aligned} b_\infty &= (E(X'X))^{-1} EX'(Xb_0 + u) \\ &= b_0 + (E(X'X))^{-1} E(X'u). \end{aligned}$$

Thus the consistency condition (9.13) is equivalent to

$$E(X'u) = 0, \tag{9.14}$$

which is interpreted as the orthogonality between the errors and the explanatory variables. Since u has mean zero, the latter condition can also be written as

$$\text{Cov}(X, u) = 0. \tag{9.15}$$

It is satisfied when Xb_0 is the population linear regression of Y on X. Thus we have the next property.

Property 9.3: *When the error term has mean zero, the OLS estimator is consistent if and only if the error term is uncorrelated with the explanatory variables.*

Definition 9.2: *A model of the form $Y_i = X_i b_0 + u_i$ with $Eu_i = 0$ is said to be seemingly linear if* $\text{Cov}(X, u) \neq 0$.

In the following subsection we give some examples of seemingly linear models.

9.3.2 Autoregressive Models With Autocorrelated Errors

Typically, the dynamic feature of an econometric model arises from temporal correlation among the disturbances or inclusion of some lagged endogenous variables among the explanatory variables. In this subsection we consider a model of which the dynamic feature is due to both reasons.

The original model is

$$Y_t = b_0 Y_{t-1} + \nu_t\ , \quad |b_0| < 1, \tag{9.16}$$

where the error term ν_t has an autoregressive representation of order one, namely

$$\nu_t = \rho_0 \nu_{t-1} + \varepsilon_t, \quad |\rho_0| < 1, \tag{9.17}$$

and $\{\varepsilon_t\}$ is a sequence of uncorrelated random variables with mean zero and identical variance $\sigma_0^2 \neq 0$. Thus the error term ν_t has mean zero.

The OLS estimator of b_0 is obtained by regressing Y_t on Y_{t-1}. It is given by

$$\hat{b}_T = \frac{\sum_{t=2}^T Y_t Y_{t-1}}{\sum_{t=2}^T Y_{t-1}^2}.$$

Although the pairs of variables (Y_{t-1}, Y_t) are not independent, it is easy to see that a necessary and sufficient condition for consistency of the ordinary least square estimator is still of the following form:

$$\mathrm{Cov}(Y_{t-1}, \nu_t) = E(Y_{t-1}\nu_t) = 0.$$

This is because

$$\hat{b}_T = b_0 + \frac{\sum_{t=2}^T Y_{t-1}\nu_t}{\sum_{t=2}^T Y_{t-1}^2},$$

which converges to

$$b_\infty = b_0 + \frac{E(Y_{t-1}\nu_t)}{E(Y_{t-1}^2)}$$

by Property B.67.

We need to compute the covariance between Y_{t-1} and ν_t. Since the parameters b_0 and ρ_0 are less than one in absolute value, we can write

$$\begin{aligned} Y_t &= b_0 Y_{t-1} + \nu_t \\ &= \sum_{i=0}^{\infty} (b_0)^i \nu_{t-i}. \end{aligned}$$

Hence

$$\begin{aligned} E(Y_{t-1}\nu_t) &= E\left(\sum_{i=0}^{\infty}(b_0)^i \nu_{t-1-i}\nu_t\right) \\ &= \sum_{i=0}^{\infty}(b_0)^i \mathrm{Cov}(\nu_{t-1-i}, \nu_t). \end{aligned}$$

Since

$$\mathrm{Cov}(\nu_{t-h}, \nu_t) = \frac{\sigma_0^2}{1-(\rho_0)^2}(\rho_0)^h \text{ for } h > 0,$$

we obtain

$$\begin{aligned} E(Y_{t-1}\nu_t) &= \sum_{i=0}^{\infty}(b_0)^i \frac{\sigma_0^2}{1-(\rho_0)^2}(\rho_0)^{1+i} \\ &= \frac{\rho_0\sigma_0^2}{(1-(\rho_0)^2)(1-\rho_0 b_0)}. \end{aligned}$$

Thus the above consistency condition is satisfied if and only if the error terms are uncorrelated, i.e.

$$\hat{b}_T \to b_0 \Leftrightarrow \rho_0 = 0. \tag{9.18}$$

This result shows that, as far as the consistency of the OLS estimator in the linear model is concerned, the lagged endogenous variables can be treated in the same way as the exogenous variables as soon as the error terms are not correlated.

9.3.3 Measurement Errors in the Variables

a) The Problem

We consider a linear model with the usual assumptions. Specifically, let

$$Y_i = b_{00} + X_i b_0 + v_i, \tag{9.19}$$

where the errors are uncorrelated, have mean zero and identical variance, and are uncorrelated with the explanatory variables, i.e., $\mathrm{Cov}(X, v) = 0$.

The variables Y and X are measured with errors. The observations Y_i^* and X_i^* satisfy

$$\begin{aligned} Y_i^* &= Y_i + \varepsilon_i, \\ X_i^* &= X_i + \eta_i, \end{aligned}$$

where ε and η denote measurement errors on Y and X. It is natural to replace the estimation of the original model by the estimation of the model

$$Y_i^* = b_{00} + X_i^* b_0 + u_i, \tag{9.20}$$

where the variables Y and X have been replaced by their observable counterparts.

Suppose that the measurement errors ε_i and η_i are independent of the variables v_j and X_j for $j = 1, \ldots, n$. Suppose also that the pairs (ε_i, η_i), $i = 1, \ldots, n$, are mutually independent and identically distributed with mean zero. Then the error term $u_i = v_i + \varepsilon_i - \eta_i b_0$ has mean zero.

The OLS estimator of b_0 is consistent if and only if the estimator of (b_{00}, b_0) is consistent (see Exercise 9.4). That is, the OLS estimator of b_0 is consistent if and only if the condition $\text{Cov}(X^*, u) = 0$ is satisfied. The latter condition can be written as

$$\text{Cov}(X + \eta, v + \varepsilon - \eta\ b_0) = 0,$$

or equivalently as

$$\text{Cov}(\eta, \varepsilon - \eta\ b_0) = 0.$$

Two special cases are of interest:

(i) Only the endogenous variable is measured with errors in which case we have $\eta = 0$ and

$$\text{Cov}(\eta, \varepsilon - \eta\ b_0) = \text{Cov}(0, \varepsilon) = 0.$$

Thus the preceding necessary and sufficient condition for consistency of the OLS estimator is satisfied.

(ii) Only the exogenous variables are measured with errors in which case we have $\varepsilon = 0$ and

$$\text{Cov}(\eta, \varepsilon - \eta\ b_0) = -b_0 V(\eta),$$

which is, in general, different from zero. Hence OLS estimation leads to an inconsistent estimator of b_0.

b) Consumption Model and Permanent Income Hypothesis

To illustrate the problem of inconsistency discussed above, we consider a consumption model where consumption at time t, denoted C_t, depends on permanent income, denoted R_t^p, which is defined as some expectation of income R_t at time $t-1$. The model is

$$C_t = a_0 R_t^p + b_0 + v_t, \tag{9.21}$$

where v_t is assumed to be independent of $R_t^p, R_t, R_{t-1} \ldots$.

We consider two cases:

(i) Being unobservable, permanent income may be replaced by income R_t which can be viewed as an approximation to permanent income. Then the estimated model is

$$C_t = a_0 R_t + b_0 + u_t,$$

where $u_t = v_t + a_0(R_t^p - R_t)$.

The above necessary and sufficient condition for consistency is

$$\text{Cov}(R, u) = 0,$$

i.e.

$$\text{Cov}(R, R - R^p) = 0.$$

Here, we suppose that expectations are optimal and given by

$$R_t^p = E(R_t \mid R_{t-1}, R_{t-2}, \cdots).$$

That is, R_t^p is the best approximation to future income given past observations on income. The corresponding prediction error is orthogonal to the prediction, i.e.

$$\text{Cov}(R^p, R - R^p) = 0.$$

Then the consistency condition is not satisfied because

$$\text{Cov}(R, R - R^p) = V(R - R^p) > 0,$$

which holds as soon as predictions are not perfect, i.e., as soon as $R^p \neq R$.

(ii) Another possibility consists in replacing the unknown value of R_t^p by $R_t^* = \hat{a}_T R_{t-1} + \hat{b}_T$, where $\hat{a}_T$ and $\hat{b}_T$ are the estimated coefficients in a linear regression of R_t on R_{t-1} and the constant term. Under weak regularity conditions, when T increases to infinity, $\hat{a}_T$ and $\hat{b}_T$ converge to the true values of the coefficients in this linear regression and R_t^* converges to the best prediction of R_t in the class of linear predictors based on past income R_{t-1} only

$$R_t^* \approx EL(R_t \mid R_{t-1}).$$

After substituting R_t^* for R_t^p in equation (9.21), the condition for consistency of the OLS estimator becomes

$$\text{Cov}(R_t^*, R_t^* - R_t^p) = 0.$$

This condition is trivially satisfied because the best prediction of R_t^p, which is a linear function of R_{t-1}, is equal to R_t^* so that the corresponding prediction error $R_t^p - R_t^*$ is orthogonal to R_t^*.

9.3.4 Simultaneous Equation Models

a) An Equilibrium Model

In equilibrium, the quantity exchanged on a market at every instant and the price of these exchanges are such that demand equals supply. To simplify, we consider some demand and supply functions that are linear in prices

$$\begin{aligned} D_t &= a_0 P_t + X_t b_0 + u_t, \quad a_0 < 0 \quad (\textit{Demand}) \\ S_t &= \alpha_0 P_t + Z_t \beta_0 + v_t, \quad \alpha_0 > 0 \quad (\textit{Supply}). \end{aligned} \tag{9.22}$$

It is assumed that the error terms u_t and v_t are uncorrelated with means zero and variance covariance matrix

$$V \begin{bmatrix} u_t \\ v_t \end{bmatrix} = \begin{bmatrix} \sigma_u^2 & \sigma_{uv} \\ \sigma_{uv} & \sigma_v^2 \end{bmatrix}.$$

The explanatory variables X_t and Z_t possibly include a constant term.

The equilibrium condition

$$D_t = S_t, \tag{9.23}$$

and the definition of the quantity exchanged

$$Q_t = D_t, \tag{9.24}$$

can be used to obtain the equilibrium quantity and price at time t as a solution to

$$\begin{aligned} Q_t^e &= a_0 P_t^e + X_t b_0 + u_t, \\ Q_t^e &= \alpha_0 P_t^e + Z_t \beta_0 + v_t. \end{aligned} \tag{9.25}$$

This system determines simultaneously the two endogenous variables Q_t^e and P_t^e. The solution is

$$
\begin{aligned}
P_t^e &= \frac{Z_t\beta_0 - X_t b_0}{a_0 - \alpha_0} + \frac{v_t - u_t}{a_0 - \alpha_0}, \\
Q_t^e &= \frac{a_0 Z_t\beta_0 - \alpha_0 X_t b_0}{a_0 - \alpha_0} + \frac{a_0 v_t - \alpha_0 u_t}{a_0 - \alpha_0}.
\end{aligned}
\tag{9.26}
$$

b) OLS Estimation of the Demand Equation

The first equation of the system (9.25), i.e.

$$Q_t^e = a_0 P_t^e + X_t b_0 + u_t$$

is linear. Thus it may seem natural to estimate the coefficient a_0 by ordinary least squares.

In general, however, the OLS estimator $\hat{a}_T$ is inconsistent. The consistency condition $\text{Cov}(P_t^e, u_t) = 0$ of this estimator is equivalent to

$$\text{Cov}(v_t - u_t, u_t) = 0.$$

Thus, even if the errors u_t and v_t are uncorrelated so that $\text{Cov}(v_t, u_t) = 0$, the above condition is not satisfied since

$$\text{Cov}(v_t - u_t, u_t) = -Vu_t = -\sigma_u^2 < 0.$$

When $X_t b_0 = b_0$, the asymptotic bias can be easily determined. It is equal to

$$
\begin{aligned}
a_\infty - a_0 &= \frac{\text{Cov}(Q_t^e, P_t^e)}{VP_t^e} - a_0 \\
&= \frac{\text{Cov}(u_t, P_t^e)}{VP_t^e} \\
&= \frac{1}{\alpha_0 - a_0} \frac{Vu_t}{VP_t^e}.
\end{aligned}
$$

It is positive. Hence a_0 is overestimated.

c) OLS Estimation of the Inverse Demand Function

The demand equation can be written with price as a function of quantity exchanged. This gives the *inverse demand function.* Specifically, from

$$Q_t^e = a_0 P_t^e + X_t b_0 + u_t,$$

we obtain

$$\begin{aligned} P_t^e &= \frac{1}{a_0} Q_t^e - \frac{X_t b_0}{a_0} - \frac{u_t}{a_0} \\ &= \bar{a}_0 Q_t^e + X_t \bar{b}_0 + \bar{u}_t, \end{aligned}$$

where $\bar{a}_0 = 1/a_0$, $\bar{b}_0 = -(b_0/a_0)$ and $\bar{u}_t = -(u_t/a_0)$.

The OLS estimator of $\bar{a}_0$, which is obtained by regressing P_t^e on (Q_t^e, X_t), is consistent if and only if

$$\operatorname{Cov}(Q_t^e, \bar{u}_t) = 0,$$

i.e., if and only if

$$\operatorname{Cov}(a_0 v_t - \alpha_0 u_t, u_t) = 0.$$

If the error terms u_t and v_t are uncorrelated, this condition reduces to

$$\operatorname{Cov}(-\alpha_0 u_t, u_t) = 0,$$

i.e.

$$\alpha_0 \sigma_u^2 = 0,$$

i.e.

$$\alpha_0 = 0. \tag{9.27}$$

Therefore the OLS estimator is consistent if the system can be written as

$$\begin{aligned} P_t^e &= \bar{a}_0 Q_t^e + X_t b_0 + \bar{u}_t, \\ Q_t^e &= Z_t \beta_0 + v_t, \end{aligned} \tag{9.28}$$

i.e., if the supply equation determines the quantity exchanged and the demand function determines the equilibrium price. Note that the simultaneous determination of P_t^e and Q_t^e is no longer present. Such a system is said to be *recursive*.

9.4 Instrumental Variable Estimation

9.4.1 Instrumental Variables

We consider a linear relation between the explained variable Y and the explanatory variables $X_1, \ldots, X_K$ of the form

$$Y_i = \sum_{k=1}^{K} X_{ik} b_{0k} + u_i, \quad i = 1, \ldots, n,$$

where $b_0 = (b_{01}, \ldots, b_{0K})'$ denotes the true value of the parameter vector. We also assume that observations on H variables $Z_1, \ldots, Z_H$ are available. These variables may include some variables among $X_1, \ldots, X_K$.

To simplify, we assume that the variables

$$(u_i, X_{i1}, \ldots, X_{iK},\ Z_{i1}, \ldots, Z_{iH})', \quad i = 1, \ldots, n$$

are independent and identically distributed and that the first two moments of their common distribution exist.

Definition 9.3:

(i) *A variable Z_h is an instrumental variable (IV) or an instrument if $E(Z_h u) = 0$.*

(ii) *The system $Z_1, \ldots, Z_H$ is a system of instrumental variables if every variable Z_h, $h = 1, \ldots, H$, is an instrument and if these variables are linearly independent.*

Let $Z = (Z_1, \ldots, Z_H)$ denote the row vector of the system of instruments. The condition of linear independence means that

$$E(Z'Z) \text{ is nonsingular.} \tag{9.29}$$

Note that the instruments have the desirable property of being uncorrelated with the error terms.

The model that was just described requires observations on the instrumental variables Z_h, $h = 1, \ldots, H$. How can such variables be found in practice? The search for instrumental variables is illustrated in the next examples.

Example 9.7: Consider a relation of the form

$$Y_i = X_{i1} b_{01} + X_{i2} b_{02} + u_i,$$

where u is an error term with mean zero, independent of the first explanatory variable X_{i1}, but possibly correlated with the second one X_{i2}. Every function $Z = g(X_1)$ of X_1 is an instrument since

$$E(g(X_1)u) = E(g(X_1))Eu = 0.$$

Example 9.8: Consider a model where the endogenous variable is explained by the expectation of its future value

$$Y_t = a_0 E(Y_{t+1} \mid Y_t, Y_{t-1}, \ldots) + u_t,$$

where u_t is an error term satisfying the usual conditions. Namely, u_t has mean zero, is homoscedastic, and is uncorrelated over time. The optimal prediction , which is unknown, can be replaced by its observable realization Y_{t+1}. This leads to the linear relation

$$Y_t = a_0 Y_{t+1} + v_t,$$

where $v_t = u_t - a_0(Y_{t+1} - E(Y_{t+1} \mid Y_t, Y_{t-1}, \ldots))$. Clearly, the error term v_t is correlated with the "explanatory" variable Y_{t+1}.

The lagged values of Y_t, namely $Y_{t-1}, Y_{t-2}, \ldots$, are instrumental variables since they are orthogonal to u_t and the prediction error

$$Y_{t+1} - E(Y_{t+1} \mid Y_t, Y_{t-1}, \ldots).$$

Example 9.9: Consider the equilibrium model

$$\begin{aligned} D_t &= a_{01} P_t + x_{1t} b_{01} + u_{1t}, \\ S_t &= a_{02} P_t + x_{2t} b_{02} + u_{2t}, \\ D_t &= S_t = Q_t. \end{aligned}$$

Many instrumental variables are available for the demand equation

$$Q_t = a_{01} P_t + x_{1t} b_{01} + u_{1t}.$$

For instance, the exogenous variables x_1 in the demand equation and x_2 in the supply equation are possible instruments. When u_{1t} and u_{2t} are uncorrelated and when there exist consistent estimators $\tilde{a}_2$ and $\tilde{b}_2$ of a_{02} and b_{02}, the residual in the supply equation

$$Q_t - \tilde{a}_2 P_t - x_{2t} \tilde{b}_2 = \tilde{u}_{2t}$$

can also play the role of an instrument.

9.4.2 Instrumental Variable Estimators

Let $Z_1, \ldots, Z_H$ be H instruments. The orthogonality conditions $E(Z_h u) = 0$, $h = 1, \ldots, H$, can be expressed in terms of the observable variables. Namely

$$E(Z_h u) = 0$$

is equivalent to

$$E(Z_h Y) = \sum_{k=1}^{K} E(Z_h X_k) b_{0k}, \quad h = 1, \ldots, H. \tag{9.30}$$

We have a linear system of H equations in the K unknowns b_{0k}, $k = 1, \ldots, K$. The quantities $E(Z_h Y)$ and $E(Z_h X_k)$ are unknown and play the role of auxiliary parameters. They can be estimated consistently by the corresponding sample moments. Then it is natural to find an estimate of b_0 by solving the system (9.30) where the population moments are replaced by their corresponding sample quantities. Three cases must be distinguished:

a) If $H < K$, i.e., if there are fewer instruments than explanatory variables, then the preceding system does not have enough equations. The method cannot be used.

b) If $H = K$, the method leads, in general, to a unique solution. Let $Z = (Z_1, \ldots, Z_K)$ and $X = (X_1, \ldots, X_K)$. The system (9.30) can be written as

$$E(Z'Y) = E(Z'X)b_0.$$

If the matrix $E(Z'X)$ is nonsingular, this gives

$$b_0 = (E(Z'X))^{-1}E(Z'Y).$$

Thus the instrumental variable (IV) estimator of b_0, denoted $\hat{b}_{IV}$, is given by

$$\hat{b}_{IV} = \left(\frac{1}{n}\sum_{i=1}^{n} Z_i'X_i\right)^{-1} \frac{1}{n}\sum_{i=1}^{n} Z_i'Y_i,$$

i.e.

$$\hat{b}_{IV} = \left(\sum_{i=1}^{n} Z_i'X_i\right)^{-1} \sum_{i=1}^{n} Z_i'Y_i. \tag{9.31}$$

A more compact expression is obtained by introducing the $n \times K$ matrices of observations on the explanatory variables and the instrumental variables. These matrices are denoted $\mathbf{X}$ and $\mathbf{Z}$, respectively. The vector of n observations on the endogenous variable is denoted Y. Then we have

$$\hat{b}_{IV} = (\mathbf{Z}'\mathbf{X})^{-1}\mathbf{Z}'Y. \tag{9.32}$$

Remark 9.2: In the classical linear model $Y_i = X_i b_0 + u_i$ where u_i has mean zero and is uncorrelated with the explanatory variables, the latter variables can be chosen as instruments. For this particular choice we have $\mathbf{Z} = \mathbf{X}$. Thus the corresponding instrumental variable estimator is the ordinary least square estimator

$$\hat{b}_{OLS} = (\mathbf{X}'\mathbf{X})^{-1}\mathbf{X}'Y.$$

c) If $H > K$, the method leads to a system in which there are more equations than unknowns. After substitution of the sample moments for the population moments, the resulting system is, in general, inconsistent. A possible solution is to select only K instruments among the H available instruments $Z_1, \ldots, Z_H$. Formally, this consists in choosing instruments defined by

$$Z^*_{\mathbf{A}} = Z\mathbf{A}, \tag{9.33}$$

where $\mathbf{A}$ is a nonrandom matrix of size $H \times K$. The components of $Z^*_{\mathbf{A}}$ are valid instruments since

$$E(uZ^*_{\mathbf{A}}) = E(uZ\mathbf{A}) = E(uZ)\mathbf{A} = 0.$$

In addition, because Z is a system of H instruments and the matrix $\mathbf{A}$ is assumed to be of full column rank K, then it is easy to see that $Z^*_{\mathbf{A}}$ constitutes a valid system of K instruments.

Note that there are as many instrumental variable estimators as possible matrices $\mathbf{A}$, i.e., an infinity. Each instrumental variable estimator is given by

$$\hat{b}_{IV}(\mathbf{A}) = (\mathbf{Z}^{*\prime}_{\mathbf{A}}\mathbf{X})^{-1}(\mathbf{Z}^{*\prime}_{\mathbf{A}}Y),$$

i.e.

$$\hat{b}_{IV}(\mathbf{A}) = [\mathbf{A}'\mathbf{Z}'\mathbf{X}]^{-1}\mathbf{A}'\mathbf{Z}'Y. \tag{9.34}$$

By construction, every instrumental variable estimator that has been introduced is a consistent estimator of b_0.

9.4.3 Asymptotic Distributions of IV Estimators

The study of the asymptotic properties of instrumental variable estimators requires additional hypotheses on the error term u. It is assumed that, conditionally on Z, the error term u has mean zero and is homoscedastic. Thus

$$E(u \mid Z) = 0, \quad V(u \mid Z) = \sigma_0^2. \tag{9.35}$$

First, we consider instrumental variable estimation when $H = K$. The instrumental variables estimator is

$$\begin{aligned}\hat{b}_{IV} &= (\mathbf{Z}'\mathbf{X})^{-1}\mathbf{Z}'Y \\ &= (\mathbf{Z}'\mathbf{X})^{-1}\mathbf{Z}'(\mathbf{X}b_0 + u) \\ &= b_0 + (\mathbf{Z}'\mathbf{X})^{-1}\mathbf{Z}'u.\end{aligned}$$

Thus

$$\sqrt{n}(\hat{b}_{IV} - b_0) = \left(\frac{1}{n}\sum_{i=1}^{n} Z_i'X_i\right)^{-1} \frac{1}{\sqrt{n}}Z_i'u_i.$$

From the Strong Law of Large Numbers we have

$$\frac{1}{n}\sum_{i=1}^{n} Z_i'X_i \to E(Z'X).$$

From the Central Limit Theorem we have

$$\frac{1}{\sqrt{n}}\sum_{i=1}^{n} Z_i'u_i \xrightarrow{d} N\left(0; \sigma_0^2 E(Z'Z)\right),$$

since

$$E(Z'u) = 0$$

and

$$\begin{aligned}E(Z'u)(Z'u)' &= E(u^2 Z'Z) \\ &= E(E(u^2 \mid Z)Z'Z) \\ &= \sigma_0^2 E(Z'Z).\end{aligned}$$

Collecting results, we obtain the following property.

Property 9.4: *When $H = K$, the instrumental variables estimator is consistent and asymptotically normally distributed with*

$$\sqrt{n}(\hat{b}_{IV} - b_0) \xrightarrow{d} N\left(0, \sigma_0^2 (EZ'X)^{-1} E(Z'Z)(EX'Z)^{-1}\right).$$

Next, we consider the general case where $H \geq K$. It suffices to replace Z by $Z\mathbf{A}$ where $\mathbf{A}$ is an $H \times K$ matrix. We obtain

Corollary 9.1: *If $H \geq K$*

$$\sqrt{n}(\hat{b}_{IV}(\mathbf{A}) - b_0) \xrightarrow{d} N(0, \mathbf{\Omega}(\mathbf{A})),$$

where

$$\boldsymbol{\Omega}(\mathbf{A}) = \sigma_0^2(\mathbf{A}'E(Z'X))^{-1}\mathbf{A}'E(Z'Z)\mathbf{A}(E(X'Z)\mathbf{A})^{-1}.$$

Remark 9.3: The consistency of the instrumental variable estimator $\hat{b}_{IV}(\mathbf{A})$ implies that the residual $\tilde{u}_i = Y_i - X_i\hat{b}_{IV}(\mathbf{A})$ is a good approximation to u_i. In particular, $\tilde{\sigma}^2 = (1/n)\sum_{i=1}^n \tilde{u}_i^2(\mathbf{A})$ is a consistent estimator of $\tilde{\sigma}_0^2$ and

$$\tilde{\boldsymbol{\Omega}}(\mathbf{A}) = n\tilde{\sigma}^2(\mathbf{A}'\mathbf{Z}'\mathbf{X})^{-1}\mathbf{A}'\mathbf{Z}'\mathbf{Z}\mathbf{A}(\mathbf{X}'\mathbf{Z}\mathbf{A})^{-1}$$

is a consistent estimator of $\boldsymbol{\Omega}(\mathbf{A})$.

9.4.4 Best Instrumental Variable Estimation

In the general case where $H \geq K$, there is an infinity of instrumental variable estimators. It is natural to ask whether there exists an estimator that dominates asymptotically any other instrumental variable estimator. The problem reduces to finding a matrix $\mathbf{A}^*$ such that

$$\boldsymbol{\Omega}(\mathbf{A}^*) \preceq \boldsymbol{\Omega}(\mathbf{A}),$$

for any other matrix $\mathbf{A}$ and for every parameter value.

Property 9.5: *There exists an optimal matrix* $\mathbf{A}^*$*. It is given by*

$$\mathbf{A}^* = E(Z'Z)^{-1}E(Z'X).$$

Then we have

$$\boldsymbol{\Omega}(\mathbf{A}^*) = \sigma_0^2[E(X'Z)E(Z'Z)^{-1}E(Z'X)]^{-1}.$$

PROOF: We need to prove that

$$[\mathbf{A}'E(Z'X)]^{-1}\mathbf{A}'E(Z'Z)\mathbf{A}[E(X'Z)\mathbf{A}]^{-1}$$
$$\succeq [E(X'Z)E(Z'Z)^{-1}E(Z'X)]^{-1},$$

or equivalently that

$$E(X'Z)(EZ'Z)^{-1}E(Z'X) \succeq E(X'Z)\mathbf{A}[\mathbf{A}'E(Z'Z)\mathbf{A}]^{-1}\mathbf{A}'E(Z'X).$$

The latter inequality is equivalent to

$$\mathbf{B}'(\mathbf{I} - \tilde{\mathbf{A}}(\tilde{\mathbf{A}}'\tilde{\mathbf{A}})^{-1}\tilde{\mathbf{A}}')\mathbf{B} \succeq 0,$$

where $\mathbf{B} = E(Z'Z)^{-1/2}E(Z'X)$ and $\tilde{\mathbf{A}} = E(Z'Z)^{+1/2}\mathbf{A}$. This is clearly verified since $\tilde{\mathbf{A}}(\tilde{\mathbf{A}}'\tilde{\mathbf{A}})^{-1}\tilde{\mathbf{A}}'$ is an orthogonal projection matrix and hence smaller than $\mathbf{I}$ in the positive definite matrix sense. □

From Property 9.5 it follows that the best instrumental variables are given by

$$Z^* = ZE(Z'Z)^{-1}E(Z'X).$$

These instruments are simply the predictors of X in the population linear regression of X on Z. Thus we obtain a simple interpretation of the best instrumental variable estimation method. Namely, the method consists in obtaining the best approximation to the variables X, which cause problems, using the variables Z which have good properties.

The original model $Y = Xb_0 + u$, which is a seemingly linear regression model (see Definition 9.2), can be rewritten as

$$Y = ZE(Z'Z)^{-1}E(Z'X)b_0 + v, \tag{9.36}$$

where

$$v = u + (X - ZE(Z'Z)^{-1}EZ'X)b_0$$

is orthogonal to Z. This is so because Z is orthogonal to u, i.e., $E(Z'u) = 0$, which follows from the fact that Z are instruments, and because Z is orthogonal to the residual in the population regression of X on Z, i.e., to

$$X - ZE(Z'Z)^{-1}EZ'X.$$

The optimal selection matrix $\mathbf{A}^* = E(Z'Z)^{-1}E(Z'X)$ cannot be used directly since it depends on the population moments $E(Z'Z)$ and $E(Z'X)$ which are unknown. It can, however, be estimated consistently by $\tilde{\mathbf{A}}^* = (\mathbf{Z}'\mathbf{Z})^{-1}\mathbf{Z}'\mathbf{X}$, i.e., by the matrix of estimated coefficients in the sample regression of X on Z.

Therefore the best instrumental variable estimator is

$$\begin{aligned}
\hat{b}_{IV} &= \hat{b}_{IV}(\tilde{\mathbf{A}}^*) \\
&= (\tilde{\mathbf{A}}^{*\prime}\mathbf{Z}'\mathbf{X})^{-1}\tilde{\mathbf{A}}^{*\prime}\mathbf{Z}'Y \\
&= [\mathbf{X}'\mathbf{Z}(\mathbf{Z}'\mathbf{Z})^{-1}\mathbf{Z}'\mathbf{X}]^{-1}\mathbf{X}'\mathbf{Z}(\mathbf{Z}'\mathbf{Z})^{-1}\mathbf{Z}'Y \\
&= (\mathbf{X}'\mathbf{P}_Z\mathbf{X})^{-1}\mathbf{X}'\mathbf{P}_Z Y,
\end{aligned}$$

where $\mathbf{P}_Z = \mathbf{Z}(\mathbf{Z}'\mathbf{Z})^{-1}\mathbf{Z}'$ is the matrix associated with the orthogonal projection on the subspace generated by the instruments. The substitution of $\tilde{\mathbf{A}}^*$ for $\mathbf{A}^*$ does not modify the properties of consistency and asymptotic normality of the estimator.

Property 9.6:

(i) The best instrumental variable (IV) estimator is given by

$$\hat{b}_{IV} = (\mathbf{X}'\mathbf{P}_Z\mathbf{X})^{-1}\mathbf{X}'\mathbf{P}_Z Y,$$

where $\mathbf{P}_Z$ is the orthogonal projection matrix on the subspace generated by the columns $Z_1, \dots, Z_H$ of $\mathbf{Z}$.

(ii) The best IV estimator is consistent and asymptotically normally distributed with

$$\sqrt{n}(\hat{b}_{IV} - b_0) \xrightarrow{d} N(0, \sigma_0^2(E(X'Z)(EZ'Z)^{-1}E(Z'X))^{-1}).$$

(iii) The best IV estimator dominates asymptotically any other instrumental variable estimator.

(iv) The asymptotic variance covariance matrix of the best IV estimator can be estimated consistently by

$$\begin{aligned} \hat{V}_{as}\sqrt{n}(\hat{b}_{IV} - b_0) &= n\tilde{\sigma}^2(\mathbf{X}'\mathbf{Z}(\mathbf{Z}'\mathbf{Z})^{-1}\mathbf{Z}'\mathbf{X})^{-1} \\ &= n\tilde{\sigma}^2(\mathbf{X}'\mathbf{P}_Z\mathbf{X})^{-1}, \end{aligned}$$

where

$$\tilde{\sigma}^2 = \frac{1}{n}\sum_{i=1}^{n}(Y_i - X_i\hat{b}_{IV})^2 = \frac{1}{n}\sum_{i=1}^{n}\tilde{w}_i^2.$$

The best instrumental variable estimator is readily computed:

a) In a first step, we regress the different explanatory variables X_k, $k = 1, \dots, K$, on the set of instrumental variables $Z_1, \dots, Z_H$. The OLS coefficient estimators obtained from these K regressions are given by $(\mathbf{Z}'\mathbf{Z})^{-1}\mathbf{Z}'X_k$.

b) Then the predicted values $\hat{\mathbf{X}}$ obtained from these regressions are given by

$$\hat{\mathbf{X}} = \mathbf{Z}(\mathbf{Z}'\mathbf{Z})^{-1}\mathbf{Z}'\mathbf{X}.$$

c) In a second step, we consider the approximate linear regression model

$$Y = \mathbf{Z}(\mathbf{Z}'\mathbf{Z})^{-1}\mathbf{Z}'\mathbf{X}b_0 + \hat{v}, \tag{9.37}$$

i.e.

$$Y = \hat{\mathbf{X}}b_0 + \hat{v}.$$

Because the usual assumptions are satisfied asymptotically in this model, we can apply ordinary least squares. This gives the estimator

$$\begin{aligned}(\hat{\mathbf{X}}'\hat{\mathbf{X}})^{-1}\hat{\mathbf{X}}'Y &= (\mathbf{X}'\mathbf{P}_Z'\mathbf{P}_Z\mathbf{X})^{-1}\mathbf{X}'\mathbf{P}_Z'Y \\ &= (\mathbf{X}'\mathbf{P}_Z\mathbf{X})^{-1}\mathbf{X}'\mathbf{P}_ZY \\ &= \hat{b}_{IV}.\end{aligned}$$

Therefore the best instrumental variable estimator can be determined by applying ordinary least squares to two successive models. For this reason, and especially when considering simultaneous equation models, this estimator is frequently called the *two-stage least squares estimator.*

Remark 9.4: Computation of the best instrumental variable estimator requires at most $K+1$ OLS regressions. In general, however, the set of instruments contains some explanatory variables of the original model. In this case, the corresponding first step OLS regression produces a vector $\hat{X}_k$ of estimated values that is identical to X_k.

Remark 9.5: Note that the residuals, the estimate of the variance of the error term, and the estimate of the variance covariance matrix obtained from the OLS regression of Y on $\hat{\mathbf{X}}$ in the second step do not coincide with the residuals $\tilde{u}_i$, the estimated variance $\tilde{\sigma}^2$, and

$$\frac{1}{n}\hat{V}_{as}[\sqrt{n}(\hat{b}_{IV}-b_0)] = \tilde{\sigma}^2[\mathbf{X}'\mathbf{P}_Z\mathbf{X}]^{-1}$$

respectively, since the vector of residuals in the second step OLS regression is $Y-\hat{\mathbf{X}}\hat{b}_{IV}$, which is different from $Y-\mathbf{X}\hat{b}_{IV}$.

Example 9.10: Consider a linear model satisfying the usual assumption of zero correlation between the error term and the explanatory variables. Then the explanatory variables $X_1, \ldots, X_K$ can be taken as instruments. The best instrumental variable estimator reduces to the OLS estimator

$$\hat{b}_{OLS} = (\mathbf{X}'\mathbf{X})^{-1}\mathbf{X}'Y,$$

since $\mathbf{P}_Z\mathbf{X} = \mathbf{X}$. Hence there is no need to improve upon the OLS estimator $\hat{b}_{OLS}$ by introducing additional instruments $Z_{K+1}, \ldots, Z_H$.

The latter property can be viewed as a consequence of the Gauss–Markov Theorem. Specifically, the other instrumental variable estimators are linear in Y and are unbiased when $Eu = 0$ since

$$E(\mathbf{Z}'\mathbf{X})^{-1}\mathbf{Z}'Y = (\mathbf{Z}'\mathbf{X})^{-1}\mathbf{Z}'EY = b_0.$$

Thus they are dominated by the OLS estimator $\hat{b}_{OLS}$.

Example 9.11: Consider a simultaneous equation model. Specifically, consider the equilibrium model

$$\begin{aligned} D_t &= a_1 P_t + x_{1t} b_1 + u_{1t}, \\ S_t &= a_2 P_t + x_{2t} b_2 + u_{2t}, \\ Q_t &= D_t = S_t. \end{aligned}$$

Instrumental variables are often chosen to be various exogenous variables appearing in the demand and supply equations.

Let K_1 denote the number of exogenous variables x_1 appearing in the demand equation and L_2 denote the number of exogenous variables x_2 in the supply equation that are not linearly related with x_1. We are interested in the estimation of a_1 and b_1. Then

$$K = K_1 + 1, \quad H = K_1 + L_2$$

Three cases can be distinguished:

(i) If $H < K$, i.e, if $L_2 = 0$, then the instrumental variable procedure is not applicable. The parameters of the demand equation are said to be *underidentified* and there does not exist a consistent estimation procedure.

(ii) If $H = K$, i.e., if $L_2 = 1$, then there exists a unique instrumental variable estimator. This case corresponds to a demand equation that is *just identified.*

(iii) In the *overidentified* case $H > K$, i.e., $L_2 > 1$, there exists an infinity of instrumental variable estimators. The best instrumental variable estimator known as the two-stage least squares estimator is obtained by regressing Q_t on $\hat{P}_t$ and x_{1t}, where $\hat{P}_t$ is the estimated value of P_t obtained from the OLS regression of P_t on x_{1t} and $\tilde{x}_{2t}$. (The variables $\tilde{x}_2$ denote the L_2 variables of x_2 that are not related to the variables x_1.)

Example 9.12: In Example 9.8, we considered replacing the model with optimal predictions

$$Y_t = aE(Y_{t+1} \mid Y_t, Y_{t-1}, \ldots) + u_t$$

by the model

$$Y_t = aY_{t+1} + v_t.$$

There we noted that the lagged variable Y_{t-1} could play the role of an instrument. The corresponding instrumental variable estimator is obtained by regressing Y_t on $\hat{Y}_{t+1}$, where $\hat{Y}_{t+1}$ is the "best" prediction of Y_{t+1} obtained from the auxiliary regression

$$Y_{t+1} = \alpha Y_{t-1} + \omega_t,$$

i.e.

$$\hat{Y}_{t+1} = Y_{t-1} \frac{\sum_{t=1}^{T-1} Y_{t-1} Y_{t+1}}{\sum_{t=1}^{T} Y_{t-1}^2}.$$

9.4.5 Two-Stage Least Squares as Best Asymptotic Least Squares

We have $E(Z'Y) = E(Z'X)b_0$. Let the auxiliary parameters be the elements of $E(Z'Y)$ and $E(Z'X)$. Note that the relationship between the parameters of interest b and these auxiliary parameters are linear in both types of parameters.

The auxiliary parameters are estimated consistently by

$$\tilde{\beta}_{1n} = \frac{1}{n} \sum_{i=1}^{n} Z_i' Y_i,$$

and

$$\tilde{\beta}_{2n} = \frac{1}{n} \sum_{i=1}^{n} Z_i' X_i.$$

The asymptotic variance covariance matrix of $u_n = \tilde{\beta}_{1n} - \tilde{\beta}_{2n} b_0$ is

$$\lim_n V(\sqrt{n} u_n) = \sigma_0^2 E(Z'Z).$$

This matrix is estimated consistently by

$$\boldsymbol{\Omega}_n = \frac{\sigma_0^2}{n} \sum_{i=1}^{n} Z_i' Z_i.$$

Thus a consistent estimator of $V_{as}(\sqrt{n}\ u_n)$ is readily available up to a multiplicative constant. It follows that the best asymptotic least squares estimator can be obtained directly without having to estimate consistently the parameter vector b in a first step. Specifically, the best asymptotic least squares estimator is

$$\begin{aligned}\hat{b} &= \left[\sum_{i=1}^{n} X_i' Z_i \left(\sum_{i=1}^{n} Z_i' Z_i\right)^{-1} \sum_{i=1}^{n} Z_i' X_i\right]^{-1} \\ &\quad \sum_{i=1}^{n} X_i' Z_i \left(\sum_{i=1}^{n} Z_i' Z_i\right)^{-1} \sum_{i=1}^{n} Z_i' Y_i \\ &= (\mathbf{X}'\mathbf{P}_Z\mathbf{X})^{-1}\mathbf{X}'\mathbf{P}_Z Y.\end{aligned}$$

Hence $\hat{b} = \hat{b}_{IV}$.

Moreover, from the optimality property of the best asymptotic least squares estimator we obtain the following result.

Property 9.7: *Because it is identical to the best asymptotic least squares estimator, the two-stage least squares estimator is best in the class of estimators that are solutions to optimization problems of the form*

$$\min_b (\mathbf{Z}'Y - \mathbf{Z}'\mathbf{X}b)'\mathbf{S}_n(\mathbf{Z}'Y - \mathbf{Z}'\mathbf{X}b).$$

The two-stage least squares estimator corresponds to the optimal choice $\mathbf{S}_n = (\mathbf{Z}'\mathbf{Z})^{-1}$.

An instrumental variable estimator associated with an $H \times K$ selection matrix $\mathbf{A}$ (see equation (9.33)) corresponds to $\mathbf{S}_n = \mathbf{A}\mathbf{A}'$. Such a matrix $\mathbf{S}_n$ is necessarily of rank K with $K \leq H$. This shows that Property 9.7 is stronger than Property 9.5.

9.5 Generalized Methods of Moments

In the previous section, the orthogonality conditions between the error terms and the instrumental variables were written as

$$EZ'(Y - Xb_0) = 0$$

so as to emphasize the relation

$$E(Z'Y) = E(Z'X)b_0$$

between the cross moments and the parameter vector b_0 of interest. However, it is not always possible to separate the parameters of interest in this fashion. For instance, consider a nonlinear regression model of the form

$$Y_i = g(X_i, b_0) + u_i, \quad i = 1, \ldots, n,$$

where the explanatory variables X are uncorrelated with the error term u. If Z denotes the set of instrumental variables then the orthogonality conditions can be written as

$$EZ' \left[Y - g(X, b_0) \right] = 0.$$

Hence it is not possible to express the parameters of interest b_0 as functions of the moments of X, Y, and Z.

In this section we consider an estimation method based on *estimating equations* that impose the nullity of the expectation of a vector function of the observations and the parameters of interest a

$$E_0 h(Y, X; a_0) = 0. \tag{9.38}$$

The function h is H-dimensional and the parameter a is of size K. This method is a *generalized method of moments.* As for the asymptotic least squares method, this method is a generalization of the method of moments. Note, however, that every asymptotic least squares estimator is not necessarily a generalized method of moments estimator, and *vice versa.*

9.5.1 Definition

The basic idea of a generalized method of moments is to choose a value for a such that the sample mean

$$\frac{1}{n} \sum_{i=1}^{n} h(Y_i, X_i; a)$$

is closest to zero.

Definition 9.4: *Let $\mathbf{S}_n$ be an $H \times H$ symmetric positive definite matrix that may depend on the observations. The generalized method of moments (GMM) estimator associated with $\mathbf{S}_n$ is a solution $\tilde{a}_n(\mathbf{S}_n)$ to the problem*

$$\min_a \left[\sum_{i=1}^{n} h(Y_i, X_i; a) \right]' \mathbf{S}_n \left[\sum_{i=1}^{n} h(Y_i, X_i; a) \right].$$

The study of the existence, consistency, and asymptotic normality of a GMM estimator is analogous to that of an ALS estimator. Thus we can be brief.

We make the following assumptions:

H1: The variables (Y_i, X_i) are independent and identically distributed.

H2: The expectation $E_0 h(Y, X; a)$ exists and is zero when a is equal to the true value a_0 of the parameter of interest.

H3: The matrix $\mathbf{S}_n$ converges almost surely to a nonrandom matrix $\mathbf{S}_0$.

H4: The parameter a_0 is identified from the constraints (9.38), i.e., $E_0 h(Y, X; a)' \mathbf{S}_0 E_0 h(Y, X; a) = 0 \Rightarrow a = a_0$.

H5: The parameter value a_0 is known to belong to a compact set $\mathcal{A}$.

H6: The quantity $(1/n) \sum_{i=1}^n h(Y_i, X_i; a)$ converges almost surely and uniformly in a to $E_0 h(Y, X; a)$.

H7: The function $h(y, x; a)$ is continuous in a.

Property 9.8: *Under assumptions H1–H7, the GMM estimator associated with $\mathbf{S}_n$ exists asymptotically and strongly converges to a_0.*

PROOF: As for the ALS method, it suffices to consider the limit problem

$$\min_a \lim_n \left[\frac{1}{n} \sum_{i=1}^n h(Y_i, X_i; a) \right]' \mathbf{S}_n \left[\frac{1}{n} \sum_{i=1}^n h(Y_i, X_i; a) \right],$$

i.e.

$$\min_a \left[E_0 h(Y, X; a) \right]' \mathbf{S}_0 \left[E_0 h(Y, X; a) \right].$$

Then it suffices to note that the unique solution to this problem is a_0 in view of Assumption H4. □

In addition to the previous assumptions, we assume:

H8: The parameter value a_0 belongs to the interior of $\mathcal{A}$,

H9: The function $h(y, x; a)$ is continuously differentiable in a.

Then the GMM estimator $\tilde{a}_n(\mathbf{S}_n)$ belongs asymptotically to a neighborhood of the true parameter value a_0. In particular, it satisfies the first-order conditions

$$\left[\frac{1}{n}\sum_{i=1}^{n}\frac{\partial h'(Y_i, X_i; \tilde{a}_n)}{\partial a}\right]\mathbf{S}_n\left[\frac{1}{n}\sum_{i=1}^{n}h(Y_i, X_i; \tilde{a}_n)\right] = 0. \qquad (9.39)$$

To establish the asymptotic normality of a GMM estimator, it suffices to take a Taylor expansion of the first-order conditions. To do so we make the next assumptions:

H10: The quantity $(1/n)\sum_{i=1}^{n}\partial h'(Y_i, X_i; a)/\partial a$ converges almost surely and uniformly in a to $E_0 \partial h'(Y, X; a)/\partial a$.

H11: $E_0\|h(Y, X; a_0)\|^2 < +\infty$.

H12: The matrix

$$\left[E_0\frac{\partial h'(Y, X; a_0)}{\partial a}\right]\mathbf{S}_0\left[E_0\left(\frac{\partial h(Y, X; a_0)}{\partial a'}\right)\right]$$

is nonsingular, which implies that $H \geq K$.

Property 9.9: *Under Assumptions H1–H12, the GMM estimator $\tilde{a}_n(\mathbf{S}_n)$ is asymptotically normally distributed with*

$$\sqrt{n}(\tilde{a}_n(\mathbf{S}_n) - a_0) \xrightarrow{d} N(0, \mathbf{\Sigma}(\mathbf{S}_0)),$$

where

$$\begin{aligned}\mathbf{\Sigma}(\mathbf{S}_0) = & \left(\left[E_0\frac{\partial h'(Y, X; a_0)}{\partial a}\right]\mathbf{S}_0\left[E_0\frac{\partial h(Y, X; a_0)}{\partial a'}\right]\right)^{-1} \\ & \left[E_0\frac{\partial h'(Y, X; a_0)}{\partial a}\right]\mathbf{S}_0 V_0[h(Y, X; a_0)]\mathbf{S}_0\left[E_0\frac{\partial h(Y, X; a_0)}{\partial a'}\right] \\ & \left(\left[E_0\frac{\partial h'(Y, X; a_0)}{\partial a}\right]\mathbf{S}_0\left[E_0\frac{\partial h(Y, X; a_0)}{\partial a'}\right]\right)^{-1}.\end{aligned}$$

PROOF: We have

$$E_0\left[\frac{\partial h'(Y, X; a_0)}{\partial a}\right]\mathbf{S}_0\frac{1}{\sqrt{n}}\sum_{i=1}^{n}h(Y_i, X_i; \tilde{a}_n) \# 0.$$

This implies

$$E_0\left[\frac{\partial h'(Y,X;a_0)}{\partial a}\right]\mathbf{S}_0$$
$$\left(\frac{1}{\sqrt{n}}\sum_{i=1}^{n} h(Y_i,X_i;a_0)+\frac{1}{n}\sum_{i=1}^{n}\frac{\partial h(Y,X;a_0)}{\partial a'}\sqrt{n}(\tilde{a}_n-a_0)\right)\ \#\ 0.$$

Hence

$$E_0\left[\frac{\partial h'(Y,X;a_0)}{\partial a}\right]\mathbf{S}_0$$
$$\left(\frac{1}{\sqrt{n}}\sum_{i=1}^{n} h(Y_i,X_i;a_0)+\left[E_0\frac{\partial h(Y,X;a_0)}{\partial a'}\right]\sqrt{n}(\tilde{a}_n-a_0)\right)\ \#\ 0.$$

Therefore

$$\begin{aligned}\sqrt{n}(\tilde{a}_n-a_0)\quad\#\quad & -\left(E_0\left[\frac{\partial h'(Y,X;a_0)}{\partial a}\right]\mathbf{S}_0\left[E_0\frac{\partial h(Y,X;a_0)}{\partial a'}\right]\right)^{-1}\\ & \left[E_0\frac{\partial h'(Y,X;a_0)}{\partial a}\right]\mathbf{S}_0\frac{1}{\sqrt{n}}\sum_{i=1}^{n}h(Y_i,X_i;a_0).\end{aligned}$$

From the Central Limit Theorem we have

$$\frac{1}{\sqrt{n}}\sum_{i=1}^{n}h(Y_i,X_i;a_0)\xrightarrow{d}N(0;V_0h(Y,X;a_0)).$$

The desired result follows. □

9.5.2 Best GMM Estimation

Does there exist an optimal choice for the sequence of matrices $\mathbf{S}_n$? Since the asymptotic variance covariance matrix of a GMM estimator depends only on the nonrandom limit matrix $\mathbf{S}_0$, this question reduces to knowing whether there exists an optimal matrix $\mathbf{S}_0$.

A proof similar to the proof of Property 9.1 gives the following property.

Property 9.10: *There exists a best GMM estimator. It is obtained when the limit matrix is*

$$\mathbf{S}_0^* = [V_0h(Y,X;a_0)]^{-1}.$$

Its asymptotic variance covariance matrix $\mathbf{\Sigma}(\mathbf{S}_0^*)$ *is equal to*

$$\left(\left[E_0\frac{\partial h'(Y,X;a_0)}{\partial a}\right][V_0 h(Y,X;a_0)]^{-1}\left[E_0\frac{\partial h(Y,X;a_0)}{\partial a'}\right]\right)^{-1}.$$

Using an argument similar to that used for instrumental variable estimators, it is easy to verify that the lower bound $\mathbf{\Sigma}(\mathbf{S}_0^*)$ can also be attained by estimators that are solutions to

$$\min_a \left[\mathbf{A}_n \frac{1}{n}\sum_{i=1}^n h(Y_i,X_i;a)\right]'\left[\mathbf{A}_n \frac{1}{n}\sum_{i=1}^n h(Y_i,X_i;a)\right], \tag{9.40}$$

where $\mathbf{A}_n$ is a $K \times H$ matrix converging almost surely to a nonrandom matrix $\mathbf{A}_0$.

An alternative way to verify the latter result is as follows. Choose a sequence of matrices $\mathbf{A}_n^*$ converging to

$$\begin{aligned}\mathbf{A}_0^* &= \left[E_0\frac{\partial h'(Y,X;a_0)}{\partial a}\right]\mathbf{S}_0^* \\ &= \left[E_0\frac{\partial h'(Y,X;a_0)}{\partial a}\right][V_0 h(Y,X;a_0)]^{-1}.\end{aligned} \tag{9.41}$$

An estimator that is a solution to the problem (9.40) associated with such a sequence $\mathbf{A}_n^*$ has an asymptotic variance covariance matrix equal to $\mathbf{\Sigma}(\mathbf{A}_0^{*\prime}\mathbf{A}_0^*)$.

To simplify the notation, let $\mathbf{C}_0 = E_0\partial h(Y,X;a_0)/\partial a'$. Noting that $\mathbf{C}_0'\mathbf{S}_0^*\mathbf{C}_0$ is a nonsingular matrix, we have

$$\begin{aligned}\mathbf{\Sigma}(\mathbf{A}_0^{*\prime}\mathbf{A}_0^*) &= \mathbf{\Sigma}(\mathbf{S}_0^*\mathbf{C}_0\mathbf{C}_0'\mathbf{S}_0^*) \\ &= (\mathbf{C}_0'\mathbf{S}_0^*\mathbf{C}_0\mathbf{C}_0'\mathbf{S}_0^*\mathbf{C}_0)^{-1}\mathbf{C}_0'\mathbf{S}_0^*\mathbf{C}_0\mathbf{C}_0'\mathbf{S}_0^*\mathbf{C}_0\mathbf{C}_0'\mathbf{S}_0^*\mathbf{C}_0 \\ &\quad (\mathbf{C}_0'\mathbf{S}_0^*\mathbf{C}_0\mathbf{C}_0'\mathbf{S}_0^*\mathbf{C}_0)^{-1} \\ &= (\mathbf{C}_0'\mathbf{S}_0^*\mathbf{C}_0)^{-1} \\ &= \mathbf{\Sigma}(\mathbf{S}_0^*).\end{aligned}$$

Note also that a consistent estimator $(\mathbf{S}_n^*)^{-1}$ of $V_0 h(Y,X;a_0)$ is $(1/n)$ $\sum_{i=1}^n h(Y_i,X_i;\tilde{a}_n)\, h(Y_i,X_i;\tilde{a}_n)'$, where $\tilde{a}_n$ is a generalized method of moments estimator of a obtained using an arbitrary sequence of matrices $\mathbf{S}_n$ such as $\mathbf{S}_n = \mathbf{I}$.

9.5.3 GMM Estimation After Linearization of the Estimating Equations

The function h appearing in the estimating equations is, in general, nonlinear in the parameters a of interest. In this subsection, we shall show that every GMM estimator is asymptotically equivalent to a two-step estimator obtained by a method of moments applied to some estimating equations that have been linearized appropriately.

We assume the existence of an estimator a_n^* that is consistent and asymptotically normally distributed for a with

$$\sqrt{n}(a_n^* - a_0) \xrightarrow{d} N(0, \mathbf{Q}_0).$$

In the neighborhood of a_n^*, and asymptotically in the neighborhood of a_0, the function $h(y, x; a)$ can be approximated by

$$h(y, x; a_n^*) + \frac{\partial h(y, x; a_n^*)}{\partial a'}(a - a_n^*).$$

This suggests the study of the behavior of the estimator $\tilde{\tilde{a}}_n(\mathbf{S}_n)$ that is a solution to

$$\min_a \sum_{i=1}^n \left[h(Y_i, X_i; a_n^*) + \frac{\partial h(Y_i, X_i; a_n^*)}{\partial a'}(a - a_n^*)\right]' \mathbf{S}_n \sum_{i=1}^n \left[h(Y_i, X_i; a_n^*) + \frac{\partial h(Y_i, X_i; a_n^*)}{\partial a'}(a - a_n^*)\right]. \qquad (9.42)$$

The objective function is quadratic in a. Thus the estimator $\tilde{\tilde{a}}_n(\mathbf{S}_n)$ can be written explicitly as a function of the observations Y_i, X_i, $i = 1, \ldots, n$, and the first-step estimator a_n^*. Specifically, we have

$$\tilde{\tilde{a}}_n(\mathbf{S}) = \left(\left[\sum_{i=1}^n \frac{\partial h'(Y_i, X_i; a_n^*)}{\partial a}\right] \mathbf{S}_n \left[\sum_{i=1}^n \frac{\partial h(Y_i, X_i; a_n^*)}{\partial a'}\right]\right)^{-1} \sum_{i=1}^n \frac{\partial h'(Y_i, X_i; a_n^*)}{\partial a} \mathbf{S}_n \sum_{i=1}^n \left[-h(Y_i, X_i; a_n^*) + \frac{\partial h(Y_i, X_i; a_n^*)}{\partial a'} a_n^*\right]. \qquad (9.43)$$

Note that this estimator is obtained from the first-step estimator a_n^* by substracting a correction term c_n, namely

$$\tilde{\tilde{a}}_n(\mathbf{S}_n) = a_n^* - c_n, \qquad (9.44)$$

where

$$
\begin{aligned}
c_n &= \left(\sum_{i=1}^{n} \frac{\partial h'(Y_i, X_i; a_n^*)}{\partial a} \mathbf{S}_n \sum_{i=1}^{n} \frac{\partial h(Y_i, X_i; a_n^*)}{\partial a'} \right)^{-1} \\
& \quad \sum_{i=1}^{n} \frac{\partial h'(Y_i, X_i; a_n^*)}{\partial a} \mathbf{S}_n \sum_{i=1}^{n} h(Y_i, X_i; a_n^*).
\end{aligned}
$$

Property 9.11: *The two-step estimator $\tilde{\tilde{a}}_n(\mathbf{S}_n)$ is asymptotically equivalent to the generalized method of moments estimator $\tilde{a}(\mathbf{S}_n)$.*

PROOF: From equation (9.43) it follows that

$$
\begin{aligned}
& \sqrt{n}(\tilde{\tilde{a}}_n(\mathbf{S}_n) - a_0) \\
&= \left(\frac{1}{n} \left[\sum_{i=1}^{n} \frac{\partial h'(Y_i, X_i; a_n^*)}{\partial a} \right] \mathbf{S}_n \left[\frac{1}{n} \sum_{i=1}^{n} \frac{\partial h(Y_i, X_i; a_n^*)}{\partial a'} \right] \right)^{-1} \\
& \quad + \left(\left[\frac{1}{n} \sum_{i=1}^{n} \frac{\partial h'(Y_i, X_i; a_n^*)}{\partial a} \right] \mathbf{S}_n \left[-\frac{1}{\sqrt{n}} \sum_{i=1}^{n} h(Y_i, X_i; a_n^*) \right. \right. \\
& \quad \left. \left. + \frac{1}{n} \sum_{i=1}^{n} \frac{\partial h'(Y_i, X_i; a_n^*)}{\partial a} \sqrt{n}(a_n^* - a_0) \right] \right) \\
& \# \left(E_0 \frac{\partial h'(Y, X; a_0)}{\partial a} \mathbf{S}_o E_0 \frac{\partial h(Y, X; a_0)}{\partial a'} \right)^{-1} \\
& \quad \left[E_0 \frac{\partial h'(Y, X; a_0)}{\partial a} \right] \mathbf{S}_0 \left[-\frac{1}{\sqrt{n}} \sum_{i=1}^{n} h(Y, X; a_0) \right] \\
& \# \sqrt{n}(\tilde{a}_n(\mathbf{S}_n) - a_0),
\end{aligned}
$$

where we have used the proof of Property 9.9. □

9.5.4 Nonlinear Two-Stage Least Squares

We consider the nonlinear model

$$
Y_i = m(X_i, a_0) + u_i, \quad i = 1, \ldots, n, \tag{9.45}
$$

where the systematic part $m(X_i, a_0)$ is *not* the population regression of Y_i on X_i. In this case, nonlinear least squares estimation of equation (9.45) leads to an inconsistent estimator. The method, however, can be readily modified when there exist instrumental variables $Z = (Z_1, \dots, Z_H)$ that are uncorrelated with the error term u_i. Specifically, we assume

$$E_0 Z' \left(Y - m(X, a_0)\right) = 0.$$

From Property 9.10, the best GMM estimator corresponds to the limit matrix

$$\begin{aligned}\mathbf{S}_0^* &= \left[V_0 Z' \left(Y - m(X, a_0)\right)\right]^{-1} \\ &= \left[V_0 (Z'u)\right]^{-1}.\end{aligned}$$

Suppose that the error u_i satisfies $E_0(u_i^2 \mid Z) = \sigma_0^2$. We have

$$\mathbf{S}_0^* = \left[\sigma_0^2 E_0 Z'Z\right]^{-1}. \tag{9.46}$$

Thus the best GMM estimator is obtained as a solution to

$$\min_a \left(\sum_{i=1}^n Z_i'(Y_i - m(X_i, a))\right)' \frac{1}{\hat{\sigma}_n^2}\left(\frac{1}{n}\sum_{i=1}^n Z_i' Z_i\right)^{-1}\left(\sum_{i=1}^n Z_i'(Y_i - m(X_i, a))\right).$$

Equivalently, using matrix notation, this estimator is obtained as a solution to

$$\min_a \, (Y - m(\mathbf{X}, a))' \mathbf{Z}(\mathbf{Z}'\mathbf{Z})^{-1}\mathbf{Z}'(Y - m(\mathbf{X}, a)), \tag{9.47}$$

where $m(\mathbf{X}, a)$, Y and $\mathbf{Z}$ denote the vectors $(m(X_1, a), m(X_2, a), \dots, m(X_n, a))'$, $(Y_1, \dots, Y_n)'$ and the $n \times H$ matrix of which the ith row is Z_i, respectively.

Definition 9.5: *The nonlinear two-stage least squares estimator is a solution to*

$$\min_a \, (Y - m(\mathbf{X}, a))' \mathbf{Z}(\mathbf{Z}'\mathbf{Z})^{-1}\mathbf{Z}'(Y - m(\mathbf{X}, a)).$$

From Property 9.10 the asymptotic variance covariance matrix can be estimated consistently by

$$\hat{\sigma}_n^2 \left(\frac{1}{n}\frac{\partial m'}{\partial a}\mathbf{Z}(\mathbf{Z}'\mathbf{Z})^{-1}\mathbf{Z}'\frac{\partial m}{\partial a'}\right)^{-1},$$

where a is replaced by its estimator $\hat{a}_n$ and where $\hat{\sigma}_n^2 = (1/n)\sum_{i=1}^n [Y_i - m(X_i, \hat{a}_n)]^2$.

9.6 Exercises

EXERCISE 9.1: Consider Example 9.4.

a) Verify that the estimator $\hat{\hat{\theta}}_n$ defined by equation (9.10) is asymptotically equivalent to

$$\tilde{\theta} = \left[\sum_{k=1}^{K} p_k(1-p_k)x_k' x_k\right]^{-1} \sum_{k=1}^{K} p_k(1-p_k)x_k' \log \frac{\hat{p}_k}{1-\hat{p}_k}.$$

b) Find the asymptotic distribution of the vector $(\hat{p}_1, \ldots, \hat{p}_K)'$. Then find the asymptotic distribution of

$$\left(\log \frac{\hat{p}_1}{1-\hat{p}_1}, \ldots, \log \frac{\hat{p}_K}{1-\hat{p}_K}\right)'.$$

c) Find the asymptotic distribution of $\hat{\hat{\theta}}_n$ Discuss the asymptotic efficiency of this estimator.

EXERCISE 9.2: Consider Example 9.3. Show that the OLS estimator, based on

(i) an auxiliary parameter vector $b(\theta) = h(p(\theta))$, where h is a bijective function of $p_k(\theta)$, $k = 1, \ldots, K$, and

(ii) the estimator $\hat{b} = h(\hat{p})$,

is asymptotically efficient for θ.

EXERCISE 9.3: Consider an autoregressive model of order 2

$$Y_t = \phi_1 Y_{t-1} + \phi_2 Y_{t-2} + \varepsilon_t,$$

where $\{\varepsilon_t\}$ is a sequence of random variables independently and identically distributed with mean zero.

a) Find the asymptotic distribution of the sample correlations coefficients $\hat{\rho}(1)$, $\hat{\rho}(2)$ and $\hat{\rho}(3)$. Hint: see Property B.67.

b) Find the asymptotic distribution of $\hat{\phi}_1$ and $\hat{\phi}_2$ defined in Example 9.6.

c) Compute $E(Y_t Y_{t-3})$. Then find a relation between ϕ_1, ϕ_2, $\rho(1)$, $\rho(2)$, and $\rho(3)$, where $\rho(3)$ appears explicitly.

d) Study the behavior of the ALS estimator based on the three independent relations between $\rho(1)$, $\rho(2)$, $\rho(3)$, ϕ_1, ϕ_2 and on the sample correlation estimators $\hat{\rho}(1)$, $\hat{\rho}(2)$, and $\hat{\rho}(3)$.

EXERCISE 9.4: Consider the seemingly linear model

$$Y_i^* = b_{00} + X_i^* b_0 + u_i,$$

where $Eu_i = 0$.

a) Show that the OLS estimator of b_0 is given by

$$b_0 = (V_{emp} X^*)^{-1} \mathrm{Cov}_{emp}(X^*, Y^*).$$

b) Derive a necessary and sufficient condition for the consistency of this estimator as an estimator of the true value b_0.

c) Compare this condition to the condition obtained in Property 9.3.

EXERCISE 9.5: Using n observations one estimates the coefficients θ_1, θ_2, ϕ_1, and ϕ_2 of the second-order polynomials

$$\Theta(z) = 1 + \theta_1 z + \theta_2 z^2$$

and

$$\Phi(z) = 1 + \phi_1 z + \phi_2 z^2.$$

The estimators used are assumed to be consistent and asymptotically normally distributed with

$$\sqrt{n}(\hat{\theta}_{1n} - \theta_1, \hat{\theta}_{2n} - \theta_2, \hat{\phi}_{1n} - \phi_1, \hat{\phi}_{2n} - \phi_2)' \xrightarrow{d} N(0, \mathbf{\Omega}).$$

One knows that the two polynomials have a common root μ_0. Let μ_1 and μ_2 denote the other two roots. Thus

$$\Theta(z) = \left(1 - \frac{1}{\mu_0} z\right)\left(1 - \frac{1}{\mu_1} z\right)$$

and

$$\Phi(z) = \left(1 - \frac{1}{\mu_0} z\right)\left(1 - \frac{1}{\mu_2} z\right).$$

a) Express the parameters θ_1, θ_2, ϕ_1, and ϕ_2 as functions of the inverses of the roots, i.e., as functions of $\tilde{\mu}_j = 1/\mu_j$, $j = 0, 1, 2$. Then suggest a method for estimating the three roots.

b) One is mainly interested in the roots μ_1 and μ_2. Show that there exists a relation between the auxiliary parameters θ_1, θ_2, ϕ_1, and ϕ_2, on the one hand, and the parameters of interest $\tilde{\mu}_1$ and $\tilde{\mu}_2$, on the other hand. Note that this relation is linear in the latter two parameters. Then propose an estimation method for μ_1 and μ_2 that is different from that obtained in a).

EXERCISE 9.6: Consider a generalized method of moments estimator of a, denoted a_n^*, based on the estimating equations $E_0 h(Y, X; a_0) = 0$. Consider another generalized method of moments estimator of a, denoted $\hat{a}_n$, based on a subsystem of the available estimating equations. It is assumed that the number of equations in the subsystem is equal to the dimension of a. Show that $\hat{a}_n - a_n^*$ is asymptotically uncorrelated with a_n^*.

EXERCISE 9.7: Suppose that some auxiliary parameters b and some parameters of interest a are related through a system of estimating equations that can be partitioned into two subsystems $g_1(b, a) = 0$ and $g_2(b, a) = 0$. Suppose also that a is identified from the first subsystem, i.e., the one associated with g_1. Are the ALS estimators based on g_1 and (g_1, g_2) asymptotically comparable?

EXERCISE 9.8: Compare the ALS estimators based on the systems $g(b, a) = 0$ and $h(g(b, a)) = 0$, where h is a bijective mapping.

EXERCISE 9.9: Propose a linearized ALS estimation method that is analogous to the linearized generalized method of moments discussed in Section 9.5.3.

9.7 References

Amemiya, T. (1974). "The Nonlinear Two-Stage Least Squares Estimator," *Journal of Econometrics*, 2, 105–110.

Amemiya, T. (1975). "The Nonlinear Limited Information Maximum Likelihood Estimator and the Modified Nonlinear Two-Stage Least Squares Estimator," *Journal of Econometrics*, 3, 375–386.

Basmann, R. (1957). "A Generalized Classical Method of Linear Estimation of Coefficients in a Structural Equation," *Econometrica*, 27, 77–83.

Berkson, J. (1955). "Maximum Likelihood and Minimum Chi-Square Estimates of the Logistic Function," *Journal of the American Statistical Association*, 50, 130–162.

Dhrymes, P. (1970). *Econometrics*, Harper and Row.

Friedman, M. (1957). *A Theory of the Consumption Function*, Princeton University Press.

Gourieroux, C., Monfort, A., and Trognon, A. (1985). " Moindres Carrés Asymptotiques," *Annales de l'INSEE*, 58, 91–122.

Hansen, L.P. (1982). "Large Sample Properties of Generalized Method of Moment Estimators," *Econometrica*, 50, 1029–1054.

Sargan, J.D. (1958). "On the Estimation of Economic Relationship by Means of Instrumental Variables," *Econometrica*, 29, 414–426.

Zellner, A. and Theil, H. (1962). " Three-Stage Least Squares: Simultaneous Estimation of Simultaneous Equations," *Econometrica*, 30, 53–78.

CHAPTER 10

Estimation Under Equality Constraints

In the preceding three chapters, we established the asymptotic normality of maximum likelihood estimators, M-estimators, asymptotic least squares estimators, and generalized method of moments estimators. The asymptotic variance covariance matrices of these estimators were derived under the assumption that the true parameter value belongs to the interior of the parameter space. In practice, the latter assumption may not be satisfied. For instance, this arises when the parameters are subject to some equality constraints. These constraints can arise in explicit, implicit, or mixed forms. These various cases are studied in the next sections. To simplify the notation, we let θ denote the function of the parameter that we wish to estimate.

10.1 Constraints

10.1.1 Explicit, Implicit, and Mixed Forms

In Chapter 1 we saw that, in some situations, a priori information could be translated in terms of equality constraints on the parameters of interest. Depending on the problem studied, such constraints can arise in various forms.

Frequently, the p-dimensional parameter vector θ of interest can be expressed as a function of a lower dimensional parameter vector $a \in \mathcal{A} \subset \mathbb{R}^q$, where $q < p$. In this case, the constraints are said to be written in an *explicit* or parametric form. Specifically, we have

$$\theta = h(a), \tag{10.1}$$

where h is a function from $\mathbb{R}^q$ to $\mathbb{R}^p$.

In other cases, equality constraints arise in an *implicit* form. That is, we have

$$g^*(\theta) = 0, \tag{10.2}$$

where g^* is a function from $\mathbb{R}^p$ to $\mathbb{R}^r$.

The preceding two formulations can be viewed as extreme cases of a more general form called the *mixed* form. Specifically, equality constraints arise in a mixed form when the components of θ satisfy some relations implying other parameters, which are called auxiliary parameters. That is, we have

$$g(\theta, a) = 0, \tag{10.3}$$

where a is a q-dimensional parameter vector and g is a function taking its values in $\mathbb{R}^r$.

Remark 10.1: The explicit form is obtained when $g(\theta, a) = \theta - h(a)$. The implicit form corresponds to an auxiliary parameter vector of dimension zero. By convention, the latter vector is taken to be equal to zero. Thus we have $g(\theta, 0) = g^*(\theta) = 0$.

Clearly, it is desirable not to impose on the parameters of interest redundant constraints, i.e., constraints that can be obtained from others. This "minimality" condition on the set of constraints can be expressed in terms of the Jacobian matrix.

For the mixed form, this condition is given by

$$\begin{cases} \partial g/\partial \theta' \text{ is of rank r}, \\ \\ \partial g/\partial a' \text{ is of rank q}. \end{cases} \tag{10.4}$$

For the special cases of the explicit and implicit forms, this condition reduces to

$$\begin{cases} \text{explicit form} : & \partial h/\partial a' \text{ is of rank q}, \\ \\ \text{implicit form} : & \partial g^*(\theta)/\partial \theta' = \partial g(\theta, 0)/\partial \theta' \text{ is of rank r}. \end{cases} \tag{10.5}$$

10.1.2 Examples

Example 10.1: Independence Constraints in a 3×2 Contingency Table

Suppose that n observations are available on two qualitative variables X and Y with three and two categories, respectively. These observations can be summarized in a 3×2 contingency table of which the n_{ij} element, $i = 1, 2, 3$, $j = 1, 2$, gives the number of observations for which the variables X and Y take the value of the ith category and jth category, respectively. Suppose that the n observations are independent and identically distributed. Then the variables (n_{ij}) follow a multinomial distribution $M(n, (p_{ij}))$, where p_{ij} is the probability that the pair (X, Y) takes the value (i, j). Let θ be the vector of p_{ij}.

Now suppose that the variables X and Y are thought to be independent. Then it is necessary to impose some constraints on θ. These constraints can be written in an explicit form by expressing the joint probabilities p_{ij} in terms of the marginal probabilities, denoted $a_{i\cdot}$ and $a_{\cdot j}$, of the variables X and Y. Specifically, we have

$$\begin{array}{ll} p_{11} = a_{1\cdot}a_{\cdot 1}, & p_{21} = (1 - a_{1\cdot})a_{\cdot 1} = (a_{2\cdot}a_{\cdot 1}), \\ p_{12} = a_{1\cdot}a_{\cdot 2}, & p_{22} = (1 - a_{1\cdot})a_{\cdot 2} = (a_{2\cdot}a_{\cdot 2}), \\ p_{13} = a_{1\cdot}(1 - a_{\cdot 1} - a_{\cdot 2}), & p_{23} = (1 - a_{1\cdot})(1 - a_{\cdot 1} - a_{\cdot 2}). \end{array}$$

There are three independent parameters, namely, $a_{1\cdot}$, $a_{\cdot 1}$, and $a_{\cdot 2}$, which can be used to express every parameter of interest as a function of them.

Alternatively, the independence constraint between X and Y can be expressed in an implicit form by requiring that the matrix

$$\begin{bmatrix} p_{11} & p_{21} \\ p_{12} & p_{22} \\ p_{13} & p_{23} \end{bmatrix},$$

is of rank one. Using determinants, this condition reduces to

$$\begin{cases} p_{11}\, p_{22} - p_{21}\, p_{12} & = 0, \\ p_{11}\, p_{23} - p_{21}\, p_{13} & = 0. \end{cases}$$

Lastly, the linear relation between the two column vectors of the above matrix can be written as

$$\begin{array}{rrcl} \exists\, a : & p_{11} & = & a p_{21}, \\ & p_{12} & = & a p_{22}, \\ & p_{13} & = & a p_{23}. \end{array}$$

That is, we have a mixed form.

Example 10.1 shows that a same constraint, which is the independence between X and Y, can be expressed in various equivalent forms. When this arises, the choice of which form to use might take into account the relative computational tractability of subsequent estimators and test statistics.

Example 10.2: In a dynamic model, the current value y_t of the endogenous variable is often expressed as a function of the present and past values of some exogenous variables. That is, y_t is expressed as a function of x_t, x_{t-1}, ... Consider the case where there is only one exogenous variable. Then we have a model of the form

$$y_t = b + w_0 x_t + w_1 x_{t-1} + \ldots, w_K x_{t-K} + u_t.$$

Suppose that the effect of the exogenous variable is exponentially decreasing with time. This suggests that the parameters w_k are constrained and satisfy

$$w_k = a\lambda^k, \text{ with } |\lambda| < 1, \quad k = 0, \ldots, K.$$

These are explicit constraints where the new parameters that determine the deterministic part of the model are b, a, and λ. A mixed form is

$$w_k - \lambda w_{k-1} = 0, \quad k = 1, \ldots, K.$$

Example 10.3: Consider a dynamic model with first-order lagged endogenous and exogenous variables

$$y_t = \theta_0 y_{t-1} + \theta_1 x_t + \theta_2 x_{t-1} + u_t, \quad t = 1, \ldots, T,$$

where the error terms are independent and identically distributed with mean zero. It is interesting to study the case where the two polynomials $1 - \theta_0 L$ and $\theta_1 + \theta_2 L$ have a common root. For, if there exists a real number a such that $\theta_1 + \theta_2 L = a(1 - \theta_0 L)$, then we can write

$$y_t - \theta_0 y_{t-1} = a(x_t - \theta_0 x_{t-1}) + u_t,$$

i.e.

$$y_t = a x_t + v_t,$$

where v_t is such that $v_t - \theta_0 v_{t-1} = u_t$. This means that the dynamic nature of the model arises only from the error term v_t.

There exist various ways for expressing the property that the above two polynomials have a common root. These are:

$$\begin{array}{ll} \text{in explicit form :} & \theta_0 = \theta_0, \theta_1 = \theta_1, \theta_2 = -\theta_1\theta_0, \\ \text{in implicit form :} & \theta_2 + \theta_1\theta_0 = 0, \\ \text{in mixed form :} & \exists\ a : \theta_1 = a \text{ and } \theta_2 = -a\theta_0. \end{array}$$

10.1.3 Relation Between Explicit and Implicit Forms

As the few examples of the previous section indicate, in some cases the constraints on the parameters can be written either in some explicit form or in some implicit form, in which cases the two forms become equivalent. This is not always possible and/or easy to do. In this section we shall consider the case where the constraints are linear. This will allow us to discuss as thoroughly as possible how these two forms are related and how one form can be obtained from the other.

a) From an Implicit Form to an Explicit Form

We consider some linear affine constraints written in an implicit form, namely $\mathbf{G}\theta = g$, where $\mathbf{G}$ and g are, respectively, a known $r \times p$ matrix of rank r and a known $r \times 1$ vector. Let $\mathbf{G}^-$ denote a generalized inverse of $\mathbf{G}$. Then we have

$$\mathbf{G}\theta = g \Leftrightarrow \exists\ \beta \in \mathbb{R}^p : \theta = \mathbf{G}^- g + (\mathbf{I} - \mathbf{G}^-\mathbf{G})\beta.$$

The β-parameterization, however, is not very convenient because the matrix $\mathbf{I} - \mathbf{G}^-\mathbf{G}$ is singular. Let $\mathbf{H}$ be a $p \times (p - r)$ matrix of which the column vectors constitute a basis of

$$\text{Ker } \mathbf{G} = \text{Im}(\mathbf{I} - \mathbf{G}^-\mathbf{G}).$$

We obtain

$$\mathbf{G}\theta = g \Leftrightarrow \exists\ a \in \mathbb{R}^{p-r} : \theta = \mathbf{G}^- g + \mathbf{H}a.$$

Hence we have obtained an equivalent explicit form in which $q = p - r$ new parameters appear where:

p = number of original parameters,

r = number of implicit constraints.

b) From an Explicit Form to an Implicit Form

Conversely, consider now some linear constraints written in an explicit form, namely, $\theta = \mathbf{H}a + h$, where a is a q-dimensional parameter vector. Hence the vector $\theta - h$ must belong to the subspace generated by the q column vectors of $\mathbf{H}$, which are assumed to be linearly independent.

This set of constraints can be written in two relatively natural implicit forms. First, since $\mathbf{I} - \mathbf{H}(\mathbf{H}'\mathbf{H})^{-1}\mathbf{H}'$ is the orthogonal projection on to the subspace that is orthogonal to the column space of $\mathbf{H}$, we have

$$\exists\ a \in I\!R^q : \theta = \mathbf{H}a + h \Leftrightarrow (\mathbf{I} - \mathbf{H}(\mathbf{H}'\mathbf{H})^{-1}\mathbf{H}')(\theta - h) = 0.$$

Note, however, that we have an implicit form in which the matrix $\mathbf{G} = \mathbf{I} - \mathbf{H}(\mathbf{H}'\mathbf{H})^{-1}\mathbf{H}'$ is not of full rank.

Second, to satisfy the full rank condition, consider some basis vectors $\tilde{\mathbf{G}}_1, \ldots, \tilde{\mathbf{G}}_{p-q}$ of the subspace orthogonal to the subspace generated by the column vectors of $\mathbf{H}$. We have

$$\begin{aligned} \exists\ a \in I\!R^q : \theta = \mathbf{H}a + h \quad &\Leftrightarrow \quad \tilde{\mathbf{G}}_k'(\theta - h) = 0, \quad k = 1, \ldots, p - q, \\ &\Leftrightarrow \quad \tilde{\mathbf{G}}'(\theta - h) = 0, \end{aligned}$$

where

$$\tilde{\mathbf{G}}' = \begin{pmatrix} \tilde{\mathbf{G}}_1' \\ \vdots \\ \tilde{\mathbf{G}}_{p-q}' \end{pmatrix}.$$

We now have an implicit form which satisfies the full rank condition. We find again the same relation between the number of implicit constraints and the number of original and auxiliary parameters, namely

r	$=$	p	$-$	q	
number of independent implicit constraints		number of original parameters		number of parameters when the constraints are satisfied	(10.6)

Remark 10.2: Deriving an implicit form from an explicit form, or *vice versa*, is straightforward when the constraints are so-called *zero constraints*. Specifically, consider a partition of the parameter vector θ into two subvectors α and β so that $\theta = (\alpha', \beta')'$. Zero constraints on α are

$$\alpha = 0.$$

This is trivially an implicit form. An explicit form can be readily obtained by treating the parameters β as auxiliary parameters. Specifically, we have

$$\alpha = 0 \Leftrightarrow \theta = \begin{pmatrix} 0 \\ \beta \end{pmatrix}.$$

10.2 An Example: Least Squares Under Linear Constraints

As an illustration of estimation under constraints, we study in this section the ordinary least squares estimation of the parameters of a linear model when the parameters are subject to some linear constraints. This example has the advantage of simplicity. In particular, the various estimators that are reviewed can be written as explicit functions of the observations. By comparing the constrained estimator to the unconstrained estimator, it follows that the study of the effects of the constraints will be relatively easy. In addition, it will be easy to assess the consequences of the form of the constraints whether these are written in an explicit or implicit form. In more complicated models, however, it is not always possible to obtain some explicit expressions for the constrained estimators. As a consequence, the properties of such estimators are difficult to derive in finite samples. Then it will be necessary to rely on an asymptotic theory. This will be the topic of Section 3 of this chapter.

10.2.1 Explicit Linear Constraints

We consider the linear model

$$y_i = x_i\theta + u_i, \quad i = 1, \ldots, n,$$

where, conditionally on the exogenous variables, the error terms have zero mean $E(u_i \mid x_i) = 0$, identical variance $V(u_i \mid x_i) = \sigma^2$, and are uncorrelated.

The parameter $\theta \in \Theta \subset \mathbb{R}^p$ is subject to some linear constraints of the form

$$\theta = \mathbf{H}a + h, \tag{10.7}$$

where $\mathbf{H}$ and h are, respectively, a known $p \times q$ matrix and a known p-dimensional vector. It is assumed that $\mathbf{H}$ is of rank q and that a varies in $\mathbb{R}^q$.

Suppose that we apply ordinary least squares subject to the above constraints. Then we must consider the optimization problem

$$\begin{cases} \min_\theta \sum_{i=1}^n (y_i - x_i\theta)^2 \\ \\ \text{subject to } \theta = \mathbf{H}a + h. \end{cases} \tag{10.8}$$

To obtain a solution to this problem, we can substitute out the constraints in the objective function and maximize the resulting objective function with respect to a. Then the constraints are used to obtain the solution in θ. That is, after substitution, the problem reduces to

$$\min_{a \in \mathbb{R}^q} \sum_{i=1}^n (y_i - x_i\mathbf{H}a - x_i h)^2.$$

This problem corresponds to the ordinary least squares estimation (without constraints) of the model

$$y_i^* = x_i^* a + u_i, \text{ with } y_i^* = y_i - x_i h, \ x_i^* = x_i\mathbf{H}.$$

The solution is

$$\hat{a}_n = \left(\sum_{i=1}^n \mathbf{H}' x_i' x_i \mathbf{H} \right)^{-1} \sum_{i=1}^n \mathbf{H}' x_i' (y_i - x_i h).$$

Using matrix notations, the solution can be written as

$$\hat{a}_n = (\mathbf{H}'\mathbf{X}'\mathbf{X}\mathbf{H})^{-1}\mathbf{H}'\mathbf{X}'(Y - \mathbf{X}h). \tag{10.9}$$

Hence the *constrained ordinary least squares estimator* of θ is

$$\hat{\theta}_n^0 = \mathbf{H}\hat{a}_n + h,$$

i.e.

$$\hat{\theta}_n^0 = \mathbf{H}(\mathbf{H}'\mathbf{X}'\mathbf{X}\mathbf{H})^{-1}\mathbf{H}'\mathbf{X}'(Y - \mathbf{X}h) + h. \tag{10.10}$$

The constrained OLS estimator can be easily expressed as a function of the unconstrained OLS estimator, which is $\hat{\theta}_n = (\mathbf{X}'\mathbf{X})^{-1}\mathbf{X}'Y$.

Property 10.1: *The estimators $\hat{a}_n$ and $\hat{\theta}_n^0$ are given by*

$$\begin{aligned} \hat{a}_n &= (\mathbf{H}'\mathbf{X}'\mathbf{X}\mathbf{H})^{-1}\mathbf{H}'\mathbf{X}'\mathbf{X}(\hat{\theta}_n - h), \\ \hat{\theta}_n^0 &= \mathbf{H}(\mathbf{H}'\mathbf{X}'\mathbf{X}\mathbf{H})^{-1}\mathbf{H}'\mathbf{X}'\mathbf{X}(\hat{\theta}_n - h) + h. \end{aligned}$$

The preceding expression for the constrained OLS estimator can be used to derive easily the first two moments of $\hat{\theta}_n^0$.

Property 10.2: *The constrained OLS estimator subject to $\theta = \mathbf{H}a + h$ is an unbiased estimator of θ with variance covariance matrix*

$$V(\hat{\theta}_n^0) = \sigma^2 \mathbf{H}(\mathbf{H}'\mathbf{X}'\mathbf{X}\mathbf{H})^{-1}\mathbf{H}'.$$

PROOF: Since $E\hat{\theta}_n = \theta = \mathbf{H}a + h$ and $V(\hat{\theta}_n) = \sigma^2(\mathbf{X}'\mathbf{X})^{-1}$ we have

$$\begin{aligned} E(\hat{\theta}_n^0) &= \mathbf{H}(\mathbf{H}'\mathbf{X}'\mathbf{X}\mathbf{H})^{-1}\mathbf{H}'\mathbf{X}'\mathbf{X}(E\hat{\theta}_n - h) + h \\ &= \mathbf{H}(\mathbf{H}'\mathbf{X}'\mathbf{X}\mathbf{H})^{-1}\mathbf{H}'\mathbf{X}'\mathbf{X}\mathbf{H}a + h \\ &= \mathbf{H}a + h \\ &= \theta, \end{aligned}$$

and

$$\begin{aligned} V(\hat{\theta}_n^0) &= \mathbf{H}(\mathbf{H}'\mathbf{X}'\mathbf{X}\mathbf{H})^{-1}\mathbf{H}'\mathbf{X}'\mathbf{X}V(\hat{\theta}_n)\mathbf{X}'\mathbf{X}\mathbf{H}(\mathbf{H}'\mathbf{X}'\mathbf{X}\mathbf{H})^{-1}\mathbf{H}' \\ &= \sigma^2\mathbf{H}(\mathbf{H}'\mathbf{X}'\mathbf{X}\mathbf{H})^{-1}\mathbf{H}'. \end{aligned}$$

□

Remark 10.3: The constrained OLS estimator $\hat{\theta}_n^0$, which takes into account information contained in the constraints $\theta = \mathbf{H}a + h$, is clearly more precise than the unconstrained OLS estimator $\hat{\theta}_n$. This can be easily verified by comparing their variance covariance matrices. We have

$$V(\hat{\theta}_n) - V(\hat{\theta}_n^0) = \sigma^2(\mathbf{X}'\mathbf{X})^{-1} - \sigma^2\mathbf{H}(\mathbf{H}'\mathbf{X}'\mathbf{X}\mathbf{H})^{-1}\mathbf{H}'$$

$$= \sigma^2(\mathbf{X}'\mathbf{X})^{-1/2}(\mathbf{I} - (\mathbf{X}'\mathbf{X})^{1/2}\mathbf{H}(\mathbf{H}'\mathbf{X}'\mathbf{X}\mathbf{H})^{-1}\mathbf{H}'(\mathbf{X}'\mathbf{X})^{1/2})(\mathbf{X}'\mathbf{X})^{-1/2}.$$

The latter matrix is positive semidefinite since

$$(\mathbf{X}'\mathbf{X})^{1/2}\mathbf{H}(\mathbf{H}'\mathbf{X}'\mathbf{X}\mathbf{H})^{-1}\mathbf{H}'(\mathbf{X}'\mathbf{X})^{1/2}$$

is an orthogonal projection matrix.

The constrained OLS estimator can be interpreted as a two-step estimator. This interpretation relies on the following property.

Property 10.3: *Consider the linear (affine) model*

$$\hat{\theta}_n = \mathbf{H}a + h + v_n,$$

where

$$Ev_n = 0, \quad Vv_n = V\hat{\theta}_n = \sigma^2(\mathbf{X}'\mathbf{X})^{-1}.$$

The estimator $\hat{a}_n$ is the generalized least squares estimator of a and $\hat{\theta}_n^0$ is the corresponding predicted value for the dependent variable in the above model.

PROOF: GLS estimation of the above model gives the estimator

$$(\mathbf{H}'(Vv_n)^{-1}\mathbf{H})^{-1}\mathbf{H}'(Vv_n)^{-1}(\hat{\theta}_n - h) = (\mathbf{H}'\mathbf{X}'\mathbf{X}\mathbf{H})^{-1}\mathbf{H}'\mathbf{X}'\mathbf{X}(\hat{\theta}_n - h).$$

This estimator is equal to $\hat{a}_n$. Property 10.3 follows. □

Thus the constrained OLS estimator $\hat{\theta}_n^0$ can be obtained from two unconstrained regressions. In a first step, a regression of Y_i on X_i gives $\hat{\theta}_n$. In a second step, a GLS regression of $\hat{\theta}_n - h$ on the columns of $\mathbf{H}$ gives $\hat{\theta}_n^0$.

Corollary 10.1: *The vectors $\hat{\theta}_n^0$ and $\hat{\theta}_n - \hat{\theta}_n^0$ are uncorrelated.*

PROOF: This a direct consequence of the interpretation of $\hat{\theta}_n^0$ and $\hat{\theta}_n - \hat{\theta}_n^0$ as the predicted value of $\hat{\theta}_n$ and the residuals, respectively, in the model of Property 10.3. □

10.2.2 Implicit Linear Constraints

Now consider the linear model

$$y_i = x_i\theta + u_i, \quad i = 1, \ldots, n,$$

where the usual assumptions are satisfied, namely, $E(u_i \mid x_1, \ldots, x_n) = 0$, $V(u_i \mid x_1, \ldots, x_n) = \sigma^2$, $E(u_iu_j \mid x_1, \ldots, x_n) = 0$,$\forall i \neq j$. Suppose that the parameters θ are constrained by

$$\mathbf{G}\theta = g, \tag{10.11}$$

where $\mathbf{G}$ and g are a $r \times p$ matrix and a r-dimensional vector, respectively, and $\mathbf{G}$ is of rank r.

The constrained ordinary least squares estimator is a solution to

$$\begin{cases} \min_\theta \sum_{i=1}^n (y_i - x_i\theta)^2 \\ \text{subject to } \mathbf{G}\theta = g, \end{cases} \tag{10.12}$$

i.e., using matrix notations

$$\begin{cases} \min_\theta (Y - \mathbf{X}\theta)'(Y - \mathbf{X}\theta) \\ \\ \text{subject to } \mathbf{G}\theta = g. \end{cases}$$

The objective function is convex in θ and the constraints are linear. Thus the above problem has a unique solution, which can be obtained by solving the first-order conditions of the Lagrangian function. Let $\tilde{\lambda}$ denote the vector of r Lagrange multipliers. The Lagrangian function is

$$\mathcal{L} = (Y - \mathbf{X}\theta)'(Y - \mathbf{X}\theta) - \tilde{\lambda}'(\mathbf{G}\theta - g).$$

The first-order conditions are

$$\begin{cases} -2\mathbf{X}'(Y - \mathbf{X}\hat{\theta}_n^0) - \mathbf{G}'\tilde{\lambda}_n = 0, \\ \mathbf{G}\hat{\theta}_n^0 = g. \end{cases}$$

From the first set of equations, we obtain

$$\begin{aligned} \hat{\theta}_n^0 &= (\mathbf{X}'\mathbf{X})^{-1}\mathbf{X}'Y + \frac{1}{2}(\mathbf{X}'\mathbf{X})^{-1}\mathbf{G}'\tilde{\lambda}_n \\ &= \hat{\theta}_n + \frac{1}{2}(\mathbf{X}'\mathbf{X})^{-1}\mathbf{G}'\tilde{\lambda}_n. \end{aligned}$$

Substituting this expression into the second set of first-order equations, we obtain the Lagrange multipliers. That is, from

$$g = \mathbf{G}\hat{\theta}_n^0 = \mathbf{G}\hat{\theta}_n + \frac{1}{2}\mathbf{G}(\mathbf{X}'\mathbf{X})^{-1}\mathbf{G}'\tilde{\lambda}_n,$$

we obtain

$$\tilde{\lambda}_n = 2(\mathbf{G}(\mathbf{X}'\mathbf{X})^{-1}\mathbf{G}')^{-1}(g - \mathbf{G}\hat{\theta}_n). \tag{10.13}$$

Therefore the constrained OLS estimator is

$$\hat{\theta}_n^0 = \hat{\theta}_n + (\mathbf{X}'\mathbf{X})^{-1}\mathbf{G}'(\mathbf{G}(\mathbf{X}'\mathbf{X})^{-1}\mathbf{G}')^{-1}(g - \mathbf{G}\hat{\theta}_n). \tag{10.14}$$

This estimator is equal to the unconstrained OLS estimator modified by an additive term that is a function of the extent $\mathbf{G}\hat{\theta}_n - g$ by which the constraints are not satisfied by $\hat{\theta}_n$.

Remark 10.4: From equations (10.13) and (10.14) and the fact that $\mathbf{G}$ is of full row rank, it follows immediately that the vectors $\tilde{\lambda}_n$, $\hat{\theta}_n - \hat{\theta}_n^0$ and $\mathbf{G}\hat{\theta}_n - g$ are in one-to-one relations.

Property 10.4: *The constrained OLS estimator subject to* $\mathbf{G}\theta = g$ *is unbiased with variance covariance matrix*

$$\begin{aligned} V(\hat{\theta}_n^0) &= \sigma^2(\mathbf{I} - (\mathbf{X}'\mathbf{X})^{-1}\mathbf{G}'(\mathbf{G}(\mathbf{X}'\mathbf{X})^{-1}\mathbf{G}')^{-1}\mathbf{G})(\mathbf{X}'\mathbf{X})^{-1} \\ & \quad (\mathbf{I} - \mathbf{G}'(\mathbf{G}(\mathbf{X}'\mathbf{X})^{-1}\mathbf{G}')^{-1}\mathbf{G}(\mathbf{X}'\mathbf{X})^{-1}). \end{aligned}$$

PROOF: This follows from equation (10.14), which expresses $\hat{\theta}_n^0$ as a function of $\hat{\theta}_n$, and from the variance covariance matrix of the unconstrained OLS estimator. □

Developing the expression for $V(\hat{\theta}_n^0)$ gives an alternative and simpler expression for the variance covariance matrix. We have

$$V(\hat{\theta}_n^0) = \sigma^2((\mathbf{X}'\mathbf{X})^{-1} - (\mathbf{X}'\mathbf{X})^{-1}\mathbf{G}'(\mathbf{G}(\mathbf{X}'\mathbf{X})^{-1}\mathbf{G}')^{-1}\mathbf{G}(\mathbf{X}'\mathbf{X})^{-1}). \tag{10.15}$$

In particular, we have

$$V(\hat{\theta}_n^0) \preceq \sigma^2(\mathbf{X}'\mathbf{X})^{-1} = V(\hat{\theta}_n).$$

That is, the constrained OLS estimator is more precise than the unconstrained OLS estimator provided, of course, that the constraints hold.

10.3 Asymptotic Properties

In general, usual estimation methods do not lead to some closed form expressions for the corresponding constrained estimators of the parameter vector. As a consequence, it is difficult to derive the exact distributions of these estimators in finite samples. As for unconstrained estimation, however, it is possible to establish some asymptotic properties under suitable regularity conditions.

These properties are studied in this section within a quite general framework that includes important estimation methods such as maximum likelihood, M-estimation, asymptotic least squares estimation, generalized methods of moments, etc. This framework is presented in the first subsection.

Under suitable regularity conditions, these various estimation methods lead to consistent estimators under constraints. This consistency property need not be established again. This is because the sufficient conditions for consistency given in Section 7.4.1, for instance, do not require that the true parameter value θ_0 belongs to the interior of the parameter space Θ. It follows that these conditions are satisfied in the constrained case as well as in the unconstrained case. On the other hand, the asymptotic variance covariance matrices of the constrained estimators are modified. In the second subsection, some Taylor expansions allow us to find some quantities that are asymptotically equivalent to our estimators. This result allows us to derive the asymptotic distributions of the various estimators in the third subsection.

10.3.1 General Framework

a) Unconstrained Problems

The various estimation methods studied in Chapters 7, 8, and 9 are all based on the optimization of some objective functions depending on the observations and the parameters of interest. The unconstrained estimator is defined as a solution to a problem of the form

$$\max_{\theta \in \Theta} L_n(\theta). \tag{10.16}$$

It is assumed that this estimator is consistent and that it satisfies the first-order conditions

$$\frac{\partial L_n(\hat{\theta}_n)}{\partial \theta} = 0. \tag{10.17}$$

Moreover, it is assumed that the objective function L_n is such that

$$\frac{1}{\sqrt{n}} \frac{\partial L_n(\theta_0)}{\partial \theta} \xrightarrow{d} N(0, \mathcal{I}_0), \tag{10.18}$$

and

$$-\frac{1}{n} \frac{\partial^2 L_n(\theta_0)}{\partial \theta \, \partial \theta'} \rightarrow \mathcal{J}_0, \text{ with probability 1,} \tag{10.19}$$

where $\mathcal{I}_0$ and $\mathcal{J}_0$ are two symmetric positive definite matrices.

Under the above conditions, it follows from a first-order Taylor expansion of $(1/\sqrt{n})\partial L_n(\hat{\theta}_n)/\partial \theta$ around θ_0 that

$$\frac{1}{\sqrt{n}} \frac{\partial L_n}{\partial \theta}(\theta_0) - \mathcal{J}_0 \sqrt{n}(\hat{\theta}_n - \theta_0) \# 0. \tag{10.20}$$

In particular, we have

$$\sqrt{n}(\hat{\theta}_n - \theta_0) \xrightarrow{d} N(0, \mathcal{J}_0^{-1} \mathcal{I}_0 \mathcal{J}_0^{-1}). \tag{10.21}$$

In general, the two matrices $\mathcal{I}_0$ and $\mathcal{J}_0$ are different. When they are equal, the asymptotic variance covariance matrix of the unconstrained estimator simplifies to

$$V_{as}\sqrt{n}(\hat{\theta}_n - \theta_0) = \mathcal{J}_0^{-1}\mathcal{I}_0\mathcal{J}_0^{-1} = \mathcal{J}_0^{-1} = \mathcal{I}_0^{-1}. \tag{10.22}$$

b) Estimation Methods

Here, we briefly review various classical estimation methods and we show how these methods fit into the preceding general framework.

(i) **Maximum Likelihood Estimation** (see Chapter 7)

We have

$$L_n(\theta) = \sum_{i=1}^{n} \log f(Y_i \mid X_i; \theta)$$

in the case of a conditional model with observations $Y_1, \ldots, Y_n$ that are conditionally independent. The matrices $\mathcal{I}_0$ and $\mathcal{J}_0$ are equal to the Fisher information matrix, i.e.

$$\begin{aligned} \mathcal{I}_0 = \mathcal{J}_0 &= E_0\left(-\frac{\partial^2 \log f(Y \mid X; \theta_0)}{\partial\theta\,\partial\theta'}\right) \\ &= V_0\left(\frac{\partial \log f(Y \mid X; \theta_0)}{\partial\theta}\right). \end{aligned} \tag{10.23}$$

(ii) **M-Estimation**

In Section 8.1.4, a quasi generalized M-estimator of θ is defined as a solution to an optimization problem of the form

$$\max_{\theta\in\Theta} \frac{1}{n}\sum_{i=1}^{n} \Psi(Y_i, X_i; \theta, \tilde{c}_n),$$

where $\tilde{c}_n$ is a function of the observations converging to a constant limit c_0.

When this estimator is consistent for θ and when the condition

$$\mathcal{H} = E_0\left(\frac{\partial^2\Psi(Y, X; \theta_o, c_0)}{\partial\theta\,\partial c'}\right) = 0 \tag{10.24}$$

is satisfied, we showed that conditions (10.18) and (10.19) are actually satisfied with

$$\begin{aligned} \mathcal{J}_0 &= E_0\left(-\frac{\partial^2\Psi(Y, X; \theta_o, c_0)}{\partial\theta\,\partial\theta'}\right), \\ \mathcal{I}_0 &= E_0\left(\frac{\partial\Psi(Y, X; \theta_o, c_0)}{\partial\theta}\frac{\partial\Psi(Y, X; \theta_o, c_0)}{\partial\theta'}\right). \end{aligned}$$

See Property 8.5.

For the special case of quasi generalized nonlinear least squares estimation (see Section 8.3.3) and quasi generalized pseudo maximum likelihood estimation (see Section 8.4.3), the two matrices $\mathcal{I}_0$ and $\mathcal{J}_0$ are equal.

(iii) **Asymptotic Least Squares Estimation**

In Chapter 9, an asymptotic least squares estimator is defined as a solution to an optimization problem of the form

$$\min_\theta k(\hat{b}_n, \theta)' \mathbf{S}_n k(\hat{b}_n, \theta), \tag{10.25}$$

where $k(b, \theta) = 0$ are the constraints linking the parameters of interest θ to the auxiliary parameters b, $\hat{b}_n$ is a consistent and asymptotically normal estimator of b with some asymptotic variance covariance matrix $\mathbf{\Omega}_0$, and $\{\mathbf{S}_n\}$ is a sequence of positive definite matrices converging to a nonsingular nonrandom matrix $\mathbf{S}_0$.

To satisfy conditions (10.16), (10.18), and (10.19) on the objective function L_n it suffices to let

$$L_n(\theta) = -\frac{n}{2} k'(\hat{b}_n, \theta) \mathbf{S}_n k(\hat{b}_n, \theta). \tag{10.26}$$

Then we have

$$\begin{aligned}
\frac{1}{\sqrt{n}} \frac{\partial L_n(\theta_0)}{\partial \theta} \quad &\# \quad -\sqrt{n} \frac{\partial k'(b_0, \theta_0)}{\partial \theta} \mathbf{S}_0 k(\hat{b}_n, \theta_0) \\
&\# \quad -\frac{\partial k'(b_0, \theta_0)}{\partial \theta} \mathbf{S}_0 \frac{\partial k(b_0, \theta_0)}{\partial b'} \sqrt{n}(\hat{b}_n - b_0).
\end{aligned}$$

It follows that

$$\mathcal{I}_0 = \frac{\partial k'}{\partial \theta} \mathbf{S}_0 \frac{\partial k}{\partial b'} \mathbf{\Omega}_0 \frac{\partial k'}{\partial b} \mathbf{S}_0 \frac{\partial k}{\partial \theta'}, \tag{10.27}$$

where all the derivatives are evaluated at the limit point (b_0, θ_0). In addition, it is easily seen that

$$\mathcal{J}_0 = \frac{\partial k'}{\partial \theta} \mathbf{S}_0 \frac{\partial k}{\partial \theta'}. \tag{10.28}$$

The two matrices $\mathcal{I}_0$ and $\mathcal{J}_0$ are equal when we consider the best asymptotic least squares estimator, i.e., when $\mathbf{S}_0$ is chosen to be

$$\left(\frac{\partial k}{\partial b'} \mathbf{\Omega}_0 \frac{\partial k'}{\partial b} \right)^{-1}.$$

Then we have

$$\mathcal{I}_0 = \mathcal{J}_0 = \frac{\partial k'}{\partial \theta}\left(\frac{\partial k}{\partial b'}\mathbf{\Omega}_0\frac{\partial k'}{\partial b}\right)^{-1}\frac{\partial k}{\partial \theta'}. \tag{10.29}$$

(iv) **Generalized Methods of Moments**

A GMM estimator is obtained by minimizing an objective function of the form

$$\min\left(\sum_{i=1}^{n} h(Y_i;\theta)\right)'\mathbf{S}_n\left(\sum_{i=1}^{n} h(Y_i;\theta)\right),$$

where h is a function that defines the estimating constraints $E_0 h(Y;\theta_0) = 0$ and $\{\mathbf{S}_n\}$ is a sequence of matrices converging to $\mathbf{S}_0$.

To satisfy conditions (10.16), (10.18), and (10.19), we let

$$L_n(Y;\theta) = -\frac{1}{2n}\left(\sum_{i=1}^{n} h(Y_i;\theta)\right)'\mathbf{S}_n\left(\sum_{i=1}^{n} h(Y_i;\theta)\right).$$

For an arbitrary sequence of matrices $\mathbf{S}_n$, the matrices $\mathcal{I}_0$ and $\mathcal{J}_0$ are, in general, different. They are, however, equal for the best GMM estimator, which corresponds to a limit of the sequence $\{\mathbf{S}_n\}$ equal to

$$\mathbf{S}_0^* = V_0(h(Y;\theta_0))^{-1}.$$

In this case, the two matrices $\mathcal{I}_0$ and $\mathcal{J}_0$ are equal and given by

$$\begin{aligned}\mathcal{I}_0 &= \mathcal{J}_0 \\ &= E_0\left(\frac{\partial h'(Y;\theta_0)}{\partial\theta}\right)(V_0 h(Y;\theta_0))^{-1}E_0\left(\frac{\partial h(Y;\theta_0)}{\partial\theta'}\right).\end{aligned} \tag{10.30}$$

c) Constrained Problems

An estimation procedure under constraints is associated with each of the estimation methods described above, i.e., with each choice of the objective function L_n. We shall assume that the constraints are written in the mixed form

$$\exists\ a \in \mathbb{R}^q,\quad g(\theta, a) = 0,$$

where g is a r-dimensional function. The constrained estimator associated with the objective function L_n and the constraints $g(\theta, a) = 0$ is defined as the vector $\hat{\theta}_n^0$ such that $(\hat{\theta}_n^0, \hat{a}_n^0)$ is a solution to the problem

$$\begin{cases}\max_{\theta,a} L_n(\theta) \\ \text{subject to } g(\theta, a) = 0.\end{cases} \tag{10.31}$$

Thus, according to the chosen objective function, we can define a constrained maximum likelihood estimator, a constrained pseudo maximum likelihood estimator, a constrained asymptotic least squares estimator, a constrained generalized method of moment estimator, etc.

If the true parameter value θ_0 is associated with a unique value a_0 of the auxiliary parameters a, then it is easy to establish consistency of $(\hat{\theta}_n^0, \hat{a}_n^0)$ to (θ_0, a_0) under suitable regularity conditions. It suffices to use an argument similar to that presented in Chapter 8.

Moreover, if (θ_0, a_0) belongs to the induced interior of $\{(\theta, a) : \theta \in \Theta, g(\theta, a) = 0\}$ and if the functions L_n and g are continuously differentiable, then the estimator $(\hat{\theta}_n^0, \hat{a}_n^0)$ satisfies asymptotically the first-order conditions. Let λ denote the vector of Lagrange multipliers associated with the constraints. The Lagrangian function is given by

$$\mathcal{L} = L_n(\theta) - g'(\theta, a)\lambda.$$

A solution $(\hat{\theta}_n^0, \hat{a}_n^0)$ and $\hat{\lambda}_n$ to this problem satisfies the first-order conditions

$$\begin{cases} \dfrac{\partial L_n(Y; \hat{\theta}_n^0)}{\partial \theta} - \dfrac{\partial g'(\hat{\theta}_n^0, \hat{a}_n^0)}{\partial \theta} \hat{\lambda}_n = 0, \\[2ex] \dfrac{\partial g'(\hat{\theta}_n^0, \hat{a}_n^0)}{\partial a} \hat{\lambda}_n = 0, \\[2ex] g(\hat{\theta}_n^0, \hat{a}_n^0) = 0. \end{cases} \tag{10.32}$$

Remark 10.5: When the constraints are written in the explicit form $\theta = h(a)$, the first-order conditions become

$$\begin{cases} \dfrac{\partial L_n(Y; \hat{\theta}_n^0)}{\partial \theta} - \hat{\lambda}_n = 0, \\[2ex] \dfrac{\partial h'(\hat{a}_n^0)}{\partial a} \hat{\lambda}_n = 0, \\[2ex] \hat{\theta}_n^0 = h(\hat{a}_n^0), \end{cases}$$

i.e.

$$\begin{cases} \hat{\lambda}_n = \dfrac{\partial L_n(Y; h(\hat{a}_n^0))}{\partial \theta}, \\[2ex] \dfrac{\partial h'(\hat{a}_n^0)}{\partial a} \dfrac{\partial L_n(Y; h(\hat{a}_n^0))}{\partial \theta} = 0, \\[2ex] \hat{\theta}_n^0 = h(\hat{a}_n^0). \end{cases}$$

The latter system is easily interpreted. When $\theta = h(a)$, it is possible to reparameterize the problem with the auxiliary parameters a. Then the estimator $\hat{a}_n^0$ is obtained by maximizing $L_n(Y; h(a))$. The second set of equations of this system corresponds to the set of first-order conditions associated with this optimization problem. The constrained estimator $\hat{\theta}_n^0$ is obtained from $\hat{a}_n^0$ by applying the transformation h. The Lagrange multiplier vector is the derivative of the objective function at the optimum value.

Remark 10.6: The other important case arises when the constraints are in some implicit form $g^*(\theta) = 0$. The corresponding first-order conditions follow directly from the system (10.32) using the convention

$$a = 0, \; g^*(\theta) = g(\theta, 0), \text{ and } \frac{\partial g'}{\partial a} = 0.$$

Then we obtain

$$\begin{cases} \dfrac{\partial L_n(Y; \hat{\theta}_n^0)}{\partial \theta} - \dfrac{\partial g^{*\prime}(\hat{\theta}_n^0)}{\partial \theta} \hat{\lambda}_n = 0, \\ \\ g^*(\hat{\theta}_n^0) = 0. \end{cases}$$

10.3.2 Taylor Expansions of the First-Order Conditions

We suppose that the functions L_n and g are twice continuously differentiable with respect to θ and a. Then we can expand the first-order conditions (10.32) in a neighborhood of (θ_0, a_0). After multiplying by the scalar $1/\sqrt{n}$ or $\sqrt{n}$, we obtain the system

$$\frac{1}{\sqrt{n}} \frac{\partial L_n(\theta_0)}{\partial \theta} + \frac{1}{n} \frac{\partial^2 L_n(\theta_0)}{\partial \theta \, \partial \theta'} \sqrt{n}(\hat{\theta}_n^0 - \theta_0) - \frac{\partial g'(\theta_0, a_0)}{\partial \theta} \frac{1}{\sqrt{n}} \hat{\lambda}_n \# 0,$$

$$\frac{\partial g'(\theta_0, a_0)}{\partial a} \frac{1}{\sqrt{n}} \hat{\lambda}_n \# 0,$$

$$\frac{\partial g(\theta_0, a_0)}{\partial \theta'} \sqrt{n}(\hat{\theta}_n^0 - \theta_0) + \frac{\partial g(\theta_0, a_0)}{\partial a'} \sqrt{n}(\hat{a}_n^0 - a_0) \# 0.$$

Now, using

$$\mathcal{J}_0 = \lim -\frac{1}{n} \frac{\partial^2 L_n(\theta_0)}{\partial \theta \partial \theta'},$$

(see equation (10.19)) and

$$\frac{1}{\sqrt{n}}\frac{\partial L_n(\theta_0)}{\partial\theta} - \mathcal{J}_0\sqrt{n}(\hat{\theta}_n - \theta_0) \# 0,$$

(see equation (10.20)), we obtain the system

$$\mathcal{J}_0\sqrt{n}(\hat{\theta}_n - \theta_0) - \mathcal{J}_0\sqrt{n}(\hat{\theta}_n^0 - \theta_0) - \frac{\partial g'(\theta_0, a_0)}{\partial\theta}\frac{1}{\sqrt{n}}\hat{\lambda}_n \# 0,$$

$$\frac{\partial g'(\theta_0, a_0)}{\partial a}\frac{1}{\sqrt{n}}\hat{\lambda}_n \# 0,$$

$$\frac{\partial g(\theta_0, a_0)}{\partial\theta'}\sqrt{n}(\hat{\theta}_n^0 - \theta_0) + \frac{\partial g(\theta_0, a_0)}{\partial a'}\sqrt{n}(\hat{a}_n^0 - a_0) \# 0.$$

It follows that $\sqrt{n}(\hat{\theta}_n^0-\theta_0)$, $\sqrt{n}(\hat{a}_n^0-a_0)$ and $(1/\sqrt{n})\hat{\lambda}_n$ are asymptotically linear functions of the unconstrained estimator $\sqrt{n}(\hat{\theta}_n - \theta_0)$ since

$$\begin{pmatrix} \mathcal{J}_0 & 0 & \frac{\partial g'(\theta_0, a_0)}{\partial\theta} \\ 0 & 0 & \frac{\partial g'(\theta_0, a_0)}{\partial a} \\ \frac{\partial g(\theta_0, a_0)}{\partial\theta'} & \frac{\partial g(\theta_0, a_0)}{\partial a'} & 0 \end{pmatrix} \begin{pmatrix} \sqrt{n}(\hat{\theta}_n^0 - \theta_0) \\ \sqrt{n}(\hat{a}_n^0 - a_0) \\ \frac{1}{\sqrt{n}}\hat{\lambda}_n \end{pmatrix}$$

$$\# \begin{pmatrix} \mathcal{J}_o\sqrt{n}(\hat{\theta}_n - \theta_0) \\ 0 \\ 0 \end{pmatrix}. \tag{10.33}$$

In particular, since $\sqrt{n}(\hat{\theta}_n - \theta_0)$ converges in distribution to a centered normal variable, then

$$\sqrt{n}(\hat{\theta}_n^0 - \theta_0),\ \sqrt{n}(\hat{a}_n^0 - a_0), \frac{1}{\sqrt{n}}\hat{\lambda}_n$$

also converge to some centered normal variables.

To find the asymptotic variance covariance matrices of these quantities, we need to solve the system (10.33). From the first set of equations we obtain

$$\sqrt{n}(\hat{\theta}_n^0 - \theta_0) \# \sqrt{n}(\hat{\theta}_n - \theta_0) - \mathcal{J}_0^{-1}\frac{\partial g'(\theta_0, a_0)}{\partial\theta}\frac{\hat{\lambda}_n}{\sqrt{n}}.$$

Using this result in the last set of equations of (10.33), we obtain

$$\frac{\partial g(\theta_0, a_0)}{\partial\theta'}\sqrt{n}(\hat{\theta}_n - \theta_0) - \frac{\partial g(\theta_0, a_0)}{\partial\theta'}\mathcal{J}_0^{-1}\frac{\partial g'(\theta_0, a_0)}{\partial\theta}\frac{\hat{\lambda}_n}{\sqrt{n}}$$

$$+\frac{\partial g(\theta_0, a_0)}{\partial\theta'}\sqrt{n}(\hat{a}_n^0 - a_0) \# 0. \tag{10.34}$$

Since the rank of $\partial g(\theta_0, a_0)/\partial\theta'$ is equal to r, the matrix

$$\frac{\partial g(\theta_0, a_0)}{\partial\theta'}\mathcal{J}_0^{-1}\frac{\partial g'(\theta_0, a_0)}{\partial\theta}$$

is nonsingular. Thus the preceding equation can be used to solve for the Lagrange multiplier vector as a function of $\sqrt{n}(\hat{\theta}_n - \theta_0)$ and $\sqrt{n}(\hat{a}_n^0 - a_0)$

$$\frac{\hat{\lambda}_n}{\sqrt{n}} \quad \# \quad \left(\frac{\partial g(\theta_0, a_0)}{\partial\theta'}\mathcal{J}_0^{-1}\frac{\partial g'(\theta_0, a_0)}{\partial\theta}\right)^{-1} \left(\frac{\partial g(\theta_0, a_0)}{\partial\theta'}\sqrt{n}(\hat{\theta}_n - \theta_0) + \frac{\partial g(\theta_0, a_0)}{\partial a'}\sqrt{n}(\hat{a}_n^0 - a_0)\right). \quad (10.35)$$

Using equation (10.35) in the second set of equations of (10.33) and solving for $\sqrt{n}(\hat{a}_n^0 - a_0)$, we obtain

$$\sqrt{n}(\hat{a}_n^0 - a_0) \quad \# \quad -\left(\frac{\partial g'}{\partial a}\left(\frac{\partial g}{\partial\theta'}\mathcal{J}_0^{-1}\frac{\partial g'}{\partial\theta}\right)^{-1}\frac{\partial g}{\partial a'}\right)^{-1} \frac{\partial g'}{\partial a}\left(\frac{\partial g}{\partial\theta'}\mathcal{J}_0^{-1}\frac{\partial g'}{\partial\theta}\right)^{-1}\frac{\partial g}{\partial\theta'}\sqrt{n}(\hat{\theta}_n - \theta_0), \quad (10.36)$$

where all the derivatives are evaluated at (θ_0, a_0). Note that the nonsingularity of the first matrix in the right-hand side follows directly from the rank condition (10.4).

Now define the projection matrix

$$\mathbf{M} \quad = \quad \frac{\partial g}{\partial a'}\left(\frac{\partial g'}{\partial a}\left(\frac{\partial g}{\partial\theta'}\mathcal{J}_0^{-1}\frac{\partial g'}{\partial\theta}\right)^{-1}\frac{\partial g}{\partial a'}\right)^{-1}\frac{\partial g'}{\partial a}\left(\frac{\partial g}{\partial\theta'}\mathcal{J}_0^{-1}\frac{\partial g'}{\partial\theta}\right)^{-1}. \quad (10.37)$$

We have

$$\frac{\partial g(\theta_0, a_0)}{\partial a'}\sqrt{n}(\hat{a}_n^0 - a_0) \;\#\; -\mathbf{M}\frac{\partial g}{\partial\theta'}\sqrt{n}(\hat{\theta}_n - \theta_0). \quad (10.38)$$

Then, using equation (10.35), we obtain

$$\frac{\hat{\lambda}_n}{\sqrt{n}} \;\#\; \left(\frac{\partial g}{\partial\theta'}\mathcal{J}_0^{-1}\frac{\partial g'}{\partial\theta}\right)^{-1}(\mathbf{I} - \mathbf{M})\frac{\partial g}{\partial\theta'}\sqrt{n}(\hat{\theta}_n - \theta_0). \quad (10.39)$$

Lastly, we obtain the constrained estimator $\hat{\theta}_n^0$ as

$$\sqrt{n}(\hat{\theta}_n^0 - \theta_0) \;\#\; \left(\mathbf{I} - \mathcal{J}_0^{-1}\frac{\partial g'}{\partial\theta}\left(\frac{\partial g}{\partial\theta'}\mathcal{J}_0^{-1}\frac{\partial g'}{\partial\theta}\right)^{-1}(\mathbf{I} - \mathbf{M})\frac{\partial g}{\partial\theta}\right)\sqrt{n}(\hat{\theta}_n - \theta_0). \quad (10.40)$$

10.3.3 Asymptotic Distributions

As noted in the previous subsection, the vector

$$\begin{pmatrix} \sqrt{n}(\hat{a}_n^0 - a_0) \\ \sqrt{n}(\hat{\theta}_n^0 - \theta_0) \\ \frac{1}{\sqrt{n}}\hat{\lambda}_n \end{pmatrix}$$

is asymptotically a linear function of $\sqrt{n}(\hat{\theta}_n - \theta_0)$ and converges in distribution to some centered normal variables. The variance covariance matrix of the asymptotic normal distribution is readily obtained from equations (10.36), (10.39), and (10.40). For instance the asymptotic variance covariance matrix of the constrained estimator $\hat{\theta}_n^0$ is

$$\begin{aligned} & V_{as}\sqrt{n}(\hat{\theta}_n^0 - \theta) \\ = & \left(\mathbf{I} - \mathcal{J}_0^{-1}\frac{\partial g'}{\partial \theta}\left(\frac{\partial g}{\partial \theta'}\mathcal{J}_0^{-1}\frac{\partial g'}{\partial \theta}\right)^{-1}(\mathbf{I} - \mathbf{M})\frac{\partial g}{\partial \theta'}\right) V_{as}\sqrt{n}(\hat{\theta}_n - \theta_0) \\ & \left(\mathbf{I} - \frac{\partial g'}{\partial \theta}(\mathbf{I} - \mathbf{M}')\left(\frac{\partial g}{\partial \theta'}\mathcal{J}_0^{-1}\frac{\partial g'}{\partial \theta}\right)^{-1}\frac{\partial g}{\partial \theta'}\mathcal{J}_0^{-1}\right) \\ = & \left(\mathbf{I} - \mathcal{J}_0^{-1}\frac{\partial g'}{\partial \theta}\left(\frac{\partial g}{\partial \theta'}\mathcal{J}_0^{-1}\frac{\partial g'}{\partial \theta}\right)^{-1}(\mathbf{I} - \mathbf{M})\frac{\partial g}{\partial \theta'}\right) \mathcal{J}_0^{-1}\mathcal{I}_0\mathcal{J}_0^{-1} \\ & \left(\mathbf{I} - \frac{\partial g'}{\partial \theta}(\mathbf{I} - \mathbf{M}')\left(\frac{\partial g}{\partial \theta'}\mathcal{J}_0^{-1}\frac{\partial g'}{\partial \theta}\right)^{-1}\frac{\partial g}{\partial \theta'}\mathcal{J}_0^{-1}\right). \end{aligned}$$

This formula, which is derived for the general case, is relatively inconvenient. It greatly simplifies, however, in important special cases.

a) Explicit Constraints

When the constraints are written in the explicit form $\theta - h(a) = 0$, we have

$$\frac{\partial g}{\partial \theta'} = \mathbf{I} \text{ and } \frac{\partial g}{\partial a'} = -\frac{\partial h}{\partial a'}.$$

Thus the asymptotically equivalent quantities of $\hat{\lambda}_n/\sqrt{n}$, $\sqrt{n}(\hat{a}_n^0 - a_0)$, and $\sqrt{n}(\hat{\theta}_n^0 - \theta_0)$ obtained previously become

$$\frac{\hat{\lambda}_n}{\sqrt{n}} \quad \# \quad \mathcal{J}_0(\mathbf{I} - \mathbf{M})\sqrt{n}(\hat{\theta}_n - \theta_0),$$

$$
\begin{aligned}
\sqrt{n}(\hat{a}_n^0 - a_0) &\;\#\; -\left(\frac{\partial h'}{\partial a}\mathcal{J}_0\frac{\partial h}{\partial a'}\right)^{-1}\frac{\partial h}{\partial a'}\mathcal{J}_o\sqrt{n}(\hat{\theta}_n - \theta_0),\\
\sqrt{n}(\hat{\theta}_n^0 - \theta_0) &\;\#\; \mathbf{M}\sqrt{n}(\hat{\theta}_n - \theta_0),
\end{aligned}
$$

where

$$
\mathbf{M} = \frac{\partial h}{\partial a'}\left(\frac{\partial h'}{\partial a}\mathcal{J}_0\frac{\partial h}{\partial a'}\right)^{-1}\frac{\partial h'}{\partial a}\mathcal{J}_0.
$$

In particular, we have

$$
V_{as}\sqrt{n}(\hat{\theta}_n^0 - \theta_0) = \mathbf{M}\mathcal{J}_0^{-1}\mathcal{I}_0\mathcal{J}_0^{-1}\mathbf{M}'. \tag{10.41}
$$

b) Implicit Constraints

In this case, the constraints are $g^*(\theta) = 0$. Asymptotically equivalent quantities are obtained using the convention

$$
a_0 = 0 \text{ (and } \hat{a}_n^0 = 0\text{) and } \frac{\partial g}{\partial a'} = 0.
$$

Equation (10.39) gives immediately

$$
\frac{\hat{\lambda}_n}{\sqrt{n}} \;\#\; \left(\frac{\partial g^*}{\partial \theta'}\mathcal{J}_0^{-1}\frac{\partial g^{*\prime}}{\partial \theta}\right)^{-1}\frac{\partial g^*}{\partial \theta'}\sqrt{n}(\hat{\theta}_n - \theta_0). \tag{10.42}
$$

Then, from equation (10.40), we obtain

$$
\begin{aligned}
&\sqrt{n}(\hat{\theta}_n^0 - \theta_0)\\
&\quad\#\left(\mathbf{I} - \mathcal{J}_0^{-1}\frac{\partial g^{*\prime}}{\partial \theta}\left(\frac{\partial g^*}{\partial \theta'}\mathcal{J}_0^{-1}\frac{\partial g^{*\prime}}{\partial \theta}\right)^{-1}\frac{\partial g^*}{\partial \theta'}\right)\sqrt{n}(\hat{\theta}_n - \theta_0).
\end{aligned}\tag{10.43}
$$

That is, equation (10.40) obtained earlier holds provided $\mathbf{M} = 0$ by convention. Note that the matrix

$$
\begin{aligned}
\mathbf{P} &= \mathcal{J}_0^{-1}\frac{\partial g^{*\prime}}{\partial \theta}\left(\frac{\partial g^*}{\partial \theta'}\mathcal{J}_0^{-1}\frac{\partial g^{*\prime}}{\partial \theta}\right)^{-1}\frac{\partial g^*}{\partial \theta'}\\
&= \mathcal{J}_0^{-1}\frac{\partial g^{*\prime}}{\partial \theta}\left(\left(\mathcal{J}_0^{-1}\frac{\partial g^{*\prime}}{\partial \theta}\right)'\mathcal{J}_0\left(\mathcal{J}_0^{-1}\frac{\partial g^{*\prime}}{\partial \theta}\right)\right)^{-1}\left(\mathcal{J}_0^{-1}\frac{\partial g^{*\prime}}{\partial \theta}\right)'\mathcal{J}_0
\end{aligned}
$$

corresponds to an orthogonal projection on to the column space of $\mathcal{J}_0^{-1}$ $\partial g^{*\prime}/\partial \theta$ with respect to the scalar product associated with $\mathcal{J}_0$. Hence the asymptotic variance covariance matrix of the constrained estimator is

$$
V_{as}\sqrt{n}(\hat{\theta}_n^0 - \theta_0) = (\mathbf{I} - \mathbf{P})\mathcal{J}_0^{-1}\mathcal{I}_0\mathcal{J}_0^{-1}(\mathbf{I} - \mathbf{P})'.
$$

c) Equality between the matrices $\mathcal{I}_0$ and $\mathcal{J}_0$

Recall that $\mathcal{I}_0 = \mathcal{J}_0$ occurs for instance when we consider maximum likelihood estimation, quasi generalized pseudo maximum likelihood estimation, best asymptotic least squares estimation, and best method of moments estimation. When such an equality holds, we can rely on a geometric interpretation in terms of orthogonal projections to establish that the constrained estimator is asymptotically uncorrelated with its difference with the unconstrained estimator.

Property 10.5: *When $\mathcal{I}_0 = \mathcal{J}_0$, the random variables $\sqrt{n}(\hat{\theta}_n^0 - \theta_0)$ and $\sqrt{n}(\hat{\theta}_n - \hat{\theta}_n^0)$ are asymptotically uncorrelated.*

PROOF: We have

$$\begin{aligned}
&\text{Cov}_{as}\left(\sqrt{n}(\hat{\theta}_n^0 - \theta_0), \sqrt{n}(\hat{\theta}_n - \hat{\theta}_n^0)\right) \\
&= \left(\mathbf{I} - \mathcal{J}_0^{-1}\frac{\partial g'}{\partial \theta}\left(\frac{\partial g}{\partial \theta'}\mathcal{J}_0^{-1}\frac{\partial g'}{\partial \theta}\right)^{-1}(\mathbf{I} - \mathbf{M})\frac{\partial g}{\partial \theta'}\right) \\
&\quad \mathcal{J}_0^{-1}\frac{\partial g'}{\partial \theta}(\mathbf{I} - \mathbf{M}')\left(\frac{\partial g}{\partial \theta'}\mathcal{J}_0^{-1}\frac{\partial g'}{\partial \theta}\right)^{-1}\frac{\partial g}{\partial \theta'}\mathcal{J}_0^{-1} \\
&= \mathcal{J}_0^{-1}\frac{\partial g'}{\partial \theta}(\mathbf{I} - \mathbf{M}')\left(\frac{\partial g}{\partial \theta'}\mathcal{J}_0^{-1}\frac{\partial g'}{\partial \theta}\right)^{-1}\frac{\partial g}{\partial \theta'}\mathcal{J}_0^{-1} \\
&\quad -\mathcal{J}_0^{-1}\frac{\partial g'}{\partial \theta}\left(\frac{\partial g}{\partial \theta'}\mathcal{J}_0^{-1}\frac{\partial g'}{\partial \theta}\right)^{-1}(\mathbf{I} - \mathbf{M})\frac{\partial g}{\partial \theta'}\mathcal{J}_0^{-1}\frac{\partial g'}{\partial \theta}(\mathbf{I} - \mathbf{M}') \\
&\quad \left(\frac{\partial g}{\partial \theta'}\mathcal{J}_0^{-1}\frac{\partial g'}{\partial \theta}\right)^{-1}\frac{\partial g}{\partial \theta'}\mathcal{J}_0^{-1}.
\end{aligned}$$

Since $\mathbf{M}$ is an orthogonal projection matrix with respect to the scalar product defined by the matrix

$$\left(\frac{\partial g}{\partial \theta'}\mathcal{J}_0^{-1}\frac{\partial g'}{\partial \theta}\right)^{-1},$$

we have

$$(\mathbf{I} - \mathbf{M})^2 = \mathbf{I} - \mathbf{M}$$

and

$$\frac{\partial g}{\partial \theta'}\mathcal{J}_0^{-1}\frac{\partial g'}{\partial \theta}(\mathbf{I} - \mathbf{M}') = (\mathbf{I} - \mathbf{M})\frac{\partial g}{\partial \theta'}\mathcal{J}_0^{-1}\frac{\partial g'}{\partial \theta}.$$

Using the preceding two equalities, we can see that

$$\left(\frac{\partial g}{\partial \theta'}\mathcal{J}_0^{-1}\frac{\partial g'}{\partial \theta}\right)^{-1}(\mathbf{I} - \mathbf{M})\left(\frac{\partial g}{\partial \theta'}\mathcal{J}_0^{-1}\frac{\partial g'}{\partial \theta}\right)(\mathbf{I} - \mathbf{M}')\left(\frac{\partial g}{\partial \theta'}\mathcal{J}_0^{-1}\frac{\partial g'}{\partial \theta}\right)^{-1}$$

$$
\begin{aligned}
&= (\mathbf{I}-\mathbf{M}')^2 \left(\frac{\partial g}{\partial \theta'}\mathcal{J}_0^{-1}\frac{\partial g'}{\partial \theta}\right)^{-1} \\
&= (\mathbf{I}-\mathbf{M}') \left(\frac{\partial g}{\partial \theta'}\mathcal{J}_0^{-1}\frac{\partial g'}{\partial \theta}\right)^{-1}.
\end{aligned}
$$

It follows immediately that

$$
\mathrm{Cov}_{as}\left(\sqrt{n}(\hat{\theta}_n^0-\theta_0), \sqrt{n}(\hat{\theta}_n-\hat{\theta}_n^0)\right)=0.
$$

□

Property 10.6: *If* $\mathcal{I}_0=\mathcal{J}_0$, *then*

$$
\begin{aligned}
V_{as}\sqrt{n}\left((\hat{\theta}_n-\hat{\theta}_n^0)\right) &= \mathcal{J}_0^{-1}\frac{\partial g'}{\partial \theta}(\mathbf{I}-\mathbf{M}')\left(\frac{\partial g}{\partial \theta'}\mathcal{J}_0^{-1}\frac{\partial g'}{\partial \theta}\right)^{-1}\frac{\partial g}{\partial \theta'}\mathcal{J}_0^{-1}, \\
V_{as}\left(\sqrt{n}(\hat{\theta}_n^0-\theta_0)\right) &= \mathcal{J}_0^{-1}-V_{as}\left(\hat{\theta}_n-\hat{\theta}_n^0)\right).
\end{aligned}
$$

PROOF: Because $\mathbf{M}$ is a projection matrix, we obtain

$$
\begin{aligned}
&V_{as}\sqrt{n}\left((\hat{\theta}_n-\hat{\theta}_n^0)\right) \\
&= \mathcal{J}_0^{-1}\frac{\partial g'}{\partial \theta}\left(\frac{\partial g}{\partial \theta'}\mathcal{J}_0^{-1}\frac{\partial g'}{\partial \theta}\right)^{-1}(\mathbf{I}-\mathbf{M})\frac{\partial g}{\partial \theta'}\mathcal{J}_0^{-1}\frac{\partial g'}{\partial \theta}(\mathbf{I}-\mathbf{M}') \\
&\quad \left(\frac{\partial g}{\partial \theta'}\mathcal{J}_0^{-1}\frac{\partial g'}{\partial \theta}\right)^{-1}\frac{\partial g}{\partial \theta'}\mathcal{J}_0^{-1} \\
&= \mathcal{J}_0^{-1}\frac{\partial g'}{\partial \theta}(\mathbf{I}-\mathbf{M}')\left(\frac{\partial g}{\partial \theta'}\mathcal{J}_0^{-1}\frac{\partial g'}{\partial \theta}\right)^{-1}\frac{\partial g}{\partial \theta'}\mathcal{J}_0^{-1}.
\end{aligned}
$$

The second equality follows from the asymptotic uncorrelation between $\sqrt{n}(\hat{\theta}_n^0-\theta_0)$ and $\sqrt{n}(\hat{\theta}_n-\hat{\theta}_n^0)$ and the equality

$$
V_{as}\left(\sqrt{n}(\hat{\theta}_n-\theta_0)\right)=\mathcal{J}_0^{-1}.
$$

□

In the case of explicit constraints, we obtain

$$
\begin{aligned}
V_{as}\left(\sqrt{n}(\hat{\theta}_n^0-\theta_0)\right) &= \mathcal{J}_0^{-1}\mathbf{M}' \\
&= \frac{\partial h}{\partial a'}\left(\frac{\partial h'}{\partial a}\mathcal{J}_0\frac{\partial h}{\partial a'}\right)^{-1}\frac{\partial h'}{\partial a}. \qquad (10.44)
\end{aligned}
$$

Remark 10.7: Equation (10.44) can be easily interpreted for maximum likelihood estimation under constraints. Let $\mathcal{P} = \{P_\theta,\ \theta \in \Theta\}$ denote the specified family of distributions. The matrix $\mathcal{J}_0$ is the Fisher information matrix of this model. Then $(\partial h'/\partial a)\ \mathcal{J}_0(\partial h/\partial a')$ is the information matrix of the nested model $\tilde{\mathcal{P}} = \{P_{h(a)}, a \in \mathcal{A}\}$, which is parameterized by a. Therefore $[(\partial h'/\partial a)\mathcal{J}_0(\partial h/\partial a')]^{-1}$ is the variance covariance matrix of the maximum likelihood estimator $\hat{a}_n^0$ of a. Then equation (10.44) results from the relation $\hat{\theta}_n^0 = h(\hat{a}_n^0)$.

When the constraints are written in the implicit form $g^*(\theta) = 0$, we have

$$\begin{aligned} V_{as}\sqrt{n}(\hat{\theta}_n^0 - \theta_0) &= (\mathbf{I} - \mathbf{P})\mathcal{J}_0^{-1}(\mathbf{I} - \mathbf{P}') \\ &= (\mathbf{I} - \mathbf{P})\mathcal{J}_0^{-1}, \end{aligned}$$

i.e.

$$\begin{aligned} &V_{as}\sqrt{n}(\hat{\theta}_n^0 - \theta_0) \\ &= \mathcal{J}_0^{-1} - \mathcal{J}_0^{-1}\frac{\partial g^{*\prime}}{\partial \theta}\left(\frac{\partial g^*}{\partial \theta'}\mathcal{J}_0^{-1}\frac{\partial g^{*\prime}}{\partial \theta}\right)^{-1}\frac{\partial g^*}{\partial \theta'}\mathcal{J}_0^{-1}. \end{aligned} \quad (10.45)$$

d) When $\mathcal{I}_0 = \mathcal{J}_0$ and the Constraints are Zero Constraints

We suppose that the parameter vector θ is partitioned into two subvectors so that $\theta = (\alpha', \beta')'$. The matrix $\mathcal{J}_0$ can be partitioned accordingly as

$$\mathcal{J}_o = \begin{pmatrix} \mathcal{J}_{0,\alpha\alpha} & \mathcal{J}_{0,\alpha\beta} \\ \mathcal{J}_{0,\beta\alpha} & \mathcal{J}_{0,\beta\beta} \end{pmatrix}.$$

Now suppose that the constraints are $\alpha = 0$. Then the constrained estimator is of the form

$$\hat{\theta}_n^0 = \begin{pmatrix} 0 \\ \hat{\beta}_n^0 \end{pmatrix}. \quad (10.46)$$

Using the explicit form $\theta = (0', \beta')'$, where β plays the role of auxiliary parameters, it follows from equation (10.44) that

$$\begin{aligned} &V_{as}\left(\sqrt{n}(\hat{\theta}_n^0 - \theta_0)\right) \\ &= \begin{pmatrix} 0 \\ \mathbf{I} \end{pmatrix}\left((0, \mathbf{I})\begin{pmatrix} \mathcal{J}_{0,\alpha\alpha} & \mathcal{J}_{0,\alpha\beta} \\ \mathcal{J}_{0,\beta\alpha} & \mathcal{J}_{0,\beta\beta} \end{pmatrix}\begin{pmatrix} 0 \\ \mathbf{I} \end{pmatrix}\right)^{-1}(0, \mathbf{I}) \\ &= \begin{pmatrix} 0 & 0 \\ 0 & \mathcal{J}_{0,\beta\beta}^{-1} \end{pmatrix}. \end{aligned}$$

Thus

$$V_{as}\left(\sqrt{n}(\hat{\beta}_n^0 - \beta_0)\right) = \mathcal{J}_{0,\beta\beta}^{-1}. \tag{10.47}$$

The same result is obtained if we interpret zero constraints as implicit constraints. Specifically, we use equation (10.45). From the partition of the matrix $\mathcal{J}_0^{-1}$

$$\mathcal{J}_0^{-1} = \begin{pmatrix} \mathcal{J}_0^{\alpha\alpha} & \mathcal{J}_0^{\alpha\beta} \\ \mathcal{J}_0^{\beta\alpha} & \mathcal{J}_0^{\beta\beta} \end{pmatrix},$$

we have

$$\begin{aligned} & V_{as}\left(\sqrt{n}(\hat{\theta}_n^0 - \theta_0)\right) \\ = \; & \mathcal{J}_0^{-1} - \mathcal{J}_0^{-1}\begin{pmatrix} \mathbf{I} \\ 0 \end{pmatrix}\left((\mathbf{I},0)\mathcal{J}_0^{-1}\begin{pmatrix} \mathbf{I} \\ 0 \end{pmatrix}\right)^{-1}(\mathbf{I},0)\mathcal{J}_0^{-1} \\ = \; & \begin{pmatrix} \mathcal{J}_0^{\alpha\alpha} & \mathcal{J}_0^{\alpha\beta} \\ \mathcal{J}_0^{\beta\alpha} & \mathcal{J}_0^{\beta\beta} \end{pmatrix} - \begin{pmatrix} \mathcal{J}_0^{\alpha\alpha} & \mathcal{J}_0^{\alpha\beta} \\ \mathcal{J}_0^{\beta\alpha} & \mathcal{J}_0^{\beta\alpha} \quad (\mathcal{J}_0^{\alpha\alpha})^{-1} \quad \mathcal{J}_0^{\alpha\beta} \end{pmatrix}. \end{aligned}$$

Hence

$$V_{as}\left(\sqrt{n}(\hat{\beta}_n^0 - \beta_0)\right) = \mathcal{J}_0^{\beta\beta} - \mathcal{J}_0^{\beta\alpha}(\mathcal{J}_0^{\alpha\alpha})^{-1}\mathcal{J}_0^{\alpha\beta}.$$

This equation is clearly identical to equation (10.47) using the inverse formula of a partitioned matrix (see Section 2.2 in Appendix A).

10.4 Constrained Two-Step Estimation

10.4.1 Methods Based on Unconstrained Estimators

When the model and the constraints are both linear, we showed that the constrained estimator $\hat{\theta}_n^0$ is readily obtained from the unconstrained estimator $\hat{\theta}_n$ (see Properties 10.1 and 10.3). This results can be easily generalized.

Let $\{\tilde{\mathcal{J}}_n\}$ be a sequence of matrices converging to $\mathcal{J}_0$.

Property 10.7: *A solution $(\tilde{\theta}_n^0, \tilde{a}_n^0)$ to the problem*

$$\begin{cases} \min_{a,\theta}(\hat{\theta}_n - \theta)'\tilde{\mathcal{J}}_n(\hat{\theta}_n - \theta) \\ \\ \text{subject to } g(\theta, a) = 0, \end{cases}$$

is asymptotically equivalent to $(\hat{\theta}_n^0, \hat{a}_n^0)$. In addition, the Lagrange multipliers $\tilde{\lambda}_n$ associated with the constraints is asymptotically equivalent to $\hat{\lambda}_n$.

PROOF: The optimization problem is of the general form studied in Section 10.3 provided we define

$$\tilde{L}_n(Y;\theta) = -\frac{n}{2}(\hat{\theta}_n - \theta)'\mathcal{J}_0(\hat{\theta}_n - \theta).$$

Then we have

$$\frac{1}{\sqrt{n}}\frac{\partial \tilde{L}_n(\theta_0)}{\partial \theta} = -\mathcal{J}_0\sqrt{n}(\hat{\theta}_n - \theta_0) \xrightarrow{d} N(0, \mathcal{J}_0\mathcal{J}_0^{-1}\mathcal{I}_0\mathcal{J}_0^{-1}\mathcal{J}_0 = \mathcal{I}_0),$$

and

$$-\frac{1}{n}\frac{\partial^2 \tilde{L}_n(\theta_0)}{\partial \theta\, \partial \theta'} \rightarrow \mathcal{J}_0.$$

Next, it suffices to note that the asymptotic equivalent quantities of

$$\frac{\hat{\lambda}_n}{\sqrt{n}},\ \sqrt{n}(\hat{a}_n^0 - a_0),\ \sqrt{n}(\hat{\theta}_n^0 - \theta_0)$$

that we obtained previously depend on the present optimization problem only through $\hat{\theta}_n$ and the matrix $\mathcal{J}_0$. But $\hat{\theta}_n$ also gives the unconstrained maximum of $\tilde{L}_n$, and $\mathcal{J}_0$ is the same for L_n and $\tilde{L}_n$. □

Property 10.7 allows us to replace the original objective function L_n, which can be relatively complex, by a quadratic function in θ which is, in general, easier to optimize. Then the constrained estimator $\hat{\theta}_n^0$ can be interpreted as a two-step estimator. In a first step, one determines the unconstrained estimator. Then, in a second step, one solves the optimization problem defined in Property 10.7.

When we consider estimation methods such as least squares, generalized method of moments, etc., Property 10.7 shows that the unconstrained estimator summarizes all information relevant to the study of the asymptotic properties of the corresponding constrained estimator.

Sometimes, it is also possible to replace the original nonlinear constraints by some linear constraints, which are more tractable.

Property 10.8: *Consider the implicit constraints $g^*(\theta) = 0$. A solution $\bar{\theta}_n^0$ to the problem*

$$\begin{cases} \min_\theta (\hat{\theta}_n - \theta)'\tilde{\mathcal{J}}_n(\hat{\theta}_n - \theta) \\ \\ \text{subject to } g^*(\hat{\theta}_n) = \dfrac{\partial g^*(\hat{\theta}_n)}{\partial \theta'}(\hat{\theta}_n)(\hat{\theta}_n - \theta), \end{cases}$$

is asymptotically equivalent to $\hat{\theta}_n^0$.

PROOF: An expression for the estimator $\bar{\theta}_n^0$ is easily obtained from the results of Section 10.2.2. Namely, we have

$$\bar{\theta}_n^0 = \hat{\theta}_n - \mathcal{J}_0^{-1} \frac{\partial g^{*\prime}(\hat{\theta}_n)}{\partial \theta} \left(\frac{\partial g^*(\hat{\theta}_n)}{\partial \theta'} \mathcal{J}_0^{-1} \frac{\partial g^{*\prime}(\hat{\theta}_n)}{\partial \theta} \right)^{-1} g^*(\hat{\theta}_n).$$

From a first-order Taylor expansion we obtain

$$\sqrt{n}(\bar{\theta}_n^0 - \theta_0) \# \sqrt{n}(\hat{\theta}_n - \theta_0)$$

$$-\mathcal{J}_0^{-1} \frac{\partial g^{*\prime}(\theta_0)}{\partial \theta} \left(\frac{\partial g^*(\theta_0)}{\partial \theta'} \mathcal{J}_0^{-1} \frac{\partial g^{*\prime}(\theta_0)}{\partial \theta} \right)^{-1} \frac{\partial g^*(\theta_0)}{\partial \theta'} \sqrt{n}(\hat{\theta}_n - \theta_0).$$

Then the desired result follows from the comparison of this expression to the asymptotic equivalent quantity (10.43) of $\sqrt{n}(\hat{\theta}_n^0 - \theta_0)$. □

10.4.2 Methods Based on the Constraints

Results similar to the previous ones can be obtained when we consider the estimation of the auxiliary parameters a.

Property 10.9: *An estimator $\tilde{a}_n^0$ that is a solution to*

$$\min_a g(\hat{\theta}_n, a)' \mathbf{S}_n g(\hat{\theta}_n, a),$$

where $\mathbf{S}_n$ is a matrix converging to

$$\mathbf{S}_0 = \left(\frac{\partial g(\theta_0, a_0)}{\partial \theta'} \mathcal{J}_0^{-1} \frac{\partial g'(\theta_0, a_0)}{\partial \theta} \right)^{-1},$$

is asymptotically equivalent to $\hat{a}_n^0$.

PROOF: A Taylor expansion of the first-order conditions

$$g(\hat{\theta}_n, \tilde{a}_n^0)' \mathbf{S}_n \frac{\partial g(\hat{\theta}_n, \tilde{a}_n^0)}{\partial a'} = 0$$

gives immediately

$$\sqrt{n}(\tilde{a}_n^0 - a_0) \# - \left(\frac{\partial g'}{\partial a} \mathbf{S}_0 \frac{\partial g}{\partial a'} \right)^{-1} \frac{\partial g'}{\partial a} \mathbf{S}_0 \frac{\partial g}{\partial \theta} \sqrt{n}(\hat{\theta}_n - \theta_0).$$

Then the desired result follows from the comparison of this expression to the asymptotic equivalent quantity (10.36) of $\sqrt{n}(\hat{a}_n^0 - a_0)$. □

Corollary 10.2: *Let $\hat{\theta}_n$ be the unconstrained maximum likelihood estimator of θ. Suppose that the constraints are written in the explicit form $\theta = h(a)$. Then the estimator $\tilde{a}_n^0$ that is a solution to*

$$\min_a (\hat{\theta}_n - h(a))'\mathbf{S}_n(\hat{\theta}_n - h(a)),$$

where $\mathbf{S}_n$ converges to $\mathcal{J}_0 = \mathcal{I}_0 = (V_{as}\sqrt{n}(\hat{\theta}_n - \theta_0))^{-1}$ is asymptotically equivalent to the maximum likelihood estimator of a.

PROOF: If $L_n(Y;\theta) = \sum_{i=1}^n \log f(Y_i;\theta)$, then we have $L_n(Y;h(a)) = \sum_{i=1}^n \log f(Y_i;h(a))$ under the constraints. Thus the estimator $\hat{a}_n^0$ is the maximum likelihood estimator of a. Then it suffices to invoke Property 10.9 noting that $\partial g/\partial\theta' = \mathbf{I}$. □

The estimation method for a proposed in Property 10.9 relies on the constraints $g(\theta, a) = 0$. In fact, the method does not depend on the actual form of the constraints.

Property 10.10: *Consider two equivalent forms of the constraints, namely, $g(\theta, a) = 0$ and $h(\theta, a, b) = 0$, where*

$$\{(\theta, a) : g(\theta, a) = 0\} = \{(\theta, a) : \exists\ b, h(\theta, a, b) = 0\}.$$

Define the estimator $\bar{a}_{0n}$ such that $(\bar{a}_{0n}, \bar{b}_{0n})$ is a solution to

$$\min_{a,b} h(\hat{\theta}_n, a, b)'\bar{\mathbf{S}}_n h(\hat{\theta}_n, a, b),$$

where $\bar{\mathbf{S}}_n$ converges to

$$\left(\frac{\partial h}{\partial\theta'}\mathcal{J}_0^{-1}\frac{\partial h'}{\partial\theta}\right)^{-1}.$$

Then $\bar{a}_{0n}$ is asymptotically equivalent to $\tilde{a}_n^0$.

PROOF: This result directly follows from Property 10.9 and the fact that the estimators $\hat{\theta}_n^0$ and $\hat{a}_n^0$ such that $(\hat{\theta}_n^0, \hat{a}_n^0, \hat{b}_n^0)$ is a solution to

$$\begin{cases} \max_{\theta,a,b} L_n(\theta) \\ \text{subject to } h(\theta, a, b) = 0, \end{cases}$$

are equal to the estimators $\hat{\theta}_n^0$ and $\hat{a}_n^0$ that solve the optimization problem

$$\begin{cases} \max_{\theta,a} L_n(\theta) \\ \text{subject to } g(\theta, a) = 0. \end{cases}$$

□

10.5 Examples

Example 10.4: The constrained model is frequently simpler than the unconstrained model. For instance, consider a logistic model where the variables Y_i, $i = 1, \ldots, n$ are dichotomous and independent conditionally on some exogenous variables $X_1, \ldots, X_n$. The model is given by

$$\begin{aligned} P(Y_i = 1 \mid X_i) &= \frac{1}{1 + \exp(\alpha X_i + \beta)}, \\ P(Y_i = 0 \mid X_i) &= \frac{\exp(\alpha X_i + \beta)}{1 + \exp(\alpha X_i + \beta)}. \end{aligned}$$

The unconstrained maximum likelihood estimator $(\hat{\alpha}_n, \hat{\beta}_n)$ of (α, β) must be obtained by numerical optimization. In contrast, the maximum likelihood estimator constrained by $\alpha = 0$ is of the form $(0, \hat{\beta}_n^0)'$ where $\hat{\beta}_n^0$ is a solution to

$$\max_{\beta} \sum_{i=1}^{n} \left(Y_i \log \left(\frac{1}{1 + \exp \beta} \right) + (1 - Y_i) \log \left(\frac{\exp \beta}{1 + \exp \beta} \right) \right).$$

The latter problem has a unique solution which is

$$\hat{\beta}_n^0 = \log \left(\frac{1 - \bar{Y}_n}{\bar{Y}_n} \right), \text{ where } \bar{Y}_n = \frac{1}{n} \sum_{i=1}^{n} Y_i.$$

Example 10.5: Consider the following linear model

$$Y_t = \begin{cases} a + b(t - t_0) + u_t, & \text{if } t \leq t_0, \\ a + c(t - t_0) + u_t, & \text{if } t > t_0, \end{cases}$$

where the error terms satisfy the usual assumptions. This model states that Y_t varies on average linearly with time with a potential change in the slope at time $t = t_0$.

Ordinary least squares estimation of b and c gives

$$\hat{b}_n = \frac{\mathrm{Cov}_1(Y, t - t_0)}{V_1(t - t_0)},$$

and

$$\hat{c}_n = \frac{\mathrm{Cov}_2(Y, t - t_0)}{V_2(t - t_0)},$$

where Cov_1, Cov_2, V_1, and V_2 denote the sample covariances and variances computed for the first and second periods, which correspond to dates $t \leq t_0$ and $t > t_0$, respectively.

If there is no change in the slope, i.e., if $b = c$, then constrained ordinary least squares estimation gives

$$\hat{b}_n^0 = \hat{c}_n^0 = \frac{\text{Cov}(Y, t - t_0)}{V(t - t_0)},$$

where the covariance and the variance are now computed using all the observations.

Example 10.6: Consider the dynamic model defined in Example 10.2, namely

$$y_t = b_0 + w_0 x_t + w_1 x_{t-1} + \ldots + w_K x_{t-K} + u_t, \ t = 1, \ldots, T,$$

where $Eu = 0$ and $Vu = \sigma^2 \mathbf{I}$.

Suppose that the parameters in this model are constrained by $w_k = a\lambda^k$, $k = 0, \ldots, K$. Equivalently, these constraints are

$$\exists \, \lambda : w_k = \lambda w_{k-1}, \ k = 1, \ldots, K.$$

From Properties 10.9 and 10.10 it follows immediately that an estimator of λ that is asymptotically equivalent to the nonlinear least squares estimator of λ is obtained as a solution to the minimization of

$$(\hat{w}_{1n} - \lambda \hat{w}_{0n}, \ldots, \hat{w}_{Kn} - \lambda \hat{w}_{K-1,n}) \mathbf{S}_n \begin{pmatrix} \hat{w}_{1n} - \lambda \hat{w}_{0n} \\ \vdots \\ \hat{w}_{Kn} - \lambda \hat{w}_{K-1,n} \end{pmatrix},$$

where $\mathbf{S}_n^{-1}$ converges to

$$V_0 \begin{pmatrix} \hat{w}_{1n} - \lambda \hat{w}_{0n} \\ \vdots \\ \hat{w}_{Kn} - \lambda \hat{w}_{K-1,n} \end{pmatrix}.$$

Hence this estimator is obtained from a quasi generalized least squares regression of $\hat{w}_{kn}$ on $\hat{w}_{k-1,n}$, $k = 1, \ldots, K$.

Example 10.7: Misspecified Constraints

Consider the linear model $Y = \mathbf{X}\theta + u$, where $Eu = 0$, and $Vu = \sigma^2 \mathbf{I}$. Let $\hat{\theta}_n^0$ denote the ordinary least squares estimator subject to the constraints $\mathbf{G}\theta = g$. From equation (10.14) this estimator is given by

$$\hat{\theta}_n^0 = \hat{\theta}_n + (\mathbf{X}'\mathbf{X})^{-1} \mathbf{G}' (\mathbf{G}(\mathbf{X}'\mathbf{X})^{-1} \mathbf{G}')^{-1} (g - \mathbf{G}\hat{\theta}_n).$$

Suppose now that the constraints are incorrect, i.e., that the true parameter value θ_0 is such that

$$\mathbf{G}\theta_0 \neq g.$$

The unconstrained OLS estimator converges to θ_0 but the constrained OLS estimator converges to

$$\lim_n \hat{\theta}_n^0 = \theta_0 + E(X'X)^{-1}\mathbf{G}'(\mathbf{G}(EX'X)^{-1}\mathbf{G}')^{-1}(g - \mathbf{G}\theta_0).$$

This quantity is, in general, different from θ_0. Thus, in general, the constrained OLS estimator subject to some misspecified constraints is inconsistent.

Nonetheless some linear functions of the parameter vector may be consistently estimated. Let $\lambda \in \mathbb{R}^p$. Then $\lambda'\hat{\theta}_n^0$ is consistent for $\lambda'\theta_0$ if and only if

$$\lambda' E(X'X)^{-1}\mathbf{G}'(\mathbf{G}E(X'X)^{-1}\mathbf{G}')^{-1}(g - \mathbf{G}\theta_0) = 0, \ \forall\ \theta_0,$$

i.e.

$$\lambda' E(X'X)^{-1}\mathbf{G}' = 0,$$

i.e.

$$\lambda \in E(X'X)\text{Ker } \mathbf{G}.$$

10.6 Exercises

EXERCISE 10.1: Consider the linear model $Y = \mathbf{X}_1\theta_1 + \mathbf{X}_2\theta_2 + u$, where $Eu = 0$, and $Vu = \sigma^2\mathbf{I}$. Verify that the OLS estimator of θ constrained by $\theta_1 = 0$ is

$$\hat{\theta}_{1n}^0 = 0,\ \hat{\theta}_{2n}^0 = \hat{\theta}_{2n} + (\mathbf{X}_2'\mathbf{X}_2)^{-1}\mathbf{X}_2'\mathbf{X}_1\ \hat{\theta}_{1n}.$$

Interpret the result.

EXERCISE 10.2: Consider a linear model $Y = X\theta + u$, $Eu = 0$, $Vu = \sigma^2\mathbf{I}$, where θ is constrained by $\theta = \mathbf{H}a + h$ (see Section 10.2.1). Characterize cases for which $\hat{\theta}_n = \hat{\theta}_n^0$ and cases for which the latter equality holds for the first component only, i.e., $\hat{\theta}_{1n} = \hat{\theta}_{1n}^0$.

EXERCISE 10.3: Constraints on the parameter vector θ can be written in various forms. Consider two equivalent forms $g(\theta, a) = 0$ and $h(\theta, \tilde{a}) = 0$, where

$$\{\theta : \exists\ a, g(\theta, a) = 0\} = \{\theta : \exists\ \tilde{a}, h(\theta, \tilde{a}) = 0\}.$$

Verify that the constrained estimator of θ does not depend on which form is chosen. Does this result hold for the Lagrange multipliers?

EXERCISE 10.4: Consider the linear model $Y_i = X_i\theta + u_i$, $i = 1, \dots, n$, where the parameter vector θ is constrained by $\mathbf{G}\theta = g$. It is assumed that the pairs (u_i, X_i), $i = 1, \dots, n$, are independent and identically distributed with $E(u \mid x) = 0$ and $V(u \mid x) = \sigma^2$. Suppose also that the matrix $E(X'X)$ is nonsingular. Using expressions for the constrained estimator $\hat{\theta}_n^0$ and the vector of Lagrange multipliers $\hat{\lambda}_n$, show directly that these statistics converge to θ_0 and zero, respectively.

EXERCISE 10.5: Consider the linear model $Y_i = X_i\theta_0 + u_i$, $i = 1, \dots, n$, where the true parameter value θ_0 does not satisfy necessarily the constraints $\mathbf{G}\theta = g$. As in Exercise 10.4, it is assumed that the pairs (u_i, X_i) are independent and identically distributed.

a) Give the expressions for the solution θ_0^* and the Lagrange multipliers λ_0^* associated with the problem

$$\begin{cases} \min_\theta \ E_0(Y - X\theta)^2 \\ \\ \text{subject to } \mathbf{G}\theta = g, \end{cases}$$

where E_0 denotes the expectation with respect to the distribution corresponding to the true value θ_0 of the parameter vector.

b) Verify that the condition $\mathbf{G}\theta_0 = g$ is equivalent to the condition $\lambda_0^* = 0$. Verify that it is also equivalent to the condition $\theta_0^* = \theta_0$.

EXERCISE 10.6: One has observations $Y_{i,k,\ell}$, $i = 1, \dots, n$, $k = 1, \dots, K$, $\ell = 1, \dots, L$ that are independent and normally distributed $Y_{i,k,\ell} \sim N(\alpha + \beta_k + \gamma_\ell, \sigma^2)$, where the parameters β_k and γ_ℓ are constrained by

$$\sum_{k=1}^{K} \beta_k = 0, \quad \sum_{\ell=1}^{L} \gamma_\ell = 0.$$

a) Interpret the parameters α, β_k, and γ_ℓ.

b) Find the maximum likelihood estimators of α, β_k, γ_ℓ, and σ^2.

EXERCISE 10.7: LOG-LINEAR PROBABILITY MODEL

Let $Y_1, \dots, Y_K$ have a multinomial distribution $M(n, p_1, \dots, p_K)$. The parameters are subject to the usual constraint $p_1 + \dots + p_K = 1$. Moreover, it is assumed that these parameters are such that the vector

$(\log p_1, \ldots, \log p_K)'$ belongs to a linear subspace $\mathcal{L}$ of $\mathbb{R}^K$ containing the vector $(1, \ldots, 1)'$.

a) Is the constrained model an exponential model?

b) Determine the first-order conditions associated with the maximum likelihood estimator under constraints.

EXERCISE 10.8: Consider the sampling model $(\mathbb{R}^2, N(\mu, \mathbf{\Omega}))^n$, where the vector $\mu' = (\mu_1, \mu_2)$ is unknown and the matrix $\mathbf{\Omega}$ is known.

a) Find the unconstrained maximum likelihood estimator of μ_1.

b) Suppose that $\mu_2 = 0$. Find the constrained maximum likelihood estimator of μ_1.

c) Find the distribution of the constrained maximum likelihood estimator of μ_1. Find the correlation between this estimator and the sample mean $\bar{Y}_2$.

EXERCISE 10.9: Consider the model

$$Y_{i,k,\ell} = \alpha + \beta_k + \gamma_\ell + \delta_{\ell k} + u_{ik\ell},$$

where the $u_{ik\ell}$'s are independent and normally distributed with mean zero and common variance σ^2. The indices i, k, and ℓ vary from 1 to n, 1 to K and 1 to L, respectively. The parameters β_k, γ_ℓ, and $\delta_{\ell k}$ satisfy the constraints

$$\sum_{k=1}^{K} \beta_k = 0, \ \sum_{\ell=1}^{L} \gamma_\ell = 0, \ \sum_{\ell=1}^{L} \delta_{\ell k} = 0, \ \forall\ k, \sum_{k=1}^{K} \delta_{\ell k} = 0, \ \forall\ \ell.$$

a) Find the maximum likelihood estimators of α, β_k, γ_ℓ, and $\delta_{\ell k}$.

b) Suppose that the constraints $\beta_k = 0$, $k = 1, \ldots, K$, are imposed. What are the consequences of these constraints on the estimation of the other parameters? Answer the same question when the consraints $\gamma_\ell = 0$, $\ell = 1, \ldots, L$ or $\delta_{\ell k} = 0$, $\ell = 1, \ldots, L$, $k = 1, \ldots, K$ are imposed.

EXERCISE 10.10: Consider again the model of Exercise 10.9. Suppose now that the index i varies from 1 to $N_{k\cdot}N_{\cdot\ell}/N_{\cdot\cdot}$, where $N_{\cdot\cdot} = \sum_{k=1}^{K} N_{k\cdot} = \sum_{\ell=1}^{L} N_{\cdot\ell}$. The coefficients are assumed to satisfy the constraints

$$\sum_{k=1}^{K} N_{k\cdot}\beta_k = 0, \ \sum_{\ell=1}^{L} N_{\cdot\ell}\gamma_\ell = 0$$
$$\sum_{k=1}^{K} N_{k\cdot}\delta_{\ell k} = 0, \ \forall\, \ell, \ \sum_{\ell=1}^{L} N_{\cdot\ell}\delta_{\ell k} = 0, \ \forall\, k.$$

Answer the questions of Exercise 10.9.

10.7 References

Burguete, J.F., Gallant, A.R., and Souza, G. (1982). "On the Unification of the Asymptotic Theory of Nonlinear Econometric Models," *Econometic Review*, 1, 151–190.

Gallant, R. (1973). "Testing a Subset of the Parameters of a Nonlinear Regression Model," *Journal of the American Statistical Association*, 70, 927–932.

Gourieroux, C. and Monfort, A. (1989). "A General Framework for Testing a Null Hypothesis in a Mixed Form," *Econometric Theory*, 5, 63–82.

Mitra, S.K. and Rao, C.R. (1968). "Some Results in Estimation and Tests of Linear Hypotheses Under the Gauss – Markov Model," *Sankhya*, A, 30, 281–290.

Newey, W.K. (1985). "Maximum Likelihood Specification Testing and Conditional Moment Tests," *Econometrica*, 53, 1047–1070.

Rayner, A.A. and Pruigle, R.M. (1967). "A Note on Generalized Inverses in the Linear Hypothesis Not of Full Rank," *Annals of Mathematical Statistics*, 38, 271–273.

Silvey, D. (1959). "The Lagrangian Multiplier Test," *Annals of Mathematical Statistics*, 30, 389–407.

Szroeter, J. (1983). "Generalized Wald Methods for Testing Nonlinear Implicit and Overidentifying Restrictions," *Econometrica*, 51, 335–348.

Theil, H. (1971) *Principles of Econometrics*, Wiley.

CHAPTER 11

Prediction

11.1 General Concepts

11.1.1 Statement of the Problem

To predict an unobserved variable is to find an approximation of it that is a function of the observations (see Chapter 2). Prediction problems are frequent in economic applications. They arise naturally in dynamic contexts when, for instance, one desires to know the level of unemployment in the next years, or when one's goal is to complete a time series of which some intermediate values are missing. Prediction problems, however, are also important in numerous other situations. For instance, a researcher wants to determine the expected change in consumption of a household whose income changes by 5%. Alternatively, one wants to find the price that would have prevailed in equilibrium on a market in desequilibrium (see Example 1.20).

We shall see in the following sections, that estimation problems and prediction problems are often closely related. As an example, consider estimation by ordinary least squares. This estimation will naturally appear when looking for an optimal prediction of a nonobserved endogenous variable by a linear function of the observed endogenous variables.

Thereafter, we let $Y_1, \ldots, Y_n$ denote the observations and W the variable to predict. To simplify, it is assumed that W takes its values in $\mathbb{R}$. A *prediction* or *predictor* of W is a function $\hat{W}(Y_1, \ldots, Y_n)$ of the observations. The *prediction error* is the discrepancy between the predicted variable and the prediction. It is defined as

$$e = W - \hat{W}(Y_1, \ldots, Y_n). \tag{11.1}$$

The prediction error is random. In general, it is assessed by its *mean squared prediction error*

$$R(\hat{W}, P_0) = E_0(W - \hat{W}(Y_1, \ldots, Y_n))^2, \tag{11.2}$$

where expectation is taken with respect to the joint distribution P_0 of $W, Y_1, \ldots, Y_n$. Given the distribution P_0, there exists an optimal prediction, i.e., a prediction that minimizes the mean squared prediction error. It is given by the expectation of W conditional upon $Y_1, \ldots, Y_n$ (see Property B.17)

$$\hat{W}_0 = E_0(W \mid Y_1, \ldots, Y_n).$$

In general, however, the joint distribution of $W, Y_1, \ldots, Y_n$ is unknown. Then it is necessary to find predictions that have good properties uniformly in the possible distributions of $W, Y_1, \ldots, Y_n$.

11.1.2 Prediction Criteria

We consider a statistical model $(\mathcal{W} \times \mathcal{Y}, \mathcal{P})$ specifying a family of joint distributions for $W, Y_1, \ldots, Y_n$.

Definition 11.1: *A predictor $\hat{W}$ (weakly) dominates another predictor W^* if and only if $\hat{W}$ is uniformly more precise than W^*, i.e.*

$$R(\hat{W}, P) \leq R(W^*, P), \ \forall \ P \in \mathcal{P},$$

or equivalently

$$E_P(\hat{W} - W)^2 \leq E_P(W^* - W)^2, \ \forall P \in \mathcal{P}.$$

An optimal predictor, that is, a predictor that dominates any other predictor exists only in the degenerate case where the conditional expectation

$$E_P(W \mid Y_1, \ldots, Y_n)$$

does not depend on $P \in \mathcal{P}$. In general, it is necessary to restrict the set of predictors considered by imposing some additional criteria. These criteria are similar to those introduced in estimation problems.

a) Unbiasedness

Definition 11.2: *A predictor $\hat{W}$ is an unbiased predictor of W if and only if*

$$E_P(\hat{W} - W) = 0, \quad \forall\ P \in \mathcal{P},$$

i.e., if and only if the associated prediction error is on average equal to zero uniformly in P.

b) Linearity

In some problems, we shall restrict predictors to be linear functions of the observations.

Definition 11.3: *A predictor $\hat{W}$ is said to be linear if it can be written as*

$$\hat{W}(Y_1, \ldots, Y_n) = \alpha_0 + \sum_{i=1}^{n} \alpha_i Y_i.$$

Linearity is frequently imposed together with unbiasedness. Then we have

$$E_P W = \alpha_0 + \sum_{i=1}^{n} \alpha_i E_P Y_i, \ \forall P \in \mathcal{P}.$$

A linear unbiased predictor exists when there exists an affine relation among the $(n+1)$-dimensional vectors $(E_P W, E_P Y_1, \ldots, E_P Y_n)'$, $P \in \mathcal{P}$, with weigths α_i independent of $P \in \mathcal{P}$. Note that it is sometimes possible to find optimal predictors in the class of linear unbiased predictors (see Section 11.2).

c) Consistency

We may also want to impose some conditions when the number of observations n increases to infinity. In this case the model concerns the joint distribution of W and the sequence $Y_1, \ldots, Y_n, \ldots$. We define sequences of predictors converging to W as follows.

Definition 11.4: *A sequence of predictors $\hat{W}_n(Y_1, \ldots, Y_n)$ converges to W*

(i) strongly if $\hat{W}_n - W$ converges almost surely to zero for every distribution $P \in \mathcal{P}$,

(ii) *in quadratic mean if* $E\left(\hat{W}_n(Y_1,\ldots,Y_n) - W\right)^2$ *converges to zero for every distribution* $P \in \mathcal{P}$.

A frequent method for finding consistent predictors is as follows. Consider a parametric model $(\mathcal{W}\times\mathcal{Y}, \mathcal{P} = \{P_\theta, \theta \in \Theta\})$. The conditional expectation of W given $Y_1, \ldots, Y_n$ depends, in general, on the parameter vector θ. Let

$$\delta_n(\theta, Y_1, \ldots, Y_n) = E_\theta(W \mid Y_1, \ldots, Y_n).$$

Such a conditional expectation cannot be used directly because of the presence of the unknown parameter vector θ. Suppose, however, that a consistent estimator $\hat{\theta}_n$ of θ is available. A natural method for predicting W is

$$\hat{W}_n = \delta_n(\hat{\theta}_n, Y_1, \ldots, Y_n) = E_{\hat{\theta}_n}(W \mid Y_1, \ldots, Y_n). \tag{11.3}$$

In equation (11.3), randomness arises both from the conditioning variables and the estimator $\hat{\theta}_n$ used. In the special case where $W = E_{\theta_0}(W \mid Y_1, \ldots, Y_n)$ (see 11.2.1.b below), $\hat{W}_n$ is a consistent predictor. In the general case, the prediction error can be decomposed as

$$\begin{aligned} & W - E_{\hat{\theta}_n}(W \mid Y_1, \ldots, Y_n) \\ = \; & (W - E_{\theta_0}(W \mid Y_1, \ldots, Y_n)) + (E_{\theta_0}(W \mid Y_1, \ldots, Y_n) \\ & -(E_{\hat{\theta}_n}(W \mid Y_1, \ldots, Y_n)), \end{aligned}$$

where θ_0 denotes the true value of the parameter vector. Thus the prediction error is the sum of the prediction error associated with the optimal prediction (equal to zero in the special case mentioned above) and an error due to the estimation of θ_0.

d) Bayesian Approach

Lastly, we can consider the Bayesian approach. Suppose that the original model is parametric $(\mathcal{W} \times \mathcal{Y}, \mathcal{P} = \{P_\theta, \theta \in \Theta\})$. Let $\Pi(d\theta)$ denote the prior distribution on the parameters θ. Then we can find the joint distribution of $W, Y_1, \ldots, Y_n$ and θ. In the Bayesian approach, all arguments are relative to this joint distribution. Thus the squared mean error in the Bayesian sense is defined as

$$R_\Pi(\hat{W}) = E_\Pi R(\hat{W}, P_\theta) = E_\Pi E_\theta(\hat{W} - W)^2. \tag{11.4}$$

From the properties of conditional expectation, it follows immediately that an optimal prediction in the Bayesian sense is

$$\hat{W} = E(W \mid Y_1, \ldots, Y_n),$$

where expectation is taken with respect to the joint distribution of $W, Y_1, \ldots, Y_n$ and θ.

11.1.3 Simulations

First, we consider the case where the joint distribution of $W, Y_1, \ldots, Y_n$ is known. Let P_0 denote such a distribution. The conditional expectation $E_0(W \mid Y_1, \ldots, Y_n)$ may be evaluated analytically. It may also be evaluated by means of a random procedure. This method is called the *simulation method* or *Monte Carlo method.* The procedure is as follows.

Let M be the number of independent drawings from the conditional distribution of W given $Y_1 = y_1, \ldots, Y_n = y_n$. Let $\omega_1, \ldots, \omega_M$ denote the resulting observed draws. From the Strong Law of Large Numbers it follows that, when M is large, the sample mean

$$\bar{\omega}_M = \frac{1}{M} \sum_{m=1}^{M} \omega_m,$$

is a good approximation to the expectation of the distribution used for the M draws, i.e., to

$$E_0(W \mid Y_1 = y_1, \ldots, Y_n = y_n).$$

Note also that the realized values of the draws (or *simulations*) can be used to approximate the prediction of an arbitrary (integrable) function of W. Specifically, the quantity

$$\overline{h(\omega)}_M = \frac{1}{M} \sum_{m=1}^{M} h(\omega_m)$$

is a good approximation to

$$E_0(h(W) \mid Y_1 = y_1, \ldots, Y_n = y_n),$$

when M is sufficiently large.

From a mathematical point of view, the preceding method adds to the original randomness due to $Y_1, \ldots, Y_n$ a new randomness ω associated with the various draws from the conditional distribution.

More generally, when the joint distribution P of $(W, Y_1, \ldots, Y_n)$ belongs to a family $\mathcal{P}$, we can give the following definition of a simulation.

Definition 11.5: *A simulation W^* of W is a random function of the observations, i.e.*

$$W^* = f(\omega, Y_1, \ldots, Y_n),$$

where the extra random variable ω has, conditionally on $(Y_1, \ldots, Y_n)$, a distribution independent of $P \in \mathcal{P}$.

The last condition in Definition 11.5 implies that simulations can be performed even though the true distribution is unknown.

The mean squared error due to the simulations is

$$R(W^*, P) = E(W^* - W)^2, \tag{11.5}$$

where expectation is taken with respect to the joint distribution of ω, $W, Y_1, \ldots, Y_n$. A simulation is said to be unbiased if

$$E(W^* - W) = 0. \tag{11.6}$$

Remark 11.1: Because the variable W is not observed, simulations are, in general, obtained independently of W conditionally on the observations $(Y_1, \ldots, Y_n)$. In this case the expression for the risk can be sometimes simplified. For instance, in the limiting case where simulations are unbiased conditionally on $(Y_1, \ldots, Y_n)$, i.e.

$$E(W^* \mid Y_1, \ldots, Y_n) = E_P(W \mid Y_1, \ldots, Y_n),$$

we have

$$\begin{aligned} R(W^*, P) &= E(W^* - W)^2 \\ &= V(W^* - W) \quad \text{(since (11.6) is satisfied)} \\ &= EV(W^* - W \mid Y_1, \ldots, Y_n) + VE(W^* - W \mid Y_1, \ldots, Y_n) \\ &= EV(W^* - W \mid Y_1, \ldots, Y_n) \\ &= EV(W^* \mid Y_1, \ldots, Y_n) + E_P V_P(W \mid Y_1, \ldots, Y_n), \end{aligned}$$

because of the conditional independence between W^* and W. Moreover, the second term is equal to

$$E_P V_P(W \mid Y_1, \ldots, Y_n) = E_P(W - E_P(W \mid Y_1, \ldots, Y_n))^2,$$

which is the optimal prediction error evaluated for the distribution P. Therefore, to this error, we must add another term that incorporates the effect of the simulations.

Remark 11.2: When the model is parameterized by θ, we have seen in equation (11.3) that a natural predictor of W is

$$\hat{W}_n = E_{\hat{\theta}_n}(W \mid Y_1, \dots, Y_n),$$

where $\hat{\theta}_n$ is a consistent estimator of θ. A similar argument can be used to obtain a simulation in the sense of Definition 11.5. Namely, a simulation is a draw from the conditional distribution of W given $(Y_1, \dots, Y_n)$ after having replaced θ by $\hat{\theta}_n$. The resulting conditional distribution, denoted $P_{\hat{\theta}_n(Y)}^{W|Y_1,\dots,Y_n}$, no longer depends on the unknown parameter θ and hence is independent of $P \in \mathcal{P}$.

Note also that because $\hat{\theta}_n$ is consistent for θ, Remark 11.1 remains asymptotically valid.

11.2 Examples

11.2.1 Predictions in the Linear Model

We consider the static linear model

$$Y_i = X_{i1}b_1 + \dots + X_{iK}b_K + u_i, \; i = 1, \dots, n, \; n+1,$$

where the error terms are centered $Eu_i = 0$, with same variance $Vu_i = \sigma^2$ and independent. The variables Y_i, $i = 1, \dots, n$, and $X_{i1}, \dots, X_{iK}$, $i = 1, \dots, n, n+1$, are assumed to be observed. The variable Y_{n+1} and the error terms $u_1, \dots, u_n, u_{n+1}$ are not observed.

Different prediction problems concerning different variables are of interest.

a) Prediction of Y_{n+1}

The variable Y_{n+1} is unobserved. It can be approximated by $x_{n+1}b = X_{n+1,1}b_1 + \dots + X_{n+1,K}b_K$, i.e., by the conditional expectation of Y_{n+1} given $Y_1, \dots, Y_n$, which is identical to the unconditional expectation of Y_{n+1} treating the x_i's as fixed. Here, we denote by x_i the $1 \times K$ row vector of exogenous variables associated with the ith observation.

Because the parameter vector b is unknown, it is natural to replace b by its ordinary least squares estimate computed from the observed variables, i.e., from $Y_1, \dots, Y_n$ and $x_1, \dots, x_n$. Specifically, we use

$$\hat{b}_n = \left(\sum_{i=1}^{n} x_i' x_i \right)^{-1} \sum_{i=1}^{n} x_i' Y_i.$$

Thus the corresponding predictor of the unobserved value of Y_{n+1} is the random variable

$$\hat{Y}_{n+1} = x_{n+1}\hat{b}_n = x_{n+1}\left(\sum_{i=1}^{n} x_i' x_i\right)^{-1} \sum_{i=1}^{n} x_i' Y_i.$$

b) Prediction of an Error Term u_i, $i = 1, \ldots, n$

The unobserved error term u_i is equal to $Y_i - x_i b$. Though b is unknown, we can approximate u_i by $\hat{u}_i = Y_i - x_i\hat{b}_n$.

Definition 11.6: *We call residuals associated with the linear model the predictions of the error terms, namely*

$$\hat{u}_i = Y_i - x_i\hat{b}_n = Y_i - x_i\left(\sum_{j=1}^{n} x_j' x_j\right)^{-1} \sum_{j=1}^{n} x_j' Y_j.$$

Residuals can be usefully pictured by means of a diagram, called the *residual diagram*, where the index of the observations is on the horizontal axis and the values of the residuals are on the vertical axis.

c) Predicted Values

The above expression for a residual shows that a residual is the difference between an observed value Y_i and its approximation $x_i\hat{b}_n$ given by the model.

Definition 11.7: *We call predicted values associated with the linear model the variables*

$$\hat{Y}_i = x_i\hat{b}_n.$$

Although the formula defining $\hat{Y}_i$ is identical to that used for defining the prediction of Y_{n+1}, there is a fundamental difference between these two types of predictions. Specifically, the predictor $\hat{Y}_{n+1}$ of the unobserved variable Y_{n+1} has some optimal properties (see Section 11.2.2). On the other hand, $\hat{Y}_i$ viewed as a predictor of Y_i, is clearly dominated by the predictor Y_i since Y_i is observed. In addition, note that $\hat{Y}_i$ cannot be interpreted as a predictor of Y_i even if Y_i is unobserved because Y_i appears in the expression for $\hat{b}_n$.

The previous examples illustrate that there are various natural predictors in the linear model. In the next subsection, we shall study their properties conditional upon the values of the exogenous variables.

11.2.2 Properties of Predictors in the Linear Model

We shall consider predicting the variable Y_{n+1} only. The reader can refer to Exercises 11.1 and 11.2 to derive properties similar to those established below for predictors of residuals and predicted values.

Property 11.1: *$\hat{Y}_{n+1}$ is an unbiased prediction of Y_{n+1}.*

PROOF: This follows from

$$\begin{aligned} E(\hat{Y}_{n+1} - Y_{n+1}) &= E(x_{n+1}\hat{b}_n - Y_{n+1}) \\ &= E(x_{n+1}(\hat{b}_n - b)) - Eu_{n+1} \\ &= 0, \end{aligned}$$

because $\hat{b}_n$ is an unbiased estimator of b and u_{n+1} has mean zero. □

Property 11.2: *The mean squared error of the predictor $\hat{Y}_{n+1}$ is*

$$E(\hat{Y}_{n+1} - Y_{n+1})^2 = \sigma^2 x_{n+1} \left(\sum_{i=1}^{n} x_i' x_i \right)^{-1} x_{n+1}' + \sigma^2.$$

PROOF: We have

$$\begin{aligned} E(\hat{Y}_{n+1} - Y_{n+1})^2 &= E(x_{n+1}(\hat{b}_n - b) - u_{n+1})^2 \\ &= V(x_{n+1}(\hat{b}_n - b) - u_{n+1}) \\ &= V(x_{n+1}(\hat{b}_n - b)) + Vu_{n+1}, \end{aligned}$$

because $\hat{b}_n$ is linear in $u_1, \ldots, u_n$, and u_{n+1} is uncorrelated with these error terms. Since the variance covariance matrix of the OLS estimator is

$$V\hat{b}_n = \sigma^2 \left(\sum_{i=1}^{n} x_i' x_i \right)^{-1},$$

it follows that

$$E(\hat{Y}_{n+1} - Y_{n+1})^2 = \sigma^2 x_{n+1} \left(\sum_{i=1}^{n} x_i' x_i \right)^{-1} x_{n+1}' + \sigma^2.$$

The second term σ^2 represents the mean squared prediction error on Y_{n+1} when b is known since, in this case, Y_{n+1} can be predicted by $x_{n+1}b$. The first term is due to the fact that b, which is unknown, is replaced by its estimator $\hat{b}_n$. □

Example 11.1: As an illustration of the above results, we consider the simple linear regression model

$$Y_i = b_0 + b_1 x_i + u_i, \ i = 1, \ldots, n+1.$$

The prediction of Y_{n+1} is

$$\begin{aligned} \hat{Y}_{n+1} &= \hat{b}_{0n} + \hat{b}_{1n} x_{n+1} \\ &= \hat{b}_{1n}(x_{n+1} - \bar{x}_n) + \bar{Y}_n, \end{aligned}$$

using the equality

$$\bar{Y}_n = \hat{b}_{0n} + \hat{b}_{1n}\bar{x}_n,$$

where

$$\bar{x}_n = \frac{1}{n}\sum_{i=1}^{n} x_i \text{ and } \bar{Y}_n = \frac{1}{n}\sum_{i=1}^{n} Y_i.$$

Thus the prediction $\hat{Y}_{n+1}$ is equal to the sample mean $\bar{Y}_n$ of the endogenous variable adjusted by a term that takes into account the distance between x_{n+1} and the sample mean $\bar{x}_n$ of the exogenous variable.

The mean squared prediction error of $\hat{Y}_{n+1}$ is equal to

$$\begin{aligned} E(\hat{Y}_{n+1} - Y_{n+1})^2 &= V(\hat{Y}_{n+1} - Y_{n+1}) \\ &= V(\hat{b}_{1n}(x_{n+1} - \bar{x}_n) + \bar{Y}_n - Y_{n+1}). \end{aligned}$$

Since $\hat{b}_{1n}$ and $\bar{Y}_n$ are uncorrelated (see Exercise 11.3) we obtain

$$\begin{aligned} E(\hat{Y}_{n+1} - Y_{n+1})^2 &= (x_{n+1} - \bar{x}_n)^2 V(\hat{b}_{1n}) + V(\bar{Y}_n) + V(Y_{n+1}) \\ &= \sigma^2 \frac{(x_{n+1} - \bar{x}_n)^2}{\sum_{i=1}^{n}(x_i - \bar{x}_n)^2} + \frac{\sigma^2}{n} + \sigma^2. \end{aligned}$$

Therefore the mean squared prediction error is an increasing function of the distance between the value x_{n+1} of the exogenous variable associated with the variable to predict and the sample mean value of the exogenous variables associated with the observed Y's.

The predictor $\hat{Y}_{n+1}$ is the best linear unbiased predictor of Y_{n+1}. This optimality property is analogous to the Gauss–Markov property of the OLS estimator (see Theorem 6.3).

Property 11.3: *The predictor $\hat{Y}_{n+1} = x_{n+1}\hat{b}_n$ is the best unbiased predictor of Y_{n+1} that is a linear function of $Y_1, \ldots, Y_n$.*

PROOF: Let $\tilde{Y}_{n+1}$ be a linear predictor of Y_{n+1}. It is of the form

$$\tilde{Y}_{n+1} = \sum_{i=1}^{n} \alpha_i Y_i.$$

The unbiasedness condition is

$$\begin{aligned} E\left(\sum_{i=1}^{n} \alpha_i Y_i\right) &= E(Y_{n+1}) \\ &= x_{n+1} b. \end{aligned}$$

The mean squared prediction error is

$$\begin{aligned} E(\tilde{Y}_{n+1} - Y_{n+1})^2 &= V(\tilde{Y}_{n+1} - Y_{n+1}) \\ &\quad \text{(from the unbiasedness condition)} \\ &= V\tilde{Y}_{n+1} + \sigma^2 \\ &= E\left(\sum_{i=1}^{n} \alpha_i Y_i - x_{n+1} b\right)^2 + \sigma^2. \end{aligned}$$

Thus the problem reduces to finding coefficients $\alpha_1, \ldots, \alpha_n$ that solve the problem

$$\min_{\alpha} E\left(\sum_{i=1}^{n} \alpha_i Y_i - x_{n+1} b\right)^2,$$

subject to thc constraints

$$E\left(\sum_{i=1}^{n} \alpha_i Y_i\right) = x_{n+1} b.$$

This is equivalent to finding the best linear unbiased estimator of $x_{n+1}b$. Since $x_{n+1}b$ is a linear function of b, it follows from the Gauss–Markov Theorem 6.3 that the solution is $x_{n+1}\hat{b}_n$ where $\hat{b}_n$ is the OLS estimator. □

Property 11.4: *The OLS estimator $\hat{b}_n$ and the predictor $\hat{Y}_{n+1}$ can be obtained simultaneously by minimizing the sum of squared errors*

$$\sum_{i=1}^{n+1} (Y_i - x_i b)^2,$$

with respect to b and Y_{n+1}.

PROOF: To solve the above optimization problem, we can proceed in two steps. First, we can minimize the objective function with respect to Y_{n+1} given an arbitrary fixed b. Then, after substitution of the solution into the objective function, we can minimize the resulting function with respect to b.

The first step gives $\tilde{Y}_{n+1}(b) = x_{n+1}b$. Substituting this solution into the objective function, the problem reduces to the minimization of $\sum_{i=1}^{n}(Y_i - x_i b)^2$ with respect to b. The solution is the OLS estimator $\hat{b}_n$. Hence the solution for Y_{n+1} is the predictor $\tilde{Y}_{n+1}(\hat{b}_n) = x_{n+1}\hat{b}_n = \hat{Y}_{n+1}$. □

The preceding properties do not require that the error terms are normally distributed. When the error terms are normally distributed, we can obtain a more precise result.

Property 11.5: *Suppose that the error terms are normally distributed. Then the predictor $\hat{Y}_{n+1}$ and the prediction error $e_{n+1} = \hat{Y}_{n+1} - Y_{n+1}$ are normally distributed with*

$$\begin{aligned} \hat{Y}_{n+1} &\sim N(x_{n+1}b, x_{n+1}V(\hat{b}_n)x'_{n+1}), \\ e_{n+1} &\sim N(0, \sigma^2 + x_{n+1}V(\hat{b}_n)x'_{n+1}). \end{aligned}$$

PROOF: Normality follows from the fact that $\hat{Y}_{n+1}$ and e_{n+1} are linear functions of the normal variables $Y_1, \ldots, Y_n$. The means and variances of $\hat{Y}_{n+1}$ and e_{n+1} are readily computed from Properties 11.1 and 11.2. □

Remark 11.3: When the parameter vector b is known, the best predictor of Y_{n+1} given $Y_1, \ldots, Y_n$ is

$$E_b(Y_{n+1} \mid Y_1, \ldots, Y_n) = \tilde{Y}_{n+1}(b) = x_{n+1}b.$$

Conditionally to the x_i's this prediction is nonrandom and, therefore, orthogonal to the prediction error $e_{n+1}(b) = Y_{n+1} - x_{n+1}b$.

When b is unknown, b is replaced by the OLS estimator $\hat{b}_n$. It is easy to verify that this substitution introduces a correlation between $\hat{Y}_{n+1} = \tilde{Y}_{n+1}(\hat{b}_n)$ and $e_{n+1}(\hat{b}_n)$. Indeed we have

$$\begin{aligned} \text{Cov}\ (\hat{e}_{n+1}, \hat{Y}_{n+1}) &= \text{Cov}\ (Y_{n+1} - x_{n+1}\hat{b}_n, x_{n+1}\hat{b}_n) \\ &= -\ V(x_{n+1}\hat{b}_n) \\ &= -\ x_{n+1}V(\hat{b}_n)x'_{n+1}. \end{aligned}$$

Note, however, that $V(\hat{b}_n)$ is close to zero when n is large so that the correlation disappears asymptotically.

11.2.3 Prediction Intervals

The form of the distribution of the prediction error e_{n+1} can be used to construct an interval that contains the value of Y_{n+1} with a given probability. Such an interval is called *a prediction interval.* For instance, consider a 95% level. With probability 0.95, it is known that the standard normal variable

$$\frac{e_{n+1}}{\sigma\sqrt{1 + x_{n+1}\left(\sum_{i=1}^{n} x_i' x_i\right)^{-1} x_{n+1}'}}$$

is between ± 1.96 since 1.96 is the 97.5%-quantile of the standard normal distribution $N(0,1)$. Hence, with probability 0.95, we have

$$Y_{n+1} \in \left(\hat{Y}_{n+1} \pm 1.96\sigma\sqrt{1 + x_{n+1}\left(\sum_{i=1}^{n} x_i' x_i\right)^{-1} x_{n+1}'}\right).$$

In practice, the unknown parameter σ^2 is replaced by its consistent estimator defined by

$$\hat{\sigma}_n^2 = \frac{1}{n}\sum_{i=1}^{n} \hat{u}_i^2,$$

or by

$$s^2 = \frac{1}{n-K}\sum_{i=1}^{n} \hat{u}_i^2.$$

Remark 11.4: The above prediction interval is only an approximate interval since the standard error σ has been replaced by an estimator. An exact prediction interval is, however, easily obtained. Specifically, the statistic

$$\frac{e_{n+1}}{s\sqrt{1 + x_{n+1}\left(\sum_{i=1}^{n} x_i' x_i\right)^{-1} x_{n+1}'}}$$

follows a Student distribution with $n - K$ degrees of freedom.

Let $t_{97.5\%}(n-K)$ denote the 97.5%-quantile of this Student distribution. With an exact probability of 0.95, we have

$$Y_{n+1} \in \left(\hat{Y}_{n+1} \pm t_{97.5\%}(n-K)s\sqrt{1 + x_{n+1}\left(\sum_{i=1}^{n} x_i' x_i\right)^{-1} x_{n+1}'}\right).$$

It is readily verified that the approximate prediction interval obtained earlier is asymptotically correct since the Student distribution $t(n-K)$ converges to the standard normal distribution $N(0,1)$ as n increases to infinity.

In the Figure 11.1, we illustrate how the prediction interval varies as a function of the value of the exogenous variable in the simple linear regression model.

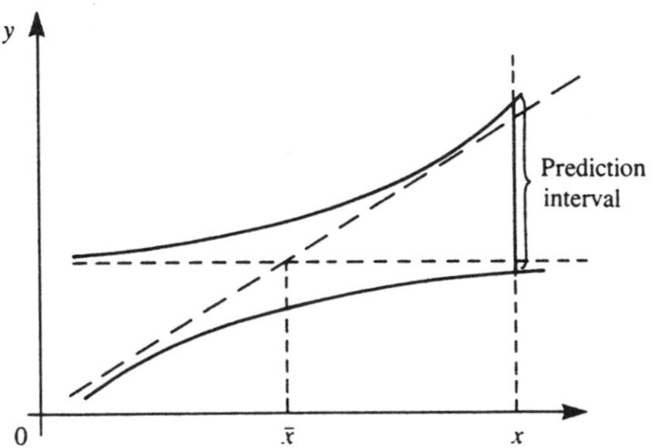

Figure 11.1: Prediction Intervals

11.2.4 Prediction of a Nonlinear Function of Y_{n+1}

To simplify, we retain the linear model framework. The problem of interest is now to predict a nonlinear function $h(Y_{n+1})$ of Y_{n+1}. A first and intuitive solution, is to propose $\hat{h} = h(\hat{Y}_{n+1})$ as a predictor. However, even if the true distribution is perfectly known, this predictor leads, in general, to a biased prediction. A better solution consists in computing

$$E_{b,\sigma^2}(h(Y_{n+1}) \mid Y_1, \ldots, Y_n) = \tilde{h}(b, \sigma^2),$$

and then in replacing b and σ^2 by some consistent estimators. Such a computation clearly requires that the distribution of the error term is completely specified up to some parameters.

To illustrate the latter method, we assume that the error terms u_i, $i = 1, \ldots, n+1$, are independent and identically distributed $N(0, \sigma^2)$. We are interested in the prediction of $\exp(Y_{n+1})$. Because of independence,

we have

$$\begin{aligned} E_{b,\sigma^2}(\exp(Y_{n+1}) \mid Y_1, \ldots, Y_n) &= E_{b,\sigma^2} \exp(Y_{n+1}) \\ &= \exp\left(x_{n+1}b + \frac{\sigma^2}{2}\right), \end{aligned}$$

where we have used properties of the normal distribution.

Thus the method consists in retaining

$$\hat{h} = \exp\left(x_{n+1}\hat{b}_n + \frac{\hat{\sigma}_n^2}{2}\right)$$

as a predictor of $\exp(Y_{n+1})$, where $\hat{b}_n$ and $\hat{\sigma}_n^2$ are the OLS estimators of b and σ^2 based on the first n observations.

11.2.5 Prediction of a Latent Variable

In Chapter 1 we saw that a latent model is frequently more interesting from the point of view of economic theory than the observable model that is derived from it. In such a situation, predicting latent variables from observed variables is frequently of interest.

Let $Y_1^*, \ldots, Y_n^*$ denote the latent variables and let $Y_1, \ldots, Y_n$ denote the observed variables. We suppose that the model is parameterized by θ. Then, in a first step, we can define predictors as

$$E_\theta(Y_i^* \mid Y_1, \ldots, Y_n),\ i = 1, \ldots, n,$$

for every given value of the parameter vector θ. Then the unknown parameter value θ can be replaced by a consistent estimator of θ in the preceding expression so as to obtain

$$E_{\hat{\theta}_n}(Y_i^* \mid Y_1, \ldots, Y_n).$$

Example 11.2: Consider the disequilibrium model defined by

$$\begin{aligned} D_t &= ap_t + b + u_t, \\ S_t &= \alpha p_t + \beta + v_t, \quad t = 1, \ldots, T, \end{aligned}$$

where u_t and v_t are independent and distributed $N(0, \sigma_u^2)$ and $N(0, \sigma_v^2)$ respectively. From the observed prices p_t and quantities exchanged $Q_t = \min(D_t, S_t)$, for $t = 1, \ldots, n$, we want to determine what is the equilibrium price p_t^e at time t. This equilibrium price, which is not observed, is given by

$$\begin{aligned} p_t^e &= \frac{b-\beta}{\alpha - a} + \frac{u_t - v_t}{\alpha - a} \\ &= p_t + \frac{D_t - S_t}{\alpha - a}. \end{aligned}$$

We need to compute

$$E(p_t^e \mid q_t) = p_t + \frac{\hat{D}_t - \hat{S}_t}{\alpha - a},$$

where $\hat{D}_t = E(D_t \mid q_t)$ and $\hat{S}_t = E(S_t \mid q_t)$. (Other observations are irrelevant to the prediction of p_t^e because of the assumed temporal independence of the observations.) We have

$$\begin{aligned} \hat{D}_t &= P(D_t > S_t \mid q_t) E(D_t \mid D_t > q_t) \\ &+ P(S_t \geq D_t \mid q_t) E(D_t \mid D_t = q_t) \\ &= \hat{\Pi}_t E(D_t \mid D_t > q_t) + (1 - \hat{\Pi}_t) q_t, \end{aligned}$$

where $\hat{\Pi}_t$ denotes the probability that there is an excess of demand conditional upon the observations. A similar computation can be followed for S. Then we obtain

$$\begin{aligned} & E(p_t^e \mid q_t) \\ = \; & p_t + \frac{(1 - 2\hat{\Pi}_t) q_t}{\alpha - a} + \frac{\hat{\Pi}_t E(D_t \mid D_t > q_t) - (1 - \hat{\Pi}_t) E(S_t \mid S_t > q_t)}{\alpha - a}. \end{aligned}$$

To obtain a useful expression for this type of prediction, it remains to determine

$$\Pi_t, E(D_t \mid D_t > q_t), E(S_t \mid S_t > q_t).$$

These quantities are easily determined using properties of the truncated normal distribution (see Exercise 11.10).

In the preceding derivation, note that other predictions were also determined, namely, the prediction of the regime $\hat{\Pi}_t = E(1_{D_t > S_t} \mid q_t)$, the prediction of the demand $\hat{D}_t$, the prediction of the supply $\hat{S}_t$, and the prediction of the demand given that there is an excess of demand $E(D_t \mid D_t > q_t)$.

11.2.6 Prediction in a Dynamic Model

The previous examples deal with models that are basically static. But the method presented above, which consists in determining first the appropriate predictor given an arbitrary parameter value and then in replacing the unknown parameter value by a consistent estimator, can also be used in a dynamic context. The dynamic models are studied in a companion book cited in reference (see also section 13.5)

Example 11.3: Suppose that observations on the endogenous and the strongly exogenous variables satisfy

$$Y_t = f(X_t, \theta) + u_t, \; t = 1, \dots, T+1,$$

where the error terms u_t follow the first-order autoregressive model

$$u_t = \rho u_{t-1} + \varepsilon_t, |\rho| < 1,$$

where ε_t's are independent with zero means and independent of the X_t's.

We have (conditionally to the process X_t):

$$\begin{aligned}
& E_{\theta,\rho}(Y_{T+1} \mid Y_1, \dots, Y_T) \\
&= E_{\theta,\rho}(f(X_{T+1}, \theta) + u_{T+1} \mid Y_1, \dots, Y_T) \\
&= f(X_{T+1}, \theta) + E_{\theta,\rho}(\rho(Y_T - f(X_T, \theta)) + \varepsilon_{T+1} \mid Y_1, \dots, Y_T) \\
&= \rho(Y_T - f(X_T, \theta)) + f(X_{T+1}, \theta),
\end{aligned}$$

because the temporal independence of the ε's gives

$$E_{\theta,\rho}(\varepsilon_{T+1} \mid Y_1, \dots, Y_T) = E_{\theta,\rho}(\varepsilon_{T+1}) = 0.$$

It remains to estimate the parameters θ and ρ. For instance, θ can be estimated consistently by the ordinary nonlinear least squares estimator $\hat{\theta}_T$ that solves $\min_\theta \sum_{t=1}^T (Y_t - f(X_t, \theta))^2$. Then ρ can be estimated consistently by the empirical correlation $\hat{\rho}_T$ of the estimated residuals

$$\hat{u}_t = Y_t - f(X_t, \hat{\theta}_T).$$

Therefore a prediction of Y_{T+1} is given by

$$\hat{Y}_{T+1} = \hat{\rho}_T(Y_T - f(X_T, \hat{\theta}_T)) + f(X_{T+1}, \hat{\theta}_T).$$

Example 11.4: The previous example focuses on the prediction of Y_{T+1}. If we assume that the model is satisfied for $t = 1, \dots, T+H$, we can also predict variables farther in the future such as $Y_{T+2}, \ldots, Y_{T+H}$. The difference between the time index h of the variable to predict Y_h and the time index T of the most recent obervation Y_T is sometimes called the *horizon of the prediction.* Clearly, the formula for an appropriate prediction depends on the horizon of the prediction.

For instance, we have

$$\begin{aligned} E_{\theta,\rho}(Y_{T+2} \mid Y_T) &= E_{\theta,\rho}(f(X_{T+2},\theta) + u_{T+2} \mid Y_1, \ldots, Y_T) \\ &= f(X_{T+2},\theta) \\ &+ E_{\theta,\rho}(\rho^2 u_T + \rho\varepsilon_{T+1} + \varepsilon_{T+2} \mid Y_1, \ldots, Y_T) \\ &= f(X_{T+2},\theta) + \rho^2(Y_T - f(X_T,\theta)). \end{aligned}$$

More generally, we have

$$E_{\theta,\rho}(Y_{T+h} \mid Y_1, \ldots, Y_T) = f(X_{T+h},\theta) + \rho^h(Y_T - f(X_T,\theta)).$$

Thus a prediction of Y_{T+h} is

$$\hat{Y}_{T+h} = f(X_{T+h},\hat{\theta}_T) + (\hat{\rho}_T)^h(Y_T - f(X_T,\hat{\theta}_T)).$$

In this example, the effect of the past on predictions arises only from the most recent observation, namely Y_T. Moreover, this effect decreases as the horizon of the prediction h increases, since $|\hat{\rho}_T| < 1$.

Example 11.5: The last formula in the preceding example gives the prediction of Y_{T+h} formulated at time T. To make the dependence on T explicit, we now denote ${}_T\hat{Y}_{T+h}$ such a prediction at time T. At time $T+1$ another observation Y_{T+1} becomes available. Thus, intuitively, the prediction of Y_{T+h} can be improved. Modifying the prediction of Y_{T+h} as more information becomes available is sometimes called *updating.*

In practice, two updating methods are used. The first method updates simultaneously theoretical predictions and estimators. That is, according to this method, the updated prediction of Y_{T+h} is

$${}_{T+1}\hat{Y}_{t+h} = f(X_{T+h},\hat{\theta}_{T+1}) + (\hat{\rho}_{T+1})^{h-1}(Y_{T+1} - f(X_{T+1},\hat{\theta}_{T+1})).$$

The second method updates theoretical predictions only. Thus we obtain

$${}_{T+1}\hat{Y}_{t+h} = f(X_{T+h},\hat{\theta}_T) + (\hat{\rho}_T)^{h-1}(Y_{T+1} - f(X_{T+1},\hat{\theta}_T)).$$

The second method is clearly simpler. Moreover, if the number of observations T is large, predictions given by the two methods do not differ substantially because $\hat{\theta}_{T+1} \approx \hat{\theta}_T$ and $\hat{\rho}_{T+1} \approx \hat{\rho}_T$.

If we use the second method, updating of the prediction of Y_{T+h} is obtained as

$$\begin{aligned} & {}_{T+1}\hat{Y}_{T+h} - {}_T\hat{Y}_{T+h} \\ &= (\hat{\rho}_T)^{h-1}(Y_{T+1} - f(X_{T+1}, \hat{\theta}_T)) - (\hat{\rho}_T)^h (Y_T - f(X_T, \hat{\theta}_T)) \\ &= (\hat{\rho}_T)^{h-1}\big[(Y_{T+1} - f(X_{T+1}, \hat{\theta}_T) - \rho_T(Y_T - f(X_T, \hat{\theta}_T)\big], \end{aligned}$$

i.e.

$${}_{T+1}\hat{Y}_{T+h} - {}_T\hat{Y}_{T+h} = (\hat{\rho}_T)^{h-1}(Y_{T+1} - {}_T\hat{Y}_{T+1}).$$

Thus the updating of the prediction of Y_{T+h} is a simple function of the prediction error associated with Y_{T+1}.

11.3 Residuals

11.3.1 Residuals in an Exponential Model

We assume that the observations $Y_1, \ldots, Y_n$ are conditionally independent given $X_1, \ldots, X_n$ with conditional densities of the exponential form

$$f(y_i \mid x_i; \theta) = \exp\left(\sum_{j=1}^{r} Q_j(x_i, \theta) T_j(y_i) + A(x_i, \theta) + B(x_i, y_i)\right). \quad (11.7)$$

Because all relevant information on the parameter vector θ is contained in the statistics $T_j(Y_i)$, $j = 1, \ldots, r$, $i = 1, \ldots, n$, it is natural to consider the regression model associated with these variables, i.e.

$$\begin{cases} T(y_i) = m(x_i, \theta) + u_i, \\ \text{with } E(u_i \mid x_i) = 0, \ V(u_i \mid x_i) = \mathbf{\Omega}(x_i, \theta), \end{cases} \quad (11.8)$$

where $T(Y_i) = (T_1(Y_i), \ldots, T_r(Y_i))'$, and $m(x_i, \theta)$ and $\mathbf{\Omega}(x_i, \theta)$ are the expectation vector and the variance covariance matrix of $T_i(Y_i)$ conditional upon $X_i = x_i$.

We can find some predictions of the error terms appearing in the second model (11.8).

Definition 11.8: *We call residuals associated with the conditional exponential model (11.7) the predictions of the error terms u_i in the associated model (11.8).*

As residuals, we can use

$$\hat{u}_i = T(Y_i) - m(x_i, \hat{\theta}_n), \tag{11.9}$$

where $\hat{\theta}_n$ is an asymptotically efficient estimator of θ. For instance, $\hat{\theta}_n$ is the maximum likelihood estimator of θ.

The use of model (11.8) and the subsequent determination of the residuals are interesting in view of the properties presented in Chapters 8 and 9.

a) For instance, Property 9.2 states that a quasi generalized least squares estimator of θ in model (11.8) is asymptotically efficient. Therefore, from an estimation point of view, we can use equivalently model (11.7) or model (11.8). In particular, we can define the residual $\hat{u}_i$ as $\hat{u}_i = T(Y_i) - m(x_i, \tilde{\theta}_n)$, where $\tilde{\theta}_n$ is a quasi generalized least squares estimator of θ.

b) From Example 7.29, the likelihood equations of model (11.7) are

$$\frac{\partial \log \ell(Y \mid x; \hat{\theta}_n)}{\partial \theta} = 0,$$

i.e.

$$\sum_{i=1}^{n} \frac{\partial Q'(x_i, \hat{\theta}_n)}{\partial \theta} \hat{u}_i = 0,$$

where $\hat{u}_i = T(Y_i) - m(x_i, \hat{\theta}_n)$ and $\hat{\theta}_n$ is the maximum likelihood estimator of θ. The likelihood equations can also be written as

$$\sum_{i=1}^{n} \frac{\partial m'(x_i, \hat{\theta}_n)}{\partial \theta} \boldsymbol{\Omega}^{-1}(x_i, \hat{\theta}_n) \hat{u}_i = 0.$$

These equations can be interpreted as orthogonality conditions between the "explanatory variables" $\partial m'(x_i, \hat{\theta}_n)/\partial \theta$ and the residuals $\hat{u}_i$ with respect to the scalar product associated with $\boldsymbol{\Omega}^{-1}(x_i, \hat{\theta}_n)$.

In general, the exact distribution of residuals is difficult to obtain. This is because residuals depend on which estimator of θ is used, such as the maximum likelihood estimator, and because the exact distributional properties of such an estimator are rarely known. On the other hand, when the model is correctly specified and when the number of observations is large, $\tilde{\theta}_n$ is consistent by definition. It follows that the properties of $\hat{u}_i$ are close to the properties of u_i. In particular, $\hat{u}_i$ has asymptotically the same distribution as u_i. A similar property holds when we consider an arbitrary subset of residuals of which the number of elements is independent of n (see Exercise 11.7).

In Figure 11.2 we give below a diagrammatical representation of residuals associated with the linear model $y_i = x_i b + u_i$, $E(u_i \mid x_i) = 0$, $V(u_i \mid x_i) = 1$. In this case, it is easily verified that Definitions 11.8 and 11.6 of residuals agree.

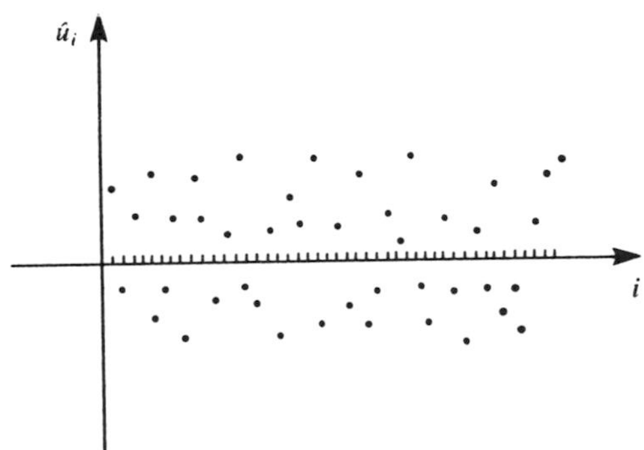

Figure 11.2: Residuals

This figure clearly shows that residuals have some properties that are similar to those of the errors u_i. For instance, on average, residuals are equal to zero, which is equal to Eu_i, for either small or large values of the index i. In addition, the variability of the residuals seems to be independent of i, which corresponds to the homoscedasticity assumption on the error terms u_i.

Diagrams similar to Figure 11.2 are frequently used for detecting possible departures from correct model specification (see Chapter 17, Vol. II).

Remark 11.5: When the error terms u_i are heteroscedastic, i.e., have different variances, it may be useful to standardize the residuals before plotting them. This leads to the notion of *standardized residuals*, which are defined as

$$v_i = V(x_i, \hat{\theta}_n)\hat{u}_i,$$

where

$$V'(x_i, \hat{\theta}_n)V(x_i, \hat{\theta}_n) = \mathbf{\Omega}^{-1}(x_i, \hat{\theta}_n).$$

11.3.2 Generalized Residuals

In this subsection we consider a model defined in two steps. Specifically, we consider a latent model which is assumed to be an exponential model with density

$$f^*(y_i^* \mid x_i, \theta) = \exp\left(\sum_{j=1}^{r} Q_j(x_i, \theta)T_j(y_i^*) + A(x_i, \theta) + B(x_i, y_i^*)\right). \tag{11.10}$$

Then, observed variables are related to latent variables by means of a mapping h so that

$$Y_i = h(Y_i^*). \tag{11.11}$$

As in Section 11.3.2, we introduce the error terms of the latent model. These error terms are defined as

$$u_i = T(Y_i^*) - m(x_i, \theta).$$

Here, however, predicting error terms is more complicated since Y_i^* is not necessarily observed. Nonetheless, we can apply the following two-step procedure:

(i) First, we compute

$$\begin{aligned} E_\theta(u_i \mid Y_1, \ldots, Y_n) &= E_\theta(u_i \mid Y_i) \\ &= E(T(Y_i^*) \mid Y_i) - m(x_i, \theta). \end{aligned}$$

(ii) Then, we replace θ in this expression by an estimator, such as the maximum likelihood estimator of θ, obtained from the estimation of the observable model.

Definition 11.9: *We call generalized residuals associated with model (11.10)–(11.11) the predictions of the error terms u_i given by*

$$\tilde{u}_i = E_{\hat{\theta}_n}(u_i \mid Y_i),$$

where $\hat{\theta}_n$ is an asymptotically efficient estimator of θ.

Remark 11.6: When the number of observations is large and when the model is correctly specified, the distribution of $\tilde{u}_i$ is no longer necessarily close to that of u_i. Here, such a distribution converges to the distribution of the prediction $E_{\theta_0}(u_i \mid Y_i)$ that is associated with the true parameter value.

Remark 11.7: The relationship between the likelihood equations and residuals mentioned earlier still holds for generalized residuals. Specifically, the score vector of the observable model is

$$\begin{aligned}
&\frac{\partial \log \ell(Y_1, \ldots, Y_n; \theta)}{\partial \theta} \\
&= E_\theta \left(\frac{\partial \log \ell(Y_1^*, \ldots, Y_n^*; \theta)}{\partial \theta} \mid Y_1, \ldots, Y_n \right) \\
&= \sum_{i=1}^{n} E_\theta \left(\frac{\partial \log f^*(Y_i^* \mid x_i; \theta)}{\partial \theta} \mid Y_i \right) \\
&= \sum_{i=1}^{n} \left(\sum_{j=1}^{r} \frac{\partial Q_j(x_i, \theta)}{\partial \theta} \left(E_\theta(T_j(Y_i^*) \mid Y_i) - m_j(x_i, \theta) \right) \right).
\end{aligned}$$

See appendix to this chapter.

Hence the likelihood equations are of the same form as in Section 11.3.1. Namely, we have

$$\sum_{i=1}^{n} \frac{\partial Q'(x_i, \hat{\theta}_n)}{\partial \theta} \tilde{u}_i = 0.$$

Example 11.6: We consider a probit model. The latent model is $Y_i^* = x_i\theta + u_i$, where the error terms u_i, $i = 1, \ldots, n$, are independent and identically distributed $N(0, 1)$. The observed variables are related to the latent variables by

$$Y_i = \begin{cases} 1, & \text{if } Y_i^* > 0, \\ 0, & \text{otherwise.} \end{cases}$$

We have

$$\begin{aligned}
E_\theta(Y_i^* \mid Y_i = 1) &= E_\theta(x_i\theta + u_i \mid x_i\theta + u_i > 0) \\
&= x_i\theta + E_\theta(u_i \mid u_i > -x_i\theta) \\
&= x_i\theta + \frac{1}{P(u_i > -x_i\theta)} \int_{-x_i\theta}^{\infty} u\phi(u)du \\
&= x_i\theta + \frac{1}{\Phi(x_i\theta)} (-\phi(u))_{-x_t\theta}^{\infty} \\
&= x_i\theta + \frac{\phi(x_i\theta)}{\Phi(x_i\theta)}.
\end{aligned}$$

A similar computation gives

$$E(Y_i^* \mid Y_i = 0) = x_i\theta - \frac{\phi(x_i\theta)}{1 - \Phi(x_i\theta)}.$$

Thus the generalized residuals are given by

$$\tilde{u}_i = x_i\hat{\theta}_n + \frac{\phi(x_i\hat{\theta}_n)}{\Phi(x_i\hat{\theta}_n)}Y_i - \frac{\phi(x_i\hat{\theta}_n)}{1 - \Phi(x_i\hat{\theta}_n)}(1 - Y_i),$$

i.e.

$$\tilde{u}_i = x_i\hat{\theta}_n + \frac{\phi(x_i\hat{\theta}_n)}{\Phi(x_i\hat{\theta}_n)(1 - \Phi(x_i\hat{\theta}_n))}(Y_i - \Phi(x_i\hat{\theta}_n)). \tag{11.12}$$

These generalized residuals can be plotted. The resulting diagram is called the *generalized residuals diagram.* We give below such a diagram when the latent model reduces to the simple linear regression model

$$Y_i^* = b_0 + b_1 x_i + u_i$$

with $b_0 = 1$ and $b_1 = 1$.

Generalized residuals are graphed against the corresponding values taken by the exogenous variable. As a consequence, the different points line up on two different curves that correspond to observations for which $Y_i = 1$ and $Y_i = 0$.

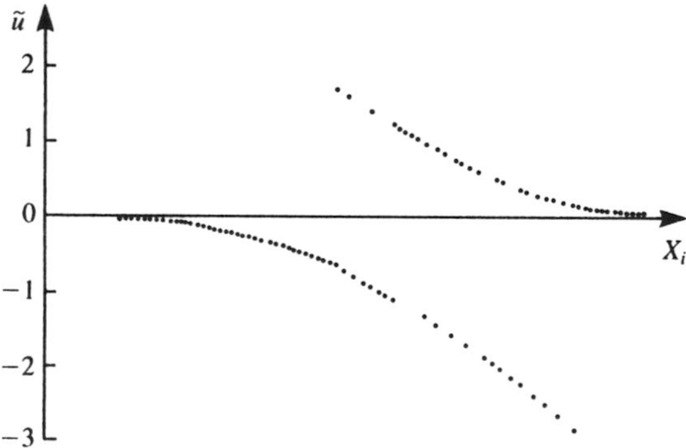

Figure 11.3: Generalized Residuals

11.3.3 Simulated Residuals

In the preceding model defined by (11.10) and (11.11) predictions of the unobserved latent variables Y_i^* (and the error terms u_i) rely on approximations based on conditional expectations. An alternative method consists in approximating the latent variables by means of simulations.

First, suppose that the parameter value θ is known. Instead of computing $E_\theta(Y_i^* \mid Y_i)$, we can draw a random variable $\check{Y}_i^*$ from the conditional distribution of Y_i^* given Y_i, denoted $P_\theta^{Y_i^* \mid Y_i}$. When the parameter value θ is unknown, a similar approach can be followed after replacing θ by a consistent estimator $\hat{\theta}_n$.

Definition 11.10: *We call simulated residuals the quantities*

$$\check{u}_i = \check{Y}_i^* - m(x_i, \hat{\theta}_n),$$

where $\check{Y}_i^*$ is drawn from the conditional distribution $P_{\hat{\theta}_n}^{Y_i^* \mid Y_i}$ and $\hat{\theta}_n$ is an asymptotically efficient estimator of θ.

There is an important distinction between simulated residuals and generalized residuals. When the model is correctly specified and when the number of observations is large, the estimator $\hat{\theta}_n$ converges to the true parameter value θ_0. Thus the variable $\check{u}_i$ is approximately a draw from the conditional distribution $P_{\theta_0}^{u_i \mid Y_i}$. Since the distribution of Y_i corresponds to the same value of the parameter, i.e., to the true value, it follows that the distribution of $\check{u}_i$ is approximately that of the error term u_i. On the other hand, in Section 11.3.2 we noted that the asymptotic distribution of a generalized residual $\hat{u}_i$ is the distribution of $E_{\theta_0}(u_i \mid Y_i)$, which is clearly not identical to that of u_i.

A Linear Latent Model

In some cases, it might be useful to introduce another notion of simulated residuals. An important case is provided by the linear latent model

$$Y_i^* = x_i b + u_i, \tag{11.13}$$

where the error terms u_i are independent and identically distributed $N(0, \sigma^2)$.

As before, let $\hat{\theta}_n$ denote a consistent estimator of θ and let $\check{Y}_i^*$ denote a random draw from the conditional distribution $P_{\hat{\theta}_n}^{Y_i^* \mid Y_i}$. Thus $\check{Y}_i^*$ constitutes a good approximation to the latent variable Y_i^*, which satisfies the linear model (11.13) by assumption. This suggests to replace the unobserved Y_i^* by its simulation $\check{Y}_i^*$. This simple method only requires standard regression packages that provide residuals among other statistics.

Specifically, a new estimate, which is in general different from the original estimator $\hat{\theta}_n$, is determined by ordinary least squares based on the simulated values. This new estimate is

$$\check{b}_n = \left(\sum_{i=1}^{n} x_i' x_i \right)^{-1} \sum_{i=1}^{n} x_i' \check{Y}_i^*.$$

Then the simulated residuals can be computed as

$$\begin{aligned} \check{\check{u}}_i &= \check{Y}_i^* - x_i \check{b}_n \\ &= \check{Y}_i^* - x_i \left(\sum_{i=1}^{n} x_i' x_i \right)^{-1} \sum_{i=1}^{n} x_i' \check{Y}_i^*. \end{aligned}$$

Definition 11.11: *When the latent model is linear, we call two-step simulated residuals the variables*

$$\check{\check{u}}_i = \check{Y}_i^* - x_i \left(\sum_{i=1}^{n} x_i' x_i \right)^{-1} \sum_{i=1}^{n} x_i' \check{Y}_i^*,$$

where each simulation $\check{Y}_i^*$ is drawn independently from the corresponding conditional distribution $P_{\hat{\theta}_n}^{Y_i^*|Y_i}$.

When the model is correctly specified and when the number of observations is large, a two-step simulated residual $\check{\check{u}}_i$ has approximately the same distribution as the error term u_i of the latent model. Such a property can be visualized by means of a *simulated residuals diagram.* The simulated residuals diagram has the same appearance as a usual residuals diagram but is quite different from a generalized residuals diagram. An example of a simulated residuals diagram is given below for the probit model considered in Section 11.3.2.

11.4 Appendix

Score Vector of the Observable Model

Consider a latent model with probability density $\ell^*(y_1^*, \ldots, y_n^*; \theta)$, also denoted $\ell(y^*; \theta)$, with respect to a measure μ^*. The observable

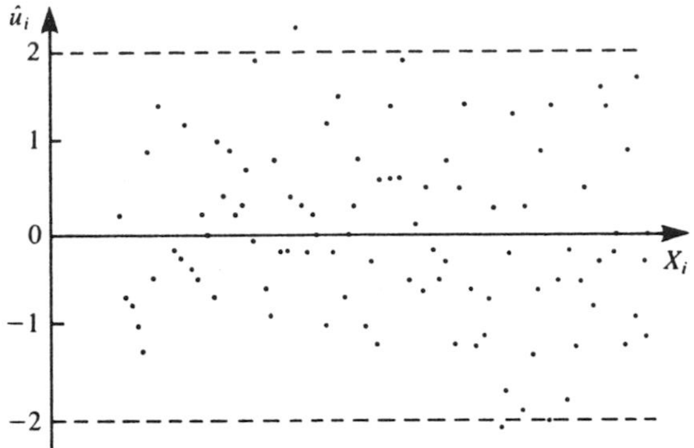

Figure 11.4: Simulated Residuals

model is derived from the latent model *via*

$$Y_i = h(Y_i^*).$$

Let $\ell(y_1, \ldots, y_n; \theta)$ or $\ell(y; \theta)$ denote the probability density of the observable model with respect to a measure denoted μ.

Lemma: We have

$$\frac{\partial \log \ell(y;\theta)}{\partial \theta} = E_\theta \left(\frac{\partial \log \ell^*(Y^*;\theta)}{\partial \theta} \mid Y = y \right).$$

PROOF: For every real function g that is integrable with respect to the distribution of $Y_1, \ldots, Y_n$, we have

$$\int_{\mathcal{Y}} g(y)\ell(y;\theta)d\mu(y) = \int_{\mathcal{Y}^*} g(h(y^*))\ell^*(y^*;\theta)d\mu^*(y^*).$$

Differentiating with respect to θ we obtain after reversing the order of differentiation and integration

$$\int_{\mathcal{Y}} g(y)\frac{\partial \ell(y;\theta)}{\partial \theta}d\mu(y) - \int_{\mathcal{Y}^*} g(h(y^*))\frac{\partial \ell^*(y^*;\theta)}{\partial \theta}d\mu^*(y^*) = 0,$$

i.e.

$$\int_{\mathcal{Y}} g(y)\frac{\partial \log \ell(y;\theta)}{\partial \theta}\ell(y;\theta)d\mu(y)$$
$$- \int_{\mathcal{Y}^*} g(h(y^*))\frac{\partial \log \ell^*(y^*;\theta)}{\partial \theta}\ell^*(y^*;\theta)d\mu^*(y^*) = 0.$$

In terms of expectations, the latter equality can be written as

$$E_\theta\left(g(Y)\left(\frac{\partial \log \ell(Y;\theta)}{\partial \theta} - \frac{\partial \log \ell^*(Y^*;\theta)}{\partial \theta}\right)\right) = 0.$$

Since the vector

$$\frac{\partial \log \ell^*(Y^*;\theta)}{\partial \theta} - \frac{\partial \log \ell(Y;\theta)}{\partial \theta}$$

is orthogonal to every function of Y, it follows from Property B.17, Volume II that

$$\frac{\partial \log \ell(Y;\theta)}{\partial \theta} = E_\theta\left(\frac{\partial \log \ell^*(Y^*;\theta)}{\partial \theta} \mid Y\right).$$

□

11.5 Exercises

EXERCISE 11.1: Consider the linear model $Y_i = x_i b + u_i$, $i = 1, \ldots, n$, where the error terms u_i are independently and identically distributed $N(0, \sigma^2)$. Verify that the residual vector $\hat{u} = (\hat{u}_1, \ldots, \hat{u}_n)'$ is a linear transformation of the error vector $u = (u_1, \ldots, u_n)'$. Show that this linear transformation is a projection. Then, find the joint distribution of $(u', \hat{u}')'$. Is $\hat{u}_i$ an unbiased prediction of u_i? Determine its mean squared prediction error.

EXERCISE 11.2: Consider Exercise 11.1 and the prediction vector $\hat{Y} = (\hat{Y}_1, \ldots, \hat{Y}_n)'$ of $Y = (Y_1, \ldots, Y_n)'$. Prove results similar to those established in Exercise 11.1 for this prediction vector.

EXERCISE 11.3: Consider the simple linear regression model $Y_i = b_0 + b_1 x_i + u_i$, $i = 1, \ldots, n$, where the error terms u_i are uncorrelated with mean zero and common variance σ^2. Verify that the OLS estimator $\hat{b}_{1n}$ of b_1 is a linear affine transformation of the centered errors $(u_i - \bar{u}_n)$, where $\bar{u}_n$ is the sample mean of the u_i's. Then show that $\bar{b}_{1n}$ is uncorrelated with $\bar{u}_n$ and hence with $\bar{Y}_n$.

EXERCISE 11.4: Let $\hat{Y}_1, \ldots, \hat{Y}_n$ be unbiased predictions of the n variables $Y_1, \ldots, Y_n$. Consider the statistic

$$V_r = \frac{\sum_{i=1}^n (Y_i - \hat{Y}_i)^2}{\sum_{i=1}^n Y_i^2}$$

as a measure of the relative mean prediction error. What is this statistic in the usual linear model where $\hat{Y}_i$ denotes the predicted value of the

ith observation on the dependent variable. Verify that $0 \leq V_r \leq 1$ and discuss the special cases $V_r = 0$ and $V_r = 1$.

EXERCISE 11.5: Consider a Tobit model where the observed variable Y_i is related to the latent variable Y_i^* by

$$Y_i = \begin{cases} Y_i^*, & \text{if } Y_i^* > 0, \\ 0, & \text{otherwise,} \end{cases}$$

where Y_i^* satisfies the linear model $Y_i^* = x_i b + u_i$, $i = 1, \ldots, n$, with u_i independently and identically distributed $N(0, \sigma^2)$. Find the predictors of Y_i^* and Y_i^{*2}.

EXERCISE 11.6: Consider the normal linear model with unknown variance

$$Y_i = x_i b + u_i, \; E(u_i \mid x_i) = 0, \; V(u_i \mid x_i) = \sigma^2.$$

a) Verify that the model is an exponential model where the statistic $T(Y_i)$ defined in (11.7) may be equal to $(Y_i, Y_i^2)'$.

b) Find some expressions for the residuals and standardized residuals.

EXERCISE 11.7 Consider the simple linear regression model $Y_i = b_0 + b_1 x_i + u_i$, $i = 1, \ldots, n$, where the error terms u_i are independently and identically distributed $N(0, \sigma^2)$. Find the distribution of $(1/\sqrt{n})(\hat{u}_1 + \ldots + \hat{u}_n)$. Compare this distribution to that of $(1/\sqrt{n})(u_1 + \ldots + u_n)$.

EXERCISE 11.8: How would you define two-step simulated residuals in a conditional latent model that is exponential? Hint: Consider the maximum likelihood estimator of θ based on the latent model where Y_i^* is replaced by some simulated value.

EXERCISE 11.9: Consider a Tobit model (see Exercise 11.5). Give an expression for its generalized residuals. When the latent model is a simple linear regression model and when the generalized residuals are plotted as functions of the corresponding values of the exogenous variable, show that a fraction of these generalized residuals lies on a curve. Find the asymptotic variance of an arbitrary generalized residual and verify that this variance depends on the value taken by the exogenous variable.

EXERCISE 11.10: Notations are those of Example 11.2.

a) Show that

$$\hat{\Pi}_t = \frac{h_{1t}}{h_{1t} + h_{2t}},$$

where

$$h_{1t} = \frac{1}{\sigma_u}\phi\left(\frac{q_t - ap_t - b}{\sigma_u}\right)\Phi\left(\frac{\alpha p_t + \beta - q_t}{\sigma_v}\right),$$
$$h_{2t} = \frac{1}{\sigma_v}\phi\left(\frac{q_t - \alpha p_t - \beta}{\sigma_v}\right)\Phi\left(\frac{ap_t + b - q_t}{\sigma_u}\right),$$

ϕ and Φ denote the density and the cumulative distribution function of the standard normal distribution. Interpret the functions h_{1t}, h_{2t} and $h_{1t} + h_{2t}$.

b) Verify that

$$E(D_t \mid p_t, D_t > q_t) = ap_t + b + \sigma_u \frac{\phi\left(\frac{q_t - ap_t - b}{\sigma_u}\right)}{1 - \Phi\left(\frac{q_t - ap_t - b}{\sigma_u}\right)}.$$

11.6 References

Brown, B.W. and Mariano, R.S. (1984). "Residual-Based Procedure for Prediction and Estimation in Nonlinear Simultaneous System," *Econometrica*, 52, 321–343.

Chesher, A. and Irish, M. (1987). "Numerical and Graphical Residual Analysis in the Grouped and Censored Normal Linear Model," *Journal of Econometrics*, 34, 33–54.

Feldstein, M.S. (1971). "The Error of Forecast in Econometric Models when the Forecast Period Exogenous Variables are Stochastic," *Econometrica*, 39, 55–60.

Goldberger, A.S. (1962). "Best Linear Unbiased Prediction in the Generalized Linear Regression Model," *Journal of the American Statistical Association*, 57, 369–375.

Gourieroux, C. and Monfort, A. (1995). *Time series and Dynamic Models*, Cambridge University Press.

Gourieroux, C., Monfort, A., Renault, E., and Trognon, A. (1987). "Generalized Residuals," *Journal of Econometrics*, 34, 5–32.

Gourieroux, C., Monfort, A., Renault, E., and Trognon, A. (1987). "Simulated Residuals," *Journal of Econometrics*, 34, 201–252.

Lancaster T. (1985). "Generalized Residuals and Heterogenous Duration Models with Applications to the Weibull Model," *Journal of Econometrics*, 28, 155–169.

Theil, H. (1971). *Principles of Econometrics*, Wiley.

Zellner, A. (1983). "Statistical Theory and Econometrics," in Z. Griliches and M. Intriligator eds. *Handbook of Econometrics*, North–Holland.

CHAPTER 12

Bayesian Estimation

12.1 The Bayesian Approach

12.1.1 Review

Let

$$(\mathcal{Y}, \mathcal{P} = \{P_\theta = \ell(y;\theta) \cdot \mu, \theta \in \Theta\}),$$

be a dominated parametric model. In the Bayesian approach a probability distribution Π, called the *prior distribution*, is defined on the set Θ of possible values of the parameter vector θ. The parameter vector θ is considered as random with prior distribution Π (see Chapter 4).

Let y be the vector of observations. After observing y, the prior distribution of the parameter vector is modified. Specifically, the observations y are used to replace the marginal distribution of θ, i.e., the prior distribution, by the conditional distribution of θ given y, called the *posterior distribution*. The posterior distribution is given by the Bayes formula

$$\pi(\theta \mid y) = \frac{\ell(y;\theta)\pi(\theta)}{\int_\Theta \ell(y;\theta)\pi(\theta)\nu(d\theta)} = \pi(\theta)\frac{\ell(y;\theta)}{\ell(y)}, \tag{12.1}$$

where $\pi(\theta)$ is the density of the prior distribution with respect to a measure ν. Then the posterior distribution has a density $\pi(\theta \mid y)$ with respect to the measure ν. Equation (12.1) shows that the posterior density is obtained by multiplying the prior density by the ratio of the conditional density of y given θ, i.e., the *likelihood of y given θ*, over the marginal density of y, called the *predictive density* of y.

Although it is interesting to know completely the posterior distribution, frequently only some characteristics of the posterior distribution are of interest. For instance, the best estimator $\hat{\theta}$ of θ in the Bayesian sense when the quadratic matrix risk function is used is the posterior mean

$$\hat{\theta} = E(\theta \mid y) \tag{12.2}$$

(see Property 5.7). Thus the determination of the Bayes estimator only requires the knowledge of the first moment of the posterior distribution. This estimator is unbiased for θ in the Bayesian sense since the expectation of $\hat{\theta}$ with respect to the distribution of y is equal to the mean of θ.

If we want to assess the precision of the Bayes estimator $\hat{\theta}$, then it suffices to note that the Bayesian risk is

$$\begin{aligned} V(\hat{\theta} - \theta) &= VE(\hat{\theta} - \theta \mid y) + EV(\hat{\theta} - \theta \mid y) \\ &= 0 + EV((E(\theta \mid y) - \theta) \mid y) \\ &= EV(\theta \mid y). \end{aligned}$$

Thus an unbiased estimator in the Bayesian sense of the risk is $V(\theta \mid y)$, i.e., the *posterior variance.* Hence the second-order central moment of the posterior distribution is useful for assessing the precision of the best estimator $\hat{\theta}$ in the Bayesian sense.

In this subsection we have briefly reviewed the principal characteristics of the Bayesian approach. The main difficulty, however, does not lie in the determination of the posterior distribution, even if the exact determination of such a distribution requires complicated mathematical derivations. Instead, the important step is the choice of an adequate prior distribution. To discuss such a choice, we now focus on this prior distribution, in particular on its interpretation and the properties that we may want to impose on it.

12.1.2 Prior Distributions

In the *classical* (or *frequentist*) approach, probability distributions are introduced by means of frequencies. For instance, the fact that empirical distributions of income are frequently close to the density of a log-normal distribution suggests the use of a log-normal distribution as an adequate distribution for the variable "income." There exist, however, other approaches to probability distributions. One of these alternative approaches is the so-called *subjective* approach, where the "probability" of an event measures the degree of beliefs in the occurence of the event according to an individual or a group of individuals. Such degrees of beliefs do exist. For instance, consider the following two events: The income elasticity of consumption is smaller than 0.5 and the income elasticity of consumption is larger than 0.5. An individual (an econometrician, say) will be often able to state which of these two events is more likely than the other one.

It is clear, however, that a probability distribution cannot be formed by questioning individuals on their beliefs only. Indeed, individuals are able to answer questions of the preceding type only for a limited number of events. Moreover, although individuals can state relatively easily which of two events is more likely to occur, individuals have, in general, more difficulties in giving a precise measure of the "probability" of each event. Lastly, individuals' answers may not satisfy the minimal coherency conditions required by a probability distribution such as the usual additivity condition. Thus, even though questioning individuals has been sometimes used to specify prior distributions on the parameter θ, especially when θ can take a few values only, such a method does not seem applicable in more complex problems.

In more complex problems one usually chooses the prior distribution in a family of probability distributions. Often, this family is a family of well-known distributions such as the family of normal, gamma, or Student distributions. A common characteristic of chosen families of distributions is that they are parameterized by a few number of auxiliary parameters α that are easily interpreted. Hence specifying a prior distribution reduces to choosing a particular value for α.

As an example, suppose that θ is a scalar parameter. It is believed that θ lies approximately between 0.2 and 0.4. If the prior distribution is chosen to be a normal distribution, then the auxiliary parameter α includes the mean m and the variance σ^2 of this normal distribution, i.e., $\alpha = (m, \sigma^2)'$. For such a normal distribution, a 95%-confidence interval is $[m - 2\sigma, m + 2\sigma]$. In view of the above prior beliefs about θ, we can choose m and σ^2 such that $m - 2\sigma = 0.2$ and $m + 2\sigma = 0.4$. Hence we can retain the normal distribution $N(0.3, (0.05)^2)$ as a prior distribution.

At this stage, we must note that the distinction between a frequentist approach and a subjective approach is not as important as it may seem at first sight. Beliefs in the most likely values of the parameter θ are frequently based on various observations or prior studies that involve the parameter θ. In such a context, the prior distribution must be updated to take into account new information. Suppose that the original prior distribution is $\Pi_0(d\theta)$ and that the variables y_0 are observed. After observing y_0, knowledge of the parameter θ is now summarized by the posterior distribution $\Pi_0(d\theta \mid y_0)$. Then the latter distribution should be used subsequently as a new prior distribution. Such a stepwise procedure is pictured below assuming, to simplify, that the observations y_0 are y_1 are independent conditionally on θ.

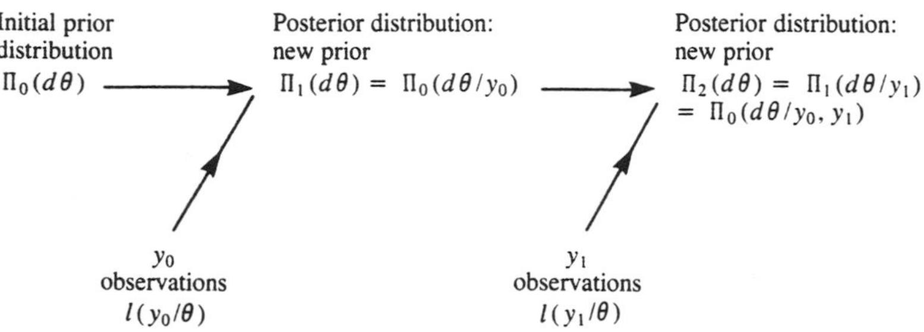

Figure 12.1: Bayesian Updating

Although the initial prior distribution depends on an individual or a group of individuals, it is intuitively clear that the importance of such a prior distribution will disappear as the number of observations increases.

Note also that, for a given statistical model $\ell(y;\theta)$ and a prior distribution chosen in a given family Π_α indexed by the auxiliary parameter α, it is desirable to obtain a posterior distribution that also belongs to the family Π_α. In this case, updating the prior distribution reduces to updating appropriately the auxiliary parameter α (see Figure 2.2).

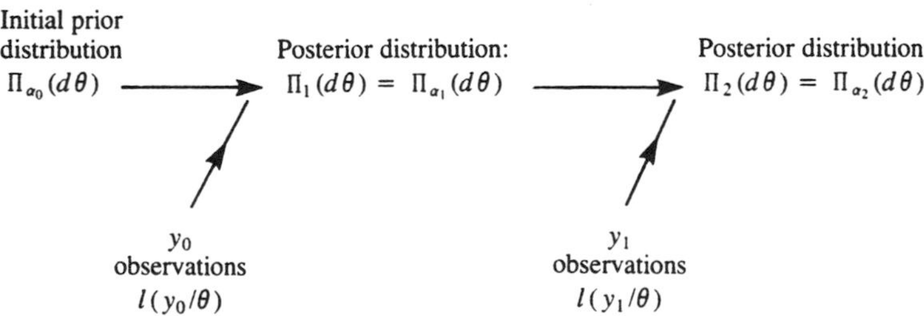

Figure 12.2: Bayesian Updating of Parameters

12.1.3 An Example of Bayesian Estimation

We consider a sample $Y_1, \ldots, Y_n$ independently and identically normally distributed $N(\theta, 1)$, where $\theta \in \mathbb{R}$ is unknown. We suppose that the prior distribution on the parameter θ is also normal with mean m_0 and variance σ_0^2, where m_0 and σ_0^2 are given. The joint distribution of $Y_1, \ldots, Y_n, \theta$ is normal as well as the conditional distribution of θ given $Y_1, \ldots, Y_n$. These distributions are characterized by their means and variance covariance matrices.

Let $Y = (Y_1, \ldots, Y_n)'$ and $e = (1, \ldots, 1)'$. By assumption, we have

(i) $E(Y \mid \theta) = \theta e,\ V(Y \mid \theta) = \mathbf{I}$,

(ii) $E\theta = m_0,\ V\theta = \sigma_0^2$.

It follows

(iii)

$$\begin{aligned}
EY &= EE(Y \mid \theta) = E(\theta e) = m_0 e, \\
VY &= VE(Y \mid \theta) + EV(Y \mid \theta) \\
&= V(\theta e) + E(\mathbf{I}) \\
&= \sigma_0^2 ee' + \mathbf{I}, \\
\operatorname{Cov}(Y, \theta) &= \operatorname{Cov}(E(Y \mid \theta), \theta) + E\operatorname{Cov}((Y, \theta) \mid \theta) \\
&= \operatorname{Cov}(\theta e, \theta) \\
&= \sigma_0^2 e.
\end{aligned}$$

Thus the joint distribution of $(Y', \theta)'$ is the normal distribution

$$N\left(\begin{pmatrix} m_0 e \\ m_0 \end{pmatrix}, \begin{pmatrix} \sigma_0^2 ee' + \mathbf{I} & \sigma_0^2 e \\ \sigma_0^2 e' & \sigma_0^2 \end{pmatrix} \right).$$

The posterior distribution, i.e., the conditional distribution of θ given Y is also normal. It is determined by its first two moments. Let $\bar{Y}$ denote the sample mean of the observations. We have

(iv)

$$\begin{aligned}
E(\theta \mid Y) &= \operatorname{Cov}(\theta, Y)(VY)^{-1}(Y - EY) + E\theta \\
&= \frac{1}{1 + n\sigma_0^2} m_0 + \frac{n\sigma_0^2}{1 + n\sigma_0^2} \bar{Y}
\end{aligned}$$

$$
\begin{aligned}
& = m_0 + \frac{n\sigma_0^2}{1+n\sigma_0^2}(\bar{Y} - m_0), \\
V(\theta \mid Y) & = V(\theta) - \mathrm{Cov}(\theta, Y)(VY)^{-1}\mathrm{Cov}(Y, \theta) \\
& = \frac{\sigma_0^2}{1+n\sigma_0^2}.
\end{aligned}
$$

We now discuss some consequences of this posterior distribution. The Bayes estimator of the parameter θ is the posterior expectation, i.e., the expectation of the posterior distribution. It is

$$
\hat{\theta} = E(\theta \mid Y) = \frac{1}{1+n\sigma_0^2} m_0 + \frac{n\sigma_0^2}{1+n\sigma_0^2}\bar{Y}. \tag{12.3}
$$

Thus $\hat{\theta}$ is a convex combination of the usual sample mean estimator $\bar{Y}$ and the prior expectation m_0 of the parameter θ. The ratio of the weigths associated with $\bar{Y}$ and m_0 is

$$
n\sigma_0^2 = \frac{\sigma_0^2}{1/n} = \frac{V(\theta)}{V(\bar{Y} \mid \theta)}.
$$

Thus this ratio depends on the prior precision on the parameter, as measured by the inverse of $V(\theta) = \sigma_0^2$, relative to the precision of the information contained in the sample only, as measured by the inverse of $V(\bar{Y} \mid \theta)$. Hence the sample mean receives a larger weight as the number of observations n increases or as prior information is less precise, i.e., as σ_0^2 increases. In the limit case, where n is infinitely large, the Bayes estimator $\hat{\theta}$ becomes equivalent to $\bar{Y}$ and prior information no longer affects the estimate.

A similar argument applies to the posterior variance, which is an estimate of the precision of the Bayes estimator. This variance is

$$
\begin{aligned}
V(\theta \mid Y) & = \frac{1}{1/\sigma_0^2 + 1/(1/n)} \\
& = \frac{1}{1/V(\theta) + 1/V(\bar{Y} \mid \theta)}.
\end{aligned}
$$

Thus the posterior variance is the inverse of the sum of the inverses of the prior variance and the variance due to the observations. As n increases to infinity, the posterior variance becomes equivalent to $1/n$. Thus, as noted earlier, prior information is no longer important.

12.1.4 Diffuse Priors

In the previous example we saw that an increase in the prior variance σ_0^2 has the effect of decreasing the importance of prior information relative to sample information. We now examine the limit case where σ_0^2 increases to infinity. Such a situation corresponds to the case where there is little prior information. We say that prior information is *diffuse* or *noninformative*.

When σ_0^2 increases to infinity, the posterior distribution converges to the normal distribution $N(\bar{Y}, 1/n)$. First, note that the mean of the prior distribution does not appear in this limiting distribution. This agrees with the intuitive idea that a diffuse prior is noninformative about the mean of the parameter. In fact, the whole posterior distribution becomes independent of the prior mean. Second, the Bayes estimator becomes identical to the usual estimator $\bar{Y}$. Hence, when σ_0^2 increases to infinity, all relevant information is contained in the observations.

We now discuss more precisely the meaning of a limit as σ_0^2 increases to infinity. Specifically, we shall discuss more rigorously the meaning of the prior distribution $N(m_0, +\infty)$. When the variance of a normal distribution increases to infinity, the ratio of its density evaluated at two points θ_1 and θ_2 converges to one since

$$\frac{\pi(\theta_1)}{\pi(\theta_2)} = \exp -\frac{1}{2\sigma_0^2}\left((\theta_1 - m_0)^2 - (\theta_2 - m_0)^2\right).$$

Thus every possible value of θ receives the same weight. This suggests that the limiting prior distribution as σ_0^2 increases to infinity has a constant density, i.e., $\pi(\theta) \propto 1$. The symbol $\propto$ means "proportional to." It is, however, well known that a uniform probability distribution cannot be defined on $\mathbb{R}$ (see Exercise 12.1).

Therefore, if we wish to follow the above approach, we must allow for prior distributions that are not probability distributions. Then we must examine whether such new prior distributions can determine unambiguously posterior distributions by Bayes rule.

Suppose that the prior distribution is

$$\pi(\theta) \propto 1. \tag{12.4}$$

Such a prior distribution is said to be *diffuse* or *noninformative*. From Bayes rule we obtain

$$\pi(\theta \mid y_1, \ldots, y_n) \propto \pi(\theta)\ell(y_1, \ldots, y_n; \theta) = \ell(y_1, \ldots, y_n; \theta),$$

i.e.

$$\pi(\theta \mid y_1, \ldots, y_n) \propto \frac{1}{(2\pi)^{n/2}} \exp -\frac{1}{2} \sum_{i=1}^{n} (y_i - \theta)^2,$$

i.e.

$$\pi(\theta \mid y_1, \ldots, y_n) \propto \exp\left(-\frac{n\theta^2}{2} + n\theta\bar{y} \right),$$

since the symbol $\propto$ means that equality holds up to a multiplicative scalar which may depend on $y_1, \ldots, y_n$. The right-hand side resembles a part of the density of the normal distribution $N(\bar{y}, 1/n)$. Thus we obtain

$$\pi(\theta \mid y_1, \ldots, y_n) = \frac{\sqrt{n}}{\sqrt{2\pi}} \exp -\frac{n}{2}(\theta - \bar{y})^2.$$

Hence, although the diffuse prior is not a probability distribution, computation of the posterior distribution is still possible. In addition, the posterior distribution is a proper probability distribution.

Lastly, note that, in the preceding example, two different interpretations of a diffuse prior were given. The first interpretation is as the limit of a proper prior as the variance σ_0^2 increases to infinity. The second interpretation is as a uniform measure on $\mathbb{R}$.

12.2 Conjugate Priors

12.2.1 Models with Sufficient Statistics of Dimension Independent of the Number of Observations

To simplify the notation, the next results are derived for unconditional models. The presence of exogenous variables does not introduce new difficulties. We consider n observations $Y_1, \ldots, Y_n$ of a random vector that are independent and identically distributed. Let $\ell_n(y_1, \ldots, y_n; \theta)$ denote the joint density of these n observations with respect to some measure $\bigotimes_{i=1}^{n} \mu(dy_i)$. If the model has a sufficient statistic

$$T^{(n)}(y_1, \ldots, y_n) = (T_1^{(n)}(y_1, \ldots, y_n), \ldots, T_{K(n)}^{(n)}(y_1, \ldots, y_n))',$$

then, using the factorization criterion (Theorem 3.1), we can write

$$\ell_n(y_1, \ldots, y_n; \theta) = h(T^{(n)}(y_1, \ldots, y_n); \theta, n)\lambda_n(y_1, \ldots, y_n).$$

In what follows, we are interested in the relation between the parameter θ and the observations $y_1, \ldots, y_n$. Then the preceding equation can be simplified as

$$\ell_n(y_1, \ldots, y_n; \theta) \propto h(T^{(n)}(y_1, \ldots, y_n); \theta, n), \tag{12.5}$$

where the symbol $\propto$ denotes, as before, that equality holds up to a multiplicative scalar that is independent of the parameter θ but that may depend on the observations.

Definition 12.1: *The model has a sufficient statistic of constant dimension if and only if we have*

$$\ell_n(y_1, \ldots, y_n; \theta) \propto h(T^{(n)}(y_1, \ldots, y_n); \theta, n),$$

where $T^{(n)}$ is a statistic whose dimension K is independent of n.

For a given model, there clearly exist many sufficient statistics and hence many decompositions of the likelihood based on the factorization criterion. According to Definition 12.1, it suffices that the condition on ℓ_n is satisfied for one of these statistics and one of these decompositions.

Example 12.1: Let $Y_1, \ldots, Y_n$ be a random sample drawn from a uniform distribution $U_{[0,\theta]}$ where $\theta > 0$. A sufficient statistic for this model is

$$T^{(n)}(y_1, \ldots, y_n) = \sup_i y_i.$$

Its dimension is equal to one. Thus it is independent of the number of observations n.

Example 12.2: Let $Y_1, \ldots, Y_n$ be a random sample drawn from a normal distribution $N(m, \sigma^2)$. A sufficient statistic with constant dimension equal to two is

$$T^{(n)}(y_1, \ldots, y_n) = (T_1^{(n)}(y_1, \ldots, y_n), T_2^{(n)}(y_1, \ldots, y_n))',$$

where

$$T_1^{(n)}(y_1, \ldots, y_n) = \frac{1}{n}\sum_{i=1}^{n} y_i, \quad T_2^{(n)}(y_1, \ldots, y_n) = \frac{1}{n}\sum_{i=1}^{n} y_i^2.$$

A useful feature of models with sufficient statistics of constant dimension is the possibility to replace standard operations on densities by operations on their statistics $T^{(n)}$. Specifically, suppose that the number of observations increases from n to $n+p$. Because the observations Y_i, $i = 1, \ldots, n+p$, are assumed independent and identically distributed, we can write

$$\ell_{n+p}(y_1, \ldots, y_n; \theta) = \ell_n(y_1, \ldots, y_n; \theta)\ell_p(y_{n+1}, \ldots, y_{n+p}; \theta).$$

Hence

$$h(T^{(n+p)}(y_1, \ldots, y_{n+p}); \theta, n+p) \propto \\ h(T^{(n)}(y_1, \ldots, y_n); \theta, n) \cdot h(T^{(p)}(y_{n+1}, \ldots, y_{n+p}); \theta, p).$$

Let $*$ denote the operation that associates $T^{(n+p)}(y_1, \ldots, y_{n+p})$ to the pair $T^{(n)}(y_1, \ldots, y_n)$ and $T^{(p)}(y_p, \ldots, y_{n+p})$. Such an operation summarizes completely how the joint density of $y_1, \ldots, y_{n+p}$ can be derived from those of $y_1, \ldots, y_p$ and $y_p, \ldots, y_{n+p}$. The next property formally states such a result.

Property 12.1: *Let $\mathcal{T}^{(n)} \subset I\!R^K$ denote the set of possible values of the statistic $T^{(n)}$. For every pair of integers n and p, there exists an operation $*$ from $\mathcal{T}^{(n)} \times \mathcal{T}^{(p)}$ to $\mathcal{T}^{(n+p)}$ such that*

$$h(T^{(n)}(y_1, \ldots, y_n); \theta, n)h(T^{(p)}(y_{n+1}, \ldots, y_{n+p}); \theta, p) \\ \propto h(T^{(n)}(y_1, \ldots, y_n) * T^{(p)}(y_{n+1}, \ldots, y_{n+p}); \theta, n+p).$$

Although the operation $*$ depends on the integers n and p, in most applications, such an operation is simply the restriction of a fixed binary operation to $\mathcal{T}^{(n)} \times \mathcal{T}^{(p)} \subset I\!R^{2K}$. This justifies that the symbol $*$ is neither indexed by n nor p.

Moreover note that the definition of the operation $*$ implies immediately that $*$ is associative and commutative.

Example 12.3: Let $Y_1, \ldots, Y_n$ be a random sample drawn from a uniform distribution $U_{[0,\theta]}$ where $\theta > 0$. We have

$$\begin{aligned} T^{(n+p)}(y_1, \ldots, y_{n+p}) &= \sup_{i=1,\ldots,n+p} (y_i) \\ &= \sup\left(\sup_{i=1,\ldots,n} y_i, \sup_{i=n+1,\ldots,n+p} y_i\right) \\ &= \sup\left(T^{(n)}(y_1, \ldots, y_n),\ T^{(p)}(y_{n+1}, \ldots, y_{n+p})\right). \end{aligned}$$

Here the operation $*$ is the operation sup.

Example 12.4: Let $Y_1, \ldots, Y_n$ be a random sample drawn from an exponential model. The distribution of Y_i has density

$$f(y_i;\theta) = \exp\left(\sum_{k=1}^{K} Q_k(\theta)T_k(y_i) + A(\theta) + B(y_i)\right).$$

The joint density of the n–tuple $Y_1, \ldots, Y_n$ is

$$\ell(y_1, \ldots, y_n; \theta) = \exp\left(\sum_{k=1}^{K} Q_k(\theta)\sum_{i=1}^{n} T_k(y_i) + nA(\theta) + \sum_{i=1}^{n} B(y_i)\right).$$

As a sufficient statistic of dimension K, we can choose the statistic

$$T^{(n)}(y_1, \ldots, y_n) = \sum_{i=1}^{n} T(y_i),$$

where $T(y_i) = (T_1(y_i), \ldots, T_k(y_i))'$. As a function h, we can choose

$$h(T^{(n)}(y_1, \ldots, y_n); \theta, n) = \exp(Q'(\theta)T^{(n)}(y_1, \ldots, y_n) + nA(\theta)).$$

Hence the operation $*$ is the usual sum operation.

12.2.2 Conjugate Priors

Given a model having a sufficient statistic of constant dimension, we now seek some forms of prior distributions that lead to simple and easily interpretable computations.

Definition 12.2: *Let $Y_1, \ldots, Y_n$ be n observations that are independently and identically distributed with a common distribution satisfying a model of the form*

$$\ell(y_1, \ldots, y_n; \theta) \propto h(T^{(n)}(y_1, \ldots, y_n); \theta, n),$$

where $T^{(n)}$ is of constant dimension and $\theta \in \Theta$. A conjugate prior distribution for the parameter θ is a distribution with density

$$\pi(\theta) \propto h(t_0; \theta, n_0),$$

where $n_0 \in \mathbf{N}^*$ and $t_0 \in \mathcal{T}^{(n_0)}$ are given.

Thus the form of a conjugate prior is similar to the form of the likelihood. Such a choice of prior distribution is not always possible. It is clear that the function h can always be chosen to be positive valued. On the other hand, if Θ denotes the set of possible values of the parameter, the function $h(t_0; \theta, n_0)$ must be integrable on Θ with respect to a measure $\nu(d\theta)$, which has been omitted from Definition 12.2. When Θ is an open subset of $\mathbb{R}^p$, one usually retains the Lebesgue measure as the dominating measure, i.e., $\nu(d\theta) = d\theta$ so that ratios $\pi(\theta_1)/\pi(\theta_2)$ can be directly interpreted as measures of relative beliefs. In this case, the function $h(t_0; \theta, n_0)$ must be integrable with respect to Lebesgue measure, i.e., the integral $\int_\Theta h(t_0; \theta, n_0) d\theta$ must exist. Then the prior density is given by

$$\pi(\theta) = \frac{h(t_0; \theta, n_0)}{\int_\Theta h(t_0; \theta, n_0) d\theta}.$$

Remark 12.1: The function h is often integrable for different choices of Θ. It is useful, when possible, to retain the largest parameter space Θ. Then, the parameter space Θ and conjugate priors are defined automatically as soon as the form of the likelihood is specified.

12.2.3 Posterior Distributions From Conjugate Priors

We suppose that the likelihood function of the model is

$$\ell_n(y_1, \ldots, y_n; \theta) \propto h(T^{(n)}(y_1, \ldots, y_n); \theta, n),$$

and that the prior distribution is of the form

$$\pi(\theta) \propto h(t_0; \theta, n_0).$$

The posterior distribution has a density which is given by

$$\begin{aligned} \pi(\theta \mid y_1, \ldots, y_n) &\propto \ell_n(y_1, \ldots, y_n; \theta)\pi(\theta) \\ &\propto h(T^{(n)}(y_1, \ldots, y_n); \theta, n) h(t_0; \theta, n_0) \\ &\propto h(T^{(n)}(y_1, \ldots, y_n) * t_0; \theta, n + n_0). \end{aligned}$$

Property 12.2: *When the conjugate prior is of the form*

$$\pi(\theta) \propto h(t_0; \theta, n_0),$$

then the posterior distribution has the same form as the prior distribution and is given by

$$\pi(\theta \mid y_1, \ldots, y_n) \propto h(T^{(n)}(y_1, \ldots, y_n) * t_0; \theta, n + n_0).$$

The posterior distribution is obtained from the prior distribution by updating appropriately the values of the auxiliary parameters t_0 and n_0. The updated values take into account information contained in the observations. Namely, we have

$$t_1 = T^{(n)}(y_1, \ldots, y_n) * t_0, \quad n_1 = n + n_0.$$

This suggests that updating can be applied iteratively. Let $Y_{n+1}, \ldots, Y_{n+p}$ be p additional observations. Then $\pi(\theta \mid y_1, \ldots, y_n) \propto h(t_1; \theta, n_1)$ can be used as the new prior distribution. It is a conjugate prior. Therefore the new posterior distribution is of the same form, namely

$$\pi(\theta \mid y_1, \ldots, y_{n+p}) \propto h(t_2; \theta, n_2),$$

where

$$\begin{aligned} t_2 &= T^{(p)}(y_{n+1}, \ldots, y_{n+p}) * t_1 \\ &= T^{(p)}(y_{n+1}, \ldots, y_{n+p}) * T^{(n)}(y_1, \ldots, y_n) * t_0 \\ &= T^{(n+p)}(y_1, \ldots, y_{n+p}) * t_0, \end{aligned}$$

and

$$n_2 = p + n_1 = n + p + n_0.$$

The form of the posterior distribution allows us to interpret the auxiliary parameters t_0 and n_0 appearing in the conjugate prior distribution. For the latter distribution, prior information can be viewed as coming from n_0 observations $Y^1, \ldots, Y^{n_0}$ such that $T^{(n_0)}(y^1, \ldots, y^{n_0}) = t_0$. Thus, *the larger n_0, the more important are prior beliefs relative to the available observations $Y_1, \ldots, Y_n$. Moreover, a suitable choice of t_0, indicates which values of θ are more likely a priori.* Such an interpretation generalizes that given in Section 12.1.3.

12.2.4 Examples

Without much difficulty, conjugate priors can be obtained for exponential models. To facilitate the interpretation of a prior distribution, however, it may be preferable to work with the usual parameterization of the model. This parameterization may not correspond to the parameterization in t_0.

a) Binomial Model

Let $Y_1, \ldots, Y_n$ be a random sample drawn from a Bernoulli distribution $B(1, p)$. We have

$$\ell_n(y; p) = p^{T^{(n)}}(1-p)^{n-T^{(n)}},$$

where $T^{(n)} = \sum_{i=1}^{n} y_i$.

A conjugate prior must have a density of the form

$$\pi(p) \propto p^{t_0}(1-p)^{n_0-t_0},$$

where $0 \leq t_0 \leq n_0$. Whenever possible, the prior must also be defined on the interval $[0, 1]$, which is the usual parameter space for p.

A distribution of the above form is a beta distribution with parameters $t_0 + 1$ and $n_0 - t_0 + 1$ (see the appendix to this chapter). Such a distribution is continuous on the interval $[0, 1]$ with density

$$\pi(p) = \frac{p^{t_0}(1-p)^{n_0-t_0}}{B(t_0+1, n_0-t_0+1)},$$

where the function beta is evaluated at $t_0 + 1$ and $n_0 - t_0 + 1$, i.e.

$$B(t_0+1, n_0-t_0+1) = \int_0^1 p^{t_0}(1-p)^{n_0-t_0} dp.$$

The corresponding posterior distribution is a beta distribution with parameters

$$t_0 + T^{(n)} + 1 \text{ and } n_0 + n - t_0 - T^{(n)} + 1.$$

Since a beta distribution with parameters α and β has a mean and a variance equal to $\alpha/(\alpha+\beta)$ and $\alpha\beta/((\alpha+\beta)^2(\alpha+\beta+1))$, respectively, we can readily determine the mean and variance of the posterior distribution. In particular, the Bayes estimator of p is

$$E(p \mid y_1, \ldots, y_n) = \frac{t_0 + T^{(n)} + 1}{n_0 + n + 2}.$$

Its precision is estimated by

$$V(p \mid y_1, \ldots, y_n) = \frac{(t_0 + T^{(n)} + 1)(n_0 + n - t_0 - T^{(n)} + 1)}{(n_0+n+2)^2(n_0+n+3)}.$$

Remark 12.2: When the number n of observations is large, the Bayes estimator satisfies approximately

$$E(p \mid y_1, \ldots, y_n) \approx \frac{T^{(n)}}{n} = \bar{y},$$

which is the usual sample mean estimator. In addition, the estimated precision of the Bayes estimator is approximately given by

$$V(p \mid y_1, \ldots, y_n) \approx \frac{T^{(n)}(n - T^{(n)})}{n^3} = \frac{\bar{y}(1-\bar{y})}{n}.$$

The latter quantity is simply the classical estimator of $p(1-p)/n$.

Remark 12.3: When n is finite, the Bayes estimator is a weighted average of the usual sample estimator $\bar{Y}$ and the prior mean of θ, which is $(t_0+1)/(n_0+2)$. Specifically, we have

$$E(p \mid y_1, \ldots, y_n) = \frac{n_0+2}{n+n_0+2}\frac{t_0+1}{n_0+2} + \frac{n}{n+n_0+2}\bar{y}.$$

b) Poisson Model

Let $Y_1, \ldots, Y_n$ be a random sample drawn from a Poisson distribution $P(\lambda)$ where $\lambda \geq 0$. The likelihood function is

$$\begin{aligned} \ell_n(y_1, \ldots, y_n; \lambda) &= \exp\left(-n\lambda + \sum_{i=1}^{n} y_i \log \lambda\right) \frac{1}{\prod_{i=1}^{n} y_i!} \\ &\propto \exp(-n\lambda)\lambda^{\sum_{i=1}^{n} y_i}. \end{aligned}$$

Thus

$$T^{(n)}(y_1, \ldots, y_n) = \sum_{i=1}^{n} y_i.$$

A conjugate prior for λ must be continuous on $\mathbb{R}^+$ with a density of the form

$$\pi(\lambda) \propto \lambda^{t_0} \exp(-n_o\lambda) \text{ with } t_0 \geq 0.$$

A gamma distribution with parameters t_0+1 and $1/n_0$ satisfies these requirements. Thus the density of a conjugate prior is

$$\pi(\lambda) = \frac{n_0^{t_0+1}\lambda^{t_0}\exp(-n_0\lambda)}{\Gamma(t_0+1)}\mathbb{1}_{\lambda>0}.$$

The corresponding posterior distribution is of the same form. It is a gamma distribution with parameters $t_0 + T^{(n)} + 1$ and $1/(n + n_0)$. Therefore

$$E(\lambda \mid y_1, \ldots, y_n) = \frac{t_0 + T^{(n)} + 1}{n + n_0}$$

and

$$V(\lambda \mid y_1, \ldots, y_n) = \frac{t_0 + T^{(n)} + 1}{(n + n_0)^2}.$$

Remark 12.4: Restricting ourselves to the first two moments of a posterior distribution clearly leads to a loss of information. In this example, when n is small, the posterior density is heavily asymmetric. Such an asymmetry might be interesting to take into account.

Remark 12.5: When n is large, the Bayes estimator becomes again approximately equivalent to the usual estimator, i.e.

$$E(\lambda \mid y_1, \ldots, y_n) \approx \frac{T^{(n)}}{n} = \bar{y},$$

while its estimated variance is

$$V(\lambda \mid y_1, \ldots, y_n) \approx \frac{\bar{y}}{n}.$$

c) Uniform Model

Let $Y_1, \ldots, Y_n$ be a random sample drawn from a uniform distribution on $[0, \theta]$. The likelihood function is

$$\ell_n(y_1, \ldots, y_n; \theta) = \frac{1}{\theta^n} \mathbb{1}_{\sup y_i \leq \theta},$$

where $T^{(n)} = \sup_{i=1,\ldots,n} y_i$.

A conjugate prior must be of the form

$$\pi(\theta) \propto \frac{1}{\theta^{n_0}} \mathbb{1}_{t_0 \leq \theta} \text{ where } t_0 > 0, n_0 > 1.$$

Thus

$$\pi(\theta) = (n_0 - 1) \frac{t_0^{n_0 - 1}}{\theta^{n_0}} \mathbb{1}_{t_0 \leq \theta}.$$

This is a Pareto distribution with parameters $\alpha = n_0 - 1$ and $A = t_0$ (see the appendix to this chapter).

The corresponding posterior distribution is also a Pareto distribution, but with parameters $\alpha_1 = n+n_0-1$ and $A_1 = \sup(t_0, T^{(n)})$. This follows from Example 12.3 where it was shown that the binary operation $*$ is the sup operation. Hence

$$\pi(\theta \mid y_1, \ldots, y_n) = (n + n_0 - 1)\frac{(\sup(t_0, T^{(n)}))^{n+n_0-1}}{\theta^{n+n_0}} \mathbb{1}_{\sup(t_0,T^{(n)})\leq\theta}.$$

The next figure represents the form of such a posterior density

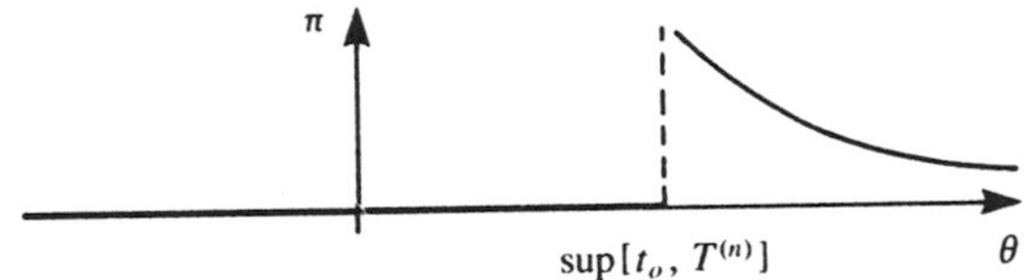

Figure 12.3: Posterior Density

The posterior mode $\tilde{\theta} = \sup(t_0, T^{(n)})$ is a natural estimator of the parameter θ. This estimator is not the Bayes estimator, which is equal to

$$\begin{aligned}
\hat{\theta} &= E(\theta \mid y_1, \ldots, y_n) \\
&= \frac{n + n_0 - 1}{n + n_0 - 2} \sup(t_0, T^{(n)}) \\
&= \frac{n + n_0 - 1}{n + n_0 - 2} \tilde{\theta}.
\end{aligned}$$

These two estimators of θ, however, become equivalent as the number n of observations increases.

The posterior variance is

$$V(\theta \mid y_1, \ldots, y_n) = \frac{n + n_0 - 1}{(n + n_0 - 2)^2(n + n_0 - 3)} \left(\sup(t_0, T^{(n)})\right)^2.$$

(see the appendix to this chapter). It is not much different from

$$\frac{\left(\sup_{i=1,\ldots,n}(y_i)\right)^2}{n^2},$$

when n is large. Note that the order of the latter quantity is $1/n^2$.

d) Gaussian Linear Model with Known Variance

Conjugate priors can also be used when the observations $Y_1, \ldots, Y_n$ are not identically distributed. A simple example is provided by the linear model.

The observation vector $Y = (Y_1, \ldots, Y_n)'$ is assumed to follow a multivariate normal distribution $N(\mathbf{X}\theta, \sigma_0^2\mathbf{I})$, where the K explanatory variables are linearly independent and the variance σ_0^2 is assumed to be known for the moment. The likelihood function is

$$\ell_n(y_1, \ldots, y_n; \theta) \propto \exp -\frac{1}{\sigma_0^2}(y - \mathbf{X}\theta)'(y - \mathbf{X}\theta).$$

Consider the OLS estimator $T^{(n)} = (\mathbf{X}'\mathbf{X})^{-1}\mathbf{X}'y$, which is a sufficient statistic. Let $\mathbf{\Omega}_{(n)} = \mathbf{X}'\mathbf{X}$ denote the *control matrix*. Then

$$\ell_n(y_1, \ldots, y_n; \theta) \propto \exp -\frac{1}{2\sigma_0^2}(T^{(n)} - \theta)'\mathbf{\Omega}_{(n)}(T^{(n)} - \theta).$$

Thus the model has a sufficient statistic $T^{(n)}$ that is of constant dimension.

The operation $*$ that associates $T^{(n+p)}$ to the pair $(T^{(n)}, T^{(p)})$ is given by

$$\begin{aligned} T^{(n+p)}(y_1, \ldots, y_{n+p}) &= \left(\sum_{i=1}^{n+p} x_i'x_i\right)^{-1} \sum_{i=1}^{n+p} x_i'y_i \\ &= \mathbf{\Omega}_{(n+p)^{-1}} \Big(\mathbf{\Omega}_{(n)}T^{(n)}(y_1, \ldots, y_n) \\ &\qquad + \mathbf{\Omega}_{(p)}T^{(p)}(y_{n+1}, \ldots, y_{n+p})\Big), \end{aligned}$$

where x_i is the ith row of $\mathbf{X}$. The operation $*$ depends on the control matrix, which is simply updated *via* the formula

$$\mathbf{\Omega}_{(n+p)}(x_1, \ldots, x_{n+p}) = \mathbf{\Omega}_{(n)}(x_1, \ldots, x_n) + \mathbf{\Omega}_{(p)}(x_{n+1}, \ldots, x_{n+p}).$$

A conjugate prior distribution for the parameter θ must be continuous on $\mathbb{R}^K$ and such that

$$\pi(\theta) \propto \exp -\frac{1}{2\sigma_0^2}(t_0 - \theta)'\mathbf{\Omega}_0(t_0 - \theta), \text{ where } \mathbf{\Omega}_0 \succ 0.$$

Thus a conjugate prior is normal with mean t_0 and variance covariance matrix $\sigma_0^2\mathbf{\Omega}_0^{-1}$.

The corresponding posterior distribution is also normal with mean $(\mathbf{\Omega}_0 + \mathbf{\Omega}_{(n)})^{-1} (\mathbf{\Omega}_0 t_0 + \mathbf{\Omega}_{(n)} T^{(n)})$, and variance covariance matrix

$$\sigma_0^2(\mathbf{\Omega}_0 + \mathbf{\Omega}_{(n)})^{-1}.$$

Thus the Bayes estimator, which is the posterior mean, is

$$\hat{\theta} = (\mathbf{\Omega}_0 + \mathbf{\Omega}_{(n)})^{-1}(\mathbf{\Omega}_0 t_0 + \mathbf{\Omega}_{(n)} T^{(n)}).$$

From this expression we obtain immediately the following property.

Property 12.3: *In a Gaussian linear model with a conjugate prior, the Bayes estimator is a convex combination of the prior mean t_0 and the OLS estimator $T^{(n)} = (\mathbf{X}'\mathbf{X})^{-1}\mathbf{X}'Y$.*

e) Gaussian Linear Model With Unknown Variance

We consider the Gaussian model $Y \sim N(\mathbf{X}\theta, \sigma^2\mathbf{I})$ where both parameters θ and σ^2 are now unknown. The likelihood function is

$$\ell_n(y_1, \ldots, y_n; \theta, \sigma^2) \propto \frac{1}{(\sigma^2)^{n/2}} \exp -\frac{1}{2\sigma^2}(y - \mathbf{X}\theta)'(y - \mathbf{X}\theta).$$

This expression can be rewritten using the control matrix $\mathbf{\Omega} = \mathbf{X}'\mathbf{X}$, the OLS estimator of $T(y) = (\mathbf{X}'\mathbf{X})^{-1}\mathbf{X}'y$ of θ, the number of explanatory variables K, and the usual variance estimator

$$V(y) = \frac{1}{n-K}\|y - \mathbf{X}T(y)\|^2. \tag{12.6}$$

Specifically, let $h = 1/\sigma^2$. We have

$$\begin{aligned}
&\ell_n(y_1, \ldots, y_n; \theta, h) \\
&\propto \; h^{n/2} \exp\left(-\frac{h(n-K)}{2}V(y) - \frac{h}{2}(T(y) - \theta)'\mathbf{\Omega}(T(y) - \theta)\right) \\
&= \; h^{K/2} \exp\left(-\frac{h}{2}(T(y) - \theta)'\mathbf{\Omega}(T(y) - \theta)\right) h^{(n-K+2)/2-1} \\
&\qquad \exp\left(-\frac{h(n-K)V(y)}{2}\right).
\end{aligned}$$

The second expression suggests the form of a conjugate prior distribution for the pair (θ, h). Namely:

(i) the marginal distribution of h is chosen in the family of gamma distributions,

(ii) the conditional distribution of θ given h is chosen in the family of normal distributions $N(t_0, (h\mathbf{\Omega}_0)^{-1})$.

Such a conjugate prior distribution for (θ, h) is said to be a *normal–gamma* distribution.

In Table 12.1, we summarize the various forms of conjugate priors (and hence of posterior distributions by construction) that are associated with some usual models.

Table 12.1
Conjugate Prior Distribution
Sampling Models

Model	θ	Θ	Prior and Posterior Distributions
$B(1,p)^{\otimes n}$	p	$(0,1)$	Beta Distribution
$P(\lambda)^{\otimes n}$	λ	$\mathbb{R}^{+}$	Gamma Distribution
$U_{[0,\theta]}^{\otimes n}$	θ	$\mathbb{R}^{+*}$	Pareto Distribution
$N(m, \sigma_0^2)^{\otimes n}$	m	$\mathbb{R}$	Normal Distribution
$N(m, \sigma^2)^{\otimes n}$	(m, σ^2)	$\mathbb{R} \times \mathbb{R}^{+*}$	Normal Gamma Distribution
Pareto $\ell(y; A_0, \alpha) = \frac{\alpha A_0^\alpha}{y^{\alpha+1}}$ for $y \geq A_0$	α	$\mathbb{R}^{+*}$	Gamma Distribution

12.3 Asymptotic Results

When the number n of observations is large, the examples of Section 11.2.4 show that:

(i) the Bayes estimator, i.e., the posterior expectation, is approximately equal to a classical estimator such as the maximum likelihood estimator,

(ii) the posterior variance is given approximately by the inverse of the estimated Fisher information matrix,

(iii) the posterior distribution converges to a normal distribution.

These asymptotic results are not specific to the use of conjugate priors. They can be established in a more general context.

12.3.1 Asymptotic Study of Posterior Distributions

To simplify the presentation, we shall not discuss explicitly the regularity conditions under which the next asymptotic arguments hold. We shall assume that the model is a conditional model of which the likelihood function for n observations is $\ell_n(y \mid x; \theta)$. Let θ_0 denote the true but unknown parameter value used to generate the observations. Thus, within a classical framework, we shall examine the posterior distributions obtained in a Bayesian framework.

It is useful to make the following assumptions where *convergence is defined in the classical sense*, i.e., with respect to the true distribution P_{θ_0} and without integrating with respect to a prior distribution.

Assumptions:

(i) The parameter space Θ is an open subset of $\mathbb{R}^p$.

(ii) The true parameter value θ_0 satisfies $\theta_0 \in \Theta$.

(iii) The specified prior distribution Π is continuous. (Hence the dominating measure is the Lebesgue measure on $\mathbb{R}^p$.) Its density is strictly positive in a neighborhood of θ_0.

(iv) The conditional likelihood function $\ell_n(y \mid x; \theta)$ is twice continously differentiable with respect to θ.

(v) The means of $(1/n) \log \ell_n(y \mid x; \theta)$, $(1/n)\partial \log \ell_n(y \mid x; \theta)/\partial\theta$ and $(1/n)\partial^2 \log \ell_n(y \mid x; \theta)/\partial\theta \, \partial\theta'$ converge P_{θ_0} – almost surely for every given θ.

(vi) The asymptotic Fisher information matrix

$$\mathcal{I}(\theta_0) = \operatorname{plim}_n \; -\frac{1}{n}\frac{\partial^2 \log \ell_n(y \mid x; \theta_0)}{\partial\theta\, \partial\theta'}$$

is nonsingular.

We also assume the existence of a maximum likelihood estimator θ_n^* of θ converging to θ_0 at the rate $1/\sqrt{n}$ and satisfying the first-order conditions $\partial \log \ell_n(y \mid x; \theta_n^*)/\partial\theta = 0$.

Property 12.4: *Under the previous assumptions, the posterior distribution of $\sqrt{n}(\theta - \theta_n^*)$ associated with the prior distribution Π converges P_{θ_0} – almost surely to the normal distribution $N(0, \mathcal{I}(\theta_0)^{-1})$.*

Sketch of the Proof: The posterior density of θ is

$$\pi_n(\theta \mid y, x) = \frac{\pi(\theta)\ell_n(y \mid x; \theta)}{\int_\Theta \pi(\theta)\ell_n(y \mid x; \theta)d\theta}.$$

Thus the posterior distribution of $z = \sqrt{n}(\theta - \theta_n^*)$ is

$$\pi_n(z \mid y, x) = \frac{\frac{1}{n^{p/2}}\pi\left(\frac{z}{\sqrt{n}} + \theta_n^*\right)\ell_n\left(y \mid x; \frac{z}{\sqrt{n}} + \theta_n^*\right)}{\int_\Theta \pi(\theta)\ell_n(y \mid x; \theta)d\theta},$$

i.e.

$$\pi_n(z \mid y, x) = \frac{\frac{1}{n^{p/2}}\pi\left(\frac{z}{\sqrt{n}} + \theta_n^*\right)\exp\left(\log \ell_n\left(y \mid x; \frac{z}{\sqrt{n}} + \theta_n^*\right) - \log \ell_n(y \mid x; \theta_n^*)\right)}{\int \pi(\theta)\ell_n(y \mid x; \theta)\exp - \log \ell_n(y \mid x; \theta_n^*)d\theta}.$$

Hence

$$\begin{aligned}\pi_n(z \mid y, x) &= K_n(y, x)\pi\left(\frac{z}{\sqrt{n}} + \theta_n^*\right) \\ &\quad\times \exp\left(\log \ell_n\left(y \mid x; \frac{z}{\sqrt{n}} + \theta_n^*\right) - \log \ell_n(y \mid x; \theta_n^*)\right),\end{aligned}$$

where $K_n(y, x)$ does not depend on the argument z.

Next, we use the fact that $z/\sqrt{n}$ converges to zero and that θ_n^* converges to θ_0. We obtain

$$\pi_n(z \mid y, x) \# K_n(y, x)\pi(\theta_0)$$
$$\times \exp\left(\frac{z'}{\sqrt{n}} \frac{\partial \log \ell_n(y \mid x; \theta_n^*)}{\partial \theta} + \frac{1}{2} \frac{z'}{\sqrt{n}} \frac{\partial^2 \log \ell_n(y \mid x; \theta_n^*)}{\partial \theta \, \partial \theta'} \frac{z}{\sqrt{n}}\right).$$

Thus

$$\pi_n(z \mid y, x) \# K_n(y, x)\pi(\theta_0) \exp\left(-\frac{1}{2} z' \left(-\frac{1}{n} \frac{\partial^2 \log \ell_n(y \mid x; \theta_n^*)}{\partial \theta \, \partial \theta'}\right) z\right).$$

Hence

$$\pi_n(z \mid y, x) \# K_n(y, x)\pi(\theta_0) \exp -\frac{1}{2} z' \mathcal{I}(\theta_0) z.$$

Finally, because the integration constant $K_n(y, z)$ must be such that $\pi_n(z \mid y, x)$ is a probability density, we obtain

$$\pi_n(z \mid y, x) \# \frac{1}{(2\pi)^{p/2}} \frac{1}{\sqrt{\det \mathcal{I}(\theta_0)^{-1}}} \exp -\frac{1}{2} z' \mathcal{I}(\theta_0) z.$$

□

12.3.2 Consequences

Various results follow immediately from Property 12.4. Some of these are:

a) The posterior distribution of θ as well as that of $\sqrt{n}(\theta - \theta_n^*)$ tend to become symmetric.

b) The posterior mean $\hat{\theta}_n = E(\theta \mid y)$ becomes approximately equal to the maximum likelihood estimator θ_n^*.

c) Since θ_n^* converges to θ_0, it follows that the Bayes estimator $\hat{\theta}_n$ also converges to θ_0.

d) The posterior variance $V(\theta \mid y)$ is such that

$$\begin{aligned} nV(\theta \mid y) &= V(\sqrt{n}(\theta - \theta_n^*) \mid y) \\ &\approx \mathcal{I}(\theta_0)^{-1}. \end{aligned}$$

e) Consistency and asymptotic efficiency properties do not depend on the chosen prior distribution, provided the prior is continuous with a strictly positive density on a neighborhood of θ_0. Then a priori information has effectively vanished due to information accumulated from the observations.

f) Since the posterior distribution can be approximated by a normal distribution, namely by

$$N\left(\theta_n^*, \frac{1}{n}\mathcal{I}(\theta_n^*)^{-1}\right),$$

we can construct, for instance, the smallest region containing approximately 95% of the probability. This region is given by the ellipsoid defined by

$$\left\{\theta : n(\theta - \theta_n^*)'\mathcal{I}(\theta_n^*)(\theta - \theta_n^*) \leq \chi^2_{0.95}(p)\right\}, \tag{12.7}$$

where $\chi^2_{0.95}(p)$ denotes the 95% quantile of the chi-square distribution $\chi^2(p)$ with p degrees of freedom. Thus, instead of considering the estimation problem of θ as a point estimation problem, we can view it as an interval estimation problem (see chapter 20).

g) The proof of Property 12.4 does not actually use the property that the specified model contains the true distribution. In fact, Property 12.4 can be readily generalized to the case where misspecification errors are present in the likelihood function. In this case, Taylor expansions are carried out around the pseudo maximum likelihood estimator θ_n^*, which converges to the pseudo true parameter value θ_0^*. Then the posterior distribution of $\sqrt{n}(\theta - \theta_n^*)$ converges P_{θ_0}-almost surely to the normal distribution $N(0, \mathcal{J}(\theta_0^*)^{-1})$, where

$$\mathcal{J}(\theta_0^*) = \text{plim} \; -\frac{1}{n}\frac{\partial^2 \log \ell_n(y \mid x; \theta_n^*)}{\partial\theta\, \partial\theta'}.$$

12.4 Diffuse Priors

12.4.1 Representations of a Noninformative Prior

In Section 12.1.4, we studied an example where the parameter θ is interpreted as a mean and where the prior distribution on this parameter is chosen in the family of normal distributions $N(m_0, \sigma_0^2)$. The variance σ_0^2 of the prior distribution intuitively measures the importance of a priori information: the larger σ_0^2, the less precise this information. When σ_0^2 increases to infinity, we showed that the posterior distribution could be viewed as being obtained from the *improper prior* $\pi(\theta)d\theta \propto d\theta$. Then we interpreted this diffuse prior as representing our noninformative prior in some way. It is important to know whether such an approach can be generalized. It is also important to provide various justifications for such noninformative priors.

a) Comparing Prior Measures of Intervals

Consider ratios of measures assigned to intervals of the form $(-\infty, a]$ and $[b, +\infty)$ according to the diffuse prior $d\theta$. For such intervals we obtain the following indeterminate result

$$\frac{\Pi((-\infty, a])}{\Pi([b + \infty))} = \frac{\int_{-\infty}^{a} d\theta}{\int_{b}^{+\infty} d\theta} = \frac{\infty}{\infty}. \tag{12.8}$$

According to Jeffreys, the existence of such an indeterminate result constitutes a formal representation of our ignorance. It is clear, however, that it is only a particular form of our ignorance, which is represented here by the limit of prior normal distributions. For instance, if we consider now intervals of the form $[a_1, a_2]$ and $[b, +, \infty)$, we obtain

$$\frac{\Pi([a_1, a_2])}{\Pi([b + \infty))} = \frac{\int_{a_1}^{a_2} d\theta}{\int_{b}^{+\infty} d\theta} = 0.$$

Hence the improper prior $d\theta$ implies that every bounded interval is infinitely less likely than an unbounded interval. In addition, it is easy to find many other improper priors satisfying property (12.8). For instance, property (12.8) is satisfied by the prior $\pi(\theta)d\theta \propto \theta^2 d\theta$. Thus condition (12.8) does not characterize completely a notion of diffuse prior.

b) Invariance With Respect to Parameterization

The Lebesgue measure $d\theta$ is invariant (up to a multiplicative factor) to linear transformations of the parameter θ. However, it is modified by nonlinear transformations of the parameter. Thus, if the Lebesgue measure is retained as a representation of a noninformative prior, it is necessary to indicate which parameterization is used.

Example 12.5: Consider the usual linear regression model $Y \sim N(\mathbf{X}b, \sigma^2\mathbf{I})$. Two types of parameters appear. There are the coefficients b of the explanatory variables, on the one hand, and the variance σ^2, on the other hand. A change of measurement units on the variables X and Y or some aggregation of explanatory variables, etc... introduce linear transformations of the parameter b. This suggests to retain the Lebesgue measure as a diffuse prior for b

$$\pi(b)db \propto db$$

since this measure is invariant by linear transformations.

If we now consider the variance σ^2, other common parameterizations are given by the standard error $\sqrt{\sigma^2}$ and the precision $h = 1/\sqrt{\sigma^2}$. These transformations are linear in $\log \sigma$. Note also that a change of measurement units on the endogenous variable leads to a translation of $\log \sigma$. This suggests the use of the Lebesgue measure as an improper prior on $\log \sigma$. This gives

$$\pi(\sigma)d\sigma \propto \frac{1}{\sigma}d\sigma,$$

after a change of variables.

Lastly, if we suppose that the two priors on b and σ^2 are independent, we obtain

$$\pi(b, \sigma)db \, d\sigma \propto \frac{1}{\sigma}db \, d\sigma.$$

Invariance issues appear to be necessary in practice. Examining such issues can be quite helpful in some simple cases. We give another example.

Example 12.6: In a Poisson process, the parameter λ is usually interpreted as the rate of occurrence of an event in the infinitely small period of time $(t, t + dt)$. Then the distribution of the number of times the event has occurred between time zero and time T is given by the Poisson distribution $P(\lambda T)$. Moreover, the length of time separating any two occurrences follows an exponential distribution with parameter $1/\lambda$. Natural changes of parameterization are $\lambda \mapsto \lambda T$ and $\lambda \mapsto 1/\lambda$. This suggests the use of the Lebesgue measure as an improper prior on $\log \lambda$. Hence

$$\pi(\lambda)d\lambda \propto \frac{1}{\lambda}d\lambda.$$

There are many diffuse priors that are compatible with some given reparameterizations. Jeffreys has proposed the following choice

$$\pi(\theta)d\theta \;\propto\; (\det \mathcal{I}(\theta))^{1/2}d\theta, \tag{12.9}$$

where $\mathcal{I}(\theta)$ denotes the Fisher Information matrix corresponding to the likelihood function of the specified model.

Property 12.5: *Let $\pi(\theta)d\theta \propto (\det \mathcal{I}(\theta))^{1/2}d\theta$ be the prior distribution and $\eta = g(\theta)$ be a continuously differentiable bijective reparameterization. The prior distribution on η induced by the mapping g and associated with $\pi(\theta)\, d\theta$ is proportional to* $(\det \mathcal{I}(\eta))^{1/2}d\eta$.

PROOF: Let $\ell(y;\theta)$ denote the likelihood function parameterized by θ. Then the likelihood function parameterized by η is $\ell(y; g^{-1}(\eta))$. Thus the Fisher information matrix associated with the model parameterized by η is

$$\begin{aligned}
\mathcal{I}(\eta) &= E_\eta\left(\frac{\partial \log \ell(Y;g^{-1}(\eta))}{\partial \eta}\frac{\partial \log \ell(Y;g^{-1}(\eta))}{\partial \eta'}\right) \\
&= \frac{\partial g^{-1}(\eta)'}{\partial \eta} E_\eta\left(\frac{\partial \log \ell(Y;g^{-1}(\eta))}{\partial \theta}\frac{\partial \log \ell(Y;g^{-1}(\eta))}{\partial \theta'}\right)\frac{\partial g^{-1}(\eta)}{\partial \eta'} \\
&= \frac{\partial g^{-1}(\eta)'}{\partial \eta}\mathcal{I}(\theta)\frac{\partial g^{-1}(\eta)}{\partial \eta'}.
\end{aligned}$$

Taking the determinant of each side of this equation gives

$$\det \mathcal{I}(\eta) = \mathbf{G}^2 \det \mathcal{I}(\theta),$$

where $\mathbf{G}$ is the Jacobian determinant of the transformation g^{-1}. Then taking the square root of each side gives

$$(\det \mathcal{I}(\eta))^{1/2} = \mathbf{G}(\det \mathcal{I}(\theta))^{1/2}.$$

Therefore $(\det \mathcal{I}(\eta))^{1/2}d\eta$ gives the prior distribution on η induced by the mapping g and associated with $\pi(\theta)d\theta$. □

Clearly, there exist many prior distributions having the preceding property. Jeffreys' solution has the advantage of giving the desired result in the case of a normal distribution.

Example 12.7: In the usual linear regression model $Y \sim N(\mathbf{X}b, \sigma_0^2\mathbf{I})$ with known variance σ_0^2, the Fisher information matrix is $\mathcal{I}(b) = (1/\sigma_0^2)$

$\mathbf{X}'\mathbf{X}$. Thus Jeffreys' diffuse prior (12.9) gives, as desired, a prior measure on b that is proportional to the Lebesgue measure.

Example 12.8: In the preceding example, suppose that the variance is unknown. The Fisher information matrix is diagonal

$$\mathcal{I}(b,\sigma^2) = \begin{pmatrix} (1/\sigma^2)\mathbf{X}'\mathbf{X} & 0 \\ 0 & n/2\sigma^4 \end{pmatrix}.$$

Computation of the determinant gives a measure that is not proportional to the expected measure $(1/\sigma)db\, d\sigma$.

c) Diffuse Priors as Limits of Conjugate Priors

In Section 12.1.4 the diffuse prior was obtained as a limit of the conjugate prior $N(m_0, \sigma_0^2)$ as σ_0^2 increases to infinity. We now examine whether such an approach is applicable to other examples. Namely, we wish to know whether a suitable limit of conjugate priors can be viewed as a diffuse prior.

Example 12.9: Let $Y_1, \ldots, Y_n$ be n random variables independently and identically distributed $N(0, \sigma^2)$. The likelihood function is

$$\ell(y,\sigma^2) \propto \frac{1}{(\sigma^2)^{n/2}} \exp -\frac{1}{2\sigma^2} \sum_{i=1}^{n} y_i^2.$$

From Section 12.2.4-e) we know that a conjugate prior on $h = 1/\sigma^2$ is a gamma distribution. Thus we have

$$\pi_{\nu,\alpha}(h) \propto h^{\nu-1} \exp -\frac{h}{\alpha}.$$

Such a prior distribution has a mean $Eh = \nu\alpha$ and a variance $Vh = \nu\alpha^2$. Hence we may hope to obtain a diffuse prior from this conjugate prior by considering sequences of auxiliary parameters such that $\nu\alpha$ converges to a finite limit and $\nu\alpha^2$ diverges to infinity. Let $\nu_n = a/\alpha_n$ where a is an arbitrary constant. As α_n increases to infinity we obtain

$$\pi(h) \propto \frac{1}{h},$$

i.e., the Lebesgue measure applied to the parameter $\log h$. Note that the "limiting prior" thus obtained does not depend on the value a.

Example 12.10: As in Section 12.2.4-a) consider a binomial model. Conjugate priors belong to the family of beta distributions

$$\pi(p) = \frac{p^{\alpha-1}(1-p)^{\beta-1}}{B(\alpha,\beta)} \mathbb{1}_{[0,1]}(p).$$

Such a distribution has a mean $Ep = \alpha/(\alpha+\beta)$ and a variance

$$Vp = \frac{\alpha\beta}{(\alpha+\beta)^2(\alpha+\beta+1)}.$$

In this case, parameter p is constrained to be in the bounded set [0, 1] and the notion of diffuse prior is non-degenerated, it is given by the uniform probability distribution on [0, 1]. It is easily seen that this distribution belongs to the previous family and that it is reached for $\alpha = 1$ and $\beta = 1$.

d) Diffuse Priors as Approximations to Prior Distributions

Lastly, a justification of diffuse priors has been given by Lindley based on robustness arguments.

Given a model $\{\ell(y;\theta), \theta \in \Theta\}$, different prior distributions lead, in general, to different posterior distributions. The " discrepancy" between two posterior distributions, however, can be much smaller than the discrepancy between the two prior distributions from which the two posterior distributions are derived. Intuitively, since a posterior distribution is given by the formula $\pi(\theta \mid y) \propto \pi(\theta)\ell(y \mid \theta)$, we can expect that changes in a prior distribution over regions where the likelihood function $\ell(y \mid \theta)$ takes small values will have little effect on the posterior distribution. Such an argument clearly depends on how the discrepancy between two distributions is measured. This argument, however, is valid if the discrepancy is based on the comparison between the means of the posterior distributions (see Section 12.6 for more precise results).

In this approach the choice of an improper prior such as Lebesgue measure constitutes a practical approximation to a prior distribution that is sufficiently flat over neighborhoods of modal values of the likelihood function.

Remark 12.6: The preceding argument assumes implicitly that the prior has a certain form in the neighborhood of the maximum likelihood

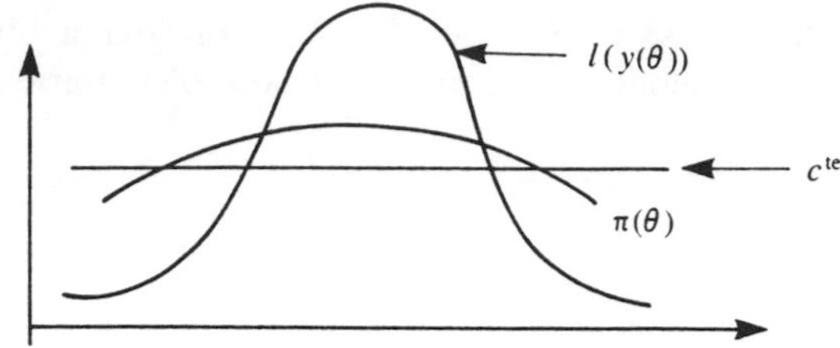

Figure 12.4: Diffuse Prior and Likelihood Function

estimator $\hat{\theta}(y)$. Since this estimator is a function of y, it follows that the prior distribution depends implicitly on the observation y. This shows that the preceding argument is not strictly a Bayesian argument.

To summarize, it seems that the notion of a diffuse prior is somewhat ambiguous. In practice, one chooses frequently some Lebesgue measures defined on appropriate transformations of the parameters so as to take into account natural parameter changes and to obtain simple forms for the posterior distributions. The above asymptotic results and robustness arguments show that such a strategy is relatively neutral to other possible choices of a prior.

12.4.2 Application to the Linear Model

a) The Model

We consider observations satisfying the linear model $y = \mathbf{X}b + u$ where the $n \times K$ matrix $\mathbf{X}$ is assumed nonrandom. To develop an estimation procedure that does not depend heavily on the normality of the errors, we assume that the errors are jointly multivariate Student distributed. The density of a multivariate Student distribution is indexed by two positive parameters $\sigma > 0$ and $\nu_0 > 0$. It is given by

$$\ell(u; \nu_0, \sigma) = \frac{K(\nu_0)}{(\sigma^2)^{n/2}} \frac{1}{\left(\nu_0 + \frac{u'u}{\sigma^2}\right)^{(n+\nu_0)/2}}, \tag{12.10}$$

where n denotes the number of observations and

$$K(\nu_0) = (\nu_0)^{\nu_0/2} \left(\nu_0 + \frac{n}{2}\right) \frac{1}{\pi^{n/2}} \frac{1}{\Gamma\left(\frac{\nu_0}{2}\right)}.$$

The mean of this distribution is zero provided $\nu_0 > 1$ and its variance covariance matrix is $E(uu') = (\nu_0\sigma^2/(\nu_0 - 2))\mathbf{I}$ provided $\nu_0 > 2$.

When ν_0 increases to infinity, this joint density converges to the density of the multivariate normal distribution $N(0, \sigma^2\mathbf{I})$. Hence the case of normal errors is contained in the above specification.

When the parameter ν_0 is finite, then u_i/σ follows a univariate Student distribution with ν_0 degrees of freedom. As ν_0 becomes small, the tails of this distribution become thicker. When $\nu_0 = 1$, this distribution is identical to the Cauchy distribution.

b) Bayesian Analysis With a Diffuse Prior

In what follows, we assume that ν_0 is fixed and that the prior distribution concerns the parameters b_k, $k = 1, \ldots, K$ and σ^2 only. Specifically, we assume that $b_1, \ldots, b_K$ and $\log \sigma^2$ follow independent diffuse priors so that

$$\pi(b, \sigma^2) \propto \frac{1}{\sigma^2}. \tag{12.11}$$

Then the posterior distribution is

$$\ell(b, \sigma^2 \mid y, \mathbf{X}, \nu_0) \propto (\sigma^2)^{-(n+2)/2} \left(\nu_0 + \frac{(y - \mathbf{X}b)'(y - \mathbf{X}b)}{\sigma^2}\right)^{-(n+\nu_0)/2},$$

i.e.

$$\ell(b, \sigma^2 \mid y, \mathbf{X}, \nu_0) \propto$$
$$\frac{(\sigma^2)^{(\nu_0/2)-1}}{(\bar{\sigma}^2)^{(n+\nu_0)/2}} \left(n + \nu_0 - K + \frac{(b - \hat{b})'\mathbf{X}'\mathbf{X}(b - \hat{b})}{\bar{\sigma}^2}\right)^{-(n+\nu_0)/2}, \tag{12.12}$$

where $\hat{b} = (\mathbf{X}'\mathbf{X})^{-1}\mathbf{X}'y$ is the OLS estimator of b

$$s^2 = \frac{1}{n-K}(y - \mathbf{X}\hat{b})'(y - \mathbf{X}\hat{b})$$

is the classical unbiased estimator of the variance, and

$$\bar{\sigma}^2 = \frac{\nu_0\sigma^2 + (n-K)s^2}{\nu_0 + n - K}.$$

The above expression for the posterior distribution gives easily the posterior marginal distribution of σ^2 and the posterior conditional distribution of b given σ^2. The latter posterior distribution is a K-multivariate Student distribution.

c) Posterior Marginal Distribution of σ^2

The posterior marginal distribution of σ^2 is proportional to

$$\frac{(\sigma^2)^{\nu_0/2-1}}{(\bar{\sigma}^2)^{(n+\nu_0-K)/2}}.$$

Hence

$$\pi(\sigma^2 \mid y, \mathbf{X}, \nu_0) \propto \left(\frac{\sigma^2}{s^2}\right)^{\nu_0/2-1} \frac{1}{\left(1+\frac{\nu_0}{n-K}\frac{\sigma^2}{s^2}\right)^{(\nu_0+n-K)/2}}. \tag{12.13}$$

Thus the variable σ^2/s^2 follows a Fisher distribution with ν_0 and $\nu = n - K$ degrees of freedom (see Property B.56). The mode of this distribution is $(\nu/\nu_0)(\nu_0 - 2)/(\nu + 2)$ provided $\nu_0 > 2$ and the posterior mean is

$$\begin{aligned} E(\sigma^2 \mid y) &= \frac{\nu}{\nu-2} \\ &= \frac{n-K}{n-K-2}, \end{aligned} \tag{12.14}$$

provided $\nu = n - K > 2$.

Remark 12.7: The Bayes estimator of σ^2 is independent of the chosen form of the distribution of the errors, i.e., of ν_0. On the other hand, the posterior distribution of σ^2 depends on ν_0. In the limiting case with normal errors, i.e., when ν_0 increases to infinity, the posterior distribution of $\sigma^2/(n-K)s^2$ converges to the inverse of a chi-square distribution with $n - K$ degrees of freedom (compare with the classical result on the distribution of $(n - K)s^2/\sigma^2$, Property 6.12 and Theorem B.6).

d) Posterior Marginal Distribution of b

Formula (12.12) shows that the posterior distribution of b conditional on σ^2 is a multivariate Student distribution. If b is the only parameter of interest, then this conditional distribution must be integrated with respect to the posterior marginal distribution of σ^2. This gives

$$\pi(b \mid y, \nu_0) \propto ((n-K)s^2 + (b-\hat{b})'\mathbf{X}'\mathbf{X}(b-\hat{b}))^{-n/2}. \tag{12.15}$$

We have a multivariate Student distribution. Note that this distribution is independent of the auxiliary parameter ν_0. The posterior mean of b is

$$E(b \mid y, \nu_0) = \hat{b}, \tag{12.16}$$

which is the OLS estimator of b.

12.4.3 Marginalizing

We consider observations on two types of variables X and Z. Let $Y = (X, Z)$. It is assumed that the joint distribution of the pair (X, Z) depends on the parameter vector $\theta = (\phi, \psi)$ and that

$$\ell(y \mid \theta) = \ell(x \mid \phi)\ell(z \mid x; \phi, \psi).$$

That is, it is assumed that the marginal distribution of X depends on θ only through ϕ.

Let π denote a prior distribution on $\theta = (\phi, \psi)$. We can always decompose π as $\pi(\phi, \psi) = \pi_1(\phi)\pi_2(\psi \mid \phi)$. Therefore the joint distribution of the observations and the parameters is

$$\ell(y \mid \theta)\pi(\theta) = (\ell(x \mid \phi)\pi_1(\phi))(\ell(z \mid x; \phi, \psi)\pi_2(\psi \mid \phi)).$$

Hence the marginal distribution of (x, ϕ) is $\ell(x \mid \phi)\pi_1(\phi)$.

Suppose now that ϕ is the parameter vector of interest. To conduct inference on ϕ, we shall first determine the (posterior) distribution of θ given y. Then we shall integrate this posterior distribution with respect to ψ so as to obtain the (posterior) distribution of ϕ given y. Such a procedure is called *marginalizing*. An example of marginalizing was given in the preceding paragraph. Here we obtain

$$\pi(\phi \mid y) = \int \frac{\ell(x \mid \phi)\pi_1(\phi)\ell(z \mid x; \phi, \psi)\pi_2(\psi \mid \phi)}{\int \ell(x \mid \phi)\pi_1(\phi)\ell(z \mid x; \phi, \psi)\pi_2(\psi \mid \phi) d\phi d\psi} d\psi.$$

When this posterior distribution depends on the observations only through x, i.e., when X is partially sufficient for ϕ so that $\pi(\phi \mid y) = \pi(\phi \mid x)$, then we can obviously determine this posterior distribution directly from the joint distribution of the pair (X, ϕ). That is, we need only the conditional distribution of X given ϕ and the marginal prior distribution on the parameter ϕ.

Marginalizing is always valid when the prior distribution is a proper probability distribution. When the prior on the parameters is an improper prior, marginalizing may not be justified. Such a difficulty is referred to as the *marginalizing paradox*. As an illustration, consider a parameterization consisting of a mean m and a standard error σ. Consider also the diffuse prior $\pi(m, \sigma)dm\ d\sigma \propto (1/\sigma)dm\ d\sigma$. Suppose that the parameter of interest is the ratio $\phi = m/\sigma$. Then we need to determine the possible improper marginal distribution π_1 of ϕ. But for every nondegenerated interval of the form (a, b), we have

$$\Pi\left(\frac{m}{\sigma} \in (a, b)\right) = \int_0^\infty \frac{1}{\sigma}\left(\int_{a\sigma}^{b\sigma} dm\right) d\sigma = +\infty.$$

Hence it is clear that marginalizing is not a possible operation here.

12.5 Best Linear Unbiased Bayesian Estimation

In the preceding sections the determination of the Bayes estimator and the posterior distribution requires that the conditional distribution of Y given θ is completely specified. Sometimes, however, a model is defined by its first two moments only. The bayesian approach is still applicable provided one restricts the class of estimators considered. We discuss such an extension within the linear model.

12.5.1 Existence and Form of the Optimal Estimator

We suppose that the observations satisfy the linear model

$$Y = \mathbf{X}b + u, \tag{12.17}$$

where $E(u \mid \mathbf{X}; b, \sigma^2) = 0$ and $V(u \mid \mathbf{X}; b, \sigma^2) = \sigma^2\mathbf{I}$. Suppose also that we restrict the class of estimators considered to the class of affine estimators, i.e., to estimators of the form

$$\tilde{b} = \mathbf{A}Y + a. \tag{12.18}$$

We can easily compute the bias in the Bayesian sense and the corresponding risk of such an estimator. We have

$$\begin{aligned} E(\tilde{b} - b) &= E(a + (\mathbf{AX} - \mathbf{I})b) \\ &= a + (\mathbf{AX} - \mathbf{I})Eb, \end{aligned}$$

and

$$\begin{aligned} &E(\tilde{b} - b)(\tilde{b} - b)' \\ &= V(\tilde{b} - b) + E(\tilde{b} - b)E(\tilde{b} - b)' \\ &= V((\mathbf{AX} - \mathbf{I})b + \mathbf{A}u) + E(\tilde{b} - b)E(\tilde{b} - b)' \\ &= VE((\mathbf{AX} - \mathbf{I})b + \mathbf{A}u \mid b, \sigma^2) + EV((\mathbf{AX} - \mathbf{I})b + \mathbf{A}u \mid b, \sigma^2) \\ &\quad + E(\tilde{b} - b)E(\tilde{b} - b)' \\ &= V((\mathbf{AX} - \mathbf{I})b) + E(\sigma^2\mathbf{AA}') + E(\tilde{b} - b)E(\tilde{b} - b)' \\ &= (\mathbf{AX} - \mathbf{I})V(b)(\mathbf{AX} - \mathbf{I})' + E\sigma^2\mathbf{AA}' + E(\tilde{b} - b)E(\tilde{b} - b)'. \end{aligned}$$

Thus, the determination of these two moments does not require a complete specification of the prior distribution. Specifically, it suffices to know the first two moments of the prior.

To simplify, we assume that $Eb = 0$. Let $\mathbf{\Omega} = Vb$ and $\eta^2 = E\sigma^2$. Then unbiasedness in the Bayesian sense, i.e.

$$E(\tilde{b} - b) = 0,$$

is equivalent to

$$a = 0.$$

Hence we can restrict ourselves to estimators without a constant term. Moreover, given the unbiasedness condition, the Bayesian risk becomes

$$E(\tilde{b} - b)(\tilde{b} - b)' = (\mathbf{AX} - \mathbf{I})\mathbf{\Omega}(\mathbf{AX} - \mathbf{I})' + \eta^2 \mathbf{AA}'.$$

Property 12.6: *There exists a unique matrix* $\mathbf{A}$ *minimizing the Bayesian risk in the positive semidefinite matrix sense. This matrix is given by*

$$\mathbf{A} = \mathbf{\Omega X}'(\eta^2 \mathbf{I} + \mathbf{X\Omega X}')^{-1}.$$

PROOF: We shall only verify that the matrix $\mathbf{A}$ must be of the above form. As an exercise, the reader may verify the converse. To establish that the above form is necessary, it suffices to consider the first-order conditions

$$(\mathbf{AX} - \mathbf{I})\mathbf{\Omega X}' + \eta^2 \mathbf{A} = 0.$$

These conditions can be written equivalently as

$$\mathbf{A}(\eta^2 \mathbf{I} + \mathbf{X\Omega X}') = \mathbf{\Omega X}',$$

i.e., as

$$\mathbf{A} = \mathbf{\Omega X}'(\eta^2 \mathbf{I} + \mathbf{X\Omega X}')^{-1}.$$

□

Note that

$$\mathbf{X}'(\eta^2 \mathbf{I} + \mathbf{X\Omega X}')^{-1} = (\eta^2 \mathbf{I} + \mathbf{X}'\mathbf{X\Omega})^{-1}\mathbf{X}',$$

since

$$\begin{aligned} &(\eta^2 \mathbf{I} + \mathbf{X}'\mathbf{X\Omega})^{-1}\mathbf{X}'(\eta^2 \mathbf{I} + \mathbf{X\Omega X}') \\ = \;& (\eta^2 \mathbf{I} + \mathbf{X}'\mathbf{X\Omega})^{-1}(\eta^2 \mathbf{I} + \mathbf{X}'\mathbf{X\Omega})\mathbf{X}' \\ = \;& \mathbf{X}'. \end{aligned}$$

Hence an alternative form for the matrix $\mathbf{A}$ is

$$\mathbf{A} = \mathbf{\Omega}(\eta^2\mathbf{I} + \mathbf{X}'\mathbf{X}\mathbf{\Omega})^{-1}\mathbf{X}',$$

i.e.

$$\mathbf{A} = (\eta^2\mathbf{\Omega}^{-1} + \mathbf{X}'\mathbf{X})^{-1}\mathbf{X}'. \tag{12.19}$$

From Property 12.6 and equation (12.19) it follows that there exists a unique best linear unbiased estimator in the Bayesian sense. This estimator is

$$\tilde{b} = (\eta^2\mathbf{\Omega}^{-1} + \mathbf{X}'\mathbf{X})^{-1}\mathbf{X}'Y. \tag{12.20}$$

Remark 12.8: From equation (12.20) and the results obtained for a Gaussian linear model with a conjugate prior (see Section 12.2.4-d)), it follows that $\tilde{b}$ is similar to the estimator obtained there. Thus, as in the classical framework, the best linear unbiased estimator is also the best estimator under normality of the error terms and under normality of the prior distribution on b.

12.5.2 Shrinkage Estimators

The estimator

$$\tilde{b} = (\eta^2\mathbf{\Omega}^{-1} + \mathbf{X}'\mathbf{X})^{-1}\mathbf{X}'\mathbf{X}(\mathbf{X}'\mathbf{X})^{-1}\mathbf{X}'Y$$

can also be written as

$$\tilde{b} = (\eta^2\mathbf{\Omega}^{-1} + \mathbf{X}'\mathbf{X})^{-1}(\mathbf{X}'\mathbf{X}\hat{b} + \eta^2\mathbf{\Omega}^{-1}0),$$

where $\hat{b}$ is the ordinary least squares estimator of b. Thus $\tilde{b}$ can be viewed as a convex combination of $\hat{b}$ and zero. Hence, when $Eb = 0$, the Bayesian estimator $\tilde{b}$ *shrinks* the OLS estimator toward zero. In general, however, shrinking is not uniform in every direction. For instance, suppose that the matrix $\mathbf{\Omega}$ is

$$\mathbf{\Omega} = (\mathbf{X}'\mathbf{X})^{-1/2}\text{diag }(\omega_k)(\mathbf{X}'\mathbf{X})^{-1/2},$$

where diag (ω_k) is a diagonal matrix with positive diagonal elements. Then we have

$$\tilde{b} = \left((\mathbf{X}'\mathbf{X})^{1/2}\text{diag}\left(\frac{\eta^2}{\omega_k}\right)(\mathbf{X}'\mathbf{X})^{1/2} + \mathbf{X}'\mathbf{X}\right)^{-1}\mathbf{X}'\mathbf{X}\hat{b},$$

i.e.

$$(\mathbf{X}'\mathbf{X})^{1/2}\tilde{b} = \text{diag }\left(1 + \frac{\eta^2}{\omega_k}\right)^{-1}(\mathbf{X}'\mathbf{X})^{1/2}\hat{b}.$$

Property 12.7: *Suppose that*

$$\mathbf{\Omega} = (\mathbf{X}'\mathbf{X})^{-1/2}\text{diag } (\omega_k)(\mathbf{X}'\mathbf{X})^{-1/2}.$$

Then the Bayesian estimator $\tilde{\gamma}$ *of the "shrinked" parameters defined as* $\gamma = (X'X)^{1/2}b$ *is obtained from the OLS estimator* via

$$\tilde{\gamma}_k = \frac{1}{1+\eta^2/\omega_k}\hat{\gamma}_k.$$

The shrinkage coefficients are equal to $1/(1+\eta^2/\omega_k)$. They are decreasing in η^2/ω_k. Hence, the larger η^2/ω_k, the more important the shrinkage and the closer to zero the Bayesian estimator.

Remark 12.9: The choice of the prior variance covariance matrix $\mathbf{\Omega}$ depends on the control matrix $\mathbf{X}'\mathbf{X}$. Thus $\mathbf{\Omega}$ depend on the observed values of the exogenous variables. Hence such a choice for $\mathbf{\Omega}$ is not strictly Bayesian.

Remark 12.10: When $\mathbf{\Omega} = \omega(\mathbf{X}'\mathbf{X})^{-1}$, then all shrinking coefficients are equal and the above estimator becomes

$$\tilde{b} = \frac{1}{1+\eta^2/\omega}\hat{b}.$$

Estimators that correspond to choices of matrices $\mathbf{\Omega}$ of the form $\mathbf{\Omega} = (\mathbf{X}'\mathbf{X})^{-1/2}\text{diag } (\omega_k)(\mathbf{X}'\mathbf{X})^{-1/2}$ are frequently called *ridge estimators.*

12.5.3 Bayesian Linear Estimators and Admissible Linear Estimators in the Classical Sense

Every linear Bayesian estimator, of which the general form was given above, is an admissible linear estimator in the classical sense. The proof of such a property is identical to the proof of Property 2.2. An interesting question is whether the converse holds, i.e., whether every linear admissible estimator is a Bayesian estimator. The answer to such a question is positive.

We shall verify this property for the special case where b is a scalar. We consider the linear model $Y = \mathbf{X}b + u$, where $\mathbf{X}$ is a $n \times 1$ matrix, $E(u \mid \mathbf{X}) = 0$, $V(u \mid \mathbf{X}) = \sigma^2\mathbf{I}$, $b \in I\!R$, and $\sigma^2 \in I\!R^{+*}$.

It is easy to see that every estimator that is a linear function of Y is dominated in the classical sense by an estimator that is a linear function of $\hat{b} = (\mathbf{X}'\mathbf{X})^{-1}\mathbf{X}'Y$. Therefore it suffices to consider estimators of the form

$$\tilde{b}(a) = a\hat{b}, \quad \text{with } a \in I\!R, \tag{12.21}$$

when searching for admissible estimators.

The classical risk of an estimator of the form (12.21) is

$$R(\tilde{b}(a); b, \sigma^2) = (a-1)^2 b^2 + a^2\sigma^2(\mathbf{X}'\mathbf{X})^{-1}. \tag{12.22}$$

Thus an estimator of the form (12.21) is inadmissible if there exists a_0 such that

$$(a_0 - 1)^2 \leq (a-1)^2 \text{ and } a_0^2 \leq a^2 \tag{12.23}$$

hold simultaneously with at least one strict inequality. Condition (12.23) is equivalent to $a < 0$ or $a > 1$. Therefore admissible estimators are of the form

$$\tilde{b}(a) = a\hat{b} \text{ with } 0 \leq a \leq 1. \tag{12.24}$$

That is, the class of admissible estimators is the class of convex combinations of zero and the OLS estimator. From the previous section it follows that such a class is exactly equal to the class of best linear estimators in the Bayesian sense.

Remark 12.11: Although estimators of the form $a\hat{b}$ are unbiased in the Bayesian sense when $Eb = 0$, such estimators are not unbiased in the classical sense with the exception of the OLS estimator which corresponds to $a = 1$.

12.6 Approximate Determination of Posterior Distributions

The posterior distribution is given by

$$\pi(\theta \mid y) = \frac{\pi(\theta)\ell(y \mid \theta)}{\int \pi(\theta)\ell(y \mid \theta)d\theta}.$$

With the exception of some simple cases such as those studied in the preceding sections, the posterior distribution is, in general, difficult to determine in practice. Therefore it is useful to find some approximations to the posterior distribution. Such approximations can be analytical, in which cases they are valid for every value of y, or they can be numerical, in which cases they are valid only for the actual observations.

12.6.1 Approximating the Prior Distribution

A first method consists in replacing the density of the prior distribution $\pi(\theta)$ by an approximation of it $q(\theta)$ such that the associated posterior distribution given by

$$q(\theta \mid y) = \frac{q(\theta)\ell(y \mid \theta)}{\int q(\theta)\ell(y \mid \theta)d\theta}$$

is readily computed. Then the approximate posterior $q(\theta \mid y)$ is used in place of $\pi(\theta \mid y)$. A similar idea was used to justify some diffuse priors (see Section 12.4).

Consequences of using an approximate prior on the posterior distribution are assessed in the next property.

Property 12.8: *We make the following assumptions.*

A.1: The approximation of the prior distribution is adequate on some subset $B \subset \Theta$, i.e.

$$\exists B \subset \Theta, \exists \beta \text{ (small)} : 1 \leq \frac{\pi(\theta)}{q(\theta)} \leq 1 + \beta, \forall\, \theta \in B.$$

A.2: The approximate prior is not significantly smaller than the original prior, i.e.

$$\exists \lambda \text{ (moderate)} : \frac{\pi(\theta)}{q(\theta)} \leq \lambda, \forall\, \theta \in \Theta.$$

Then, under these assumptions, we have

$$\frac{\Pi(B \mid y)}{1+\beta} \leq \frac{\pi(\theta \mid y)}{q(\theta \mid y)} \leq \frac{1+\beta}{Q(B \mid y)}, \forall\, \theta \in B,$$

and

$$\frac{\pi(\theta \mid y)}{q(\theta \mid y)} \leq \frac{\lambda}{Q(B \mid y)}, \forall\, \theta \in \Theta.$$

PROOF: We shall establish only one of the above inequalities, namely

$$\frac{\pi(\theta \mid y)}{q(\theta \mid y)} \leq \frac{\lambda}{Q(B \mid y)}.$$

The other inequalities are proved similarly. We have

$$\begin{aligned}
\frac{\pi(\theta \mid y)}{q(\theta \mid y)} &= \frac{\pi(\theta)}{q(\theta)} \frac{\int q(\theta)\ell(y \mid \theta)d\theta}{\int \pi(\theta)\ell(y \mid \theta)d\theta} \\
&\leq \lambda \frac{\int q(\theta)\ell(y \mid \theta)d\theta}{\int \pi(\theta)\ell(y \mid \theta)d\theta} \quad \text{(using A.2)} \\
&\leq \lambda \frac{\int q(\theta)\ell(y \mid \theta)d\theta}{\int_B \pi(\theta)\ell(y \mid \theta)d\theta} \\
&\leq \lambda \frac{\int q(\theta)\ell(y \mid \theta)d\theta}{\int_B q(\theta)\ell(y \mid \theta)d\theta} \quad \text{(using A.1)} \\
&= \frac{\lambda}{Q(B \mid y)}.
\end{aligned}$$

□

Property 12.8 holds even when the approximate prior q is improper. Hence, in Assumption A.1, it is always possible to choose the value one as a lower bound for $\pi(\theta)/q(\theta)$.

Example 12.11: Consider a random sample $Y_1, \ldots, Y_n$ drawn from the normal distribution $N(m, 1)$. Suppose that the prior distribution on m is the shifted exponential distribution

$$\pi(m) = \begin{cases} b\exp(-b(m-a)), & \text{if } m > a, \\ 0, & \text{otherwise.} \end{cases}$$

The presence of a threshold leads to a posterior distribution that depends on the cumulative distribution function Φ of the standard normal distribution.

Suppose that we approximate the above prior by the improper prior

$$q(m) = b(\exp -b(m-a)), \ \forall \ m \in I\!R.$$

We have

$$q(m \mid y) = \sqrt{n}\phi\left(\sqrt{n}\left(m - \bar{y} + \frac{b}{n}\right)\right)$$

and

$$\pi(m \mid y) = \frac{q(m \mid y)}{\Phi\left(\sqrt{n}\left(\bar{y} - a - \frac{b}{n}\right)\right)} \mathbb{1}_{m>a},$$

where ϕ and Φ denote the density and the cumulative distribution functions of the standard normal distribution $N(0, 1)$.

Property 12.8 can be applied with $B = (a, +\infty)$, $\beta = 0$ and $\lambda = 1$. We have

$$Q(B \mid y) = \Phi\left(\sqrt{n}\left(\bar{y} - a - \frac{b}{n}\right)\right).$$

It follows that

$$\frac{\pi(m \mid y)}{q(m \mid y)} \leq \frac{1}{\Phi\left(\sqrt{n}\left(\bar{y} - a - \frac{b}{n}\right)\right)}, \quad \forall\, m,$$

and

$$1 \leq \frac{\pi(m \mid y)}{q(m \mid y)}, \quad \forall\, m > a.$$

12.6.2 Direct Approximations to Posterior Distributions

Another method, which is frequently used, consists in selecting a family of possible distributions for the posterior distribution and in retaining a distribution in this family that has some characteristics common to the exact posterior distribution. For instance, if the family of normal distributions is selected, then the exact posterior distribution could be replaced by a normal distribution with the same mode and the same curvature at the modal value. Alternatively, when conjugate priors arise naturally, we can base approximations to the exact posterior distribution on families of conjugate priors or on mixtures of such conjugate priors.

Remark 12.12: The idea of using mixtures of distributions arises essentially from the study of models derived from latent models for which there exist conjugate priors. Specifically, consider a latent model whose likelihood is $\ell^*(y^* \mid \theta)$ and for which a conjugate prior is $\pi(\theta)$. By definition, the corresponding posterior distribution, which is $\pi^*(\theta \mid y^*) \propto \ell^*(y^* \mid \theta)\pi(\theta)$, belongs to the same family as the conjugate prior.

Suppose now that the observed variable Y is related to the latent variable Y^* by $Y = h(Y^*)$. The posterior distribution $\pi(\theta \mid y)$ is obtained from the joint distribution of the pair (Y, θ). We have

$$\pi(\theta \mid y) = \frac{\int_{h^{-1}(y)} \pi^*(\theta \mid y^*)\ell^*(y^*)dy^*}{\int_{h^{-1}(y)} \ell^*(y^*)dy^*},$$

and

$$\ell(y, \theta) = \int_{h^{-1}(y)} \ell^*(y^* \mid \theta)\pi(\theta)dy^*.$$

To simplify the notation, we have implicitly assumed that Y is discrete valued. The posterior distribution is

$$\pi(\theta \mid y) \propto \int_{h^{-1}(y)} \ell^*(y^* \mid \theta)\pi(\theta)dy^*,$$

or

$$\pi(\theta \mid y) \propto \int_{h^{-1}(y)} \pi^*(\theta \mid y^*)\ell^*(y^*)dy^*.$$

Hence the posterior distribution appears as a mixture of conjugate priors $\pi^*(\theta \mid y^*)$.

Example 12.12: It may happen that the resulting mixture is a particular conjugate distribution.

(i) Consider independent pairs of independent variables (Y_{1i}^*, Y_{2i}^*), $i = 1, \ldots, n$. Suppose that the parameter θ appears only in the distribution of the variables Y_{1i}^*. Assume also that the variables Y_{1i}^* are identically exponentially distributed with density

$$\ell(y_{1i}^* \mid \theta) = \theta \exp(-\theta y_{1i}^*) \mathbb{1}_{y_{1i}^* > 0}.$$

Thus the joint distribution of the variables $(Y_{1i}^*, Y_{2i}^*, i = 1, \ldots, n)$ has density

$$\exp(-\theta S(Y) + n \log \theta), \text{ with } S(Y) = \sum_{i=1}^{n} Y_{1i}^*,$$

with respect to a dominating measure of the form

$$\mu_2(dy_2^*) \prod_{i=1}^{n} (\mathbb{1}_{y_{1i}^* > 0} dy_{1i}^*).$$

If the variables $(Y_{1i}^*, Y_{2i}^*, i = 1, \ldots, n)$ are observed, then a prior on θ could be the conjugate gamma distribution

$$\pi(\theta) \propto \exp(-\theta\lambda + k \log \theta),$$

where $\lambda > 0$ and $k > -1$ are two auxiliary parameters.

(ii) Suppose now that the variables $Y_{1i}^*, i = 1, \ldots, n$, which can be interpreted as survival times, are not always observed. Namely, observation of the phenomenon stops at time given by Y_{2i}^*. That is, we observe Y_{1i} and Y_{2i} given by

$$Y_{1i} = \min(Y_{i1}^*, Y_{i2}^*),$$

and

$$Y_{i2} = \mathbb{1}_{Y_{i1}=Y_{i1}^*}.$$

The likelihood function is proportional to

$$\ell(y \mid \theta) \propto \exp(-\theta S_{+1} + S_{+2} \log \theta),$$

where

$$S_{+1} = \sum_{i=1}^{n} Y_{i1}, \quad S_{+2} = \sum_{i=1}^{n} Y_{i2}.$$

Hence, if the prior distribution is a conjugate prior for the latent model, then it is readily seen that the corresponding posterior distribution is a gamma distribution with parameters $\lambda^* = \lambda + S_{+1}$ and $k^* = k + S_{+2}$.

12.6.3 Numerical Integration

To determine the posterior expectation of a function $g(\theta)$ of the parameter we need to determine

$$E(g(\theta) \mid y) = \frac{\int_\Theta g(\theta)\ell(y \mid \theta)\pi(\theta)d\theta}{\int_\Theta \ell(y \mid \theta)\pi(\theta)d\theta}.$$

The main practical difficulties encountered in the explicit determination of such a posterior moment arise from the presence of integrals. These integrals, however, can be evaluated numerically for the observed value y. A method that enables such an evaluation is the so-called *integration method by Monte Carlo.*

Let $q(\theta \mid y) = \ell(y \mid \theta)\pi(\theta)$. Consider the numerator

$$M = \int_\Theta g(\theta)q(\theta \mid y)d\theta.$$

If $p(\theta)$ denotes a probability density on Θ, then this integral can be written as

$$M = \int_\Theta \frac{g(\theta)q(\theta \mid y)}{p(\theta)} p(\theta)d\theta. \tag{12.25}$$

Property 12.9: *The Monte Carlo integration method consists in drawing n independent values $\theta_1, \ldots, \theta_n$ from the distribution given by $p(\theta)d\theta$ and in approximating M by*

$$\hat{M}_n = \frac{1}{n}\sum_{i=1}^{n} g(\theta_i)\frac{q(\theta_i \mid y)}{p(\theta_i)}.$$

The density p used for the draws is called an importance function.

Thus the Monte Carlo integration method consists in approximating the integral M by the quantity $\hat{M}_n$. Since $\hat{M}_n$ is an estimator of M, it is important to study its properties.

Property 12.10:

a) *$\hat{M}_n$ is a consistent estimator of M.*

b) *$\hat{M}_n$ is unbiased.*

c) *The variance of $\hat{M}_n$ is*

$$V\hat{M}_n = \frac{1}{n}\left(\int_\Theta g^2(\theta)\frac{q^2(\theta \mid y)}{p(\theta)}d\theta - M^2\right).$$

PROOF:

a) Consistency of $\hat{M}_n$ directly follows from the Strong Law of Large Numbers provided the integral M exists. (The latter condition is assumed to be satisfied.)

b) Since every variable θ_i follows the distribution given by $p(\theta)d\theta$, we have

$$\begin{aligned} E\hat{M}_n &= E_p\left(g(\theta)\frac{q(\theta \mid y)}{p(\theta)}\right) \\ &= \int_\Theta g(\theta)\frac{q(\theta \mid y)}{p(\theta)}p(\theta)d\theta \\ &= M. \end{aligned}$$

c) Lastly, because the draws are independent, we have

$$\begin{aligned} V\hat{M}_n &= \frac{1}{n}V_p\left(g(\theta)\frac{q(\theta \mid y)}{p(\theta)}\right) \\ &= \frac{1}{n}\left(\int_\Theta g^2(\theta)\frac{q^2(\theta \mid y)}{p(\theta)}d\theta - M^2\right). \end{aligned}$$

□

Note that the variance of the approximation based on the Monte Carlo integration method depends on the choice of the importance function p. Thus an appropriate choice of p should lead to the smallest possible variance. Consider the extreme case where $V\hat{M}_n = 0$. Then it is easily seen that it is the case if p is a density proportional to $g(\theta)q(\theta \mid y)$. Such an optimal choice supposes that the sign of $g(\theta)q(\theta \mid y)$ remains constant. Moreover, such a choice is not useful in practice since it gives

$$p(\theta) = \frac{g(\theta)q(\theta \mid y)}{\int_\Theta g(\theta)q(\theta \mid y)d\theta},$$

where the denominator is precisely unknown. Nonetheless, the previous argument suggests that the choice of an importance function approximately proportional to $g(\theta)q(\theta \mid y)$ leads to a good approximation $\hat{M}_n$.

12.7 Appendix

SOME COMMON PROBABILITY DISTRIBUTIONS

a) Pareto Distribution

A Pareto distribution with parameters $\alpha > 0$ and $A > 0$ is a continuous distribution on $\mathbb{R}$ with density

$$f(y; \alpha, A) = \frac{\alpha A^\alpha}{y^{\alpha+1}} \mathbb{1}_{y \geq A}. \tag{12.26}$$

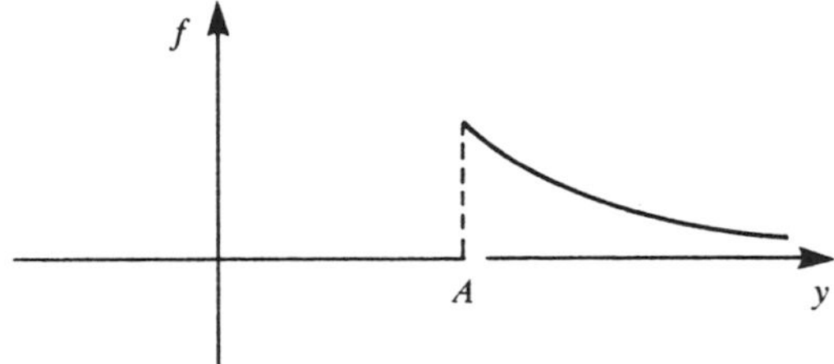

Figure 12.5: Pareto Density

The mean of a Pareto distribution exists provided $\alpha \geq 1$, in which case it is given by

$$E_{\alpha,A} Y = \alpha A^\alpha \int_A^\infty \frac{dy}{y^\alpha} = \frac{\alpha}{\alpha - 1} A. \tag{12.27}$$

When the parameter α is strictly larger than 2, the variance exists. The second-order raw moment is

$$E_{\alpha,A}Y^2 = \alpha A^\alpha \int_A^\infty \frac{dy}{y^{\alpha-1}} = \frac{\alpha}{\alpha-2}A^2.$$

Then we obtain the variance as

$$V_{\alpha,A}Y = \frac{\alpha}{\alpha-2}A^2 - \frac{\alpha^2}{(\alpha-1)^2}A^2,$$

i.e.

$$V_{\alpha,A}Y = \frac{\alpha A^2}{(\alpha-2)(\alpha-1)^2}. \tag{12.28}$$

b) Beta Distribution

A Beta distribution with parameters α and β restricted to be both strictly positive is a continuous distribution on $[0,1]$ with density

$$f(y;\alpha,\beta) = \frac{y^{\alpha-1}(1-y)^{\beta-1}}{B(\alpha,\beta)}\mathbb{1}_{[0,1]}(y), \tag{12.29}$$

where the constant $B(\alpha,\beta)$ is such that the integral of the density is equal to one. Thus $B(\alpha,\beta)$ is given by

$$B(\alpha,\beta) = \int_0^1 y^{\alpha-1}(1-y)^{\beta-1}dy.$$

It can be expressed in terms of the gamma function Γ as

$$B(\alpha,\beta) = \frac{\Gamma(\alpha)\Gamma(\beta)}{\Gamma(\alpha+\beta)}. \tag{12.30}$$

The density of a beta distribution with parameters α and β both stricly larger than one is represented in the next figure.

The mean of a beta distribution is

$$\begin{aligned} E_{\alpha,\beta}Y &= \frac{\int_0^1 y^\alpha(1-y)^{\beta-1}dy}{B(\alpha,\beta)} \\ &= \frac{B(\alpha+1,\beta)}{B(\alpha,\beta)} \\ &= \frac{\Gamma(\alpha+1)}{\Gamma(\alpha)}\frac{\Gamma(\alpha+\beta)}{\Gamma(\alpha+\beta+1)}, \end{aligned}$$

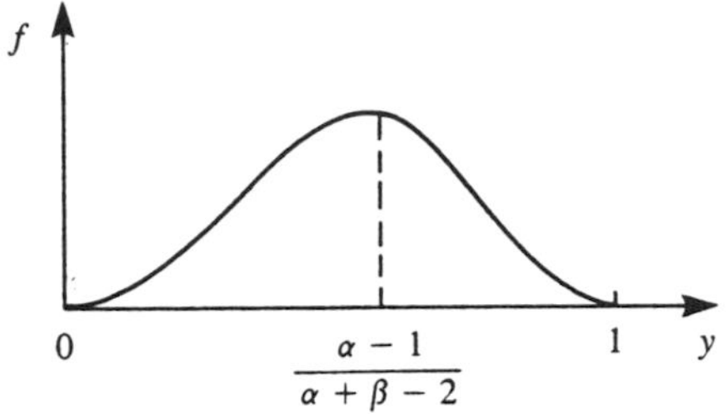

Figure 12.6: Beta Density

i.e.

$$E_{\alpha,\beta}Y = \frac{\alpha}{\alpha+\beta}, \tag{12.31}$$

where we have used the recursion relation $\Gamma(\alpha+1) = \alpha\Gamma(\alpha)$.

The second-order raw moment is computed similarly. We have

$$\begin{aligned} E_{\alpha,\beta}Y^2 &= \frac{B(\alpha+2,\beta)}{B(\alpha+\beta)} \\ &= \frac{\Gamma(\alpha+2)}{\Gamma(\alpha)}\frac{\Gamma(\alpha+\beta)}{\Gamma(\alpha+\beta+2)} \\ &= \frac{(\alpha+1)}{\alpha+\beta+1}E_{\alpha,\beta}Y. \end{aligned}$$

Then we obtain the variance as

$$\begin{aligned} V_{\alpha,\beta}Y &= E_{\alpha,\beta}Y\left(\frac{\alpha+1}{\alpha+\beta+1} - E_{\alpha,\beta}Y\right) \\ &= \frac{\alpha}{\alpha+\beta}\left(\frac{\alpha+1}{\alpha+\beta+1} - \frac{\alpha}{\alpha+\beta}\right), \end{aligned}$$

i.e.

$$V_{\alpha,\beta}Y = \frac{\alpha\beta}{(\alpha+\beta)^2(\alpha+\beta+1)}. \tag{12.32}$$

12.8 Exercises

EXERCISE 12.1: We consider a measure defined on $I\!R$ with density $f(y) = a$ with respect to Lebesgue measure. Verify that the condition $\int_{-\infty}^{+\infty} f(y)dy = 1$ implies that $a = 0$. Conclude that there does not exist a uniform probability distribution on $I\!R$.

EXERCISE 12.2: Let $\hat{\theta} = E(\theta \mid Y)$ be the Bayes estimator of θ, where θ is a scalar. Let $\delta(Y)$ be another estimator. Verify that the Bayesian risk of δ is given by

$$R_\pi(\delta) = R_\pi(\hat{\theta}) + \int \left(\delta(y) - \hat{\theta}(y)\right)^2 \ell(y \mid \theta)\pi(\theta)d\mu(y)d\nu(\theta).$$

Deduce the optimality of $\hat{\theta}$.

EXERCISE 12.3: Consider the Gaussian linear model $Y \sim N(\mathbf{X}\theta, \sigma^2\mathbf{I})$ where θ and σ^2 are unknown. Suppose that the prior on (θ, σ^2) is a conjugate prior.

a) Give formulae for updating the auxiliary parameters appearing in the prior distribution as the number of observations increases.

b) Find the Bayes estimators of θ and σ^2. Give an estimate of their precision.

c) What happens to the preceding formulae when the number n of observations increases to infinity assuming that the control matrix is such that $(1/n)\mathbf{X}'\mathbf{X}$ converges to a nonsingular matrix?

EXERCISE 12.4: Consider a random sample drawn from the Pareto distribution

$$\ell(y; A, \alpha) = \frac{\alpha A^\alpha}{y^{\alpha+1}} 1_{y \geq A},$$

where A is known but α is unknown.

a) Determine the likelihood function and conclude that a sufficient statistic is the geometric mean, denoted G, of the observations.

b) Suppose that the prior distribution on α corresponds to the diffuse prior on $\log \alpha$ given by $\pi(\alpha) = 1/\alpha$, where $\alpha > 0$. Verify that the posterior distribution of α is a gamma distribution. Determine its parameters. Show that the corresponding Bayes estimator of α is $1/\log(G/A)$.

EXERCISE 12.5: Can a same family such as the family of gamma distributions (say) be a family of conjugate priors for two different models?

EXERCISE 12.6: Suppose that the prior distribution on $\log \sigma$ is improper and proportional to the Lebesgue measure. What is the prior distribution on σ^p?

EXERCISE 12.7: Let $Y_1, \ldots, Y_n$ be a random sample drawn from the normal distribution $N(\theta, 1)$. Consider prior distributions of the form $\pi_{\sigma_0} = N(m_0, \sigma_0^2)$ on the parameter θ including the limit case of the diffuse prior π_∞ (see Section 12.1.4). Determine the value of the Kullback discrepancy between the posterior distributions associated with π_{σ_0} and π_∞. Verify that such a discrepancy measure depends on the observations. How will you interpret the convergence of the posterior distributions as σ_0 increases to infinity?

EXERCISE 12.8: To measure the amount of information contained in a continuous distribution on $[-A, +A]$ with density $f(x)$, Shannon has proposed the quantity

$$I(f) = \int_{-A}^{A} f(x) \log f(x) dx.$$

Study the properties of such a measure. In particular, verify that it is minimized when the distribution is uniform on $[-A, +A]$. Interpret the latter result in terms of a diffuse prior.

12.9 References

Anscombe, F.J. (1961). "Bayesian Statistics," *American Statistician*, 15, 21–24.

Box, G.E.P and Tiao, G.C. (1973). *Bayesian Inference in Statistical Analysis*, Addison-Wesley.

Cox, D.R. and Hinkley, D.V. (1974). *Theoretical Statistics*, Chapman and Hall.

De Groot, M.H. (1970). *Optimal Statistical Decision*, New York, MacGraw Hill.

Dreze, J.H. (1976). "Bayesian Limited Information Analysis Using Poly-*t* Densities," *Journal of Econometrics*, 6, 329–354.

Jeffreys, H. (1961). *Theory of Probability*, Oxford.

Lindley, D.V. (1965). *Introduction to Probability and Statistics from a Bayesian Viewpoint*, Cambridge University Press.

Raiffa, H. and Schlaifer, R. (1961). *Applied Statistical Decision Theory*, Harvard University Press.

Richard, J.F. (1973). *Posterior and Predictive Densities for Simultaneous Equation Models*, Springer-Verlag.

Rothenberg, T.J. (1975). "The Bayesian Approach and Alternatives," in S.E. Fienberg and A. Zellner eds., *Studies in Bayesian Econometrics and Statistics*, Amsterdam, North Holland, pp. 55–67.

Zellner, A. (1971). *An Introduction to Bayesian Inference in Econometrics*, Wiley.

CHAPTER 13

Numerical Procedures

In the previous chapters we studied various estimators obtained by minimization of some criteria such as maximum likelihood estimators, least squares estimators, pseudo maximum likelihood estimators, method of moments estimators, asymptotic least squares estimators, etc. The numerical determination and updating of such estimators as well as various predictions as new observations become available are, however, questions that are frequently difficult to solve analytically. Such questions can be approached by means of numerical procedures. In this chapter we present various classical numerical procedures used in statistics and we discuss their respective advantages and disadvantages.

13.1 Numerical Optimization

To begin with, we consider the problem of maximizing a scalar function $V(\theta)$ defined on a subset Θ of $\mathbb{R}^p$ with a nonempty interior. When the function is twice continuously differentiable, the local maxima of the function $V(\theta)$ in the interior of Θ can be characterized by the first and second partial derivatives. Thereafter, to simplify the notation, we let $g(\theta) = \partial V(\theta)/\partial\theta$ and $\mathbf{G}(\theta) = \partial^2 V(\theta)/\partial\theta\partial\theta' = \partial g(\theta)/\partial\theta'$ denote the gradient and the Hessian, respectively, of the function V at θ.

A local maximum $\hat{\theta}$ of V satisfies the first-order conditions

$$g(\hat{\theta}) = \frac{\partial V(\hat{\theta})}{\partial\theta} = 0.$$

Moreover, except in some degenerated case, $\hat{\theta}$ is such that the matrix

$$\mathbf{G}(\hat{\theta}) = \frac{\partial^2 V(\hat{\theta})}{\partial\theta\,\partial\theta'}$$

is negative definite.

The various numerical optimization algorithms presented in this section can determine local maxima in some favorable cases. If a global maximum of the function V is desired, then it is, in principle, necessary to find all local maxima and to determine among these local maxima the one that gives the highest value to the function V.

Note, however, that a consistent M-estimator may be obtained at a local maximum of the criterion function. Thus, the fact that usual numerical optimization algorithms determine local maxima can also be useful.

13.1.1 Gradient Methods

a) Introduction

A numerical optimization algorithm is an iterative procedure that allows generation of sequence of approximations $\theta^{(0)}, \theta^{(1)}, \ldots, \theta^{(k)}, \ldots, \theta^{(K)}$ to the desired local maximum $\hat{\theta}$. It is defined by:

(i) the method for choosing the *initial condition* $\theta^{(0)}$,

(ii) the *iteration formula* describing how the approximation $\theta^{(k+1)}$ at the $(k+1)$th step is computed from the approximation $\theta^{(k)}$ obtained in the preceding step,

(iii) the *stopping rule* defining the maximum number of iterations of the algorithm.

The central piece of an algorithm is clearly the iteration formula. In general, this formula is of the form

$$\theta^{(k+1)} = \theta^{(k)} + \mu^{(k)}\, d^{(k)}, \ \mu^{(k)} \in I\!R^{+}, \ d^{(k)} \in I\!R^{p}. \tag{13.1}$$

Hence $\theta^{(k+1)}$ can be viewed as being determined in two steps. First, an appropriate *direction* $d^{(k)}$ *of search* is chosen for the function V. Then an appropriate *step* or *stepsize* $\mu^{(k)}$ along this direction is chosen so as to maximize the increase in the function V.

INCREASING DIRECTION OF SEARCH

Definition 13.1: *A vector d is an increasing direction of search for the function V at the point θ if and only if $V(\theta + \mu d)$ is an increasing function of μ for μ positive and sufficiently small.*

From a Taylor expansion of V in a neighborhood of $\mu = 0$ we obtain

$$V(\theta + \mu d) \# V(\theta) + \mu g'(\theta) d.$$

From this relation we obtain the following characterization of increasing directions.

Property 13.1: *A vector d is an increasing direction of search for the function V at a point θ where the gradient $g(\theta)$ is nonzero if and only if $g'(\theta)d > 0$.*

Such directions always exist when $g(\theta)$ is nonzero. For instance, we can choose $d = g(\theta)$ since

$$g'(\theta)d = g'(\theta)g(\theta) = \|g(\theta)\|^2 > 0.$$

We can also easily characterize increasing directions in terms of the gradient (see Exercise 13.1). We have

Property 13.2: *If $g(\theta)$ is nonzero, then increasing directions of search are of the form $d = \mathbf{Q}g(\theta)$, where $\mathbf{Q}$ is a symmetric positive definite matrix.*

Thus, if we want to have an increasing numerical algorithm, i.e., an algorithm such that $V(\theta^{(k+1)} \geq V(\theta^{(k)}), \forall k = 0, \ldots, K-1$, it suffices to consider an increasing direction with a suitable stepsize. This is equivalent to replacing the iteration formula (13.1) by

$$\theta^{(k+1)} = \theta^{(k)} + \mu^{(k)} \mathbf{Q}^{(k)} g(\theta^{(k)}), \tag{13.2}$$

where $\mathbf{Q}^{(k)}$ is a symmetric positive definite matrix.

Definition 13.2: *A gradient method is a a numerical optimization algorithm based on an iteration formula of the form (13.2).*

DETERMINATION OF THE STEPSIZE

A suitable choice of direction produces an increasing algorithm. The purpose of an adequate choice of stepsize is to obtain a *convergent algorithm*, i.e., an algorithm such that $\lim_{k\to\infty} \theta^{(k)} = \hat{\theta}$, on the one hand, and to increase the speed of convergence, on the other hand.

There are many ways to choose the stepsize $\mu^{(k)}$.

(i) Optimal Stepsize

A natural idea consists in choosing $\mu^{(k)}$ so as to maximize the increase in the function V along the direction $d^{(k)}$. The optimal size is given by solving the optimization problem

$$V\left(\theta^{(k)} + \mu^{(k)}\mathbf{Q}^{(k)}g(\theta^{(k)})\right) = \max_{\mu \geq 0} V\left(\theta^{(k)} + \mu\mathbf{Q}^{(k)}g(\theta^{(k)})\right). \quad (13.3)$$

We are led again to solve an optimization problem, which in practice must be solved numerically. This maximization problem, however, is with respect to a scalar parameter μ. This allows the application of simpler algorithms and methods such as a grid search method (see Section 13.1.3).

(ii) Optimal Stepsize by Quadratic Approximation

Instead of solving directly the optimization problem (13.3), we can consider an approximate problem. Specifically, from a second-order Taylor expansion of the function V around $\mu = 0$ we obtain

$$\begin{aligned} V\left(\theta^{(k)} + \mu\mathbf{Q}^{(k)}g(\theta^{(k)})\right) \quad \# \quad & V(\theta^{(k)}) + \mu g'(\theta^{(k)})\mathbf{Q}^{(k)}g(\theta^{(k)}) \\ & + \frac{1}{2}\mu^2 g'(\theta^{(k)})\mathbf{Q}^{(k)}\mathbf{G}(\theta^{(k)})\mathbf{Q}^{(k)}g(\theta^{(k)}). \end{aligned}$$

Thus maximization of this approximation with respect to μ gives, after solving the corresponding first-order condition

$$\mu^{(k)} = -\frac{g'(\theta^{(k)})\mathbf{Q}^{(k)}g(\theta^{(k)})}{g'(\theta^{(k)})\mathbf{Q}^{(k)}\mathbf{G}(\theta^{(k)})\mathbf{Q}^{(k)}g(\theta^{(k)})}. \quad (13.4)$$

Replacing the original criterion function by a quadratic approximation may lead to undesired effects on the algorithm. For instance, when the function V has a positive definite Hessian at $\theta^{(k)}$, then it is readily seen that $\mu^{(k)}$ is negative and corresponds to a minimum of the quadratic approximation. However a quadratic approximation is clearly useful when the Hessian is negative definite, which is the case in the neighborhood of a local maximum.

(iii) There exist many other methods for determining the stepsize. The method presented next allows us to achieve convergence of the algorithm (see Goldstein (1967) for a proof).

Property 13.3: *Consider a gradient method*

$$\theta^{(k+1)} = \theta^{(k)} + \mu^{(k)}d^{(k)} \text{ with } d^{(k)} = \mathbf{Q}^{(k)}g(\theta^{(k)}),$$

where for every k:

(i) the direction $d^{(k)}$ is such that there exists a scalar $\alpha \in (0,1)$ satisfying

$$\frac{d^{(k)}g(\theta^{(k)})}{d^{(k)\prime}d^{(k)}} > \alpha,$$

(ii) the stepsize $\mu^{(k)}$ is such that

$$\mu^{(k)} = 1 \text{ if } \frac{V(\theta^{(k)} + d^{(k)}) - V(\theta^{(k)})}{d^{(k)\prime}g(\theta^{(k)})} \geq \delta,$$

and

$$\delta \leq \frac{V(\theta^{(k)} + \mu^{(k)}d^{(k)}) - V(\theta^{(k)})}{\mu^{(k)}d^{(k)\prime}g(\theta^{(k)})} \leq 1 - \delta \text{ otherwise},$$

where δ is a scalar belonging to $(0, 1/2)$.

Then $g(\theta^{(k)})$ converges to zero as k increases to infinity.

Such a convergence theorem clearly shows that a limit point of the algorithm satisfies the first-order conditions of the optimization problem. This limit point, however, may correspond to a local minimum or a saddle point. This is because the chosen value of the stepsize does not ensure that the algorithm is increasing.

STOPPING RULES

From a practical point of view it is important to make a distinction between a theoretical convergence property of an algorithm such as Property 13.3 and a numerical convergence of the algorithm. It is the later concept that determines the maximum number K of iterations. It is recommended to stop the algorithm, i.e., to fix indirectly the maximum number K of iterations when several conditions are satisfied *simultaneously*. Examples of such conditions are the following:

(i) The convergence of the sequence $\theta^{(k)}$ must hold numerically. Thus the difference between two successive values $\theta^{(k)}$ and $\theta^{(k+1)}$ must be sufficiently small (e.g., smaller than a given tolerance level ε_1) before stopping the algorithm

$$\|\theta^{(k+1)} - \theta^{(k)}\| \leq \varepsilon_1.$$

(ii) The values of the criterion function must not differ significantly before stopping the algorithm. This motivates a condition of the form

$$|V(\theta^{(k+1)}) - V(\theta^{(k)})| \leq \varepsilon_2.$$

(iii) The value of the gradient must be close to zero, i.e.

$$\|g(\theta^{(k)})\| \leq \varepsilon_3.$$

Then the maximum number of iterations could be, for instance, the smallest index k for which the preceding three inequalities hold simultaneously.

Note that all three preceding criteria are satisfied asymptotically when theoretical convergence is achieved at a saddle point or at a local minimum. Therefore it seems necessary, at the end of the numerical algorithm, to compute the Hessian $\mathbf{G}(\theta^{(K)})$ so as to verify that the second-order conditions for a local maximum are satisfied.

b) Method of Steepest Ascent

This algorithm consists in retaining the increasing direction that ensures the steepest ascent. To determine such an optimal direction, it is necessary to introduce a norm on the space $I\!R^p$. We assume that such a norm corresponds to a symmetric positive definite matrix $\mathbf{B}$.

Locally around θ we have

$$V(\theta + \mu d) \# V(x) + \mu g'(\theta) \cdot d,$$

for every direction d of norm equal to one.

Then the optimal direction is obtained as a solution to

$$\begin{cases} \max_d g'(\theta) \cdot d \\ \\ \text{subject to } d'\mathbf{B}d = 1. \end{cases} \tag{13.5}$$

The solution is readily obtained by introducing a Lagrange multiplier associated with the constraint. The solution is given by

$$\tilde{d} = \frac{\mathbf{B}^{-1} g(\theta)}{(g'(\theta)\mathbf{B}^{-1} g(\theta))^{1/2}}. \tag{13.6}$$

The simplest choice of a norm corresponds to $\mathbf{B} = \mathbf{I}$. In this case we obtain the iteration formula

$$\theta^{(k+1)} = \theta^{(k)} + \frac{\mu^{(k)}}{\|g(\theta^{(k)})\|} g(\theta^{(k)}). \tag{13.7}$$

Remark 13.1: Although the increasing property of the algorithm is ensured by an appropriate choice of the stepsize $\mu^{(k)}$, the locally "optimal" direction of steepest ascent may turn out to be relatively inefficient.

For instance, suppose that the isocurves of the function V are of the form represented in the next figure in a neighborhood of a local maximum $\hat{\theta}$.

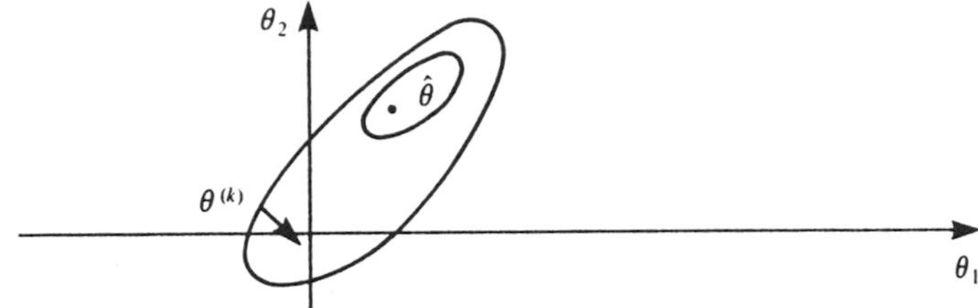

Figure 13.1: Steepest Ascent Method

The steepest ascent direction at $\theta^{(k)}$ is orthogonal to the tangent to the isocurve passing through $\theta^{(k)}$. In Figure 13.1, such a direction is almost orthogonal to the desired direction $(\theta^{(k)}, \hat{\theta})$. Hence, the method of steepest ascent may lead to a large number of iterations.

c) Newton Method

The basic idea of the Newton method is to replace the function V by its quadratic approximation in a neighborhood of $\theta^{(k)}$ at every step. At step k, a quadratic approximation gives

$$V(\theta^{(k)} + d) \# V(\theta^{(k)}) + g'(\theta^{(k)}) \cdot d + \frac{1}{2} d' \mathbf{G}(\theta^{(k)}) d.$$

To determine the vector $d^{(k)}$ that maximizes such an approximation, it suffices to solve the first-order conditions. This gives

$$d^{(k)} = -\mathbf{G}(\theta^{(k)})^{-1} g(\theta^{(k)}). \tag{13.8}$$

Hence we obtain an iteration formula of the form

$$\theta^{(k+1)} = \theta^{(k)} - \mu^{(k)} \mathbf{G}(\theta^{(k)})^{-1} g(\theta^{(k)}). \tag{13.9}$$

Remark 13.2: The preceding argument is clearly valid only if the vector $d^{(k)}$ given in equation (13.8) corresponds to a local maximum of the quadratic approximation. This is true when the Hessian $\mathbf{G}(\theta^{(k)})$ is negative definite. Thus the Newton method will behave properly when the objective function V is globally concave. When V is not globally concave, it will be necessary to modify the algorithm. Also note that using formula (13.4) to obtain $\mu^{(k)}$ we obtain $\mu^{(k)} = 1$ as expected.

Remark 13.3: When the objective function V is globally concave, the Newton method can be interpreted as a method of steepest ascent where the matrix defining the norm used at step k is given by $\mathbf{B}^{(k)} = -\mathbf{G}(\theta^{(k)})$.

Remark 13.4: Another interpretation of the Newton method, based on geometrical arguments, is obtained from the first-order conditions. Recall that these conditions are $g(\hat{\theta}) = 0$. To simplify, consider the case $p = 1$. Then, finding $\hat{\theta}$ is equivalent to finding a zero of the function g. At the kth iteration we can replace the function g by its tangent at $\theta^{(k)}$. Correspondingly, we can replace $\hat{\theta}$ by the value of θ where this tangent intersects the horizontal axis. Hence, when $p = 1$, the Newton algorithm can be represented geometrically as in Figure 13.2.

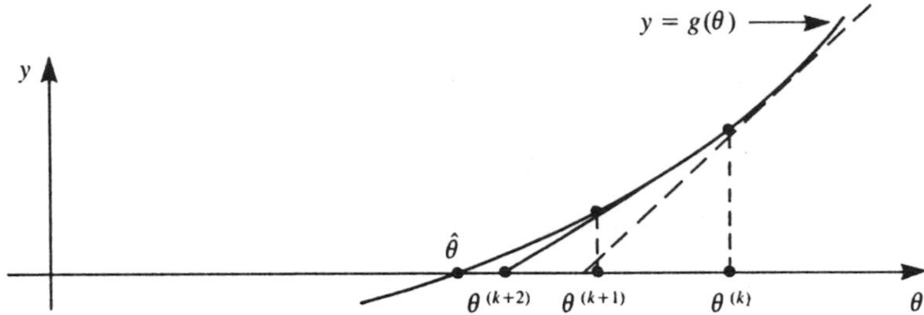

Figure 13.2: Newton Method

The equation of the tangent at $\theta^{(k)}$ to the curve defined by $y = g(\theta)$ is

$$y - g(\theta^{(k)}) = \frac{\partial g(\theta^{(k)})}{\partial \theta}(\theta - \theta^{(k)}) = \mathbf{G}(\theta^{(k)})(\theta - \theta^{(k)}).$$

The intersection point of this tangent with the horizontal axis is determined by the value $\theta^{(k+1)}$ satisfying

$$-g(\theta^{(k)}) = \mathbf{G}(\theta^{(k)})(\theta^{(k+1)} - \theta^{(k)}).$$

Thus

$$\theta^{(k+1)} = \theta^{(k)} - (\mathbf{G}(\theta^{(k)}))^{-1} g(\theta^{(k)}).$$

This is simply the iteration formula of the Newton algorithm.

d) Quasi Newton Methods

We noted that a Newton algorithm may exhibit undesired properties when the Hessian is not negative definite (see Remark 13.2). Some modifications to this algorithm, which have been proposed, consist in replacing the Hessian $\mathbf{G}(\theta^{(k)})$ by a negative definite matrix $\bar{\mathbf{G}}^{(k)}$ that approximates $\mathbf{G}(\theta^{(k)})$.

(i) Levenberg–Marquardt Algorithm

In this algorithm a scalar matrix is added to the Hessian so that

$$\bar{\mathbf{G}}^{(k)} = \mathbf{G}(\theta^{(k)}) + \gamma^{(k)}\mathbf{I}. \tag{13.10}$$

The scalar $\gamma^{(k)}$ is chosen to be negative and sufficiently small so that $\bar{\mathbf{G}}^{(k)} \prec 0$. It suffices to choose $\gamma^{(k)}$ smaller than minus the largest eigenvalue of $\mathbf{G}(\theta^{(k)})$.

In practice, one avoids in general to compute the eigenvectors and eigenvalues of the Hessian. A common procedure is to select a value $\gamma^{(k)}$ in a more or less heuristic fashion so as to increase the value of the criterion function V.

(ii) Davidson–Fletcher–Powell Algorithm

In this algorithm, an approximation to $\mathbf{G}(\theta^{(k)})^{-1}$ is computed recursively at every step. Let $\mathbf{H}^{(k)}$ denote such an approximation. Then the algorithm is as follows:

(i) A direction $d^{(k)}$ is determined according to $d^{(k)} = -\mathbf{H}^{(k)} g(\theta^{(k)})$.

(ii) An optimal size $\mu^{(k)}$ is obtained as a solution to the maximization of $V(\theta^{(k)} + \mu d^{(k)})$.

(iii) A new value of θ is obtained according to $\theta^{(k+1)} = \theta^{(k)} + \mu^{(k)}\, d^{(k)}$.

(iv) The matrix $\mathbf{H}$ is updated according to

$$\begin{aligned} \mathbf{H}^{(k+1)} = \mathbf{H}^{(k)} & \\ & - \frac{\mathbf{H}^{(k)} \left(g(\theta^{(k+1)}) - g(\theta^{(k)})\right) \left(g(\theta^{(k+1)}) - g(\theta^{(k)})\right)' \mathbf{H}^{(k)}}{\left(g(\theta^{(k+1)}) - g(\theta^{(k)})\right)' \mathbf{H}^{(k)} \left(g(\theta^{(k+1)}) - g(\theta^{(k)})\right)} \\ & + \frac{\mu^{(k)} d^{(k)} d^{(k)\prime}}{(g(\theta^{(k+1)}) - g(\theta^{(k)}))' d^{(k)}}. \end{aligned}$$

e) Approximate Derivation

The various gradient methods presented above rely on the gradient function $g(\theta) = \partial V(\theta)/\partial\theta$. In practice, it may be difficult to differentiate the function V analytically. Then $g(\theta^{(k)})$ can be replaced by an approximate value. Specifically, a partial derivative such as the jth component of $g(\theta^{(k)})$ is the slope of a tangent. Hence it can be approximated naturally by the slope of an approximate line. Let e_j denote the vector whose components are all equal to zero with the exception of the jth component which is equal to one. Let h be a positive scalar. Two natural approximations to $g(\theta^{(k)})$ are

$$g_j^{(k)} = \frac{V(\theta^{(k)} + he_j) - V(\theta^{(k)})}{h},$$

or

$$\bar{g}_j^{(k)} = \frac{V(\theta^{(k)} + he_j) - V(\theta^{(k)} - he_j)}{2h}. \tag{13.11}$$

In general, the value $V(\theta^{(k)})$ is computed within the algorithm when determining, for instance, the stepsize or when checking the increase of the objective function. Then it is readily seen that the above second approximation requires twice as many evaluations of the function V. In general, however, $\bar{g}_j^{(k)}$ is a more accurate approximation to the jth partial derivative than $g_j^{(k)}$. For such reasons the first approximation is frequently used in the first steps of the algorithm while the second approximation is used when the algorithm is close to convergence.

13.1.2 Gradient Methods and ML Estimation

In this section, we shall see how gradient methods can be used to determine estimators obtained by maximizing or minimizing some criterion functions. To simplify, we restrict ourselves to estimation by maximum likelihood. It is, however, easy to adapt the results and discussions presented below to other estimation methods.

We assume that n independent and identically distributed observations (Y_i, X_i), $i = 1, \ldots, n$, are available. The conditional density of Y_i given X_i is assumed known up to some parameter vector θ with density $f(y_i \mid x_i; \theta)$. A conditional maximum likelihood estimator of θ corresponds to a maximum of the conditional likelihood function

$$\log \ell(y \mid x; \theta) = \sum_{i=1}^{n} \log f(y_i \mid x_i; \theta).$$

Thus we have

$$\begin{aligned} V(\theta) &= \log \ell(y \mid x; \theta) \\ &= \sum_{i=1}^{n} \log f(y_i \mid x_i; \theta). \end{aligned} \tag{13.12}$$

The first and second partial derivatives are

$$\begin{aligned} g(\theta) &= \frac{\partial \log \ell(y \mid x; \theta)}{\partial \theta} = \sum_{i=1}^{n} \frac{\partial \log f(y_i \mid x_i; \theta)}{\partial \theta}, \\ \mathbf{G}(\theta) &= \frac{\partial^2 \log \ell(y \mid x; \theta)}{\partial \theta\, \partial \theta'} = \sum_{i=1}^{n} \frac{\partial^2 \log f(y_i \mid x_i; \theta)}{\partial \theta\, \partial \theta'}. \end{aligned}$$

Before introducing some algorithms designed for the determination of $\hat{\theta}$, it is useful to make three remarks:

(i) From a practical point of view, the estimator $\hat{\theta}$ is not the only object of interest. In particular, its precision is of interest. Thus it is desirable to have algorithms that can also provide an estimated value of this precision.

(ii) An algorithm will be more efficient the closer the initial value $\theta^{(0)}$ is to the desired value $\hat{\theta}$. This is because, in the neighborhood of $\hat{\theta}$, the function V is approximately concave, which is a property useful to many algorithms such as the Newton method. In addition, by starting from an initial value close to $\hat{\theta}$, we can expect that the number of steps required for numerical convergence of the algorithm will be smaller.

Clearly, the main difficulty is to find a close value to $\hat{\theta}$ since $\hat{\theta}$ is unknown. In general, such a difficulty is resolved as follows. Suppose that a simple consistent estimator $\tilde{\theta}$ of θ_0 is available, where θ_0 denotes the true value of the parameter θ. Then, provided the number of observations is large, we have $\tilde{\theta} \# \theta_0$ and $\hat{\theta} \# \theta_0$. Hence $\tilde{\theta} \# \hat{\theta}$ so that we can choose $\theta^{(0)} = \tilde{\theta}$ as an initial value.

Thus, the determination of the ML estimator is often done in two steps:

— In a first step, a consistent but frequently imprecise estimator that is easy to compute is determined.

— In a second step, this preliminary estimate is used as an initial value for some algorithm that determines the maximum likelihood estimator.

The second step, which is heavier computationally than the first step, allows us to improve the precision of the original estimator $\tilde{\theta}$ since the estimator $\hat{\theta}$ is not only consistent but also asymptotically efficient.

(iii) A case quite favorable to algorithms such as the Newton algorithm is when the log-likelihood function is concave in the parameters. In Chapter 7 we noted that concavity is satisfied in some important models when the model is suitably reparameterized. Thus, a suitable reparameterization of a model is useful not only because it may simplify the proofs of some properties (see Chapter 7) but also because it is desirable from a numerical point of view.

a) Newton–Raphson Algorithm

This algorithm is a direct application of the Newton method. The iteration formula is

$$\theta^{(k+1)} = \theta^{(k)} - \mu^{(k)} \left(\frac{\partial^2 \log \ell(y \mid x; \theta^{(k)})}{\partial \theta \, \partial \theta'} \right)^{-1} \frac{\partial \log \ell(y \mid x; \theta^{(k)})}{\partial \theta}. \tag{13.13}$$

The method presents the same disadvantage as the Newton method. Namely, the matrix

$$\mathbf{G}(\theta^{(k)}) = \frac{\partial^2 \log \ell(y \mid x; \theta^{(k)})}{\partial \theta \, \partial \theta'}$$

is not necessarily negative definite.

Note that, when the algorithm converges to $\hat{\theta}$, the matrix premultiplying the score vector in equation (13.13) converges to

$$\begin{aligned} -(\mathbf{G}(\hat{\theta}))^{-1} &= -\left(\frac{\partial^2 \log \ell(y \mid x; \hat{\theta})}{\partial \theta \, \partial \theta'} \right)^{-1} \\ &= \left(-\sum_{i=1}^{n} \frac{\partial^2 \log f(y_i \mid x_i; \hat{\theta})}{\partial \theta \, \partial \theta'} \right)^{-1}. \end{aligned}$$

From Section 7.5.3 it follows that the premultiplying matrix in equation (13.13) is, up to a scalar factor, an estimator of

$$E\left(-\frac{\partial^2 \log f(Y \mid X; \theta_0)}{\partial \theta \, \partial \theta'} \right)^{-1},$$

i.e., of the inverse of the Fisher information matrix associated with one observation. It follows that $-(\mathbf{G}(\hat{\theta}))^{-1} \# V_{as}\hat{\theta}$. Hence an estimate of the precision of the ML estimator is determined at the last step of the algorithm.

b) Score Algorithm

The preceding interpretation in terms of precision can be used to modify the Newton–Raphson algorithm. Namely, at the true parameter value θ_0, it follows from the Strong Law of Large Numbers that

$$-\frac{1}{n}\sum_{i=1}^{n}\frac{\partial^2 \log f(y_i \mid x_i;\theta_0)}{\partial\theta\,\partial\theta'} \# E_{\theta_0}\left(-\frac{\partial^2 \log f(Y \mid X;\theta_0)}{\partial\theta\,\partial\theta'}\right).$$

This suggests to approximate minus the Hessian by

$$-\frac{\partial^2 \log \ell(y \mid x;\theta)}{\partial\theta\,\partial\theta'} \# -nE_{\theta}\left(\frac{\partial^2 \log f(Y \mid X;\theta)}{\partial\theta\,\partial\theta'}\right).$$

Because observations are assumed independent and identically distributed, the latter quantity is equal to

$$E_{\theta}\left(-\frac{\partial^2 \log \ell(Y \mid X;\theta)}{\partial\theta\,\partial\theta'}\right),$$

i.e., to the Fisher information matrix $\mathcal{I}(\theta)$ corresponding to the conditional model. Then the score algorithm is a quasi Newton method where the Hessian is replaced by $-\mathcal{I}(\theta)$. The iteration formula is

$$\theta^{(k+1)} = \theta^{(k)} + \mu^{(k)}(\mathcal{I}(\theta^{(k)}))^{-1}\frac{\partial \log \ell(y \mid x;\theta^{(k)})}{\partial\theta}. \tag{13.14}$$

Note that the matrix premultiplying the score vector is now symmetric positive semidefinite.

c) Berndt–Hall–Hall–Hausman Algorithm

Consider again the true parameter value θ_0. We know that the Fisher information matrix admits two equivalent forms, which are

$$E_{\theta_0}\left(\frac{-\partial^2 \log f(Y \mid X;\theta_0)}{\partial\theta\,\partial\theta'}\right)$$

and

$$E_{\theta_0}\left(\frac{\partial \log f(Y \mid X;\theta_0)}{\partial \theta}\frac{\partial \log f(Y \mid X;\theta_0)}{\partial \theta'}\right).$$

In addition, from the Strong Law of Large Numbers we have for n large

$$\begin{aligned} & E_{\theta_0}\left(\frac{\partial \log f(Y \mid X;\theta_0)}{\partial \theta}\frac{\partial \log f(Y \mid X;\theta_0)}{\partial \theta'}\right) \\ & \quad \# \frac{1}{n}\sum_{i=1}^{n}\frac{\partial \log f(y_i \mid x_i;\theta_0)}{\partial \theta}\frac{\partial \log f(y_i \mid x_i;\theta_0)}{\partial \theta'}. \end{aligned}$$

This suggests to approximate minus the Hessian by

$$\sum_{i=1}^{n}\frac{\partial \log f(y_i \mid x_i;\theta_0)}{\partial \theta}\frac{\partial \log f(y_i \mid x_i;\theta_0)}{\partial \theta'}.$$

The Berndt–Hall–Hall–Hausman (BHHH) algorithm is a quasi Newton method of which the iteration formula is

$$\begin{aligned} \theta^{(k+1)} &= \theta^{(k)} + \mu^{(k)}\left(\sum_{i=1}^{n}\frac{\partial \log f(y_i \mid x_i;\theta^{(k)})}{\partial \theta}\frac{\partial \log f(y_i \mid x_i;\theta^{(k)})}{\partial \theta'}\right) \\ & \quad \times \frac{\partial \log \ell(y \mid x;\theta^{(k)})}{\partial \theta}. \end{aligned} \tag{13.15}$$

As before, the matrix premultiplying the score vector is positive semidefinite.

Remark 13.5: An important advantage of the BHHH algorithm is that it requires the analytical or numerical computation of the first partial derivatives only. In particular, it does not require the determination of the second partial derivatives.

d) Application to a Gaussian model

As an illustration, we consider the conditional Gaussian model defined by

$$y_i = g(x_i,\theta) + u_i,$$

where the error terms u_i are independently and identically distributed $N(0,1)$. Maximum likelihood estimation is here equivalent to nonlinear least squares estimation. We have

$$\log \ell(y \mid x;\theta) = -\frac{n}{2}\log 2\pi - \frac{1}{2}\sum_{i=1}^{n}(y_i - g(x_i,\theta))^2.$$

The first and second partial derivatives are

$$\begin{aligned}
\frac{\partial \log \ell(y \mid x;\theta)}{\partial \theta} &= \sum_{i=1}^{n} \frac{\partial g(x_i,\theta)}{\partial \theta}(y_i - g(x_i,\theta)),\\
\frac{\partial^2 \log \ell(y \mid x;\theta)}{\partial \theta\, \partial \theta'} &= \sum_{i=1}^{n} \frac{\partial^2 g(x_i,\theta)}{\partial \theta\, \partial \theta'}(y_i - g(x_i,\theta))\\
&\quad - \sum_{i=1}^{n} \frac{\partial g(x_i,\theta)}{\partial \theta}\frac{\partial g(x_i,\theta)}{\partial \theta'}.
\end{aligned}$$

The Fisher Information matrix is

$$\mathcal{I}(\theta) = \sum_{i=1}^{n} \frac{\partial g(x_i,\theta)}{\partial \theta}\frac{\partial g(x_i,\theta)}{\partial \theta'}.$$

We can determine explicitly the various algorithms presented above. The iteration formulae are as follows.

Newton–Raphson Algorithm:

$$\theta^{(k)} = \theta^{(k)} - \mu^{(k)} \left(\sum_{i=1}^{n} \frac{\partial^2 g(x_i,\theta^{(k)})}{\partial \theta\, \partial \theta'}(y_i - g(x_i,\theta^{(k)})) \right.$$

$$\left. - \sum_{i=1}^{n} \frac{\partial g(x_i,\theta^{(k)})}{\partial \theta}\ \frac{\partial g(x_i,\theta^{(k)})}{\partial \theta'} \right)^{-1} \sum_{i=1}^{n} \frac{\partial g(x_i,\theta^{(k)})}{\partial \theta'}(y_i - g(x_i,\theta^{(k)})).$$

Score Algorithm:

$$\begin{aligned}
\theta^{(k+1)} &= \theta^{(k)} + \mu^{(k)} \left(\sum_{i=1}^{n} \frac{\partial g(x_i,\theta^{(k)})}{\partial \theta}\frac{\partial g(x_i,\theta^{(k)})}{\partial \theta'} \right)^{-1}\\
&\quad \sum_{i=1}^{n} \frac{\partial g(x_i,\theta^{(k)})}{\partial \theta}(y_i - g(x_i,\theta^{(k)})).
\end{aligned}$$

BHHH Algorithm:

$$\theta^{(k+1)} = \theta^{(k)} + \mu^{(k)} \left(\sum_{i=1}^{n} \frac{\partial g(x_i,\theta^{(k)})}{\partial \theta}\frac{\partial g(x_i,\theta^{(k)})}{\partial \theta'}(y_i - g(x_i,\theta^{(k)}))^2 \right)^{-1}$$

$$\sum_{i=1}^{n} \frac{\partial g(x_i,\theta^{(k)})}{\partial \theta}(y_i - g(x_i,\theta^{(k)})).$$

In this example the simplest procedure is the score algorithm. In addition, its iteration formula has an interesting interpretation based on a linearization of the original nonlinear econometric model with respect to the parameters (see Exercise 13.2). Relative to the score algorithm, the BHHH algorithm is obtained by weighting the terms

$$\frac{\partial g(x_i, \theta^{(k)})}{\partial \theta} \frac{\partial g(x_i, \theta^{(k)})}{\partial \theta'}$$

by the squares of the residuals $(y_i - g(x_i, \theta^{(k)}))^2$. Moreover, it can be seen that these estimation residuals are implicitly computed at every step of the algorithm. Hence their values are readily retrieved.

13.1.3 Direct Search Methods

Direct search methods evaluate the criterion function at various points and retain a point that gives the largest value of the criterion function. In general, direct search methods are not based on theoretical justifications and can be computationally intensive especially when the dimension of the parameter θ is large. Direct search methods, however, present the advantage of not requiring the determination of the derivatives of the criterion function. In addition, direct search methods are frequently used for determining the stepsize $\mu^{(k)}$ arising in gradient type procedures.

a) Grid Search

To begin with, suppose that the criterion function V depends on a scalar parameter θ so that $p = 1$. A grid search consists in choosing a set of values θ_j of possible values for θ, for instance, -5, -4, -3, -2, -1, 0, 1, 2, 3, 4, and 5, and in evaluating the value $V(\theta_j)$ of the criterion at every of these points θ_j. Because the number of chosen points is finite, there exists a point for which the criterion function is maximized. For instance, suppose that

$$V(2) \geq V(\theta_j), \ \forall \ j, \text{ with } \theta_j \neq 2.$$

Hence $V(2) \geq V(3)$ and $V(2) \geq V(1)$. Thus, if the function V is continuous, then V has a local maximum on the interval $(1, 3)$. Then another grid search is pursued on the interval $(1, 3)$ so as to obtain a more precise approximation to the local maximum. For instance, the function V can be evaluated at the points 1.0, 1.1, 1.2, ..., 2.9, and 3.0. If one desires, the procedure can be pursued further. When θ is a scalar parameter, this method is clearly simple and requires a relatively small number of function evaluations, thirty in our example.

A grid search method, however, is not as appealing when the dimension p of the parameter θ is large. This is because a grid search must be based on all the components of θ simultaneously. For instance, if 10 possible values are selected for each component of θ in a first grid search, then there will be 10^p function evaluations. Then, if twenty values are used for each component in a second grid search, then there will be 20^p additional function evaluations. Table 13.1 gives an idea of the overall computational costs as the size p of the parameter increases.

Table 13.1

Size p	1	2	3	p
Number of Evaluations	30	500	9000	$10^p + 20^p$

It is clear that computational costs constitute an important limitation to a grid search method.

b) Random Grid Search

The number of function evaluations can be decreased substantially when a grid search is not undertaken systematically. This is the case for a random search. A random grid search, however, does not produce necessarily a local maximum.

An example of a random grid search is as follows. At the kth step, one has an approximation $\theta^{(k)}$ and p scalars $\alpha_j^{(k)}$, $j = 1, \ldots, p$, that reflect the quality of the approximation $\theta^{(k)}$ along the p components of θ. Then q_k independent values from the p-dimensional uniform distribution on $(-1, +1)^p$ are drawn. Let $(r_{i1}, \ldots, r_{ip})'$, $i = 1, \ldots, q_k$, denote the observed values of these draws. Next, among the points $(\theta_j^{(k)} + r_{ij}\alpha_j^{(k)})$, $i = 1, \ldots, q_k$, one determines the point that gives the largest value for the citerion function V.

This point is retained as a new approximation $\mu^{(k+1)}$. The "errors"

$\alpha_j^{(k)}$ are decreased by a factor a priori given

$$\alpha_j^{(k+1)} = (1-\varepsilon)\alpha_j^{(k)}, \text{ with } 0 < \varepsilon < 1.$$

13.2 Fixed Point Methods

13.2.1 Principles

One is led frequently to solve an equation of the kind $V(\theta) = \theta$ where V is a mapping from $\Theta \subset \mathbb{R}^p$ to $\Theta \subset \mathbb{R}^p$. This problem is equivalent to finding a *fixed point* of the mapping V.

A fixed point is often determined by means of the so-called *Gauss–Seidel algorithm*, which is defined by

$$\theta^{(k+1)} = V(\theta^{(k)}). \tag{13.16}$$

If V is a continuous mapping and if the sequence of values $\theta^{(k)}$ converges to a limit $\hat{\theta}$, then we must have

$$\hat{\theta} = \lim_{k\to\infty} \theta^{(k+1)} = \lim_{k\to\infty} V(\theta^{(k)}) = V(\lim_{k\to\infty} \theta^{(k)}) = V(\hat{\theta}).$$

Hence $\hat{\theta}$ is a fixed point as required.

Clearly, convergence of the sequence $\theta^{(k)}$ is not ensured. If the mapping V is arbitrary, the sequence $\theta^{(k)}$ may not converge or may cycle indefinitely. Some sufficient conditions for convergence are known. The next property gives one of these.

Property 13.4: *Suppose that the mapping V is such that there exists a scalar α, with $0 \le \alpha < 1$ and*

$$\forall \theta,\ \bar{\theta} \in \Theta : \|V(\theta) - V(\bar{\theta})\| \le \alpha\|\theta - \bar{\theta}\|.$$

Then the algorithm (13.16) converges.

PROOF:

We have

$$\|\theta^{(k+1)} - \theta^{(k)}\| = \|V(\theta^{(k)}) - V(\theta^{(k-1)})\| \le \alpha\|\theta^{(k)} - \theta^{(k-1)}\|.$$

By induction, it follows that

$$\|\theta^{(k+1)} - \theta^{(k)}\| \le \alpha^k\|\theta^{(1)} - \theta^{(0)}\|.$$

The sequence $\theta^{(k)}$ is such that the series with general term $\theta^{(k+1)} - \theta^{(k)}$ converges normally because $\|\theta^{(k+1)} - \theta^{(k)}\|$ is dominated by the general term of a convergent series. Hence the series with the general term $\theta^{(k+1)} - \theta^{(k)}$ also converges, i.e.

$$\sum_{k=0}^{K} (\theta^{(k+1)} - \theta^{(k)}) = \theta^{(K+1)} - \theta^{(0)}$$

converges. □

In practice, fixed point algorithms may be applied to the first-order conditions associated with M-estimators. For instance, consider the maximum likelihood estimator $\hat{\theta}$. It satisfies the first-order conditions

$$\frac{\partial \log \ell(y \mid x; \hat{\theta})}{\partial \theta} = 0.$$

In some cases, such conditions can be rewritten as

$$\hat{\theta} = V(y \mid x; \hat{\theta}),$$

which corresponds to a fixed point problem.

13.2.2 An Example: The Fair Algorithm

We consider a simple Tobit model. The latent variables Y_i^* are assumed to satisfy a Gaussian linear model $Y_i^* = x_i b + u_i$ where the error terms u_i are independent and identically distributed $N(0, \sigma^2)$. The observed endogenous variables are related to the latent variables by

$$Y_i = \begin{cases} Y_i^*, & \text{if } Y_i^* \geq 0, \\ 0, & \text{otherwise.} \end{cases}$$

Let J_0 and J_1 denote the subsets of indices corresponding to $Y_i = 0$ and $Y_i = 1$, respectively. The likelihood equations are

$$\frac{\partial \log \ell}{\partial b} = -\sum_{J_0} \frac{1}{\sigma} \frac{\phi(x_i b/\sigma)}{\Phi(-x_i b/\sigma)} x_i' + \frac{1}{\sigma^2} \sum_{J_1} (y_i - x_i b) x_i' = 0,$$

and

$$\frac{\partial \log \ell}{\partial \sigma^2} = \frac{1}{2\sigma^2} \sum_{J_0} \frac{x_i b}{\sigma} \frac{\phi(x_i b/\sigma)}{\Phi(-x_i b/\sigma)} - \frac{n_1}{2\sigma^2} + \frac{1}{2\sigma^4} \sum_{J_1} (y_i - x_i b)^2 = 0,$$

where n_1 denotes the number of "complete" observations, i.e., the number of elements of J_1. These first-order conditions can be rewritten as

$$b = \left(\sum_{J_1} x_i' x_i\right)^{-1} \sum_{J_1} x_i' y_i - \sigma \left(\sum_{J_1} x_i' x_i\right)^{-1} \left(\sum_{J_0} \frac{\phi(x_i b/\sigma)}{\Phi(-x_i b/\sigma)} x_i'\right)$$

and

$$\sigma^2 = \frac{1}{n_1} \sum_{J_1} (y_i - x_i b) y_i.$$

These equations are of the form

$$\begin{cases} b = V_1(b, \sigma^2), \\ \sigma^2 = V_2(b). \end{cases}$$

Fair algorithm follows as

$$\begin{cases} b^{(k+1)} = V_1(b^{(k)}, \sigma^{2(k)}), \\ \sigma^{2(k+1)} = V_2(b^{(k)}). \end{cases}$$

Fair algorithm may not converge. It is, however, easily applied. In addition, the preceding formulae can be readily interpreted. For instance, the first equation shows that $b^{(k+1)}$ is the sum of the OLS estimator of b using the complete observations, i.e., $\left(\sum_{J_1} x_i' x_i\right)^{-1} \sum_{J_1} x_i' y_i$, and a term correcting the OLS bias

$$-\sigma^{(k)} \left(\sum_{J_1} x_i' x_i\right)^{-1} \left(\sum_{J_0} \frac{\phi(x_i b^{(k)}/\sigma^{(k)})}{\Phi(-x_i b^{(k)}/\sigma^{(k)})} x_i'\right).$$

13.3 EM Algorithm

The Expectation Maximization (EM) algorithm is used for the numerical determination of the maximum likelihood estimator when the observable model is derived from a latent model. When the latent model is exponential, the iteration formula defining the EM algorithm takes a simple form, which is easily interpreted.

13.3.1 Definition

The latent variables $Y^* = (Y_1^*, \ldots, Y_n^*)'$ are assumed to have a density $\ell^*(y^* \mid x; \theta)$, where x denotes the values taken by some exogenous variables. The observed endogenous variables $Y = (Y_1, \ldots, Y_n)'$ are related to the latent variables through a mapping h so that $Y_i = h(Y_i^*)$, $i = 1, \ldots, n$. The observed endogenous variables have a density denoted $\ell(y \mid x; \theta)$. Thereafter the parameter vector θ is assumed to be identified in the observable model and, therefore, identified in the latent model.

If the latent variables $Y_1^*, \ldots, Y_n^*$ were observable, the maximum likelihood estimator of θ would be obtained as a solution to the maximization of $\log \ell^*(y^* \mid x; \theta)$. Because the variables $Y_1^*, \ldots, Y_n^*$ are not observed, one may consider replacing the original criterion function by its best approximation based on the observed variables $Y_1, \ldots, Y_n$. This leads to the maximization of the conditional expectation of the latent log-likelihood function given the observed variables. Such an optimization problem, when solved directly, does not lead, however, to satisfactory results (see Exercise 13.4). As a consequence, the actual method will be based on a iterative procedure.

Specifically, the following function is introduced

$$Q(\theta, \tilde{\theta}) = E_{\tilde{\theta}} \left(\log \ell^*(Y^* \mid x; \theta) \mid Y = y \right). \tag{13.17}$$

Note that the conditional expectation is evaluated at value $\tilde{\theta}$ that may differ from the value θ appearing in ℓ^*. Also, the expectation is taken conditional on $X = x$.

Every iteration of the EM algorithm consists of two steps, which are an evaluation of the expectation (the E step) followed by a maximization (the M step). If $\theta^{(q)}$ denotes the approximate value obtained at the qth iteration, then the approximation $\theta^{(q+1)}$ at the following iteration is obtained after

$$\left\{ \begin{array}{ll} \text{Step E :} & \text{Evaluation of } Q(\theta, \theta^{(q)}), \\ \text{Step M :} & \text{Determination of } \theta^{(q+1)} \text{as a solution to} \\ & \text{the maximization of } Q(\theta, \theta^{(q)}). \end{array} \right. \tag{13.18}$$

The EM algorithm is especially interesting from a numerical point of view when the optimization of $Q(\theta, \theta^{(q)})$ is much simpler than the optimization of $\log \ell(y \mid x; \theta)$.

13.3.2 Application to Exponential Latent Models

In this subsection we consider the special case where the latent model is exponential with density of the form

$$\ell^*(y^* \mid x;\theta) = \exp(\theta' T(y^*,x) + B(y^*,x) + C(\theta,x)). \tag{13.19}$$

Hence, the prediction of the latent log-likelihood function is obtained directly as

$$\begin{aligned} Q(\theta,\tilde{\theta}) &= E_{\tilde{\theta}}(\log \ell^*(Y^* \mid x;\theta) \mid Y = y) \\ &= \theta' E_{\tilde{\theta}}(T(Y^*,x) \mid Y = y) + E_{\tilde{\theta}}(B(Y^*,x) \mid Y = y) + C(\theta,x). \end{aligned}$$

Therefore, at the $(q+1)$th iteration, we are led to maximize the quantity

$$\theta' E_{\theta^{(q)}}(T(Y^*,x) \mid Y = y) + C(\theta,x) \tag{13.20}$$

with respect to θ. The first-order conditions are

$$E_{\theta^{(q)}}(T(Y^*,x) \mid Y = y) = -\frac{\partial C}{\partial \theta}(\theta^{(q+1)},x). \tag{13.21}$$

Hence, when the latent model is exponential, the E step only requires the determination of the prediction of the canonical statistic $E(T(Y^*,x) \mid Y = y)$.

Remark 13.6: For an exponential family of the form considered above, we know that

$$E_\theta \frac{\partial \log \ell^*(Y^* \mid x;\theta)}{\partial \theta} = 0,$$

i.e.

$$\int \left(T(y^*,x) + \frac{\partial C}{\partial \theta}(\theta,x) \right) \ell^*(y^* \mid x;\theta) d\mu(y^*) = 0,$$

i.e.

$$E_\theta T(Y^*,x) + \frac{\partial C}{\partial \theta}(\theta,x) = 0.$$

It follows that the first-order conditions are equivalent to equating the conditional and unconditional expectations of the canonical statistic. That is, we have

$$E_{\theta^{(q)}}(T(Y^*,x) \mid Y = y) = E_{\theta^{(q+1)}}(T(Y^*,x)). \tag{13.22}$$

Example 13.1: The EM algorithm can take even a simpler form when the latent model is a particular exponential model. As an illustration, we consider the usual Gaussian linear model, where the variance of the error term is assumed to be equal to one. Hence the latent model is $Y_i^* = x_i b + u_i$, where the error terms u_i are independently and identically distributed $N(0,1)$. The observed variables are related to the latent variables by $Y_i = \mathbb{1}_{Y_i^* \geq 0}$.

The latent log-likelihood function is

$$\begin{aligned}\log \ell^*(y^* \mid x; b) &= -\frac{n}{2}\log 2\pi - \frac{1}{2}\sum_{i=1}^{n}(y_i^* - x_i b)^2 \\ &= -\frac{n}{2}\log 2\pi - \frac{1}{2}\sum_{i=1}^{n} y_i^{*2} + \sum_{i=1}^{n} y_i^* x_i b - \frac{1}{2}\sum_{i=1}^{n}(x_i b)^2.\end{aligned}$$

The prediction of the latent log-likelihood function is

$$\begin{aligned}Q(b;\tilde{b}) &= -\frac{n}{2}\log 2\pi - \frac{1}{2}E_{\tilde{b}}\left(\sum_{i=1}^{n} Y_i^{2*} \mid Y = y\right) \\ &\quad + E_{\tilde{b}}\left(\sum_{i=1}^{n} Y_i^* x_i b \mid Y = y\right) - \frac{1}{2}\sum_{i=1}^{n}(x_i b)^2.\end{aligned}$$

In this case, the first-order conditions at the $(q+1)$th iteration reduce to

$$E_{b^{(q)}}\left(\sum_{i=1}^{n} Y_i^* x_i' \mid Y = y\right) = \sum_{i=1}^{n} x_i' x_i b^{(q+1)},$$

i.e.

$$b^{(q+1)} = \left(\sum_{i=1}^{n} x_i' x_i\right)^{-1} \sum_{i=1}^{n} x_i' E_{b^{(q)}}(Y_i^* \mid Y_i).$$

Thus the approximate value $b^{(q+1)}$ is simply the coefficient estimate in an OLS regression of the predictions $E_{b^{(q)}}(Y_i^* \mid Y_i = y_i)$ on the explanatory variables x_i. Since these predicitions are

$$E_{b^{(q)}}(Y_i^* \mid Y_i = y_i) = x_i b^{(q)} + \phi(x_i b^{(q)})\left(\frac{y_i}{\Phi(x_i b^{(q)})} - \frac{1 - y_i}{1 - \Phi(x_i b^{(q)})}\right),$$

the iteration formula becomes

$$b^{(q+1)} = b^{(q)}$$

$$+\left(\sum_{i=1}^{n} x_i' x_i\right)^{-1} \sum_{i=1}^{n} x_i' \phi(x_i b^{(q)})\left(\frac{y_i}{\Phi(x_i b^{(q)})} - \frac{1 - y_i}{1 - \Phi(x_i b^{(q)})}\right). \quad (13.23)$$

13.3.3 Properties

Property 13.5: *The EM algorithm is an increasing algorithm, i.e.*

$$\forall\, q,\ \log \ell(y \mid x; \theta^{(q+1)}) \geq \log \ell(y \mid x; \theta^{(q)}).$$

PROOF:

Let $L(\theta) = \log \ell(y \mid x; \theta)$. Define the function

$$H(\theta, \tilde{\theta}) = E_{\tilde{\theta}}(\log \ell(Y^* \mid Y, x; \theta) \mid Y = y),$$

which is the prediction of the conditional log-likelihood of Y^* given $Y = y$.

From

$$\log \ell^*(y^* \mid x; \theta) = \log \ell(y^* \mid y, x; \theta) + \log \ell(y \mid x; \theta),$$

it follows that

$$\begin{aligned} & E_{\tilde{\theta}}(\log \ell(Y^* \mid x; \theta) \mid Y = y) \\ & \quad = \quad E_{\tilde{\theta}}(\log \ell(Y^* \mid Y, x; \theta) \mid Y = y) + \log \ell(y \mid x; \theta). \end{aligned}$$

That is

$$Q(\theta, \tilde{\theta}) = H(\theta, \tilde{\theta}) + L(\theta).$$

Therefore

$$\begin{aligned} L(\theta^{(q+1)}) - L(\theta^{(q)}) \quad = \quad & \left(Q(\theta^{(q+1)}, \theta^{(q)}) - Q(\theta^{(q)}, \theta^{(q)})\right) \\ & + \left(H(\theta^{(q)}, \theta^{(q)}) - H(\theta^{(q+1)}, \theta^{(q)})\right). \end{aligned}$$

The first term in the right-hand side is positive since $\theta^{(q+1)}$ gives the maximum of the function $Q(\theta, \theta^{(q)})$ with respect to θ. Moreover, from Kullback inequality (see Property 1.1) we have $H(\theta, \tilde{\theta}) \leq H(\tilde{\theta}, \tilde{\theta}),\ \forall\, \theta, \tilde{\theta}$. Hence the second term in the right-hand side is also positive. These imply that $L(\theta^{(q+1)}) - L(\theta^{(q)}) \geq 0,\ \forall\, q$. Hence the EM algorithm is increasing. □

Property 13.6: *Suppose that the latent log-likelihood function is continuously differentiable. Suppose also that expectation and differentiation can be interchanged so that*

$$\frac{\partial}{\partial \theta} E_{\tilde{\theta}}(\log \ell^*(Y^* \mid x; \theta) \mid Y = y) = E_{\tilde{\theta}}\left(\frac{\partial}{\partial \theta} \log \ell^*(Y^* \mid x; \theta) \mid Y = y\right).$$

Lastly, suppose that the latter derivative is continuous in $(\theta, \tilde{\theta})$. *Then every limit point* $\theta^{(\infty)}$ *of the sequence* $\theta^{(q)}$ *satisfies the first-order conditions*

$$\frac{\partial \log \ell(y \mid x; \theta^{(\infty)})}{\partial \theta} = 0.$$

PROOF:

The approximate value $\theta^{(q+1)}$ satisfies the first-order conditions

$$\left(\frac{\partial Q(\theta, \theta^{(q)})}{\partial \theta} \right)_{\theta = \theta^{(q+1)}} = 0,$$

i.e.

$$E_{\theta^{(q)}} \left(\frac{\partial \log \ell^*(Y^* \mid x; \theta^{(q+1)})}{\partial \theta} \mid Y = y \right) = 0.$$

When q increases to infinity, we have

$$E_{\theta^{(\infty)}} \left(\frac{\partial \log \ell^*(Y^* \mid x; \theta^{(\infty)})}{\partial \theta} \mid Y = y \right) = 0.$$

since both $\theta^{(q)}$ and $\theta^{(q+1)}$ converge to θ^{∞}. Then it suffices to note that the conditional expectation of the latent score vector is equal to the observed score vector (see the appendix to Chapter 11). Hence

$$\frac{\partial \log \ell(Y \mid x; \theta^{(\infty)})}{\partial \theta} = 0.$$

□

Because the EM algorithm is increasing by Property 13.5, every limit point is necessarily a local maximum or a saddle point. It remains to study when the sequence $\theta^{(q)}$ is converging. In fact, convergence is not ensured and the simplest way to know when it occurs is to analyze the problem numerically (see Exercise 13.6 for some results).

13.4 Kalman Filter

The Kalman filter and the Kalman smoothing procedure studied in this section are algorithms that can be used to compute conditional expectations in a relatively general framework. This framework is called the *state space* framework.

13.4.1 State Space Models

We consider a model defined by the equations

$$\beta_{t+1} = \mathbf{F}_t \beta_t + \varepsilon_t, \tag{13.24}$$

and

$$z_t = \mathbf{H}_t' \beta_t + \eta_t, \quad t \geq 1, \tag{13.25}$$

where β_t is a random k-dimensional vector, called the *state vector* at time t. It is assumed that β_1 follows a normal distribution $N(m, \mathbf{P})$ and that the k-dimensional vectors ε_t, $t \geq 1$, are independently and identically distributed $N(0, \mathbf{Q})$. The $k \times k$ matrix $\mathbf{F}_t$, called the *transition matrix*, is nonrandom (see however Remark 13.11). Equation (13.24), called the *state equation*, defines completely the distribution of β_t for every $t \geq 1$.

The vector z_t, called the *measurement vector*, is of dimension n. The vectors η_t are mutually independent of ε_t (see Remark 13.9 for a generalization) and identically distributed $N(0, \mathbf{R})$. Equation (13.25), called the *measurement equation*, allows to define the distribution of z_t, $t \geq 1$. Together, equations (13.24) and (13.25) clearly determine the distribution of the process (β_t, z_t), $t \geq 1$, which is Gaussian.

The $n \times k$ matrix $\mathbf{H}_t$ is nonrandom (see Remark 13.11). It is called the *measurement matrix*. To simplify the notation, the matrices $\mathbf{Q}$ and $\mathbf{R}$ are assumed to be independent of t. Such an assumption is not necessary (see below).

Note that an important distinction between z_t and β_t is that z_t is observed while β_t is, in general, partially observed or unobserved. In any case, the information available at time t is $z_1, \ldots, z_t$.

Problems that we shall study within a state space framework are problems that involve the numerical determination of conditional expectations. Three kinds of such problems can be distinguished. Filtering problems focus on the computation of $E(\beta_t \mid z_1, \ldots, z_t)$, which is the optimal approximation to β_t given information available at time t. Smoothing problems focus on the computation of $E(\beta_s \mid z_1, \ldots, z_t)$ in the case where $s < t$. Hence these problems focus on the optimal approximation to β_s at a time $t > s$. Thirdly, prediction problems deal with the numerical determination of $E(\beta_s \mid z_1, \ldots, z_t)$ or $E(z_s \mid z_1, \ldots, z_t)$ where $s > t$. Before studying such problems, we now give some examples of state space models.

Example 13.2: Consider the second-order autoregressive model

$$z_t - \phi_1 z_{t-1} - \phi_2 z_{t-2} = u_t,$$

where u_t is a Gaussian white noise process with variance σ^2.

Let

$$\beta_t = \begin{pmatrix} z_t \\ z_{t-1} \end{pmatrix},$$

we have

$$\begin{cases} \beta_{t+1} = \begin{pmatrix} \phi_1 & \phi_2 \\ 1 & 0 \end{pmatrix} \beta_t + \begin{pmatrix} u_{t+1} \\ 0 \end{pmatrix}, \\ z_t = (1, 0)\beta_t. \end{cases}$$

Hence the model can be written in a state space form. Note that here the state vector is observed and that the error term η_t is zero. This form is sometimes called the *companion form.*

Example 13.3: Consider the first-order moving average model

$$z_t = u_t + \phi u_{t-1},$$

where u_t is a Gaussian white noise process with variance σ^2.

Let

$$\beta_t = \begin{pmatrix} z_t \\ \phi u_t \end{pmatrix},$$

we have

$$\begin{cases} \beta_{t+1} = \begin{pmatrix} 0 & 1 \\ 0 & 0 \end{pmatrix} \beta_t + \begin{pmatrix} u_{t+1} \\ \phi u_{t+1} \end{pmatrix}, \\ z_t = (1, 0)\beta_t. \end{cases}$$

Hence the measurement error is again zero. On the other hand, the state vector β_t is partially observed.

Example 13.4: Linear Model with Time Varying Coefficients

Consider the model

$$\begin{cases} z_t = x_t \beta_t + \eta_t, \\ \beta_{t+1} = \mathbf{F}\beta_t + \varepsilon_t, \end{cases}$$

where η and ε are independent Gaussian white noise processes of dimension one and k, respectively. The model is already in a state space form. Note that if $\mathbf{F} = \mathbf{I}$ and $\mathbf{Q} = V(\varepsilon_t) = 0$, then we obtain the classical linear model with constant coefficients over time. Note, however, that the parameter vector $\beta = \beta_t = \beta_1$ is considered as random and distributed $N(m, \mathbf{P})$. The latter distribution can be viewed as a prior distribution on β.

13.4.2 Kalman Covariance Filter

The Kalman covariance filter is an algorithm that is used to compute recursively the "filtered" state vector

$$\hat{\beta}_{t|t} = E(\beta_t \mid z_1, \ldots, z_t).$$

We introduce the following notation. Let

$$\begin{aligned}
\hat{\beta}_{t|t-1} &= E(\beta_t \mid z_1, \ldots, z_{t-1}), \\
\hat{z}_{t|t-1} &= E(z_t \mid z_1, \ldots, z_{t-1}), \\
\mathbf{\Sigma}_{t|t} &= E((\beta_t - \hat{\beta}_{t|t})(\beta_t - \hat{\beta}_{t|t})'), \\
\mathbf{\Sigma}_{t|t-1} &= E((\beta_t - \hat{\beta}_{t|t-1})(\beta_t - \hat{\beta}_{t|t-1})'), \\
\mathbf{M}_{t|t-1} &= E((z_t - \hat{z}_{t|t-1})(z_t - \hat{z}_{t|t-1})'), \\
\tilde{z}_t &= z_t - \hat{z}_{t|t-1} = z_t - \mathbf{H}_t'\hat{\beta}_{t|t-1}.
\end{aligned}$$

Then $\hat{\beta}_{t|t-1}$ and $\hat{z}_{t|t-1}$ are the predictions of β_t and z_t formed at time $t-1$. The matrices $\mathbf{\Sigma}_{t|t}$, $\mathbf{\Sigma}_{t|t-1}$ and $\mathbf{M}_{t|t-1}$ are the mean squared prediction errors and $\tilde{z}_t$ is the OLS residual in the regression of z_t on its past values.

Property 13.7: Kalman Covariance Filter

We have the following relations:

(i) $\hat{\beta}_{t|t} = \hat{\beta}_{t|t-1} + \mathbf{K}_t\tilde{z}_t$, *where the* gain *of the filter is*

$$\mathbf{K}_t = \mathbf{\Sigma}_{t|t-1}\mathbf{H}_t(\mathbf{H}_t'\mathbf{\Sigma}_{t|t-1}\mathbf{H}_t + \mathbf{R})^{-1}$$

(i') $\mathbf{\Sigma}_{t|t} = (\mathbf{I} - \mathbf{K}_t\mathbf{H}_t')\mathbf{\Sigma}_{t|t-1}$,

(ii) $\hat{\beta}_{t+1|t} = \mathbf{F}_t\hat{\beta}_{t|t}$,

(ii') $\mathbf{\Sigma}_{t+1|t} = \mathbf{F}_t\mathbf{\Sigma}_{t|t}\mathbf{F}_t' + \mathbf{Q}$,

(iii) $\hat{z}_{t+1|t} = \mathbf{H}_{t+1}'\hat{\beta}_{t+1|t}$,

(iii') $\mathbf{M}_{t+1|t} = \mathbf{H}_{t+1}'\mathbf{\Sigma}_{t+1|t}\mathbf{H}_{t+1} + \mathbf{R}$.

PROOF:

(i) We have

$$\begin{aligned}
\hat{\beta}_{t|t} &= E(\beta_t \mid z_1, \ldots, z_t) \\
&= E(\beta_t \mid z_1, \ldots, z_{t-1}, \tilde{z}_t).
\end{aligned}$$

In view of the identity between conditional expectation and linear regression with normal errors (see Property B.43), we have

$$\begin{aligned}\hat{\beta}_{t|t} &= E(\beta_t \mid z_1, \ldots, z_{t-1}) + E(\beta_t \mid \tilde{z}_t) - E\beta_t \\ &= \beta_{t|t-1} + E(\beta_t \mid \tilde{z}_t) - E\beta_t\end{aligned}$$

(see Frisch–Waugh Theorem B.3). Then, from the formula for a conditional expectation with normal errors (see Property B.43), we obtain

$$E(\beta_t \mid \tilde{z}_t) = E\beta_t + \operatorname{Cov}(\beta_t \mid \tilde{z}_t)(V(\tilde{z}_t))^{-1}\tilde{z}_t.$$

On the other hand, we have

$$\begin{aligned}\operatorname{Cov}(\beta_t, \tilde{z}_t) &= \operatorname{Cov}(\beta_t, \mathbf{H}_t'(\beta_t - \hat{\beta}_{t|t-1}) + \eta_t) \\ &= \mathbf{\Sigma}_{t|t-1}\mathbf{H}_t,\end{aligned}$$

and

$$\begin{aligned}V(\tilde{z}_t) &= V(\mathbf{H}_t'(\beta_t - \hat{\beta}_{t|t-1}) + \eta_t) \\ &= \mathbf{H}_t'\mathbf{\Sigma}_{t|t-1}\mathbf{H}_t + \mathbf{R}.\end{aligned}$$

Hence

$$\hat{\beta}_{t|t} = \hat{\beta}_{t|t-1} + \mathbf{\Sigma}_{t|t-1}\mathbf{H}_t(\mathbf{H}_t'\mathbf{\Sigma}_{t|t-1}\mathbf{H}_t + \mathbf{R})^{-1}\tilde{z}_t.$$

(i') We have

$$\mathbf{\Sigma}_{t|t} = V(\beta_t - \hat{\beta}_{t|t}).$$

But from (i) we have

$$\beta_t - \hat{\beta}_{t|t} = \beta_t - \hat{\beta}_{t|t-1} - \mathbf{\Sigma}_{t|t-1}\mathbf{H}_t(\mathbf{H}_t'\mathbf{\Sigma}_{t|t-1}\mathbf{H}_t + \mathbf{R})^{-1}\tilde{z}_t.$$

Since $\beta_t - \hat{\beta}_{t|t}$ and $\tilde{z}_t$ are uncorrelated it follows that

$$\mathbf{\Sigma}_{t|t} + V\left(\mathbf{\Sigma}_{t|t-1}\mathbf{H}_t(\mathbf{H}_t'\mathbf{\Sigma}_{t|t-1}\mathbf{H}_t + \mathbf{R})^{-1}\tilde{z}_t\right) = \mathbf{\Sigma}_{t|t-1},$$

i.e.

$$\begin{aligned}\mathbf{\Sigma}_{t|t} &= \mathbf{\Sigma}_{t|t-1} - \mathbf{\Sigma}_{t|t-1}\mathbf{H}_t(\mathbf{H}_t'\mathbf{\Sigma}_{t|t-1}\mathbf{H}_t + \mathbf{R})^{-1}\mathbf{H}_t'\mathbf{\Sigma}_{t|t-1} \\ &= (\mathbf{I} - \mathbf{K}_t\mathbf{H}_t')\mathbf{\Sigma}_{t|t-1}.\end{aligned}$$

(ii) This is an immediate consequence of equation (13.24).

(ii') We have

$$\begin{aligned}\mathbf{\Sigma}_{t+1|t} &= V(\beta_{t+1} - \hat{\beta}_{t+1|t}) \\ &= V(\mathbf{F}_t(\beta_t - \hat{\beta}_{t|t}) + \varepsilon_t) \\ &= \mathbf{F}_t \mathbf{\Sigma}_{t|t} \mathbf{F}_t' + \mathbf{Q}.\end{aligned}$$

(iii) This is an immediate consequence of equation (13.25) written at time $t+1$.

(iii') We have

$$\begin{aligned}\mathbf{M}_{t+1|t} &= V(z_{t+1} - \hat{z}_{t+1|t}) \\ &= V(\mathbf{H}_{t+1}'(\beta_{t+1} - \hat{\beta}_{t+1|t}) + \eta_{t+1}) \\ &= \mathbf{H}_{t+1}' \mathbf{\Sigma}_{t+1|t} \mathbf{H}_{t+1} + \mathbf{R}.\end{aligned}$$

□

Equations (i) and (i') of the Kalman filter are called the *measure updating equations.* Equations (ii) and (ii') are called the *time updating equations.* Equations (iii) and (iii') are called the *prediction equations* for the observations.

To apply the Kalman filter (Property 13.7) some *initial values* are required. More precisely, to apply formuale (i) and (i') at time $t = 1$, we need $\beta_{1|0}$ and $\mathbf{\Sigma}_{1|0}$. Intuitively, $\beta_{1|0}$ is the optimal prediction of β_1 based on no information. Thus $\beta_{1|0}$ is equal to the mean m. Then we have $\mathbf{\Sigma}_{1|0} = \mathbf{P}$. Such an intuitive solution is confirmed by the exact evaluation of $\hat{\beta}_{1|1} = E(\beta_1 \mid z_1)$. Applying the formula for a conditional expectation with normal errors, we find easily that

$$\hat{\beta}_{1|1} = m + \mathbf{P}\mathbf{H}_1(\mathbf{H}_1'\mathbf{P}\mathbf{H}_1 + \mathbf{R})^{-1}(z_1 - \mathbf{H}_1'm).$$

This equation agrees with formula (i) with $\beta_{1|0} = m$ and $\mathbf{\Sigma}_{1|0} = \mathbf{P}$. Similarly, we have $V(\beta_1 - \hat{\beta}_{1|1}) = \mathbf{P} - \mathbf{P}\mathbf{H}_1(\mathbf{H}_1'\mathbf{P}\mathbf{H}_1 + \mathbf{R})^{-1}\mathbf{H}_1'\mathbf{P}$, which is formula (i') with $\mathbf{\Sigma}_{1|0} = \mathbf{P}$.

Various remarks can be made on the Kalman filter.

Remark 13.7: The formulae giving the variance covariance matrices, i.e., Property 13.7–(i'), (ii'), and (iii'), do not involve the observations z_t. Thus these formulae can be used independently of any observations provided the matrices $\mathbf{F}_t$ and $\mathbf{H}_t$ are known.

Remark 13.8: Suppose that equation (13.24) is replaced by

$$\beta_{t+1} = \mathbf{F}_t\beta_t + \mathbf{G}_t u_t + \varepsilon_t,$$

where $\mathbf{G}_t$ is a nonrandom matrix and u_t is either a nonrandom vector or a function of $z_1, \ldots, z_t$. Then it is easy to see that only formula (ii) of the Kalman filter is modified. Specifically this formula is replaced by

$$\hat{\beta}_{t+1|t} = \mathbf{F}_t \hat{\beta}_{t|t} + \mathbf{G}_t u_t.$$

Remark 13.9: Suppose that ε_t and η_t are correlated with $E(\varepsilon_t \eta_t') = \mathbf{S}$. Let $\varepsilon_t^* = \varepsilon_t - \mathbf{S}\mathbf{R}^{-1}\eta_t$. Then

$$\beta_{t+1} = \mathbf{F}_t \beta_t + \varepsilon_t^* + \mathbf{S}\mathbf{R}^{-1}\eta_t.$$

Hence

$$\begin{cases} \beta_{t+1} = (\mathbf{F}_t - \mathbf{S}\mathbf{R}^{-1}\mathbf{H}_t')\beta_t + \mathbf{S}\mathbf{R}^{-1} z_t + \varepsilon_t^*, \\ z_t = \mathbf{H}_t' \beta_t + \eta_t, \end{cases}$$

where $E(\varepsilon_t^* \eta_t') = 0$ and $V(\varepsilon_t^*) = \mathbf{Q} - \mathbf{S}\mathbf{R}^{-1}\mathbf{S}'$. Therefore, Remark 13.8 applies. Hence the Kalman filter is still applicable.

Remark 13.10: When the error terms ε_t and η_t are not normally distributed but have finite second-order moments, the formulae of the Kalman filter remain valid provided the concept of conditional expectation is replaced by that of linear regression.

Remark 13.11: Suppose that the matrices $\mathbf{H}_t$ and $\mathbf{F}_{t-1}$ are functions of $z_1, \ldots, z_{t-1}$ and that the errors are not normal. Then the formulae of the Kalman filter still hold provided the various variance covariance matrices are viewed as conditional upon the variables used in the conditioning of the relevant expectations. In particular, this implies that the process (β_t, z_t) is no longer normal although the conditional distributions of these variables given the past are normal. This is because the expectations of these conditional distributions are no longer linear in the conditioning variables and their variance covariance matrices are no longer independent of the conditioning variables.

Remark 13.12: From formulae (i) and (ii) we can easily obtain an equation linking $\hat{\beta}_{t+1|t}$ to $\hat{\beta}_{t|t-1}$. Similarly, from formulae (i') and (ii'), we can obtain an equation linking $\mathbf{\Sigma}_{t+1|t}$ to $\mathbf{\Sigma}_{t|t-1}$. Such equations are the *direct prediction updating* equations.

From the same formulae, we can also derive an equation linking $\hat{\beta}_{t+1|t+1}$ to $\hat{\beta}_{t|t}$ and an equation linking $\mathbf{\Sigma}_{t+1|t+1}$ to $\mathbf{\Sigma}_{t|t}$. The resulting equations are the *direct filter updating* equations.

13.4.3 Information Filter

The basic formulae of the covariance filter are given in Property 13.7–(i), (i'), (ii), and (ii'). This set of formulae is equivalent to another set of formulae, which is called the *information filter.* The basic idea of the information filter is to base the induction not on

$$\hat{\beta}_{t|t}, \mathbf{\Sigma}_{t|t}, \hat{\beta}_{t+1|t} \text{ and } \mathbf{\Sigma}_{t+1|t}$$

but on

$$\hat{a}_{t|t} = \mathbf{\Sigma}_{t|t}^{-1}\hat{\beta}_{t|t}, \mathbf{\Sigma}_{t|t}^{-1},$$

and

$$\hat{a}_{t+1|t} = \mathbf{\Sigma}_{t+1|t}^{-1}\hat{\beta}_{t+1|t} \text{ and } \mathbf{\Sigma}_{t+1|t},$$

assuming that the relevant matrices are nonsingular.

Property 13.8: Information Filter
We have the following relations:

(I–i) $\hat{a}_{t|t} = \hat{a}_{t|t-1} + \mathbf{H}_t\mathbf{R}^{-1}z_t,$

(I–i') $\mathbf{\Sigma}_{t|t}^{-1} = \mathbf{\Sigma}_{t|t-1}^{-1} + \mathbf{H}_t\mathbf{R}^{-1}\mathbf{H}_t',$

(I–ii) $\hat{a}_{t+1|t} = (\mathbf{I} - \mathbf{B}_t)\mathbf{F}_t'^{-1}\hat{a}_{t|t},$

(I–ii') $\mathbf{\Sigma}_{t+1|t}^{-1} = (\mathbf{I} - \mathbf{B}_t)\mathbf{A}_t,$

where

$$\mathbf{A}_t = \mathbf{F}_t'^{-1}\mathbf{\Sigma}_{t|t}^{-1}\mathbf{F}_t^{-1},$$

and

$$\mathbf{B}_t = \mathbf{A}_t(\mathbf{A}_t + \mathbf{Q}^{-1})^{-1}.$$

PROOF:
(I–i') The formula of the inverse of a partitioned matrix

$$\begin{pmatrix} \mathbf{A} & \mathbf{B} \\ \mathbf{C} & \mathbf{D} \end{pmatrix},$$

where $\mathbf{A}$ and $\mathbf{D}$ are nonsingular, implies the matrix inversion equality

$$(\mathbf{D} - \mathbf{C}\mathbf{A}^{-1}\mathbf{B})^{-1} = \mathbf{D}^{-1} + \mathbf{D}^{-1}\mathbf{C}(\mathbf{A} - \mathbf{B}\mathbf{D}^{-1}\mathbf{C})^{-1}\mathbf{B}\mathbf{D}^{-1}$$

(see Property A.4). Applying this equality with $\mathbf{A} = \mathbf{R}$, $\mathbf{B} = \mathbf{H}'_t$, $\mathbf{C} = -\mathbf{H}_t$, and $\mathbf{D} = \boldsymbol{\Sigma}_{t|t-1}^{-1}$ shows that

$$\left(\boldsymbol{\Sigma}_{t|t-1}^{-1} + \mathbf{H}_t\mathbf{R}^{-1}\mathbf{H}'_t\right)^{-1} = \boldsymbol{\Sigma}_{t|t-1} - \boldsymbol{\Sigma}_{t|t-1}\mathbf{H}_t\left(\mathbf{R} + \mathbf{H}'_t\boldsymbol{\Sigma}_{t|t-1}\mathbf{H}_t\right)^{-1}\mathbf{H}'_t\boldsymbol{\Sigma}_{t|t-1}.$$

Hence Property 13.7–(i') is equivalent to

$$\boldsymbol{\Sigma}_{t|t} = \left(\boldsymbol{\Sigma}_{t|t-1}^{-1} + \mathbf{H}_t\mathbf{R}^{-1}\mathbf{H}'_t\right)^{-1},$$

which is (I–i').

(I–ii') Property 13.7–(ii), which is

$$\boldsymbol{\Sigma}_{t+1|t} = \mathbf{F}_t\boldsymbol{\Sigma}_{t|t}\mathbf{F}'_t + \mathbf{Q},$$

is equivalent to

$$\boldsymbol{\Sigma}_{t+1|t} = \mathbf{A}_t^{-1} + \mathbf{Q},$$

where $\mathbf{A}_t^{-1} = \mathbf{F}_t\boldsymbol{\Sigma}_{t|t}\mathbf{F}'_t$. Hence

$$\begin{aligned}\boldsymbol{\Sigma}_{t+1|t}^{-1} &= (\mathbf{A}_t^{-1} + \mathbf{Q})^{-1} \\ &= (\mathbf{I} + \mathbf{A}_t\mathbf{Q})^{-1}\mathbf{A}_t.\end{aligned}$$

Then, applying again the inversion matrix equality given previously, this equation is equivalent to

$$\boldsymbol{\Sigma}_{t+1|t}^{-1} = (\mathbf{I} - \mathbf{B}_t)\mathbf{A}_t,$$

where

$$\mathbf{B}_t = \mathbf{A}_t(\mathbf{A}_t + \mathbf{Q}^{-1})^{-1},$$

which is (I–ii').

(I–ii) Property 13.7–(ii) is equivalent to

$$\hat{a}_{t+1|t} = \boldsymbol{\Sigma}_{t+1|t}^{-1}\mathbf{F}_t\boldsymbol{\Sigma}_{t|t}\hat{a}_{t|t},$$

we have

$$\begin{aligned}\boldsymbol{\Sigma}_{t+1|t}^{-1}\mathbf{F}_t\boldsymbol{\Sigma}_{t|t} &= (\mathbf{I} - \mathbf{B}_t)\mathbf{A}_t\mathbf{F}_t\boldsymbol{\Sigma}_{t|t} \\ &= (\mathbf{I} - \mathbf{B}_t)\mathbf{F}_t'^{-1}.\end{aligned}$$

This establishes the equivalence between (I–ii) and Property 13.7–(ii).

(I–i) Property 13.7–(i) can be written as

$$\hat{\beta}_{t|t} = \mathbf{\Sigma}_{t|t-1}\hat{a}_{t|t-1} + \mathbf{\Sigma}_{t|t-1}\mathbf{H}_t(\mathbf{H}_t'\mathbf{\Sigma}_{t|t-1}\mathbf{H}_t + \mathbf{R})^{-1}(z_t - \mathbf{H}_t'\mathbf{\Sigma}_{t|t-1}\hat{a}_{t|t-1}).$$

Then, using Property 13.7–(i'), this is equivalent to

$$\hat{\beta}_{t|t} = \mathbf{\Sigma}_{t|t}\hat{a}_{t|t-1} + \mathbf{\Sigma}_{t|t-1}\mathbf{H}_t(\mathbf{H}_t'\mathbf{\Sigma}_{t|t-1}\mathbf{H}_t + \mathbf{R})^{-1}z_t,$$

i.e., to

$$\hat{a}_{t|t} = \hat{a}_{t|t-1} + \mathbf{\Sigma}_{t|t}^{-1}\mathbf{\Sigma}_{t|t-1}\mathbf{H}_t(\mathbf{H}_t'\mathbf{\Sigma}_{t|t-1}\mathbf{H}_t + \mathbf{R})^{-1}z_t.$$

Right multiplying Property 13.7–(i') by $\mathbf{H}_t\mathbf{R}^{-1}$, we obtain easily

$$\mathbf{\Sigma}_{t|t}\mathbf{H}_t\mathbf{R}^{-1} = \mathbf{\Sigma}_{t|t-1}\mathbf{H}_t(\mathbf{H}_t'\mathbf{\Sigma}_{t|t-1}\mathbf{H}_t + \mathbf{R})^{-1}.$$

Hence a form equivalent to Property 13.7–(i) is

$$\hat{a}_{t|t} = \hat{a}_{t|t-1} + \mathbf{H}_t\mathbf{R}^{-1}z_t,$$

i.e., (I–i). □

If the variance covariance matrix of β_1, denoted $\mathbf{P}$, is nonsingular, then the initial conditions of the covariance filter $\hat{\beta}_{1|0} = m$ and $\mathbf{\Sigma}_{1|0} = \mathbf{P}$ are equivalent to the *initial conditions of the information filter*

$$\hat{a}_{1|0} = \mathbf{P}^{-1}m \text{ and } \mathbf{\Sigma}_{1|0}^{-1} = \mathbf{P}^{-1}.$$

An interesting feature of the information filter is that it allows for the consideration of an initial "diffuse" distribution on β_1 obtained when all the eigenvalues of the matrix $\mathbf{P}$ increase to infinity, i.e., when $\mathbf{P}^{-1}$ converges to zero. In this case, one takes $\hat{a}_{1|0} = 0$ and $\mathbf{\Sigma}_{1|0}^{-1} = 0$ as initial conditions. Such initial conditions correspond to an initial "diffuse" or "vague" knowledge of β_1. Hence they are appropriate to some Bayesian type estimations.

Remark 13.13: The formulae of Property 13.8 require that the matrices $\mathbf{R}$, $\mathbf{Q}$, and $\mathbf{F}_t$ are nonsingular. If $\mathbf{Q} = 0$, however, it is easy to see that formulae (I–i) and (I–i') are unchanged while formulae (I–ii) and (I-ii') become $\hat{a}_{t+1|t} = \mathbf{F}_t'^{-1}\hat{a}_{t|t}$ and $\mathbf{\Sigma}_{t+1|t}^{-1} = \mathbf{A}_t$, respectively.

Remark 13.14: Using $\mathbf{\Sigma}_{t|t}^{-1}$ and $\mathbf{\Sigma}_{t+1|t}^{-1}$ does not actually require that these matrices are nonsingular. In general, these matrices are singular in the first iterations when the filter is initialized at $\hat{a}_{1|0} = 0$ and $\mathbf{\Sigma}_{1|0}^{-1} = 0$.

13.4.4 Kalman Filter and Computation of Likelihood Functions of State Space Models

We consider the state space framework of Section 13.4.1. In view of Remark 13.9, we may assume that the error terms ε_t and η_t are correlated. Let $\mathbf{S} = E(\varepsilon_t \eta_t')$. In addition, the vector m and the matrices $\mathbf{F}_t, \mathbf{H}_t, \mathbf{P}, \mathbf{Q}, \mathbf{R}, \mathbf{S}$ are no longer necessary known and may depend on an unknown parameter vector $\theta \in \Theta \subset I\!R^p$.

Our goal is to evaluate the likelihood function of the model, i.e., the density of the observations $z_1, \ldots, z_T$ viewed as a function of θ. This will allow estimation of θ by maximum likelihood provided sufficient regularity conditions are satisfied so that the desired asymptotic properties of ML estimation hold.

For every given θ, the Kalman filter can be used to compute the value of the likelihood function. The next property is used.

Property 13.9: *The log-likelihood function of the state space model (13.24)-(13.25) is*

$$L_T(\theta) = -\frac{nT}{2} \log 2\pi - \frac{1}{2} \sum_{t=1}^{T} \log |\mathbf{M}_{t|t-1}| - \frac{1}{2} \sum_{t=1}^{T} \tilde{z}_t' \mathbf{M}_{t|t-1}^{-1} \tilde{z}_t,$$

where $\tilde{z}_t = z_t - \hat{z}_{t|t-1}$, $\mathbf{M}_{t|t-1} = V(z_t - \hat{z}_{t|t-1})$ *and* $\hat{z}_{1/0} = Ez_1$, $\mathbf{M}_{1/0} = V(z_1)$.

PROOF:

The joint density of the vector $(z_1', \ldots, z_T')$ can be decomposed as

$$f(z_1, \theta) f(z_2 \mid z_1; \theta) \ldots f(z_t \mid z_1, \ldots, z_{t-1}; \theta) \ldots f(z_T \mid z_1, \ldots, z_{T-1}; \theta).$$

Every conditional density is a normal density. Specifically, we have

$$\begin{aligned} &\log f(z_t \mid z_1, \ldots, z_{t-1}; \theta) \\ = \quad & -\frac{n}{2} \log 2\pi - \frac{1}{2} \log |\mathbf{M}_{t|t-1}| - \frac{1}{2} \tilde{z}_t' \mathbf{M}_{t|t-1}^{-1} \tilde{z}_t. \end{aligned}$$

Since $\hat{z}_{t|t-1}$ and $\mathbf{M}_{t|t-1}$ are, respectively, the conditional expectation and the conditional variance covariance matrix of z_t given $z_1, \ldots, z_{t-1}$, the desired result follows. □

Because $\hat{z}_{t|t-1}$ and $\mathbf{M}_{t|t-1}$ are determined by the Kalman filter, the log-likelihood function at θ can be readily obtained by applying this filter. Then we can use one of the maximization algorithms presented earlier to determine the maximum likelihood estimator.

Remark 13.15: The initial values $\hat{z}_{1|0} = Ez_1$ and $\mathbf{M}_{1|0} = V(z_1)$ can be obtained from Property 13.7–(iii) and (iii') of the Kalman filter at $t = 0$ with $\hat{\beta}_{1|0} = m$ and $\mathbf{\Sigma}_{1|0} = \mathbf{P}$.

Remark 13.16: If the two summations in the formula of Property 13.9 start at $t = \tau$, and if the constant term of this formula is replaced by $-(n/2)(T - \tau + 1)\log 2\pi$, then we obtain the log-likelihood function conditional on $z_1, \ldots, z_{\tau-1}$. In particular, if the Kalman filter (Property 13.7) is applied starting from equations (i) and (ii') at $t = 1$ with $\beta_{1|0} = m$ and $\mathbf{\Sigma}_{1|0} = \mathbf{P}$, we obtain $\tilde{z}_t$ and $\mathbf{M}_{t|t-1}$ for $t \geq 2$ only. In this case, the formula of Property 13.9, hence modified, gives the log-likelihood function conditional on z_1.

Remark 13.17: If $\mathbf{F}_{t-1}$ and $\mathbf{H}_t$ are functions of $z_1, \ldots, z_{t-1}$, then Property 13.9 remains valid in view of Remark 13.11 since the proof of Property 13.9 involves conditional distributions only.

Example 13.5: Consider again the first-order moving average

$$z_t = u_t + \phi u_{t-1},\ Eu_t = 0,\ V(u_t) = \sigma^2,\ |\phi| < 1$$

(see Example 13.3).

A corresponding state space model is

$$\begin{cases} \beta_{t+1} = \begin{pmatrix} z_{t+1} \\ \phi u_{t+1} \end{pmatrix} = \begin{pmatrix} 0 & 1 \\ 0 & 0 \end{pmatrix} \beta_t + \begin{pmatrix} u_{t+1} \\ \phi u_{t+1} \end{pmatrix}, \\ z_t = (1, 0)\beta_t. \end{cases}$$

Here we have

$$\hat{z}_{1|0} = Ez_1 = 0 \text{ and } \mathbf{M}_{1|0} = V(z_1) = \sigma^2(1 + \phi^2).$$

Similarly

$$\hat{\beta}_{1|0} = E\beta_1 = \begin{pmatrix} 0 \\ 0 \end{pmatrix},\ \mathbf{\Sigma}_{1|0} = V(\beta_1) = \sigma^2 \begin{pmatrix} 1+\phi^2 & \phi \\ \phi & \phi^2 \end{pmatrix}.$$

On the other hand

$$\hat{\beta}_{t|t-1} = \begin{pmatrix} \hat{z}_{t|t-1} \\ 0 \end{pmatrix},\ \mathbf{\Sigma}_{t|t-1} = \begin{pmatrix} \mathbf{M}_{t|t-1} & \phi\sigma^2 \\ \phi\sigma^2 & \phi^2\sigma^2 \end{pmatrix}.$$

Hence the prediction updating equations obtained from Property 13.7–(i) and (ii), which are

$$\hat{\beta}_{t+1|t} = \mathbf{F}_t \hat{\beta}_{t|t-1} + \mathbf{F}_t \mathbf{K}_t \tilde{z}_t,$$

imply that

$$\hat{z}_{t+1|t} = 0 + (0,1)\mathbf{K}_t\tilde{z}_t,$$

where

$$\mathbf{K}_t = \frac{1}{\mathbf{M}_{t|t-1}}\begin{pmatrix} \mathbf{M}_{t|t-1} & \phi\sigma^2 \\ \phi\sigma^2 & \phi^2\sigma^2 \end{pmatrix}\begin{pmatrix} 1 \\ 0 \end{pmatrix} = \begin{pmatrix} 1 \\ \phi\sigma^2/\mathbf{M}_{t|t-1} \end{pmatrix}.$$

Hence we obtain the recursion formula

$$\hat{z}_{t+1|t} = \frac{\phi\sigma^2}{\mathbf{M}_{t|t-1}}\tilde{z}_t,$$

i.e.

$$\tilde{z}_{t+1} = z_{t+1} - \frac{\phi\sigma^2}{\mathbf{M}_{t|t-1}}\tilde{z}_t. \tag{13.26}$$

Similarly, from Property 13.7–(i') and (ii') imply

$$\mathbf{M}_{t+1|t} = -\frac{\phi^2\sigma^4}{\mathbf{M}_{t|t-1}} + \phi^2\sigma^2 + \sigma^2. \tag{13.27}$$

Equations (13.26) and (13.27) are used to determine $\tilde{z}_{t+1}$ and $\mathbf{M}_{t+1|t}$, recursively. Hence, the likelihood function can be easily evaluated.

Note also that, in this example, we can determine explicitly the scalar $\mathbf{M}_{t+1|t}$. Let

$$\mathbf{N}_{t+1} = \frac{1}{\mathbf{M}_{t+1|t} - \sigma^2} + \frac{1}{\sigma^2(1-\phi^2)}.$$

It is easy to see that equation (13.27) leads to the recursion formula

$$\mathbf{N}_{t+1} = \frac{1}{\phi^2}\mathbf{N}_t.$$

It follows that

$$\mathbf{M}_{t+1|t} = \sigma^2 + \sigma^2\frac{(1-\phi^2)\phi^{2(t+1)}}{1-\phi^{2(t+1)}}.$$

Note, however, that, even in this simple example, the explicit determination of $\tilde{z}_{t+1}$ is difficult. This illustrates the usefulness of a recursive method.

13.5 Prediction and Smoothing in State Space Models

13.5.1 Prediction

We consider the general state space model defined by (13.24) and (13.25), i.e.

$$\begin{aligned} \beta_{t+1} &= \mathbf{F}_t \beta_t + \varepsilon_t, \\ z_t &= \mathbf{H}_t' \beta_t + \eta_t. \end{aligned}$$

The hypotheses of Section 13.4.1 are maintained. In particular, ε_t and η_t are assumed uncorrelated.

We observe $z_1, \ldots, z_t$ and we want to predict β_{t+h} and z_{t+h}, $h \geq 1$. That is, we want to determine

$$\begin{aligned} \hat{\beta}_{t+h|t} &= E(\beta_{t+h} \mid z_1, \ldots, z_t), \\ \hat{z}_{t+h|t} &= E(z_{t+h} \mid z_1, \ldots, z_t), \end{aligned}$$

as well as the variance covariance matrices of the prediction errors. When $h = 1$, the optimal predictions of β_{t+1} and z_{t+1} as well as the variance covariance matrices of the corresponding prediction errors are given by Property 13.7–(ii), (ii'), (iii), and (iii') of the Kalman filter.

More generally, writing equations (13.24) and (13.25) at time $t + h$, we obtain

$$\beta_{t+h} = \mathbf{F}_{t+h-1} \beta_{t+h-1} + \varepsilon_{t+h-1}, \tag{13.28}$$

$$z_{t+h} = \mathbf{H}_{t+h}' \beta_{t+h} + \eta_{t+h}. \tag{13.29}$$

Taking conditional expectation given $z_1, \ldots, z_t$, this system becomes

$$\beta_{t+h|t} = \mathbf{F}_{t+h-1} \hat{\beta}_{t+h-1|t}, \tag{13.30}$$

$$\hat{z}_{t+h|t} = \mathbf{H}_{t+h}' \hat{\beta}_{t+h|t}. \tag{13.31}$$

Substracting (13.30) from (13.28) and (13.31) from (13.29) we obtain

$$\begin{aligned} \beta_{t+h} - \hat{\beta}_{t+h|t} &= \mathbf{F}_{t+h-1} (\beta_{t+h-1} - \hat{\beta}_{t+h-1|t}) + \varepsilon_{t+h-1}, \\ z_{t+h} - \hat{z}_{t+h|t} &= \mathbf{H}_{t+h}' (\beta_{t+h} - \hat{\beta}_{t+h|t}) + \eta_{t+h}. \end{aligned}$$

The latter formulae express the predictions errors at horizon h as functions of the prediction errors at horizon $h - 1$. Then we can readily obtain the variance covariance matrices of the prediction errors. These are

$$\boldsymbol{\Sigma}_{t+h|t} = \mathbf{F}_{t+h-1}\boldsymbol{\Sigma}_{t+h-1|t}\mathbf{F}'_{t+h-1} + \mathbf{Q}, \quad (13.32)$$

$$\mathbf{M}_{t+h|t} = \mathbf{H}'_{t+h}\boldsymbol{\Sigma}_{t+h|t}\mathbf{H}_{t+h} + \mathbf{R}. \quad (13.33)$$

The preceding equations show that

$$\beta_{t+h|t}, \hat{z}_{t+h|t}, \boldsymbol{\Sigma}_{t+h|t}, \mathbf{M}_{t+h|t}$$

are easily obtained by applying the Kalman filter (Property 13.7). Specifically, after using (iii'), it suffices to follow the sequence of formulae (ii) and (ii'), where $\hat{\beta}_{t|t}$ and $\boldsymbol{\Sigma}_{t|t}$ are replaced by $\hat{\beta}_{t+1|t}$ and $\boldsymbol{\Sigma}_{t+1|t}$, respectively, and to iterate this operation $h-1$ times. Of course, the values of $\hat{\beta}_{t+1|t}$ and $\hat{\boldsymbol{\Sigma}}_{t+1|t}$ must be kept so as to continue the algorithm at (i) and (i') for time $t+1$.

Remark 13.18: From Remark 13.9, we know how to modify the equation giving $\hat{\beta}_{t+1|t}$ when ε_t and η_t are correlated, The remaining equations are unchanged. In particular, the system (13.30)–(13.33) is unchanged for $h \geq 2$.

Remark 13.19: When $\mathbf{H}_t$ and $\mathbf{F}_{t-1}$ are functions of $z_1, \ldots, z_{t-1}$, we saw that the Kalman filter equations of Property 13.7 remain valid provided the various variance covariance matrices are interpreted as conditional on the information used in the computation of the conditional expectations (see Remark 13.11). In contrast, when the prediction horizon h is larger than two, i.e., $h \geq 2$, then formulae (13.30)–(13.33) can no longer be used. This is because the matrices $\mathbf{F}_{t+h-1}$ and $\mathbf{H}'_{t+h}$ are now random conditional on $z_1, \ldots, z_t$.

13.5.2 Smoothing

We consider the general state space model defined by

$$\begin{aligned} \beta_{t+1} &= \mathbf{F}_t\beta_t + \varepsilon_t, \\ z_t &= \mathbf{H}'_t\beta_t + \eta_t, \end{aligned}$$

where the variance covariance matrix of the vector $w_t = (\varepsilon'_t, \eta'_t)'$ is

$$\begin{pmatrix} \mathbf{Q} & \mathbf{S} \\ \mathbf{S}' & \mathbf{R} \end{pmatrix}.$$

We observe $z_1, \ldots, z_T$ and we want to determine the optimal prediction $\hat{\beta}_{t|T} = E(\beta_t \mid z_1, \ldots, z_T)$ of β_t, $t \in (1, \ldots, T)$, as well as the variance covariance matrix of $\beta_t - \hat{\beta}_{t|T}$, denoted $\mathbf{\Sigma}_{t|T}$.

Property 13.10: *We have the recursion formulae*

(i) $\hat{\beta}_{t|T} = \hat{\beta}_{t|t} + \mathbf{C}_t(\hat{\beta}_{t+1|T} - \hat{\beta}_{t+1|t})$, *where* $\mathbf{C}_t = \mathbf{\Sigma}_{t|t}\mathbf{F}_t'\mathbf{\Sigma}_{t+1|t}^{-1}$,

(ii) $\mathbf{\Sigma}_{t|T} = \mathbf{\Sigma}_{t|t} + \mathbf{C}_t(\mathbf{\Sigma}_{t+1|T} - \mathbf{\Sigma}_{t+1|t})\mathbf{C}_t'$.

PROOF: (i) Let $E(\beta_t \mid I_t)$ denote the conditional expectation

$$E(\beta_t \mid z_1, \ldots, z_t,\ \beta_{t+1} - \hat{\beta}_{t+1|t},\ w_{t+1}, \ldots, w_T).$$

Each variable z_{t+i+1}, $i = 0, \ldots, T-1$, is a function of the conditioning variables in the above expectation since

$$\begin{aligned} z_{t+i+1} &= \mathbf{H}_{t+i+1}'\beta_{t+i+1} + \eta_{t+i+1}, \\ \beta_{t+i+1} &= \mathbf{F}_{t+i} \ldots \mathbf{F}_{t+1}\beta_{t+1} + \varepsilon_{t+i} \\ &\quad + \mathbf{F}_{t+i}\varepsilon_{t+i-1} + \ldots + \mathbf{F}_{t+i} \ldots \mathbf{F}_{t+2}\varepsilon_{t+1}, \\ \beta_{t+1} &= \beta_{t+1} - \hat{\beta}_{t+1|t} + \hat{\beta}_{t+1|t}, \end{aligned}$$

and $\hat{\beta}_{t+1|t}$ is a function of $z_1, \ldots, z_t$. Hence

$$\hat{\beta}_{t|T} = E(\beta_t \mid z_1, \ldots, z_T) = E(E(\beta_t \mid I_t) \mid z_1, \ldots, z_T),$$

(see formula B.45).

We now compute $E(\beta_t \mid I_t)$. Since errors are normal, then $E(\beta_t \mid I_t)$ is a random vector of which the components are orthogonal projections in the L_2 sense on the subspace generated by the variables of I_t and 1. This subspace is the sum of three mutually orthogonal subspaces, which are

$$\begin{aligned} I_{1t} &= (z_1, \ldots, z_t, 1), \\ I_{2t} &= (\beta_{t+1} - \hat{\beta}_{t+1|t}), \\ I_{3t} &= (w_{t+1}, \ldots, w_T). \end{aligned}$$

Hence $E(\beta_t \mid I_t)$ can be decomposed as

$$\begin{aligned} E(\beta_t \mid I_t) &= \hat{\beta}_{t|t} + (E(\beta_t \mid \beta_{t+1} - \hat{\beta}_{t+1|t}) - E\beta_t) \\ &\quad + (E(\beta_t \mid w_{t+1}, \ldots, w_T) - E\beta_t). \end{aligned}$$

The third term is equal to zero while the second term can be written as

$$\begin{aligned}
&E(\beta_t \mid \beta_{t+1} - \hat{\beta}_{t+1|t}) - E\beta_t \\
&= \text{Cov}(\beta_t, \beta_{t+1} - \hat{\beta}_{t+1|t})\mathbf{\Sigma}_{t+1|t}^{-1}(\beta_{t+1} - \hat{\beta}_{t+1|t}) \\
&= \text{Cov}(\beta_t, \mathbf{F}_t(\beta_t - \hat{\beta}_{t|t}) + \varepsilon_t)\mathbf{\Sigma}_{t+1|t}^{-1}(\beta_{t+1} - \hat{\beta}_{t+1|t}) \\
&= \mathbf{\Sigma}_{t|t}\mathbf{F}_t'\mathbf{\Sigma}_{t+1|t}^{-1}(\beta_{t+1} - \hat{\beta}_{t+1|t}) \\
&= \mathbf{C}_t(\beta_{t+1} - \hat{\beta}_{t+1|t}).
\end{aligned}$$

Hence we have

$$E(\beta_t \mid I_t) = \hat{\beta}_{t|t} + \mathbf{C}_t(\beta_{t+1} - \hat{\beta}_{t+1|t}).$$

Then, taking expectation conditional on $z_1, \ldots, z_T$, we obtain

$$\hat{\beta}_{t|T} = \hat{\beta}_{t|t} + \mathbf{C}_t(\hat{\beta}_{t+1|T} - \hat{\beta}_{t+1|t}),$$

as desired.

(ii) Substracting β_t from each side of the preceding equation and multiplying by minus one, we obtain

$$\beta_t - \hat{\beta}_{t|T} = \beta_t - \hat{\beta}_{t|t} - \mathbf{C}_t\hat{\beta}_{t+1|T} + \mathbf{C}_t\hat{\beta}_{t+1|t},$$

i.e.

$$(\beta_t - \hat{\beta}_{t|T}) + \mathbf{C}_t\hat{\beta}_{t+1|T} = (\beta_t - \hat{\beta}_{t|t}) + \mathbf{C}_t\hat{\beta}_{t+1|t}.$$

Each side of this equation is decomposed as a sum of two uncorrelated terms. Hence we have

$$\mathbf{\Sigma}_{t|T} + \mathbf{C}_t V(\hat{\beta}_{t+1|T})\mathbf{C}_t' = \mathbf{\Sigma}_{t|t} + \mathbf{C}_t V(\hat{\beta}_{t+1|t})\mathbf{C}_t',$$

i.e.

$$\mathbf{\Sigma}_{t|T} = \mathbf{\Sigma}_{t|t} + \mathbf{C}_t(V(\hat{\beta}_{t+1|t}) - V(\hat{\beta}_{t+1|T}))\mathbf{C}_t'. \tag{13.34}$$

On the other hand, we have the identity

$$(\beta_{t+1} - \hat{\beta}_{t+1|t}) + \hat{\beta}_{t+1|t} = (\beta_{t+1} - \hat{\beta}_{t+1|T}) + \hat{\beta}_{t+1|T}.$$

Each side of this equation is again decomposed as a sum of two uncorrelated terms. Hence

$$\mathbf{\Sigma}_{t+1|t} + V(\hat{\beta}_{t+1|t}) = \mathbf{\Sigma}_{t+1|T} + V(\hat{\beta}_{t+1|T}),$$

i.e.

$$V(\hat{\beta}_{t+1|t}) - V(\hat{\beta}_{t+1|T}) = \mathbf{\Sigma}_{t+1|T} - \mathbf{\Sigma}_{t+1|t}.$$

Then, using equation (13.34), the desired result follows. □

Property 13.10 shows that $\hat{\beta}_{t|T}$ and $\mathbf{\Sigma}_{t|T}$ can be obtained by first applying the Kalman filter, which provides $\hat{\beta}_{t|t}$, $\hat{\beta}_{t+1|t}$, $\mathbf{\Sigma}_{t|t}$ and $\mathbf{\Sigma}_{t+1|t}$, and then using Property 13.10–(i) and (ii) starting from $t = T - 1$.

13.6 Recursive Least Squares and Recursive Residuals

The preceding results can be straightforwardly applied to the linear model. Consider the linear model

$$y_t = x_t \beta + \eta_t, \; t = 1, \ldots, T,$$

where the error terms η_t are independently and identically distributed $N(0, \sigma^2)$.

The model can be written in the state space form

$$\begin{cases} \beta_{t+1} = \beta_t \; (= \beta) \\ y_t = x_t \beta + \eta_t. \end{cases}$$

Hence we have $\mathbf{F}_t = \mathbf{I}$, $\mathbf{H}_t' = x_t$, $\mathbf{Q} = 0$, $\mathbf{S} = 0$ and $\mathbf{R} = \sigma^2$.

The information filter with $\mathbf{Q} = 0$ (see Remark 13.13) is:

(I–i) $\hat{a}_{t|t} = \hat{a}_{t|t-1} + x_t' y_t / \sigma^2$,

(I–i') $\mathbf{\Sigma}_{t|t}^{-1} = \mathbf{\Sigma}_{t|t-1}^{-1} + x_t' x_t / \sigma^2$,

(I–ii) $\hat{a}_{t|t-1} = \hat{a}_{t|t}$,

(I–ii') $\mathbf{\Sigma}_{t|t-1}^{-1} = \mathbf{\Sigma}_{t|t}^{-1}$.

In view of equations (I–ii) and (I–ii'), we can simplify the notation by letting

$$\begin{array}{lll} \hat{a}_t & = \hat{a}_{t|t} & = \hat{a}_{t|t-1}, \\ \mathbf{\Sigma}_t^{-1} & = \mathbf{\Sigma}_{t|t}^{-1} & = \mathbf{\Sigma}_{t|t-1}^{-1}. \end{array}$$

Then the information filter can be written as

$$\hat{a}_t = \hat{a}_{t-1} + \frac{x_t' y_t}{\sigma^2}, \tag{13.35}$$

$$\mathbf{\Sigma}_t^{-1} = \mathbf{\Sigma}_{t-1}^{-1} + \frac{x_t' x_t}{\sigma^2}. \tag{13.36}$$

In particular, if we use a diffuse prior, i.e., if $\hat{a}_{1|0} = 0$ and $\boldsymbol{\Sigma}_{1|0}^{-1} = 0$, then we have

$$\boldsymbol{\Sigma}_T^{-1} = \frac{1}{\sigma^2}\sum_{t=1}^{T} x_t' x_t,$$

and

$$\hat{a}_t = \frac{1}{\sigma^2}\sum_{t=1}^{T} x_t' y_t.$$

Hence

$$\hat{\beta}_T = \hat{\beta}_{T|T} = \left(\sum_{t=1}^{T} x_t' x_t\right)^{-1} \sum_{t=1}^{T} x_t' y_t.$$

Hence we obtain the least squares formula. This agrees with Property 12.3 where $\Omega_0 = 0$.

The information filter with a diffuse prior is equivalent to the covariance filter when $t \geq \tau$ and $\boldsymbol{\Sigma}_\tau^{-1} = 1/\sigma^2 \sum_{t=1}^{\tau} x_t' x_t$ is nonsingular, which is in general satisfied when $t \geq k$, where k is the number of components of x_t. In this case, the updating equations of the covariance filter Property 13.7–(i) and (i') can be used. Here these are

$$\hat{\beta}_t = \hat{\beta}_{t-1} + \mathbf{K}_t \tilde{y}_t,$$

i.e.

$$\hat{\beta}_t = \hat{\beta}_{t-1} + \boldsymbol{\Sigma}_{t-1} x_t' \left(x_t \boldsymbol{\Sigma}_{t-1} x_t' + \sigma^2\right)^{-1} \tilde{y}_t, \tag{13.37}$$

and

$$\frac{\boldsymbol{\Sigma}_t}{\sigma^2} = \frac{\boldsymbol{\Sigma}_{t-1}}{\sigma^2} - \frac{\boldsymbol{\Sigma}_{t-1}}{\sigma^2} x_t' \left(x_t \frac{\boldsymbol{\Sigma}_{t-1}}{\sigma^2} x_t' + 1\right)^{-1} x_t \frac{\boldsymbol{\Sigma}_{t-1}}{\sigma^2}. \tag{13.38}$$

The gain of the filter, which is

$$\mathbf{K}_t = \boldsymbol{\Sigma}_{t-1}(x_t' \boldsymbol{\Sigma}_{t-1} x_t' + \sigma^2)^{-1},$$

can be written as

$$\mathbf{K}_t = \frac{1}{\sigma^2}\boldsymbol{\Sigma}_t x_t',$$

using Property 13.7–(i'). Hence equation (13.37) becomes

$$\hat{\beta}_t = \hat{\beta}_{t-1} + \frac{\boldsymbol{\Sigma}_t x_t'}{\sigma^2} \tilde{y}_t,$$

i.e.

$$\hat{\beta}_t = \hat{\beta}_{t-1} + \left(\sum_{i=1}^{t} x_i' x_i \right)^{-1} x_t' \left(y_t - x_t \hat{\beta}_{t-1} \right). \tag{13.39}$$

This equation used in conjunction with equation (13.38) allows to update the so-called *recursive least squares estimates*, which are the least squares estimates based on t observations.

In particular, equation (13.39) shows that the change $\hat{\beta}_t - \hat{\beta}_{t-1}$ in the least squares estimate is proportional to the residual $y_t - x_t \hat{\beta}_{t-1}$. Conditionally or unconditionally to β the variance of the residual $y_t - x_t \hat{\beta}_{t-1}$ appearing in equation (13.39) is

$$\sigma^2 \left(1 + x_t \left(\sum_{i=1}^{t} x_i' x_i \right)^{-1} x_t' \right).$$

The "normalized" residuals

$$w_t = \frac{y_t - x_t \hat{\beta}_{t-1}}{\left(1 + x_t \left(\sum_{i=1}^{t} x_i' x_i \right)^{-1} x_t' \right)^{1/2}}$$

are called *recursive residuals*.

By construction, recursive residuals are distributed $N(0, \sigma^2)$. Moreover, it is easy to see that these residuals are mutually independent since $\forall\, r < s$

$$\begin{aligned}
\text{Cov}\,(w_r, w_s) &= E \left(\eta_r - x_r \left(\sum_{i=1}^{r-1} x_i' x_i \right)^{-1} \sum_{i=1}^{r-1} x_i' \eta_i \right) \\
&\quad \left(\eta_s - x_s \left(\sum_{j=1}^{s-1} x_j' x_j \right)^{-1} \sum_{j=1}^{s-1} x_j' \eta_j \right) \\
&= -x_s \left(\sum_{j=1}^{s-1} x_j' x_j \right)^{-1} x_r' \\
&\quad + x_r \left(\sum_{i=1}^{r-1} x_i' x_i \right)^{-1} \left(\sum_{i=1}^{r-1} x_i' x_i \right) \left(\sum_{j=1}^{s-1} x_j' x_j \right)^{-1} x_s' \\
&= 0.
\end{aligned}$$

13.7 Exercises

EXERCISE 13.1:

a) Consider two nonzero vectors u and v of $I\!R^n$ such that $u = \mathbf{Q}v$, where $\mathbf{Q}$ is a symmetric positive definite matrix. Show that $u'v > 0$.

b) Let v be the vector $(1, 0, 0, \dots, 0)'$. Characterize the vectors u such that $u'v > 0$.

c) Consider a vector $u = (u_1, \dots, u_n)'$ such that $u_1 > 0$. Find a symmetric positive definite matrix $\mathbf{Q}$ such that u' is the first row of $\mathbf{Q}$. Deduce property 13.2.

EXERCISE 13.2: Consider the nonlinear regression model $y_i = g_i(\theta) + u_i$, $i = 1, \dots, n$. One wants to determine the nonlinear least squares estimator $\hat{\theta}$ of θ. Thus the criterion function is

$$\sum_{i=1}^{n} (y_i - g_i(\theta))^2 = V(\theta).$$

a) Find a linear approximation to $g_i(\theta)$ in the neighborhood of $\theta^{(k)}$. When $g_i(\theta)$ is replaced by this approximation in the criterion function, verify that the criterion function becomes

$$\tilde{V}(\theta) = \sum_{i=1}^{n} \left(y_i - g_i(\theta^{(k)}) - \frac{\partial g_i}{\partial \theta'} (\theta - \theta^{(k)}) \right)^2 .$$

b) Determine the value $\theta^{(k+1)}$ at which the function $\tilde{V}$ is minimized.

EXERCISE 13.3: Compare the Newton–Raphson and BHHH algorithms when the model is the linear model $y_i = x_i\theta + u_i$ and the errors are independently and identically distributed $N(0, 1)$.

EXERCISE 13.4: Consider a random sample $Y_1^*, \dots, Y_n^*$ drawn from a distribution with density $\theta \exp(-\theta y^*) \mathbb{1}_{I\!R^+}(y^*)$. We observe Y_i where $Y_i = Y_i^* \mathbb{1}_{(y_i^* < 1)}$.

a) Find the log-likelihood function of the latent model.

b) Find the conditional expectation of this log-likelihood function given the Y_i's.

c) Find the limit of the estimator obtained by maximizing the function in b) with respect to θ.

EXERCISE 13.5: Determine the iteration formula of the EM algorithm for a Tobit model where the latent model is linear and Gaussian. That is, the latent model is $Y_i^* = x_i b + u_i$ where the errors u_i are independently and identically distributed $N(0, \sigma^2)$. The observed variables Y_i are related to the latent variables by $Y_i = Y_i^* \mathbb{1}_{(Y_i^* \geq 0)}$.

EXERCISE 13.6: Consider applying the EM algorithm to a model where

(i) the log-likelihood function $L(\theta)$ is bounded above,

(ii) there exists a strictly positive scalar λ such that

$$Q(\theta^{(q+1)}, \theta^{(q)}) - Q(\theta^{(q)}, \theta^{(q)}) \geq \lambda \|\theta^{(q+1)} - \theta^{(q)}\|^2,$$

where Q is defined in equation (13.17).

a) Use the proof of Property 13.5 to show that

$$\sum_q \|\theta^{(q+1)} - \theta^{(q)}\|^2 < +\infty.$$

Conclude that there exists a converging subsequence $\theta^{(q)}$.

b) Suppose that the latent model is a Gaussian model defined by $Y_i^* = x_i \theta + u_i$, $i = 1, \ldots, n$, where the error terms u_i are independently and identically distributed $N(0, 1)$. Show that

$$Q(\theta^{(q+1)}, \theta^{(q)}) - Q(\theta^{(q)}, \theta^{(q)}) = (\theta^{(q+1)} - \theta^{(q)})' \mathbf{X}' \mathbf{X} (\theta^{(q+1)} - \theta^{(q)}).$$

Conclude that a condition of type (ii) above is satisfied.

c) Consider observations such that

$$\begin{pmatrix} Y_1 \\ Y_2 \end{pmatrix} = \begin{pmatrix} Y_1^* \\ Y_2^* \end{pmatrix} \sim N\left(\begin{pmatrix} \theta_1 \\ \theta_2 \end{pmatrix}, \mathbf{I} \right).$$

Take as initial values

$$\begin{pmatrix} \theta_1^{(0)} \\ \theta_2^{(0)} \end{pmatrix} = \begin{pmatrix} y_1 + 2 \\ y_2 \end{pmatrix}.$$

First, verify that

$$\begin{cases} \theta_1^{(q)} = y_1 + r_q \cos \alpha_q, \\ \\ \theta_2^{(q)} = y_2 + r_q \sin \alpha_q, \end{cases}$$

where

$$r_q = 1 + \frac{1}{1+q} \quad \text{and} \quad \alpha_q = \sum_{k=1}^{q} \frac{1}{1+k}.$$

Second, verify that

$$\begin{pmatrix} r_{q+1} \\ \alpha_{q+1} \end{pmatrix} = M(r_q, \alpha_q),$$

where

$$M(r,\alpha) = \begin{pmatrix} 2 - \frac{1}{r} \\ \alpha + 1 - \frac{1}{r} \end{pmatrix} \mathbb{1}_{r>1} + \begin{pmatrix} r \\ \alpha + 1 - \frac{1}{r} \end{pmatrix} \mathbb{1}_{r \leq 1}.$$

Conclude that the limit points of the sequence $\theta^{(q)}$ are all the points on a circle with radius one centered at (y_1, y_2). Conclude that the sequence $\theta^{(q)}$ does not converge.

EXERCISE 13.7: Generalize Example 13.2 to a pth order autoregressive model defined by

$$z_t - \phi_1 z_{t-1} - \cdots - \phi_p z_{t-p} = u_t.$$

In particular, verify that we can let $\beta_t' = (z_t, \ldots, z_{t-p+1})$ so that the transition matrix $\mathbf{F}$ is

$$\begin{pmatrix} \phi_1 \cdots \phi_p \\ \mathbf{I}_{p-1} \quad 0 \end{pmatrix}.$$

EXERCISE 13.8: Generalize Example 13.3 to a qth-order moving average defined by

$$z_t = u_t - \theta_1 u_{t-1} \cdots - \theta_q u_{t-q}.$$

In particular, show that we can let β_t be the $q+1$ dimensional vector defined by

$$\beta_t = (z_t, -\theta_1 u_t - \cdots - \theta_q u_{t+1-q}, \ldots, -\theta_q u_t)'.$$

Show that the transition matrix **F** becomes

$$\begin{pmatrix} 0 & \mathbf{I}_q \\ 0 & 0 \end{pmatrix}.$$

EXERCISE 13.9: Consider an ARMA(p, q) defined by

$$z_t - \phi_1 z_{t-1} - \cdots - \phi_p z_{t-p} = u_t - \theta_1 u_{t-1} - \cdots - \theta_q u_{t-q}.$$

Show that a state space representation of this model is obtained by letting the state vector be the $p + q$ dimensional vector defined by

$$\beta_t = (z_t, z_{t-1}, \ldots, z_{t-p+1}, \varepsilon_t, \varepsilon_{t-1}, \ldots, \varepsilon_{t-q+1})'.$$

Show that the transition matrix **F** is the $(p + q) \times (p + q)$ matrix

$$\begin{pmatrix} \phi_1 \cdots \phi_p & -\theta_1 \cdots - \theta_q \\ \mathbf{I}_{p-1} \;\; 0 & 0 \\ & 0 \cdots 0 \\ 0 & \\ & \mathbf{I}_{q-1} \;\; 0 \end{pmatrix}.$$

EXERCISE 13.10: Consider the linear system

$$y_t = x_t \beta, \; t = 1, \ldots, T,$$

where β is an unknown vector of dimension K. Show that the Kalman covariance filter can be used to solve this system. Interpret geometrically the recursion formulae of the filter when $\hat{\beta}_{1|0} = 0$ and $\mathbf{\Sigma}_{1|0} = \mathbf{I}_K$.

13.8 References

Anderson, B.D. and Moore, J.B. (1979). *Optimal Filtering*, Prentice Hall.

Berndt, E.K., Hall, B.H., Hall, L.R.E., and Hausman, J.A. (1974). "Estimation and Inference in Nonlinear Structural Models," *Annals of Economic and Social Measurement*, 3, 653–666.

Boyles, R. (1983). "On the Convergence of the Optimization," *Journal of the Royal Statistical Society*, B, 45, 47–50.

Brown, R.L., Durbin, J., and Evans, J.M. (1975). "Techniques for Testing the Constancy of Regression Relationships Over Time," *Journal of the Royal Statistical Society*, Series 13, 37, 149–192.

Dempster, A.P.N., Laird, N.M., and Rubin, D.B. (1977). "Maximum Likelihood from Incomplete Data Via the E.M. Algorithm," *Journal of the Royal Statistical Society*, B 39, 1–38.

Fair, R. (1977). "A Note on the Computation of the Tobit Estimation," *Econometrica*, 45, 1723–1727.

Fletcher, R. (1980). *Practical Methods of Optimization*, Wiley.

Fletcher, R. and Powell J. D. (1963). "A Rapidly Convergent Descent Method for Minimization", *Computer Journal*, 6, 163–168

Fletcher, R. and Reeves, C. (1964). "Function Minimization by Conjugate Gradients," *The Computer Journal*, 7, 149–153.

Goldfeld, S.M. and Quandt, R.E. (1972). *Nonlinear Methods in Econometrics*, North-Holland.

Goldfeld, S., Quandt, R.E., and Trotter, H. (1966). "Maximization by Quadratic Hill-Climbing," *Econometrica*, 34, 541–551.

Goldstein, (1967). *Constructive Real Analysis*, Harper Row.

Gourieroux, C. and Monfort A. (1995). *Time Series and Dynamic Models*, Cambridge University Press.

Marquardt, D. W. (1963). "An Algorithm for Least Squares Estimation of Nonlinear Parameters ", *SIAM Journal*, 11, 431–441

Phillips, G.D.A. and Harvey, A.C. (1974). "A Simple Test for Serial Correlation in Regression Analysis," *Journal of the American Statistical Association*, 69, 935–939.

Powell, M. (1964). "An Efficient Method for Finding the Minimum of a Function of Several Variables Without Calculating Derivatives," *The Computer Journal*, 7, 155–162.

Quandt, R.E. (1983). "Computational Problems and Methods," *Handbook of Econometics*, Vol 1, North-Holland.

Theil, H. (1971). *Principles of Econometrics*, Wiley.

Table 1

Cumulative Distribution Function of the Standard Normal Distribution

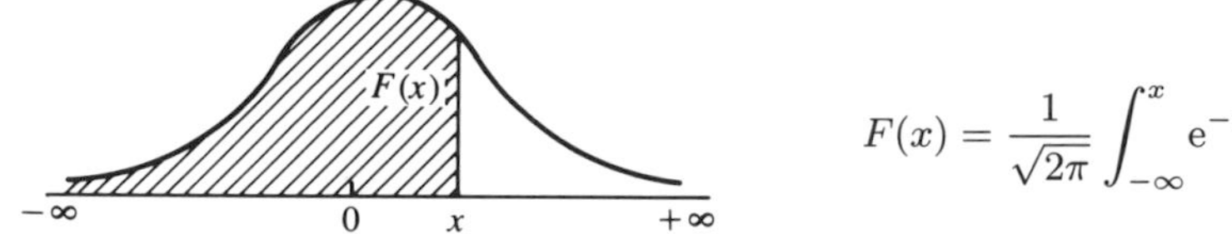

$$F(x) = \frac{1}{\sqrt{2\pi}} \int_{-\infty}^{x} \mathrm{e}^{-u^2/2} \mathrm{d}u$$

x	0.00	0.01	0.02	0.03	0.04	0.05	0.06	0.07	0.08	0.09
0.0	0.500 00	0.503 99	0.507 98	0.511 97	0.515 95	0.519 94	0.523 92	0.527 90	0.531 88	0.535 86
0.1	0.539 83	0.543 80	0.547 76	0.551 72	0.555 67	0.559 62	0.563 56	0.567 50	0.571 42	0.575 35
0.2	0.579 26	0.583 17	0.587 06	0.590 95	0.594 84	0.598 71	0.602 57	0.606 42	0.610 26	0.614 09
0.3	0.617 91	0.621 72	0.625 52	0.629 30	0.633 07	0.636 83	0.640 58	0.644 31	0.648 03	0.651 73
0.4	0.655 42	0.659 10	0.662 76	0.666 40	0.670 03	0.673 65	0.677 24	0.680 82	0.684 39	0.687 93
0.5	0.691 46	0.694 97	0.698 47	0.701 94	0.705 40	0.708 84	0.712 26	0.715 66	0.719 04	0.722 40
0.6	0.725 75	0.729 07	0.732 37	0.735 65	0.738 91	0.742 15	0.745 37	0.748 57	0.751 75	0.754 90
0.7	0.758 04	0.761 15	0.764 24	0.767 31	0.770 35	0.773 37	0.776 37	0.779 35	0.782 30	0.785 24
0.8	0.788 14	0.791 03	0.793 89	0.796 73	0.799 55	0.802 11	0.805 11	0.807 85	0.810 57	0.813 27
0.9	0.815 94	0.818 59	0.821 21	0.823 81	0.826 39	0.828 94	0.831 47	0.833 98	0.836 46	0.838 91
1.0	0.841 34	0.843 75	0.846 14	0.848 50	0.850 83	0.853 14	0.855 43	0.857 69	0.859 93	0.862 14
1.1	0.864 33	0.866 50	0.868 64	0.870 76	0.872 86	0.874 93	0.876 98	0.879 00	0.881 00	0.882 98
1.2	0.884 93	0.886 86	0.888 77	0.890 65	0.892 51	0.892 35	0.896 17	0.897 96	0.899 73	0.901 47
1.3	0.903 20	0.904 90	0.906 58	0.908 24	0.909 88	0.911 49	0.913 09	0.914 66	0.916 21	0.917 74
1.4	0.919 24	0.920 73	0.922 20	0.923 64	0.925 07	0.926 47	0.927 86	0.929 22	0.930 56	0.931 89
1.5	0.933 19	0.934 48	0.935 74	0.936 99	0.938 22	0.939 43	0.940 62	0.941 79	0.942 95	0.944 08
1.6	0.945 20	0.946 30	0.947 38	0.948 45	0.949 50	0.950 53	0.951 54	0.952 54	0.953 52	0.954 49
1.7	0.955 43	0.956 37	0.957 28	0.958 19	0.959 07	0.959 94	0.960 80	0.961 64	0.962 46	0.963 27
1.8	0.964 07	0.964 85	0.965 62	0.966 38	0.967 12	0.967 84	0.968 56	0.969 26	0.969 95	0.970 62
1.9	0.971 28	0.971 93	0.972 57	0.973 20	0.973 81	0.974 41	0.975 00	0.975 58	0.976 15	0.976 70
2.0	0.977 25	0.977 78	0.978 31	0.978 82	0.979 32	0.979 82	0.980 30	0.980 77	0.981 24	0.981 69
2.1	0.982 14	0.982 57	0.983 00	0.983 41	0.983 82	0.984 22	0.984 61	0.985 00	0.985 37	0.985 74
2.2	0.986 10	0.986 45	0.986 79	0.987 13	0.987 45	0.987 78	0.988 09	0.988 40	0.988 70	0.988 99
2.3	0.989 28	0.989 56	0.989 83	0.990 10	0.990 36	0.990 86	0.991 11	0.991 11	0.991 34	0.991 58
2.4	0.991 80	0.992 02	0.992 24	0.992 45	0.992 66	0.992 86	0.993 05	0.993 24	0.993 43	0.993 61
2.5	0.993 79	0.993 96	0.994 13	0.994 30	0.994 46	0.994 61	0.994 77	0.994 92	0.995 06	0.995 20
2.6	0.995 34	0.995 47	0.995 60	0.995 73	0.995 85	0.995 98	0.996 09	0.996 21	0.996 32	0.996 43
2.7	0.996 53	0.996 64	0.996 74	0.996 83	0.996 93	0.997 02	0.997 11	0.997 20	0.997 28	0.997 36
2.8	0.997 44	0.997 52	0.997 60	0.997 67	0.997 74	0.997 81	0.997 88	0.997 95	0.998 01	0.998 07
2.9	0.998 13	0.998 19	0.998 25	0.998 31	0.998 36	0.998 41	0.998 46	0.998 51	0.998 56	0.998 61

Table 2

Quantiles of the Standard Normal Distribution ($u =$ value of Z such that $Pr(\mid Z \mid > u) = \alpha$)

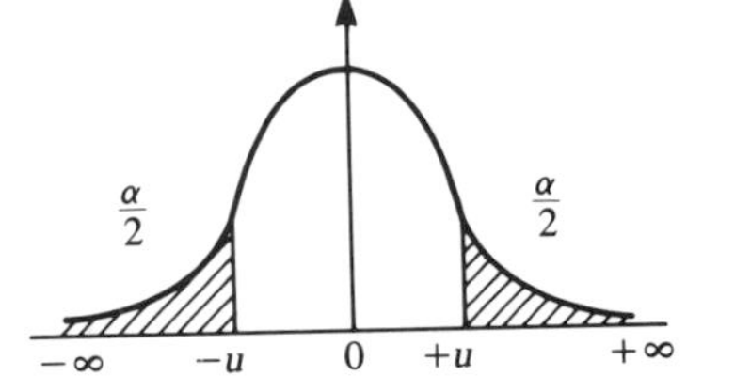

α	0.00	0.01	0.02	0.03	0.04	0.05	0.06	0.07	0.08	0.09
0.0	∞	2.5758	2.3263	2.1701	2.0537	1.9600	1.8808	1.8119	1.7507	1.6954
0.1	1.6449	1.5982	1.5548	1.5141	1.4758	1.4395	1.4051	1.3722	1.3408	1.3106
0.2	1.2816	1.2536	1.2566	1.2004	1.1750	1.1503	1.1264	1.1031	1.0803	1.0581
0.3	1.0364	1.0152	0.9945	0.9741	0.9542	0.9346	0.9154	0.8965	0.8779	0.8596
0.4	0.8416	0.8239	0.7892	0.8064	0.7722	0.7554	0.7388	0.7255	0.7063	0.6903
0.5	0.6745	0.6588	0.6433	0.6280	0.6128	0.5978	0.5828	0.5681	0.5534	0.5388
0.6	0.5244	0.5101	0.4959	0.4817	0.4677	0.4538	0.4399	0.4261	0.4125	0.3989
0.7	0.3853	0.3719	0.3585	0.3451	0.3319	0.3186	0.3000	0.2924	0.2793	0.2663
0.8	0.2533	0.2404	0.2275	0.2147	0.2019	0.1819	0.1764	0.1637	0.1510	0.1383
0.9	0.1257	0.1130	0.1004	0.0878	0.0753	0.0627	0.0502	0.0376	0.0251	0.0125

Table 3

Quantiles of the Chi–Square Distribution with ν Degrees of Freedom

($x =$ value of χ^2 such that $Pr(\chi^2 > x) = \alpha$)

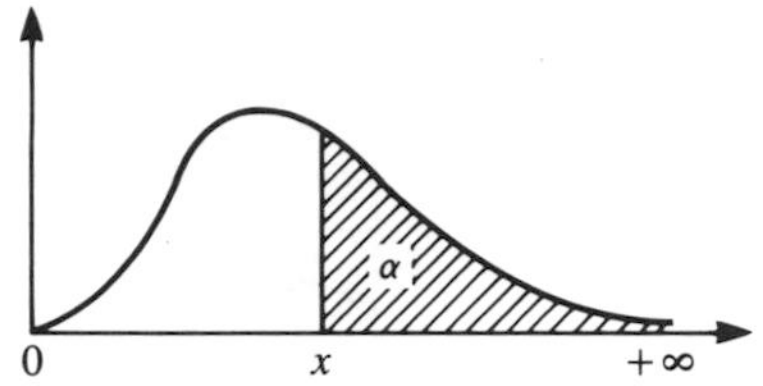

ν \ α	0.990	0.975	0.950	0.900	0.100	0.050	0.025	0.010	0.001
1	0.000 2	0.001 0	0.003 9	0.015 8	2.71	3.84	5.02	6.63	10.83
2	0.02	0.05	0.10	0.21	4.61	5.99	7.38	9.21	13.82
3	0.12	0.22	0.35	0.58	6.25	7.81	9.35	11.34	16.27
4	0.30	0.48	0.71	1.06	7.78	9.94	11.14	13.28	18.47
5	0.55	0.83	1.15	1.61	9.24	11.07	12.83	15.09	20.52
6	0.87	1.24	1.64	2.20	10.64	12.59	14.45	16.81	22.46
7	1.24	1.69	2.17	2.83	12.02	14.07	16.01	18.47	24.32
8	1.65	2.18	2.73	3.49	13.36	15.51	17.53	20.09	26.13
9	2.09	2.70	3.33	4.17	14.68	16.92	19.02	21.67	27.88
10	2.56	3.25	3.94	4.87	15.99	18.31	20.48	23.21	29.59
11	3.05	3.82	4.57	5.58	17.27	19.67	21.92	24.72	31.26
12	3.57	4.40	5.23	6.30	18.55	21.03	23.34	26.22	32.91
13	4.11	5.01	5.89	7.04	19.81	22.36	24.74	27.69	34.53
14	4.66	5.63	6.57	7.79	21.06	23.68	26.12	29.14	36.12
15	5 .23	6.26	7.26	8.55	22.31	25.00	27.49	30.58	37.70
16	5.81	6.91	7.96	9.31	23.54	26.30	28.84	32.00	39.25
17	6.41	7.56	8.67	10.08	24.77	27.59	30.19	33.41	40.79
18	7.01	8.23	9.39	10.86	25.99	28.87	31.53	34.80	42.31
19	7.63	8.91	10.12	11.65	27.20	30.14	32.85	36.19	43.82
20	8.26	9.59	10.85	12.44	28.41	31.41	34.17	37.57	45.32
21	8.90	10.28	11.59	13.24	29.61	32.67	35.48	38.93	46.80
22	9.54	10.98	12.34	14.04	30.81	33.92	36.78	40.29	48.27
23	10.20	11.69	13.09	14.85	32.01	35.17	38.08	41.64	49.73
24	10.86	12.40	13.85	15.66	33.20	36.41	39.37	42.98	51.18
25	11.52	13.12	14.61	16.47	34.38	37.65	40.65	44.31	52.62
26	12.20	13.84	15.38	17.29	35.56	38.88	41.92	45.64	54.05
27	12.88	14.57	16.15	18.11	36.74	40.11	43.19	46.96	55.48
28	13.57	15.31	16.93	18.94	37.92	41.34	44.46	48.28	56.89
29	14.26	16.05	17.71	19.77	39.09	42.56	45.72	49.59	58.30
30	14.95	16.79	18.49	20.60	40.26	43.77	46.98	50.89	59.70

when $\nu > 30$. then $\sqrt{2\chi^2} - \sqrt{2\nu - 1}$ is approximately $N(0.1)$.

Table 4

Quantiles of the Student Distribution with ν Degrees of Freedom

(t = value of T such that $Pr(|\, T \,| > t) = \alpha$)

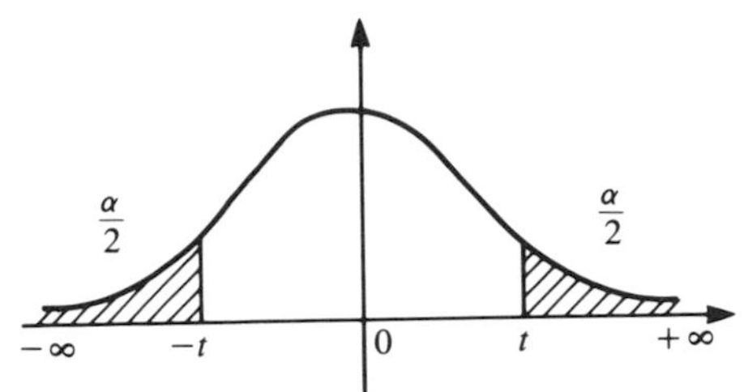

ν \ α	0.90	0.80	0.70	0.60	0.50	0.40	0.30	0.20	0.10	0.05	0.02	0.01	0.001
1	0.158	0.325	0.510	0.727	1.000	1.376	1.963	3.078	6.314	12.706	31.821	63.657	636.619
2	0.142	0.289	0.445	0.617	0.816	1.061	1.386	1.886	2.920	4.303	6.965	9.925	31.598
3	0.137	0.277	0.424	0.584	0.765	0.978	1.250	1.638	2.353	3.182	4.541	5.841	12.929
4	0.134	0.271	0.414	0.569	0.741	0.941	1.190	1.533	2.132	2.776	3.747	4.604	8.610
5	0.132	0.267	0.408	0.559	0.727	0.920	1.156	1.476	2.015	2.571	3.365	4.032	6.869
6	0.131	0.265	0.404	0.533	0.718	0.906	1.134	1.440	1.943	2.447	3.143	3.707	5.959
7	0.130	0.263	0.402	0.549	0.711	0.896	1.119	1.415	1.895	2.365	2.998	3.499	5.408
8	0.130	0.262	0.399	0.546	0.706	0.889	1.108	1.397	1.860	2.306	2.896	3.355	5.041
9	0.129	0.261	0.398	0.543	0.703	0.883	1.100	1.383	1.833	2.262	2.821	3.250	4.781
10	0.129	0.260	0.397	0.542	0.700	0.879	1.093	1.372	1.812	2.228	2.764	3.169	4.587
11	0.129	0.260	0.396	0.540	0.697	0.876	1.088	1.363	1.796	2.201	2.718	3.106	4.437
12	0.128	0.259	0.395	0.539	0.695	0.873	1.083	1.356	1.782	2.179	2.681	3.055	4.318
13	0.128	0.259	0.394	0.538	0.694	0.870	1.079	1.350	1.771	2.160	2.650	3.012	4.221
14	0.128	0.258	0.393	0.537	0.692	0.868	1.076	1.345	1.761	2.145	2.624	2.977	4.140
15	0.128	0.258	0.393	0.536	0.691	0.866	1.074	1.341	1.753	2.131	2.602	2.947	4.073
16	0.128	0.258	0.392	0.535	0.690	0.865	1.071	1.377	1.746	2.120	2.583	2.921	4.015
17	0.128	0.257	0.392	0.534	0.689	0.863	1.069	1.333	1.740	2.110	2.567	2.898	3.965
18	0.127	0.257	0.392	0.534	0.688	0.862	1.067	1.330	1.734	2.101	2.552	2.878	3.922
19	0.127	0.257	0.391	0.533	0.688	0.861	1.066	1.328	1.729	2.093	2.539	2.861	3.883
20	0.127	0.257	0.391	0.533	0.687	0.860	1.064	1.325	1.725	2.086	2.528	2.845	3.850
21	0.127	0.257	0.391	0.532	0.686	0.859	1.063	1.323	1.721	2.080	2.518	2.831	3.819
22	0.127	0.256	0.390	0.532	0.686	0.858	1.061	1.321	1.717	2.074	2.508	2.819	3.792
23	0.127	0.256	0.390	0.532	0.685	0.858	1.060	1.319	1.714	2.069	2.500	2.807	3.767
24	0.127	0.256	0.390	0.531	0.685	0.857	1.059	1.318	1.711	2.064	2.492	2.797	3.745
25	0.127	0.256	0.390	0.531	0.684	0.856	1.058	1.316	1.708	2.060	2.485	2.787	3.725
26	0.127	0.256	0.390	0.531	0.684	0.856	1.058	1.315	1.706	2.056	2.479	2.779	3.707
27	0.137	0.256	0.389	0.531	0.684	0.855	1.057	1.314	1.703	2.052	2.473	2.771	3.690
28	0.127	0.256	0.389	0.530	0.683	0.855	1.056	1.313	1.701	2.048	2.467	2.763	3.674
29	0.127	0.256	0.389	0.530	0.683	0.854	1.055	1.311	1.699	2.045	2.462	2.756	3.649
30	0.127	0.256	0.389	0.530	0.683	0.854	1.055	1.310	1.697	2.042	2.457	2.750	3.656
40	0.127	0.255	0.388	0.529	0.681	0.851	1.050	1.303	1.684	2.021	2.423	2.704	3.551
80	0.126	0.254	0.387	0.527	0.679	0.848	1.046	1.296	1.671	2.000	2.390	2.660	3.460
120	0.126	0.254	0.386	0.526	0.677	0.845	1.041	1.289	1.658	1.980	2.358	2.617	3.373
∞	0.126	0.253.	0.385	0.524	0.674	0.842	1.036	1.282	1.645	1.960	2.326	2.576	3.291

Table 5

Quantiles of the Fisher–Snedecor Distribution with ν_1 and ν_2 Degrees of Freedom

(f = value of F such that $Pr(F > f) = \alpha$)

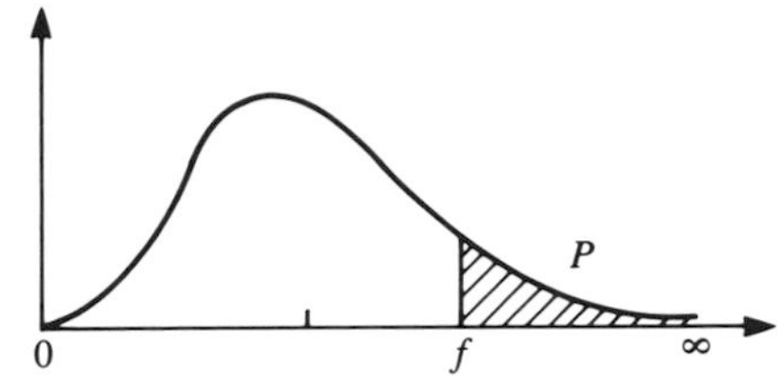

ν_2	$\nu_1 = 1$		$\nu_1 = 2$		$\nu_1 = 3$		$\nu_1 = 4$		$\nu_1 = 5$	
	$P = 0.05$	$P = 0.01$	$P = 0.05$	$P = 0.01$	$P = 0.05$	$P = 0.01$	$P = 0.05$	$P = 0.01$	$P = 0.05$	$P = 0.01$
1	161.4	4 052	199.5	4 999	215.7	5 403	224.6	5 625	230.2	5 764
2	18.51	98.49	19.00	99.00	19.16	99.17	19.25	99.25	19.30	99.30
3	10.13	34.12	9.55	30.81	9.28	29.46	9.12	28.71	9.01	28.24
4	7.71	21.20	6.94	18.00	6.59	16.69	6.39	15.98	6.26	15.52
5	6.61	16.26	5.79	13.27	5.41	12.06	5.19	11.39	5.05	10.97
6	5.99	13.74	5.14	10.91	4.76	9.78	4.53	9.15	4.39	8.75
7	5.59	12.15	4.74	9.55	4.35	8.45	4.12	7.85	3.97	7.45
8	5.32	11.26	4.46	8.65	4.07	7.59	3.84	7.01	3.69	6.63
9	5.12	10.56	4.26	8.02	3.86	6.99	3.63	6.42	3.48	6.06
10	4.96	10.04	4.10	7.56	3.71	6.55	3.48	5.99	3.33	5.64
11	4.84	9.65	3.98	7.20	3.59	6.22	3.36	5.67	3.20	5.32
12	4.75	9.33	3.88	6.93	3.49	5.95	3.26	5.41	3.11	5.06
13	4.67	9.07	3.80	6.70	3.41	5.74	3.18	5.20	3.02	4.86
14	4.60	8.86	3.74	6.51	3.34	5.56	3.11	5.03	2.96	4.69
15	4.54	8.86	3.68	6.36	3.29	5.42	3.06	4.89	2.90	4.56
16	4.49	8.53	3.63	6.23	3.24	5.29	3.01	4.77	2.85	4.44
17	4.45	8.40	3.59	6.11	3.20	5.18	2.96	4.67	2.81	4.43
18	4.41	8.28	3.55	6.01	3.16	5.09	2.93	4.58	2.77	4.25
19	4.38	8.18	3.52	5.93	3.13	5.01	2.90	4.50	2.74	4.17
20	4.35	8.10	3.49	5.85	3.10	4.94	2.87	4.43	2.71	4.10
21	4.32	8.02	3.47	5.78	3.07	4.87	2.84	4.37	2.68	4.04
22	4.30	7.94	3.44	5.72	3.05	4.82	2.82	4.31	2.66	3.99
23	4.28	7.88	3.42	5.66	3.03	4.76	2.80	4.26	2.64	3.94
24	4.26	7.82	3.40	5.61	3.01	4.72	2.78	4.22	2.62	3.90
25	4.24	7.77	3.38	5.57	2.09	4.68	2.76	4.18	2.60	3.86
26	4.22	7.72	3.37	5.53	2.98	4.64	2.74	4.14	2.59	3.82
27	4.21	7.68	3.35	5.49	2.96	4.60	2.73	4.11	2.57	3.70
28	4.20	7.64	3.34	5.45	2.95	4.57	2.71	4.07	2.56	3.75
29	4.18	7.60	3.33	5.42	2.93	4.54	2.70	4.04	2.54	3.73
30	4.17	7.56	3.32	5.39	2.92	4.51	2.69	4.02	2.53	3.70
40	4.08	7.31	3.23	5.18	2.84	4.31	2.61	3.83	2.45	3.51
60	4.00	7.08	3.15	4.98	2.76	4.13	2.52	3.65	2.37	3.34
120	3.92	6.85	3.07	4.79	2.68	3.95	2.45	3.48	2.29	3.17
∞	3.84	6.64	2.99	4.60	2.60	3.78	2.37	3.32	2.21	3.02

Table 5 Continued

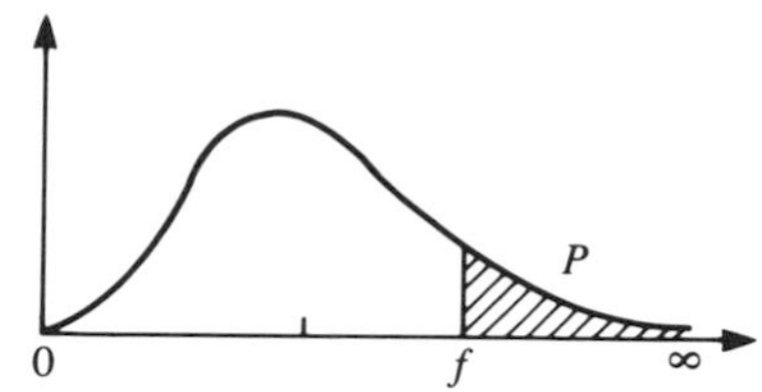

ν_2	$\nu_1 = 6$		$\nu_1 = 8$		$\nu_1 = 12$		$\nu_1 = 24$		$\nu_1 = \infty$	
	$P = 0.05$	$P = 0.01$	$P = 0.05$	$P = 0.01$	$P = 0.05$	$P = 0.01$	$P = 0.05$	$P = 0.01$	$P = 0.05$	$P = 0.01$
1	234.0	5 859	238.9	5 981	243.9	6 106	249.0	6 234	254.3	6 366
2	19.33	99.33	19.37	99.36	19.41	99.42	19.45	99.46	19.50	99.50
3	8.94	27.91	8.84	27.49	8.74	27.05	8.64	26.60	8.53	26.12
4	6.61	15.21	6.04	14.80	5.91	14.37	5.77	13.93	5.63	13.46
5	4.95	10.67	4.82	10.27	4.68	9.89	4.53	9.47	4.36	9.02
6	4.28	8.47	4.15	8.10	4.00	7.72	3.84	7.31	3.67	6.88
7	3.87	7.19	3.73	6.84	3.57	6.47	3.41	6.07	3.23	5.65
8	3.58	6.37	3.44	6.03	3.28	5.67	3.12	5.28	2.93	4.86
9	3.37	5.80	3.23	5.47	3.07	5.11	2.90	4.73	2.71	4.31
10	3.22	5.39	3.07	5.06	2.91	4.71	2.74	4.33	2.54	3.91
11	3.09	5.07	2.95	4.74	2.79	4.40	2.61	4.02	2.40	3.60
12	3.00	4.82	2.85	4.50	2.69	4.16	2.50	3.78	2.30	3.36
13	2.92	4.62	2.77	4.30	2.60	3.96	2.42	3.59	2.21	3.16
14	2.85	4.46	2.70	4.14	2.53	3.80	2.35	3.43	2.13	3.00
15	2.79	4.32	2.64	4.00	2.48	3.67	2.29	3.29	2.07	2.87
16	2.74	4.20	2.59	3.89	2.42	3.55	2.24	3.18	2.01	2.75
17	2.70	4.10	2.55	3.79	2.35	3.45	2.19	3.08	1.96	2.65
18	2.66	4.01	2.51	3.71	2.34	3.37	2.15	3.00	1.92	2.57
19	2.63	3.94	2.48	3.63	2.31	3.30	2.11	2.92	1.88	2.49
20	2.60	3.87	2.45	3.56	2.28	3.23	2.68	2.86	1.84	2.42
21	2.57	3.81	2.42	3.51	2.25	3.17	2.05	2.80	1.81	2.36
22	2.55	3.76	2.40	3.45	2.23	3.12	2.03	2.75	1.78	2.31
23	2.53	3.71	2.38	3.41	2.20	3.07	2.00	2.70	1.76	2.26
24	2.51	3.67	2.36	3.36	2.18	1.03	1.98	2.66	1.73	2.21
25	2.49	3.63	2.34	3.32	2.16	2.99	1.96	2.62	1.71	2.17
26	2.47	3.59	2.32	3.29	2.15	2.96	1.95	2.58	1.69	2.13
27	2.46	3.56	2.30	3.26	2.13	2.93	1.93	2.55	1.67	2.10
28	2.44	3.53	2.29	3.23	2.12	2.90	1.91	2.52	1.65	2.06
29	2.43	3.50	2.28	3.20	2.10	2.87	1.90	2.49	1.64	2.03
30	2.42	3.47	2.27	3.17	2.09	2.84	1.89	2.47	1.62	2.01
40	2.34	3.29	2.18	2.99	2.00	2.66	1.79	2.29	1.51	1.80
60	2.25	3.12	2.10	2.82	1.92	2.50	1.70	2.12	1.39	1.60
120	2.17	2.96	2.01	2.66	1.83	2.34	1.61	1.95	1.25	1.38
∞	2.09	2.80	1.94	2.51	1.75	2.18	1.52	1.79	1.09	1.00

Index